INTERPRETING THE NEW TESTAMENT

INTERPRETING THE NEW TESTAMENT

*An Introduction to the Principles
and Methods of N.T. Exegesis*

Hans Conzelmann and Andreas Lindemann
Translated by Siegfried S. Schatzmann
From the 8th rev. German edition

HENDRICKSON
PUBLISHERS
PEABODY, MASSACHUSETTS 01961-3473

Translated from *Arbeitsbuch zum Neuen Testament*, 8th revised edition, 1985, J.C.B. Mohr (Paul Siebeck) Tübingen

ISBN 0–913573–80–9

TABLE OF CONTENTS

PART TWO: CONTEMPORARY HISTORY OF THE NT—
THE ENVIRONMENT OF PRIMITIVE CHRISTIANITY

TRANSLATOR'S PREFACE

This translation of the *Arbeitsbuch zum Neuen Testament* is based on the 8th revised edition. Whenever possible, quotations from German sources follow the already available English translations. With the German publisher's permission the bibliography in most sections was supplemented with salient English works.

Both editors and publisher of the English translation are to be congratulated for making this text accessible to a broader audience. The rewards will ultimately be found in informed exegesis of the New Testament.

Siegfried S. Schatzmann
Oral Roberts University
Tulsa, Oklahoma

PREFACE TO THE EIGHTH EDITION

In the 7th edition much was revised or expanded and the index of Greek and Hebrew words (p. 379f.) was added. Now the entire book has been revised once more and augmented in some instances; the bibliography has been brought up to date once again.

Göttingen and Bethel
October 27, 1985
Hans Conzelmann
Andreas Lindemann

PREFACE

Currently biblical exegesis, and especially New Testament exegesis, do not appear to be in vogue. In part this may be due to waning interests in history in general. But to a much greater extent it is due to the fact that the exegetical methods meanwhile have become so refined and specialized that only the "initiates" seem to comprehend them. For the student, the multiplicity of methods and especially of findings raises the impression that NT exegesis contributes more to a general uncertainty than to understanding.

In some places, therefore, this had led to the call for a reduction in the extent of critical work and thereby regain more "positive" results. Such an effort, however, would not represent a further development of the work of exegesis, but a regression. Therefore a different approach is chosen in this book: We have endeavored to present the methods and results of critical exegesis in such a way that the individual steps leading to these results become lucid and can be retraced critically, either to adopt or to reject them. In any case, it is important to observe that questions of methodology must in no wise be regarded as questions of world view; instead, the validity of a method has to be demonstrated rationally, that is, in the object of investigation alone. On this premise, perhaps, it is possible for the unity of NT exegesis, if not indeed for the unity of NT theology, to become visible.

Of course, a presentation of the methods and results cannot take place *sine ira et studio*. A Workbook, too, has its own particular position. We began with the assumption that the historical-critical interpretation of the

NT cannot be an end in itself but is to contribute especially to the clarification of what is Christian belief. To this extent historical work is up to date in interest.

At this point we express our gratitude to Mrs. Margitta Stein for her careful work in typing the manuscript, as well as to Mr. Frank Herkommer, stud. theol. and Mr. Hartmud Plath, stud. theol., for their help in proofing. In connection with the presentation of Judaism, Dr. Berndt Schaller has made significant contributions; for this we are especially indebted to him.

Göttingen, February 14, 1975
Hans Conzelmann
Andreas Lindemann

INSTRUCTIONS ON HOW TO USE THIS BOOK

Interpreting the New Testament is not intended to be read from beginning to end, in one sitting. Rather, its intent is to serve as a guide for individual study and as an introduction to the methods and results of the exegesis of the NT. To the beginning student of the NT, this text is to give instructions on finding his way through the entire task of exegesis. Hence, to the undergraduate and graduate student of the NT, the book may be a tool for successful independent study. For those anticipating theological examinations, it is designed to help test the application of principles studied.

The various parts of the book may be worked through independently of one another, for instance, as parallel reading to augment lectures or exercises or to supplement one's study. In any case, however, it is advisable to begin with the methodology (Part One).

The suggested exercises and readings are arranged so that they can be completed in a relatively brief period of time, using the generally easily available tools as indicated.

The bibliographic references are limited to essentials. To that degree they serve to establish the student's own NT library. Since most cited literature contains further bibliographic references, a comprehensive and complicated bibliography could be avoided here.

Three important abbreviations require attention:

Barrett: C. K. Barrett, *The NT Background: Selected Documents* (New York: Harper & Row, 1961).

L-G: J. Leipoldt and W. Grundmann, eds., *Umwelt des Urchristentums II. Texte zum neutestamentlichen Zeitalter,* [3]1972.

H-S: E. Hennecke and W. Schneemelcher, eds., *New Testament Apocrypha,* 2 vols., translated and edited by R. McL. Wilson (London: Lutterworth, 1963–65).

All other abbreviations correspond with those of the *Journal of Biblical Literature* (JBL) and of the *Theological Dictionary of the NT* (TDNT).

PART 1:
METHODOLOGY

§ 1   Overview of NT Studies

Bibliography: *Section 1*: R. Bultmann, "The Problem of Hermeneutics," in *Essays Philosophical and Theological*, 1955, and "Ist voraussetzungslose Exegese möglich?" *Glauben und Verstehen III*, 142–150; G. Ebeling, *The Study of Theology*, ET 1978, 13–25. *Section 2*: G. Ebeling, "The Significance of the Critical Historical Method for Church and Theology in Protestantism," *Word and Faith*, ET 1963, 17–61. *Section 3*: W. G. Kümmel, *The NT: The History of the Investigation of its Problems*, ET 1972; D. Lührmann, *Auslegung des Neuen Testaments*, 1984; P. Ricoeur, *Essays in Hermeneutics*, 1974; G. Strecker, ed., *Das Problem der Theologie des Neuen Testaments*, WdF 367, 1975. *Section 4*: E. Preuschen, *Analecta. Kürzere Texte zur Geschichte der alten Kirche und des Kanons II*, 1910; H. v. Campenhausen, *The Formation of the Christian Bible*, ET 1977; Ph. Vielhauer, *Geschichte der urchristlichen Literatur*, 1975, 774–786.

1. Basic concepts

Exegesis, the interpretation of the NT text, constitutes the most important task of the study of the NT.

This task is facilitated by certain supporting disciplines, e.g., the crystallization of the characteristics of NT Greek, the illumination of NT history as a specific era in the hellenistic-Roman and Jewish history, and the description of the social conditions in Palestine at the time of Jesus, etc.

The "text" is given in the form of the NT writings whose significance is found in their special prominence that the Christian church accords them as "sacred writings." The use of the NT in the church is the primary reason for integrating the subject "New Testament" in the theological discipline rather than in the realm of the science of classical antiquity, for instance. Despite the New Testament's particular theological position, the methods used in NT studies are those governing the interpretation of other historical texts.

The goal of exegesis is the *understanding* of the text. Before this, however, one must ask about the conditions to which basic understanding is to be subjected. The general discipline concerned with understanding is known as *hermeneutics*. As a method, hermeneutics is necessary because text and reader never encounter one another directly; rather, they are always separated from one another by a distance determined by time and subject matter. There is no unmediated, let alone "direct," understanding; indeed, mediation is always the primary prerequisite. The reader needs to be informed about the language in which the text is written.

He should further be acquainted with the particular historical, social, and cultural conditions under which the text was written. As far as it is possible, he must also know the recipients, including their relationship to the author of the text.

Another presupposition of proper exegesis concerns the place of the exegete himself. He must ask (or be asked) about the presuppositions he brings to the text. What tradition is in his background? What questions does he expect the text to answer? Why indeed does he even deal with this text? It would be wrong to move the encounter between exegete and text to a "neutral zone," as if there were, on the one side, a text of timeless value (at any rate) and devoid of history (possibly) and, on the other side, an exegete who approaches the text free of all presuppositions. There is no exegesis without presuppositions. Each interpretation is at least influenced by the exegete's own historical setting. Therefore, he must first of all be clear about the presuppositions he brings along.

One should not understand this in terms of psychological introspection. Rather, it is essential to determine one's own position, so that the exegete does not yield to an inappropriate identification between what the text says and the exegete's predetermined expectations (cf. R. Bultmann, *Glauben und Verstehen III*, 142–150.)

An important aspect of exegesis based on scientific criteria is the knowledge and application of *methods* that aid the explication of what the text says. In principle, the object (text) determines the method and not vice versa; methods are means to an end, never ends in themselves.

This principle is to be maintained against criticism from the "right" as well as from the "left." The "right," i.e., fundamentalism, argues the point that personal faith is presuppositional for proper exegesis—a faith that a priori excludes certain "critical" results. The "left," represented for instance by Marxism's ideology of history, argues that the only true interpretation—even of religious texts—is Marxist. However, the latter interpretation leads to the inevitable conclusion that religion is unscientific and represents an exclusive projection of human longings, predicated upon society or a metaphysical world to come. Both positions refuse to scrutinize their own presuppositions.

2. Methods

In terms of method, the biblical texts are to be treated no differently than other literary sources, especially those of antiquity. The scientific study of the Bible utilizes the same formal methods as those used in the study of antiquity, namely, classical philology, archaeology, and ancient history.

For the beginner in this discipline, this observation may already cause initial problems to surface. Anyone who expects "edification" from his encounter with the OT and the NT is at once confronted with the questions of authenticity, unity, and historical reliability. He has to ask whether the certainty of his own faith may be jeopardized by questioning the historical reliability of certain traditions concerning Jesus, or whether such danger can be avoided on the premise that faith and historical insight belong to two fundamentally different levels.

The Bible distinguishes itself from other ancient witnesses through its message. It is a collection of specific historical documents that attest to and present the Jewish, as well as the Christian faith, according to a great variety of theological opinions. The only—and for the time being pre-liminary—presupposition for the exegesis of these witnesses is the as-sumption that their expressions are somehow meaningful and that it is therefore worthwhile to pay attention to them. With regard to method, it would be untenable to require the exegete to accept (or reject) the con-tent of these texts a priori.

This also applies particularly to P. Stuhlmacher's argument of a "hermeneutic of agreement (*Einverständnis*) with biblical texts" in *Vom Verstehen des Neuen Testaments*, 205–225. Stuhlmacher feels that "the rash 'know-it-all' attitude of the scholarly community needs to be eliminated in order to make room for a new search of those energies in the tradition that are truly life-giving and enduring." But this search is precisely the task of *critical* exegesis because it cannot be es-tablished a priori what those "life-giving energies" are. The standard cannot be derived from the tradition; rather, it needs to come exclusively from the NT it-self. Stuhlmacher shows strong tendencies toward harmonizing and even stan-dardizing the theological streams of the NT on the premise of predetermined dogmatic considerations.

Historical texts essentially can be interpreted from two different vantage points: (1) they can be read for the sake of their own content; (2) they can be understood and interpreted as sources, that is, they can aid in re-constructing historical events.

For example, one can read Plato's works, in the sense that their philosophy is in-tellectually accepted, in order to learn to be a better philosopher. But his works can also serve as a source for understanding the history of Greek thought. Like-wise, one may read Karl Marx to analyze and criticize more adequately the con-temporary social situation. Yet, Marx can also be read in order to be informed regarding the social movement in the 19th century.

To be sure, the two perspectives should not be taken as alternatives; rather, they belong together. On the one hand, in order to understand the text, it has to be correctly classified historically. On the other hand, in order to use the text as a historical source, its content must first be analyzed. Certainly, one or the other perspective will generally domi-nate. In the NT, the whole issue is best exemplified in the Gospels. They are practically the only *sources* for the life and ministry of Jesus, but they are also *theological documents* with their own pertinent claim. If it were presupposed methodologically that the value of one of the two perspec-tives is to be minimized, the result would be an a priori reduction in the findings of the exegesis.

3. Specific Disciplines

The interpretation of a text, i.e., the exegetical task itself, requires certain preconditions: the wording of the text must be established; the meaning of the words then needs to be ascertained; the literary characteristics of the text must be recognized and defined; the historical locus of the text must be determined as narrowly as possible. The questions regarding the theology of the text can be addressed only after these issues are settled.

(1) *Textual criticism* deals with the handwritten transmission of the text and seeks to reconstruct the "original" text, that is, the text which comes closest to the autographs. The student needs to consider, however, that not a single original manuscript (autograph) is available today.

(2) In the *translation* it must be observed that the Greek terms used in the NT can only be understood properly in the context of the ancient patterns of language and thought. For instance, a systematic translation that ignores the development of the Greek language from the earlier classical era to the hellenistic era cannot do justice to the Greek text. Equally problematic would be an attempt to exegete the translation instead of the original form of the text. The sense of a word is often obscured, rather than clarified, by the translation. Thus, the English concept of "spirit" does in no way correspond consistently with the Greek concept of πνεῦμα.

In order to comprehend the range of meaning, consider the number of nuances for the term "spirit": intelligence, imagination, genius, ghost, essence.

For a proper understanding of the Greek text, one needs to conduct a careful analysis of the concrete cultural, political, and social setting of the era of that text. In other words, the determination of the meaning of a particular concept requires both a careful analysis of the context and a lexical classification.

(3) In the determination of the *literary "Gattung"* (form, type, genre), the same factors need to be considered. A correct evaluation of the historical reliability of a Gospel text, for instance, is only possible if one pays careful attention to the literary *Gattung* to which that text belongs. Thus, if a miracle story is read like an actual account, one necessarily misses the intent of the former because a miracle story is not drawn up like a record of the facts, but represents a literary product of its own kind.

(4) The historical classification of a text is the task of introductory studies (*Einleitungswissenschaft*); these build the external foundations by inquiring into authorship, recipients, historical situation, and literary unit of that text. It is important for the task of exegesis to know, for instance, whether a certain NT letter is the only literary witness that we possess of its author, or whether we could possibly interpret this letter in conjunction with other letters or writings by the same author. It is crucial to know whether the author of a particular writing knows the recipients and their specific situation, or whether he addresses the text to the church at large. The methodological problem of such introductory studies is their circular reasoning. Information about a text's historical locus can only be derived from that text itself because possible extracanonical sources dealing with the same matter are very scant.

An "introduction to the NT" presents the historical problems of the respective NT writings (usually in canonical sequence). The descriptions of early Christian literary history inform us about the preliterary forms, as well as about the early Christian writings in the process of their formation. Such descriptions necessarily exceed canonical bounds.

(5) A more detailed determination of the historical situation of a text also encompasses the knowledge of the political, social, and cultural conditions of its environment. In the case of the NT, this involves the conditions of the first-century world (*Spätantike*) in which early Christianity arose. It is the task of NT history to draw out these insights. Closely associated is the history of early Christianity, i.e., the so-called apostolic era. Here again one encounters the problem already observed in the "introduction to the NT," namely, that the NT texts are but secondary sources for historical events. In other words, the history of the early church can at best be reconstructed indirectly. Rarely is one fortunate enough (as in the case of the Apostolic Council) to possess, next to the Lukan description in Acts 15, a divergent account of Paul as "eyewitness" of the event (Gal 2), so that both descriptions can be compared with one another and a certain appraisal made of their historical credibility.

(6) The actual goal of NT exegesis is the explanation of the texts' theological content. Indeed, these texts are especially characterized by a certain theological assertion or claim that ultimately must be worked out and elucidated. Hence, the subcategory "theology of the NT" receives special significance because it attempts to summarize the theological idea of the NT writings, either following the systematic structure of particular themes (e.g., Christology, theology), or following the historical sequence (e.g., theology of Paul, of the Synoptics).

R. Bultmann provides a fine overview of the history, function, and problem of NT theology in the epilogue of his *Theology of the* NT, 2 vols., ET 1951–55, II, 237–251.

4. Collection of the NT Writings (Formation and theological significance of the canon)

(1) The NT was not written as "canonical" writings; that is to say, they were not, from the start, intended for the entire church's continual use. The letters of Paul, for instance, were "occasional" (though not private) letters, far removed from the notion that they were "sacred" writings. The subsequent canonization of certain texts served two purposes: One, it represented a collection of "classical" writings, and two, it led to the separation of the nonaccepted, hence "apocryphal" writings.

The pattern for the formation of the NT canon was found in the Jewish canon of the OT, finalized after the Jewish War of A.D. 70. Christianity adopted both the term "sacred writings" and the idea of their "inspiration" (2 Tim 3:16f.). Two relatively early stages in the formation of the NT canon can be traced. First, at the beginning of the second century the tendency to collect the letters of Paul emerges. Thus, the Roman writer of 1 Clement (ca. A.D. 100) knows of Paul's 1 Corinthians, as does Ignatius, who wrote his letters shortly after A.D. 100. In 2 Peter (shortly before A.D. 150?) a collection of Pauline writings is already presupposed (2 Pet 3:15f.) without divulging anything about its scope. Second, the canon of the "heretic" Marcion (ca. A.D. 150) is significant; it comprised two parts, namely "the Gospel" (Luke) and "the Apostle" (Paul's letters without the Pastorals). It is debatable whether Marcion should be viewed as originator of the idea of a Christian canon (following Harnack and Campenhausen), or whether he already followed certain models. One thing is certain: Marcion was the first to publish a collection or list of authoritative Christian writings.

The scope of the canon and the sequence of its writings were debated for a long time. Especially the fourfold Gospel presented a problem. While Marcion canonized only Luke's Gospel, Tatian, from Syria and a student of Justin Martyr, established a harmony of all four Gospels—the Diatessaron (ca. A.D. 175), which was widely recognized by the church. By the time of Irenaeus (ca. A.D. 200), however, the paralleling of Matthew, Mark, Luke, and John was firmly established while their precise order remained fluid. Codex D (see p. 20), for instance, places Matthew and John first because each bears the name of an apostle. Likewise, in the second part of the canon, writings attributed to the apostles, certain ones continued to be questioned. Hebrews, James, the Petrine letters, and 3 John are not found in the Muratorian canon (a list of writings [ca. A.D. 200] accepted as authoritative by the Catholic church). The definitive and commonly accepted NT canon was not settled until the fourth century.

(2) Even today there exists no such thing as a general and normative arrangement of writings in the canon. For example, Luther relegated Hebrews, James, and Jude to the end of the NT in his German Bible, together with the Revelation of John, thereby expressing his bias concerning these writings. In the other major German translation, the Zürich Bible, Hebrews and James conversely introduce the collection of non-Pauline letters, following the tradition of the Latin Vulgate, without thereby attaching a special, positive value to them.

It need not be especially emphasized that neither the historical sequence of the formation of the NT texts nor their systematic-theological value can be derived from their place in the canon. On the other hand, of course, it is not by accident that the Gospel of Matthew—highly esteemed by the early church—was placed at the beginning of the canon, while the disputed Apocalypse was placed at the end. Likewise, Romans does not "accidentally" introduce the series of Paul's writings.

(3) The NT writings were held to have been written by believers of the earliest church on account of their (alleged) authors' names (Peter, Jude, James, etc.). But the emergence of historical criticism has shown that not all of the NT books originated in the earliest Christian era. Some canonical writings (Johannine letters, 2 Peter) are definitely of more recent origin than some writings that were left out of the canon (1 Clement, Didache; see § 45). The preference of the former over the latter cannot be assessed adequately on theological grounds. Nevertheless, it must be noted that the selection of the canonical writings was generally based on sound theological judgment. In any case, the question of the canon constitutes one of the unique theological problems of NT studies in particular and of Christian theology in general. Can it be convincingly argued that exegesis should be confined to the canon, although the criteria that once led to the formation of precisely this canon can no longer be retraced theologically? If neither the idea of inspiration nor the motive of historical originality are considered viable, how does one, after all, justify any work in the NT as a relatively unified body of material?

At this juncture, we can at best attempt to point in the direction of an answer to the question of the canon. The authority of the NT canon must not be understood as formal authority. Neither 2 Peter nor Romans are accorded greater formal authority, on an a priori basis, than other theological witnesses in the history of the church. The special significance of the former arises exclusively from their message, i.e., the revelation of God in Christ, and from their treatment of this message. The criterion for the evaluation of biblical assertions must be found in the question of whether or not they explain the meaning of such revelation to the individual as well as to the world. Thus, there exists a canon within the canon. Luther asserted that the doctrine of justification represents such a canon within the canon, not necessarily in terms of formal categories but at least in terms of its theological structure. His well-known formula that "what promotes Christ" (*was Christum treibet*) is canonical should be understood in the same way (see his preface to James). In the study of the NT, then, the interpreter is confronted with the problem of whether or not this κανών, this standard, is theologically relevant. At any rate, any attempt to systematize and harmonize the NT assertions would in no way be adequate.

Suggestions for further reading:

The historical and theological problem of the canon is discussed extensively in the collection of essays by E. Käsemann, *Das Neue Testament als Kanon*, 1970; idem,

"The Canon of the New Testament and the Unity of the Church," in *Essays on New Testament Themes*, 1964. See also W. G. Kümmel, "Notwendigkeit und Grenze des NT Kanon," (*NT als Kanon*), 62–97; H. v. Campenhausen, *Formation of Bible*, 147–209; G. Ebeling, *The Word of God and Tradition*, ET 1968, 102–147. Compare with D. Lührmann, "Gal. 2:9 und die katholischen Briefe. Bemerkungen zum Kanon und zur regula fidei," ZNW 72 (1981): 65–87.

§ 2 *Tools for the Scholarly Study of the* NT

1. *Primary sources*

(1) The best convenient edition of the NT is Nestle's *Novum Testamentum Graece*, since 1979 available in its 26th edition, fully revised and edited by B. and K. Aland.

The earlier editions of the Nestle Greek text were based on the major critical editions of the 19th century; for details, see Nestle[25], 3–6. The new edition draws directly upon current manuscript research.

In the critical apparatus of the text, Nestle[26] lists almost all important variant readings of the NT manuscripts so that the reader is able to evaluate the textual decisions made by the editors and to reach his own reasonable text-critical conclusion.

Among the older editions, a Greek-Latin edition (Vulgate) and a Greek-German (Luther's 1912 translation) edition are also available.

The *Greek New Testament* (UBS[3], edited by K. Aland et al.), represents a new endeavor; it cites the textual variants in relatively few places and is, therefore, not suitable for study purposes. The *text* of UBS[3] and Nestle[26] is identical.

A *synopsis* (of the first three Gospels) that prints the texts in parallel form is indispensable for exegetical work in the first three Gospels. Currently available are two modern editions: One, the *Synopsis Quattuor Evangeliorum*, [13]1984, edited by K. Aland, contains a wealth of supplemental material (e.g., the complete Gospel according to Thomas, in an appendix) and includes the entire Gospel of John; two, the 13th edition of A. Huck's *Synopsis of the First Three Gospels* (1981), completely revised by H. Greeven, which renders the Johannine passages only where actual parallels with the Synoptics exist. Greeven also offers the parallel passages found in the apocryphal gospels, as well as the parallel texts in the Gospel according to Thomas, for which he gives his own Greek translation (from Coptic). The text in Aland's synopsis is identical with that of Nestle[26], as are the text-critical symbols used. The text in Greeven's synopsis differs not infrequently from Nestle[26]. While the textual apparatus is to a degree more elaborate than in Aland's, it is more difficult to decipher. Greeven's edition has revived the text-critical discussion.

Before making the inevitable purchase of one of the two synopses, both should be carefully compared in a test passage, including their arrangement and print.

(2) The NT writers often refer to the OT, generally using its most common Greek translation, the Septuagint (LXX) (see p. 137). A convenient edition is available in A. Rahlf's set of two volumes ([7]1962); the large critical edition with a comprehensive apparatus, the "Göttingen LXX," is currently being published (19 vols. since 1926). Besides the Hebrew Bible, the Septuagint also contains the OT Apocrypha. The latter, together with other ancient extracanonical Jewish writings (Pseudepigrapha), are collected in German, in E. Kautzsch, *Die Apokryphen und Pseudepigraphen des AT*, [2]1962. The Pseudepigrapha with additional texts are also available in P. Riessler, *Altjüdisches Schrifttum ausserhalb der Bibel* ([2]1966). Riessler's edition, in contrast to that of Kautzsch, contains but few brief comments. The collection of "Jüdische Schriften aus hellenistisch-römischer Zeit," edited by W. G. Kümmel and others, is available with commentary since 1973.

(3) A certain knowledge of the texts of the Jewish sect of Qumran, from the Dead Sea area, is indispensable. The most pertinent texts have been collected in E. Lohse's Hebrew-German edition of *Die Texte aus Qumran*, [2]1971. An acquaintance with the difficult rabbinic writings is made easier with the aid of R. Mayer's anthology, *Der babylonische Talmud* (1963; Goldmann pocket book, religion series 1902, cf. p. 110f. below).

(4) The study of the NT frequently also requires a glimpse into later Christian sources. The NT Apocrypha are collected in the two-volume set of E. Hennecke and W. Schneemelcher (vol. 1: gospels, vol. 2: apocalypses etc.). Editions of the writings of the "Apostolic Fathers" are cited in § 45 (on Gnosis, see § 22).

2. Translation tools

(1) The normative modern dictionary for the entire scope of the (ancient) Greek language is H. G. Liddell—R. Scott, *A Greek-English Lexicon* ([9]1940, updated 1968). Indispensable, especially for NT studies, is W. Bauer, W. F. Arndt, F. W. Gingrich, and F. Danker, *A Greek-English Lexicon of the New Testament and Other Early Christian Literature* (ET [2]1979). For the purpose of detailed studies, J. H. Moulton—G. Milligan, *The Vocabulary of the Greek Testament Illustrated from the Papyri and Other Non-Literary Sources* (1929) is especially helpful. This work does not contain the entire vocabulary of the NT; nevertheless, when the comparative materials are cited, in contrast to Bauer, it not only provides the source but also cites the text itself.

(2) *The Theological Dictionary of the New Testament* (10 vols., 1964–78, incl. index), originated by G. Kittel and, since 1954, edited by G. Friedrich, is not a dictionary proper; rather, it represents a collection of monographs

and essays on significant theological terms in the NT. Each article provides an elaborate overview of the usage of the respective term in the secular Greek world, in the OT and in Judaism, in the NT, as well as in the patristic era. The emphasis invariably rests on the delineation of the theological significance. Much briefer is the *Exegetische Wörterbuch zum neuen Testament* (ed. H. Balz and G. Schneider; 3 vols., 1980–83). In English one might consider *The New International Dictionary of New Testament Theology* (ed. C. Brown; 3 vols., 1975).

(3) An essential tool for translating and exegeting difficult passages is *A Greek Grammar of the New Testament and Other Early Christian Literature*, by F. Blass, A. Debrunner, and R. W. Funk (1961). The extensive index facilitates the usefulness of this book greatly.

(4) With the help of a concordance the student is able on his own to gain an overview of the frequency and usage of the words found in the NT. The *Handkonkordanz zum griechischen NT*, by A. Schmoller (⁷1938 and several reprints since then) is not comprehensive, yet is generally adequate. A comprehensive one is W. F. Moulton and A. S. Geden's *A Concordance to the Greek Testament* (⁴1963). It is based on the Westcott-Hort text instead of on the Nestle text. K. Aland's *Vollständige Konkordanz zum griechischen NT* (2 vols., incl. tables and outlines) is also quite extensive. A two-volume reprint edition is also available for the LXX, *A Concordance to the Septuagint and Other Greek Versions of the OT*, by E. Hatch and H. E. Redpath (1975). For the writings of the Apostolic Fathers, H. Kraft and U. Früchtel have compiled a concordance, the *Clavis Patrum Apostolicorum*, 1963.

3. Literature

(1) The two most important reference works are the following: *Die Religion in Geschichte und Gegenwart* (ed. K. Galling; 3rd revised ed. 1957–65; 6 vols., incl. indices; abbreviated RGG³), and the Roman Catholic *Lexikon für Theologie und Kirche* (ed. J. Hofer and K. Rahner, ²1957–67; 10 vols., incl. indices; abbreviated LThK²). For information on Palestine's geography, history, religion, culture, and literature, one should consult the *Biblisch-Historische Handwörterbuch* (ed. B. Reicke and L. Rost, 1962–79, 4 vols., incl. indices and a very detailed historical-archaeological map of Palestine; abbreviated BHH). Also available since 1976 are several volumes of the 30-volume set of the *Theologische Realenzyklopädie* (TRE).

(2) The most significant type of literature in the realm of NT studies are the commentaries (generally in series) on the individual books of the NT. The outstanding German series is the *Kritisch-exegetischer Kommentar über das Neue Testament*, originated in 1832 by H. A. W. Meyer and currently edited by F. Hahn (now abbreviated KEK, earlier as MeyerK). The individual volumes in this series are continually revised and updated to represent the current status of interpretation; they offer a high degree of historical and theological information. A wealth of philosophical and religio-historical material is found in the *Handbuch zum NT*, originated by H. Lietzmann in 1907 (from 1949 to 1982 ed. by G. Bornkamm and since then by A. Lindemann; abbreviated HNT); its theological interpretation is generally held to a minimum, in keeping with the nature and intent of the series. "Meyer" and "Lietzmann" are used most often in exegetical study. For the purpose of more intensive studies, one is well advised to consult *Herders Theologischer Kommentar zum NT* (Catholic; ed. A. Vögtle and R. Schnackenburg; abbreviated HThK), which is in process of publication since 1953. Its individual volumes are very extensive and thus provide a fine overview of the current discussion. Also available since 1975 is the *Evangelisch-katholische Kommentar* (EKK).

Next to the series discussed above, we recommend two works for more in-depth work: the *Kommentar zum NT* (ed. Th. Zahn, 1903ff.; abbreviated KNT), available as a reprint set, thus no longer revised; and the *Theologischer Handkommentar zum NT* (rev. and ed. by E. Fascher, abbreviated ThHK), published in the Democratic Republic of Germany (DDR). Both works are theologically very conservative; yet, "Zahn" generally has made very meticulous philological contributions. The most important commentary series in English is the *International Critical Commentary* (ICC), first published in 1895, and is, in part, being rewritten. The most important French commentary is the *Commentaire du Nouveau Testament* (CNT, since 1949); in addition, the Catholic series Etudes Bibliques is known for its elaborate exegetical commentaries. Designed for the beginning student and lay person are the series *Das Neue Testament Deutsch* (NTD; since 1932, ed. G. Friedrich and P. Stuhlmacher), the *Zürcher Bibelkommentare* (ZBK; revisions since 1978, ed. H. H. Schmid and S. Schulz), as well as the Catholic series *Regensburger NT* (RNT; since 1938, now ed. by J. Eckert and O. Koch). Additional commentaries, particularly those not in series, are listed in W. G. Kümmel's *Introduction to the NT*.

(3) The *Kommentar zum NT aus Talmud und Midrasch*, by P. Billerbeck (6 vols.; vols. 1–4 [5]1969, vols. 5–6 [3]1969), is to be understood as an indispensable collection of material from the rabbinic literature, rather than as a commentary proper. In catalogues and bibliographies this source is generally listed as Strack-Billerbeck. Whereas H. L. Strack made possible its publication, the work itself is exclusively that of P. Billerbeck.

(4) The substantive framework of the relevant literature is contained in the special studies, on specific text passages or on special topics (monographs). Similar to commentaries, most of these monographs are published in series and generally are found in the same location in a library (though this is not necessarily true in American libraries, transl.). The characteristics of the individual series are not uniform, so that any

blanket assessment of the degree of importance of each series is inappropriate. In the following, therefore, we will present a selection of currently available monograph series in strictly alphabetical order (incl. customary abbreviations; see section on abbreviations below).

Abhandlungen zur Theologie des Alten und Neuen Testaments—AThANT—Theologischer Verlag, Zürich

Beiträge zur Historischen Theologie—BHTh—J. C. B. Mohr (Paul Siebeck), Tübingen

Biblische Studien—BSt—Neukirchener Verlag, Neukirchen

Beiträge zur Wissenschaft vom Alten und Neuen Testament—BWANT—Kohlhammer, Stuttgart

Beihefte zur Zeitschrift für die Neutestamentliche Wissenschaft—BZNW—de Gruyter, Berlin

Forschungen zur Religion und Literatur des Alten und Neuen Testaments—FRLANT—Vandenhoeck & Ruprecht, Göttingen

Neutestamentliche Abhandlungen—NTA—Aschendorff, Münster

Society for New Testament Studies Monograph Series—SNTSMS—Cambridge University Press

Supplements to Novum Testamentum—Nov Test Suppl—E. J. Brill, Leiden

Studien zum Alten und Neuen Testament—StANT—Kösel-Verlag, Munich

Studien zum Neuen Testament—StNT—Gütersloher Verlagshaus Gerd Mohn

Studien zur Umwelt des Neuen Testaments—StUNT—Vandenhoeck & Ruprecht, Göttingen

Stuttgarter Bibelstudien—SBS—Katholisches Bibelwerk, Stuttgart

Texte und Untersuchungen—TU—Akademie-Verlag, Berlin (GDR)

Wissenschaftliche Untersuchungen zum Neuen Testament—WUNT—J. C. B. Mohr (Paul Siebeck), Tübingen

Wissenschaftliche Monographien zum Alten und Neuen Testament—WMANT—Neukirchener Verlag, Neukirchen.

(5) From among the many scholarly journals we are able to cite only the most important. The leading German journal is the *Zeitschrift für die neutestamentliche Wissenschaft und die Kunde der älteren Kirche* (ZNW, since 1900), while the journal *Biblische Zeitschrift* (BZ, new series since 1957) represents the leading Catholic contribution. Among the best international journals, with articles written in English, German, and French, are to be mentioned *New Testament Studies* (NTS, since 1954), *Novum Testamentum* (NovTest, since 1956) and *Biblica* (Bibl, since 1920), the voice of the Pontifical Bible Institute, Rome. The *Journal of Biblical Literature* (JBL, since 1881) is one of the journals published in the U.S. The Catholic *Revue Biblique* (RB, since 1894) is the leading journal in matters pertaining to biblical archaeology and is published in France.

New publications in all theological disciplines are reviewed, in part quite extensively, in the *Theologische Literaturzeitung* (*ThLZ*, since 1876), as well as in the (Catholic) *Theologische Revue* (*ThRv*, since 1902). Scholarly contributions are published in the *Theologische Rundschau* (*ThR*, new series since 1929) and in *Verkündigung und Forschung* (*VF*, since 1941), appearing semi-annually. Essays on NT themes can be found, among other theological journals, for instance, in *Evangelische Theologie* (*EvTh*, since 1934), *Kerygma und Dogma* (*KuD*, since 1955), *Zeitschrift für Theologie und Kirche* (*ZThK*, since 1891), and *Theologische Zeitschrift* (*ThZ*, since 1945).

(6) A comprehensive bibliography of new publications of books and essays is provided by the *Elenchus bibliographicus biblicus* (EBB). Essays, and recently also books, dealing with the Old and New Testament and related disciplines are listed in the annual publication of *Internationale Zeitschriftenschau für Bibelwissenschaft und Grenzgebiete* (IZBG, since 1951), with brief content summaries. More comprehensive synopses drawn from a smaller, but nevertheless adequate selection of journals are found in the *New Testament Abstracts* (since 1956). In similar fashion, *ZNW* and *ThLZ* (cited above) discuss newly published essays and books. Bibliographic references relative to specific topics can generally be obtained in the bibliographies of new dissertations and NT commentaries.

4. *Abbreviations*

The ability to read scholarly writings and to prepare one's own research papers requires of the student a certain expertise in knowing the common abbreviations of the biblical books or of the classical writers and their works on the one hand, and of the commentary and monograph series on the other. A fairly exhaustive compilation of abbreviations has been established by S. Schwertner in the *Theologische Realenzyklopädie*. Likewise, the tables of abbreviations in every volume of the RGG, the TDNT (only in vols. 1 and 10), and the LThK, continue to be useful. While they complement one another in certain ways, they also are divergent in the use of abbreviations. It must be noted that many journals and periodicals have devised their own system of abbreviations, in consideration of articles in foreign languages.

Suggested exercises:

1. Decode p. 1 of the TDNT, vol. 6 (incl. footnote 4) with the aid of the list of abbreviations in vol. 1.

2. Decipher the references given in Haenchen's commentary on Acts 26:28 (E. Haenchen, *The Acts of the Apostles*, ET 1971, 689, n. 2). You should also look up the three respective references in the library.

§ 3 The Language of the New Testament

Bibliography: A. Debrunner, *Geschichte der griechischen Sprache* II, 1954 (Collection Göschen 114); E. Norden, *Die antike Kunstprosa* (II), [5]1958, 451–510; C. F. D. Moule, *An Idiom Book of New Testament Greek*, [2]1959; J. H. Moulton and W. F. Howard, *A Grammar of New Testament Greek*, vol. 1, *Prolegomena*; vol. 2, *Accidence and Word Formation*, 1908, 1929; L. Radermacher, *Neutestamentliche Grammatik*, HNT 1/1, [2]1925.

1. General observations

The writings collected in the NT are representative, not so much of the formal or artistic, but of the popular type of literature. According to the renowned philologist E. Norden, the Gospels are "entirely removed from the artistic literature." The language used in the NT books is not the classical Greek, but the vernacular of that era, namely "Koine," which had developed into a global language in the wake of the worldwide expansion of Greek tradition during the period of "Hellenism" (see below, p. 112ff.). Within Koine Greek, various levels of language quality emerge; thus it is fairly easy to distinguish between vulgar and refined ways of speech, and between the colloquial language of the marketplace and literary language. Numerous examples of colloquial language use are extant in private correspondences of antiquity, as A. Deissmann has shown in his book, *Light from the Ancient East*, ET 1927. This popular language has been the deliberate literary vehicle in the diatribes of Epictetus, the philosopher of ca. A.D. 50–138.

2. Unique features of Koine Greek

Koine Greek derives largely from the Attic dialect; the spoken language changed, however, especially when it lost its distinct enunciation (this is known as itacism, i.e., the tendency to pronounce η, ει like an *i* sound). Verb forms are becoming mixed; for instance, the α of the first aorist form filters into the second aorist (εἶπαν, instead of εἶπον), and μι-verbs take on some characteristics of ω-verbs (ἐτίθουν, instead of ἐτίθεσαν). In prepositional constructions the definite article often is missing (cf. Rom 1:1— εἰς εὐαγγέλιον θεοῦ—"for *the* gospel of God," rather than "for *a* gospel of God"). The sharp distinction made in the meaning of prepositions is no longer maintained—an important factor even for the exegesis of biblical texts. For instance, the virtual synonymity of περί and ὑπέρ means for exegesis that there is no essential difference between the expressions that Christ died ὑπέρ τῶν ἁμαρτιῶν (1 Cor 15:3) or περὶ ἁμαρτιῶν (1 Pet 3:18). The use of the cases together with the individual prepositions is no longer strictly maintained; thus ὑπό with the accusative case also responds to the question of "where" (cf. Rom 6:14—ὑπὸ νόμον does not mean "under a law" but "under the law"; on the use of the article, see above). Similar observations apply to παρά and πρός; in John 1:1, καὶ ὁ λόγος ἦν πρὸς τὸν θεόν does not mean "the λόγος was (orientated) towards God," but "he was with God." Even εἰς and ἐν are not always distinguished (Mk 1:9—ἐβαπτίσθη εἰς τὸν Ἰορδάνην—is rendered "he was baptized in the Jordan," not "dipped into the Jordan"). Typical in Koine Greek is the sharp decline in the use of the optative mood as well as the diminishing distinction made between the imperfect and aorist tenses. Following a ἵνα one may find the indicative mood (cf. BAGD, s. v. ἵνα), and, in addition to the normal notion of finality, ἵνα is capable of carrying a consecutive significance. At any rate, final clauses and consecutive clauses often become virtually indistinguishable logically—a circumstance that sometimes has theological connotations in the NT in that God's purpose and its result cannot be separated from one another. Sentence construction becomes less compact; complete sentences are less frequent, as the NT use of the genitive absolute and of the infinitive with an accusative subject shows (cf. Bl-Debr §§ 423; 406). More complex sentences are found almost exclusively in Hebrews and occasionally in the Lukan writings. Conversely, semitisms, i.e., Hebrew and Aramaic echos, begin to penetrate the Greek. In this regard, it is striking to observe the use of the pleonastic setting of the personal pronoun (Mk 7:25—γυνή, ἧς εἶχεν τὸ θυγάτριον αὐτῆς πνεῦμα ἀκάθαρτον), as well as the use of εἰς in conjunction with εἶναι (Mt 19:5—ἔσονται εἰς σάρκα μίαν; cf. Bl-Debr §§ 297; 145). In terms of syntax one also notices—especially in Mark—the frequent stringing together of several sentences by using the simple conjunction καί (ἐγένετο), in keeping with both the average popular language and with Hebrew style. It must be noted that many semitisms cannot be traced back as much to the Hebrew or Aramaic languages as to the influences of the semitically tinted language of the LXX; thus one speaks of "septuagintisms."

A special linguistic feature in NT Greek is the prominence and the shift in meaning of certain terms; for instance πίστις with the definite meaning of "the faith," or κύριος meaning "the Lord" (i.e., Christ), became for Paul almost technical terms with great theological significance. In these and other examples one notices that the Christian community, though on a limited scale, developed its own new mode of expression.

The linguistic level varies greatly in the NT. While Mark uses very simple Greek, Matthew and Luke improve his style in many instances. Next to the writer of Hebrews, according to Blass, Debrunner, and Funk, Luke's Greek is formulated most carefully, especially in the introductions (Lk 1:1-4; Acts 1:1-3) and in the Pauline speeches in Acts. While "Paul shows a good, sometimes select vernacular Greek," the Apocalypse of John, for instance, is totally outside this parameter; the latter is largely written semitically with Greek expressions (cf. Bl-Debr § 3.4).

3. Semitisms

The semitic coloration of many parts of the NT is explained by some scholars with the assumption that this is "translated Greek"; in other words, it is asserted that these texts were originally written in Hebrew or Aramaic and only later were they translated into Greek. It is undeniably true that Jesus spoke a semitic language and that the sayings he handed down were translated into Greek at some point in time. However, this original wording of Jesus' words can no longer be reconstructed unambiguously.

Examples: One can submit this to the test of attempting to translate the Greek words back into Aramaic.

(1) According to Lk 10:11 (Mt 10:7—parallel) Jesus announces: ἤγγικεν ἡ βασιλεία τοῦ θεοῦ, which is generally translated as, ". . . has come nigh." C. H. Dodd (*The Parables of the Kingdom*, 1935; revised ed., 1961) has pointed to the semitic character of this phrase, namely, that in the LXX the Hebrew נגע or the Aramaic מטא are rendered by ἐγγίζειν as well as by φθάνειν, hence the meaning of the words of Jesus cited above is equivalent with Lk 11:20—ἔφθασεν ἐφ' ὑμᾶς ἡ βασιλεία τοῦ θεοῦ (". . . has arrived among you"). Consequently, the conclusion must be drawn that Jesus himself taught that the kingdom of God was already realized in his person; the plain meaning was made unclear only in the Greek translation. Dodd's interpretation, however, is predicated upon the assumption that Lk 10:11 and 11:20 have the same Aramaic word behind them—a notion that lacks every kind of support. Even if the assumption were correct, the question of what that Aramaic word was, would still be unanswered. In this example, the method of retranslation yields no progress at all; instead, it merely points up the opinion of the person retranslating.

(2) What does the word ἐπιούσιος mean in the fourth request of the Lord's Prayer? Jerome explains in his commentary on Matthew that he had found the reading מחר, meaning "give us today tomorrow's (i.e., future) bread"; he claimed to have found this reading in the "Hebrew gospel" (no doubt he meant the Gospel of the Nazaraeans; cf. H-S I, 147). Yet, this reference likewise contributes nothing to the original meaning of the prayer uttered by Jesus, since the Gospel of the Nazaraeans did not retain the original language in which Jesus' words were spoken, but itself represents a Hebrew translation from the Greek.

(3) In Mt 7:6a the saying has been handed down, "Do not give dogs what is sacred; do not throw your pearls to pigs" (NIV). J. Jeremias, (*Abba*, 1966) has pointed out that the Aramaic קדישא can mean both "the sacred thing" and "the ring"; hence the original sense of this saying is "do not put a ring on a dog; do not fasten your pearls (to the neck of) pigs." One needs to ask here whether the retranslation contributes anything to the understanding of this saying.

It is quite plausible that individual sources used by NT writers were written in a semitic language. In the case of entire books, however, it is difficult to establish that they were not composed in Greek originally. At any rate, semitic coloring of the language does not prove the point of a translation since semitisms are also found, for instance, when a semitic author writes in Greek. For the purpose of exegesis, this observation means that one must always come to grips with the currently available— Greek—text. Admittedly, a proper understanding of numerous NT concepts requires us to know the semitic equivalents and their background because the meaning of such NT concepts as ἀλήθεια, for instance, is determined more by Jewish traditions than by those of Greek philosophy. Yet, the recourse to an assumed originally semitic composition of entire text pericopae is fraught with such serious uncertainties that it is generally wiser to forego the attempt. The problem becomes very plain, for instance, in Bultmann's endeavor to find an original semitic composition behind the Logos hymn in Jn 1:1–18 (see below, p. 99f.).

§ 4 The Text of the New Testament

Bibliography: *Sections 1 and 2*: K. and B. Aland, *The Text of the New Testament*, ET 1987, 3–180; B. M. Metzger, *A Textual Commentary on the Greek NT*, 1971; B. F. Westcott and F. J. A. Hort, *Introduction to the New Testament in the Original Greek*, reprint, 1988. *Section 3*: K. and B. Aland, *The Text of the NT*, 275–311; H. Zimmermann, *Neutestamentliche Methodenlehre*, [7]1982, 28–76.

Preliminary remark:

   This chapter contains references for practicing one's own text-critical work; most of all, however, it is to provide help in using commentaries. One should become capable of reconstructing and evaluating the text-critical arguments in commentaries. For in-depth information we refer to the above text by K. and B. Aland which is designed to aid especially in working with the *Novum Testamentum Graece* (Nestle[26]).

1. Transmission of the NT text

The NT books, like all literature of antiquity, are transmitted only in manuscript form. It is true that we do have available a very large number of NT manuscripts of variable age and quality. The task of *textual criticism* has as its goal the possible reconstruction of the original text (*Urtext*) by classifying and evaluating these manuscripts. Because this goal remains largely elusive, one searches (a) for the oldest transmitted manuscript and (b) for the "best" reading likely for the text.

The oldest known text is not necessarily also the best text; a later manuscript can plausibly be either based on a very good, but now lost copy (*Vorlage*) or represents a careful reconstruction of the original reading. Blanket judgments must by all means be avoided in textual criticism.

The first printed Greek NT was published by the humanist Erasmus of Rotterdam in 1516; however, his edition was based on inferior manuscripts and was, all things considered, a careless effort. A better attempt, already completed in 1514 (OT: 1517), was the "Complutensian Polyglot," yet it received the printing permission from Pope Leo X no earlier than 1520. Next to the Greek text it also contained the Latin text of the NT, the Vulgate (hence the name Polyglot, i.e., "multilingual"). Until the 18th century these text editions were commonly used as a "textus receptus." The first critical editions, that is, those which cite several variant readings in a given passage, were edited by J. A. Bengel (1734) and J. J. Wettstein (1751/52). Alongside the textual variants, Wettstein's reprint edition of 1962 offers a large number of parallels from Greek, Latin, and Jewish sources; thus it continues to be valuable for exegetical purposes.

The modern methodology in textual criticism emerged in the 19th century and was most vividly demonstrated in the NT editions of Tischendorf—his "Editio octava critica major" was published in 1869/72—Westcott-Hort, and von Soden. Citing the manuscript evidence available to them, they all offer their own reconstructed text with critical apparatus.

2. NT *manuscripts*

(1) Textual criticism has as its first task the approximate determination of the age of a manuscript. In this respect, palaeography has already led to fairly well-established results. The first part of the investigation pertains to the styles of writing, especially the difference between uncials (capital letters) and minuscules (cursive or small letters). In distinction to the ancient personal correspondence, literary works (books) were written in capital letters, placed side by side, without spaces to divide words, punctuation, or accents, that is, in the so-called scriptio continua. The common script of antiquity, cursive script, which uses small letters written continuously (similar to our modern handwriting), became dominant only from the 8th to 10th century on. Palaeography has also established a number of additional observations, making possible a more precise dating of manuscripts. On the basis of the shape of certain letters, of abbreviations for frequently repeated words (e.g., $\overline{\Theta\Sigma}$ for $\Theta E O \Sigma$, $\overline{\Pi N}$ for $\Pi NEYMA$, and $\overline{K\Sigma}$ for $KYPIO\Sigma$), and of writing materials used, the age of a manuscript can be determined with relative ease.

Dating a manuscript further requires consideration—at least in theory—of the form of the manuscript. Two forms were known in antiquity, the scroll and the codex. In the older form, the scroll, individual papyrus sheets were glued together and rolled up on a rod; the writing was in columns, allowing the text to be read by rolling the scroll from one end to the other. In contrast, a codex was made by folding leaves, stacking them in layers, and then binding them, a procedure still followed in making books today (cf. details in K. and B. Aland, *The Text of the* NT, 75f.). Since NT manuscripts, including the oldest known papyrus fragment, P^{52} (which dates back to the early second century), are available only in codex form, the form of the manuscript cannot serve as criterion in textual criticism of the NT.

Egyptian papyrus was the common writing material. Papyrus was relatively cheap, yet also susceptible to external conditions. Hence papyri have been discovered in arid Egypt almost without exception. Only later and with increasing affluence could churches afford expensive parchment; therefore, it is generally correct to say that papyri are very old.

Modern textual criticism identifies the papyri with the letter P and superscript numerals that refer not to the age of the papyri but to the listing sequence. Only small papyrus fragments were extant by 1930; since then numerous papyrus manuscripts have been discovered. Among them are the third-century Chester-Beatty papyri, P^{45} (Gospels), P^{46} (Pauline letters), and P^{47} (Apocalypse), as well as the exceptionally well-preserved Bodmer papyri of which P^{66} (ca. A.D. 200, containing the Gospel of John) and P^{75} (also from the early 3rd century, containing the Gospels of Luke and John) are particularly significant. The condition of these papyri, named after their owners, can easily be observed from the available photographs. Textual criticism has received new impetus as a result of these and other papyrus finds.

The bulk of extant manuscripts are of the parchment codex type. Traditionally the uncials that have been known for some time are identified with Latin and Greek capital letters, while Codex Sinaiticus carries the Hebrew letter ℵ (Aleph).

All of these uncial manuscripts, as well as those discovered since then, are also distinguished by consecutive numbers (with a preceding zero, i.e., 01, 02, etc., to differentiate them from the minuscules). A virtually comprehensive overview of the Greek NT manuscripts with their respective age and content is available in Nestle[26], pp. 684–711. These manuscripts are discussed in detail in K. and B. Aland, *The Text of the NT*, 83–102 (papyri), 102–125 (parchment uncials), 125–155 (minuscules). Also particularly helpful is the categorization of the manuscripts according to their quality (cf. overview, 155–160).

The four most important uncials originally contained the entire OT and NT; today, however, they show considerable lacunae in some instances.

ℵ=01 "Sinaiticus"—4th century; the name is derived from Tischendorf's discovery of the codex in a monastery at Sinai. In the old Huck-Lietzmann synopsis the symbol for Sinaiticus was not ℵ but S;

A=02 "Alexandrinus"—5th century;

B=03 "Vaticanus"—ca. A.D. 350;

C=04 "Codex Ephraemi rescriptus"—5th century.

Codex C is a "palimpsest": because parchment was costly, a text was often erased and another written over it—in this case the works of the Syrian Father Ephraem.

All other uncials contain only parts of the NT, either the Gospels, the letters of Paul, or others.

In the case of these partial manuscripts, the same letter symbol is sometimes used more than once. While the one Codex D contains the Gospels and Acts, the second Codex D contains the Pauline letters; both come from the 6th century. Therefore, one is well advised to remember the names or the numbers: D^e represents Codex Bezae (Cantabrigiensis) and is given the number 05; it used to belong to Theodor Beza, the reformer of Geneva, and is today preserved in Cambridge. D^p, assigned the number 06, stands for Codex Claromontanus because it had been kept in the monastery of Clermont, France for some time (it too used to belong to Beza).

The minuscule manuscripts are numbered continuously. The majority of them originated in the 10th/11th century (see above, p. 18) or later and are therefore considerably less significant than the papyri and uncials. Nevertheless, some of them deserve attention: the best known is minuscule 33, the "queen of the cursives," which has textual affinities with Codex Vaticanus; in the Pauline letters, minuscule 1739 (together with P^{46}) enjoys a certain key position. Two "families" of related minuscules are also noteworthy, namely, the "Lake family" and the "Ferrar family," so called in memory of their discoverers (Nestle abbreviates these as f^1 and f^{13}).

Next to the Greek manuscripts, the early versions are also important for textual criticism. Most significant are the Syriac, the Egyptian Coptic and the Latin versions (for more information see K. and B. Aland, *The Text of the NT*, 182–200; cf. with Greeven, *Synopsis*, pp. XIX–XXVI.) Finally, the Scripture citations in the church fathers yield additional material to be evaluated in textual criticism; one needs to be aware, of course, that the Fathers do not always cite verbatim and that the transmission of their writings is generally in worse condition than that of the NT (cf. K. and B. Aland, *Text of the NT*, 166–180).

The chapter division of the biblical texts was not made until the 13th century. Luther cites "the end of Matthew" (*Matthäi am Letzten*) without versification, which was introduced no earlier than 1551 by the Parisian printer Estienne.

Finally, some significance has to be attributed to the lectionaries, those collections of pericopae that were used in the communal Scripture readings.

A special problem is the text of Luke and the Pauline letters that originated with Marcion, known in church history as an archheretic. Marcion changed the texts extensively because, in his opinion, they had earlier been falsified in conformity with Judaism and therefore had to be purged and restored to their "original" meaning.

For instance, Marcion excised the entire fourth chapter of Romans (Abraham's righteousness by faith) and elsewhere he achieved radically different meanings of texts by making some minor changes in the wording of the text. Thus he removes the words καὶ θεοῦ πατρός from Gal 1:1, so that it now reads that it was not God who raised Jesus Christ from the dead, but that he raised himself. The motive for such changes was his tendency to distinguish sharply between the God of the OT as (imperfect) creator of an evil world and the "unknown" God of grace, revealed through Christ.

It would be wrong to dismiss summarily Marcion's readings as tendentious. His text originated very early (ca. 150) and for this reason requires attention. Yet, since we know him only through the writings of some of the church fathers (especially Tertullian), a reliable reconstruction is not possible.

Suggested exercise

Make a text-critical analysis of Eph 3:9. What intention can be observed in the variant readings?

(2) Investigations conducted by text critics have shown that many manuscripts are clearly related to one another; consequently, several "text families" can be observed:

(a) The most important group is the Egyptian or, more specifically, Alexandrian text and is supported primarily by the ancient uncials א, B, and C cited above, and, outside the Gospels, also by A.

It must be noted that a manuscript does not need to represent one text type consistently. The scribe could conceivably have used one text in the Gospels and quite another in the letters of Paul. In the four Gospels, Codex A belongs to the Byzantine text family.

The significance of the Alexandrian text type has been further increased through the discovered papyri (P[46,66,75] and, with certain exceptions, also P[45]).

According to the tradition of Jerome, this text type is the result of the methodical labor of a certain Hesychius; hence the occasional references to the "Hesychian" text (cf. the symbol 𝕳 in the earlier editions of the Nestle text).

(b) The second group is the so-called Western text and bears this name because it is supported, among others, by the Old Latin versions. The Western text type was widespread also in Syria and, somewhat earlier, in Egypt, as P[38,48] as well as some altered readings in P[46,66] indicate. While the designation "Western" has established itself, it is nevertheless an unfortunate one. The main witnesses of this text type are the codices Bezae Cantabrigiensis (D[e]) and Claromontanus (D[p]). These variants contain considerable peculiarities, and are, in places, of excessive length; in the synoptic Gospels the tendency to harmonize the text of the individual Gospels is quite apparent.

(c) The majority of manuscripts supports the "Byzantine" text type, also known as the "Majority Text" (*Reichstext*) or, more commonly, as the Koine text. This text type contains numerous changes, namely, attempts at improvement as well as additions. They are of inferior text-critical value; yet, generalizations are again to be avoided. In the earlier editions of Nestle the Koine text type was given the symbol $\mathfrak{K}$.

3. Methods of Textual Criticism

In order to begin the actual text-critical task, one begins with the external attestation of a reading, paying greater attention to the quality of the manuscripts than to their quantity. Primary attention must be given to the papyri and codices of the Alexandrian text type, which are generally preferred over later manuscripts, even if the latter outweigh the former in quantity. When the variants have been properly diagnosed and provisionally categorized, then follows the second step in the investigation, that of evaluating the "internal evidence." The reading assumed to be the earliest and most likely original must yield a reasonable meaning that corresponds with the context and must be able to explain the origin of other variants through textual changes. In the pursuit of this task, one needs to distinguish between (1) the unintentional scribal and reading errors and (2) the intentional changes in the text.

(1) Unintentional scribal and reading errors can arise because of optional reading possibilities of the uncial script (cf. p. 18) so that the recourse to the earliest manuscripts does not help at all. E.g., in Mk 10:40 we read, τὸ δὲ καθίσαι . . . ΔΟΥΝΑΙΑΛΛΟΙΣΗΤΟΙΜΑΣΤΑΙ. The last letters can rendered as "ἀλλ' οἷς ἡτοίμασται," that is, "for whom it is meant" (with the completion "they will be given"); this is the rendering given in most NT editions and, correspondingly, the Vulgate translated "sed quibus paratum est." But those letters can also be rendered as "ἄλλοις ἡτοίμασται," "it is meant for others"; for instance, the Syriac version (syr^s) opted for this reading, as did E. Klostermann (*Mark*, 108). The final decision, in this case, rests not with the external evidence of the uncial manuscripts which is identical in both cases, but with the meaning of the text.

Some problems are directly related to pronunciation at the time Koine Greek was spoken: The reading ἔχωμεν in Rom 5:1 is preferred by most; yet it is important to remember that o and ω were pronounced identically in Koine, so that a copyist could not rely on sound differences between the two words. The final decision can only be made on the basis of the context of Paul's theology, which makes it plausible that the original reading did not say ἔχωμεν ("we might have peace with God") but instead said ἔχομεν ("we have peace"). Likewise the phenomenon of itacism in Koine Greek could lead to writing errors: εἶδε, ἴδε, and ἤδη were pronounced virtually identically and therefore were easily confused. A frequent cause of unintentional errors was the accidental omission (haplography) or the accidental duplication (dittography) of words or entire parts of a sentence. Thus only the contextual meaning can answer the question of whether 1 Thes 2:7 should read ἐγενήθημεν ἤπιοι ("we were gentle"), or whether this should be considered haplography and originally read ἐγενήθημεν νήπιοι ("we were foolish"). If the former possibility is taken to be original, the assumption would have to be made that the second reading originated as a result of dittography. Not infrequently one encounters a homoeoteleuton (identical endings of words and lines of text) which occasionally leads to the omission of a word or even of entire lines. This is the reason why some manuscripts of Matthew omit an entire verse, namely 12:47, because both v 46 and v 47 end with the identical word λαλῆσαι. This passage also supports the earlier argument that generalizations concerning the value of individual manuscripts easily leads to erroneous conclusions. Mt 12:47 is not extant in Vaticanus, nor in the original hand of Sinaiticus, whereas the verse is handed down in the Byzantine, as well as in the Western texts—clearly the original reading. A similar case can be made with regards to Jn 21:25; the original hand of Codex ℵ does not contain this verse, evidently on account of its proximity to Jn 20:30.

(2) Of greater interest are the intentional changes that a scribe made. For instance, in the synoptic texts there is an acute tendency to harmonize the Gospels; compare, for instance, the manuscript evidence in Mk 8:31; 9:31; 10:34 with the respective parallels in Mt and Lk. In this case, the best reading is probably the one with the least correspondence between the parallel texts. Frequently a text is also completed with supplemental material from the parallel accounts, especially from Mt. The textual transmission of the Lord's Prayer in Lk (11:2–4), compared to that found in Mt (6:7–13) is a good example; the shorter tradition in the Lukan manuscripts has obviously been supplemented with the Matthean text.

Two rules of thumb are worth remembering: (1) The shorter reading is generally to be preferred, since copyists tended to add to rather than subtract from the text (formula: "lectio brevior potior"). Example: The doxology in the Lord's Prayer would not likely have been eliminated had it belonged to the prayer from the beginning; rather, since it was not extant in the original text, it was added subsequently because of its liturgical use. The text-critical conclusion is that the reading without the doxology is the better one. (2) Obscure text statements were clarified or adjusted to conform to the changed dogmatic condition. Thus the statement of Jn 7:39 ("the Spirit was not yet") was changed to conform to the trinitarian theology, "the Holy Spirit was not yet given." Here the rule of "lectio difficilior" is to be applied, namely, that the more difficult, offensive text is generally to be preferred, as long as it is not "difficult" to the point of being absurd. J. A. Bengel, therefore, articulated it more accurately: proclivi praestat ardua.

The least feasible text-critical expedient is conjecture. Only when no extant manuscript reading yields a sensible meaning may one cautiously attempt to determine what the original text might have said. In NT exegesis today, conjectures are postulated only in the rarest of cases, as in Acts 4:25, for instance, where no extant reading yields a reasonable meaning.

Practice example: Text-critical evaluation of Mk 1:4.

The text-critical task is executed in three steps: (1) categorization of the manuscripts into the respective text families; (2) evaluation of the individual readings; (3) the actual text-critical assessment with its goal of reconstructing the history of the text.

(1) The manuscript evidence (following Nestle[26]):

I. Codex B (Vaticanus), minuscule 33, a few other Greek witnesses, as well as some Bohairic (a Coptic dialect) manuscripts support the reading: ἐγένετο Ἰωάννης ὁ βαπτίζων ἐν τῇ ἐρήμῳ κηρύσσων βάπτισμα.

II. Codex ℵ (Sinaiticus), L and Δ, as well as a few other Greek witnesses, plus most of the Bohairic manuscripts support the reading: ἐγένετο Ἰωάννης ὁ βαπτίζων ἐν τῇ ἐρήμῳ καὶ κηρύσσων βάπτισμα.

III. Codices A (Alexandrinus) and W (Freerianus), the minuscule families f¹ and f¹³, the "Majority Text" 𝔐 (i.e., codices K [017], P [024], [036], minuscules 565, 1010, 1241, 1424, plus the majority of the remaining minuscules), a Syriac version, and apparently also the Sahidic (Coptic dialect) tradition attest to the reading: ἐγένετο Ἰωάννης βαπτίζων ἐν τῇ ἐρήμῳ καὶ κηρύσσων βάπτισμα.

Decoding the sigla 𝔐 is somewhat complicated: On p. 50* (in Nestle[26]) one finds a listing of the manuscripts which 51 generally are included in 𝔐 and are cited specifically only when they differ from 𝔐. The application of the procedure given on p. 47* leads to the following observation: Codex Δ (037) and minuscules 28, 33, 700 are cited under different variant readings; codices N (022) and Q (026) do not contain Mk 1:4 (cf. overview, p. 684ff.); what remains is the uncials cited above and the minuscules listed on p. 711. In the earlier printings of Nestle[26] uncial 0133 was erroneously cited as a "consistent witness."

VI. Codices D (Bezae, Cantabrigiensis) and Θ (Koridethi), minuscules 28 and 700, the Old Latin version in part (plus the Vulgate), and the Syriac Peshitta attest to the reading: ἐγένετο Ἰωάννης ἐν τῇ ἐρήμῳ βαπτίζων καὶ κηρύσσων βάπτισμα.

(Vulgate: Fuit Ioannes in deserto baptizans et praedicans baptismum).

(2) Evaluation: Variant I is quantitatively weak, but fairly well attested qualitatively, since B is the main witness of the Egyptian text type. Variant II is well attested, both quantitatively and qualitatively, with all the uncials cited belonging to the Egyptian text type. Variant III has the support of the bulk of the witnesses; however, these are largely of the Byzantine text type (Codex A, minuscules) and of the "Western" texts. Variant

IV is attested by the main witness each of the "Western" (see p. 21 above) and of the "Caesarean" text; caution needs to be exercised especially with regards to D, but in view of the antiquity of this text type, originality cannot be excluded a priori. Conclusion: the external evidence does not permit a definitive text-critical evaluation.

(3) We must endeavor, therefore, to reconstruct the history of the text, in order to find the earliest possible wording from which all other variants can be derived.

(a) We begin with the hypothetical assumption that variant III, with its overall strongest quantitative attestation, was the original reading (so Greeven in his *Synopsis*). Then we ask whether the rise of the other variants can be explained under this assumption. This is certainly the case with variant IV; D and the other witnesses have smoothed out the text by rearranging the word order. It cannot be explained, however, why the writers of variants I and II inserted the article ὁ in front of the participle βαπτίζων, especially since the article disturbs the grammatical construction.

(b) Therefore, we assume the priority of variant II; ℵ is an excellent manuscript and the unusual title ὁ βαπτίζων is surely original, especially since ℵ agrees with B. Apart from this, variant II (ὁ βαπτίζων . . . καὶ κηρ.) is "more difficult" than variant I which lacks καί; but since the awkward sequence of a finite verb with a participle closed by καί is otherwise foreign to Mark, one may have to decide against the rule of "lectio difficilior" (contrary to Nestle[26]).

(c) One needs to examine whether the history of the text can be explained by the assumption that variant I offers the earliest form of the text (so Nestle[25]). In this case, the scribe of variant II would have combined the two participles βαπτίζων and κηρύσσων, while forgetting to eliminate the awkward article before βαπτίζων. But it is also conceivable that variant III is derived directly from variant I and that variant II represents a mixture of both. In any case, variant IV is the most recent reading.

Conclusion: The textual history of Mk 1:4 may best be explained with the assumption that the earliest extant reading is preserved in Vaticanus.

Suggested exercises:

1. Read a paragraph in an uncial text available on photographic prints (numerous illustrations in K. and B. Aland, *The Text of the NT*, 1987), or on facsimiles (cf. the edition of the Bodmer papyri Bibliotheca Bodmeriana, 1956ff.).

2. Read Jn 11:31–37 in P[66] (Bodmer II, 111), together with the explanations by H. Zimmermann (see bibliography), 84–88.

3. Study the critical apparatus in Nestle, pp. 170f. (Lk 5:39–6:9), observing especially the types of harmonizations (particularly in codex D) and additions.

4. Do a text-critical analysis of Mk 1:1.

5. For more extensive reading, consult H. Zimmermann (see bibliography), 59ff.

6. Instructive is also the material of B. Aland, "Neutestamentliche Textkritik heute," *VF* 21 (2/1976) 3–22.

§ 5 Literary Genres of the NT

Bibliography: *Section 1*: W. Schneemelcher, "Gospel," in H-S I, 71–81; C. H. Talbert, *Literary Patterns, Theological Themes and the Genre of Luke–Acts*, SBLMS 20, 1974. *Section 2*: W. G. Doty, *Letters in Primitive Christianity*, 1973; P. Wendland, *Die urchristlichen Literaturformen*, HNT 1/3, 1912; O. Roller, *Das Formular der paulinischen Briefe*, BWANT IV/6, 1933; the article on "Epistolographie," in: *Der Kleine Pauly II*, 1967, 324–327. *Section 3*: M. Dibelius, *Aufsätze zur Apg*, FRLANT 60, [5]1968 (esp. the article on "Der erste christliche Historiker," 108–119). *Section 4*: Ph. Vielhauer, "Apocalyptic," in H-S II, 579–601.

Preliminary remark:

The NT writings can be divided into four literary types (*Gattungen*):

1. The genre of "gospel"
2. The genre of "letter"
3. The genre of "historical monograph"
4. The genre of "apocalypse"

Except for the gospel genre, these literary types were not created by the NT writers but were already available to them and served the early church in its theological endeavor.

1. Gospel

The term εὐαγγέλιον did not initially describe a particular literary type but signified the good news of salvation itself (e.g., Gal 1:11; the phrase ἀρχὴ τοῦ εὐαγγελίου in Mk 1:1 probably has in mind the "disclosure of the message" of Jesus Christ). The concept εὐαγγέλιον became the designation of a literary genre since the written Gospels contain the accounts of the events of salvation. According to Justin Martyr, the writings concerning Jesus are called εὐαγγέλιον. The former meaning, however, continued to persist, for the manuscripts consistently witness to the εὐαγγέλιον κατὰ Μάρκον ("Gospel *according to* Mark") and not to "the Gospel *of* Mark" etc.

There are no parallels to the NT literary type "Gospel." A comparison with certain literary types of antiquity, such as the biography and the historical monograph, demonstrates this. The substantial difference to the classical biography, such as that of Plutarch or Suetonius, is made clear especially in the Gospel of Mark: The person of the author cannot be recognized and the action of the "hero," namely of Jesus of Nazareth, is not presented biographically. Apparently the issue is not at all a continuous description of the life of Jesus or a presentation of his character; instead, the primary focal point is the work of Jesus as the revealer sent by God, as seen in his deeds, teaching, and passion. Events are of interest only from this vantage point. Literary demands come into vogue gradually (at best), beginning with Luke, particularly as the dedication of Lk 1:1-4 shows. He endeavors a more emphatically biographical development and thus precedes his Gospel with a series of infancy narratives (Lk 1-2)—perhaps even adding this to his Gospel later (see below). Probably the closest parallel to the gospel genre is provided in the traditions of the sayings and experiences of the rabbis (cf. the Mishnah tractate *Aboth*, i.e., "Fathers"), as well as in the popular Greek stories of the deeds of famous men, called their πράξεις. Even so, the Gospels represent a genre all their own because they unfold the tradition of Jesus directly from the viewpoint of faith in him as the redeemer; hence it was the intention of the respective writers that these Gospels be understood not only as narrative, but at the same time and especially as proclamation. This point is made quite lucid in Jn 20:31. Conversely, of course, the Gospels also contain a certain biographical framework: the tension increases from Jesus' baptism in Jordan (in Matthew and Luke even from the announcement of Jesus' birth) to the point of his crucifixion in Jerusalem. Nevertheless, the passion and death of Jesus are not primarily the biographical finale, but first of all the theological goal of their presentation. There is not even a trace of a development of the self-consciousness and character of Jesus.

Suggested exercises:

1. Read A. Dihle, "Die Evangelien und die biographische Tradition der Antike," *ZThK* 80, 1983, 33–49.

2. Read one of the apocryphal gospels, e.g., the "Proto-Gospel of James" or the "Gospel of Nicodemus" (H-S I, 370ff., 444ff.). A comparison with the NT ("canonical") Gospels shows clearly the extent to which apocryphal gospels have been permeated with fictional and, to a degree, with fantastic and bizarre traits, so that one can hardly address these in terms of the genre of "gospel" as described above.

2. Letter

(1) A letter in antiquity conspicuously distinguished itself in its form from the modern letter. At its beginning one finds the sender's name, followed by that of the recipient, and then the greeting: ᾿Απίων ᾿Επιμάχω τῶι πατρὶ καὶ κυρίω πλεῖστα χαίρειν (A. Deissmann, *Light from the An-*

ͨ̃ient East, 179f.). Next one may find an appeal to the gods in terms of gratitude or of a request for the welfare of the recipient: καὶ διὰ πάντω[ν] εὔχομαί σαι ὑγειαίνειν. Τὸ προσκύνημά σου [ποι]ῶ κατ' αἰκάστην ἡμαί-ραν παρὰ τῷ κυρίῳ [Σερ]άπειδει (Deissmann, 187). At the end of the let-ter is the conveyance of greetings: [ἀ]σπάζεταί σε ἡ σύμβιός [μου Α]ὐ-φιδία καὶ [Μ]άξιμος [ὁ υἱός μ]ου κτλ. (Deissmann, 184).

(2) In terms of the form of the prescript, the Greek letter must be clearly distinguished from the oriental one: the Greek prescript is based on the term χαίρειν and represents a single clause or phrase (compare the ex-ample cited above). In the NT it can be found in Acts 15:23, 23:26, Jas 1:1 and corresponds to the Latin form of greeting "salutem (dicit)." The orien-tal form of greeting has two parts; here the sentence structure is inter-rupted with the greeting expressed in direct speech. Dan 4:1 (following Theodotion, not the LXX) says: Ναβουχοδονοσορ ὁ βασιλεὺς πᾶσι τοῖς λαοῖς, φυλαῖς καὶ γλώσσαις τοῖς οἰκοῦσιν ἐν πάσῃ τῇ γῇ Εἰρήνη ὑμῖν πληθυνθείη (for the translation of these citations, see p. 380).

Paul consistently uses the oriental form and most of the early Chris-tian literature follows his example. It is important to know this pattern because it already yields some preliminary perspectives important in exe-gesis. First one needs to isolate the broad structure (sender—recipient—greeting), then one analyzes the complementary details surrounding the broad structure.

(a) The sender, in this case Paul, almost invariably adds to his name a reference to his official status, here a reference to his apostleship: Παῦλος ἀπόστολος. In most cases, this reference is then further explained. In the letter to the Galatians, for example, Paul points to the origin of his po-sition because his apostleship is being attacked in Galatia. Conversely, the designation ἀπόστολος does not occur in Philippians, since Paul does not have to fear any such misunderstanding in Philippi. An official func-tion is also expressed by the term δοῦλος; Paul's self-description as "servant" of God corresponds with that of OT men of God (the concept "his servants the prophets" is a standard expression in the Qumran writ-ings). The fact that Paul wrote to the churches in Rome, Corinth, and other cities not as a private citizen but in the exercise of his calling is under-scored by the truly private letter to Philemon in which the terms ἀπόστολος and δοῦλος do not occur (δέσμιος refers to the situation of his imprisonment and is not to be construed as a title). The official pur-pose of the major letters is further emphasized by the naming of other co-senders who are not, however, co-writers, since Paul writes mostly in the first person singular. But even where Paul employs the plural form, he uses it stylistically, meaning himself (cf. 2 Cor 10, esp. vv 7–16).

(b) The recipients are addressed as Christian communities, but here, too, nuances show up whose intent agrees with the broader content of the letter. Whereas in the polemical letter to the Galatians, for example, Paul considers it sufficient to address them as ταῖς ἐκκλησίαις τῆς Γαλατίας, in 1 Corinthians the address is quite elaborate.

(c) The basis of the greeting must be sought in the Jewish שלום. In Jewish letters it can be expanded as well; for instance 2 Bar 78:2 has "mercy and peace be unto you" (cf. 1 Tim 1:2). Except in 1 Thes, Paul consistently writes χάρις ὑμῖν καὶ εἰρήνη ἀπὸ θεοῦ πατρὸς ἡμῶν καὶ κυρίου Ἰησοῦ Χρ. Hence he alludes to the normal verb χαίρω and at the same time, even in the introductory lines of his letters, he brings to bear the concept of χάρις, so vital to his theology.

The introductory greeting should be translated "from God our father, and from the Lord," and not "from God, the father of the Lord Jesus Christ, and ours," although the latter is not factually incorrect (cf. 2 Cor 1:3). Paul's intent in this greeting is not to stress that God is the father of Jesus Christ, but rather that grace and peace come from both God and Christ, as 1 Thes 1:1 shows.

Another foundational aspect is found in Galatians where Paul is concerned with the question whether Christ might have "died in vain" (2:21). Even at the outset he refers to this problem by enlarging the greeting christologically (1:4) and by adding a doxology (1:5).

(d) A further routine component of Pauline letters, following the initial greeting, is the proem, formulated either as thanksgiving or as praise to God. The characteristic key terms are εὐχαριστέω and—in Paul only in 2 Cor—εὐλογέω. Both expressions are taken from the Jewish cultic language, and the proems in general show their indebtedness to the Jewish style of liturgy. The proem is sometimes clearly delineated (1 Cor 1:4–9) and at other times it filters into the rest of the letter (e.g., 1 Thes). An exception to this can be observed in Ephesians which contains two pericopae of thanksgiving—apparently as a result of an intensified repetition of the Pauline style of letter writing, one using the verb εὐλογέω and the other εὐχαριστέω. Typically, the exception in the opposite direction, again, is Galatians where no thanksgiving at all is found; in view of the Galatian situation, there is, for Paul, no room for thanksgiving.

(e) At the end of the letter, Paul expresses good wishes, generally preceded by more greetings. The peculiarity of Galatians is underscored once again by the absence of these final greetings. Among the typical concluding phrases one finds for instance, ὁ δὲ θεὸς τῆς εἰρήνης μετὰ πάντων ὑμῶν (Rom 15:33; cf. 16:20; 1 Cor 16:24), or λοιπὸν ἀδελφοὶ χαίρετε (2 Cor 13:11; Phil 3:1); occasionally a summons to prayer also occurs at the end of a letter (Rom 15:30; Phil 4:6).

Suggested exercises:

1. Is there evidence for considering Rom 15:33 originally to have been a conclusion to the letter?

2. Analyze the ending of 1 Thes.

(3) The fixed forms of the letter described above apply to the private letter as well as to the formal letter, which was intended for publication to start with, and which, following Deissmann's suggestion, is also called "epistle." These epistles were by no means a rarity in antiquity. The LXX has a fictitious letter that in reality is a didactic writing (a polemic against idols), namely the Epistula Jeremiae, allegedly written to the Jews exiled in Babylon but in reality written sometime between the fourth and the second century B.C. This letter must in no way be confused with the (genuine?) letter of the prophet Jeremiah found in Jer 29:4ff. In Rome, Seneca drew up philosophical essays in letter form around A.D. 60. So-called letters sometimes constitute a special stylistic device and are inserted into more comprehensive historical works, such as the Maccabees (1 Macc 10:24ff.; 12:5ff.; 2 Macc 1f.) or the Lukan history of Acts (15:23ff.; 23:25ff.). In the interpretation of the Pauline letters, and even more in order to understand his apostleship, it is not unimportant how one views these writings, either as private letters or as epistles. For a long time they were read primarily as formal doctrinal writings, especially Romans. Then the personal-private character was recognized, which is not really missing in Romans (Rom 9:1-5), so that Paul's letters came to be understood as documents concerning his person, piety, and personal faith. Thus A. Deissmann discovered in 2 Corinthians "all the varied emotions that succeeded and encountered one another in his capacious soul," and "deep contrition and thankfulness towards God, the reformer's wrath, irony and trenchant candor towards the vicious" (*Light from the Ancient East*, 237). Hence he claimed that the exegesis of the letters of Paul had to become a "psychological reproduction," since his letters did not point up a theological system but that their uniqueness was to be found in their "non-systematic piety" (241). But this one-sided argument ignores the theological character of Paul's letters. He does not inform about his own personhood; rather he establishes, in thesis or polemic, his own theological position as an apostle.

Suggested exercise

Read ancient letters, reproduced photographically, with text and translation in A. Deissmann, *Light from the Ancient East*. Additional translations of ancient (private) letters are found in Barrett, 38ff.; L-G II, 61ff.

3. Historical monograph

The literary genre known as πράξεις (Acts), in which loosely sequenced events and deeds of famous men are recounted, is represented in the NT exclusively by the Acts of the Apostles. The latter, however, does not fully correspond with the literary works belonging to the genre of πράξεις, for the specific historical and theological views of the author shape not only the content, but also the form of the writing. In terms of style, Luke demonstrates a masterful command of the "dramatic episode" ("*dramatischer Episodenstil*," Haenchen) in the presentation of the sequence of events, just as it can be found in historical works and novels contemporary with Luke. The individual events are collected into a meaningful and reasonable account, so much so that a unified action with a specific goal can be discerned—in spite of the different kinds of materials Luke used.

Likewise comparable with ancient historiography is the insertion of speeches in Acts. Yet, the character of these speeches is unlike that known in Greek historiography; rather, in Acts the theological intention is prominent. Biographical elements are almost entirely absent. Instead, the speeches are shaped as proclamation of the gospel.

Suggested reading:

For the literary, theological, and historical significance of Acts, see E. Haenchen, *The Acts of the Apostles*, ET 1971, 81–99.

4. *Apocalypse*

This genre likewise occurs only once in the NT, in the Revelation of John. Originally this was a Jewish literary genre; the oldest such work is the book of Daniel. Apocalyptic literature blossomed especially in the NT era.

Jewish apocalypses are altogether pseudepigraphical, i.e., they are based on the fictitious notion that they were written by famous people of antiquity, such as Daniel, Ezra, Enoch, and Baruch. They claim to have received "revelations" from God, in other words, insights into the future, up until the end of the world. In reality, however, the authors of apocalyptic writings present past events in the form of earlier prophecy and then add a "genuine" prophecy that usually refers to the actual situation. For example, at the end of the book of Daniel one finds a prophecy about the end of King Antiochus IV; since the prediction of Dan 11:40ff. did not come to pass, the book must have been written shortly before the events described (a Syrian military campaign against Egypt). The assumption can be made, therefore, that the book of Daniel was written prior to the death of Antiochus, ca. 165 B.C.

The literary genre of the apocalypse is an expression of a particular understanding of history. The apocalyptic writer begins with the idea that history proceeds according to a plan determined by God in times past. This plan can be read out of past events and makes possible the knowledge of the present time. An example of such a plan is found in the apocalypse of the ten weeks in Ethiopic Enoch 93; 91:12–17. In the apocalypse,

the present is understood as "the last times" in which tribulation intensifies and the hardships of the faithful escalate. Nevertheless, in the end
there is salvation for those who are now suffering. It is the purpose of
the "revelations" to admonish God's people to remain faithful.

These writers endeavor to delineate specific time periods in history past, in
order to "calculate" the dates of eschatological events. In contrast to the OT
understanding of history, the apocalyptic writer does not reckon with the
possibility of God's contingent acts in history. The world view of apocalypticism is analogous to the writer's historical consciousness that the world
is abandoned to evil powers. Mythical visions, speculation with numbers,
and astrology are to aid in understanding and coping with the present.

With regards to the content and understanding of the NT Apocalypse of John,
which to some degree departs drastically from the Jewish apocalypses described
above, see § 44.

Suggested exercises:

1. Read Daniel and the apocryphal 4 Ezra (English text in J. H. Charlesworth,
ed., *The OT Pseudepigrapha*, 2 vols., 1984).

2. Compare the mythical animals described in Daniel and in the Revelation of
John: Who is meant? What ways did the authors choose in presenting them? (Tools:
Commentaries in the NTD, ATD, and ICC).

§ 6 Exegetical Methods

Bibliography: G. D. Fee, *New Testament Exegesis. A Handbook for Students and Pas-
tors*, 1983; H. Zimmermann, *Neutestamentliche Methodenlehre. Darstellung der his-
torisch-kritischen Methode*, [7]1982.

1. Scholarly doubt

The general starting point for the contemporary exegetical work in the
NT is the scholarly doubt by which historical investigation questions the
ancient ecclesiastical tradition regarding the Bible. (1) Were the NT books
in fact written by the men in whose name they have been handed down?
(2) Does the presentation, especially of the words and deeds of Jesus,
align with historical reality; in other words, should the Gospels be understood as reminiscences of eyewitnesses of the story of Jesus?

(1) There are certain writings in the NT in which the author mentions
his name explicitly, such as the letters of Paul, James, Peter, or of Jude.
If these are to be considered historically reliable statements, all of these
letters would have to come from roughly the same time (between A.D.

40 and 70). One gets the impression, however, that these individual letters are predicated upon very divergent church situations. Besides, the careful reader will notice that some of Paul's letters, in comparison with others of the same writer, reflect peculiarities in language, thought, and in the objective situation of the letter. Is there justification, therefore, for regarding some, or possibly even all of these letters as pseudonymous?

Some writings contain no name of an author at all, such as the four Gospels and Hebrews. In this case one needs to ask whether the church traditions that attribute these writings to John, Mark, etc., contain pertinent observations or whether these traditions are mere fiction. At any rate, what can be known about the writers of the Gospels if we do not even know their names?

Scholarly investigation harbors doubts concerning the authorship of

(a) a number of Pauline letters (Pastoral letters, Colossians, Ephesians, 2 Thessalonians);

(b) all seven "catholic" letters (James, Jude, Johannine letters, Petrine letters)—they are given this designation because they apparently are addressed to the entire church (καθολικὴ ἐκκλησία), rather than to specific churches or individuals;

(c) all of the Gospels, as well as Acts;

(d) the Revelation of John.

(e) The writer of Hebrews is totally unknown. Church tradition attributes it to Paul, a position already questioned by Origen on the basis of its literary style. Indeed, the assumption of the Pauline tradition lacks any evidence (see below, § 40).

Result: It is quite possible that, apart from Paul, we do not know a single NT author by name.

(2) The four Gospels transmit words and deeds of Jesus whose presentation cannot be harmonized. In addition, we are told several incidents which, in the very nature of things, cannot have been experienced by immediate witnesses, such as Jesus' trial before Pilate or his prayer in Gethsemane. Should one then conclude that at least in such instances the author was carried away by his imagination? Can the differences between the Gospels be traced back to the different subjective recollection of the authors? The same question needs to be raised with regards to the accounts in the Acts of the Apostles. Did Luke write accurate historical accounts of the history of the early church, based on authentic source material; or is his account more like a novel, so that no historical knowledge can be drawn from it?

Questions such as these belong to the *methodological principles* characteristic not only for working with NT texts, but with all literary witnesses of antiquity.

2. *Advice for specific historical-critical problems*

I. Examples of inquiry into the authorship of a NT writing.

(1) Pastoral letters:

Both letters to Timothy and the letter to Titus were written by Paul, according to their own witness. What possibilities do we have to test the reliability of such witness? The following questions need to be posed and must be answered satisfactorily:

(a) Did the ancient church anywhere either doubt or even contest the Pauline authorship?

(b) Do the Pastoral letters parallel theologically the other letters of Paul? Are terms and concepts evident which are otherwise not found in Paul at all, at least not in his earlier letters? Is the meaning of terms found in both instances the same or are there certain shifts in meaning?

(c) Does the presupposed self-understanding of Paul in the Pastoral letters correspond with that found in the other Pauline letters?

(d) Can the situation in the life of Paul which is described in the Pastoral letters, be verified?

(2) Colossians and Ephesians:

According to Col 1:1 and Eph 1:1, both of these letters have also been written by Paul. Questions (a) and (d), posed under the Pastoral letters, apply here as well with even sharper distinctions:

(a) Does the language, that is sentence structure and conceptuality, correspond with that of the other letters?

(b) Are the theological concepts, as in ecclesiology, for instance, identical? In particular, is the notion of Christ as the "head" of his body, the church, that found in the ecclesiology of the other Pauline letters?

(c) What is the situation in the history of the church and of theology? In Eph 2:20 apostles and prophets are viewed as a closed group: Is this to be regarded as Paul's view into the future, or as a retrospective glance, and therefore as the perspective of a "forger"?

(3) 2 Peter:

The situation here is different from that described under (1) and (2) in that we possess only 1 Peter next to the second letter, leaving us with considerably less suitable material for comparison. An analysis is further complicated by the fact that many scholars question the genuineness of 1 Peter. At any rate, the following questions pertain to 2 Peter:

(a) If this were indeed a letter of the disciple Simon Peter, when would it have to have been written? Is the theological-historical situation presupposed in this letter (cf. e.g., 3:14ff.) even conceivable during Peter's lifetime?

(b) How can the unique parallelism between 2 Peter and Jude be explained?

Since we present only the methodological principle of scholarly doubt in this part of § 6, and we are not seeking to answer the theological and historical questions regarding the content, it is sufficient here to raise the questions as such. This does not mean that an attempt at finding appropriate answers could not already be made at this point, especially keeping the usefulness in mind of the respective §§ in Part Three (especially §§ 31–33, 43).

II. The examples cited above pertained to the fundamental questions regarding complete NT writings. In the following we shall present some examples of individual questions concerning specific text passages, endeavoring to answer them by means of the critical methods.

(1) Acts 17:22. Paul opens his speech on the Aereopagus with an endorsement of the δεισιδαιμονία of the Athenians. What does that mean essentially? The term has two meanings: on the one hand it can mean "religion, fear of God," on the other, "superstition." Bauer's lexicon shows that both meanings are supported in the realm of the Greek language. The real question is, which of the two meanings is more pertinent to the issue of the text: Does Paul express a *captatio benevolentiae*, that is, does he emphasize, "you are pious?" Or does he chide the Athenians as superstitious, perhaps because of their idolatry?

In the attempt of an answer, one should not begin by asking what *Paul* could have meant; rather, at least provisionally, one must begin by asking what the *writer* of Acts ("Luke") allows Paul to say. Even if Paul in fact did speak on the Areopagus in Athens, it should be clear that Acts 17 does not present a verbatim account of that speech. In order to understand the speech correctly, therefore, one must ask about its form and purpose in the present context. Thus it becomes clear that "Paul" relates positively to a certain Athenian altar inscription; therefore, he attests to the Athenians' subjective honesty in their religious activity. Hence, in Acts 17:22, δεισιδαίμων does not mean "superstitious," but "pious, religious," in a positive sense.

(2) Acts 18:13. The Jews accuse Paul before Gallio, the Roman proconsul of Achaia, of having transgressed against "the law." Against what law? Against the Jewish (OT), or against the Roman (the state) law? If the accusation relates to the Jewish law, one needs to ask why the Roman proconsul even bothered with it. If it relates to the Roman law, Gallio's refusal to intervene is incomprehensible. The solution to this problem emerges when, as in the first example above, the literary character of the text is considered. In no way is the question allowed to be, "What did the Jews mean?" but rather, "What did Luke have them say?" Then it becomes evident that the accusation of the Jews was deliberately ambiguous: Gallio was supposed to take action against Paul, although the controversy over the law had nothing to do with him.

(3) Jesus' sermon in Nazareth (Mk 6:1–6; Mt 13:54–58; Lk 4:16–30) is presented with much greater precision by Luke than by Mark and Matthew. Some exegetes conclude from this that in this case Luke was historically more reliable and gave a better account than the two other evangelists. In view of this argument, it is good to remember an observation known as the "Karl May rule" (a German novelist of American Indian culture, transl.), i.e., that an accurate description of the milieu and/or the broad rendition of verbatim speech proves nothing at all relative to the historicity or "exactness" of the events told.

3. *Practical exercises in exegesis*

(1) General remarks:

(a) It is best to begin with a provisional translation by using a lexicon and a grammar. At the same time it should be observed whether the critical apparatus notes substantial variant readings from the printed text, with the possibility of making certain decisions against the text proposed by the editors. Then one attempts to retrace the actions or the train of thought. What is the scene? What persons emerge? What is the aim of the action? En route to that goal, are there gaps and breaks, or is everything constructed logically?

(b) Prior to the exegesis proper it is essential to be clear about one's own inquiry: What do I really want to learn? What do I expect the text to say? Am I hoping to gain information about the history, that is, about the life of Jesus? In view of the miracle accounts, am I eager to learn something about belief in miracles in antiquity in general, or specifically about belief in miracles in a Christian context? Or am I inquiring less about the historical reality than about the portrayal of Jesus or about the understanding of faith on the part of the respective evangelist?

These questions do not have to be treated as alternatives; as guiding perspectives they may all be significant at the same time. It is important, though, to formulate the questions in such a way that in the answers the text is elucidated and thus some primary exegetical results can be formulated. For instance, What does the narrative of the birth of Jesus in Lk 2 look like, if I seek to understand it as a historical account? What does the text represent if I leave the question of historicity open?

(c) Only when these questions have been cleared up, should other bibliographic sources be consulted: What kinds of questions are contained in the commentaries? What historical and theological information do they offer? Where and for what reasons do they contradict my results thus far?

(2) Examples:

(a) Exegesis of a synoptic text (Mk 1:21–28)

(i) Following the avenue recommended above, we begin with the translation, textual criticism, and grammatical explanation.

21 And they are entering Capernaum.	Historical present. The Old Syriac version (Sinaitic) omits this sentence. Can this reading claim originality?
And immediately on the Sabbath	Why does the Greek text have the plural τοῖς σάββασιν?
he went into the synagogue and taught.	Change of tense (now imperfect). ℵ and other Alexandrian witnesses do not have εἰσελθών and offer a different word order. Could this be original? Can the εἰς in Mark mean "in" in the sense of ἐν? Tool: Concordance.
22 The people were astonished at his teaching; for he taught them as one who had authority, and not as the scribes.	ἦν διδάσκων is a popular phrase. On the periphrastic construction, see Bl-Debr. §§ 352–356.
23 And immediately there was in their synagogue	The words εὐθύς and αὐτῶν are not found in some manuscripts (see the apparatus in Aland's *Synopsis*). Were they missing originally? Which reading is better stylistically? What result does a comparison with the Lukan parallel yield?
a man	For the translation of ἄνθρωπος consult Bauer's lexicon.
with an unclean spirit and he cried out,	ἐν="with": Bl-Debr. § 198.2. What does Luke's text show here?
24 saying, "What do you want with us, Jesus, you Nazarene? Have you come to destroy us? I know who you are:	ℵ has the plural (οἴδαμεν) corresponding with ἡμῶν and ἡμᾶς in v 24. Is this original? (Recall the rule of § 4: proclivi praestat ardua.)

the Holy One of God."

Or is the nominative here to be taken as a vocative: "You holy one of God!" (cf. Bl-Debr. §147)? Control question: *What* does the demon know (in the narrative)?

25 And Jesus rebuked him, saying, "Be quiet and come out of him!"

Some manuscripts have a longer text here. Which one was original? Regarding the apparatus in Nestle: What does (D) mean? For information, see Nestle's introduction, p. 45ff.

26 And the unclean spirit shook him violently and shrieked aloud and came out of him.

According to some manuscripts, the order of events is different (see apparatus in Aland's *Synopsis*). What better sequence of events can be feasible? Again the text-critical decision applies: proclivi praestat ardua.

27 And they all were so amazed that they asked one another: "What is this? A new teaching with authority! And he even gives orders to the unclean spirits and they obey him."

28 And the news about him spread quickly over the whole region of Galilee.

(ii) Before reaching for the secondary sources, such as the commentaries, one should try to formulate a provisional analysis of the text. Initial indications for the exegesis emerge by gathering up the difficulties in the text in order to understand the latter:

V 21 *They*, specifically Jesus and the disciples, go to Capernaum, but only *he*, Jesus, enters the synagogue. Why do the disciples not join him? What does "immediately on the Sabbath" mean? The Sabbath began Friday evening, while public worship was held Saturday morning (Billerbeck IV/1, 153ff.). Could the εὐθύς refer to the temporal gap between the entrance into Capernaum and the visit in the synagogue?

V 22 The reader learns something about the reaction of those who heard Jesus' teaching, as well as about his didactic method; however, he learns nothing at all about *what* Jesus taught.

Vv 23f. *Who* cries out—the man or the demon ("the unclean spirit")? What is the explanation for the plural ("we") and the subsequent change to the singular ("I know")?

V 27 Why are the bystanders at first astonished not about Jesus' exorcism but about his teaching—and that as a direct reaction to the miracle?

V 28 The reference to the dissemination of the "news about Jesus" breaks up the unity of space and time, otherwise presupposed in the sequence of events; thus 1:29 does not connect to v 28 but to the situation described in vv 23–27. How is that to be explained?

Additional observations are made in the endeavor to order the entire text according to formal perspectives: V 21 contains references to place (Capernaum, synagogue) and time (Sabbath) of the action which, of course, are not absolutely essential for a proper understanding. In vv 21–22 the narrator points to the authoritative teaching of Jesus and to the reaction of the hearers in his presence (is the substantiation of v 22b the content of their amazement or the narrator's comment?). Both indicators are appropriate to the scene of the synagogue but carry no weight in the understanding of the action in vv 23–26; not until v 27 does the narrative return to the former. To begin with, the reference to the locus "synagogue" is repeated in v 23; then, without further preparation we are told that a demoniac had been there who (v 24) cried out at Jesus (direct address). Jesus reacts, also in direct address, with a twofold command that the narrator describes in commentary fashion as a "rebuke" of the demon (v 25). After this, the demon comes out of the ill man with visible and audible signs (v 26), thereby closing the event proper. The amazed reaction of the bystanders (v 27; direct address) refers first of all to the authoritative teaching of Jesus (cf. v 22) and then to his exorcisms (plural!). The narrator adds (v 28) that everywhere in Galilee people spoke about Jesus—hence not only about this one deed.

One may ask now whether the conspicuous references about Jesus' authoritative teaching were later inserted into an earlier briefer account; if they are bracketed for the sake of experiment, the narrative becomes at least smoother and more cohesive. The geographical references (v 21a: Capernaum; v 28: "all of Galilee") clearly connect the pericope as a whole with the immediate and broader context of the Gospel. The passage is preceded by the calling of the first disciples at the "Sea of Galilee" (1:16), that is Lake Gennesaret, along whose northern shore Capernaum is situated (cf. 1:29). "All of Galilee" is the territory in which Jesus had begun his preaching ministry (1:14f.) and where he will remain (8:26) until the end of his public ministry (for details, see § 34).

With regards to the lake, the town, and the area one should consult J. Dalman, *Orte und Wege Jesu*, [4]1967, or the respective articles in the BHH, even if this data contributes little to the understanding of the text.

These observations lead to the preliminary result that Mark evidently had used an available source (*Vorlage*) which included the incident of the healing of a demoniac (in a synagogue?). Mark supplemented this narrative with references to Jesus' teaching (about the content of which he had informed his readers already in 1:14f.) and fitted it into the total framework of his Gospel with geographical and terse chronological pointers.

If one inquires into the intent (*Tendenz*) of the message of the narrative, one notices that apart from Jesus himself no one else is mentioned specifically; even the demon-possessed man remains anonymous and we learn nothing at all about him except for his illness. In particular, nothing is told about his own reaction to his healing: does he gain a special relationship to Jesus, or does he perhaps in gratitude even join him? Or does no change occur at all for him, apart from the healing? Strangely, his fate remains shrouded in darkness. From this observation, confirmed by other narratives using the same style, the following conclusion can be drawn for exegesis and proclamation: Healing stories are obviously not to be construed as conversion stories.

(iii) In order to penetrate deeper into the text's understanding, it is essential to obtain information about the synagogue and Sabbath, about teaching in the synagogue, and about the group known as scribes. In addition, one needs to be informed about belief in demons in antiquity, views of demon possession, as well as about the ancient practices of exorcism. Some initial information can be found in the two excursuses in E. Klostermann's commentary on Mark; some of the evidence cited should be looked up, and then consult further secondary source material. First off, it would be wise to consult a form-critical presentation (for details, see § 9) to test one's own preliminary analysis. Only afterwards should one look into commentaries on Mark and other literature as well.

Bultmann (*History of the Synoptic Tradition*, 223) includes our pericope among the miracle stories. He is of the opinion that the references to the "teaching" of Jesus were originally not part of the narrative. Rather, Mark added them when he joined the text he received to his Gospel. If one excises these "redactional" additions of the evangelist, a stylistically pure miracle story (exorcism) emerges.

Quite apart from whether or not Bultmann's analysis is accepted, our passage does indeed deal with the presentation of a miracle; therefore, to test this assertion, we shall ask the commentaries to be consulted how they interpret the demon and its exclamation. We restrict the consultation to the following well-known commentaries:

J. Gnilka, *Das Evangelium nach Markus,* EKK II/1,2, 1978/79.

W. Grundmann, *Das Evangelium nach Markus,* ThHK 2, [8]1980.

E. Haenchen, *Der Weg Jesu. Eine Erklärung des Markus-Evangeliums und der kanon-ischen Parallelen,* [2]1968.

E. Klostermann, *Das Markusevangelium,* HNT 3, [5]1971.

E. Lohmeyer, *Das Evangelium des Markus,* KEK I/2, [17]1967.

R. Pesch, *Das Markusevangelium,* HThK II/1,2, [3,2]1980.

W. Schmithals, *Das Evangelium nach Markus,* OTK 2, GTB 503/4, 1979.

E. Schweizer, *The Good News According to Mark,* ET [3]1976

V. Taylor, *The Gospel According to St. Mark,* 1953.

G. Wohlenberg, *Das Evangelium des Markus,* KNT 2, [3]1930.

Other English commentaries that might be consulted include: W. Lane, *The Gospel of Mark,* NIC, 1974; A. Plummer, *The Gospel According to St. Mark,* 1914; V. K. Robbins, *Jesus the Teacher: A Socio-rhetorical Interpretation of Mark,* 1984.

In the following discussion the commentaries are used in chronological order, as far as possible.

Wohlenberg (59f.) offers the following comments concerning the interpretation of the demon and its address directed to Jesus: (a) The expression ἅγιος τοῦ θεοῦ is found in the OT (meaning, of course, its Greek translation, the Septuagint, LXX) and in secular Greek and is a special honorific title. This is objective information important for an understanding of the text and can easily be verified. (b) The demon's confession is displeasing to Jesus because Jesus wanted his nature to be grasped with sober reason. This is not information, but interpretation which can likewise be tested critically: Is it gained from the text itself, or is it derived from general considerations about the nature of Jesus, that is, about the nature of religion in general? And most of all: does Wohlenberg's interpretation square at all with the flow and the whole intent of the text?

Lohmeyer (36) thinks that the demon attempts to use his power against Jesus: it knows Jesus' name and this knowledge lends it a certain power over him ("*Rumpelstilzchen-Motif*"); the demon *threatens* Jesus. However, in light of this argument it is necessary to ask if it corresponds with the tendency of expression in the narrative: From the very beginning the narrative presupposes that Jesus is superior to the demon; therefore, the latter *cannot* possibly threaten him.

Klostermann (20) points out that the demon does not want to adjure Jesus; rather, the demon's expression contains the confession that Jesus is the Messiah. The demons know that they are going to be annihilated in the messianic era. Taylor maintains a similar position (174f.).

Haenchen (87) psychologizes the event by arguing that Jesus did not heal the demoniac out of compassion but "in order not to become known in his essence." This tendency in the narrative also explains why "the hearers apparently take note only of the healing act of Jesus, rather than of the words of the demon."

Haenchen also draws attention to the fact that 1:21ff. should not be attached to 1:16 in strict temporal sequence; the introductory remark "immediately on the Sabbath" (v 21) does not mean that the preceding call of the disciples also took place on a Sabbath. This observation also sheds light on the shift from plural to singular in v 21, which at first appears to be unintelligible. Evidently, in the original narrative only Jesus was discussed; when the healing story was attached to the story of the call of the disciples, an adjustment became necessary: the disciples had to be mentioned once again. Since they played no further role in the following narrative, the older text persisted; hence Jesus alone enters the synagogue.

Grundmann (59ff.) equates demon possession with insanity. The individual "hallucinates" that he is being possessed by a demon. This human being who became the property of an unclean spirit, attempts to implement a magic spell against the Lord "who puts an end to this possession." The plural of v 24 is reminiscent of the "speech pattern of a schizophrenic who combines his real ego and his imaginary ego under the 'we.' " Ultimately the words of Jesus prove to be powerful: "The sick person appears to be well and free of the demon. The pathologically enslaved ego . . . had rediscovered itself." Grundmann obviously seeks for a rational, "medical" explanation for the events described. Here again the control question is to be asked: What does the *text* say? Does it not presuppose the miracle in its magnitude?

Schweizer (23f.) likewise argues similarly to Grundmann: In the assumption of antiquity that sickness was predicated upon evil spirits lies the reality that sickness ultimately represents that which God did not want. Schweizer argues that such healings "without doubt" did take place and that these healings "surely could also be explained psychologically," although "that in itself does not yet express anything about the secret of Jesus' authority." Decisive is not the specific miracle, "but that he teaches with such authority that something happens."

Pesch (121f.) emphasizes that the demon wanted to combat Jesus by means of a "counter spell." The Christian narrator then used this defensive gesture for the purpose of a "christological presentation" (*Inszenierung*). Pesch assumes that the narratives of exorcisms were based upon "historical presuppositions from the life of Jesus" (p. 125) and demonstrated "the liberating power of the reign of God, the miracle of man's whole existence in splendid communication, free of fear (because free of dominion)" (p. 127).

According to *Gnilka* (80), the cry of the demon encompassed both "defence and confession," knowing that the mission of Jesus "has as its goal the abolition of the demonic"; but by using such knowledge, the demon attempted "to gain authority over Jesus with a spell, as it were." Gnilka argues that there is no historical detail behind the narrative, rather "a general reminiscence of (Jesus') activity of exorcism" (p. 127).

Schmithals, who argues for his own literary hypothesis concerning the origin of Mark (see below, p. 61), views 1:21–28 as an original unit of material. The miracle describes the content of Jesus' new teaching (p. 120). The possessed serves "as an example of the person in need of the help of Jesus in general" (hence the plural in v 24). The narrator leaves open the question whether it is the demon or the man who speaks—evil is powerful only where man makes room for it. Furthermore, irony is clearly to be found in the word, since the demon itself desperately sought to adjure Jesus (p. 121f.).

After the critical reading of the commentaries, one should consult the other secondary sources (cf. D.-A. Koch, *Die Bedeutung der Wundererzählungen für die Christologie des Markusevangeliums*, 1975, 43f.; see further bibliography there).

With regards to the secondary sources, the controlling question is whether their assertions take their orientation from the text, and so take into account its wording, or whether additional arguments are inserted. It is foundational to begin exegesis by accepting the text as literary witness and interpreting it as such. The question is not what the demon or the patient meant to say, but what the narrator has him say. It is the narrator who desires to give the reader a message, and the meaning of the entire narrative lies in this message. If this is taken into account, it becomes clear that the accounts about Jesus serve the proclamation of faith in him. Where Jesus appears, demons are finished (in keeping with the world view of that time, of course); they have to confess their impotence before the "Holy One of God." It would be wrong, therefore, to interpret the address of v 24 as a threat. Regardless of whether the narrative contains a historical nucleus or not, it was shaped after the death of Jesus; it presupposes faith in the resurrected one. In the final analysis, the narrative is concerned with the present power of the one whom the church confesses as the "Holy One of God." Adding the formerly bracketed statements (p. 39) to the narrative, one notices that Mark endeavors a further actualization of the text: What Jesus previously did in the synagogue of Capernaum is still being experienced in the power of his teaching. In view of this teaching of Jesus, the reader is to join in with the chorus of the bystanders.

The interpretation of this Markan text has to be followed by the comparison with the synoptic parallels: Where in Luke does one find agreements with Mark, and what differences are there? How can the situation in the Matthean text be explained? What are the possibilities of dependence between Luke and Mark? Is there evidence for a literary priority of the one or the other? Compare § 7.

(b) Advice with reference to work on a Pauline text:
Questions and perspectives regarding 1 Thes 4:13–18 (5:11, respectively).

At this point we forego translation and textual criticism and suggest your own independent procedure, following the pattern outlined on p. 24f., and p. 36ff.

A fundamental condition for the exegesis of this passage is an initial and general orientation to 1 Thessalonians, which can be obtained in Kümmel's *Introduction* or from the introductory materials in commentaries. The most important aspects are also found in § 24 of our presentation; hence a general reference will suffice at this point.

Paul knows the community in Thessalonica (northern Greece); he himself founded it and they must be familiar with the basic features of his theology. The first letter Paul addresses to the church is concerned in part with issues that apparently needed further clarification. It appears that Paul's co-worker Timothy brought a list of questions from his stay in Thessalonica that Paul now answers in writing. One of these questions is the theme of what happens to those church members who die, or who have already died, before the parousia of Jesus. Paul begins with the phrase, οὐ θέλομεν δὲ ὑμᾶς ἀγνοεῖν. The new topic is signalled by the preposition περί: "Concerning those who are asleep" (cf. 5:1, "concerning times and dates"). Paul addresses two related complex issues: (a) 4:13ff.: resurrection of the dead and parousia of Jesus; (b) 5:1ff.: time of the parousia and consequences for the present. The community's question that Paul answers can be inferred from the type of answer given; it may have been formulated as follows: "Do those believers who die before the parousia of Jesus also enter into eternal life?" An interesting feature of this question is the very fact that it was asked at all. In his ministry in Thessalonica, Paul had apparently not addressed this subject; perhaps it is not even decisive in connection with his theology. The question of the community contains several specific, relevant presuppositions: (a) The recognition of the apocalyptic world view; (b) the essential existence of the belief in the resurrection; (c) the expectation of a relatively imminent parousia.

Paul answers the question altogether within the framework of the given world view: The dead will also be raised—they will indeed be the first to meet the Lord, even prior to those still alive. Nobody knows the date of the parousia, nor does anyone need to know it. Yet, it is not sufficient to recognize the message of Paul's answer; in addition, the methodology in Pauline argumentation needs to be observed, for the latter can yield further significant aspects for understanding the text. The following insights can thus be gained:

(a) The issue in Pauline argumentation is not the formal prescience of future events, but the hope of those alive (v 13). When Paul describes the believers as those who hope, in contrast to the "rest of men who have no hope," he does not mean that in his opinion and outside of Christianity, there are no concepts and anticipations of a beyond; rather, he means that the latter do not possess the true, well-founded hope. These assertions, therefore, are not formulated based on his world view, but from a strictly christological vantage point. The salvation event of the death and resurrection of Christ is the reason for the Christians' hope.

(b) The point of entry is not a visionary projection of the future (although Paul would have been quite capable of that as well, cf. 2 Cor 12:1ff.); rather, it is the expression of the confession of faith: "Jesus died and has been raised" (v 14). The truth of this statement needs no further substantiation since it is not being questioned in Thessalonica at all: εἰ γὰρ πιστεύομεν. . . (εἰ is here, as often in the NT, used with the indicative mood, denoting reality: "if—and it is indeed so—"; cf. Bl-Debr § 372.1). From the destiny of Jesus arise certain consequences for believers; their destiny is wrapped up with the destiny of Jesus, quite independent from whether or not they experience the parousia. Christian existence, determined by hope, finds its orientation in the work of redemption.

(c) Paul further appeals to a saying of Jesus (v 15). In this connection several things are unclear: (1) What is the extent of that saying? (2) Where did Paul get it? This leads to the further questions: (3) How often (and for what purpose) does Paul cite sayings of Jesus? (4) Outside of the NT, where else have sayings of Jesus been handed down? J. Jeremias provides an overview of this material in "Isolated Sayings of the Lord," in H-S I, 85–90. (5) What are the criteria for evaluating the "authenticity" of such a saying (see p. 306f.)?

From the creedal statement and the saying of Jesus, Paul draws the following conclusion: He expects to witness the parousia personally in his lifetime (v 17). Yet physical death in no way affects salvation. Paul makes no attempt at an apocalyptic calculation of the parousia (5:1ff.); his main point is that the Lord comes suddenly.

The portrait of the parousia developed in 1 Thes 4:13–18 may be compared with the "apocalypses" in the synoptic Gospels, especially with Mk 13. In this connection, the question of agreements and divergences almost inevitably leads to the problem of the essential theological relevance of apocalyptic conceptions. In the case of 1 Thes 4:13–18, the following exegetical results emerge:

(i) Paul works with traditional material, i.e., with confessional elements, with apocalyptic images, and with some Jesus tradition whose origin is unclear.

(ii) Paul organizes this material in such a way that the reference to hope and faith is at the beginning, that is, for him the decisive element is the determination of the present Christian existence.

(iii) The confirmation (v 18) is found in the result (5:11): the goal is the mutual exhortation, comfort, and upbuilding of Christians among themselves (the key term is παρακαλέω).

Suggested exercise:

Exegete a Pauline text according to the features demonstrated in instruction and example above. Possible texts are: Rom 12:1–2; 13:1–7; 1 Cor 8:1–6.

Tools: Grammar, lexicon, articles in the TDNT, and only then the commentaries.

§ 7 *Literary Criticism of the Synoptic Gospels*

Bibliography: *Section 1:* R. Bultmann, "Die Erforschung der synoptischen Evangelien," *Glauben und Verstehen* IV, 1–41; H. Koester, "One Jesus: Four Primitive Gospels," in *Trajectories through Early Christianity*, 1971; W. Schmithals, *Einleitung in die drei ersten Evangelien*, 1985. *Section 2:* W. G. Kümmel, *Introduction to the NT*, ET 1980, 42–80. *Section 3:* W. A. Beardslee, *Literary Criticism of the New Testament*,

1970; N. Freye, *Anatomy of Criticism*, 1967; N. Petersen, *Literary Criticism for New Testament Critics*, 1978; H. Zimmermann, *Neutestamentliche Methodenlehre*, [7]1982, 79–84.

1. General Observations

Since the 18th century the first three Gospels have been referred to as "synoptic," because they are closely related to one another and by all means should be "viewed together." Literary criticism is concerned first of all with the question of whether and how these three Gospels are connected to one another as literary works.

To begin with, there are several possibilities: (1) One author may have copied the other; this leads to the further question of who used whose writing as a source. (2) All three evangelists could have independently drawn from one another and from common literary and oral traditions.

Literary criticism cannot determine whether a certain tradition possibly goes back to Jesus himself or whether it represents the creation of the church. Finding the solution to that problem is the task of form criticism (cf. § 9). Literary criticism does not examine the individual passages of tradition; rather, it evaluates the different traditions in Matthew, Mark, and Luke *in their relationship* to one another, notwithstanding the importance of placing a paragraph (pericope), alongside its actual message, within the structure of the gospel.

The peculiar problem faced by literary criticism in the synoptic Gospels is the fact that, on the one hand, they contain considerable similarities while, on the other hand, there also are substantial differences in the wording of the tradition. The crucial question is how this twofold evidence can be explained.

Further, literary criticism also holds a certain implication for the possible reconstruction of the history of Jesus: Which one is the oldest extant source? Which one is most reliable? The answer is not necessarily the same in both cases, since a later writer could certainly have achieved more precise results on account of more intensive investigation (cf. Lk 1:1–4).

A glance at the older hypotheses relative to the synoptic problem helps elucidate the problem of literary criticism. To be sure, it is not necessary to keep in mind each individual hypothesis; nevertheless, one should be familiar with them since a number of formulations of the questions asked by the older inquiries are still important today.

(1) Tradition hypothesis (representatives were J. G. Herder and J. C. L. Gieseler): Independently of one another, all the evangelists drew from oral tradition.

This hypothesis perceives something that is correct (see below, § 9); however, it is unable to shed sufficient light on the interrelationship of the

Gospels: it fails to explain both the verbal agreement in particular instances, and the agreement in the order of the narratives and of the words of Jesus.

(2) Utilization hypothesis (represented by J. J. Griesbach): One evangelist has used one or several other Gospels.

But who used which one as a source? Traditionally, the Gospel of Matthew was held to be the earliest, and in the more recent investigation, this view continues to be maintained by Zahn and Schlatter. In the meantime, however, the assumption of Markan priority has been—and continues to be—adopted. The weakness of the utilization hypothesis is its inability to explain adequately the differences between the Gospels; still, some of this theory's elements continue to be applicable today in the two-document hypothesis (see below, § 8).

(3) Ur-Gospel hypothesis (D. F. Michaelis; G. E. Lessing): All three synoptic writers used a no longer extant "Ur-gospel." This hypothesis cannot explain how the agreements between Matthew and Luke, over against Mark, could have arisen. It appeals to the further assumption that Mark had only an abridged form of the Ur-gospel available. But such "secondary hypotheses," which are contingent upon prior hypotheses and which seek to prove the latter at the same time, must be approached with the utmost of suspicion, although they are not uncommon in historical investigations.

(4) Fragment hypothesis (F. D. E. Schleiermacher): The Gospels are constructed from a large number of initially independent small collections of separate stories.

In the case of this hypothesis, the agreement in the overall framework of the Gospels remains unexplained. Conversely, the question of possible older collections within the Gospels is posited again today and is answered partly in the affirmative.

2. Problem of mutual dependence

Conspicuous is the fact that the three synoptic Gospels are of different length. In the printed text of Nestle, Mark comprises roughly 1500 lines, while Matthew has already more than 2400 and Luke, finally, more than 2600. If the hypothetical assumption is made that somehow there was bound to be a literary relationship between these Gospels, the question of priority becomes inevitable: Can these three Gospels be based upon a common literary source (Ur-gospel hypothesis)? At first glance, the agreements in the overall framework, as well as of the verbal parallels in the individual pericopae, appear to favor this notion. Conversely, one is hard pressed to explain why Mark offers so much less material than the other writers. Did he cut out some things, e.g., the entire Sermon on the Mount? Or did the others have access to additional material on a large scale, and if so, from where? To begin with, it is indeed more likely that Lk and Mt used sources in addition to Mk, for there is no reason for Mk to have reduced the material to such an extent. With the assumption of the opposite development, it is easier to explain the situation: the shortest Gospel, Mark, was the basis for Matthew and Luke; the latter made a few stylistic and theological "improvements" of the Markan material and added further material—literary sources and/or oral traditions.

Clearly, the decision of priority can only be made between Matthew and Mark, since Luke expressly presupposes the existence of other gospel accounts (Lk 1:1-4).

(2) Let us now test the soundness of the provisional hypothesis that Mark was the basis of Matthew (or one of them).

(a) The healing of the paralytic is recounted in Mt 9:1-8 and in Mk 2:1-12, as well as in Lk (5:17-26). Especially at the beginning of the narrative, the Matthean and Markan rendering show marked differences. According to Mk, Jesus has been in Capernaum for several days already. One gains the impression that the crowded village of Capernaum is to be viewed as part of the substance of the development of the narrative. In Matthew, however, the crowd scene is missing altogether; apparently the story begins immediately upon Jesus' arrival in the town, and nothing is said about any kind of difficulty in approaching Jesus. Yet, besides such differences there are also major agreements between the two versions of the account (cf. esp. Mk 2:8ff. and Mt 9:4ff.), rendering the total literary independence rather unlikely. The test question is: Which rendering can more easily be derived from the other? This question makes clear that Mt abbreviates what appeared to him to be unimportant to the actual core of the narrative. The picturesque situation bothered him; instead he wanted to accentuate the didactic content. The result is that in Mk the people show their faith in Jesus by overcoming a considerable obstacle in coming to him, while according to Mt their faith is seen already in the fact that they come to Jesus in the first place. Especially fruitful is a comparison between Mt 9:3f. and Mk 2:6ff.: in Mk what is concretely related to the scene—the rebuke of the scribes, as well as Jesus' reply—in Mt becomes a general moral rebuke, and one that functions reciprocally as well. On the one hand, then, Mt smoothed out the somewhat awkward style of the Markan rendition; on the other hand, he has simplified the essential problem at hand by eliminating the fundamental question, "Who can forgive sins except God?" (Mk 2:7).

One striking proof of literary dependence is the agreement in the sentence construction of Mt 9:6/Mk 2:10. In both instances we find an anacoluthon. Theologically significant is the difference at the end. While Mk, true to style, ends with the statement, "We have never seen anything like this," Mt points to the ἐξουσία that God has given *to people*—which, in the context of the Gospel, can only refer to the church that has the authority to forgive sins (and the power to heal miraculously?).

The comparison between Mk and Lk is simple: the differences, in the Lukan sense, are improvements: The opponents are already introduced and described more fully at the very beginning; their appearance in v 21, therefore, is not as abrupt as in Mk. Yet, it is precisely v 21 that shows that Lk had the Markan text before him, since he refers here to the γραμματεῖς as does Mk (and not to the νομοδιδάσκαλοι, as one would expect on the basis of v 17).

(b) The parable of the mustard seed is given in Mk 4:30–32 as well as in Mt 13:31f. and in Lk 13:18f. It is striking that Mk and Lk begin with a double question, while Mt formulates thematically: ἄλλην παραβολὴν . . . (cf. v 24). The literary relationship between Mk and Mt is obvious: μικρότερον . . . πάντων τῶν σπερμάτων . . . μεῖζον τῶν λαχάνων . . . ὥστε . . . τὰ πετεινὰ τοῦ οὐρανοῦ . . . κατασκηνοῦν. At the same time, there are essential differences. While Mk draws a picture ("If one plants a mustard seed, it happens that . . ."), Mt first begins to tell a story ("A man sowed . . .") but then does not continue in a narrative style (such as: "and when it sprouted . . ."); instead, he proceeds in the style of Mark: "When it sprouts, it. . . ." The Lukan presentation, which initially parallels Mk in part (see above), aligns with Mt in the ὁμοία ἐστίν of the introduction of the parable. Like Mt, he tells a story, with the difference, of course, that he consistently uses the narrative style. In terms of word order, there are clear agreements between Mt and Lk against Mk: For both, the word is αὐξάνειν; they also have in common the statement that the seed becomes a tree, as well as the reference that the birds would nest in its branches. On the other hand, Luke does not compare the mustard seed with other seeds, and he especially does not describe it as the smallest of all seeds; only the seed at the beginning and the tree at the end are placed over against one another.

The situation here is therefore considerably more complicated than in the first example: Mk and Lk differ; but Mt parallels Mk against Lk, and sometimes he also parallels Lk against Mk. This circumstance, too, is most easily explained from the vantage point of the Markan priority, since the structure in Mk can hardly have emerged from the text either in Lk or in Mt. Conversely, Lk does not seem to have had access to Mk at all; rather, he may have used a tradition independent from Mk, one that contained the same parable, though in a different form. Mt appears to have known this second form as well, for his text clearly shows the attempt to merge both forms with one another, without thereby achieving a genuine balance.

Nevertheless, it is to be noted that the Markan priority that we assert pertains only to the *literary* relationships; the question whether the Markan framework or indeed the Lukan framework was (more) original, i.e., the older one in terms of the history of tradition, cannot be answered by literary criticism. Rather, this is the task of form criticism (see § 9).

Literary criticism can only ascertain that the parable of the mustard seed was known to Mk in one framework, whereas Mt had it available in two forms, one of which evidently was the Markan text. Luke also knew both forms but preferred the non-Markan version.

(3) The supposition that the Gospel priority belongs to Mk and that both Mt and Lk used him as basis or source is strengthened by a comparison of the overall framework of the Gospels (already a glimpse into the table of contents of a Synopsis is instructive). One might try to explain the agreements in the order of presentation of the events by arguing for the rendering of historical incidents, but that would make the divergences inexplicable, such as the presentation of Jesus' appearance in his hometown Nazareth. These findings need to be explained in a different way.

When we compare the format of Mt and Mk, the following pericopes run parallel:

Mt 3:1–6 and	Mk 1:1–6
Mt 3:7–10	without parallel in Mk, but cf. Lk (3:7–9)
Mt 3:11–12	Mk 1:7–8
Mt 3:13–17	Mk 1:9–11
Mt 4:1–11	Mk 1:12–13, cf. also Lk (4:1–13)
Mt 4:12–17	Mk 1:14–15
Mt 4:18–22	Mk 1:16–20

In Mk there follow narratives of healings, then a comprehensive summary (1:32–34, 35–38, 39), then more healings, and finally, several "disputes." In contrast, Mt ends ch 4 with a summary, followed by the Sermon on the Mount in chs 5–7; then he narrates miracle stories in chs 8 and 9, with Mt 9:1 corresponding to Mk 2:1. Hence we see that Mt adduces considerably more material than Mk. It is also to be assumed that Mk likely did not suppress material known to him, but instead that Mt had more material at his disposal than the writer of the Gospel of Mark.

Now it is important that the material in Mt that exceeds that of Mk is to a large extent also found in Lk. The comparison between Mk and Lk leads to similar findings as that between Mk and Mt: The content of Mk 1:1–6, 44 is also found in Lk, agreeing extensively; only for Mk 3:20f. and 4:26–29 are no parallels found. On the other hand, in Lk the calling of the first disciples (Mk 1:16–20) is preceded by Jesus' first public appearance in Nazareth (4:16ff.), and the calling itself is given in an entirely different version in Lk 5:1–11, hence Luke's subsequent omission of the incident of Mk 6:1–6. Particularly striking is the fact that Mk 6:45–8:26 is not paralleled at all in Lk; therefore one refers to this as the so-called great omission, (see below). For the purpose of control it is helpful to compare Mt and Lk. We notice that both contain a lot more material than Mk. But they insert it into the material taken from Mk, always in differing places respectively. An agreement in the structure of the Gospel between Mt and Lk—with a few exceptions (see below)—is found only where both also agree with Mk. Example: Mt adds the Sermon on the Mount behind Mk 1:39, while Lk has his Sermon on the Plain, corresponding to the Sermon on the Mount, after Mk 3:19. However, the healing of the paralytic, the calling of Levi, and the question of fasting in Mt 9:1-8, 9–13, 14–17, are placed parallel to Lk 5:17–26, 27–32, 33–39, thus corresponding entirely with the Markan text (2:1–12, 13–17, 18–22). From these observations the assumption can be drawn that Mt and Lk worked independently of one another. The only remaining question is where they obtained the material common to both.

The following preliminary result can be maintained: (a) The Gospel of Mark was available as a source to Mt and Lk; hence it is the oldest of the three synoptic Gospels. (b) Evidently there is no literary connection between Lk and Mt. (c) It is possible that Lk and Mt have used a source independently of one another, one that was unknown to Mk.

This hypothesis, the so-called two-document hypothesis, contains some points of weakness:

(1) How is it to be explained that Mk has some, albeit few, pericopae which have identically *not* been taken up by Mt and Lk (e.g., Mk 4:26–29; 8:22–26)? Could Mt and Lk possibly have read a shorter "Ur-Mark" in which the special material mentioned was missing?

(2) If Mt and Lk are literarily independent from one another, how can one explain that they agree against the Markan text in many places, although the substance of those texts comes from Mk? Here one refers to the "minor agreements"—the (English) term is attributed to the Anglo-Saxon research that has raised this issue. For instance, Mt and Lk omit certain "psychological" references of Mk (cf. e.g., Mk 1:41 and parallels). Once again the question arises whether a possible "Ur-Mark" perhaps did not yet contain these references. Or did Mt and Lk not work independently of one another after all? Or did they have the same idea—independently of one another? Mk 9:14–29 (and parallels) is a particularly impressive example. The similarity between Mt and Lk is especially strong in the abridgements, so much so that this phenomenon can hardly be explained without the assumption of a literary relationship (nothing is gained with a reference to oral tradition, since both used the Markan text in any case).

Representatives of the two-document hypothesis have correctly pointed out that most minor agreements between Mt and Lk in most cases are concerned with grammatical and stylistic improvements that are also found in those instances where Mt and Lk do not harmonize. In favor of the assumption of the mutual independence of Mt and Lk is the fact that the minor agreements never contain *entire sentences* beyond Mk. A third argument follows: If Lk did know the Gospel of Matthew, it would have to be explained why he never inserted the common material at the same place in Mk as Mt did.

The notion argued from time to time that the section 6:45–8:26 (see above) was lacking in the copy of Mark available to Lk, that Mt and Lk did not use the current Gospel of Mark but a revised "Deutero-Mark," is altogether unlikely. The complete Gospel of Mark would then have to have existed in three forms ([1] the text canonized later; [2] the text available to Mt; [3] that available to Lk), without the slightest trace of such abridged, more recent (!) renditions of Mk in the transmission of the text.

At this point it is necessary to emphasize once more that no theology is perfect, no hypothesis is capable of explaining adequately all of the problems, and that there are always open questions. But it does appear that the two-document hypothesis is adequate to answer satisfactorily most problems arising in conjunction with the synoptic problem.

3. Relationship of textual and literary criticism

The ending of Mk (16:9–20), as well as the final chapter in Jn (21) are disputed. In both cases the question must be asked: Is the final pericope to be considered an original part of the book or not? Although the formal question is the same in both cases, the methodology in answering the question in both cases is entirely different. Mk 16:9–20 is a case to be treated by textual criticism: The pericope is missing in B, ℵ, sy^s, among others, while other manuscripts are handing down a totally different ending. This indicates that the passage represents a later addition to the Gospel of Mark. This supposition is further supported by the literary observation that the passage leaves the impression of being a subsequent and artificial construction of a number of other references. On the other hand, the case of John 21 does not pertain to textual criticism, for there is no indication at all that this chapter was ever missing from any manuscript of the Gospel of John. Nevertheless, both Jn 20:30f. and Jn 21:24f. indicate that this chapter is an appendix to the finished Gospel. The doubts of its originality are not based on textual criticism, but exclusively on literary criticism.

Suggested exercise: Exegesis of Mt 1:16

The genealogy of Jesus in Mt 1 is constructed according to the following schema: "Abraham begat Isaac" etc. This schema is broken in v 16 because, in the opinion of the evangelist, Joseph was not the father of Jesus; therefore it says: "Jacob begat Joseph, the husband of Mary, of whom was born Jesus, called the anointed one." The Sinaitic Syriac translation (sy^s), however, has the following interesting rendering (in a reverse translation into Greek): Ἰωσὴφ δέ, ᾧ ἐμνηστεύθη παρθένος Μαρία, ἐγέννησεν Ἰησοῦν τὸν λεγόμενον Χριστόν. Many exegetes consider this text to be original, arguing that it shows that the genealogy had originally pointed to Joseph as the father of Jesus—after all, Jesus was a descendant of David via Joseph, not via Mary.

At this juncture it is essential to distinguish sharply between textual and literary criticism: Naturally, the genealogy of Jesus, which makes sense only if Jesus indeed leads back to David, must originally have said, "Joseph begat Jesus from Mary"; but this form cannot possibly ever have been part of the Gospel of Matthew, since Mt is concerned with the fact that Jesus is the son of David and *at the same time* the son of the virgin. Thus Mt had to change the form available to him when he inserted it into his Gospel. If one still insists that the Syriac reading preserves the original Matthean text, the following issues require explanation: (a) how could Mt reconcile this wording with his theological conviction? and (b) why is the text, outside of sy[s], consistently handed down in a different rendering.

Alternatively one can of course ask whether the Syriac translation perhaps intended to deny the doctrine of the virginal conception of Jesus; such a tendency cannot a priori be ruled out entirely in the early Eastern church in Syria. Yet, a glance at the Syriac text of Mt 1 and 2 (as well as Lk 1:2) shows that the Sinaitic Syriac in no way denied the virgin birth (Mt 1:18–23; Lk 1:34f.). At the back of this formulation of Mt 1:16 apparently lies the writer's concern to present Jesus, not as the physical son, but as the legal son of Joseph, in order to demonstrate in this fashion that Jesus was a Davidite.

§ 8   Major Agreements Between Matthew and Luke: The Logia Source (Q)

Bibliography: M. E. Boring, *The Sayings of the Risen Jesus*, SNTSMS 46, 1982; A. v. Harnack, *The Sayings of Jesus: The Second Source of St. Matthew and St. Luke*, ET 1908; P. Hoffmann, *Studien zur Theologie der Logienquelle*, NTA NF 8, [3]1982; J. S. Kloppenborg, *The Formation of Q: Trajectories in Ancient Wisdom Collections*, 1987; idem, *Q Parallels*, 1988; W. G. Kümmel, *Introduction to the NT*, ET 1975, 26–53; D. Lührmann, *Die Redaktion der Logienquelle*, WMANT 33, 1969; T. W. Manson, *The Sayings of Jesus*, reprint 1949; A. Polag, *Fragmenta Q. Textheft zur Logienquelle*, 1979; S. Schulz, *Q—Die Spruchquelle der Evangelisten*, 1972; Ph. Vielhauer, *Geschichte der urchristlichen Literatur*, 1975, 268–280, 311–329.

1. Relationship between Matthew and Mark

It has already been mentioned in § 7 that there are also agreements between Mt and Lk where a Markan parallel (*Vorlage*) is lacking. How is this circumstance explained, if the observation that Mt and Lk are literarily independent of one another is valid?

(1) A comparison between Mt 3:1–12 and Lk 3:1–18 shows: Both rely first on Mk (1:2–6) but then go beyond Mk, rendering the content of the penitential sermon of John the Baptist. While the addressees are not identical (Mt 3:7—Pharisees and Sadducees; Lk 3:7—people), in both cases the message of the sermon is given in almost identical wording. The agreement in the word order of Mt 3:7–10 and Lk 3:7–9 is explicable only un-

der the assumption that both had access to a second source besides Mk. This assumption is further strengthened when one notices that Mt 3:11 and Lk 3:16 are indeed paralleled in Mk 1:7f., that is, they are evidently predicated upon Mk, but that Mt 3:12 and Lk 3:17, without Markan parallel, once again agree almost verbatim. Likewise, frequent verbal agreement is evident in the temptation account of Mt 4:1-11 and Lk 4:1-13.

In the sermon of the Baptist, Lk adds a supplement beyond Mt (Lk 3:10-14). The origin of this addition is not clear. Did he have another source that was unavailable to Mt? Or did Lk himself create it? Certain criteria for the solution may be derived both from the style and from the content.

(2) A comparison between Lk 6:20-49 (Sermon on the Plain) and Mt 5-7 (Sermon on the Mount) shows:
Lk 6:20-23 corresponds with Mt 5:3, 6, 11ff.
Lk 6:27-30 corresponds with Mt 5:44, 39-42
Lk 6:32-36 corresponds with Mt 5:46f., 45, 48
Lk 6:37f. corresponds with Mt 7:1f.
Lk 6:41-49 corresponds with Mt 7:3-5, 16-21, 24-27.
If one begins with Lk, the Sermon on the Mount appears to be an expansion of the Sermon on the Plain. In any case, the agreements between the two compositions cannot be purely accidental, since there are also agreements in the format—of special importance is the position of the beatitudes at the beginning. Conversely, if one begins with Mt, it is striking that a large part of those sentences found in the Sermon on the Mount, but not in the Sermon on the Plain, are nevertheless found in the Gospel of Luke, albeit in completely different places and contexts.

The simplest explanation for this situation is the assumption that there existed a source that Mt and Lk used independently of one another, without regularly adhering to the presentation (sequence of the individual logia and scenes) in that source. However, this second source in addition to Mk can only be deduced hypothetically; no such manuscript has been handed down. One speaks of the two-document hypothesis because one designates the second source with the letter Q [German, *Quelle*] or— though rarely—with the letter L (for "logia source"). The primary content of Q are logia (sayings) of Jesus, but some narrative material is also found.

Suggested exercises:
1. Sort out those logia that appear both in the Sermon on the Mount and in the Gospel of Luke, but which appear in a different context. Tool: Synopsis.
2. Make an analysis of the transmission of the Lord's Prayer by comparing it in the Lukan and Matthean settings.

2. Character of the logia source Q

The assumption that Q was a literary source, is sometimes disputed:

(1) It could have been a fluid layer of oral tradition; otherwise it cannot be explained why the wording of the sayings from Q individually differ so widely from one another.

There are indeed such divergences that cannot be construed as deliberate alterations by the respective evangelist because they demonstrate neither the typical style nor the particular theological interest of the one or the other evangelist. For instance, Mt 5:25f./Lk 12:57–59 and Mt 5:43–48/Lk 6:27f., 32–36, evidently contain the same sayings, and yet one wonders whether Mt and Lk indeed used the same form of the logia. Did "Q" actually exist only in oral tradition? Or must it be assumed that there were different editions of the (written) logia source being used in the churches?

(2) Second, the written form of Q is contested by pointing out that Mt and Lk take up and incorporate into their Gospels the Q-material, common to both, in quite a different sequence.

This observation is indeed appropriate. In distinction from Mt who arranges the sources before him from a systematic vantage point, Lk gathers the material from Q (and the material unique to him) in two blocks and seems to have adhered to the order of the material before him.

It is alleged to be unlikely that Mt and Lk could have assimilated one and the same source so differently. At the very least, this would be in stark contrast to the way in which they used the Gospel of Mark. With but few exceptions, they both left unchanged the order of the latter.

Against this argument, a number of counter arguments are cited: (a) In the face of all the differences in the treatment of Q, there are nevertheless substantial agreements in the *word order*. If one begins with the consideration that the words of Jesus have been translated from Aramaic into Greek, it becomes necessary for a Greek source which contained the words of Jesus to have existed in *written* form, otherwise Mt and Lk could not have the identical word order in many instances. (b) If Q were nothing but scattered, oral tradition without a solid framework, it would be hard to explain how Mt and Lk could scoop up so much *in common* from this tradition. (c) It is essential to point out that the agreement in the order in which the Q-material has been adopted is by no means as marginal as it is sometimes claimed—the table in Kümmel's *Introduction to the NT* (p. 65f.) is quite informative in this regard. (d) Notice, finally, that there are some "doublets" here and there in Mt and Lk, where the identical saying of Jesus is found in two different places in the same Gospel. Here it is consistently the case that one saying is supported in Mk, from whom the two other writers took it up, and the other saying must have been found once again in the written form of Q; otherwise it is unlikely that Mt and Lk would have adopted it almost mechanically. Hence, in ch 8:16–18 Lk follows Mk (4:21f., 24f.); in other words, he adopts the three individual sayings in the given sequence. There are differences in the exact word order, however, that do not point to special Lukan characteristics. A prime example is the saying of Lk 8:16 (par Mk 4:21), which is found a second time in Lk 11:33. Luke contains a larger number of individual sayings that are also found in Mt—though in a different place, and which therefore presumably come from Q. The saying handed down in Lk 11:33 has been incorporated into the Sermon on the Mount by Mt (5:15). When Lk found the identical logion in Mk 4:21 and incorporated it into his Gospel (8:16), he adapted it according to the Q form; he phrased it from the perspective of the person's activity (ὁ λύχνος is not the subject of the sentence, as in Mk), and, in particular, he did not adopt the interrogative form.

Further examples show the same situation: Lk 8:17 (par Mk 4:22) is also found in Lk 12:2; the word order of the latter is almost identical with that of Mt 10:26.

Lk 8:18 (par Mk 4:25) is found again in Lk 19:26, though in the form of a participial clause, rather than a relative clause. Mt likewise has this saying twice (13:12; 25:29), once again (a) in the Markan form (i.e., as a relative clause) and (b) in the Q form as a participial clause.

Suggested exercise:

Analyze	Mk 8:34f.	Mt 16:24f.	Lk 9:23f.
		Mt 10:38f.	Lk 14:27; 17:33
	Mk 8:38	Mt 16:27	Lk 9:26
		Mt 10:32f.	Lk 12:8f.
	Mk 13:9, 13	Mt 24:9, 13	Lk 21:12, 17, 19
		Mt 10:19f.	Lk 12:11f.

Besides the *sayings doublets* addressed already, there are also entire *discourse doublets*. For example, the beginning of the extensive commissioning discourse in Mt 10 has its antecedent in Mk 6:7–13, where, after giving some brief instructions, Jesus sends the disciples on their mission. In his overall framework, however, Mt has the discourse in a different place than Mk. Luke has *two* commissionings, with Lk 9 essentially paralleling the Markan text, while Lk 10 essentially follows the Matthean text. This circumstance is best explained with the assumption that there were two accounts of the sending out of the disciples, i.e., Mk and Q. While Lk adopted both accounts, Mt worked them together and, with the help of some material unique to him, created a single long discourse.

One can test this by endeavoring to separate the layers from one another within Mt 10. Thus it appears that Mt combined here, as in other discourses elsewhere, materials from Q, Mk, and material unique to Mt into larger units (cf., e.g., the eschatological discourse in Mt 24f.).

These references favor the assumption that the logia source Q had been handed down in writing. Even so, several problems remain unresolved: The original text of Q can only be reconstructed with great difficulty. In the vicinity of Q one has to reckon constantly with strong influences of oral tradition. Even the environment of the logia source can only be determined tentatively at best. The component parts of Q that can be regarded as certain are found in those instances where Mt and Lk agree—beyond Mk (especially in the case of larger compositions, such as the Sermon on the Mount or the Sermon on the Plain respectively). On the other hand, it is also feasible that Mt or Lk omitted something from Q, so that the respective logion or a certain narrative can only be found in *one* of the evangelists and that it is no longer possible to ascertain whether the material comes from Q or from a special tradition (*Sonderüber-lieferung*). It is to be noted, of course, that the evangelists generally did not tend to omit material that they knew; it can be considered probable, therefore, that Q did not contain much more material than what we can ascertain on the basis of Mt and Lk.

3. *Q as a literary source*

Attempts at comprehensive reconstructions of the logia source Q have been made, among others, by A. v. Harnack, S. Schulz, and A. Polag. Harnack found 7 narratives, 11 parables, 13 speech groups (*Sprachgruppen*), and 29 sayings. Schulz presented a comprehensive analysis and interpretation of the entire material of the tradition attributed to the logia source. For him, Q originated in Jewish-Christian communities in the Syrian-Palestinian border area, and that over an extended period of time. Part of the oldest layer of the source, according to Schulz, is the prophetic-enthusiastic sayings tradition (*Spruchgut*) in which the tendency to "kerygmatize" the ministry of the earthly Jesus is not yet apparent. On the other hand, in the younger Q tradition are found not only new literary forms (historical narrative, parables, apophthegms, apocalyptic materials), but the "I-sayings" as well, which viewed the entire earthly ministry of Jesus retrospectively. Here the earthly life of Jesus is interpreted kerygmatically, which could possibly be attributed to the influence of older Markan traditions.

It is doubtful, of course, that there ever existed a "non-kerygmatic" Jesus tradition in a Christian community. Furthermore, it is advisable to remain cautious with regard to an overly detailed determination of both extent and content of the logia source. Nevertheless, several relatively unassailable observations are appropriate:

(1) Besides the logia, Q also contains narrative material, such as the temptation account and the story of the centurion of Capernaum.

(2) Q is not a gospel in the literary sense, for it obviously contains no passion narrative; this does not allow the conclusion, however, that Q did not know the kerygma of the passion at all. Q was a book for the edification of the church, familiar with the kerygma of the cross and the resurrection.

(3) The ordering of the individual logia in Q was certainly not random; rather, in part one finds collected "speeches": the Sermon on the Plain in Lk 6:20ff. is a sort of early Christian mini-catechism. Similarly the framework of Q that can plausibly be reconstructed from Lk shows the existence of a meaningful arc spanning from the appearance of John the Baptist to the eschatological discourse of Jesus.

From Lk and Mt the following approximate content of Q can be derived:

John the Baptist's sermon	(Lk 3:7-17;	Mt 3:7-12)
Temptation of Jesus	(Lk 4:2-13;	Mt 4:2-11)
Sermon on the Plain	(Lk 6:20-49;	Mt 5-7)
Centurion of Capernaum	(Lk 7:1-10;	Mt 8:5-13)
John the Baptist	(Lk 7:18-35;	Mt 11:2-19)
Expression of woe and joy	(Lk 10:13-15, 21f.;	Mt 11:21-27)
Beelzebub	(Lk 11:14-23;	Mt 12:22-30)
Return of the evil spirit	(Lk 11:24-26;	Mt 12:43-45)
Against the Pharisees	(Lk 11:39-51;	Mt 23:4, 23-25, 29-36)
Woe over Jerusalem	(Lk 13:34f.;	Mt 23:37-39)
Discourse on last things	(Lk 17:22-37;	Mt 24:26-28, 37-41)
Parable of the talents	(Lk 19:12-27;	Mt 25:14-30)

By the way, eschatology was not only the final didactic element in Q; it is also placed at the end in Mark's presentation of Jesus' teaching (Mk 13) as well as in the Didache. Even in the Pauline letters one notices the tendency to move the treatment of the eschatological themes to the end (cf. 1 Cor 15; 1 Thes 4:5).

(4) Just as the logia source has no passion narrative, neither does it contain an explicit passion kerygma. Hence it never uses the title Messiah for Jesus, which early Christianity understood especially in the context of the suffering of Jesus (see below, § 56). Q preserves the previous teaching of Jesus on the one hand, authenticated by his resurrection, and anticipates the parousia of Jesus on the other, without further elaboration on the specifics.

(5) The place and date of origin are unknown. Yet, there is some evidence relative to both aspects. Since Chorazin, Bethsaida, Capernaum, and Jerusalem are mentioned as places of Jesus' ministry, it is possible to view Galilee and especially the Jewish territory on the Lake of Gennesaret as the geographical point of origin of Q. The fact that the imminence of the parousia of Jesus is no longer assumed in Q (Mt 24:48 par Lk 12:45) and at the same time that Christians have to reckon with more intensive persecutions (Mt 23:35 par Lk 11:50), leads to the conclusion that the logia source came into being not much earlier than, for instance, Mk—in other words, shortly before the destruction of Jerusalem in A.D. 70.

(6) A special problem is the relationship of Q to Mk: Did Mk know the logia source? In favor of such an assumption is the fact that they have some sayings in common; however, the extent of this common material is so scant that one may be dealing with little more than with common oral tradition. These findings are discussed in Polag, pp. 92–98.

§ 9 Form Criticism in the Synoptic Gospels

Bibliography: *Section 1*: K. L. Schmidt, *Der Rahmen der Geschichte Jesu*, 1919 ([5]1969). *Section 2*: E. Güttgemanns, *Candid Questions Concerning Gospel Form Criticism*, ET 1979; V. Taylor, *The Formation of the Gospel Tradition*, [2]1960; E. F. McKnight, *What is Form Criticism?* 1969. *Section 3*: R. Bultmann, *The History of the Synoptic Tradition*, ET 1963. *Section 4*: M. Dibelius, *From Tradition to Gospel*, ET 1965.

Preliminary remark:

Exegetical analysis of the synoptic Gospels requires three operations:

(1) Isolation of the individual narratives and words processed in the now extant Gospels (separation of "tradition" and "redaction").

(2) Determination of the form (*Gattung*) of the isolated narratives and words for the purpose of understanding and interpreting them as self-contained individual texts.

(3) Interpretation of the text in the present redactional context of the entire Gospel.

1. Analysis of the literary ''framework'': Example Mk 1

The first perspective for the analysis is the question of how the individual scenes are tied together in time and space (cf. § 7 above). In the introduction of the Gospel of Mark the appearance and proclamation of John the Baptist are described in brief (Mk 1:[1]2–8); in vv 9–11 we are told of Jesus' baptism and in v 12f. of the temptation of Jesus in the wilderness. In this account the temporal references are maintained very vaguely: That Jesus had been baptized by John "in those days" (i.e., when the Baptist was at the Jordan), still makes relatively good sense; but that he was led into the wilderness "at once" (εὐθύς) after the baptism, sounds somewhat strange (hence the parallels made a change at this point). It appears as if the baptism and temptation stories had been tied together quite closely by Mark himself, with the tying together of the two accounts made with a terse and inclusive καὶ εὐθύς, which surely comes from the hand of the evangelist.

A consultation of the concordance shows how frequently the term καὶ εὐθύς (or εὐθέως) occurs in Mk, especially in comparison with Mt and Lk.

A "summary" follows in 1:14f.—the proleptic and summarizing formulation of the overall theme of the teaching of Jesus. At this point the time reference, which is again given in general terms ("after John was put in prison"), is obviously meant to underscore the appearance of the one *after* the other. It is hard to imagine that the imprisonment of John occurred immediately following the temptation of Jesus.

The narrative proper in the Markan Gospel begins in 1:16: Jesus calls his first disciples. Strangely enough, no time reference is to be found here, nor is there any connection to the preceding summary. Apparently Mk wants to create the impression that the calling of the disciples took place before Jesus even began his public ministry. The scene at the lake described in 1:16–20 could stand just as well at an entirely different place in the Gospel; there is no relationship either to what preceded or to what follows. On the basis of the present context, one gains the impression that in vv 21–28 (cf. p. 36ff. above) we are told of Jesus' first stay in Capernaum—and yet nothing at all is said about it in the narrative itself. We have already addressed the problem of the time references (see above, p. 39f.); in any case it is clear that this passage is not intended to unfold the life of Jesus in the biographical sense. The subsequent text of vv 29–31 is again connected with the context via the indeterminate καὶ εὐθύς; the reference to the synagogue also establishes a certain factual connection. On the other hand, the narrative would itself remain altogether understandable if it began only with ἦλθον εἰς τὴν οἰκίαν.

The passages of vv 32–34, 35–39, again, are not narratives but summaries by means of which Mk provides an overall impression of Jesus; but at the same time he appears to want to create the impression that the events recounted beginning with 1:16 were the happenings in the course of one day.

The healing narrative told in 1:40–45 contains neither a reference to time nor place. No gap at all remains in the flow of the action if this narrative is bracketed and 2:1 is joined to 1:39.

Suggested exercise:

Analyze Mk 2 and 3, observing the perspectives utilized thus far (temporal and spatial connections).

Consequently, from our walk through Mk 1 it surfaces that the Gospel of Mk is obviously comprised of a number of originally self-contained narratives (i.e., traditions) that Mk has connected more or less skillfully with one another with connecting incidental remarks, especially with reference to place and time, and then supplemented them with the summaries created by him (redaction).

Only now is it possible to take up the two remaining tasks cited above (p. 59), the first being the form-critical analysis and interpretation of each narrative on the first level of the tradition (that is, the interpretation of the smallest, self-contained units of narrative). The second step, the interpretation of the narratives in the present framework of the Gospel by working out the special theological interest of the evangelist, is presented in § 10 below.

2. *Form-critical analysis of small units*

(1) The task of *form criticism* is the analysis and interpretation of the individual narratives, and that on the oldest level of tradition. Therefore one searches for the smallest, self-contained unit because the addition of material in the process of transmission is considered more probable than the opposite. Hypothetically, therefore, the smallest unit capable of being interpreted is considered the starting point of the tradition, while it remains to be seen whether this smallest unit was handed down already in written or whether it was still in oral form.

W. Schmithals (bibliographic ref. in § 7; cf. also p. 42 above) questions the successful application of the form-critical method in the exegesis of the synoptic Gospels. He argues that Mk is based on a "basic written account" (*Grundschrift*), formulated initially by an individual writer as a *literary unit*; all narratives are traceable back to this writer. A prior oral level cannot be shown. Yet the assumption that this postulated "basic written account" was a pure desk-top product without out a previous tradition of narration is highly unlikely. The narrative forms suggest the assumption that what we have before us are individual traditions whose origin and history of transmission are to be probed.

The fundamental question asked by form criticism will be elucidated with the example of the miracle stories. In the era of theological orthodoxy, the miracle stories of the Gospels were regarded as historically reliable accounts of events that had indeed happened. In this pursuit, appeal was made to the verbal inspiration, i.e., the "inerrancy" of the Bible, in order to substantiate the dogma. A new leaf was turned over with the Enlightenment in which the application of the principle of reason to the biblical texts led to an altogether new assessment of the theological and especially the historical value of the Bible, and particularly of its miracle narratives.

Lessing pronounced the theologically based verdict that a rational truth could be neither confirmed nor refuted by a miracle. The rationalistic explanation of miracles established the argument that it was impossible to break through the laws of nature and that the alleged miracles were to be explained as natural processes. In this fashion the calming of the storm (Mk 4:35–41) was explained by saying the boat had rounded a cape and thus had suddenly moved into the leeside. Jesus' walking on the lake means that Jesus had mastered the art of treading water, and so on.

Clearly such an interpretation of the miracle narratives runs counter to their very intent, for these narratives want to report miracles and not at all events that can be explained naturally. It was the methodological error of rational theology that it failed to investigate the NT miracle accounts with regards to their style: Is it a question of an eyewitness account? What function is particularly accorded to the miracle itself within the whole narrative? A change was signalled in the "Life of Jesus" by David Friedrich Strauss. He emphasized that the miracle stories were to be taken as myths, the "story-like wrapping of religious ideas." The accounts of the Gospels were not so much shaped as historical reminiscences, as they were created under the impression of the idea of the incarnation that was awakened by Jesus. It was not permissible to trace back to a "rational" core what is inexplicable in the Gospels; rather, the mythical character of the narratives was to be acknowledged. On the other hand, it was clearly evident that all of what is narrated had to be ahistorical because it contradicted reason. For exegesis, Strauss's argument meant some considerable progress. One cannot eliminate the miracle from the miracle story in order to retain the historical core, because precisely the miracle itself is the message of the miracle narrative.

We recall that the Gospels are made up of self-contained, small units of tradition. Brief scenes (dialogues, miracles), sayings, and parables are tied together with terse "redactional" links. It is highly probable that these passages were handed down orally. Form criticism investigates these small preliterary units concerning their external narrative form, their special content character, and their theological purpose; the laws of the formation of oral transmission are of special importance here. The transition from oral to written form did not take place without interruption but led to the abridgment of the oral narratives (on this, consult Güttgemanns [see bibliography], esp. 69–166).

(2) Form criticism uses two differing methods—one is a rather aesthetic analysis and the other a rather sociological one, since it is concerned with both the determination of the external form of a text and especially with the place, i.e., the situation in which the text emerged. It is on account of these two approaches, which are not to be viewed as optional but which may receive varying emphasis, that there is no generally acknowledged, uniform terminology in form criticism, and, correspondingly, no standard analysis of the material.

Dibelius and Bultmann construe form criticism in the first place as sociological analysis by asking for the life setting ("*Sitz im Leben*") in the case of each tradition. Dibelius is more inclined to determine the forms of the tradition on the basis of forms (cf. *Tradition to Gospel*, 1–8), whereas Bultmann argues more on the basis of content (cf. *History of the Synoptic Tradition*, 4–8). This finds its expression in their terminology: Dibelius speaks of tales, paradigms, etc. as literary types (*Gattungen*), while Bultmann, in keeping with the content of the texts, speaks of miracle stories, disputes, etc. The objection sometimes raised against Bultmann's procedure, that the determination of the *form* should not be allowed to be based on the *content*, is not valid, especially since form criticism is interested precisely in the relationship of form and content in the historical place of its shaping. Form criticism begins with the observation that a specific narrated content corresponds with a specific form of narration; therefore, Bultmann's procedure is methodologically legitimate. The fact that there are two terminologies in the realm of form criticism does not even need to bother the beginner. The question whether Bultmann's classification or Dibelius' was the "correct" one is superfluous, because the concern is first of all not the adoption of the terminology, but the form-critical method of operation. In any case, the "forms" (*Formen*) are ideal types that may occur with far less "purity" in each concrete instance than in theory.

In determining the form, the following question is to be answered first of all: Is this a historical narrative or a legend, poetry or prose, an anecdote, a parable, and so on? But such a classification according to external perspectives alone does not yet lead to the actual essence of form-critical analysis; rather, the sociological aspect also needs to be considered. Every tradition, especially those handed down orally, stands in an immediate relationship with the community that shapes tradition, thus reflecting the social conditions and the religious, political, and philosophical ideas of the latter. In other words, the tradition itself allows certain inferences about the particular situation in the formation of tradition. The sociological task of form criticism, therefore, is the question of the "Sitz im Leben."

Form-critical work has been developed especially by H. Gunkel in the area of the OT. The phenomenon of the "Sitz im Leben" emerges much more clearly there than in the NT. For instance, the legends of the patriarchs in the Pentateuch intend to substantiate the existence of certain social and political associations in Israel, such as the "house of Joseph." The legends of institution relative to some sanctuaries are meant to endorse the validity, that is, especially the antiquity of the cultus celebrated there (cf., e.g., the cult legend of Bethel, Gen 28:10–22).

(3) Within the units of tradition that have been analyzed form critically, certain rules of style can be recognized:

(a) A strict unity of place and time dominates, i.e., the individual narrative contains only one scene and not a longer action sequence or the psychological development of a person. In the narrative of the plucking of wheat on the Sabbath (Mk 2:23–28), it is not important to know how this stroll came about, how long it lasted, what was its particular destination, and what was possibly planned afterwards. Only the fact of the path "through the fields" is picked up, obviously for the set purpose of providing a narrative framework for a dialogue (vv 24–27). This main characteristic of the spatial-temporal unity also applies to the somewhat longer "tales," such as the narrative of the demoniac of Gadara (Mk 5:1–20). Here the description of the milieu—at least in comparison with the brevity of other stories—is relatively detailed, and there are two actions: The encounter with the demoniac and the tragic fate of the herd of pigs. And yet, only *one* story is told, since the second action is not independent but dependent upon what precedes.

It is different in those instances where an extended action is narrated; in those cases a secondary, literary shaping exists to be begin with. This is shown in the group of legends in Lk 1 and 2 as well as in the passion narrative, within which are found interlocking scenes (trial of Jesus and, at the same time, Peter's denial) that cannot have been handed down orally in this form.

(b) One scarcely hears of any details (Dibelius speaks of the "lack of a portrait"). In the simplest type of narrative, such as the miracle stories, the name of the sick person healed is not mentioned (an exception is Blind Bartimaeus, Mk 10:46); specific references concerning place and time are often lacking (cf. Mk 1:40–45); and the description of the setting is extremely terse or is lacking altogether, except when the setting is significant for the narrated action itself. No mention is made of the psychological motives of the actors or of what the healed person feels afterwards. When reference is made to faith or joy, it has to do with the behavior of the bystanders, not with that of the one healed (cf., e.g., Mk 2:5). Therefore, the miracle story summons the hearer to faith and does not turn the fate and behavior of the one healed into an edifying example. It is well to remember the key statement: Stories of healing are not conversion stories.

However, this changes later on; the extensive narrative of the Sabbath-day healing of the man born blind (Jn 9) ends with the confession of Jesus as the Son of man by the one healed (9:38).

(c) In the dialogue scenes there are usually only two partners facing one another (individuals or also groups, e.g., "the Pharisees"); other persons, even if they are among the audience, do not enter the conversation directly. The relatively complicated scene in Mk 2:1–12 demonstrates this: Present are Jesus, the people, the patient and his companions, as well as some scribes. In spite of this, the "conversation" is limited to Jesus' directly addressing the patient (who did not say anything himself) and to Jesus' brief "debate" with his opponents. The duality of the scene, therefore, remains even here.

Greater differentiation in the narration is again not found until the Gospel of John, as the narrative of Jn 9, cited above, shows.

(d) The suppression of all details in the NT narrative allows the main point for which the narratives have been shaped in the first place to emerge more strongly. This *point*, in any case, is generally Jesus himself, specifically the now exalted Jesus in whom the church believes. Jesus is presented as the miracle worker, as the mighty Savior who shows himself as the authoritative Son of God through his deeds; but he is also presented as teacher whose teaching is still being heard, comprehended, and believed, and who is himself present in his teaching.

3. Forms of the synoptic tradition (according to R. Bultmann)

A preliminary overview of the material can be gained through formal classification. There is (A) narrative material and (B) sayings material. However, this division does not fully work out, since there are also secondary forms: (1) parables are stories of Jesus in which an action is described; systematically, however, they are part of the sayings material. (2) Still subject to debate is the form-critical classification of those narratives concerning Jesus in which the main point is a saying of Jesus; Bultmann incorporates these texts—he calls them apophthegms—in the sayings material, whereas Dibelius considers them to be part of the narratives.

Before dealing more closely with Bultmann, a basic opening remark concerning the use of his book on the "history of the synoptic tradition" is called for. If one consults the book for the purpose of analyzing a particular pericope, the immediate impression is that the author makes apodictic decisions about the text without even as much as an attempt at substantiation. This, however, is not the case at all. If one begins to read each chapter in light of its end, as it were, the criteria upon which Bultmann has established his arguments become clear. Only in this way is it possible either to retrace his decisions or to criticize them.

In the part I A, for instance, Bultmann analyzes the apophthegms individually (pp. 19–39); only then follows the basic section concerning the "form and history of the apophthegms" (pp. 39–69) in which the characteristics of style and thereby also the essential criteria of form-critical assessment are cited and discussed. This format, which at first seems rather strange, is based on Bultmann's endeavor to proceed analytically, that is, by beginning with the text itself and thus to gain the general standards and criteria for the determination of the type. Conversely, in the individual analysis he already presupposes the basic knowledge presented in the second part. It is essential to be aware of this, in order to understand and use Bultmann's book correctly.

(A) Narrative material

Among the *narrative materials* are to be found (a) the miracle stories, divided into healing miracles and nature miracles, and (b) the historical narratives and legends.

(1) The concept *miracle story* is to be understood strictly form critically; in other words, only those stories belong to this group in which the communication of the miracle proper is the actual purpose of the narrative. Miracle narratives whose main point is not located in the miracle as such, but rather in a saying or in a teaching, belong to the apophthegms.

In terms of the general characterization of the style, Bultmann's category of miracle story almost coincides with Dibelius' tale, but it also has some affinities with the paradigms.

The differing evaluation of individual pericopae can be seen in two examples: Mk 1:23(!)–28, for Dibelius, is a "paradigm of a less than pure type" (p. 40), but for Bultmann is clearly a miracle story (on the pre-Markan level, of course); Mk 2:1–12 for Dibelius is a fairly pure paradigm, while Bultmann maintains that, in its present form, it is an apophthegm, grounded in a miracle story.

Miracle stories have a typical structure observable with particular clarity in the example of the casting out of the demon ("exorcism"):

(a) Exposition: Brief description of the situation of the sick (perhaps: reference to the duration or severity of the illness).

(b) The demon notices the exorcist.

(c) The demon is commanded to depart from the ill person.

(d) The effect on the ill person is seen. The demon departs with a demonstration that portrays the success (to the reader) vividly: The victim is being pulled around; the demon screams loudly or knocks down an object while departing (the latter, however, does not occur in any NT miracle story). In the case of a healing miracle without exorcism, the demonstration can also consist of the former paralytic taking up his bed and going home on his own.

(e) The effect upon the bystanders is important: they praise either God or the miracle worker (Dibelius: "choral ending"); thereby the reader is encouraged to join in the amazement.

In spite of the substantial agreements between the synoptic miracle stories on the one hand and the Jewish or hellenistic miracle stories on the other (Bultmann gives a large number of such examples), there is a distinct difference between the two: the miracles of Jesus were not miracles for show, but always miracles of help. Of course, the tendency to heighten the miraculous can also be observed in the Synoptics, as a comparison of the stories of the feeding of the multitudes will show easily.

Recommended further reading for advanced students:

G. Theissen, *The Miracle Stories of the Early Christian Tradition*, ET 1983.

(2) Among the type (*Gattung*) *"historical narratives and legends"* are the narratives of baptism, transfiguration, as well as the birth, passion, and Easter stories. Especially concerning the passion narrative, Bultmann's opinion differs sharply from that of Dibelius. While Dibelius by and large sees it as a unit, Bultmann suspects that it originally contained only a meager basic message (apprehension, conviction, execution) which had subsequently been filled up with further scenes.

Among the Easter stories, Bultmann again distinguishes two further groups: the grave stories and the appearance stories.

He designates as grave stories those narratives relating directly to the (empty) grave. A special problem in this connection is the question of whether the grave stories were originally ascension stories, that is, whether they presuppose that Jesus is already in heaven. Or were they created afterwards in order to support the appearance stories? Bultmann assumes the latter to be correct, and, if one opts to support the former, it becomes indeed necessary to explain the unavoidable rivalry among the appearance stories.

The second group is the appearance stories, among which it is necessary to distinguish between those narratives whose main point is a saying of the resurrected one—such as the Great Commission—and narratives in which the main point is the appearance of the resurrected one himself.

The location of the appearances is also significant for the interpretation. According to Mt the resurrected one appears to the women in Jerusalem (28:9f.), but to the disciples in Galilee (28:16-20). In Lk, he appears only in Jerusalem. Jn 20 narrates the appearances in Jerusalem, and the appended ch 21 reports those in Galilee. (The Gospel of Mark contains no appearance stories at all.)

(B) Sayings material

Among the *sayings material* Bultmann included (a) the "apophthegms," broken down into controversy dialogues and scholastic dialogues, as well as so-called biographical apophthegms, and (b) the dominical sayings in which Jesus appears as teacher of wisdom, as proclaimer of prophetic and apocalyptic sayings, and as creator of community regulations. Of course (c) the parables also belong to the dominical sayings, but on account of their special significance the parables need to be discussed separately.

(1) The term "apophthegm" occurs in the Greek history of literature as well as in the patristic writings; it characterizes anecdotes about philosophers, saints, or monks, climaxing in an emphatic expression. In the synoptic Gospels, therefore, the term refers to stories whose climactic utterance is a saying of Jesus.

Within the apophthegms, the most important group is the controversy dialogues and scholastic dialogues that highlight Jesus in argumentation with opponents or in answering certain questions—generally concerning problems in the experience of the community. The impetus can be provided by a miracle (as in Mk 3:1-6) or by a question addressed to Jesus (Mk 2:23-28) in which it is a fixed trait that Jesus responds with a counter question, in true rabbinic fashion. The "biographical apophthegms" (e.g.,

Mk 1:16–20; 6:1–6; 10:13–16) are sermon paradigms; "they help to present
Jesus as a living contemporary" (*History of the Synoptic Tradition*, 61).

Suggested exercises:

1. Mk 3:1–6 is an apophthegm while Mk 1:21–27 (28) is a miracle story. What are
the characteristic differences in their respective styles?

2. In Mk 2:1–12 there is a secondary transformation of a miracle story into an
apophthegm. What was the scope of the original miracle story?

The disputes mainly involve a question or rebuke, followed by the appropriate answer of Jesus; there is therefore practically never a true altercation. Generally the life situation is located in the apologetic and
polemic of the Christian community that bases its religious practice on
Jesus and so defends itself against the critics. Therefore, the situations
presented in the apophthegms do not reflect genuine events that transpired in the life of Jesus, but, according to Bultmann, they are almost
always—and in the case of the controversy dialogues and scholastic dialogues almost exclusively—"ideal situations." Bultmann distinguishes between organic and inorganic apophthegms: In the former, word and scene
are formed in one sweep, and only in the framework of the scene is the
word clear and meaningful (Mk 3:1–6). In the inorganic apophthegms,
however, the original word will likely have existed independently and the
scene was then created to provide a suitable framework for the isolated
word handed down by Jesus (Mk 2:15f.; 2:18; 7:1f.). Hence Mk 1:16–20,
for instance, is not a genuine "story" at all; rather, the narrative may have
been spun out of the originally independent saying of Jesus about fish-
ers of men for the purpose of illustrating this saying. In similar fashion,
the story of Jesus' appearance in Nazareth may have originated from the
saying about the prophet who is regarded without honor in his hometown.

The blessing of the little children in Mk 10:13–16 serves as an example of the change
of an apophthegm. In this pericope which, in its form, is undoubtedly an apophthegm, Jesus gives two explanations that do not fully harmonize: for one, he says
that *children* enter the kingdom of God, and for another, he says that one enters
the kingdom of God by being *like* a little child—addressed to adults, of course.
But v 15 can be isolated from the scene without losing the clarity of the pericope,
while conversely the same verse can also be understood as a self-contained saying apart from the context. If the control test is made by attempting to separate
v 14, it becomes evident that this is impossible—v 14 organically belongs to the
narrative. This analysis indicates that an originally organic apophthegm had been
expanded by including v 15 and thereby became an inorganic apophthegm. It
is interesting to note that Matthew took v 15 out of its setting and placed in a
different one (cf. Mt 19:13–15 with 18:3).

The form-critical analysis of the apophthegms has certain consequences
for the theological interpretation. In our example of Mk 10:13–16 (see

above), the story must first of all be interpreted without v 15: The kingdom of God is intended for little children; it is a complete gift which one receives without personal effort beforehand. After this, v 15 needs to be considered on its own. Here the condition for entrance into the kingdom of God is formulated—it must be accepted "like a child," i.e., without being entitled to it. Clearly the combination of both elements was quite obvious and step three, the interpretation of the entire passage now at hand, confirms this observation.

Suggested exercises:

1. The "path" of this tradition can be pursued further by probing the context of Mk 10:13–16 and the incorporation by Mt and Lk. Does the meaning change, or instead is the former interpretation underscored when the pericope is compared in Mk, Mt, and Lk in their respective contexts? Compare A. Lindemann, "Die Kinder und die Gottesherrschaft," *WuD* NF 17, 1983, 77–104.

2. The comparison between Mk and Mt is impressive: The form of the miracle stories is polished in order to give prominence to a particular main point.

In Mt the apophthegms as such are changed into legal debates. Given these perspectives, a comparison is especially informative between Mk 3:1–6 and Mt 12:9–14; Mk 2:23–28 and Mt 12:1–8; Mk 10:17ff. and Mt 19:16ff.

(2) The dominical sayings constitute the second group of sayings material. We have already observed above that the *sayings of Jesus* were first handed down as self-contained sayings, that is, without a broader association. This can be seen in their placement in widely divergent places within the respective outlines of the synoptic Gospels (cf. Mk 10:15 with Mt 18:3; Mk 13:9–12 with Mt 10:17–21). "Discourses" of Jesus consistently prove to be secondary arrangements of originally separate sayings, such as that seen in an analysis of Mk 8:34–9:1. Vv 34, 35, 36f., 38; 9:1 are individual units of meaning, similar to proverbs (for their interpretation, see below, p. 70). In this connection, a comparison between the Sermon on the Mount in Matthew and the Lukan Sermon on the Plain is profitable. From the observation that Matthew generally constructs longer speeches than Lk, the working hypothesis arises that the Sermon on the Mount represents an expansion of the Sermon on the Plain, or better still: the logia source is the older composition foundational for both.

Example: The pericope on loving one's enemies in Lk 6:27–36 corresponds with Mt 5:38–48, but the "golden rule" of Lk 6:31 is found in an entirely different place in Mt, only in 7:12. Who has changed the order? Lk 6:34f. has no parallel in Mt; has the latter therefore truncated, or has Lk expanded? Compare this with p. 54 above.

Suggested exercise:

Continue the analysis of the Sermon on the Mount and the Sermon on the Plain beyond Lk 6:37 in the direction indicated above. Use Bultmann's *History of the Synoptic Tradition* to aid in this endeavor (table of contents). The leading question must be the following: Are the individual pericopae in the Sermon on the Mount and in the Sermon on the Plain consistent from a *literary* vantage point or only in terms of their content?

Bultmann divides the sayings of Jesus according to the criteria of content and form. In the category of content, four groups emerge:

(a) The "logia" in the strict sense (i.e., wisdom sayings), in the form of an assertion (e.g., Mt 12:34), a question (Mt 6:27), or a command (Mt 10:16).

Bultmann's terminology is not unambiguous at this point. On the one hand, generally all logia or sayings are words of Jesus; on the other hand, more strictly only the wisdom or proverbial sayings are words of Jesus.

(b) Prophetic and apocalyptic sayings, such as the statements of salvation and of woe (Lk 6:20ff.).

(c) Legal sayings (e.g., Mt 10:11f.).

(d) "I" sayings (e.g., Mt 10:34–36; cf. Lk 12:51–53).

With reference to the form, Bultmann distinguishes between unitary (Lk 10:17), two-part (Mk 8:35), and three-part sayings (Mt 7:1–5).

The model for the logia is to be found in OT and Jewish wisdom sayings, such as those collected in Proverbs or in Jesus ben Sirach. The parallels are multitudinous, as seen in the comparison of Mt 6:34 with *Sanh* 100b: "Do not concern yourself with tomorrow's care, for you do not know what the day will bring forth! Who knows whether you are still here tomorrow and you have toiled for a world which is no longer of concern to you," or with *Berakh* 9b: "(Moses speaks to God:) Lord of the world, sufficient for the hour is the need thereof" (documentation in Billerbeck I, 441).

Likewise, the interpretation of the logia must be carried out in two steps. First one needs to ask about the meaning of the saying in and of itself apart from its context. The second question is: What does it mean in its present context?

Reading Dibelius, *Die Botschaft von Jesus Christus* (Siebenstern Paperback 99) serves as a useful and interesting exercise relative to the first question; there the sayings are printed like isolated aphorisms.

Mk 8:34–9:1 serves as an exercise. We have already pointed out above that the individual sayings can easily be understood in isolation from the context; now we inquire into the meaning:

1. What does v 34 mean in a situation in the life of Jesus? What does the verse mean in the situation of the community?

2. If one brackets the words ἕνεκεν ἐμοῦ καὶ τοῦ εὐαγγελίου of v 35 for testing purposes, one gets a "wisdom precept" (*Weisheitsregel*) which occurs in ancient historical accounts, for instance, in speeches made by generals before a battle. The soldier who flees thereby risks his life. What is the meaning of this sentence when it is a Christian precept?

3. Into what situation do v 38 and 9:1 fit?

4. How is the "speech" of 8:34–9:1 to be understood in the context of the Gospel of Mark? Why does it follow immediately after the first prediction of his passion?

The following rules can be ascertained for the collection of the logia in the Gospels:

(*a*) They are inserted into situations that are already existing or that have been created ad hoc, so that apophthegms are formed (example: Mk 10:15; cf. above, p. 69).

(*b*) They are placed into a "suitable" context; thus Mk 4:21–25 is to be read together with v 11 in the understanding of the evangelist—the statement then elucidates the nature of the secret of the kingdom of God.

(*c*) Individual logia are connected with one another via key words.

(*d*) Series of content-related logia are formed (cf. the Beatitudes).

(*e*) Entire "catechisms" are formed, some shorter (cf. Mk 9:37ff.) and some longer (Sermon on the Plain, Sermon on the Mount).

The form-critical analysis also yields certain criteria relative to the question of which logia are to be regarded as "authentic," i.e., which can be traced back to the preaching of the historical Jesus. As soon as they are divested from their altogether Christian (i.e., post-Easter) framework, the question can be raised objectively whether the logion per se originated in the teaching of the community, whether it fits the traditionally alleged Jewish framework, or whether neither is the case and it can be assumed, therefore, that it is very likely an authentic saying of Jesus. (The problem is delineated in detail in § 52 below.)

(3) Without a doubt, the most important part of the sayings material are the *parables*, for here the likelihood of finding "authentic" material is particularly high. For one, this assumption is based on the comparison with Jewish parables, and, second, it takes into consideration the observation that the production of parables within the church is carried out only on a small scale. The third and most important criterion is the assertion that most parables are to be understood as coming from the pre-Easter situation, that is, from the immediate context of the life of Jesus. For example, they forcefully connect the present actions of Jesus with their future effectiveness (cf. Mk 4:3–8); they teach to comprehend the coming kingdom of God; and, most of all, they contain no explicit teaching about the person of Jesus, and they do not presuppose an organized church. Doubts concerning the "authenticity" of a parable are in order

as soon as one of the criteria mentioned is not met, as for instance when the parable contains a distinct Christology, when constitutional problems of a church seem to be addressed, and so on.

For the purpose of the reconstruction of the teaching of Jesus, the parables are all the more important, since the problem of translation from Aramaic (the language of Jesus) into Greek is not posed as clearly here. Whereas individual words, or even entire logia can be changed considerably in the translation as well as in the transition from the oral to the written form, the picture of a parable as a whole may well remain intact, even when many changes are possible in the details.

The general stylistic characteristics of the parables correspond with those of other forms of narrative:

1. The presentation is brief; in other words, only those persons and circumstances relevant to the action are mentioned (e.g., in the parable of the prodigal son, no mention is made of the prodigal's mother).

2. As a rule, only two acting persons appear; when a possible group is mentioned, such as the "wicked tenants of the vineyard," it is treated as a unit.

Yet Mk 12:1ff. is concerned with the formation of the church, at least in the passage's present setting. The characteristic elements of style are the same, however.

3. The action is unilateral and pursues a clear goal.

4. The emphasis rests on the conclusion of the parable; for this reason the parables are to be deciphered in reverse (one speaks of the law of the "weight of the stern" [*Achtergewicht*]).

The material predominantly used in the parables comes from the rural milieu of Palestine: The peasant and his servant(s), the baking housewife, the neighbors in the village, house construction and fishing, children playing, trade, vine-growing, and other occupations of life are drawn upon as illustrative material. The same holds true for the persons acting: Pharisees, tax collectors, Samaritans are encountered in their typical, and yet, in part, also in atypical behavior patterns.

In terms of material and partly also in intent (*Tendenz*), there are similarities, of course, between the synoptic and the Jewish parables. Nevertheless, it can be said that synoptic texts are arranged with more color than the rabbinic parables, which are usually somewhat monotonous.

Excursus I: Concerning the History of the Investigation of Parables

The principles of the interpretation of parables can be established more easily by first overviewing some of the decisive stages in the recent scholarly research.

Bibliography:

A. Jülicher, *Die Gleichnisreden Jesu*, ²1910.

C. H. Dodd, *The Parables of the Kingdom*, (1935), 1961.

J. Jeremias, *The Parables of Jesus*, ET ²1963.

W. Harnisch, ed., *Gleichnisse Jesu. Positionen der Auslegung von Adolf Jüli-cher bis zur Formgeschichte*, WdF 367, 1982.

The special merit of Adolf Jülicher lies in the fact that he overcame the allegorical interpretation of the parables common until then (see also Excursus II). He argued that parables are pictures focusing on one main point. This methodological axiom has been widely adopted. However, Jülicher's interpretation of the parabolic message is being questioned, for he categorically aims at deriving one general truth from the respective parable. Thus, the parable of the entrusted talents teaches that only effort will be rewarded—and the entire narrative serves to present this truth.

Charles Harold Dodd opposed the interpretations of Jülicher by charging that they were too general and moralistic. The decisive issue in the correct interpretation is the mooring of the parables in the concrete situation of Jesus. Of course Dodd is not concerned to show biographical incidents as framework for the parables, but to base each parable upon the context of the self-understanding of Jesus in the framework of the overall situation of the world. Dodd explained that Jesus proclaims a "realized eschatology," that is to say, Jesus was convinced that the kingdom of God had entered this world in his person; what transpires in the present is only the crisis precipitated by the kingdom. It was *this* situation that the parables of Jesus sought to interpret. On this basis Dodd interprets the parable of the mustard seed in Lk 13:18f. (Dodd considers this version to be original, rather than that of Mk 4:30–32): "Jesus is asserting that the time has come when the blessings of the Reign of God are available for all men" (*Parables*, 153).

Joachim Jeremias continues where Dodd stops. But he is of the opinion that parables ought to be interpreted based on their *biographical* situation. For instance, if a parable speaks of a thief, it was told in the wake of a theft which actually happened (Jeremias, *Parables*, 48f.). The multiplicity of the images used has its reason in Jesus' constant references to actual events. As a whole, the parables do not show an eschatology that is realized but one which is being realized.

In the parables Jesus points out that the end approaches irresistibly and the time of the final decision has come. However, the analysis of the parables shows that the original narrative situation is in no sense handed down; indeed, what is characteristic is precisely that the parables were actually handed down without any special reference to the situation and yet remain fully intelligible.

In his standard work, *Die Gleichnisreden Jesu*, which has not been re-placed to date, Jülicher has undertaken a more detailed classification of the parables.

In this endeavor, he draws from the concepts of Aristotelian rhetoric. Against this procedure the objection is raised that these categories are not relevant to the parables of Jesus, since these are not shaped after the Greek model of style, but after the Jewish one. However, in exegesis one needs to observe fundamentally that the concrete interpretation alone can determine the usefulness of specific types of concepts. One needs to evaluate the feasibility of working with Jülicher's categories; if they are workable, the terminology is less important than the correct designation of the content of the various narratives.

(a) The pre-form of the parabolic narrative is the *similitude* (e.g., Mt 5:14—a city on a hill cannot be hidden).

(b) Comparative forms of the word picture are the *hyperbole* (Mt 5:29—if your eye offends you, pluck it out!) and the *paradox* (Mk 8:35—whoever wants to save his life will lose it).

(c) Quite rarely the simple *comparison* (as . . . so) occurs, as in Mt 10:16, for instance: Be as shrewd as snakes. . . .

(d) The abbreviated comparison is known as *metaphor* (cf. e.g., Mt 7:13f.—the "narrow gate," the "narrow way") and needs to be decoded ("translated").

The parabolic narratives which Jülicher expounds, are divided into four types:

(e) The *parable* in the strict sense of the term, namely, a similitude; the topic is a frequently observed circumstance, such as the making of sour-dough, the growth of the mustard seed, etc. The hearer is personally called upon to observe, so that he can arrive at a certain conclusion. This is seen especially in those parables introduced with the question, "Who among you is . . . ?" The point of comparison between the picture presented and the issue intended lies in one particular place, and it is the task of the exegete to find this singular point of comparison.

(f) The *parable* as a "story" that one is told, a specific and individual action (e.g., the story of the prodigal, Lk 15:11–32). Yet there are over-laps: the saying of the mustard seed, for instance, is a parable [in the sense of the similitude, transl.] and is narrated as such by Mark (in the present tense); in Q, however, it was handed down in the form of a parable [in the sense of story, transl.], as the Lukan form shows: "There was a man who. . . ." The narrative difference is seen very clearly in Mt. There the text begins in the form of a parable but is then continued in the same form as in Mark (not: it grew . . ., but: it grows . . .). In the parable as story as well, there is only one point of comparison.

(g) A unique event is also reported in the *example story*, but in distinc-tion to the parable (see [f]), a certain exemplary demeanor is described directly, rather than in pictorial disguise. One can illustrate the difference between the parable and the example story by comparing Lk 16:1–8 with Lk 10:30–35: The unjust steward in the parable, of course, is no moral example in his practical action—the only exemplary thing is his quick grasp of the situation; on the other hand, the behavior of the good Samaritan is presented as direct example: Everyone is to act this way.

(h) A type which departs completely from all those mentioned heretofore is the *allegory,* which is best understood as a stringing together of metaphors. There are *several* points of comparison in the allegorical narrative—not only one. In any case, most if not all of the specifics cited have a symbolic meaning; in other words, the narrative has to be decoded piece by piece. The action sequence is not natural but is construed to point more or less clearly to the symbolic meaning, whereas the specifics in the similitude and in the story are not transposed allegorically but are to be understood in the literal sense.

Example: The story of the good Samaritan takes place between Jerusalem and Jericho. If it were to be interpreted allegorically, the following transfers of meaning would occur: Jerusalem would be the city of God; Jericho, which is "down," the city of sin. Whoever leaves the city of God falls into the hands of "robbers" and would perish if a "rescuer" did not appear. However, the fact that the narrative, in its literal sense, makes perfectly good sense and contains a readily meaningful sequence of events, shows that this is not an allegory.

The picture part of the allegory (the narrated action) is constructed in such a way that only the main issue, (what is actually meant) is expressed, while the picture part always contains either a clear break or an exaggeration in content that is unintelligible as normal action.

Excursus II: Comments on the Determination of the Allegory

Bibliography: H.-J. Klauck, *Allegorie und Allegorese in synoptischen Gleichnistexten,* NTA NF 13, 1978.

The question whether or not a certain parable to be exegeted should be understood as an allegory is of special significance because it is also important in connection with the problem of origin.

Jülicher postulated that the parables of Jesus were *never* to be construed as allegories. When they do contain allegorical traits, these are secondary, and the formation of pure allegories is always to be attributed to the church. This proposition is contested by some exegetes with the question why Jesus should not occasionally have taught in allegories. The answer to this question emerges quickly, however, by observing that the allegories in the synoptic Gospels consistently presuppose a higher Christology or ecclesiology than is conceivable in the proclamation of Jesus. Furthermore, it is unlikely that Jesus used a form of speech that was entirely unintelligible apart from a special hermeneutical key.

(1) It is striking that the evangelists themselves offer a more or less allegorical interpretation of two parables:

(a) The parable of the sower, Mk 4:1ff. with parallels (incl. *Gospel according to Thomas*, logion 9), is interpreted in such a way in Mk 4:13–20 that individual features of the picture are "translated" symbolically. This interpretation is not original, for it shows characteristics belonging to a later era. For instance, the absolute use of ὁ λόγος, which refers to the sermon, is a technical term of the church's language of proclamation. But the decisive observation is that the parable and its interpretation do not match at all in terms of content; the interpretation that the birds are representative of the devil is quite forced. Notice that the meaning of the seed changes abruptly in the middle of the text—at first the seed is "the word," then suddenly the meaning changes to people who hear the word. The pure parable becomes an allegory and the promise turns into an exhortation. While the plentiful harvest from the "good soil" is in the foreground in the parable itself, the frequent failure of the seed becomes the central interest in the interpretation. Even the interpretation of the parable's point itself (thirtyfold etc.) is dispensed with. Evidently the church's experience is mirrored in the interpretation in that the proclamation often lacks a positive response (in addition, cf. p. 84ff.).

(b) Likewise in the interpretation of the parable of the tares (Mt 13:24–30 and 36–43) the picture is changed into an allegory. Whereas the parable itself emphasizes that tares and wheat were not to be separated, the interpretation focuses on the evil fate of the transgressors of the law—once again, the promise becomes an exhortation and a warning.

(2) It can also be observed that an original parable itself is later allegorized. This is seen, for instance, in the parable of the wedding feast, Mt 22:1–10 par Lk 14:16–24: The Matthean form contains an allegorical streak from the beginning; for, the central character is not "someone," as in Luke, but a king. Nor does it concern just any feast (as in Luke), but the wedding feast of the son of a king. From the beginning, therefore, the thought emerges that the point of discussion is God and his Son. The one-time mission of a servant in Luke is juxtaposed by the repeated mission in Matthew—evidently he thinks of the prophets who call upon rebellious Israel. In the context of the illustration, the torture and murder of the servants is absurd. It can be explained from the viewpoint that the prophets in Israel had been killed. Utterly grotesque is the continuation: While the feast is pending, the king leads a battle against "the city" of the rebellious guests, obliterates the city and then invites new guests to the apparently still imminent wedding feast. The idea in mind is obviously the destruction of Jerusalem in A.D. 70, which is interpreted as punishment for the rejection of the Christian message. Beyond what is found in Luke, the Matthean form contains an additional scene: one of the new

guests does not wear a wedding garment. But how could he, since he was invited to come off the street? Apparently it is intended to present allegorically the condition for participating in salvation. Thus, in Matthew this parable is an abstract of salvation history. If the disruptive features are bracketed, it is possible to come closer to the original parable—and now the agreements with the Lukan form also become clear. In Luke, the former action is quite natural: invitation, rejection, other guests. Yet, even here a certain interruption in the development is found. Although there are now all kinds of people from the city in the banqueting hall, there is still more room available; hence the servant leaves once more to bring in people off the streets. Since Matthew has no doubling here, it appears that it was Luke who has allegorized at this point. Whereas in Matthew Israel and the new people of God confronted one another, in Luke it was Israel and the church, comprised of Jews and Gentiles, that is, of "the inhabitants of the city" and of those "from outside." Therefore, if one brackets the allegorical features in Matthew and Luke respectively, a basic core common to both results: The parable (of Jesus) taught that salvation comes to those who did not appear to be predestined for it. Out of this, Matthew shapes the picture of the confrontation of the church with Israel, and Luke shapes that of the universal mission.

An exegetical detail observation: Who actually speaks in v 24? Originally, it was likely the host—in that case it fits the picture. In the context of Luke, however, Jesus speaks directly, of course—in that case it refers symbolically to the heavenly banquet.

(3) It seems that the parable of the wicked tenants (Mk 12:1-12) is on the borderline between parable and allegory. On several occasions and in vain the master sends his servants to collect the rent. After the servants have been ignored and some even murdered, he sends his son, who is killed as well and thrown out of the vineyard. But with this act the evildoers call down their doom; the vineyard is given to others. It is disputed whether the murdered son is a reference to Jesus and whether this feature of the parable, therefore, is to be interpreted allegorically. If the parable presupposes the death of Jesus (thus Bultmann, Kümmel), it has its origin in the church. In contrast, Jeremias and Hengel, among others, argue that the "beloved son" is also to be interpreted nonallegorically in the framework of the parable; if the traces of allegorical revision, especially in v 5, are bracketed, one gains a parable of Jesus true to style. It concerns the concrete social setting in Galilee: The farmlands (Lat. *Latifundia*) are in the possession of foreigners, which leads to unrest among the rural population as well as to acts of violence. The *Gospel according to Thomas*, logion 65, still shows the original form. But even if v 5 were excised, the text would remain an allegory. After all that transpired before-

hand, the sending of the "beloved son" is incomprehensible within the illustration—but it is clear to the hearer *who* this son is in reality.

The situation is similar in the narrative of the wise and foolish virgins (Mt 25:1–13): Can the action per se be understood, or does it require an allegorical interpretation? At the same time the question of origin needs to be raised again. If it deals with a normal wedding, the parable can be attributed to Jesus himself. But if the bridegroom refers to Christ in his parousia, the parable is the product of the church.

Suggested exercise:

Gather viewpoints and work toward a solution for Mt 25:1–13, using the contributions of Jülicher, Bultmann, Jeremias, and Weder (see below).

Excursus III: Unique Problems in the Interpretation of Parables

(1) The so-called growth parables (sower, seed growing on its own, tares among the wheat, mustard seed, fig tree) represent a unique problem for the theological interpretation. The scenes they contain suggest to the reader first of all that they deal with the growth, that is, with the organic and continuous development of the kingdom of God in the world. A number of different solutions have therefore been offered for the interpretation of Mk 4:26–29: (a) The kingdom grows within man; (b) it grows and develops in the world; (c) it is an eschatological entity, hence it is like the *harvest*; (d) the kingdom is neither a process of the inner life nor a future apocalyptic catastrophe, but a present crisis (Dodd: realized eschatology); (e) the main point of the parable is the certainty of the fulfillment of the promise. All of these interpretive attempts disregard that the growth parables are not at all intended to describe a development, but on the contrary, they precisely want to set forth a contrast. The parable of the mustard seed points this out with special clarity; the insignificant beginning is juxtaposed to an overwhelming end.

(2) Another unique problem is the introductory phrase of the kingdom of God parables. This phrase says (with some variants): ὁμοία ἐστὶν ἡ βασιλεία τοῦ θεοῦ . . . (cf. the somewhat divergent formulations in Mk 4:26, 30; Mt 13:24, 33; Lk 13:20), and parallels the Hebrew אמשל לך משל למה הדבר דמה ל or, in brief, משל ל. It does not mean, "the kingdom of God is like (a merchant, owner of a vineyard etc.)," but rather, "the matter of the kingdom of God is like that of . . ." (Mt 13:45); in other words, the kingdom of God is not compared to the person but to the entire process. Yet, it must be asked again whether the parable introduced thus at its core indeed deals with the kingdom of God, or whether the introductory phrase might not possibly be secondary and therefore only reflects the interpretation of the church or of the evangelist. Hence, according to Bultmann, the parables of the seed growing of itself, of the

mustard seed, and of the leaven did not originally pertain to the kingdom of God; the initial meaning can thus no longer be known (*History of the Synoptic Tradition*, 173).

(3) At the conclusion of many parables one finds an application (cf. Mk 13:29; Lk 14:33; 15:7, 10); here as well one must determine on a case by case basis whether these are not secondary additions that miss the original meaning of the respective parable.

From our observations we draw the following conclusions relative to the interpretation of parables:

(a) The parables were handed down without reference to the situations in which they were originally told. Therefore, it is not appropriate to try to explain them in conjunction with a particular situation in the life of Jesus; they are only able to be understood and interpreted in the light of the totality of Jesus' teaching.

(b) The most important methodological criterion of the interpretation of parables is the question of the main point to which the whole narrative is directed. It is to be noted, of course, that the parables of Jesus do not intend to present the reign of God merely in the form of an image or of a comparison; they are not illustrations of something that Jesus could easily have said in a speech proper. Rather, in them the reign of God itself is presented "as parable." Therefore, besides the question of the main point, it is necessary to consider, too, the multiplicity of the images and themes used.

(c) Understanding the meaning of a parable can be facilitated by means of a crucial question: Is its intent to console or to exhort, i.e., to warn? One is to disregard, of course, the present context and secondary expansions because the general tendency of understanding the parables as words of exhortation of the church predominates. However, the alternative mentioned is not to be pushed to its extreme either; in the parables Jesus indeed communicates God's unconditional salvation; consequently they are positive illustrations of the promise. But this message becomes a message of judgment where salvation is not accepted; in a sense, the parables are thus at once consolation and admonition.

More recent literature for the interpretation of parables:

J. Breech, *The Silence of Jesus*, 1983.

C. E. Carlston, *The Parables of the Triple Tradition*, 1975.

J. D. Crossan, *In Parables*, 1973.

G. Eichholz, *Gleichnisse der Evangelien. Form, Überlieferung, Auslegung*, [2]1975.

R. W. Funk, *Parables and Presence*, 1982.

W. Harnisch (ed.), *Die neutestamentliche Gleichnisforschung im Horizont von Hermeneutik und Literaturwissenschaft*, WdF 575, 1982.

E. Jüngel, *Paulus und Jesus*, HUTh 2, [5]1979, 139–174.

E. Linnemann, *Parables of Jesus. Introduction and Exposition*, ET 1966.

N. Perrin, *Jesus and the Language of the Kingdom*, 1976.

B. B. Scott, *Hear Then the Parables*, 1988.

D. O. Via, Jr., *The Parables. Their Literary and Existential Dimension*, 1967.

H. Weder, *Die Gleichnisse Jesu als Metaphern*, FRLANT 120, ³1984.

A. N. Wilder, *Early Christian Rhetoric*, 1964.

4. Forms of the synoptic tradition (according to M. Dibelius)

Dibelius distinguishes between (A) the narratives on the one hand, and (B) paraenesis, that is, the teaching of Jesus, on the other.

(A) Dibelius suggests the separation of the narrative material into five groups: (1) paradigm, (2) tale, (3) legend, (4) myths; (5) the passion is accorded special status. These need to be discussed in more detail since the categories of Dibelius differ more sharply at this point than those of Bultmann in the paraenesis. The life situation in the narratives, according to Dibelius, is the sermon, the "testimony of salvation." But only part of the narrative is of noteworthy significance for the sermon, that of the passion story. The remaining forms merely serve as illustrative examples of the sermon, as paradigms in the broad sense. The paraenesis has a different life situation from the start; it belongs to the realm of catechetical instruction.

(1) Among the *paradigms* are, for instance, the story of the healing of the man with the withered hand (Mk 3:1–6) and the narrative of the blessing of the little children (Mk 10:13–16). Dibelius point out the following characteristics of style: The paradigms are units of thought complete in themselves and are intelligible by themselves (Dibelius here speaks of a "rounding-off"); therefore they originally existed as self-contained narratives.

They are told in simple terms; colorful details, especially the description of persons, their character, etc. are lacking (Dibelius: "portraits"). The style is that of the devotional language.

The sayings of Jesus are clearly brought to prominence; at the conclusion there may be an affirming "choral ending" by the audience which, of course, is addressed to the hearers.

Note that Bultmann includes those narratives containing sayings of Jesus among the speech material (see above).

The typical conclusion of a paradigm for Dibelius is an idea that is useful in the sermon.

(2) In the group known as *tales*, Dibelius includes, among others, the narrative of the demoniac and the pigs (Mk 5:1ff.) and the story of the feeding of the five thousand (Mk 6:35ff.).

Dibelius mentions the following stylistic features here: Like the paradigms, tales are individual, self-contained stories; but they are laid out more broadly than the paradigms and contain more details.

Tales are comparable to the miracle stories of antiquity; it is their aim to present Jesus as miracle worker. In other words, they are epiphany stories in which Jesus appears as a man equipped with divine powers. For this reason tales contain more detailed references to specifics, such as references to the special healing technique (touching, smearing on of spittle, uttering an effective phrase). /

Dibelius assumes that tales are expansions of paradigms; by picking up secular motifs, they reflect a certain inward development of Christianity that has moved closer to "the world" in the meantime.

Tales are not intended as sermon illustrations. "By then neither the preaching of salvation could be explained nor the knowledge of salvation increased," but "the pre-eminence of the 'Lord Jesus' could be demonstrated and all other rival gods who were worshipped driven from the field" (Dibelius, *Tradition to Gospel*, 96).

(3) *Legends*, according to Dibelius, are stories such as that of the twelve-year-old Jesus in the temple (Lk 2:41–52). In the birth and infancy narratives in Matthew and Luke, several motifs typical for "legends of personnel" are found: the miraculous birth of a hero, the recognition of the child as the redeemer to come, his being in danger and miraculous preservation, his early maturity. Such legendary features are in agreement with those found in the biographies of many significant personalities in antiquity. Therefore, Dibelius speaks of the "law of biographical analogy"—analogy because a direct dependence is nonexistent.

Similarly to the paradigm, the legend has a distinctly devotional quality. In contrast to the former, the latter does not emphasize the sermon, the kerygma in word and deed, "but the religiousness and sanctity of the hero together with the protection granted him by God" (Dibelius, *Tradition to Gospel*, 108).

(4) The *myth*, as Dibelius understands it, surfaces only very rarely in the Gospels; it is used with great reticence. Only the story of the baptism, temptation, and transfiguration of Jesus are "myths," according to Dibelius. These texts are mythical because an otherworldly person is seen in action or because a mythical, i.e., outside the realm of reality, event is recounted. By "myth" Dibelius means a story of the gods such as those not infrequently found in the history of religion; hence his concept of myth is quite different from that of Bultmann.

(5) The *passion narrative* is a special case because of the predetermined, definitive sequence of scenes—and necessarily so, of course; the arrest *must* precede the trial, and the trial must precede the condemnation, etc. The established outline corresponds with the christological kerygma (cf. 1 Cor 15:3–5), the assertions of which are replete with meaning. The passion narrative, for Dibelius, has immediate salvific meaning; in other words, it is not meant to be a report, but proclamation of the purpose of God in what happened in the passion of Jesus. For this reason refer-

ence is also made quite frequently to the Old Testament; the passion is in accordance with the will of God that is recognized in the Bible. Some specific features of the passion narrative can only be traced back to the fact that the Old Testament was read as prophecy regarding Christ. For instance, it is from the Old Testament that we know the amount which Judas received for his betrayal (Mt 26:15).

Suggested exercises:

1. Analyze a paradigm, e.g., Mk 3:1-6, following the criteria outlined by Dibelius: Do the characteristics cited by Dibelius fit, even with regards to the use in the sermon?

2. Analyze a tale, e.g., Mk 5:1-20 (following the same directives).

(B) Dibelius formally divides paraenesis, that is, the tradition of the sayings of Jesus, into six groups:

1. maxims (proverbs, gnome)
2. metaphor
3. parabolic narrative
4. prophetic call (beatitude, woe, eschatological preaching)
5. short commandment
6. extended commandment (with basis, promise, or threat).

According to Dibelius, all of these types need to be included among the paraenetic texts, although only the last two groups contain imperative formulation. Even the parables, for Dibelius, consistently have paraenetic meaning.

Suggested exercise:

We forego a more detailed delineation of the position of Dibelius and, instead, recommend the reading of Dibelius, *Tradition to Gospel*, 233-265.

§ 10 Redaction-critical Formulation of the Question

Bibliography: H. Conzelmann, *The Theology of St. Luke*, ET 1960; W. Marxsen, *Mark the Evangelist*, ET 1969; N. Perrin, *What is Redaction Criticism?* 1969; J. Rohde, *Rediscovering The Teaching of the Evangelists*, 1968; G. Strecker, *Der Weg der Gerechtigkeit. Untersuchungen zur Theologie des Matthäus*, FRLANT 82, [3]1971; "Redaktionsgeschichte als Aufgabe der Synoptikerexegese," in *Eschaton und Historie. Aufsätze*, 1979, 9-32; H. Zimmermann, *Neutestamentliche Methodenlehre*, [7]1982, 215-238.

1. General Observations

It is the task of redaction criticism to work out the theological position of each of the synoptic Gospels. What were the criteria by which the evangelist selected and compiled his material? How did he work the individual fragments of tradition into the overall context of his gospel? Which theological tendency (*Tendenz*) and intention underlie his gospel in general? Of course, these issues are dealt with primarily in part 3 of this book (see § 34–36). Nevertheless, they need to be addressed already at this point; for, while the methodology used by redaction criticism is no different from that used in form criticism, it represents in the exegesis of the Synoptics a methodologically necessary step that extends form criticism.

The earliest representatives of form criticism regarded the authors of the synoptic Gospels first of all "only to the smallest extent as authors" and "principally as collectors, vehicles of tradition, editors" (Dibelius, *Tradition to Gospel*, 3), who joined together small units and who gave a certain framework to all of the material handed down. K. L. Schmidt (*Der Rahmen der Geschichte Jesu*, 317) argued rather summarily: Mark does little more than "basically placing individual pericopae side by side." In the last part of his *History of the Synoptic Tradition*, Bultmann already placed greater emphasis on the special theological interests of the individual evangelists, thereby lending greater prominence to the argument that Matthew, Mark, and Luke were also theological "authors" and not merely "collectors." Yet Bultmann did not venture to speak of a "theology of Mark"; there is no specific chapter in his presentation of the theology of the New Testament in which the theology of the Synoptics is discussed. Meanwhile, however, a new tendency has gained acceptance. The question is now asked about the theological position and the particular theological interest of the first three evangelists, as well as about the extent to which this position shapes the structure and content of each Gospel. Thus Conzelmann's *An Outline of the Theology of the NT* includes an albeit brief main part concerning the synoptic kerygma and, within it, a chapter devoted to "the theology of the three Synoptics" (cf. also E. Lohse, *Grundriss der neutestamentlichen Theologie*, 1974, § 26–28). It almost appears now as if there were a certain reaction following the prime of the form-critical method; redaction-critical work seems almost to have displaced form-critical method. The fact of the matter is, however, that the two methods do not compete against, but complement one another. It was form criticism that made it possible to recognize the framework created by the authors of the Gospels and established the criteria for distinguishing the individual layers of tradition. Yet, it is correct to say that it is inappropriate to stop with the analysis of the small units. Furthermore, we are not allowed to dismiss as "secondary" and virtually meaningless those "additions" made by the evangelists in their traditional material. Rather, it is important to observe in the exegesis that the special theological interest of the evangelist is seen precisely at those points. Conversely, the same applies where a synoptic comparison shows that Matthew or Luke characteristically changed or omitted altogether certain pericopae from the Markan material. An example of this type of interpretation is Mt 15:29–31, where the miracle of the healing of a deaf-mute narrated in Mk 7:31–37 is changed so radically that the narratives can hardly be recognized as parallels. Following the Markan text, the healing is brought about by means of certain magical practices: Jesus places his fingers in the ears of the sick and touches his tongue with saliva. He uses magic words (ἐφφαθά) and obtains power from heaven. Luke has not included this narrative at all, whereas Matthew took it up only with drastic corrections; all the magical practices are omitted. At the outset it is merely stated that Jesus had healed "the lame, the crippled, the blind, the deaf, and many others" that were brought to him. These changes by Matthew, or the excision by Luke, are not accidental but are theologically motivated. Matthew and Luke also omit the narrative of the healing of the blind man from Bethsaida (Mk 8:22–26)—apparently because this story was likewise characterized by the mention of magic practices.

2. Synoptic comparison—The presupposition of the redaction-critical approach

An overview of the theology of the individual synoptic Gospels will be given in § 34–36.

The redaction-critical approach can be ascertained simply by comparing the three synoptic Gospels with one another. Two goals are to be met. On the one hand, the respective overall theological interest of the Gospels needs to be worked out; on the other hand, the detailed synoptic comparison is essential. If one presupposes the two-document hypothesis, the special redactional interests of Matthew and Luke can be pointed out with relative facility by investigating where the two vary from Mark. An attempt is made to explain the possible reasons for such variations. Are the reasons of a purely stylistic-linguistic nature, or is there a theological concept hidden behind them?

More difficult is the situation when there is no Markan parallel, that is, when a unit of tradition likely comes from Q. In this case the individual instance needs to be examined as to whether or not the differences between Matthew and Luke can be traced back to the special interest of the one or the other evangelist, or—theoretically possible—whether Q was available in two divergent recensions (p. 112ff.).

The Markan chapter of parables (4), together with its parallels, serves as an example: An overview indicates that Matthew and Luke have adopted the major components of Mk 4:1–20. Only Luke parallels Mk 4:21–25, while the parable of the seed growing by itself (Mk 4:26–29) has been omitted by both Matthew and Luke. In its place Matthew has inserted the parable of the weeds among the wheat which he found in the material unique to him. At the point of Mk 4:30–32, all three synoptic writers harmonize, though Luke does not add this parable until 13:18f.

The form-critical analysis of Mk 4:1–9 indicates that vv 1 and 2 are creations of the evangelist; this is pointed out by the strong emphasis of the typically Markan key terms διδάσκειν and διδαχή. But the remaining verses constitute a stylistically genuine parable (without application) which ends with the appeal to "hear!" By characterizing this parable as "teaching" to begin with, Mark apparently wants to avoid a novel-like misunderstanding of the parable.

Matthew omits the key term "teaching" but retains the broader setting at the sea (13:1–9). For the rest, he makes stylistic improvements and in v 8 reverses the order of the numbers: the greatest result is found at the beginning.

Luke proceeds differently. He combines the settings of Jesus teaching the multitudes standing along the shore as he sits in a boat with that of Peter's catch (5:1ff.; his own material), so that the only thing remaining from the Markan material in Lk 8:4 is the reference to Jesus' teaching outside the town. In the parable itself there are a number of linguistic and logical improvements.

The parable of the sower is followed by the so-called purpose of parables theory (Mk 4:10–12). In its present form it is clearly a redactional feature of Mark, who in this way replaced an originally existing connection between v 9 and v 13. In the tradition the parable was followed immediately by the hearers' question concerning the interpretation of the parable, then followed the interpretation itself (4:13ff.). Mark has altered the question of the hearers into one posed by the *disciples* alone (the old form is still shining through dimly in v 10, ἠρώτων αὐτὸν οἱ περὶ αὐτόν), which Jesus then answers via the theory of parables. This theory denotes that only the disciples of Jesus, the church, can understand the parables correctly as God's pledge of salvation. οἱ ἔξω the non-Christians, are hearing only ἐν παραβολαῖς, which in this case clearly means enigmatic speech (*Rätselrede*). As a confirmation, v 12 loosely cites Is 6:9f., although a determination of the immediate textual source (LXX, Hebrew text, or targum) is no longer possible. By means of the theory of parables, Mark gave an entirely different function to the parables which were meant to explain and elucidate the meaning of the message of Jesus precisely to the "outsiders"; now they separate the church from the world. First of all, Matthew and Luke have smoothed out the clumsy introduction of Mark (4:10; cf. Mt 13:10—Why do you speak with *them* in parables?) The tendency (*Tendenz*) found in Mark is further strengthened in Matthew by the reference that the others had no knowledge at all of the mysteries, i.e., the revelations of the kingdom of God (13:11). Therefore, Matthew already includes at this point (v 12) the saying of Mk 4:25 ("Whoever has will be given more") and allows the parable of Jesus to become the fulfillment of the OT prophecy (ἀναπληροῦται αὐτοῖς ἡ προφητεία). Finally, there follows the disciples' beatification in vv 16, 17; in contrast to the others, they "see" and "hear."

This macarism comes from Q; Luke uses it in 10:23f. in connection with the sending and the return of the disciples.

Beginning with 4:13, Mark returns to his source. This is already noticeable in that the answer of v 13 does not fit the question of v 10, since Mark had altered the question for the purpose of generalization in v 10 and thus used the plural (τὰς παραβολάς), whereas in v 13 the singular (τὴν παραβολὴν ταύτην) is used again. The Markan text contains a distinct rebuke of the disciples: How will you understand the other parables, if this one is already too lofty for you? In contrast, Matthew and Luke simply add the interpretation of the parable and thereby strengthen their purpose, which is to position the disciples, from the beginning, on the side of those understanding.

Over against the parable itself, its interpretation is secondary because some of its details do not fit at all. In the allegorical interpretation the central point is not the seed as word of proclamation but, beginning with Mk 4:16 and parallels, the focus is exclusively on the hearers. The parable no longer deals with the destiny of the word, the sermon, but with the reaction of the individual hearer. Here the heightening of the psychological aspects in Matthew, over against Mark, is recognized in Matthew's consistent reference to the hearers in the singular where Mark still used the plural. Beyond this, Luke expanded the interpretation of the parable through specific additions, which shed light on the situation in the history of the church and, at the same time, show the special theological interest of the evangelist. Thus the work of the devil (v 12) is interpreted by indicating that people do not believe and therefore will not be "saved"; others believe for a certain time, but in the time of temptation they depart from the faith (v 13). For Luke, therefore, the important thing is to "persevere" in the present situation. This is underscored almost paradigmatically in v 15; those in the good soil are the people who *keep* the word and bring fruit with *persistence*. By means of this exhortation to persistence and steadfastness in the faith, Luke addresses the hearers: the kingdom of God is not imminent; it is essential to remain true to the faith.

Suggested exercise:

Some of the stylistic improvements in the interpretation of the parable in Lk 8:11–15, improvements which Luke himself made in the parable, have been "forgotten." What are the contradictions? How are they to be explained?

A clear correction of the Markan text by the two other synoptic writers can be observed in that neither included the parable of the seed growing by itself (Mk 4:26–29); Matthew replaced it with the parable of the weeds among the wheat. The intended purpose is clearly discernible; the eschatological focus of the inevitable coming of the judgment and of its nearness is pushed back. Matthew emphasizes that the separation of good and evil is not yet allowed to occur (in the church); Luke omits the eschatological thought altogether at this point.

Suggested exercise:

Draw a synoptic comparison between Mk 8:31–9:1 and its parallels. Concerning the form-critical and redaction-critical analysis of the Markan text: Which special theological interests of the evangelist can be observed?

What peculiarities in Matthew and Luke does the synoptic comparison point out? What is the content relationship of the Lukan text?

Tools: Conzelmann, *Theology of Luke*, 55ff.; Strecker, *Weg* (see biblio.), index; Strecker, *Eschaton* (see biblio.), 52–75.

§ 11   *Literary Criticism Outside the Gospels*

Bibliography: *Section 3*: K. Aland, "The Problem of Anonymity and Pseudonymity in Christian Literature of the First Two Centuries," *JTS* 12, 1961, 39–49; N. Brox (ed.), *Pseudepigraphie in der heidnischen und jüdisch-christlichen Antike*, Wege der Forschung 484, 1977.

1. Literary relationships between specific NT writings

(1) The literary-critical methods presented in § 7 and § 8 in principle are applied outside the Gospels just as they are within critical studies of the Gospels. If there are conspicuous agreements between the writings of different authors, for instance, the question to be asked in both cases is how these agreements can be explained. Three possibilities lend themselves in answer to that question to begin with:

(a) The authors were eyewitnesses of the same events (it is to be observed, however, that *verbal* agreements cannot be explained thereby).

(b) One author knows the other (which calls for an answer to the question of who copied from whom).

(c) Both authors used the same source independently of one another.

An example from classical philology: The description of the Roman emperors Galba, Otho, and Vitellius corresponds so clearly in the historical accounts of Plutarch, Tacitus, and Suetonius that the assumption of a literary relationship is inevitable; either the authors knew one another, or they in part used the same sources.

(2) Within the NT letters, a comparison between 2 Peter and Jude best illustrates this point. Both letters are indeed attributed to different au-

thors. But there are so many instances of content agreements and, in part, even of verbal agreements that one cannot circumvent the notion of a literary relationship. Conversely, the two letters are so different in style and thought that it is highly unlikely for both letters to have come from the same author (cf. § 43).

Suggested Exercises:

Follow the parallels cited by Nestle and compare them in both directions. How does 2 Peter read, assuming it is based on Jude? Conversely, how does Jude read, assuming it is based on 2 Peter?

Check questions: Where do the two letters agree, and where do they not agree? To which parts of the letters and to which themes are the agreements limited? Did one of the authors condense the content? Or did the other expand? Hence, which letter served as source of the other?

Further references in this respect:

(a) Jude cites apocryphal writings (e.g., Eth. Enoch or the Assumption of Moses) while 2 Peter does not.

(b) In Jude the OT examples are not cited in the biblical order, whereas in 2 Peter they follow the order of the canonical texts. In the case of both (a) and (b) the question is: Which procedure presupposes a more developed use of the Bible?

(c) The subject matter in 2 Peter is broader than that of Jude. How significant is this in the dating of the two letters?

(3) A comparison between Ephesians and Colossians is instructive, although the evidence is more involved to the extent that both letters bear the name of the same author, Paul. If this is considered historically reliable, one needs to ask whether Paul perhaps used one letter as a basis for the other. On the other hand, if the reference to the author is regarded as incorrect, four possibilities arise:

(a) One of the letters comes from Paul, while the other is an imitation by a disciple (which requires the question to be answered of which letter should then be considered as "authentic").

(b) Both letters come from the same disciple of Paul (which causes us to ask, as in the case of the authenticity of both letters, how the verbal agreements can be explained).

(c) While the letters are written by different authors, both make use of the same realm of language, form, and thought (which raises the question of whether the most distinct agreements are found precisely in the realm of concrete formulae).

(d) Both letters come from different authors, with one using the other as a source (which again requires the additional question of who used whom).

Suggested exercises:

Compare 1 and 2 Thessalonians, or compare Col 2:6–19 with the parallels in Ephesians given by Nestle.

References for continuing your own work:

1. Which ideas and concepts in Col and Eph correspond and which ones do not? Are the agreements found primarily in passages where traditional material, such as hymns, is cited, so that both authors could have picked up the same material independently of one another? Or are the agreements found in the "redactional" passages, that is, in those which have definitely been the product of the respective author?

2. Extensive verbal agreements are found in early Christian writings outside the NT, such as the Didache and the letter of Barnabas, both of which belong to the writings of the so-called Apostolic Fathers. But these, too, in some instances contain such enormous differences that a direct dependence is highly unlikely. The most feasible assumption is, therefore, that both writings in part used the same source independently of one another.

3. Certain similarities also exist between Eph, Jas, and 1 Pet (such as are listed in the table in C. L. Mitton, *The Epistle to the Ephesians*, 1951). Upon closer examination, it appears that the agreements pertain only to the paraenesis. Typically, very common and frequent expressions and formulations in the paraenesis occur repeatedly in the most divergent texts, without a literary relationship between them.

2. Literary problems within NT writings

Occasionally, certain contradictions in the account or breaks in the train of thought can be found within a writing. Some graphic examples of this are contained especially in Acts.

One needs to bear in mind that literary criticism is more complex here than in the synoptic Gospels. In the latter, the parallelism of three related writings provides a handle for determining the source relationships, whereas in Acts one is dependent exclusively on internal criteria.

Examples:

(1) In Acts 15:22ff. Paul and Barnabas are said to be accompanied as far as Antioch by Judas and Silas; then, v 33 says that Judas and Silas had left Antioch again and returned to Jerusalem. And yet, it is reported in v 40 that Paul had taken Silas (!) along to begin his second missionary journey. How can this discrepancy be explained? Is there evidence of a mere negligence on the part of the author, who merely had forgotten to mention in v 33 that Silas had indeed remained in Antioch? In fact, some manuscripts try to smooth it out (v 34). Or is it possible to recognize the seam of two different sources at this point?

(2) The apostolic decree of 15:23ff. is addressed to Gentile Christians not only in Antioch and Syria, but also to Gentile Christian communities

in Cilicia. But up to this point nothing has been said in Acts about the existence of such churches in the vicinity of Tarsus in Asia Minor. Is it necessary to see an internal conflict in this tension which forces us to suspect a citation from a source in vv 23–29? Or is this the result merely of literary carelessness?

(3) The Pentecost narrative of Acts 2 leaves an ambivalent impression. On the one hand, it is recorded that every hearer understood the sermon in his own language; in other words, the account deals with a miracle of languages. On the other hand, those filled with the Spirit are suspected of drunkenness, that is, they apparently speak unintelligibly "in tongues" and are in ecstasy. How is this contradiction to be resolved? Is it possible to dissect the present narrative—for instance, into two originally self-contained accounts (miracle of languages; mass ecstasy with glossolalia)? Or did a core narrative exist that was reworked by Luke (which leads to the further question of which is the core narrative and which is the reworked material)?

(4) The narrative of Stephen's martyrdom is also strangely two-layered. According to 6:11–15, it seems to be a matter of legal proceedings in the Sanhedrin; however, 7:54–58 points to a popular uprising, so that the stoning (v 59) does not appear to be the sentence, but mob justice. Did Luke have two sources containing divergent aspects?

(5) The accounts of Acts 4 and 5 are conspicuously parallel and furthermore, Acts 5 and 12 also show connections. Has the author included different sources in which the same event was told? Or do they deal with different incidents, thereby rendering the parallelism accidental?

Suggested exercise:

Analyze the references in Acts mentioned above and attempt to answer the questions posed.

Tools: Commentaries on Acts.

Literary problems are also found in some Pauline letters, especially in 2 Corinthians.

(6) There is a curious break between 2 Cor 2:13 and 2:14. Psychologically it could be explained by arguing that Paul interrupted the dictation after v 13 and then continued with v 14 the following day. But such ideas are eliminated quickly when it is realized that the account of 2:13 has a direct continuation in 7:5. The solution of the problem, therefore, may be found in a literary hypothesis; the two segments originally came from different letters, written in entirely different situations and only subsequently were worked into one single letter. Finally, chs 10–13 pose another special literary problem (see below, § 29.4).

Similar hypotheses of partition are also suggested for other Pauline letters (see below, § 26 and 28).

(7) A further problem within 2 Corinthians, though somewhat different from those mentioned under (6) above, is section 6:14–7:1. The pattern of thought in this passage differs so sharply from that of its context
and linguistically corresponds only marginally with the usual style of the
Pauline letters that one may have to consider the possibility of an insertion by a later hand, i.e., an "interpolation" (another term would be
"gloss"). Of course, the origin of this insertion and the identity of its in-
stigator must remain an open issue to begin with. At any rate, it appears
that 2 Cor 6:14–7:1 clearly has parallels in the Qumran texts. Some scholars are looking for similar secondary interpolations in Romans and in the
Gospel of John; in the latter's case, Bultmann is of the opinion that it was
an "ecclesiastical" redactor who sought to adapt John's Gospel to the common theology of the church and especially to its eschatology.

(8) Syntactical difficulties may also suggest a second hand that inter-
fered with the text at a later point; indications to that effect are found
e.g., in Jn 4:1f.; 13:1f.; Jas 2:1.

3. Concerning the authenticity of NT writings

The "question of authenticity" also forms part of the realm of literary problems. The question is whether there are criteria which help to determine
whether or not a writing was actually written by the author whose name
it bears. Extreme caution is necessary in the discussion of the
"authenticity" of a writing. The burden of proof rests on the one con-
testing the authenticity. Yet, the problem cannot be removed by arguing
that forgeries could in no wise be attributed to Christians of the first and
second century, let alone to the authors of biblical writings. Clearly,
pseudonymity and anonymity occurred not infrequently in Judaism, as
seen in the apocryphal writings, and in Christianity, as evidenced by the
apocryphal gospels and acts of the apostles.

The question why there was such a large number of anonymous and especially
pseudonymous writings in early Christianity is discussed frequently (see bibliography). Two observations are important: (a) Those, for instance, who wrote letters by using fictitious authorial references wanted to utilize the authority of their
pseudonym, such as Paul's, but at the same time they intended to dupe their
readers. (b) They also wanted to increase the authority of their pseudonym; thus
the author of 1 Peter obviously wishes to promote the ecclesiastical-theological
heritage of Peter.

The first question to be asked always is: Does the author mention his
name? If the author's name is only passed on by tradition (this is the case,
for instance, in the Gospels and in Hebrews), one has to inquire into the
age of this tradition as well as the authorities supporting it. Is their information based on available sources, or are the references more or less
fanciful? The best known example is Papias, bishop of Hierapolis (ca. A.D.

140, possibly earlier), who claimed to know special details concerning the origin of the Gospels (cf. Huck-Greeven, *Synopsis*, p. VIII; Aland, *Synopsis*, 531f.).

The issue becomes more difficult when the name of the author is in fact mentioned in the writing, as seen in all of the NT letters, except Hebrews and the Johannine letters. Is the reference to be taken as reliable or fictitious? Did a disciple attribute the writing to his master in order to rely on the authority of the latter?

Suggested exercises:

1. Evaluate the Pauline authorship of Colossians and Ephesians. Note the following: (a) The style of an author may change in the course of time. One needs to ask, however, whether Colossians and Ephesians are still within the realm of the apostle (and theologian) Paul's assumed ability to change. A comparison between the uncontested, genuine letters of Paul (1 Thes, Gal, 1 Cor, 2 Cor, Rom, Phil, Phlm) on the one hand and the contested letters (2 Thes, Col, Eph, Pastoral letters) on the other is very instructive.

(b) The appearance of new ideas or concepts per se is less suspicious than when an author's most used concepts suddenly appear with a different meaning or in a new combination. In the case of Ephesians and Colossians it is to be asked whether or not the altered ecclesiological conceptuality still represents a viable variant within the theology of Paul.

For advanced students:

(c) Is the "world view" of Ephesians congruent with that found in the other Pauline letters? Compare, for instance, Eph 2:2; 2:7; 4:8–10; 6:10ff. with related statements by Paul.

(d) What is the situation concerning the eschatology and the understanding of history in Colossians and Ephesians?

Tools: H. Conzelmann, *An Outline of the Theology of the NT,* ET 1969, 344–347; A. Lindemann, *Die Aufhebung der Zeit*, 1975, 26–48, 237–259.

2. Especially significant is the question of which situation in the history of the church and of theology is presupposed in a letter. Can this situation still be accommodated in the life of the alleged author? This question is particularly urgent in the Pastoral letters.

§ 12   Minor Forms Outside the Gospels

Bibliography: O. Cullmann, *The Earliest Christian Confessions*, ET 1949; R. P. Martin, *Carmen Christi: Philippians 2:5–11 in Recent Interpretation and in the Setting of Early Christian Worship*, SNTSMS 4, 1967; V. H. Neufeld, *Earliest Christian Confessions*, NTTS 5, 1963; Ph. Vielhauer, *Geschichte der urchristlichen Literatur*, 1975, 9–57; K. Wengst, *Christologische Formeln und Lieder des Urchristentums*, StNT 7, 1972. Section 1: H. Conzelmann. "Was glaubte die frühe Christenheit?" *Gesammelte Aufsätze*, BEvTh 65, 1974, 106–119. Section 2: D. Lührmann, *Das Offenbarungsverständnis bei Paulus und in paulinischen Gemeinden*, WMANT 16, 1965, 124–133. Section 3: R. Deichgraber, *Gotteshymnus und Christushymnus in der frühen Christenheit. Untersuchungen zu Form, Sprache und Stil der frühchristlichen Hymnen*, 1967. Section 5: A. Vögtle, *Die Tugend- und Lasterkataloge im NT*, NTA 16, 4/5, 1936; S. Wibbing, *Die Tugend- und Lasterkataloge im NT*, BZNW 25, 1959.

Minor forms—confessions, hymns, fixed schemas—are found not only in the Gospels but also in the remaining NT literature, especially in the collection of letters.

1. Confessions

The confessions represent the oldest layer of NT tradition; they constitute the beginning of the Christian theology in general. While there is no fixed wording to be observed yet in the NT confessions, certain models have found a definite embodiment in the letters.

(1) Criteria for reconstruction

(a) Occasionally a letter states explicitly that what is cited is "tradition," or *paradosis* (1 Cor 15:1ff.); this is indicated by the typical key words παραλαμβάνειν and παραδιδόναι, both of which are technical terms for the transmission of school traditions. The corresponding Jewish concepts are קבל מן and מסר ל. In the tradition of the Lord's Supper, 1 Cor 11:23ff., the shape of the tradition is further confirmed in the occurrence of the same text in Mark (and in the parallels).

(b) The key words πιστεύειν and ὁμολογεῖν are also capable of pointing to traditional material (Rom 10:9; 1 Jn 1:9; 2:23; 4:2f.); confessions and statements of faith—or parts of them—are introduced by these verbs.

(c) Certain external characteristics of style may favor the assumption that the text, in particular instances, has not been formulated loosely but is based on tradition:

(i) Parallelismus membrorum (Rom 4:25; 1 Cor 15:3–5)

(ii) Relative clauses (Rom 3:25; 4:25)

(iii) Participial clauses (Rom 1:3f.)

(iv) Unusual vocabulary; substantial evidence for this is found in cases where words and expressions occur copiously which an author normally does not use at all or only in exceptional cases (Rom 1:3f.; 3:25: πνεῦμα ἁγιωσύνης, ἱλαστήριον, πάρεσις τῶν προγεγονότων ἁμαρτημάτων).

(d) Likewise, an out-of-place statement within a passage may be evidence of traditional material; for example, given the context of Rom 1:3f., it is difficult to grasp why Paul inserts these pertinent christological statements at this point. The focus becomes clearer only when it is realized that Paul cites an already existing confession; by means of this apparently well-known formula, he desires to point out the commonality of the faith to the church in Rome which is still unknown to him.

Suggested exercise:

1 Cor 15:3–5 can be reduced to a basic statement: "Christ died and was raised." Look for other instances where this formula occurs (Tool: Concordance).

(2) Results of reconstruction attempts

Confessional statements in the NT may be classified in a variety of ways.

(a) Confessions (key word: ὁμολογέω) relating to the person of Jesus, such as "Jesus is Lord"; a pure form of such a "homology" is found in Phil 2:11.

(b) Statements of faith (key word: πιστεύω) relating to the "work of redemption," such as "God has raised Christ from the dead" (Rom 8:11). The best passage to remember is Rom 10:9 where both types are combined, namely, the homology and the "creed."

Most of the NT confessions are comprised of only one "article": the christological one. These may be formulated in terms of content, that of the redemptive work, or in terms of the person, specifically Jesus himself. Next to these, there are confessions with two articles: *"one* God and *one* Lord (=Christ)" (1 Cor 8:6). Of course, the latter are of later origin; whereas the doctrine of the one God did not need to be emphasized in Judaism, it had to be formulated specifically in the realm of the Gentile mission.

The tendency to expand the statements of faith can be observed already in the NT. 1 Cor 15:3–5 is the best known example of an expanded statement; likewise the "statement of work" (*Werkaussage*) in Rom 4:25 is enlarged: παρεδόθη . . . διὰ τὰ παραπτώματα ἡμῶν . . . καὶ ἠγέρθη . . . διὰ τὴν δικαίωσιν ἡμῶν. Particularly instructive is 1 Thes 1:9f. where Paul gives a brief outline of the Christian doctrine and then clearly inserts a christological formula (v 10b).

The development of the confessions of faith can be traced from the brief statements in the NT all the way to the Apostles' Creed. This material is available in E. v. Dobschütz, *Das Apostolicum*, 1932.

Suggested exercises:

1. Analysis: Find the confession formula in (a) the prediction of Jesus' passion in Mk 8:31 (taking also into consideration the parallels in Mk 9 and 10); (b) the

trial of Jesus before the Jewish council in Mk 14:53ff., and parallels; (c) the Lazarus story in Jn 11:20ff. Note: The confession statement can be embedded in the context so firmly that the formulaic character is no longer readily noticed.

2. Theological interpretation: In his letters Paul cites confession formulae and then interprets them contextually; it is possible to observe this in the following pericopae: 1 Thes 4:13ff.; Rom 3:21ff.; 4:25ff.; 14:1–9. Which conclusions are emphasized in the confession? Which ones are omitted?

3. Polemical application: In the first letter of John the author combats the opponent with a reference to the confession. But the problem is that both parties maintain the same confession: "Jesus is the Son of God." What is the theological difference between the two parties?

2. *Revelation schema*

The "revelation schema" is a special mode of expression. It represents a fixed form in which two divergent statements about the relationship of the revelation (Latin: *revelatio*) to the world are juxtaposed: (a) God's plan of redemption has been veiled until now; (b) God's plan of redemption is now made manifest. The recipients and the redemptive significance of this revelation are always given special mention and emphasis.

The foundational content of this schema may be expanded, for instance, by describing in more detail the present unveiling of the mystery. The revelation comes to pass today through God's representatives, thus through the apostles or the prophets. In its fully developed form, the revelation schema is not found until Colossians and Ephesians, as well as in the other post-Pauline writings.

Suggested exercises:

1. Look up the revelation schema in Colossians, Ephesians, in the Pastoral letters (1, 2 Tim; Tit), and in 1 Peter. How is it treated? What special function does it serve in its respective context? What is the relationship of the schema to statements such as the one in Heb 1:1–4?

2. Suggested exercise for the advanced student: Analyze Rom 16:25–27 (a) text critically; (b) literarily (issue of authenticity!); (c) theological interpretation.

Tools: W. Schmithals, *Der Röm. als historisches Problem*, 1975, 108 124.

3. *Hymns*

(1) Another group of fixed forms in the NT are the hymns. Of course, they do not always stand out clearly; on the contrary, in a number of cases the analysis is actually very tenuous. The fact that Christian poetry existed from the beginning is attested by Col 3:16, Eph 5:19, and earlier in 1 Cor 14:26.

Early Christianity was acquainted with a living poetry in the stylistic tradition of the OT. This is evident, for instance, in the "Psalms of Solomon" from the first century B.C., found in the Septuagint (an English translation is found in J. H. Charlesworth, ed., *The Old Testament Pseudepigrapha*, 2 vols., 1983/85), as well as in the Qumran hymns (*hodayoth*).

The NT contains two hymns of the psalm style which can be easily recognized: The Magnificat in Lk 1:46–55 and the Benedictus in Lk 1:68–79 (the names are taken from the first word in the Vulgate). For instance the Magnificat compares favorably with the psalm of Hannah in 1 Sam 2:1–10. Both hymns of Lk 1 possibly are Christian adaptations of hymns that originated among the adherents of John the Baptist.

Unfortunately, other hymns handed down in the NT cannot be reconstructed with equal facility. While there are certain indications for their parameters, the decision must necessarily remain uncertain in many cases. The following may denote signs of a possible hymn: elevated style, a certain strophic structure, a special linguistic rhythm, and a content-oriented, emphatic position in the context. Nevertheless, there are practically no strophes constructed with absolute consistency, and there is not a fixed rhythm. The style of the NT hymns in no way conforms with that found in Greek poetry, whose rhythm we only find in the few citations of Greek poetic literature, namely in 1 Cor 15:33; Tit 1:12; Acts 17:28.

(2) In the following, four hymns will be analyzed and briefly interpreted: 1 Tim 3:16; Phil 2:6–11; Col 1:15–20; Jn 1:1 . . . 18.

(a) 1 Tim 3:16 represents the only hymn with consistent structure in the NT; the only inconsistency is the missing word ἐν in line three.

One recognizes, to begin with, that vv 14–16 in 1 Tim 3 interrupt the continuity. Furthermore, v 16 is also set off through the solemn introduction. The text corresponds to the Egyptian enthronement ritual (cf. E. Norden, *Agnostos Theos*, ⁴1956, 254ff.): The six lines are arranged in pairs, the front position of the verbs is not Greek. Lohmeyer's analysis differs, however. He argues for two stanzas of three lines each, with the first stanza dealing with the historical aspects, whereas the second stanza addresses the accomplished, eschatological fact.

The following special style elements of the hymn catch the eye: (a) The linking relative pronoun by which the citation is inserted into the context; (b) the he-form; (c) the front position of the verb; (d) the force that the form exerts on the content: below/above (flesh/Spirit); above/below (angels/nations); below/above (world/glory), paying attention to the chiastic structure.

The term chiasm is drawn from the Greek letter χ and signifies the position of the clauses of the sentence, following the order of a-b-b-a.

Further style elements of the hymn are (e) the absence of the article and (f) the purposeful construction of the whole. According to the content, this hymn is an example of the revelation schema (see above) in poetic form, with the redemptive event depicted as enthronement of the revealer in the realm of the world and eternity. Both the revealer and the revelation are mentioned, as are the realm and the recipients of the revelation, and finally, the proclamation of the latter.

(b) Phil 2:6–11: The unique vocabulary is the first indication of the fact that Paul is quoting here; he uses not only unique individual words, but also an entire cluster of words and content. Although there is no regular rhythm, one senses a certain rhythmic development. A certain hiatus within the text is conspicuous: The acting subject changes (at first Christ, then God), thus leaving the distinct impression that the hymn has two stanzas. For the purpose of an experiment, the text may be written line by line:

> [ἐν Χριστῷ ᾽Ιησοῦ]
> ὃς ἐν μορφῇ θεοῦ ὑπάρχων
> οὐχ ἁρπαγμὸν ἡγήσατο τὸ εἶναι ἴσα θεῷ,
> ἀλλὰ ἑαυτὸν ἐκένωσεν
> μορφὴν δούλου λαβών,
> ἐν ὁμοιώματι ἀνθρώπων γενόμενος
> καὶ σχήματι εὑρεθεὶς ὡς ἄνθρωπος
> ἐταπείνωσεν ἑαυτὸν
> γενόμενος ὑπήκοος μέχρι θανάτου θανάτου δὲ σταυροῦ
> διὸ καὶ ὁ θεὸς αὐτὸν ὑπερύψωσεν
> καὶ ἐχαρίσατο αὐτῷ τὸ ὄνομα τὸ ὑπὲρ πᾶν ὄνομα,
> ἵνα ἐν τῷ ὀνόματι ᾽Ιησοῦ πᾶν γόνυ κάμψῃ
> ἐπουρανίων καὶ ἐπιγείων καὶ καταχθονίων,
> καὶ πᾶσα γλῶσσα ἐξομολογήσηται
> ὅτι κύριος ᾽Ιησοῦς Χριστὸς
> εἰς δόξαν θεοῦ πατρός.

In terms of rhythm, the reference to the cross at the end of the first half appears to be excessive and disturbs the content. The notion that not the death of Jesus as such had redemptive meaning, but that precisely the specific kind of death, namely the cross, was fundamental for the understanding of faith, is Pauline (Gal 3:13) and thus far removed from the hymn itself. Evidently Paul had inserted the words θανάτου δὲ σταυροῦ into the hymn he had before him.

The analysis of the hymn is disputed in the details. The discussion first of all involves the original extent of the hymn and, in particular, whether there are other supplements, in addition to Paul's insertion. G. Strecker (*ZNW* 55, 1964, 71f.) brackets v 8 as Pauline; G. Friedrich (NTD 8, loc. cit.) regards v 10b and v 11b as Pauline additions. But here, as elsewhere, the general guideline applicable in the analysis of such texts is that the simplest analysis usually is also the most plausible, unless there are convincing arguments to the contrary. In our case it will indeed suffice to consider as insertion the three words θανάτου δὲ σταυροῦ. The meaning then becomes clear: The hymn deals with a preexistent divine being who demonstrates obedience to God in descent, incarnation, and death. The latter responds with exaltation, induction into the position of Kyrios, and presentation to all beings in all realms of the cosmic structure. Through the hymn the hearer is informed that he may share in salvation by joining in the final acclamation, that is, through the acknowledgment of Jesus as Lord.

Clearly, the issue is not the adoption of a particular hypothesis of arrangement of the details. Rather, it is important to recognize the content observations and, in our case, especially the break prior to v 9, which produces the division into two parts.

(c) Col 1:15–20: In a sense, vv 12, 13–20 noticeably interrupt the thought pattern; they contain a thematic christological explanation. Yet, from the linguistic perspective, vv 13 and 14 are also set off from what follows; both verses contain the standard language of the community ("forgiveness of sins . . ."), whereas vv 15ff. are dominated by an otherwise uncommon cosmological terminology. Furthermore, v 15 has the sentence beginning with a relative clause (ὅς ἐστιν), which we encountered already in other pre-formed elements. It is very likely, therefore, that the hymn begins with v 15. The conclusion can be defined more easily: The author reiterates his address to the readers in v 21, indicating that the hymn likely extended to v 20.

The point of departure for the analysis is the observation that there are two parallel sentences: V 15 ὅς ἐστιν εἰκὼν τοῦ θεοῦ . . . πρωτότοκος and v 18b ὅς ἐστιν ἀρχή, πρωτότοκος. . . . We may, therefore, tentatively divide it into two stanzas: (1) the "picture," namely, that the Son of the Creator, as mediator of the creation and as Lord of the world, is the revealer; (2) the Son, as mediator of the reconciliation through his resurrection, is the redeemer. But then it is apparent quickly that the form (two stanzas) and the content (two acts of the Son: creation and redemption) do not correspond exactly, since allusion to the redemption is already made in the first stanza in the reference to the church as the body of the revealer. This incongruence between form and content can be overcome when it is assumed that the author of Colossians augmented the hymn he had available which, in turn, means that Col 1:15ff. does not represent the original form. If one brackets the words τῆς ἐκκλησίας in the first stanza, v 18 still belongs entirely to the first stanza's content; in this case, the σῶμα of the mediator of the creation does not refer to the church but to the cosmos. Given this assumption, the content and form of the arrangement are congruent. By means of the supplemental reference to the church, the author pursued the goal of connecting more securely both parts of the hymn: The church is the body of the mediator of creation and, thereby, creation and redemption belong together directly. The assumption that Col 1:15ff. was reworked is confirmed by a further observation relative to the second stanza: The statement διὰ τοῦ αἵματος τοῦ σταυροῦ αὐτοῦ does not fit the context in terms of style and content; if they are bracketed provisionally, a smooth expression results: εἰρηνοποιήσας δι' αὐτοῦ εἴτε . . . εἴτε. . . . Similar to v 18, the author's addition intends to recall the historical work of redemption by interpreting the mythological content of the hymn via reference to the historical death of Jesus. The same tendency is also seen in v 21f. where the application of the hymn follows in the context.

More subtle analyses are also available for Col 1:15ff., such as beginning with the assumption that both stanzas originally had to have had the same shape. But this can only be "demonstrated" through fairly deliberate deletions.

(d) Jn 1:1 . . . 18: The special character of the Johannine "prologue" is noticeable already in the two clearly distinct forms of style within Jn 1:1ff., those of poetry and prose. The poetic style begins with v 1, with interspersed sentences formulated in pure prose (vv 6–8, 15). In keeping with this observation, considerable differences in content become apparent; whereas the poetry deals with a divine being, the Logos, the prose texts speak of a historical human being, John the Baptist. Awkward stylistic features are also evident: v 9 is unfitting after v 8, since the subject of the sentence in v 9 cannot be the Baptist. It appears as if v 9 connected with v 5, so that the prose section of vv 6–8 can be bracketed.

The text contains two problems, one of form and the other of content. How far does the hymn extend? Where is the transition from the pre-existence to the historical appearance of the Logos? It is quite clear that something entirely new begins with v 19 and the hymn has to end with v 18. Yet already vv 17, 18 are rendered in prose, which means that they, too, should be excluded from the hymn. On the basis of these assumptions, Bultmann has argued that the hymn extended as far as v 16 (while the further reference to John in v 15, of course, is also an addition; see above). On the other hand, Käsemann locates the end of the hymn in v 12, ignoring, of course, that v 15 is a clear intrusion between v 14 and v 16 and that these verses cannot, for that reason, have come from the evangelist himself but had to have been extant in the frame of the hymn available to him. The question of the parameters of the hymn has considerable theological significance; for, it is a question of whether v 14—the incarnation—belongs to the hymn or whether it was appended as interpretation by the evangelist. This further ties in with the issue of whether the original hymn was Christian at all, or whether it was a pre-Christian hymn that the author included in the Gospel and, in the process, Christianized. When Bultmann regards the hymn to have been Jewish originally, including v 14, he ignores that the idea of the incarnation of a divine being is without parallel in Judaism. Neither is it clear why Käsemann considers the hymn to be Christian while maintaining that v 14 is the evangelist's creation. The following assertion can be made at any rate: V 14 belongs to the hymn (with Bultmann, contra Käsemann) but the latter is Christian (with Käsemann, contra Bultmann).

The second question is much more difficult to answer: At first glance one has the impression that the topic of the incarnation does not begin until v 14. But that immediately raises the question of how v 5 ("the light shines in the darkness") and v 9 ("the light came into the world") are to be understood. Here Bultmann perceives a clear distinction between the hymn and the evangelist: the former intended to show the transition only in v 14, while the evangelist related the historical appearance of the Logos already in v 5 and thus inserted the reference to the Baptist already at this point. However, Käsemann is of the opinion that both the hymn and the evangelist in v 5 had in mind the historical appearance, so that the significance of v 14 is not to be overestimated in any way.

Suggested exercise:

Interpret the text following the analyses of Bultmann and Käsemann, in R. Bultmann, *The Gospel of John*, ET 1971, 13–83; E. Käsemann, "Aufbau und Anliegen des johanneischen Prologs," *Ex. Versuche und Besinnungen* II, 155–180.

Additional exercise for the advanced: How are the tenses to be understood? Is it necessary to argue that the evangelist changed them (e.g., in v 5), as Bultmann claims?

(3) The hymns in the Apocalypse are a special case. The contention is over whether or not they are to be understood as Jewish-Christian *church* tradition, or whether they were created by the *author* of the Apocalypse himself. The decision encompasses the following criteria:

(a) Is the style of the hymns different from that of the context?

(b) What is the content relationship of the hymns to the context; do they possibly harmonize with the latter?

Both questions may have to be answered with the conclusion in mind that they are poetical interludes in the text created by the author himself (cf. e.g., Acts 4:11; 5:9–12).

There are a number of other texts considered by some exegetes as songs or hymns, such as Eph 1:3–12; 1:20–23; 2:14–18; 1 Pet 2:21–24. But in these instances, the evidence is by far not as unambiguous as in the examples we considered above. At any rate, caution is necessary lest one characterizes a text as "hymn" too quickly.

4. Other forms

(1) The early Christian community makes use of some liturgical sayings.

(a) The Aramaic acclamation *maranatha* מרנאתא occurs in 1 Cor 16:22 and Did 10:6. Two divergent translations are possible: (i) the indicative, "our Lord comes" and (ii) the imperative, "our Lord, come!" Generally the imperative sense is preferred; but even then it remains an open question whether the acclamation requests the eschatological coming of Christ, that is, the parousia, or whether it has in mind the coming of Christ to the gathered community.

(b) The early church adopts the Jewish form of the doxology: "Blessed be God for ever, Amen" (Rom 1:25; 9:5 et al.).

(2) In the proclamation and teaching some forms have been developed that may be understood and interpreted as expression of the Christian comprehension of salvation.

(a) The "formerly-now form" which places in juxtaposition the deplorable past of the individual, and his present, new life in Christ, becomes almost paradigmatic in Rom 7:5f.; in this case Rom 7:7ff. may be viewed as commentary of the "formerly" and Rom 8 as commentary of the "now." Further instances can easily be located in the concordance (the simplest method is to look up the key words ποτέ and νῦν; yet, in some instances these words may be missing.) In the theological interpretation it is to be noted that it does not mean "Formerly we were—now we are," because this would indicate that the individual is occupied with a psychological self-examination based on his present position of grace. Rather, it means: "Formerly we were—now we are made (by God)"; in other words, the theme of the formerly-now form is God's gracious act in man, and not man who has been pardoned.

(b) The relationship between the act of redemption and its ethical implication is shown by means of the relationship between the "indicative" and the "imperative." The emphasis lies upon the indicative, i.e., the granting of salvation, which precedes the imperative of Christian ethics. The fulfillment of ethical demands is not the prerequisite but the consequence of salvation. This form is reflected clearly in the development of some of the NT letters: The first part deals with the act of redemption, while the second part addresses the resultant moral consequences (cf. Rom 1–11; 12–15; Gal 1–4; 5–6; Eph 1–3; 4–6).

Suggested exercises:

1. Examine the structure of Romans, Galatians, Ephesians, and Colossians, and determine the themes.

2. (For the advanced:) Examine the structure of Hebrews and 1 John. How are the christological and the ethical (paraenetic) segments conjoined with one another?

Note: The indicative-imperative form, like the formerly-now form, can serve as a guideline for the contemporary sermon. However, it is not suitable as a sermon *model* when it is used as a fixed norm. Christian preaching that ends with the moral-ethical appeal, ultimately rescinds the affirmation of the redemptive act ("without works of the law") and ends up—despite the good intention—in legalism. Some instructive examples, warnings, and instructions are given by M. Josuttis, *Die Gesetzlichkeit in der Predigt der Gegenwart*, [2]1969.

5. Forms of paraenesis

The forms mentioned above, those related to Christian teaching and preaching, already introduce us to the realm of paraenesis. In this case, too, early Christianity uses fixed forms that essentially come from the world around it.

Early Christianity's adoption of already available forms as well as its message of moral instruction reflects the basic understanding of early Christian ethics to begin with. There is a general consensus with the Jewish as well as with the pagan environment concerning what is good and to be practiced by man. The moral values Paul lists in Phil 4:8 are in no sense specifically Christian virtues; rather, they are universally recognized. What is new is the substantiation of the ethical demand; ethics is not the presupposition, but the consequence of the redemptive event and of the resultant eschatological hope (cf. Phil 4:5, ὁ κύριος ἐγγύς).

In terms of form, the following are found in the NT letters:

(a) *Proverbial ethics* (*Spruchethik*), which follow the Jewish pattern (cf., e.g., the Proverbs and the book Jesus ben Sirach) are found in the synoptic Gospels (see above). In the exegesis of such materials, even within the letters, it is to be observed that the individual proverbs must be interpreted as self-contained units. Every proverb contains a complete thought designed to be convincing by itself. Therefore, proverbs are not logically connected; and even when certain groupings, ordered by content, do occur, there exists no consistent thought pattern. Neither is it permissible to read into the text a reciprocal interpretation of the individual proverbs.

Suggested exercises:

1. Analyze Rom 12 and the paraenesis of Ephesians (proverbial ethics).

2. (for the advanced:) Analyze the paraenesis of James (Tools: M. Dibelius, *James*, ET 1976).

(b) *Catalogue of virtues and vices* whose prototype is to be found in hellenistic Judaism (Wisdom of Solomon, Philo) but which may also have originated in Stoicism. A paradigm of this type is Gal 5:16–23, where a catalogue of vices is juxtaposed to a catalogue of virtues (cf. also Col 3:5–

14). As far as content is concerned, all catalogues contain a relatively fixed, common core of listed virtues and vices, which leads to the conclusion that the assertions of the catalogues are not to be taken as actual, that is as reaction to particular situations. Therefore, it is inappropriate to deduce from Gal 5:16ff. that precisely these vices were prevalent in Galatia in Paul's time. Rather, these catalogues are to be read and interpreted as universally applicable summaries of moral teaching. Hence, even the specifically cited vices are not to be defined too sharply (e.g., robbery and theft, avarice and covetousness denote practically the same thing).

Suggested exercise:

On the basis of Gal 5:16ff., determine the core of the catalogues of virtues and vices by means of a concordance.

(c) The *household codes* (*Haustafeln*) are also of hellenistic origin. Their basic idea is encountered as early as in Aristotle's philosophical-political writings in which the "house" and its rules (*oikonomia*) denote the embryo and pristine concept of the state. The Christian "house rules" contain an indirect political claim in the sense that they are concerned with the order and organization of the Christian community and with the relational conduct of Christians. Nevertheless, what applies to the catalogues of virtues and vices is equally true of the household codes, expressly, that the observance of their regulations in no sense represents the precondition for salvation.

The concrete function of the household codes can be ascertained by beginning with the analysis of the simplest example (Col 3:18ff.) and then observing the enlargement of the form in Ephesians on one hand and in 1 Peter on the other.

Suggested reading

D. Lührmann, "Wo man nicht mehr Sklave oder Freier ist. Überlegungen zur Struktur frühchristlicher Gemeinden," *WuD* NF 13, 1975, 53–83 (esp. 71–83).

W. Schrage, "Zur Ethik der neutestamentlichen Haustafeln," *NTS* 21, 1975, 1–22.

6. Appendix: Application of the form-critical method in Acts

M. Dibelius has shown that in Acts, too, similar to the synoptic Gospels, individual traditional stories and a redactional frame can be recognized. At first it remained an open issue whether the frame originated in the Lukan redaction or already in the pre-Lukan tradition. Dibelius himself assumed that the frame of Acts was an "itinerary," that is, a type of diary regarding the individual stages of the journeys, written by Paul's fellow travellers. Into the particular places mentioned in this travel diary, Luke then inserted accounts of Paul's experiences with which he was familiar from the tradition. In this fashion he had thus woven the story of the healing of the lame man into the account of the stay in Lystra (14:8ff.) and the Aereopagus speech into the account of the stay in Athens (17:16ff.). But this itinerary hypothesis is not tenable. More feasible is the opposite assumption that the frame is the work of the author of Acts. Evidently it was Luke himself who took the individual extant accounts originating in the various towns and connected them through the subsequent organization of the travel route, thus creating the impression of "missionary journeys." In Acts 13 and following, for instance, it is quite possible to separate the frame, that is, the references to the route, from the individual stories: 13:4–6a—redactional frame; vv 6b–12—miracle story; vv 13–15—frame; vv 16–43—Paul's address in Antioch (presumably Luke's own work) etc. Conspicuous is the correspondence between the respective closure of the individual sections (13:12; 13:48f.) and that found in the synoptic miracle stories ("choral ending").

Suggested reading

M. Dibelius, "The Acts of the Apostles as an Historical Source," in *Studies in the Acts of the Apostles*, ET 1956, 91–95.

W. W. Gasque, *A History of the Criticism of the Acts of the Apostles*, 1975; idem, "A Fruitful Field: Recent Study of the Acts of the Apostles," *Int* 42, 1988, 117–131;

E. Grässer, "Acta-Forschung seit 1960," *ThR* NF 41, 1976, esp. 186–194.

M. Hengel, *Acts and the History of Earliest Christianity*, ET 1979.

U. Wilckens, *Die Missionsreden der Apostelgeschichte. Form- und traditionsgeschichtliche Untersuchungen*, WMANT 5, ³1974.

PART TWO: CONTEMPORARY HISTORY OF THE NT—THE ENVIRONMENT OF PRIMITIVE CHRISTIANITY

§ 13 Concerning Methodology

1. General matters

A knowledge of the forms of life and thought pertaining to the time in which Jesus and the early church lived is indispensable for the historical analysis and the theological interpretation of the NT. At the same time, this knowledge is presuppositional to understanding early Christianity as a historical phenomenon in antiquity rather than as an abstract entity—such as an ideal church.

The following examples are intended to clarify the necessity of this task:

(1) The story of the tax coin (Mk 12:13ff.) becomes plain only if the political conditions in Palestine at that time are known.

(2) The meaning of the Lukan account of the birth of Jesus (Lk 1f.) can only be grasped with a knowledge of the historical individuals and times mentioned: Who was Herod? Who was Augustus? What happened in Palestine after the death of Herod? How is the census mentioned in Lk 2 to be understood in the context of the Roman system of government?

(3) Numerous ideas and concepts that play a significant part in the NT (kingdom of God, Messiah, Son of man, righteousness of God, law) are Jewish, that is, they are of Jewish origin. Their significance can be ascertained only by observing the larger religious and ideological framework in which they are used.

(4) Gaining an appropriate understanding of the trial of Jesus presupposes not only the mastery of the formal exegetical methods (literary criticism, form criticism, etc.), but much more requires also an overview of both the Roman practice of provincial government and Roman and Jewish criminal law.

(5) An accurate knowledge of the environment of the NT is also essential in recognizing which themes and problems the NT virtually omitted. Totally lacking are the ideology and terminology of Greek philosophy, such as ontology, logic, psychology, and aesthetics. This means that those NT concepts also important in Greek philosophy (e.g., νόμος, θεός, δικαιοσύνη, ψυχή) cannot be explained by the latter. Also omitted in the NT are Greek political science, systematic ethics (but not the popular philosophical ethics), as well as the entire Greek cosmology. With this in mind, it is relatively simple to answer the question of what impression the NT writings must have made on the educated Greeks and Romans.

2. Literature

(1) H. Koester, *Introduction to the NT*, 2 vols., ET 1982, esp. vol. 2.

J. Leipoldt and W. Grundmann, eds., *Umwelt des Urchristentums* I (Darstellung), ³1971; II (Ausgewählte Quellen), ³1972; III (Bilder zur Religionsgeschichte), ³1973.

E. Lohse, *NT Environment*, ET 1976.

E. Schürer, *The History of the Jewish People in the Age of Jesus Christ*, 3 vols. (German); 3 vols., ET rev. 1973, 1986, 1987.

Brief but instructive is R. Bultmann, *Das Urchristentum im Rahmen der antiken Religionen*, ⁴1976.

Collections of documents:

C. K. Barrett, *The NT Background. Selected Documents*, 1956, and Leipoldt-Grundmann II (see above; in the following cited as L-G). See also in English: H. C. Kee, *The Origins of Christianity, Sources and Documents*, 1973; D. R. Cartlidge and D. L. Dungan, *Documents for the Study of the Gospels*, 1980.

(2) The required basic understanding of dates, facts, and persons of the environment of early Christianity can be gained by observing, first of all, the traditional principles of organization that are dominant in literature. Generally, the following categories are addressed:

(a) The history of hellenistic-Roman antiquity, encompassing both the political history and the history of religion and ideas related to the former.

(b) The cultural world of the Roman Empire and, embedded in it,

(c) The status of Judaism at this time. As a rule one distinguishes between Palestinian Judaism and Diaspora Judaism.

The individual presentations of NT history arrange these three thematic blocks with considerable variation; either they move from the general (Roman Empire) to the specific (Judaism, religions, etc.), or conversely they move from Judaism and its history via Hellenism to the delineation of the history and politics of Rome.

Suggested exercise:

Read an entire presentation of the history of the NT and, alongside, consult a collection of sources, e.g., E. Lohse, *NT Environment*, and Barrett or L-G II.

§ 14 Concerning Sources

Preliminary remarks:

The task of achieving historical expertise is based upon and at the same time greatly facilitated by the exhaustive and critical materials of the primary sources.

The pertinent source materials may be grouped into various categories: those categories determined by content ("religious" or "profane" [i.e., secular, transl.] texts) and those determined by external characteristics (inscriptions or literary sources). Of course, such grouping has no significance with regards to principles involved; it has only "technical" significance. For instance, there are collections of inscriptions or of papyri with radically diverse content.

We distinguish between hellenistic and Jewish sources. But even here the lines of separation should not be drawn sharply. For instance, the historian Josephus is Jewish and yet is a hellenistic author, since he writes in Greek and for non-Jewish readers.

The most important sources from the entire realm of antiquity, those from the Greek, Roman, and Jewish domain, are found in the source collections by Barrett and L-G cited above.

1. Hellenistic sources

(1) Apart from Barrett and L-G, English translations of *religious sources* may be found in M. P. Nilsson, *A History of Greek Religion*, 2nd ed., ET 1949, and in K. Latte, *Die Religion der Römer*, ²1927, which also contains sources pertaining to Greco-Roman syncretism (gnosis, mystery religions). Religious sources in Greek are found in the collection of *Pantheion* (³1965).

(2) Significant are also the presentations of *historical events*. With regard to Roman history, one should be familiar with the works of Tacitus and with the biographies of the Caesars by Suetonius; concerning Jewish history, one should have a working knowledge of the works of Josephus. In his *Annals* and *Histories,* Tacitus describes the history of the emperors to the end of the first century and endeavors to show a high degree of scholarly accuracy, considering its antiquity. Suetonius offers the biographies of the Roman emperors from Caesar to Domitian; however, the value of his presentations is not to be compared with that of Tacitus. In his *Jewish Antiquities (Ant.)*, Josephus presents Jewish history from creation to the Jewish War and then describes the latter again at length in his second extensive work, *The Jewish War (War)*; (for a Greek-English edition, see *Josephus*, 10 vols., Loeb Classical Library (Cambridge, Mass.: Harvard, 1976). In addition, mention is to be made of the biographer and philosopher Plutarch, who wrote in Greek and who is of interest to us on account of his description of the mystery religions. Critical editions are available on all of the works cited; however, they are also available in English translations, in part even in paperback editions.

(3) Of great significance are the *inscriptions*, which provide information about the religious as well as the political traditions. They are gathered in enormous, almost countless volumes.

A representative selection of such inscriptions is found in W. Dittenberger's *Sylloge Inscriptionum Graecarum* (4 vols., ³1915–1924) and in the collection *Orientis Graeci Inscriptiones Selectae* (2 vols., 1903–5). A basic introduction is found in R. Helbing's volume, *Auswahl aus griechischen Inschriften* (in the Göschen collection, nr. 757, 1915), which also has the German translation of the inscriptions. A commentary on these texts, but no translation, is offered by G. Pfohl, *Inschriften der Griechen*, 1972.

The two source collections of Barrett and L-G which have already been mentioned several times, contain significant and interesting inscriptions (Barrett, 48–53; L-G 84, 113, 114); among them is to be found perhaps the most significant of the preserved inscriptions, namely the "Monumentum Ancyranum," the account of Augustus (excerpts in Barrett, 1ff.).

(4) The large number of *papyrus texts* found in Egypt are predominantly documents such as official decrees, judicial complaints, protocols, business contracts, marriage certificates, and divorce documents; private letters have also been discovered. The manufacturing process is described by the Roman scholar C. Pliny the Elder (text in Barrett, 19). The magical papyri are especially important for the history of religions.

In one of the magical papyri is found the comprehensive so-called liturgy of Mithras (L-G 125). Originally this text was held to be a liturgical formula of the mithraic cult (hence the current name), but further research has shown since then that it represents a text of magic.

Suggested exercise:

Read the so-called liturgy of Mithras.

Information concerning the papyri's general significance for the study of the language and environment of the NT, is offered in A. Deissmann, *Light from the Ancient East*, ET 1965.

Relevant texts are found in Barrett (e.g., 20, 24, 27, 31, 34, 41, 45) and L-G 71ff.

(5) The *philosophical* writings of antiquity are likewise significant sources. *The* typical philosophical orientation of the NT era is Stoicism, especially in its popular form. When one deals with the paraenetic passages of the NT writings, it is helpful to have a general conception of Stoic ethics and at least of the teachings of Epictetus (cf. § 21).

Considerable selections of the writings of Epictetus and of Plutarch have been published as paperbacks. In any case, one should read the philosophical texts reproduced in Barrett and L-G in order to gain a general impression not only of the content, but also of the structure.

2. Jewish Sources

Of particular importance for the study of the NT is the religious source material of Judaism. It is difficult, of course, to survey the material.

The source collections of L-G and Barrett contain an abundance of texts from ancient Judaism (partly in excerpts); it is necessary, however, to be able to work with the sources independently of these collections on account of their frequent citation in the literature (on the text editions, see above, p. 19).

(1) First off, it is essential to know in general the most important genres of Jewish literature:

(a) Proverbial wisdom; in the OT, the book of Proverbs belongs to this genre. The book Jesus ben Sirach, which has been incorporated into the LXX, and, for instance, the Mishnah tractate (see below) *Aboth*, "Sayings of the Fathers," originated in later Judaism.

(b) Likewise, Baruch and the Wisdom of Solomon are wisdom writings; but in contrast to the proverbial wisdom, these are not mere collections of proverbs, but rather more thematically oriented discussions.

(c) Psalms; in the NT era the "Psalms of Solomon" and especially the Qumran hymns (*hodayoth*, 1 QH) belong to this genre.

(d) History finds its reflection, for example, in the apocryphal books of the Maccabees (1, 2 Macc).

(e) Among those writings which belong to the genre of narrative or novella are the books of Tobit and Judith; the writing "Joseph and Aseneth" is a romance.

(f) Apocalypses; the book of Daniel in the OT is representative. From a later era, 4 Ezra is typical of this kind of literature (this book should be read in its entirety).

(g) Finally, there is the genre known as "testament," which is indebted to the blessing of Jacob in Gen 49. Characteristic is the "Testament of the Twelve Patriarchs."

(2) The texts of the Jewish sect of Qumran from the Dead Sea are especially significant for our understanding of ancient Judaism. In part they render very detailed information about the life and teaching of this religious group outside official Judaism at the time of Jesus (cf. § 19.6). The manuscripts are primarily from the first century B.C. and A.D.; in other words, they are the oldest available writings of this era.

Since these texts are frequently called upon as parallels of the NT, it is necessary to know the most common editions of the Qumran writings, and especially their method of citation.

The most accessible and easiest to use is the edition of E. Lohse which offers a German translation with brief notes next to the pointed Hebrew text. More extensive comments are found in the two-volume edition of *Die Texte vom Toten Meer* (ed. J. Maier, 1960). [In English see A. Dupont-Sommer, *The Essene Writings from Qumran*, 1973.]

Meanwhile a unified method of citing the Qumran writings has been adopted in scholarship. The first numeral represents the cave in which the manuscripts were found (the numeration follows the sequence in which they were discovered); then follows the letter Q and finally another letter which designates the actual writing. In the citation of the reference (generally in roman and arabic numerals) it is to be noted that they are not concerned with chapter and verse but that they denote column and line—in contrast to the early Christian literature, the Qumran community wrote on *scrolls* (cf. above, p. 39f.).

Therefore, 1 QS I 1 denotes the following: Cave 1 (discovered first) of Qumran, book Serek (generally: community rules), column 1, line 1. 1 QM XI 3: Cave 1, book Milhama (war of the children of light against the children of darkness; in brief, called War Scroll), column 11, line 3.

The abbreviation 1 QH designates the book Hodayoth (hymns).

The abbreviation 1 QpHab denotes a pesher (commentary) on the prophet Habakkuk.

In addition to these major books which generally have been very well preserved, the caves contain countless smaller fragments; they are numbered consecutively in arabic numerals, after the reference to the cave number, for instance 1 Q 27 etc.

It is of paramount significance for OT scholarship and especially for textual criticism that some of the oldest available manuscripts of OT books in Hebrew were also found. The abbreviations 1 QIs^a, 1 QIs^b etc. designate the respective manuscripts of Isaiah found in cave 1.

The Damascus Document also belongs to the Qumran writings. A complete manuscript that originated in medieval times was found in 1896; this book is usually identified as "Cairo Document" (abbreviated CD), in keeping with the place of its discovery (occasionally the abbreviation Dam is also used in literary works). Fragments of this writing were also discovered at Qumran.

(3) The "rabbinic literature" is comprised of (a) the Talmud, (b) the Midrash and (c) targumic writings. They are not altogether written by individual rabbis; in some cases they represent monumental collections of traditions, based upon a process encompassing several centuries. Commonly the following groupings of rabbinic tradition are identified: The oldest tradents were the Tannaim (until A.D. 220), followed by the Amoraim (until ca. A.D. 500), the Saboraim (until ca. 600), and the Geonim (until ca. 1000).

(a) The most important collection is the Talmud ("teaching") and contains primarily the interpretation of the law; but beyond that it also represents a type of encyclopedia of ancient Jewish learning from all realms of life. It consists of two parts: The *Mishnah*, written in Hebrew, and the *Gemarah*, mostly in Aramaic. Foundational to the entire work is the Mishnah, which was compiled around A.D. 200 (the name is derived from the Hebrew שנה [to repeat, teach, learn]) and which is comprised of 63 "tractates," arranged in six groups, each ordered according to subject matter. The Gemarah is the collection of the rabbinic doctrinal debates on the Mishnah.

It is to be noted that the Gemarah does not contain exclusively later materials but also some dogmas which, in terms of the history of tradition, are on the same level as the Mishnah (here one refers to the so-called baraita propositions).

The Gemarah on the Mishnah collected by the Palestinian rabbis, together with the Mishnah itself, constitutes the Palestinian or Jerusalem
Talmud (Yerushalmi). Its significance is marginal in comparison with the
Babylonian Talmud (Babli), which resulted from the work of the scholars
serving in the rabbinic academies of Babylon. Jewish thought has been—
and continues to be—shaped decisively by the Babylonian Talmud.

A multi-volume English translation of the Babylonian Talmud has been made available by I. Epstein, ed.; popular introductions are found in R. Mayer, *Der babylonische Talmud* (see above, p. 9), and in G. Stemberger, *Der Talmud. Einführung,
Texte, Erläuterungen*, 1982. One should survey the Talmud in its original form in
a library at least once.

The Yerushalmi as well as the Babli follow the outline of the Mishnah,
while omitting numerous tractates.

The Mishnah is referenced by citing the tractate, chapter and paragraph;
thus M *Shab(bat)* III, 1 (or 3,1) is the Mishnah tractate about the Sabbath,
ch 3, § 1.

The M is often omitted, as does Billerbeck, because the form of citation indicates
that it concerns the Mishnah.

If one cites from the Gemarah of the Babylonian Talmud rather than the
Mishnah, the tractate and page number—identical pagination has been
adopted in all editions—are given (with additional distinctions between
recto and verso). In addition, a lower case b sometimes precedes the tractate (not in Billerbeck, however) for the sake of clarity. Therefore, b*Shab*
30a denotes: Babylonian Talmud, tractate *Shabbat*, page 30, recto (30b, correspondingly, would be verso). If the Jerusalem Talmud is cited, the following are given: Tractate, chapter, page, column and line and, for clarity's
sake, a lower case p or j. Hence p*Berakh* 2, 5d, 10 means: Jerusalem Talmud, tractate *Berakhoth*, chapter 2, page 5 verso, left hand column, line 10.

In order to be able to consult references in Billerbeck and in other
secondary literature, it is essential to be acquainted with this method of
citation.

A work paralleling the Mishnah is the Tosephta ("completion") which
not only intends to complement the Mishnah but actually stands independently at its side. The Tosephta did not attain popular recognition but
is very significant historically and theologically. The form of its citation
follows that of the Mishnah, but with a prefaced capital T (hence: T *Shab*
III,1).

(b) Very important is also the rabbinic interpretive literature in which
one generally distinguishes between Halakah (from הלך "to walk") and
Haggadah (from הגיד "to tell"). The Halakah is concerned with the interpretation and new formation of legal codes; the Haggadah interprets narrative materials and is, therefore, more colorful and multifaceted than the
Halakah.

Among the halakic writings, for instance, are the midrashim (commentaries) on the legal texts of the Pentateuch; among the haggadic writings are to be found the predominantly devotional midrashim of the Pentateuch and of other biblical books. A famous one is the Midrash Rabba ("Great Midrash"), particularly its book Genesis Rabba.

On the editions, see the article "Rabbinische Literatur" in *Der Kleine Pauly* IV, 1323–1326. Extensive information is offered in H. L. Strack, *Introduction to the Talmud and Midrash*, ET [4]1976.

(c) The targumic literature arose out of the necessity to translate the Hebrew Bible into the colloquially used Aramaic. The Targum Onkelos was the official Aramaic translation of the Bible (with a second century A.D. origin in Babylon). Next to it there were Palestinian targums, representing not so much a translation as a free paraphrase with numerous comments and elucidating embellishments. These targums also play a certain role in OT textual criticism.

Suggested Exercises:

1. Look up the tractate *Shabbat* in the Babylonian Talmud and observe the layout of a page. Relevant explanations are found in R. Mayer, *Der Babylonische Talmud*, 22f.

2. Decode some paragraphs in Billerbeck, e.g., I, 616–618, concerning the problem of the Sabbath.

(4) The most important source for our understanding of hellenistic Judaism, apart from some writings of the Greek OT (e.g., the "Wisdom of Solomon"), is the voluminous work of Philo, the religious philosopher of Alexandria. A selection of his writings is found in L-G 292–324 (see below, p. 137).

§ 15 Political and Social Setting of the Hellenistic Era

Bibliography: M. I. Finley, *The Ancient Economy*, 1973; U. Kahrstedt, *Kulturgeschichte der römischen Kaiserzeit*, [2]1958; H. C. Kee, *Christian Origins in Sociological Perspective*, 1980; F. Taeger, *Charisma. Studien zur Geschichte des antiken Herrscherkults*, 2 vols., 1957/60; W. W. Tarn and G. T. Griffith, *Hellenistic Civilization*, [3]1959; C. B. Welles, *Die hellenistische Welt*, PWG III/2, 1976, 401–571.

1. The concept of "Hellenism"

"Hellenism" is a modern term. It was coined by 19th-century historians and generally designates the post-classical Greek history after Alexander the Great. According to the definition of J. G. Droysen, the encounter and blending of the Greek and oriental culture are characteristic of Hellenism.

The close of the hellenistic era is determined differently by individual historians. Tarn views the era of the Roman Empire as a decisively new epoch and therefore does not consider it as belonging to the hellenistic era. For Bengtson, however, the term "Hellenism" encompasses the entirety of post-classical antiquity up to the end of ancient paganism. Of course, the choice of one's definition of "Hellenism" is not crucial for the account of the environment of early Christianity, since it can hardly be contested that the realm of the eastern Mediterranean has to be understood as part of the hellenistic cultural realm in the NT era.

The term "Hellenism" is often associated with the notion that this was an era of decline, devoid of its own creative, cultural contribution. At the back of this conception was the picture of the "classical" era which was understood to have ended with Alexander the Great. His successors were nothing more than "diadochoi" and "epigonoi," until Rome finally intervened with its new order. This picture needs considerable correction and has undergone many modifications. The truth of the matter is that the hellenistic era had its own vitality; it produced remarkable political, cultural, and even technical accomplishments, as well as progress in the areas of trade and administration. One only needs to peruse a major historical atlas (e.g., *Grosser Historischer Weltatlas*, 20–22, or Westermann's *Geschichtsatlas*, 20, 22f., 26f., 28f.) to recognize that a virtually worldwide network of economic and cultural connections was forged between states and nations during this era.

2. Hellenistic culture, society, and politics

(1) Hellenism represents a "cultural mix." It can be viewed as a synthesis of two opposite movements. Under Alexander the Great and his successors, Hellenism presses eastward, but at the same time oriental thought and culture gain influence in the West. This explains, for example, the rise of a blending of gods and myths in the religious realm: stories of Greek gods take on oriental traits, while oriental deities are identified as Greek gods (a so-called *interpretatio Graeca*). In this manner emerges a worldwide syncretistic culture and religiosity in the era of Hellenism.

Greek cities are established in remote eastern territories and there form economic and cultural centers, the most significant of which are Alexandria in Egypt and Antioch in Syria. Soon Alexandria owns the most voluminous library of antiquity and becomes the center for philological learning. Commentaries on classical literary works are produced here, as well as text-critical editions of literary works. Antioch on the Orontes, which plays a prominent role in the history of early Christianity because the earliest Gentile-Christian community was established here, develops into the most significant trade center of the Roman Empire, next to Rome and Alexandria.

Externally, hellenistic cities are characterized by the typical hallmarks of Greek culture: Everywhere one encounters temples, theaters, and educational centers; in the streets one finds countless statues and inscriptions honoring important personalities of the city (cf. 1 Macc 1:10–15; 2 Macc 4:7–17). However, in contrast with the traditional culture of cities of the classical Greek era, these hellenistic cities are no longer *politically* "autonomous." Their only remaining freedom is *communal*, that is, it is restricted to internal affairs. In the same way, the citizen no longer has the old liberties, such as those typical of the Athenian democracy.

(2) Consequently, the endeavor to improve the condition of the private life of the individual citizen becomes more prominent. At the same time, the concept of freedom is depoliticized and individualized; the question is no longer one of external political liberty but now one of "inner," intellectual liberty. This idea of an inner freedom that is accessible to everyone—including the slave—contributes, along with other factors, to the continuation of slavery. The latter is mitigated only by the slave owner's economic interests which require a better treatment of the slaves; it is further mitigated by the emerging humanitarian ideal which, unlike earlier tradition, leads to numerous emancipations of slaves, yet does not lead to the abolition of slavery (for emancipation documents, see Barrett, 52f.).

This explains why practically no societal changes occur during this time. The idea of the individual's inner freedom virtually eliminates the search for the external freedom of society. While social unrest and uprisings of slaves occur here and there, and communist utopias can be found in the literary works, the structure of hellenistic society as a whole remains firm until the great influx of people from the east that took place during the Roman era, in the course of which that structure collapses almost suddenly.

Land owners undoubtedly enjoy the highest degree of prestige in the hellenistic society. Ranking behind them is the financial aristocracy (merchants, ship owners). Laborers and craftsmen are essentially insignificant. Tax collectors are hated by all (cf. below, p. 123). There are certain philosophical groups, such as the Cynics (see below), who regard wealth and class distinctions as secondary, but this attitude has no concrete social consequences whatsoever.

The deplorable state of affairs socially has serious effects, especially on the family of the lower social stratum. Abandonment of children—especially of girls—is extremely frequent because it was feared that larger families might suffer starvation. The wages paid to the free laborer or craftsman were very low; sometimes the standard of living among the slaves was even higher than among the freedmen. There was no organized social welfare; however, wealthy citizens were often prepared to donate large sums of money for grain supplies or public buildings because it increased their prestige.

(3) Concerning the role of the woman in the hellenistic era, some stereotypes are well known. It is asserted, for example, that women were more or less without rights and, in principle, did not enjoy any public standing. This image is not entirely appropriate. There were female rulers who enjoyed extraordinary success as politicians; many queens gained great fame and political influence at the side of their husbands. It is true, however, that generally women were excluded from public activity per se; yet they were in no way without rights in the private, civil sector. They were able to acquire property which was fully at their disposal. In certain religious associations they were able to function as priestesses. Nevertheless, it was indeed always only the minority of women which could capitalize on these rights.

It is noteworthy that there was a high degree of equality and liberality in the realm of marital laws. Marriage and divorce were enacted by simple contract or by both partners' common declaration to that effect. According to Greek and Roman law, a divorce could be asked for by both partners (according to Jewish law, only the husband had this right). Monogamy alone was the common type of marriage.

Suggested exercises:

1. Compare a hellenistic marriage or divorce contract (Barrett, 31, 34) with the Jewish marriage law (Billerbeck I, 318).

2. Exegete and evaluate the legal history of Mk 10:1–12 par. Tool: E. Klostermann, *Das Markusevangelium*, HNT 3, loc. cit.

(4) In comparison with classical antiquity, the socio-political situation that presents itself in the new hellenistic conception of the state has changed. The territorial state has taken the place of the independent city-state (see above) which no longer exists in its old form. At its helm stands the deified dictator. In fact, it is true to say that the cult of the ruler is one of the hallmarks of Hellenism. Behind this cult is the notion that God became manifest in the ruler. Of course, the popular title rulers used, "*Sōtēr*," also points out that the ruler recognized his responsibility to take seriously the welfare of the people. In general, the rulers' names make very clear the claims of royalty: Antiochus Soter, Antiochus Theos, Antiochus Epiphanes. The recurring, severe altercations between the hellenistic rulers of the Near East and the Jews were altogether inevitable; for, the cult of the ruler and Jewish monotheism were mutually exclusive. The effective imprint of the hellenistic cult of the ruler can be read out of the unfolding of the history of the Roman emperor; when the control of the East was assumed by the Roman Empire, there was an immediate introduction of the cultic veneration of the respective ruling emperor. Under Augustus this still took the shape of the veneration of

the deified Rome and of the ruler as an institution; later on this was turned into a cult of the person of the ruling emperor. Numerous inscriptions attest to this.

Suggested exercise:

Read some of the inscriptions relative to the cult of the ruler in L-G II, 126, 128–131 and especially the hymn to Demetrios Poliorketes, L-G II, 127.

§ 16 Political Structure of the Roman Empire

Bibliography: O. Cullmann, *The State in the New Testament*, ET 1957; N. Lewis and M. Reinhold, eds., *Roman Civilization: Sourcebook II: The Empire*, 1966; E. Meyer, *Römischer Staat und Staatsgedanke*, ³1964.

While the Roman Empire at the time of Jesus formally remains a republic, factually it is to be understood as a monarchy, or more precisely, a "principate." On the one hand, this means concretely that the emperor position is not hereditary and, on the other hand, that the emperor, more correctly the princeps, is indeed the first citizen. As such he enjoys far-reaching authority and decisive political importance, but he is by no means almighty. His special position is predicated upon the fact that he unites numerous important offices in his person. He commands the Roman troops outside of Italy and has the immediate control over those provinces in which troops were stationed ("imperial provinces" in distinction to "senatorial provinces"). As permanent tribune of the people he claims immunity and, in this capacity, moreover has the power of veto against all measures of the authorities. In fact, in all judicial matters pertaining to Roman citizens he is the highest and final court of appeal.

The Roman Empire was not a centralized state in the modern sense; indeed, even the technical prerequisites—such as the communications system—were lacking. One only needs to picture that it took weeks for authorities in the eastern part of the Empire to receive an official directive from Rome in response to a pertinent inquiry. As a result, the ruling governors in the provinces enjoyed extensive authority. Roman citizenship was not associated with the empire but with cities. Certain privileges to which the *cives Romani* (Roman citizens) were entitled, could only be exercised in Rome (e.g., the right to vote in the election of Roman officials). Roman citizens outside of Rome enjoyed a special legal protection; they were not allowed to be flogged without court verdict and, in the case of a trial, had the right of appeal to Caesar. Since non-Romans in many cases were declared Roman citizens, their former home town citizenship could be combined with that of Rome. In Acts Paul is depicted as a Roman citizen and, at the same time, as a citizen of the city of Tarsus.

Within the empire, the city of Rome, as well as Italy, maintained a special status. For instance, no troops—except the imperial Praetorian guard—were allowed to be stationed in the city. Otherwise, the empire was divided into provinces, obviously with widely varying characteristics. At the helm of the province was the governor; in the senatorial provinces (e.g., Asia, that is, western Asia Minor) he was a proconsul or *propraetor* (with the title of "proconsul"), while in the imperial provinces (e.g., Syria), he was a *legatus Augusti pro praetore*.

Provinces of a lower rank were merely under a *praefectus* (prefect) or a procurator. The province of Judea had this type of status since A.D. 6 and thus was under the superintendence of the governor of Syria.

Within the territory of the provinces there were free cities. Officially, their inhabitants were not regarded as subjects but as allies, on a variety of levels, of course. They enjoyed a largely communal autonomy upon which the Roman administration was built, so that the final decision always belonged to the Roman governor. The example of Ephesus in Acts 19 shows how a city official might intervene in a particular instance. Next to the free cities, there were also Roman colonies, which were cities inhabited by Roman citizens. A well-known example from Acts is the city of Philippi in northern Greece (Acts 16:12; cf. p. 174 below).

Finally, there were also the so-called client states (*Klientel-Fürstentümer*) allied with the empire who were granted extensive internal independence and, in some cases, even their own military. However, they were not permitted to determine their own foreign policy and, in fact, depended more or less on the good graces of Rome. Palestine serves as an example: The inheritance of King Herod the Great is at the disposal of Augustus in Rome (see below, p. 119f.). If one reads contemporary accounts of Roman history, such as the works of Tacitus, it appears that the events are consistently seen from Rome's perspective. Yet, in reality the Roman administration in the provinces continued with a fair degree of stability, even when the insanity of Caligula and Nero at times caused chaotic conditions in Rome itself. Of course, the civil wars in connection with the battles for the succession to the throne affected the empire as a whole.

Likewise, much of what happened in the provinces had little immediate correlation with the events in Rome. The Jewish War, precipitated by the cessation of the offerings for Caesar in the temple of Jerusalem in A.D. 66, had nothing to do with the politics of Nero in Rome. The status of the Jews elsewhere in the empire was not endangered by the defeat in Palestine.

(2) In this connection, Rome's policy concerning religion is of interest. Augustus attempted to revive the veneration of the inherited deities of Rome, but, like all such attempts at restoration, this one too was doomed to failure. Furthermore, Rome introduced the veneration of the deceased ruler as *divus*; the first one to be bestowed such divine honor was Caesar,

namely as *divus Iulius*. In the provinces, especially in the east, the veneration of the goddess Roma and of the living potentate was soon added (see above). But in general, the common populous had nothing to do with this entire development; these were official cults of the state and not elements of popular piety.

The tolerance that pervades the religious realm is significant. The official Roman religion was not propagated as imperial religion; rather, the practice of the various religions remained free. Here Judaism was even treated as a special case. On account of Jewish monotheism, the cult of the ruler was intolerable for the Jews and therefore was not imposed upon them. It was simply agreed that the Jews would bring sacrifices *on behalf of* the emperor without revering him as God (see p. 119 below). Tolerance in the religious realm had been stretched to its limits when, in the judgment of the police authorities, a cult was threatening public safety. Thus the mystery religions were readily suspected of clandestine alliances; hence the mystery associations resident in Rome were controlled by the police. The famous letter of Pliny the Younger to the emperor Trajan (Text: Conzelmann, *History of Primitive Christianity*, ET 1973, p. 168ff.) indicates that the actions taken against Christians were also defended primarily by appealing to concerns of security.

§ 17 Palestine Under Roman Rule

Bibliography: S. Benko and J. J. O'Rourke, eds., *The Catacombs and the Colosseum: The Roman Empire as the Setting of Primitive Christianity*, 1971; W. Grundmann, "Das palästinensische Judentum," in L-G I, ³1971, 143–194; M. Hengel, *Die Zeloten*, AGSU 1, ²1976; idem, *Judaism and Hellenism*, 2 vols., ET 1974; J. Jeremias, *Jerusalem in the Time of Jesus*, ET 1969; E. Lohse, *The NT Environment*, ET 1976; R. Meyer, Σαδδουκαῖος, TDNT VII, 35–54; R. Meyer/ H.-F. Weiss, Φαρισαῖος, TDNT IX, 11–48.

1. Developments until the Roman take-over

The assumption that Palestine existed outside the realm of the direct influence of the hellenistic culture is erroneous. Nevertheless, Judaism in Palestine intermixed less with hellenistic elements than in other areas of the empire.

After the death of Alexander the Great, Palestine at first belonged politically to Egypt under the Ptolemies; subsequently they were governed by Syria, under the Seleucids. 1 and 2 Maccabees (see above), as well as Daniel, are documents attesting to this phase in the development of hellenistic Palestine. Several hellenistic cities were established during that era. At the time of Jesus, the best known among them were Caesarea Maritima, which served as residence for the Roman procurator and Sebaste (also known as Augustus-Sebastos), the former city of Samaria. Among other hellenistic settlements were also most of the cities of the Decapolis (the "ten cities" east of the Jordan river); particularly well known was Gadara (cf. Mk 5:20; 7:31).

Under the Seleucids even Jerusalem, the center and symbol of Judaism, was greatly hellenized. The struggle of the Maccabees was in part directed against these attempts at hellenization. But even after the Maccabean victory Jerusalem remained a city influenced by Hellenism, just as the Jewish state as a whole, under the Maccabees as well as under their successors the Herods, for all intents and purposes remained a hellenistic construct. Only the cult in Jerusalem remained strictly Jewish and thus devoid of hellenistic traits.

During the final pre-Christian century Palestine was conquered by Rome; in 63 B.C. Pompey occupied the country, including Jerusalem, and incorporated it into the province of Syria (L-G 139). The horror and indignation of this event are reflected in the Psalms of Solomon 2. In 40 B.C. the country regained limited independence: As an act of favor, Rome gave it to Herod as a client kingdom. After his death (4 B.C.) Palestine was at first divided among his sons, but soon in A.D. 6 the south (Samaria, Judea, and Idumea) was subjected to the Roman administration.

2. Political conditions in Palestine in the early church era

(1) The external condition of Palestine is determined by the relationship with Rome. The subject kings (tetrarchs) enjoy a certain freedom of movement; even in the province of Judea (see above) there is a certain Jewish self-government. The Palestinian Jews are benefitting from the empirewide recognition of the Jews as a special nation. The privileges granted by Caesar (L-G, 247) were ratified by Augustus and Tiberius; accordingly, the Jews were neither obligated to participate in the cult of the ruler, nor were they to be forced to participate in other cults. Foreign cults were simply out of the question in Jerusalem (excluding, of course, the territory of the Roman garrison). Even after the Jewish War this special status did not change for the Jews.

(2) At the helm of the Jewish self-government in Judea is the high priest, who represents the people before the Roman procurator on the one hand and supervises the cult in Jerusalem on the other. Furthermore, he presides over the Sanhedrin, comprised of 70 members (English translation: Jewish Council). In the NT as well as in Josephus, the point is made that there were several high priests at one and the same time (cf. Mt 26:14); however, most likely this is merely a reference to the members of the Sanhedrin who belonged to the high priestly families, that is, to current and former high priests and to the relatives of the most prominent priestly families (cf. Bauer, *Greek-English Lexicon*, 112). Moreover, the Sanhedrin was comprised of representatives of the aristocracies both of the priests and of the laity, plus the group of the scribes. The council's jurisdiction was restricted to Judea; of course, its prestige encompassed all of Judaism, for it was entrusted with the administration of the temple to which every Jew in the world contributed an annual tax of two drachma.

This temple tax was discontinued after the fall of Jerusalem in A.D. 70; it was replaced by the "fiscus Iudaicus," a mandatory tax designated for the Jupiter Capitolinus. This measure was continually met with opposition and encouraged later Jewish uprisings. However, it remained in force practically until the end of the cult of Jupiter practiced in Rome (cf. Barrett, 19ff.).

In certain cases the Sanhedrin was allowed to intervene outside of Judea through special representatives; nevertheless, there is no literary evidence for a law of the Sanhedrin as presupposed in Acts 9:2. Also controversial is the question whether capital punishment was under the jurisdiction of the Sanhedrin, that is, whether the execution of Jesus could have been carried out on the basis of a corresponding verdict handed down by the Sanhedrin (in this connection, see p. 332f. below).

(3) Within Palestinian Judaism there were several groups, sometimes labeled as "parties," with divergent religious conceptions and, in part, with contrasting political ideals (Josephus, *War* II, 119ff.; cf. Barrett, 124ff.):

(a) The group of the *Pharisees* was a closed society; while its leadership was in the hands of the scribes, its composition was essentially from the laity. In the second century B.C. they united under the Hasmoneans (Maccabean dynasty) with the intent to separate themselves from the masses of the people—the *'am ha-'aretz*—through special religious efforts. Their aim was to realize the priestly ideal in day-to-day life (cf. Barrett, 163f.). At the same time, they also promoted the development of Jewish thought and endeavored not to forsake the traditions (see also p. 130f. below). Pharisaism was cautious in its relationship with the Romans, since the Pharisees anticipated the restoration of Israel through God's imminent intervention and not through political, military action.

(b) Until the Jewish War, the order of the *Sadducees*—the party of the priestly aristocracy—was politically influential. They adhered strictly to the letter of the law and therefore denied both "modern" metaphysics and postbiblical traditions (see also p. 132 below). Politically the Sadducees were striving to attain a balanced relationship with Rome. This party was completely annihilated in the Jewish War, leading to the ultimate victory of the Pharisees. The latter, therefore, appear as the most important Jewish party in the synoptic Gospels.

(c) The *Zealots* are distinguished sharply from the two groups mentioned thus far. As far as their religious conviction was concerned, they were more closely aligned with the Pharisees and also sought to distinguish themselves through adherence to the law. But for them this adherence was connected with a revolutionary program. They rendered a political interpretation to the dictum that God alone was the Lord of Israel; hence they were in irreconcilable opposition to the Roman occupation. Thus their efforts almost inevitably led to insurrection (Josephus, *Ant.* XX, 167ff.; *War* II, 258ff.).

(d) The *Essenes* constituted a fourth group. The primary contrast to the three other groups was that they retreated into the desert and thus separated from the world as well as from Judaism in general (see also p. 138ff. below).

(4) The tensions between Rome and the Jewish population intensified during the administration of the procurator Pontius Pilate (Barrett, 123f.). The situation came to a climax when the emperor Caligula ordered the erection of his statue in the temple in Jerusalem by disregarding Jewish privileges. However, the Syrian governor Petronius was able to delay the carrying out of the order until Caligula's successor, Claudius, retracted the command (cf. Barrett, 11ff.).

Some exegetes maintain that the "little apocalypse," 2 Thes 2 (v 3!) is based on Caligula's order; others connect the "abomination of desolation" in Mk 13 with the same. But this cannot be ascertained. In any case, extreme caution is necessary in attempting to explain apocalyptic texts historically.

Herod Agrippa I once more achieved a considerable degree of independence for Palestine (from A.D. 41 to 44 he even claimed the title of royalty for himself); yet after his death the whole country was finally subjected to Roman procurators. The degree of unrest continued to escalate (Barrett, 127), especially on account of the actions of the Zealots and of the "sicarii" (dagger bearers) who did not even shrink back from political murder. Finally, in A.D. 66 the general revolt against Rome erupted. This revolt, the "Jewish War," ended in total defeat in A.D. 70; Palestine now became a common Roman province (Barrett, 130–133). What little room remained for Jewish self-government was used by the Pharisees to reform Judaism systematically in accordance with their conception. This development was led by Rabbi Johanan ben Zakkai.

Into this phase of the history of Palestinian Judaism belongs the demarcation of the biblical canon and the systematic collection of tradition by the rabbis influenced by Pharisaism. Matthew reflects this situation: For him the Pharisees are *the* representatives of the Jewish people; while he still knows of the existence of the Sadducees, who played an important role at the time of Jesus, he is no longer personally acquainted with them.

3. Geographical conditions in Palestine

(1) Information can be obtained from the presentations of "biblical geography" which are based upon archaeological finds and upon descriptions by classical writers.

G. Dalman, *Orte und Wege Jesu,* [4]1967 (=1924).

O. Keel, M. Küchler, Chr. Uehlinger, *Orte und Landschaften der Bibel. Ein Handbuch und Studienreiseführer zum Heiligen Land,* vol. 1: *Geographisch-geschichtliche Landeskunde,* 1984; vol. 2: *Der Süden,* 1982.

The following Bible atlases provide insights into the political and geographical conditions of Palestine:

Y. Aharoni and M. Avi-Yonah, *The Macmillan Bible Atlas,* 1977.

H. Guthe, *Bibelatlas,* [2]1926.

H. G. May, *Oxford Bible Atlas,* 1962.

G. E. Wright and F. V. Filson, *The Westminster Historical Atlas to the Bible,* 1945.

Maps of Palestine at the time of Jesus and of early Christianity are also found in the *Grosser Historischer Weltatlas* and in Westermann's *Geschichtsatlas.*

When studying Bible atlases, with the exception of Guthe, it is necessary to note that they represent a description of biblical history that is no longer tenable from a scholarly perspective. For instance, in the realm of the OT one invariably finds a description of the "historical" route that Israel took through the wilderness under Moses' leadership, or of the route of the patriarchal journeys. Almost all atlases and most maps depict the routes of the journeys of the apostle Paul without recognizing that we possess only the data of Acts and not that of the actual routes. Even with the information of Acts we are not able to construct their sequence without gaps; one needs to supplement the data with the help of assumptions.

(2) The salient points concerning the situation in Palestine can be drawn from the *Grosse Historische Weltatlas* (p. 27):

(a) Under Herod the Great all of Palestine is united.

(b) After his death the country is divided among his sons (as tetrarchs).

(c) The south (Judea) becomes a Roman province in A.D. 6.

(d) The whole country is once again united under Herod Agrippa I (during A.D. 41–44).

(e) After the Jewish War, i.e., after A.D. 70, Palestine becomes a Roman province.

In order to comprehend the Gospel presentation of the travels of Jesus, an approximate understanding of the location of the respective Palestinian territories is essential.

(a) Under the Seleucids Galilee belonged to Syria; under the Hasmoneans this territory was systematically re-Judaized. Herod Antipas ruled here and in Perea (see below) in the time of Jesus, while northeastern Galilee was governed by his brother Philip.

(b) Perea was the territory east of the Jordan; in its northernmost region was the "Decapolis," a confederation of free hellenistic cities. During the time of Jesus the Jews considered this Transjordan territory as "heathen country."

(c) Samaria was the homeland of the Samaritans—separated from the remaining Jews—with their own sanctuary on Mt. Gerizim (see p. 140f. below). The capital was Samaria, which Herod the Great rebuilt as a hellenistic city and named Sebaste. After Herod's death, Samaria was initially governed by his son Archelaus. Together with Judea it became a Roman province in A.D. 6.

(d) Judea, with Jerusalem as its capital, was the heart of Palestine.

(e) To the extreme south was Idumea, ancient Edom, which was converted into Jewish territory by the Hasmoneans. The family of Herod the Great (see below) had its roots here.

4. *Economic conditions in Palestine*

The dominant types of industry can be derived from the parables, for they reflect the social and economic situation of the "plains" during the time of Jesus.

Agricultural home production constituted the basis for the economic and living conditions. Yet, there were also larger agricultural units in Judea; likewise, in the fertile areas of Galilee as well as in the lowlands of the Jordan, large estates are known to have existed (cf. Jeremias, *Parables*, 74f.). The latter was usually in the possession of the royal and high priestly families, yet to a large extent also in the hands of (imperial) foreigners. Two statements by Josephus underscore this: In Palestine, wheat is stored for the emperor (*Life*, 71). Although living in Rome, Josephus himself receives real estate in Palestine (422, 425, 429). The great landowners enjoyed considerable economic and political influence on account of the volume of the crops, especially wine, oil, and wheat, and because they employed a sizable workforce. Real estate was often leased out, which, in many cases, led to the impoverishment of the tenant due to high lease payments; Josephus offers information in this regard too (*War* II, 84f.; *Ant*. XVII, 304ff.). In contrast to the towns, craftsmanship was virtually undeveloped in the rural areas. Likewise, trade was marginal at best; bartering was the norm.

Skilled labor was centralized in Jerusalem. Impoverished families often expected a betterment in their economic situation by moving to the city and thus left the "plains."

Taxes and dues were a constant source of tension and unrest. In all of the provinces there were two kinds of direct taxes: a tax based on the agricultural yield and a poll-tax. At the time of Jesus the collection of these taxes was not sublet in Palestine; instead, it was the responsibility of the local authorities to collect them. Indirect taxes or dues, on the other hand, were sublet. Of particular importance was the *portorium* (customs duty and transit payments associated with streets and bridges etc.). The state's lessees (tax collectors) were extremely unpopular because the citizens— often justifiably—felt they were cheated.

Further reading:

Detailed information concerning the system of taxation is found in O. Michel's article on τελώνης in the TDNT VIII, 88–105.

§ 18 *Personalities in the History of the* NT

Bibliography: *Section 1:* H.-G. Pflaum, *Das römische Kaiserreich*, PWG IV/2, 1976, 317–428.

Preliminary remarks:

It is necessary to be acquainted with those personalities in the NT and in the environment of early Christianity that played an important part. Of course, this chapter is not concerned with a detailed biographical portrait of these personalities; rather, it deals with those facts and figures significant for the exegesis of the NT.

1. Roman Emperors

(1) *Augustus* (absolute monarch from 31 B.C. to A.D. 14) is mentioned in Lk 2:1 in connection with a worldwide census. Whether this census did indeed take place in this form is debatable (see p. 291f. below).

Information pertaining to the rule of Augustus is found in the Monumentum Ancyranum (Barrett, 1; L-G, 17) and in the biography by Suetonius. For many contemporaries the reign of Augustus seemed like an ushering in of the golden era; the emergence of such "messianic" sentiments is reflected in the Fourth Eclogue of Virgil (written in 40 B.C.; see text in Barrett, 8–10 and in L-G, 132) and in the *carmen saeculare* of Horace (Barrett, 6–8). The idealization of Augustus led to the engendering of legends about his birth and childhood (miraculous signs relative to his birth, the child's rescue from persecution, remarkable intellectual aptitude; L-G, 135); it also led to the development of the cult of Augustus (L-G, 130f.). But Augustus was not yet an absolute dictator in the style of some of his successors. His position as princeps was predicated to a large extent upon his actual, personal authority and upon his amalgamation of several important offices (see above), rather than upon the brute force of his dominion.

(2) *Tiberius*, the successor to Augustus (A.D. 14–37), is cited in Lk 3:1, which, incidentally, contains the only concrete dating for the life of Jesus (likely the year A.D. 28). Tacitus and Suetonius offer information on Tiberius (see texts in Barrett, 10f.). The crucifixion of Jesus occurred during his tenure; yet Rome does not even take note of Jesus' execution. (In Roman literary works, the first reference to Jesus is found in Tacitus).

Occasionally the assertion is made that Sejanus, one of Tiberius' minions until
A.D. 31 and an opponent of the Jews, had influenced the position of the Judean
procurator Pilate. The deposition of Pilate had been connected with the removal
of Sejanus. But this is highly improbable: In spite of the downfall of Sejanus,
Pilate maintained his office until the end of A.D. 36 (or 37); there is no evidence
for a rupture in his polity (see below).

(3) *Gaius* (Caligula), who reigned from 37–41, is not mentioned in the
NT. However, his rule is of significance for the historical development of
Palestine, for he was the first Roman emperor to promote vigorously the
cult of the emperor. Thus, in spite of the friendship between Caligula and
Herod Agrippa, the rise of tension was inevitable (see above, p. 119f.).
Philo wrote an apologetic of Judaism in his *Legatio ad Gaium* (cf. L-G, 251).

(4) *Claudius* (41–54) is mentioned in Acts 11:28 and 18:2. Classical literature distorts his image (cf. the texts in L-G, 26–28). All things considered, his reign was an epoch of internal consolidation. Acts 11:28 refers
to a worldwide famine during his tenure of office. Other sources at least
speak of occasional food scarcity, though not of a *general* famine. Claudius
issued an edict according to which the Jews were expelled from Rome
(the edict is referenced in Acts 18:2; concerning its dating, see p. 339f.
below). Suetonius attributes the occasion of the edict to disturbances
among the Jews in Rome, caused by a certain "Chrestus" (Barrett, 14).
It is possible that this presentation conceals a vague allusion to the pene-
tration of Christianity into Rome; in this case, of course, Suetonius must
have had a totally false conception of this event (i.e., Jesus in Rome).
Claudius also intervened in the Jewish disturbances in Alexandria, as his
letter to the city indicates (L-G, 269).

(5) *Nero* (54–68), during whose reign the Jewish War began, is not explicitly mentioned in the NT, although for Christians he became virtually
the archetype of the apocalyptic tyrant, due to the persecution of Christians
subsequent to the fire of Rome. Yet, this persecution did not encompass
the whole empire but was limited to the city of Rome (Barrett, 15f.).

The idea of an apocalyptic Nero redivivus was a later development. In this connection it is to be noted that the primary reason why Christians regarded Nero
as the apocalyptic monster was not his altogether dictatorial reign. Rather, they
considered his attack against the Roman church as a criminal act. Furthermore
Tacitus, with his commitment to the ideal of the Republic, does not categorically
condemn *this* particular action of Nero.

When Paul (according to Acts) appeals to Caesar during his trial as a
privilege of his Roman citizenship, the reference must be to Nero. However, Acts withholds the outcome of the process.

The frequently discussed question of whether Rev 13 contains a cryptic reference to Nero will likely continue to elude a definitive answer.

(6) *Vespasian* (69–79) and *Titus* (79–81) are not mentioned in the NT, despite their major significance both for Jewish and for Christian history. To begin with, Vespasian was a Roman general, commissioned by Nero to crush the Jewish revolt in Palestine (Barrett, 18f.). While still there, the troops proclaimed him emperor, after which he returned to Italy and secured power. His son Titus concluded the war victoriously by conquering Jerusalem in A.D. 70. In the NT, Mt 22:7 and Lk 21:20ff. are reminiscent of these events. The arch of Titus in Rome depicts temple utensils, such as the seven-branched lampstand, which had been carried along in the triumphal procession. Both the conquest of Jerusalem and the destruction of the temple were severe blows for Judaism; for the first community of Jerusalem, which had likely escaped from the city shortly before the siege began, it signalled the definitive end. However, the Jewish status as a privileged group in the Roman empire was practically unaffected by this defeat (see above, pp. 117, 119).

(7) During the reign of *Domitian* (81–96) the first more extensive persecutions of Christians occurred, the traces of which are found in 1 Peter, in the Apocalypse, and in 1 Clement, though without citing the name of the emperor. Domitian intensified the cult of the ruler; for the first time the living emperor received the title "Deus et Dominus noster" (Barrett, 19). The statue of Domitian in Ephesus is characteristic of Domitian's style of rulership (BHH III, plate 50b).

The government of the later Roman emperors was not reflected in the NT.

2. Herods

(1) *Herod* "the Great" is mentioned in the birth narrative of Jesus. He ruled Palestine from 37 to 4 B.C. (Josephus renders two detailed accounts of his life; cf. Barrett, 118–122). He was of Idumean origin (see above, p. 123), therefore the Jews did not accept him as a legitimate Jew. His dominion over Palestine was handed to him by Rome; he maintained it skillfully throughout the vicissitudes of the Roman civil wars until his death. His political achievements as ruler are uncontested; his methods, however, were often dubious. The murder of the infants of Bethlehem (Mt 2) may not be historical. Nevertheless, it is not accidental that he was held capable of such deeds.

In Palestine Herod emerged as the promoter of Judaism by his extensive remodeling of the temple and by his significantly enlarging the Antonia fortress. In addition, he built a new large royal palace. The dimensions of these buildings can be seen on the maps of the old city of Jerusalem (cf. the accounts of Josephus in L-G, 142, 143). Herod is also famed for the fortresses of Masada and Machaerus.

Outside his own country, however, Herod was a thoroughly hellenistic ruler without respect for the Jewish religion. Thus he built Samaria/Sebaste and Caesarea as hellenistic cities, including a temple for the emperor (cf.

L-G, 143). After the death of Herod, the country was divided up among his sons Archelaus, Herod Antipas, and Philip. They were not accorded the title of royalty, however; instead, Archelaus was known as an ethnarch and Herod Antipas and Philip were tetrarchs (in the NT, of course, they are also called kings occasionally).

(2) *Archelaus*, ethnarch of Judea, Samaria, and Idumea, is mentioned in Mt 2:22. Josephus describes him as a brutal and unfair ruler (see also Barrett, 123). He was exiled ten years after his accession to office.

(3) *Herod Antipas* was tetrarch of Galilee and Perea from 4 B.C. to A.D. 39 and thus the country's ruler in Jesus' time. In the NT, his marriage to Herodias, a niece of Herod the Great, is very important because it contradicted the law. In A.D. 39 he was deposed and exiled.

(4) Until his death in A.D. 34, *Philip* reigned over the eastern Jordanian region, an area barely inhabited by Jews. He is mentioned in Lk 3:1 and Mk 6:17 par. (see above), but he has no role to play in the history of early Christianity.

(5) (Herod) *Agrippa I*, the brother of Herodias, became the successor to Antipas and reigned until A.D. 44. Gradually he succeeded in bringing all of Palestine under his domain. In A.D. 41 he was given royalty status. His death is described in legendary form in Acts 12.

(6) His son, *Agrippa II*, ruled from approx. A.D. 50–100 over Transjordan and is mentioned in Acts 25f.

3. Governors/procurators

Among the governors of Syria and Palestine in the era of the NT, four are cited: Quirinius, Pilate, Felix, and Festus.

(1) Publius Sulpicius *Quirinius* became governor of Syria in A.D. 6/7; after the removal of Archelaus, he conducted a census in Judea.

According to Lk 2:2, this census took place in the time of the birth of Jesus (concerning its dating, see § 48). But this cannot be harmonized with the known dates of the tenure of office of Quirinius; according to his time of office, this census could not have taken place prior to A.D. 6 or 7. For this reason it is argued that Quirinius held the office of governor of Syria twice, at different times. But this assumption remains unsubstantiated.

(2) *Pontius Pilate* was procurator (*praefectus*) of Judea ca. A.D. 26–36. According to Jewish testimonials he was cruel and unjust. Lk 13:1 speaks of the slaughter of several Galileans; according to Josephus (*Ant.* XVIII, 85ff.), in A.D. 36 Pilate raided Samaritans who had gathered at Mt. Gerizim and later had them executed. In direct reaction to this incident the Syrian governor deposed him and sent him to Rome to give an account for his actions. He did not adhere to the privileges accorded to the Jews either; for instance, he allowed Roman troops to enter Jerusalem carrying the standards which bore the effigies of Caesar (Barrett, 123f.). How-

ever, his conduct in the trial of Jesus was in keeping with the established legal guidelines (in this context, cf. pp. 332f. below).

(3) *Antonius Felix* was procurator of Palestine (not only of Judea) in ca. A.D. 52–56. He was a freedman and as such received his position, which ordinarily was reserved for equestrians, by some opportune political constellation in Rome. Tacitus (*History* V, 9) describes him as cruel and unjust. However, in Acts he is depicted as ambivalent: according to ch 24:25, when he heard Paul preach on righteousness and judgment, he was gripped by fear; yet v 26 shows that he expected to be paid a bribe by Paul. At the back of this account, however, there is probably no historically accurate characterization of Felix to be found. In this way, apparently, Luke is simply delineating why Paul had not been released by Felix, despite evidence of his innocence.

(4) *Porcius Festus*, the successor of Felix, was governor of Palestine from A.D. 56 to 60 (?). He assumed the trial against Paul from Felix and comes across as an upright individual. One also gains this impression from Acts 25f.

4. High priests

In the NT three high priests are mentioned by name:

(1) *Annas*, who held the office from A.D. 6 to 15, was the first high priest appointed by Rome. In Lk 3:2 and Acts 4:6 Luke mentions him as the ruling high priest in the time of Jesus, but these references are erroneous.

Five of the sons of Annas later became high priests themselves, so that the "house of Annas" was one of two leading high priestly families.

(2) *Caiaphas* (Joseph Qajjaph/Kaiaphas), who played a major role in the passion story, held the office of high priest in about A.D. 18–37; according to Jn 18:13 he was the son-in-law of Annas. John probably based this on the assumption that the office of the high priest was filled or confirmed annually. But this assertion does not measure up to what we know from Jewish sources.

(3) *Ananias*, who was significantly involved in the trial against Paul, according to Acts 23:2; 24:1, officiated from A.D. 48 to approximately 55. He was murdered by the revolutionaries at the onset of the Jewish War in A.D. 66.

The two other individuals mentioned in Acts 4:6, John and Alexander, were not high priests at all (see above, p. 119f.); nothing is known of a high priest named Sceva (Acts 19:14).

Suggested reading:

Information concerning the original position of the high priests is found in 1 Macc 14:25–49 and in Josephus (see texts in Barrett, 115–118).

§ 19 Judaism

Bibliography: D. E. Gowan, *Bridge between the Testaments*, PTMS 14, 1976; J. Maier, *Geschichte der jüdischen Religion*, 1972, 7–211; J. Maier and J. Schreiner, eds., *Literatur und Religion des Frühjudentums*, 1973; Section 2: M. Limbeck, *Die Ordnung des Heils. Untersuchungen zum Gesetzesverständnis des Frühjudentums*, 1971. Section 3: W. Foerster, *From the Exile to Christ: A Historical Introduction to Palestinian Judaism*, ET 1964; F. C. Grant, *Ancient Judaism and the New Testament*, 1959; J. N. Lightstone, *The Commerce of the Sacred: Meditations of the Divine among Jews in the Greco-Roman Diaspora*, Brown Judaic Series 59, 1986; J. Maier, "Tempel und Tempelkult," in J. Maier and J. Schreiner, 371–390; J. Neusner, *Judaism in the Beginning of Christianity*, 1984; S. Sandmel, *Judaism and Christian Beginnings*, 1978; P. Schäfer, "Der synagogale Gottesdienst," in J. Maier and J. Schreiner, 391–413. Section 4: P. D. Hanson, *The Dawn of Apocalyptic*, 1975; K. Müller, "Die Ansätze der Apokalyptik," in J. Maier and J. Schreiner, 31–42; D. S. Russell, *The Method and Message of Jewish Apocalyptic*, 1964; J. Schreiner, "Die apokalyptische Bewegung," in J. Maier and J. Schreiner, 214–253; P. Volz, *Die Eschatologie der jüdischen Gemeinde*, ²1934 (⁵1966). Section 5: P. Borgen, *Philo, John, and Paul: New Perspectives on Judaism and Early Christianity*, Brown Judaic Series 131, 1987; H. Hegermann, "Das griechisch-sprechende Judentum. Philon von Alexandria," in J. Maier and J. Schreiner, 328–369; J. Neusner, "Babylonisches Judentum während der Zeit des 2. Tempels," ibid., 321–327. Section 6: "Esserer," in *Kleiner Pauly*, II, 1967, 375–378; "Essenes," *IDB* II, 143–149; "Qumran," ibid., IV, 1972, 1316–1322; F. M. Cross, *The Ancient Library of Qumran*, 1961; J. Maier and K. Schubert, *Die Qumran-Essener*, 1973. Section 7: H. G. Kippenberg, *Garizim und Synagoge*, RGVV 30, 1972; J. MacDonald, *The Theology of the Samaritans*, 1964.

1. General matters—The concept of God

(1) At the time of Jesus, Judaism was no homogeneous entity. While the Pentateuch is generally recognized as the religious foundation, its interpretation is debated. Furthermore, the canonical scope is still fluid. Only the dicta that God is *one* and that he elected Israel to be his people are construed as theologically binding. This inseparable unity between people and religion is the general characteristic of Judaism. Anyone who separates himself from the history of Israel and from belonging to the Jewish people is no longer a Jew (a well-known case was Tiberius Alexander, Philo's nephew). Everyone entering Judaism as a proselyte also becomes a member of the Jewish race (with some restrictions).

(2) Its worldwide expansion and the existence of diverse groups are characteristic of Judaism in the NT era.

(a) It is possible to distinguish geographically between the predominantly Aramaic-speaking Palestinian Judaism on the one hand and the Greek-speaking diaspora Judaism on the other hand. There is also a large Aramaic-speaking diaspora in Mesopotamia (Babylon).

(b) The whole nation is divided cultically into four groups: Priests, Levites, "Israelites," and proselytes. In terms of theological education, the distinction is made between scribes and laity, the echo of which is found in the NT.

(c) Within Judaism there are different religious groups ("parties"): Pharisees, Sadducees, and Zealots; the Essenes and Samaritans represent special cases (see below, pp. 138–141). These groups are representative of different convictions, not only in terms of political issues (see above, p. 121), but also in terms of fundamental theological questions (see below, pp. 132, 134ff.).

Judaism of the NT era is often called "late Judaism." This is not a legitimate concept; it creates the impression that Judaism, existing alongside the church, is an anachronism up to the present time. Equally erroneous is the apologetic designation "early Judaism," which creates the impression that the OT is not part of Judaism. It is best to speak of Judaism in late antiquity or of Judaism in the hellenistic-Roman era.

(3) The two main pillars of Jewish religion are: (a) confession of the one God, the Creator, who chose Israel to be his people and who will yet redeem it; (b) obedience to the law, the record of the covenant between God and Israel. Such strict obedience concerns the cult and conduct of life; however, there remains a certain tolerance in the interpretation of the commandments.

The temple in Jerusalem constitutes the visible token of the unity of Judaism as its only cultic center. Therefore, if the Samaritans have their own temple, it means their separation from Judaism.

Sometime between 170 B.C. and A.D. 71 there was another Jewish temple in Leontopolis (Egypt), which was established by Onias, the high priest's son who fled from Jerusalem. This temple was not considered illegal but, at the same time, it did not have any great significance beyond its immediate surroundings.

Some theological issues, however, are subject to differing and in part even conflicting positions. Eschatology, for example, is not an integral part of Jewish teaching: the Sadducees reject apocalyptically understood eschatology, as well as all metaphysics over and above faith in God (cf. Acts 23:8). The Pharisees, on the other hand, and others like them, maintain the idea of a resurrection from the dead (see also p. 135) In any case, there are signs of an emerging tendency to emphasize the notion of the world to come: The transcendence of God becomes more and more prominent; God is farther and farther removed from the world, as it were. Thus it is deemed essential to mediate between a distant God and this world, and corresponding functions are accorded to angels and hypostases (see p. 200f.).

2. Law

(1) The law was the center of Jewish life and thought. Traditionally the opinion is held that the Jews considered the observance of the law as an oppressive and unbearable burden. But this assessment is inaccurate: Of the 613 commandments and prohibitions (Billerbeck I, 900ff.), many had long since become common tradition.

(2) Jewish obedience to the law must not be misinterpreted: The issue is not formal obedience but the attitude behind that obedience. What matters is not the human efforts alone, but the disposition to obedience. Even if one hopes for a reward for keeping the commandments, it is not permissible at all to use the law selfishly.

Therefore, the law is not to be construed as motivation for external legalism and, especially for the Jew, is not a nuisance (though this appears to be the case for Luke, the Gentile Christian; Acts 15:10). The pious Jew is proud of the law and of his ability to keep the commandments (Phil 3:2ff.; Barrett, 151–153). Obedience, therefore, does not come about mechanically and his primary motivation is not fear but his love of God, the acknowledgement of God's honor. By measuring his efforts against God's will, man is made aware of his sinfulness and realizes his dependence upon forgiveness. Thus obedience leads to humility.

The rabbinic debates concerning the correct interpretation of the law are typical of the method of their theological pursuit. At the time of Jesus and of the early church the most prominent schools were those of Shammai and Hillel. While Shammai maintained a strict interpretation of the law, Hillel's was more lenient (cf. Barrett, 140).

According to Acts 23:8, Paul was a student of Gamaliel I, known as a Hillelite, (cf. also p. 357).

(3) Since the will of God, as documented in the law, is consistent, the rabbis are able to summarize the law in one sentence. Rabbi Hillel made the statement: "What you do not like, do not do to anyone else; this is the whole Torah and everything else is explanation: go and learn" (Billerbeck I, 460). This "golden rule" is also found in the NT (Mt 7:12). But there is an objective difference—not a formal one (see below, p. 316f.)—between the two: Whereas the love commandment in the NT is intended to eliminate casuistry, the latter is indeed reinforced in the statement found in the rabbinic tradition. The questions posed because of the commandment of love, namely, "Who is my neighbor?" and "What does 'to love' mean?" are answered casuistically (cf. Lk 10:25–29; Billerbeck I, 354–370) and not, as in the case of Jesus, by referring to the concrete situation (cf. Lk 10:30–37).

(4) Special significance was given to the discussion of the correct interpretation of the Sabbath commandment, the echo of which is also found in the NT (cf. Mk 3:1–6). Originally, the Sabbath was meant as a day of rest;

only gradually did it evolve into the day devoted to the synagogal worship service. Among the scribes the commandment of the Sabbath rest became the object of a broadly developed casuistry. It was interpreted as a strict prohibition against doing any work. The tractate *Shabbath* contains what was allowed and what was prohibited on a Sabbath (Barrett, 154–155). Jewish criticism of Jesus very likely erupted because he transgressed the Sabbath commandment time after time. Of course the law, even according to Jewish teaching, required interpretation that had in mind its application to various spheres of life. But this interpretation was consistently casuistic, for obedience was to be practiced very meticulously. This was the task for which the guild of the scribes emerged.

(5) One of the fundamental topics in theological discussion was the question of what rank of prominence was to be given to the scribal traditions themselves. In contrast to the Pharisees, the Sadducees were not prepared to recognize pharisaic scribal interpretation as normative next to the law. While they also interpreted the law, they did not make the interpretation part of the teaching that was considered to be binding. The assertions in Mt 23 that are directed against the Pharisees already reflect the post-70 A.D. situation of the pharisaic hegemony in the interpretation of the law. The seven principles of interpretation attributed to R. Hillel, are famous (*Middoth*; cf. Barrett, 146); among these the first two are given special significance.

The first principle is known as *qal waḥomer* (light and heavy) and points to the conclusion of *a minori ad maius*, that is from the less to the greater and vice versa. Paul employed this principle in Rom 5:15 and 5:9f. (numerous parallels are cited in Billerbeck III, 223ff.). The second principle is called *gezerah shewah* (analogous argument); it denotes the analogical conclusion.

Example: In Pes 66a (the Pesikhta is a haggadic midrash on the teachings of the major Jewish festivals) the question is raised whether the Passover sacrifice was also permitted on the Sabbath, that is whether it would "displace" the Sabbath. Num 28:2 seems to indicate that the *tamid* sacrifice was indeed to be presented on the Sabbath. Yet, the latter has the expression במועדו "at its festive time;" the same term is also used with regard to the Passover in Num 9:2. Conclusion: What applies there is also applicable here.

Paul uses this principle, e.g., in connection with Rom 4:1–12.

(6) It may be argued that Judaism as a whole was a religion anchored in the law. For the Jew, the law was the unambiguous sign of God's covenant with Israel and assured him of the hope of its restoration as a state. The law also prevented Israel from being absorbed among the nations; for it established a mark of distinction between the Jew and the nations via circumcision, Sabbath, and purity code.

Suggested exercises:

1. Become familiar with the names of the most important Jewish scribes and read some of the rabbinic literature. On Shammai and Hillel, see Barrett, 140f. and L-G, 234; on Gamaliel, cf. L-G, 240, 241; on Johanan ben Zakkai, see Barrett, 142; on Akiba, see Barrett, 142f.

2. Read the tractate *Aboth*, produced in full in I. Epstein, ed., *The Babylonian Talmud*, ET 1935–48, 1–91.

3. Familiarize yourself with the basic features of the teachings of Judaism. On the Sabbath commandment, see Barrett, 153–155; on judicial procedure, see Barrett, 169–172; on the Passover, see Barrett, 155–157. Rabbinic parables are cited in Barrett, 148f.

4. Compare the Eighteen Benedictions (L-G, 244; cf. Barrett, 162–163) with the Lord's Prayer.

3. Cult and festivals

(1) The cult is the very heart of Jewish worship. Cultic sacrifices were offered exclusively at the temple which had been reinstituted by Ezra in the post-exilic era. Herod the Great later remodeled and expanded it considerably.

(a) Just as in OT times, the temple itself was divided into the holy place and the holy of holies; the ark of the covenant, however, was no longer in the most holy place.

Non-Jews were only permitted to enter the outer court of the temple; trespassing the inner boundary meant capital punishment (for the text of the warning signs, see Barrett, 50). Inside this inner boundary were several courts: The court of women was accessible to Jewish women, while Jewish men were allowed to enter the "court of Israel." The actual temple court was reserved for the priests. Located here were the altar of burnt offering on which the official sacrifices were brought twice daily and the temple proper. Only the high priest was allowed to enter the holy of holies, and only once each year on the Day of Atonement (see below).

A detailed sketch of the lay-out of the temple is found in J. Jeremias, *Jerusalem in the Time of Jesus*, ET 1969, p. 80; see also E. Lohse, *The NT Environment*, ET 1976, p. 150f. On the excavations, see B. Mazar, *Der Berg des Herrn*, 1979 (contains extensive documentation).

(b) The weekly Jewish worship service in the synagogue does not involve the offering up of sacrifices; it centers strictly on the Word (*Wortgottesdienst*). It is comprised of four segments: (i) The Shema ("Hear O Israel," Billerbeck IV/1, 189ff.) as a prayer and, at the same time, as confession of the one God, according to Dt 6:4ff. (ii) The Eighteen Benedictions (Billerbeck IV/1, 208ff.). (iii) A scripture reading from the Torah and from the prophetic books, with a subsequent free translation into Aramaic, i.e., their vernacular (in the Diaspora, therefore, into Greek). (iv) The sermon on the text; in this connection, every male adult Jew might be granted permission to speak (cf. Lk 4:16ff.).

(2) In the course of the year, the major pilgrimage festivals were especially significant.

(a) The *Passover* was held in the evening of the 14th Nisan (month of spring) and began with the slaying of the Passover lambs at the temple (since the temple's destruction, there is no more Passover lamb). This was followed by the week of unleavened bread (*mazzoth*), commemorating the hurried exodus from Egypt (in Mk 14:12 the two events are merged). Together with the Mazzoth festival, the Passover signalled the beginning of the harvest festival.

Barrett, 155f., offers some excerpts from the tractate *Pesaḥim*; it is also worthwhile to read the account in Billerbeck IV/1, 41–76.

(b) The *festival of Weeks* (Pentecost) was celebrated fifty days after the Passover. Originally this festival was significant as a harvest thanksgiving festival; in the course of time it took on the meaning of salvation history, namely, as the festival of covenant ratification at Sinai (cf. Billerbeck II, 598–602).

(c) The *Day of Atonement* (*yom kippur*) was an important fall festival, celebrated as a day of fasting. Only on this particular day did the high priest enter the holy of holies in the temple for the purpose of asking God for forgiveness of sins (Barrett, 159–162). As a token of atonement, he sacrificed a he-goat on the altar of burnt offering for his own sins; then, he symbolically imposed the people's sins upon a second he-goat and chased it into the wilderness. After A.D. 70 the celebration of this ritual was no longer possible; since then the people commemorate the Day of Atonement as a day of repentance.

The precise instructions for this festival are given in the Mishnah tractate *Yoma* (and are partly reproduced in Barrett, 159–162).

(d) The epitome of festivals was the *Feast of Tabernacles* which followed Yom Kippur and, as a vintage festival, was celebrated with a particularly ostentatious rite (the text describing this ritual is found in Barrett, 157f.). A salvation-historical connotation was attached to it because, in commemoration of the exodus from Egypt, the Jews lived in booths for seven days.

4. Eschatology

(1) For Judaism in the NT era, eschatology was of decisive significance. The origin of eschatology, that is its development within Judaism, is a point of debate in scholarship. Fundamentally two types of Jewish eschatology are discerned:

(a) On one side there is the national, this-worldly hope in the liberation of Israel, understood as continuous with the prophetic proclamation of salvation in the OT.

(b) On the other side there is the universal, apocalyptic anticipation of the end of the world, of the resurrection of the dead, and of judgment, together with the hope of the world to come. These notions are likely the result of Iranian influence, since they are nonexistent in pre-exilic as well as in early post-exilic Judaism, and thus in the bulk of the OT.

At times the eschatological hope is connected with the anticipation of a savior; usually this is either the messiah as national savior (who is always understood as a human being), or it is the "Son of man," a transcendent figure who ushers in the apocalyptic kingdom.

(2) The concept of national hope and that of apocalyptically oriented eschatology cannot be sharply distinguished from one another: Apocalypticism, too, remains tied up with the Jewish nation and speaks primarily of the future of Israel (Daniel, 4 Ezra); on the other hand, the concept of the "messiah," contrary to its usual meaning, is also applicable to the transcendent savior (4 Ezra). Certain OT structures also persist in apocalypticism, even if they do not fit systematically. Thus it is possible to find the prophetic idea of "the remnant" alongside the apocalyptic idea of the general resurrection of the dead. Not all the dead will be raised; only the good remnant of the people, or of mankind, will be spared in the judgment and experience the new world.

The apocalypticist understands his teaching as comfort for the assailed people. In a time of distress and travail, it is necessary to affirm that these events are in line with God's will and that God will bring them to an end imminently. In addition, the concept of the equalizing justice plays an important part. The present suffering of the nation and of the individual will be transformed into joy in the world to come, while the enemy who is presently triumphant will then be crushed.

In apocalypticism the idea of hope is heavily "spiritualized" and individualized. Salvation is expected to come from the "world beyond" and thus no longer from the hope within the context of history. In fact, the individualization of piety is a general trait of Judaism in the NT era and is not only reflected in apocalypticism, but also in the wisdom orientation (see p. 108f.).

Suggested further reading:

1. The notion of the two ages is extensively documented: in "this age" it is the hostile, evil powers that are reigning, while the righteous are suffering; in the "age to come" the reverse will be true, and this hope means consolation for the righteous (4 Ezra 7:45–61; Barrett, 239ff.). The eschatological idea of judgment focuses on this aspect: In the judgment that God metes out, these powers will

be abolished; then God will establish his righteous reign (in this regard, the Assumption of Moses 10 is particularly instructive; for its text, see Barrett, 242f.).

2. The concept of resurrection and judgment is twofold: individual and corporate. The story of the rich man and poor Lazarus (Lk 16:19ff.) presupposes an individualized understanding of resurrection and judgment taking place immediately upon death. More frequent, however, is the notion that there will be a general resurrection of the dead at the end of time (so for Christians, 1 Cor 15). In this context, consult Billerbeck IV/2, 1166–1198.

3. The concept of the messianic era and the expectation of the coming Son of man are particularly important in 4 Ezra (text in Charlesworth, *OT Pseudepigrapha*, I, 525–559). The messianic era is also described in 2 (Syriac Apocalypse of) Baruch (excerpts in Barrett, 245ff.), and the coming of the Son of man is found in 1 (Ethiopic Apocalypse of) Enoch (Barrett, 252–255).

5. Peculiarities of Diaspora Judaism

(1) More Jews, by far, lived in the Diaspora than in Palestine. The table of nations in Acts 2:9–11 is illustrative of just how pervasive Judaism was at that time. It must be noted, however, that the Diaspora and hellenistic Judaism were not identical. There were Jews living in the Orient; a large group lived in Mesopotamia. The Babylonian Talmud attests to their theological endeavor (see above, p. 110f.). Alexandria, Philo's place of residence, was the most important spiritual and economic center of hellenistic Diaspora Judaism (cf. Barrett, 136f.; L-G, 245). In Alexandria, as well as in Cyrene (Lybia) Jews formed autonomous political entities.

It is conceivable that the Jews were generally given the status of the *peregrini* (non-citizens) in the Roman Empire. They enjoyed a certain autonomy, as well as the special protection of their religion. In their "pagan" environment, the Jews were particularly conspicuous because of their religious exclusiveness. They were the only people for whom the participation in foreign cults was altogether inconceivable. The cult's total lack of images was characteristic and, for their environment, simultaneously surprising and strange. Finally, the observance of the Sabbath was likewise conspicuous (Juvenal addresses this in his *14th Satire* 96–106; L-G, 265).

A Roman view of the Jews is found in Tacitus, *History* V, 3–5 (L-G, 274).

The mission of Judaism among non-Jews was typical; two groups of converts can be discerned:

(a) The proselytes, who converted to Judaism, were circumcised and kept the whole law; (b) the so-called God-fearers accepted the fundamental Jewish confession of the one true God, but did not specifically adopt Jewish legal regulations.

(2) Hellenistic Judaism has contributed a wealth of literature that has been preserved exclusively in post-NT Christian tradition, whereas within Judaism itself it was completely superseded by the rabbinic literature.

(a) The translation of the Bible into the Greek language was an outstanding achievement. The legend of the miraculous formation of this so-called Septuagint (LXX) is preserved in the Epistle of Aristeas (Barrett, 213ff.; L-G, 275). The truth of the matter is, however, that the LXX developed through a lengthy process of tradition which comes to expression in the divergent text tradition and in the canon deviates from the Hebrew Bible. Without a doubt, the LXX was extremely important in the spiritual development of hellenistic Judaism. It was held to be as inspired as the original Hebrew text. However, the fact that early Christianity accepted the LXX as holy Writ and interpreted it christologically caused Judaism to replace it with other translations in the second century (Aquila, Symmachus, Theodotion).

The structure and composition of the LXX in places differ significantly from the Hebrew canon (and thus also from the standard translation of the OT). Nestle[26] offers a detailed overview of these differences, p. 739ff. On the LXX editions, see above, p. 9.

(b) The apologetic writings of hellenistic Judaism defended monotheism and were directed polemically against polytheism, especially against the veneration of icons. Noteworthy among these are the Wisdom of Solomon (excerpts in L-G, 281–286), the novel of Joseph and Aseneth (English translation in Charlesworth, OT Pseudepigrapha II, 202–247), the work of Josephus Against Apion (excerpts in L-G, 271–273), and especially the works of Philo (see below).

The book of 2 Maccabees represents one of the witnesses of the conflict between Judaism and Hellenism; it is expressly critical of the tendency to establish a synthesis between the two cultural realms, especially in the area of religion.

Hence the limelight belongs to the criticism against the Syrian kings Seleucus and Antiochus Epiphanes (L-G, 278–280).

Suggested reading:

2 Macc is also a typical example of the devotional writings, legends and tractates of hellenistic Judaism (B. M. Metzger, *The Oxford Annotated Apocrypha*, 1965, 1977, 263–293.). In addition, Kautzsch offers a selection from the Sibylline Oracles (Sib Or) by means of which Judaism imitated pagan oracles (II, 184ff.; Eng.: Charlesworth, *OT Pseudepigrapha* I, 335ff.)

(3) The most important figure in hellenistic Judaism was Philo, the theologian and philosopher of religion resident in Alexandria; he was a contemporary of Jesus (ca. 15/10 B.C. to A.D. 40). His political prominence came in A.D. 40 when he led a delegation of Alexandrian Jews before Emperor Caligula (Gaius), in protest against the anti-Jewish measures of the Alexandrians and in order to secure the inherited Jewish privileges (cf.

the *Legatio ad Gaium,* an apologetic writing of Philo; for excerpts, see L-G, 309–314). He wrote a comprehensive allegorical commentary on Genesis (which is handed down in various individual writings, e.g.: *Allegorical Laws [Leg All]; Concerning the Giants [Gig],* etc.), as well as some brief commentaries on the Pentateuch (partially preserved). Philo also wrote systematic treatises on creation and on the giving of the law by Moses, among others. Finally, his historical-apologetic writings are significant; in these he focused especially on Moses as the unique and ideal ruler and lawgiver and Judaism as the true religion, that is, the true philosophy. Allegory was his key method of biblical interpretation: He transposed the OT narratives into the language and ideology of hellenistic philosophy and interpreted the patriarchal figures as ethical models. Nevertheless, Philo held fast to Judaism, to its foundational dogmatic teaching, and to the law.

Suggested reading:

A knowledge of at least some of Philo's writings is indispensable. They are repeatedly used as parallel texts for NT writings and, in addition, provide insight into the theology and hermeneutical principles used by hellenistic Judaism in its interpretation of the Bible. In any case, one ought to read the selections from the Philonic writings, including the brief introductory remarks preceding each selection (see L-G, 292–324).

6. Essenes (Qumran community)

(1) As a group the Essenes lived at the fringes of official Judaism. Yet fundamentally they had not severed their relationship and were not considered heretical. They were convinced that they represented the true Israel; therefore, their adherents were striving to adhere meticulously to the entire purity code mandated by the law. While they essentially recognized the temple in Jerusalem as the cultic center of the Jews, they held it to be desecrated and thus did not participate in the sacrificial rituals or in the traditional Jewish festivals.

Ancient writers have made widely divergent assertions concerning the way of life and outlook of the Essenes (cf. art. "Essener," in *Kleiner Pauly* II, 375–378; "Essenes," *IDB* II, 143–149).

(2) Some of the Essenes also retreated territorially from the rest of the Jews and lived in a type of monastic order in the desert along the Dead Sea (Qumran).

Extensive digging has taken place at Qumran since the discovery of numerous scrolls in 1947. As a result we know more about the Qumran community than about any other Jewish group, although they are not directly mentioned in the NT. In particular, a voluminous library was discovered which affords a glimpse into the cult, theology, and daily life of the community.

The following represent the most important categories of Qumran writings (regarding the method of citing them, see above, pp. 109f.): (a) community regulations, i.e., the Damascus Document (see p. 110) and the Manual of Discipline; (b) commentaries on biblical books; (c) religious poetry (collections of psalms) and (d) the eschatological writing of the "war of the children of darkness against the children of light."

The center of the teaching of Qumran was the principle that all demands of the law had to be kept fully; in terms of concrete practice, this happened when the novice accepted the community regulations at the time of admittance into the community. The group demanded the relinquishing of all personal possessions and also intensified the purity code.

The eschatological conceptions of the Qumran community are dualistic in character. Light and darkness are in conflict with one another; now the children of light are being separated from the children of darkness, and every individual ultimately must decide his allegiance to either of the two groups (cf. 1 QS III concerning the two spirits and their ways). At the end of time, after the last war between the two spirits, God's kingdom will break in. In this regard, the eschatology of Qumran has two messianic figures: in the first place, the priestly messiah, and in the second place, the political messiah. The ranking of these two messiahs also reflects the hierarchy of the Qumran community as it is seen in their external organization as well as in the ordering of the community meal.

(3) Frequently the question is raised concerning the relationship of the teaching of Jesus and of the early church (especially in view of the antitheses of the Sermon on the Mount) to the theology of the Qumran community. There are indeed clear agreements in specific subject areas: In both cases man is challenged to make a fundamental decision; in both cases there is a dualistic understanding of light vs. darkness; Qumran and early Christianity have in common the idea of predestination. But the crucial difference between them is in the interpretation of the law. Jesus' antithetical appeal to intensify the Torah is not as much stating principle as it is taking its orientation from the concrete situation of the neighbor, whereas in Qumran the rigorous ethical demands apply in principle. Jesus does not demand the relinquishing of possessions in principle (cf. Mk 10:17-31) because he does not make human effort the precondition for the grace of God. In the concrete situation of the individual, obedience to God's claims may be demonstrated in voluntary poverty; yet, Jesus does not establish this as a principle. The relationship between Paul and Qumran is similar: Both know the concept of *sola gratia*; but while Paul draws the inference from it that Christ is the end of the law (Rom 10:4), the law is intensified precisely through this understanding of grace in Qumran. Both the Christian and the Qumran community base their existence upon a historical founder, i.e., Jesus and the "Teacher of Right-

eousness" respectively. But it is significant that Christianity views Jesus as the redeemer, while the Teacher of Righteousness has essentially the function of the teacher of the law.

Suggested exercises:

1. The hermeneutical principles of the Qumran community's interpretation of the OT are seen in 1 QpHab: The OT statements actually refer to the Teacher of Righteousness and to the community; in other words, this writing is to be interpreted eschatologically for the present. How does that relate to early Christian interpretation of Scripture?

2. What are the consequences of the divergent understanding of the Teacher of Righteousness and of Jesus for the theology of their respective communities? Tool: G. Jeremias, *Der Lehrer der Gerechtigkeit*, 1963, 319–353.

3. How is it possible to reconcile Qumranian dualism with monotheism? Tool: J. Becker, *Das Heil Gottes*, 1964, 74–83.

4. What is the connection between consciousness of sin and justification? To what extent are there agreements with Pauline theology? What are the differences? Tool: J. Becker, *Heil Gottes*, 238–279.

7. Samaritans

The Samaritans virtually lived outside the parameters of official Judaism; they were viewed as heretics.

The reasons for the rise of this Jewish separatist community are largely unknown. The establishment of their own sanctuary on Mt. Gerizim (presumably at the close of the 4th century B.C.) was decisive in the separation from the rest of Judaism. Since they acknowledged only the Pentateuch as Holy Scripture, until the post-NT era they rejected both the idea of a resurrection of the dead and of apocalypticism altogether. Their confession encompassed four main assertions: There is *one* God; Moses and the law are the religious foundation; Mt. Gerizim is the place where God is worshipped; hope focuses on a day of vengeance and reward to come.

The first evidence that the Samaritans also had a messianic expectation is found in Jn 4; however, it is also conceivable that John merely presupposed such an expectation. Only later on did Samaritan sources address the issue of hope in a "prophet like Moses" (following Dt 18:15–19), called *Ta'eb*.

The translation of the term *ta'eb* is controversial. The following are possible renderings: (a) "the restorer" (of the cult); (b) "the one who leads back" (i.e., the one who leads people to repentance); (c) simply, "the returning one."

The *Ta'eb* is not a supernatural figure, and certainly not a redeemer; rather, he remains part of the priestly order.

Scholarship maintains differing views on the relationship between the Samaritans and the remaining Jews in the NT era. J. Jeremias argues that the relationship was subject to very serious fluctuations, but it is appropriate to say that at the time of Jesus, "the Jewish attitude to the Samaritans was very much the same as their attitude to Gentiles" (*Jerusalem in the Time of Jesus*, ET 1969, 358). On the other hand, H. G. Kippenberg argues that despite the segregation of Jews and Samaritans from the Maccabean era until well into the second century A.D., some rabbis were still fully cognizant of the fact that the Samaritans were Israelites and not Gentiles (Kippenberg, *Garizim und Synagogue*, 137–143).

§ 20 Non-Jewish Religions of the Hellenistic Era

Bibliography: R. Bultmann, *Das Urchristentum im Rahmen der antiken Religionen*, [4]1976, 109–187; F. Cumont, *Oriental Religions in Roman Paganism*, ET 1956; F. C. Grant, ed., *Ancient Roman Religion*, 1957; idem, ed., *Hellenistic Religions*, 1953; G. Haufe, "Hellenistische Volksfrömmigkeit. Die Mysterien," in: L-G I, [3]1971, 68–126; H. C. Kee, *The Origins of Christianity: Sources and Documents*, 1973, 54–99; M. P. Nilsson, *Geschichte der griechischen Religion II. Die hellenistische und römische Zeit*, HAW V/2, [2]1961; A. D. Nock, *Conversion*, 1933; M. J. Vermaseren, ed., *Die orientalischen Religionen im Römerreich*, 1981.

1. Overview

Through Alexander the Great, Hellenism spread extensively in the East. During the Roman era, conversely, the influx of people from the eastern part of the Empire into the west (Italy) became a factor in the religious development that gained increasing significance. The political, economic, and cultural changes associated with this migration also led to changes in world view and philosophy of life. Granted, the traditional cult of the Roman and Greek deities enjoyed unprecedented popularity; the official cult at major festivals was dedicated to them. Nevertheless, only infrequently is it still associated with a genuinely religious effort, an authentic belief in Apollo or Athena, in Jupiter or Diana. The proliferation of religions and the formation of communities in every part of the Empire were typical characteristics of the era.

In this way the old religions were influenced by new elements, thus bringing about a "syncretism" (i.e., a "*Theokrasie*"). The trademark of this syncretism was the identification of the Greek deities with those of the east (*interpretatio Graeca*). The stories of the gods (myths) and their respective functions become mingled. For instance, Aphrodite was identified with the Egyptian goddess Isis; in aretalogy she was celebrated as the promoter of culture and justice (Barrett, 97ff.; L-G, 124). Hermes, formerly a messenger of the gods and god of the merchants, was identified with the Egyptian deity Thot and thus became "Hermes Trismegistos," the all-wise Logos, the redeemer and, at the same time, patron of a widespread corpus of devotional literature (cf. the *Corpus Hermeticum*, especially the tractate of *Poimandres*; Barrett, 80–90). Zeus (Baal) of Heliopolis in Syria became the universal god who encompassed in himself all other gods.

The tendency toward monotheism became a characteristic of these identifications of deities and corresponds with the development in philosophy (see § 21 below). The existence of many gods was not denied in this process; rather, a certain proclivity arose to understand these diverse gods as manifestations of the one divine power. An impressive piece of documentation is found in a text of one of the Orphic fragments: εἷς Ζεύς, εἷς ῎Αδης, εἷς ῞Ηλιος, εἷς Διόνυσος, εἷς θεὸς ἐν πάντεσσιν (cf. E. Peterson, ΕΙΣ ΘΕΟΣ, 1926, 241f.).

2. Types of religions

It is necessary to distinguish between the different types of deities as well as between the different types of cults.

(1) (a) The astral religions, i.e., veneration of astral deities, were popular especially in Babylon and Syria. The Syrian Baals, well known from the OT, had originally been fertility gods, but developed into astral deities under the Chaldean influence. There was even a tendency to view them as universal deities.

Belief in astral deities arose as a result of the reinterpretation of ancient fatalism which viewed man as tied up with Ananke or Heimarmene (oppressive cosmic fate). Now the stars were considered to be the rulers of the world; the former deities became cosmic forces and with that also received the power to deliver man from the unrelenting Heimarmene. Now man was no longer hopelessly abandoned to fate; through belief in the astral deities he could be delivered and saved.

Ultimately, this notion was also the basis for magic and especially for Gnosticism (see § 22 below).

(b) Also widespread was the belief in the "dying and rising gods." Originally they symbolized the cycle of nature but later were individualized. In the East, these were partly known as national deities (such as Isis), but as soon as they moved west, they lost their national character and became cultic lords in communities of a new sociological type whose adherents had a common bond without regard for nationality (see below).

The rise of the mystery religions was particularly characteristic: It was the purpose of the mysteries of antiquity to deliver the actual being of man from the grip of demonic powers by granting the adherent participation in the fate of the cult deity through the mystery. "Be of good courage, you adherents of the mystery, the deity is delivered; thus we, too, shall find deliverance from suffering" (cf. L-G, 116). This appeal from the cult of the dying and rising Osiris (L-G: Attis) is characteristic of the essence of this piety. In the initiation ceremony the old life of the adherent died and the new life of redemption began.

The most common was the veneration of Isis. She is regarded as the mistress of the cosmos, the omniscient one; she is wisdom personified. The whole world reveres her *"numen unicum multiformi specie, ritu vario, nomine multiiugo"* (Apuleius met XI 5). In the cult she is addressed as *"una quae es omnia"* (cf. E. Peterson, ΕΙΣ ΘΕΟΣ, 235).

Next to the cult of Isis and Osiris (Barrett, 92ff.), those of Attis and of Adonis (Barrett, 95f.; L-G, 118) are also representative of this type of deity. In this regard, it is to be remembered that the mystery cults were not exclusive; it was possible to be initiated into several cults. At the same time it is significant that the mystery religions did not form any supraregional organization or a "church."

It would be erroneous to see behind the various mystery religions a uniform theology or anthropology. But in comparison to the classical era, their great popularity demonstrates the fundamental change in the understanding of existence, namely, the tendency to the mystical and irrational.

(c) Manticism, astrology, and belief in miracle workers were also significant. One consulted the oracle (L-G, 96); a father inquires with the god Serapis about his son's willingness to agree with him (Barrett, 31). The outstanding figure among the miracle workers of that era was the peripatetic philosopher Apollonius of Tyana; among other things, raisings from the dead (L-G, 86) and exorcisms (Barrett, 77) were attributed to him.

(d) In addition, mention has to be made of certain manifestations of the religious substratum. Magical formulae and practices flourished in the second century B.C. It was thought that the gods could be induced to perform or to refrain from certain actions by using appropriate means. Some of the countless magical papyri are printed in L-G, 87–92; cf. H. C. Kee, *The Origins of Christianity: Sources and Documents*, 1973, 84–89.

(2) In the realm of piety, the hellenistic culture has produced not only new content, but also new forms. To a great extent this is related to the fact that the cult of the new deities was no longer associated with the cult of the nation or the state, but with the cult of a community, which in some cases, might be scattered around the world, but which freely gathers without national and social barriers in order to serve the deity.

(a) In contrast to the festivals of the official religions, the mystery religions are characterized by a cult behind closed doors, inaccessible to non-initiates. The motto of such a mystery society is copied in L-G, 113. But besides secret processions they also held public festivals, which, of course, were used for propaganda and thus contributed to the expansion of the cult. Prudentius describes the initiation of a priest of the Great Mother (Barrett, 96f.).

(b) Initiation, that is, the consecration of the initiate by the mystagogue, is the most important ritual of the mystery religions. In strict secrecy the novice had to undergo certain purification rituals, followed by the handing over of the symbol and finally by the viewing of the deity. Clearly, an emphatically sexual symbolism was important, especially in the cult of the female deities.

(c) Furthermore, these initiation rituals, as well as the strict shielding of the activities of the mysteries from the public, were reason enough for the Roman Senate to ban the cult of Isis. During the reign of Augustus several laws against the mysteries were passed (Dio Cassius 53: 2,4); Tacitus notes the expulsion of the cult of the Sacra Aegyptica et Judaica from Rome (*Annals* II, 85). Nevertheless, in the long run these cults proved to be stronger—already Caligula had erected an Isis temple on the Field of Mars.

Suggested reading:

Details of the cult of Isis and of its associated festivals are given by Apuleius in the eleventh book of his *Metamorphoses* (*The Golden Ass*); the text is printed, in part, in L-G, 123). The extraordinary regard for Isis can be deduced from Kyme's aretalogy of Isis (L-G, 124).

On the cult of Cybele and of Attis, see L-G, 115.

The rather dissolute cult of Dea Syriaca is described by Apuleius (met VIII; cf. L-G, 117).

On the mystery cult of Andania, consult L-G, 114.

§ 21   Philosophy of the Hellenistic Era

Bibliography: O. Gigon, *Grundprobleme der antiken Philosophie*, 1959; *Die antike Kultur und das Christentum*, 1966; H. C. Kee, *The Origins of Christianity*, 231–383; A. A. Long and D. N. Sedley, *The Hellenistic Philosophers*, 2 vols., 1987; A. J. Malherbe, ed., *The Cynic Epistles, A Study Edition*, SBLSBS 12, 1977; M. Pohlenz, *Die Stoa. Geschichte einer geistigen Bewegung*, [4]1970/72.

1. General matters

Alongside the political and social development of the hellenistic era (see above, p. 112ff.), the upper crust of the population also underwent a spiritual reorientation. It was no longer the *polis* that shaped the horizons of thought and consciousness, but the world, the cosmos; it is quite appropriate to say that a cosmopolitan awareness had taken shape within Hellenism. This can be seen, for instance, in the etymology of certain political concepts; in the political and philosophical literature of Hellenism, the terms ἐλευθερία and νόμος no longer designate the freedom of the citizen of the autonomous city, nor the laws that the free city accords to itself; instead they address the individual's status in the world. However, both concepts thereby lose their concrete political function and significance; the individual's search for inner freedom becomes central.

The cosmopolitan tendency and the turning away from the concrete questions pertaining to the societal situation find their expression in philosophy. Man seeks self-understanding in nature and in the cosmos; thereby philosophy develops the notion that the laws of the cosmos are at once also the laws of man.

2. *Philosophical schools*

It is essential to be familiar with the four most important philosophical schools:

1. Plato—the Academicians
2. Aristotle—the Peripatetics
3. Stoa; the Cynics, whose founder was Diogenes, are in many ways related to the Stoics.
4. Epicurus—the Epicureans.

These four schools will be introduced briefly, at least to the degree that they are important for the history of the NT. For more comprehensive studies, consult the available literary treatments, especially that of O. Gigon (see bibliography).

The common denominator for all four orientations is the development toward individualism, as previously indicated, as well as toward cosmopolitanism. The dominant theme is the question of the individual's appropriate formation of life, while pure theory is pushed back. The beginning of all reflection is the conviction that virtue is attainable and makes man happy. The tendency toward monotheism is typical in the development of philosophy, as expressed in the pseudo-Aristotelian writing *De mundo*, for instance (cf. L-G, 350).

But then there were also some fundamental differences between these schools. Their partly juxtaposed presuppositions persisted (such as the tension between the first three schools who appealed to Socrates and the Epicureans who refused to be aligned with the Socratic tradition) and continued to be significant in the subsequent development.

(1) Although it had moved away from its origins by then, the Platonic school continued to insist on the fundamental significance of idealism; that is, the parallelism of the world of ideas/archetype and of the

world/reflection to be experienced physically remained decisive. Among the Platonists of the first century was to be found, among others, Plutarch (A.D. 50–120), who is known especially for writing his "parallel biographies" of famous Greeks and Romans, as well as some moralistic literature. As a whole, Platonism maintained an Academic existence and did not concentrate on a popular orientation. Some effects are found in Cicero and Philo, but the Academy did not regain substantial influence until Neoplatonism (Plotinus). There are no genuine points of contact between the latter and the NT; in other words, assertions and concepts of the NT must in no wise be interpreted with the aid of "Platonic" categories.

(2) The Peripatetics, like Aristotle himself, were given to empirical learning. Both their philosophical system and their ethics were influenced thereby. Peripatetic philosophy was built upon a system comprised of six central assertions: *God* is the primal unmoved mover of the cosmos; *this cosmos* is eternal; the world of *man* is removed from the immediate influence of God. The cycle is the ideal of cosmic movement, hence Plato's *ideology* is refuted. The tension that is already a factor in Aristotle persists in *psychology*: It is possible to view the soul either as uncorporeal, divine, or as tied to the body in a temporal, material fashion. Finally, Peripatetic *ethics* consistently understands virtue as the center between two extremes, such as courage as the center between avarice and wastefulness etc. Echoes of this are found in the NT household codes. All in all, however, Aristotelianism also remains within the bounds of the Academic.

(3) The monotheistic tendency of the time becomes particularly tangible in the Stoa. There is only one thing divine that permeates the entire cosmos without being identical with it. Yet, the Stoic system was able to accommodate the most diverse mythologies and conceptions of deity.

The unity of the view of life and ethics was characteristic of Stoic thought. In the foreground was the endeavor to provide answers to the practical questions of life, demonstrating thereby the harmony of natural law and moral law. The cosmos is permeated by the Logos and between this macrocosm and the microcosm (man) there is harmony. Hence nature is viewed as lawgiver for all the ethical problems; in other words, insofar as man lives in full harmony with nature, he has achieved the highest degree of virtue, while his conscience continually spurs him on to examine his own perfection.

In the early Christian era, Seneca and Epictetus were representatives of the Stoa. They claimed that the wise man is to make every effort to be freed from the emotions and thus to be free even with regard to death. That which influences him from without is not under the control of the wise man, but the inner conquest of self belongs to his own domain of power. "In our power are thought, impulse, will to get and will to avoid, and, in a word, everything which is our own doing. Things not in our power include the body, property, reputation, office, and, in a word, everything which is not our own doing. Things in our power are by nature free, unhindered, untrammeled; things not in our power are weak, servile, subject to hindrance, dependent on others. . . . Make it your study then to confront every harsh impression with the words, 'You are but an impression, and not at all what you seem to be.' Then test it by those rules that you possess; and first by this—the chief test of all—'Is it concerned with what is in our power or with what is not in our power?' And if it is concerned with what is not in our power, be ready with the answer that it is nothing to you" (Epictetus, *Manual* I, L-G, 332; English transl. in W. J. Oates, *The Stoic and Epicurean Philosophers*, 1940, p. 468).

Suggested Exercises:

1. Compare 1 Cor 3:21-23 with the corresponding Stoic assertions.

2. Compare 1 Cor 4:9-13 with the corresponding Stoic motives. Tool: H. Conzelmann, *1 Corinthians; A Commentary on the First Epistle to the Corinthians*, Hermeneia, ET 1975, pp. 88-90.

The Stoic concept that human life and the being of the cosmos are determined by divine providence is important for NT theology (L-G, 334). Of significance is also the Stoic "eschatology," which expects a conflagration of the cosmos, in the wake of which there will be a new world; there are connections here with the apocalyptic conceptions of Judaism and of early Christianity.

(4) The three philosophical schools cited first present a contrast to the teaching of Epicurus, who distanced himself deliberately from the Socratic tradition. He himself summarized the main characteristics of the Epicurean teaching in forty statements of his "Principal Doctrines" (*Kyriai doxai*):

"I. The blessed and immortal nature knows no trouble itself nor causes trouble to any other, so that it is never constrained by anger or favour. For all such things exist only in the weak.

II. Death is nothing to us: for that which is dissolved is without sensation; and that which lacks sensation is nothing to us.

III. The limit of quantity in pleasures is the removal of all that is painful. Wherever pleasure is present, as long as it is there, there is neither pain of body nor of mind, nor of both at once.

IV. Pain does not last continuously in the flesh, but the acutest pain is there for a very short time, and even that which just exceeds the pleasure in the flesh does not continue for many days at once. But chronic illnesses permit a predominance of pleasure over pain in the flesh.

V. It is not possible to live pleasantly without living prudently and honourably and justly, nor again to live a life of prudence, honour, and justice without living pleasantly. And the man who does not possess the pleasant life, is not living prudently and honourably and justly, and the man who does not possess the virtuous life, cannot possibly live pleasantly. . . .

XII. . . . A man cannot dispel his fear about the most important matters if he does not know what is the nature of the universe but suspects the truth of some mythical story. So that without natural science it is not possible to attain our pleasures unalloyed" (L-G, 325; Engl. transl. Oates, *Stoic and Epicurean Philosophers*, pp. 35, 36).

For Epicurus the fact is that the gods have no association with the created order and, therefore, that hope or fear are absurd with regard to an intervention of the gods in the affairs of men. Likewise, he is convinced that the cosmos is not eternal but temporally limited, and that all conceptions of a life to come are to be rejected. For the Epicureans it was a matter of course that man could be liberated from fear by rational enlightenment and thus did not need religion. In sharp contrast to the Stoics, they rejected any notion of a resurrection.

Suggested exercises:

1. Readings:

On Platonism: L-G, 350–352; the two texts on the spirit and on the soul by Plotinus are particularly insightful (L-G, 353, 354).

On Stoicism: Zeno's argument about stuff as the substance of all being (Barrett, 62), the notion of the *nomos* of the world (Barrett, 62) and the pantheism of the Hymn of Cleanthes (Barrett, 63). Also consult L-G, 327–349 (texts of Seneca, Epictetus and Marcus Aurelius; ET see Oates, *Stoic and Epicurean Philosophers*, 1940).

On Epicureanism: Apart from the texts of Epicurus (Barrett, 73–75; L-G, 325f.; ET see Oates, *Stoic and Epicurean Philosophers*, 1940), it is good to read the paragraph on Epicurus in *De rerum natura* by Lucretius (Barrett, 72, 73). This pericope is a typical example of the pathos of the Epicurean enlightenment (see above).

2. *Exercises:*

(1) Read H. Schlier, ἐλευθερία, TDNT II, 487–502; H. Kleinknecht, νόμος (A. Greek world and Hellenism), TDNT IV, 1022–1035, with the following question in mind: How are the Stoic and the NT understandings of the two terms related to one another? Then, based on the insights gained, conduct a brief exegesis of 1 Cor 6:12; 8:1ff.

(2) Translate Rom 1:18–3:20; in this connection, read M. Pohlenz, "Paulus und die Stoa," ZNW 42, 1949 (on the life of Paul in recent scholarship, 522–569), and G. Bornkamm, "Die Offenbarung des Zornes Gottes. Röm. 1–3," *Ges. Auf.* I, 9–33.

(3) Exegete the formula of Rom 11:36.

(4) Exegete the Areopagus speech, Acts 17.

Tool: H. Conzelmann, "Die Rede des Paulus auf dem Areopag," *Ges. Auf.*, 91–105.

§ 22   Gnosis

Bibliography: General: R. Bultmann, *Primitive Christianity in its Contemporary Setting*, ET 1956, 162–171; R. M. Grant, *Gnosticism and Early Christianity*, ²1966; H. Jonas, *Gnosis und spätantiker Geist* I, FRLANT 51, ³1964; II, FRLANT 63, 1954; idem, *The Gnostic Religion; The Message of the Alien God and the Beginnings of Christianity*, 2nd rev. ed., ET 1963; E. Pagels, *The Gnostic Gospels*, 1981; J. M. Robinson, ed., *The Nag Hammadi Library in English*, 1978; K. Rudolph (ed.), *Gnosis und Gnostizismus*, 1975 (Collection with additional bibliographic references); idem, *Gnosis. The Nature and History of Gnosticism*, ET 1983; H.-M. Schenke, "Die Gnosis," in L-G I, ³1973, 371–415. *Section 1*: U. Bianchi (ed.), *Le Origini dello Gnosticismo*, 1967; C. Colpe, *Die religionsgeschichtliche Schule*, FRLANT 78, 1961; R. Haardt, "Zur Methodologie der Gnosisforschung," in K.-W. Tröger (ed.), *Gnosis und Neues Testament*, 1973, 183–202; C. W. Hedrick and R. Hodgson, Jr., eds., *Nag Hammadi, Gnosticism, and Early Christianity*, 1986; H. Jonas (see above) I, 1–91. *Section 2*: W. Foerster et al., *Die Gnosis*, vols. 1–3, 1969/1980 (vol. 1, 2 ET 1972/74); R. Haardt, *Gnosis: Character and Testimony*, ET 1971; H. Leisegang, *Die Gnosis*, 1924; W. Völker, *Quellen zur Geschichte der christlichen Gnosis* (Greek). *Sections 3 and 4*: (see general section). *Section 5*: K. W. Tröger (ed.), *Gnosis und NT*, 1973; R. McL. Wilson, *Gnosis and NT*, 1968.

1. Problem of definition

(1) The meaning of "gnosis," that is, the particular religious phenomenon to be designated as gnosis, is a matter of controversy in scholarship. Since there are differing definitions used in the various presentations of gnosis, a brief overview of definitions is essential here.

At a colloquium held in Messina in 1966, experts on the concept of gnosis endeavored to find agreement concerning its linguistic usage. They differentiated between gnosis and Gnosticism and defined "gnosis" as knowledge of divine mysteries reserved for an elite group. In contrast, the concept of "Gnosticism" was to denote the developed gnostic systems of the second century (cf. C. Colpe, in "Christentum und Gnosis," BZNW 37, 1969, 129–132). However, no true, objective clarification of the problem was achieved.

(2) Hence, it is important to be acquainted with the older definitions as well.

(a) A. v. Harnack defined gnosis as the "acute secularization or hellenization of Christianity" (*History of Dogma* I, 237ff.). Harnack explains that this hellenization represents a fundamental development in the dogmatics of the ancient church and could be discerned from the church's forms of life and thought, but especially from the rise and development of ecclesiastical dogmas (trinitarian doctrine, doctrine of the two natures). Of special significance is Harnack's distinction of two divergent forms of hellenization: (i) Where Christianity and Hellenism coalesced in a slow process there emerged the ecclesiastical dogma that is acknowledged as normative to this day. (ii) Where Christianity and Hellenism merged quickly, like a chemical reaction ("acute hellenization"), there emerged gnosis, namely, a Christian philosophy of religion.

(b) W. Bousset (*Hauptprobleme der Gnosis*, 1907) offered his definition in the presuppositional context of the "history of religions school." Central for him is the mystery of redemption, that is, the understanding that people are delivered by an other-worldly, heavenly redeemer who is understood as archetypal man (*Urmensch*). Bousset was of the opinion that Gnosticism emerged out of the convergence of the Iranian and the Babylonian religion; in the wake of the Persian conquest of Babylon, the Babylonian gods, especially the astral deities who ruled the world, had been reduced to the status of gnostic astral demons. Therefore, the history of religions school understood gnosis as a pre-Christian phenomenon which, from the beginning, contained the basic features of the mythology that was developed later. C. Colpe has levelled his critique against this argument, especially against the "archetypal man myth" (see bibliography).

(c) A fundamentally different perspective is offered by H. Jonas (see bibliography). He argues that Harnack and Bousset attempted to explain the rise of gnosis in a causal-genetic manner which ultimately amounts to superimposing scientific categories upon historical phenomena without doing justice to the latter ("alchemy of ideas"). In addition, Harnack made the mistake of constructing his theory on the premise of the major Christian-gnostic systems of Basilides and Valentinus, rather than on the popular forms, in other words, on the mythical oriental materials. Bousset's notion of the degradation of the Babylonian astral deities ignores that the planets continue to be masters of the world even in gnosis— but now as devilish, evil powers.

Jonas considers it to be the fundamental weakness in the previous definitions that they sought to fathom the essence of gnosis by examining its historical roots. But before the latter can be ascertained, one needs to know the meaning of gnosis. Hence, a phenomenological determination of the essence of gnosis is necessary: A definition must begin with a fully developed gnostic system, namely, with a non-Christian form, such as the Mandaean religion. An analysis of the Mandaean texts and their comparison with other gnostic systems leads to the observation that the decisive issue in gnosis is not the myths but the special gnostic self-understanding of man. Therefore, by "gnosis" Jonas means a particular comprehension of the world and man that can be objectivized in many given forms; in other words, it can be shaped into differing views of life or myths. At any rate, the gnostic self-understanding, in its essence, is the mindset of late antiquity. It is for this reason that the phenomenon of gnosis has so many layers and that there could be a Jewish as well as a Christian gnosis, for instance.

The view that gnosis is *the* mindset late antiquity, is being contested today. It is nevertheless true to say that Jonas' work represented a significant step forward in the scholarly investigation and has remained irreplaceable for the description of the phenomenon of gnosis.

(d) H.-M. Schenke (cf. bibliography) rejects the three definitions of the concept of gnosis cited above. He explains: "Gnosis represents a religious liberation movement of the early Christian era in which the possibility of a negative interpretation of the world and of existence is apprehended in a particular and unmistakable manner. This possibility then solidified into a thoroughgoing world view which negates the world, which, in turn, yields its characteristic expression to the shaping of words, imagery, and artistic myths" (L-G I, 374). By means of this broad definition Schenke attempts to summarize the immensely diverse systems and conceptions.

Schenke categorically rejects the concept of "Gnosticism." It is demeaning and belongs "basically to the terminology of those fighting heretics" (L-G I, 375).

2. Gnostic sources

Two distinct groups of sources exist:

(1) The primary sources, i.e., gnostic manuscripts.

(2) The secondary sources, i.e., the descriptions of gnosis from the pen of their opponents, especially from the church fathers who compiled, in part, some rather extensive excerpts of gnostic writings.

The sources are reflected in the multi-volume work *Die Gnosis* (see bibliography): Vol. 1 (*Gnosis—A Selection of Gnostic Texts*, ET 1972) contains patristic witnesses; vol. 2 (ET 1974) contains Nag Hammadi writings and Mandaean texts; vol. 3 (1980) contains Manichaean texts (in German translation).

(1) Of the primary sources, the following are among the most comprehensive:

(a) The *Corpus Hermeticum*, especially tractates 1 (*Poimandres*) and 13. These texts indicate no Christian influence; it is also to be noted that not all of the tractates of the *Corpus Hermeticum* are gnostic.

(b) The Mandaean writings emerged relatively late; nevertheless, they reflect some very early traditions. The most important texts were translated by M. Lidzbarski, whose edition and sequence are generally followed: Ginza (i.e., "the treasure"), the book of John and the Mandaean liturgies.

(c) The Nag Hammadi (Nile) texts, written in the Coptic language, contain witnesses attesting to a Christian Gnosis, as well as those indicating a Gnosis retouched with only a slight Christian taint. The Gospel according to Thomas and the Gospel according to Philip are to be consulted in the exegesis of the synoptic Gospels. Some writings related to the Nag Hammadi texts, such as the Pistis Sophia, have been known for some time.

An English translation of the entire collection of the Nag Hammadi texts is available in James Robinson, *Nag Hammadi Library in English,* New York: Harper and Row, 1981.

(d) The Christian-Gnostic autographs apart from the Nag Hammadi Library constitute a further group. The Thomas documents and the Odes of Solomon are representative of this group.

(e) The Manichaean writings represent a late stage of the fully developed Gnosis but also contain some ancient tradition in many instances. Worthy of note are such writings as the Kephalaia, the Manichaean Homilies, and the Manichaean Psalter.

(2) The portrayal of Gnosis by the church fathers and their excerpts from gnostic writings are significant sources, especially with regard to the major Christian-gnostic systems. Of special importance are Irenaeus' *Adversus Haereses,* the *Refutatio Omnium Haeresium* by Hippolytus, and the *Panarion* by Epiphanius. It is assumed that these excerpts are largely authentic; yet one needs to bear in mind that misunderstandings and distortions— even of a deliberate nature—are possible (cf. for instance, the question of the possible existence of a libertine Gnosis, p. 153f.).

Suggested reading:

Examples of all the above categories of writings are found in L-G, 355–365. One should be familiar with at least some of the Odes of Solomon and especially with the Hymn of Pearls in the Acts of Thomas.

3. Bases of gnostic thought

(1) Gnosis (γνῶσις) signifies knowledge, specifically knowledge of the truth of human existence. This is expressed with particular clarity in a text of the Valentinian Gnosis, preserved by Clement of Alexandria (*Exc ex Theod* 78,2; ET in *Gnosis* I, 230):

> . . . the knowledge: who were we? what have we become?
> where were we? into what place have we been cast?
> whither are we hastening? from what are we freed?
> what is birth? what is rebirth?"

The questions posed in this text are not inherently gnostic; only via the implied Valentinian answer do they become gnostic, through the realization that the knowledge of the origin and the destination of man also denotes his deliverance out of the cosmos.

(2) As a rule, this understanding of existence is described by the unfolding of a mythical view of the world and of man. The typically gnostic thought can therefore be explained with their cosmology and their anthropology.

(a) Cosmology. Philosophy developed the view which pictured the cosmos as a globe (the globe representing a perfect form). The heavenly bodies which move in spheres (circles), in keeping with unalterable laws, point to the reliability and harmony of the entire cosmic structure into which man has been placed as a microcosm. Gnosticism was able to adopt formally this world view; in this pursuit, however, it undertook a radical revaluation: The cosmos actually is not man's sheltering home; rather, it is a hostile power. Its laws are thoroughgoing evil because they are meant to destroy man. The reason for man's dismay is to be found precisely in the orderly constitution of the cosmos. The firmament is a wall that bars us from the world of light beyond, our home, with the stars being the guardians that keep us imprisoned in the hollow cosmic globe. The ascent of the human self into the world of light beyond occurs en route through the various spheres encompassing and dominating the cosmos. The difference between the ancient philosophical world view and that of Gnosticism can be summarized as follows: Whereas in the former *heimarmene* (fate) and *pronoia* (providence) are united, in the latter they break apart, since *heimarmene* is plainly evil. This view has consequences for the gnostic understanding of God: God is identical with the light beyond. As pure being he is absolutely transcendent and does not share in the cosmos at all. Hence, the decisive element in the gnostic world view is not the cosmic concept itself but the special gnostic appraisal of the cosmos: Its division into the "alien" world as an active, banishing power on the one hand, and into the otherworldly realm of salvation, which is our true homeland, on the other. This gnostic dualism, therefore, is not static but dynamic.

(b) The process delineated under cosmology is the same in anthropology. Gnosticism is able to assume the Greek perspective that man is composed of body and soul, but assigns new meaning to this perspective: Man, including his soul, belongs altogether to the world; in other words, as man he is the prison of his true self. The soul is actively evil because it deceives the true self with the false hope of the beauty of the world. Its intention is to keep the self imprisoned in this world and to kindle in him the love of the world in which it [the self] is lost. As a consequence, the notion of the soul's heavenly journey is reinterpreted; it is not the soul that ascends into heaven as a shaped form, but the ego, man's true being finds his liberation by becoming one with the world of light beyond, thus liberation is identical with the dissolution of the individual. This understanding of the world and of liberation by Gnosticism also has consequences for ethics. Since liberation consists of the termination of man's individuality, and since the world is inherently evil, there can be no individual responsibility for the world on the part of man. Theoretically, two extreme potentialities of existence present themselves: Either radical asceticism, that is, the retreat from the world into subjectivity, or total libertinism. Such libertinism is not mentioned in the gnostic autographs; it is attributed to them in part, however, by the church fathers (cf. *Gnosis*, I, 313–325). As a rule, gnostics renounced a concrete life with regard to the world. Yet, remarkably, next to this radical individualism in which every one pursues his own knowledge and solipsistically follows his own path, there also is the tendency to establish communities in which the enlightened members exhort one another with knowledge (gnosis) of a higher plane, as it were. Gnostic poetry and devotional literature had its origin in such communities.

4. Aspects of gnostic mythology

It is the intent of gnostic mythology to answer the question of why man is searching for deliverance. The answer is as follows: Man carries in himself, in his ego, a spark of the original light (*Urlicht*); this spark yearns to return to its place of origin, to its homeland.

Instead of a spark, one may also speak of a pearl or something similar, which man has lost and wants to find again.

But why did this spark even enter the realm of matter? There are two kinds of answers to this question. Either it is argued that the spark had descended from or "fallen" out of the realm of light. Or it is asserted that through an uprising from below, matter had seized some particles of light from the world beyond (in Manichaeism, for instance). In the world these sparks of light are numbed by the noise of the world; they forget where they came from—they are dead. The drama of deliverance begins at this point. God—more correctly, the ur-light (since God is without form)—or the (foreign) light sends the deliverer, the caller who raises the dead spark of light to new life (such a call to awaken is found in Eph 5:14). In this context it is characteristic that this gnostic call actually has no specific content; the light itself does not need to be called upon for a particular gnosis. Rather, as soon as it awakens, it recognizes both itself and its true origin in the deliverer. In the back of this is the ancient philosophical idea that like is only recognized by like. Man's self is only capable of recognizing the deliverer because both are light. As soon as man's self has recognized the deliverer, it has the ability to reach the world of light beyond, past the cosmic guardians (the stars).

Thus the decisive statement of gnostic mythology is the following: Man is identical with the deliverer; through the liberation man does not, as in the mystery religions, become something which he had not been before, but he "becomes" what he had always been since his point of origin.

Suggested exercises:

1. Compare the parable of the pearl in Mt 13:45f. with the corresponding rendering in the Gospel according to Thomas (Log 76) and with the hymn of the pearl in the Acts of Thomas (L-G, 465).

Tools: H. Jonas, *Gnosis* I, 320ff.; A. Adam, *Die Psalmen des Thomas und das Perlen-Lied als Zeugnisse vorchristlicher Gnosis*, 1959, 55–83).

2. Read the *Corpus Hermeticum* I (*Poimandres*) in Barrett, 82–90.

5. Gnosis and the NT

In the relevant literature this topic is frequently discussed and, in general as well as in particular, it is subject to controversy. Many scholars note gnostic influence especially in John and in Ephesians as well as in Paul. Conversely, others point to the fact that there was no evidence yet of a fully developed Gnosis at the time of their writing; therefore, it is not permissible to speak of gnostic influence at this point. For instance, those texts cited as parallels of John are invariably more recent than John; hence they cannot be adduced as possible sources for John.

But in the topic of Gnosis and the New Testament, the question is not so much whether or not there is evidence of a direct dependence of John upon a particular type of Gnosis. It is quite possible to observe in several instances that certain motifs which are typical in Mandaean texts are also encountered in John. This is of special interest because the Mandaean texts originated without Johannine influence.

A careful distinction is necessary between demonstrable relationships and mere convergences. One speaks of a "convergence" when the same motif is found in different religions without evidence of any connection between them.

Furthermore, it is essential to observe that there are, on the one hand, actual gnostic ideas, and on the other hand, ideas and conceptions which are not gnostic per se but which have been taken up by Gnosticism. For example, certain mythical redeemer doctrines, the dualism of light and darkness, speculative wisdom, and especially the principle of "like recognizes like" (see below), play a crucial role in Gnosticism. But all of these phenomena are not genuinely gnostic; they were merely assumed by Gnosticism. If these ideas are also found in the NT in a similar form, it is not for this reason appropriate to speak of a connection between Christianity and Gnosis. The complicated relationship between gnostic and NT texts may be clarified with a negative example: The Christ *mythos* on which Phil 2:6ff. is based is *not gnostic*, although the picture of the descent and the ascent of the redeemer occurs there. But it could readily be gnosticized if the contemplating ego (a) would identify with the redeemer, that is, (b) if it would discover its own heavenly origin in the redeemer and,

at the same time (c) would view existence in this world as imprisonment. Precisely at the point of their attitude towards the world, Gnosis
and the Christian faith are distinguished sharply. The cosmos is no longer
the place of the redemptive event in Gnosticism, rather it is the hostile
power out of which the ego calls for deliverance (cf. the Naassene Psalm
in H-S II, 807f.). It can hardly be overlooked that the Johannine sayings
which are related to this cosmology (cf. concordance, s.v. κόσμος), do
show a certain factual affinity to the gnostic statements.

However, in all comparisons in the history of religions, it is necessary
to observe that the historical etymology may aid the understanding but
it is in no wise tantamount to the understanding itself. Conversely, the
recognition of historical contingencies in no way constitutes a value judgment. In theology one occasionally encounters the attempt to prove simultaneously a historical novelty in Christian ideas and its truth. But over
against this, it must be maintained that historical originality does not constitute evidence of truth. If certain mythological statements of John can
be attributed to gnostic influence, this does not yet represent a verdict
about the truth of these statements; theology has no cause to defend itself apologetically against such an awareness.

Suggested exercise:

The principle of knowledge known as "like with like" plays an important role
in the entire ancient history of philosophy and of religion. Examples:

Democritus (Diels 68, Fragment B 164): It is an ancient opinion that "like is recognized by like." This is substantiated with examples from the animate and in-
animate nature where like always attracts its own kind.

Plato, Laws IV, 716c: "Then what life is agreeable to God, and becoming in his
followers? One only, expressed once for all in the old saying that 'like agrees with
like, with measure measure,' but things which have no measure agree neither
with themselves nor with the things which have (the right measure).

Cicero, Tusc. IV, 57: ". . . wisdom is the knowledge of things divine and human
and acquaintance with the cause of each of them, with the result that wisdom
copies what is divine, whilst it regards all human concerns as lower than virtue."

Epictetus, Diss II, 14: Man must know "the true nature of the gods. For whatever
their nature is discovered to be, he that is to please and obey them must needs
try, so far as he can, to make himself like them. If God is faithful, he must be
faithful too; if free, he must be free too. . . ."

Philo, Mut Nom 6: "And so when you hear that God was seen by man, you must
think that this takes place without the light which the senses know, for what belongs to the mind can be apprehended only by the mental powers."

Corpus Hermeticum XI, 20: "If you do not adapt yourself to God, you cannot
know God, for like can (only) be known by like."

This principle is also known in the NT writings, e.g., with Paul, in 1 Cor 2:11 and in the Gospel of John (3:3ff.). In a distinctly gnostic form it is encountered in the Hymn of Pearls and in the Acts of Thomas, especially Logion 112 (H-S II, 502f.).

In terms of interpretation it is to be noted that this idea becomes specifically gnostic only when it is interpreted in the sense of an identity of substance between the act of knowing and that which is known.

Suggested reading:

O. Gigon, *Grundprobleme der antiken Philosophie*, 1959, 243–256. C. W. Müller, *Gleiches zu Gleichem. Ein Prinzip frühgriechischen Denkens*, 1965.

PART THREE: THE NEW TESTAMENT WRITINGS— AN OVERVIEW

I. THE LETTERS OF PAUL

Bibliography: G. J. Bahr, "Paul and Letter Writing in the First Century," *CBQ* 28, 1966, 465–77; W. G. Doty, *Letters in Primitive Christianity*, 1973; L. E. Keck and V. P. Furnish, *The Pauline Letters*, 1984; W. G. Kümmel, *Introduction to the NT*, 1980, 247–252; B. Rigaux, *The Letters of St. Paul; Modern Studies*, ET 1968; C. J. Roetzel, *The Letters of Paul*, ²1982; A. Suhl, *Paulus und seine Briefe*, StNT 11, 1975.

Preliminary Remarks

In the following paragraphs, the sequence in which the letters of Paul will be discussed follows the probable date of writing. For reasons of methodology explained below, an exception is made with regard to the second letter to the Thessalonians. Of course, uncertainties cannot be avoided altogether.

A very controversial point in scholarship is whether all of the letters attributed to Paul are "genuine," that is, whether they actually were written by Paul. Therefore, those letters which can safely be claimed as authentic are treated in the first section, while those whose authenticity is questioned and which, in the opinion of this writer, are definitely not authentic, are treated in the following section. Of course, other positions on the issue of authenticity are referenced in the discussion of the individual letters.

There are certain concepts used in Pauline studies under which certain letters of Paul are gathered into particular groups. The four most extensive letters are known as the Pauline "main letters" (*Hauptbriefe*), which are Romans, 1 and 2 Corinthians, and Galatians; they are commonly acknowledged as authentic. The letters which, following their own presentation, Paul wrote while in prison, are called "prison letters"; yet, in this regard the following distinctions need to be made, contingent on one's view of authenticity:

1. If all of the extant letters of Paul are considered authentic, Ephesians, Philippians, Colossians, 2 Timothy, and Philemon are designated as prison letters.

2. Since the letters to Timothy and Titus clearly emerge from the Pauline corpus as a group of their own (they are called pastoral letters), many exegetes do not consider them to be authentic.

Consequently, if they are excluded, the prison letters in the narrower sense are comprised of Ephesians, Philippians, Colossians, and Philemon.

3. The authenticity of Ephesians and Colossians is yet to be discussed; if it is negated, only two letters remain as "genuine" prison letters, namely Philippians and Philemon.

§ 23   Character and Style of Pauline Letters

Bibliography: W. G. Kümmel, "Paulusbriefe," RGG V, 195–198; C. J. Roetzel, *The Letters of Paul*, ²1982.

(1) We have already referred earlier (§ 5) to the question of whether the letters of Paul ought to be understood as private correspondence with specific characteristics of a letter or as "epistles," artistic writings which merely use the external form of a letter. In the final analysis, the latter alternative is inappropriate.

In one sense, the authentic letters of Paul (see below for more discussion on this issue) are actual letters. They address specific recipients and not merely an "audience" in general. They have specific purposes and deal with questions and concrete conditions in the churches. They contain personal messages, such as travel plans, and convey personal greetings.

Philemon is a typical example of a personal letter, a so-called letter of recommendation (cf. p. 178 below) which was commonly known as a regular type in ancient epistolography (for examples, cf. A. Deissmann, *Light from the Ancient East*, p. 170ff.). An example of an ongoing correspondence between Paul and his churches is 1 Corinthians in which Paul deals with a number of inquiries addressed to him by the Corinthians (e.g., 7:1).

In connection with the current issues of discussion, Paul also refers to the theological foundations. His letters contain numerous didactic pericopae which transcend current questions and problems and likely were not merely formulated in an ad hoc fashion but which are based on preparatory work or perhaps on group discussions.

Thus in Thessalonica, for instance, the question had been raised whether those Christians who die prior to the (imminent) parousia also receive eternal life. Paul answers this question with a brief treatise in which he develops the basic features of his eschatology in two rounds (4:13ff.; 5:1ff.). Examples of this same procedure are found especially in 1 Cor (10:1ff.; 11; 13; 15).

Galatians and Romans are theological discussions and yet, at the same time, actual letters. The development of both letters, which does not follow the style of a letter but apparently rather that of the development of a sermon (using the indicative of the affirmation of salvation and the imperative of the ethical consequences), shows clearly that they are not as much occasional letters as carefully worked-out treatises. In this connection it is instructive to compare 1 Cor 8–10 with Rom 14f.; for both texts deal with virtually identical problems. The problem of the day in Corinth was whether it was permissible to eat meat sacrificed to idols; in 1 Cor the problem is handled accordingly. In Romans Paul refers to his earlier discussions in principle, but in this case without reference to possible problems which currently existed in Rome (of which Paul likely knew nothing since he did not know the church); rather, he treats the topic in a more pronounced didactic form.

(2) Paul's argument is largely dialogical, in other words, he has an imaginary partner raise objections which he then dismisses; this method of style is found especially in Romans (cf. the frequently recurring phrase τί οὖν ἐροῦμεν?). Often Paul poses rhetorical questions to the reader, or he argues directly *ad hominem* (Rom 2:1, 21f.). Likewise the *captatio benevolentiae* occurs quite frequently; in it the reader, with deliberate flattery, is supposed to have a certain understanding relative to the problem being discussed (Rom 7:1 etc.). The phrase οὐκ οἴδατε . . . should be understood the same way, i.e., in the sense of "Surely you know that . . ." (e.g., 1 Cor 9:24). All of these devices are stylistic elements of ancient discussions in popular philosophy, particularly the diatribe in which the writer takes up an assumed dialogue with the reader (typical examples are the diatribes of Epictetus).

Paul uses additional rhetorical devices, such as the play on words (as in 1 Cor 8:2f. with the term γινώσκειν), parallelism (Rom 12:4–8), antithesis (1 Cor 7:29–31), and the "chain," or climax respectively (Rom 5:3–5). Though not always with great skill, he also takes up pictures and comparisons from all kinds of possible realms in order to illustrate a point. He refers to agriculture and building in 1 Cor 3 and Rom 11:16–19, to sports in 1 Cor 9:24f., to the military in 1 Cor 9:7 and to the soldier's armour in 1 Thes 5:8.

§ 24   1, 2 Thessalonians (Also a methodological exercise for the study of a Pauline letter; 1 Thes)

A. First Letter

Bibliography: E. Best, *A Commentary on the First and Second Epistles to the Thessalonians*, HNTC, 1986; R. F. Collins, *Studies on the First Letter to the Thessalonians*, BETL 66, 1984; M. Dibelius, *An die Thessalonicher I. II.*, HNT 11, ³1937; E. v. Dobschütz, *Die Thessalonicherbriefe*, KEK, ⁷1909 (reprint 1974); R. Jewett, *The Thessalonian Correspondence*, 1986; W. G. Kümmel, "Das literarische und geschichtliche Problem des ersten Thessalonicherbriefes," in *Ges. Auf.*, 1965, 406–416; A. J. Malherbe, *Paul and the Thessalonians*, 1987; W. Marxsen, *Der erste Brief an die Thessalonicher*, ZBK NT 11.1, 1979; W. A. Meeks, *The First Urban Christians: The Social World of the Apostle Paul*, 1983.

Those perspectives important for the exegesis and the theological understanding of the letter should be acquired in the reading materials along the way.

1. Schema of a letter

The prescript (cf. p. 27f. above) is remarkably brief. The proem (see p. 29 above) clearly begins with v 2 (εὐχαριστοῦμεν); however its closing cannot be ascertained easily. One can only say that it appears to have ended at the end of ch 1, since 2:1 seems to introduce the correspondence proper. Here Paul reminds both himself and the recipients of the letter of his stay in Thessalonica. Nevertheless, in 2:13 the keyword εὐχαριστέω appears once again—the reference has the effect of a resumption of the proem, and the content of the following statements is consistent with the latter. It may be said, therefore, that evidently the boundaries of the proem are not clearly established.

There is another explanation for the findings described above: 1 Thes is the later composite of (at least two) originally independent letters and in this process both proems had been incorporated in the text. But in order to assume a hypothesis of division, the most important piece of evidence is lacking: It is impossible to identify with certainty the various underlying situations in the respective parts of the letter.

In continuation of the correspondence (ch 2f.), paraenesis and eschatology are dealt with thematically in 1 Thes 4f. At the close of the letter (5:23–28) are good wishes, greetings, and the request to read the letter in the gathering of the community. 1 Thes thus contains all of the elements in the schema of the Pauline letters.

2. About the historical situation: place and time of writing

The primary question in the scholarly study of the background is always the following: When and from where was the letter written? Explicitly we hear nothing about the time and place of writing, but there are several indications which render an answer feasible. From 1:1 we learn that Silvanus and Timothy are with Paul. 1:5–9 indicates that Paul had worked in Thessalonica some time earlier and then had left the city and territory of Thessalonica. When did that happen?

In order to answer this question, one requires geographical and historical information which can be gathered from maps, lexicons, commentaries, and especially from a concordance. The key words Thessalonica, Silas

(=Silvanus), and Timothy lead us to Acts 17:1ff. which recount the stay and arrest in Thessalonica. According to 17:10ff. Paul flees from there via Berea to Athens, while Silas and Timothy at first remain in Macedonia. Paul proceeds from Athens to Corinth where the two catch up with him again (18:5). This presentation of the events in Acts is largely in agreement with Paul's own presentation in 1 Thes 3:1–6: Paul left Athens and wrote the letter from Corinth after Timothy's return from Thessalonica. Nevertheless, there are some differences between 1 Thes 3:1f. and Acts 17; following the Acts account Paul travels alone from Berea, via Athens, to Corinth and is only then reunited with his co-workers. Following 1 Thes 3, however, Paul sends Timothy back to Thessalonica from Athens, which means that the latter had to have accompanied Paul to Athens, or he (Paul) must have already met him in Athens (and not only in Corinth), whereupon Paul must have sent him straight back to Thessalonica. The reference to Timothy's final return to Paul in 3:6 shows clearly that Corinth is the place where the letter was written.

The objection could be raised that Acts does not mention this letter, therefore, Paul could hardly have written it from Corinth. It is important to note, however, that Acts does not mention Paul's letters at all. Hence, its silence at this point cannot be used as an argument. Furthermore, the comparison of 1 Thes 3 and Acts 17 points to an important factor to recognize in the use of Acts as historical source: Acts presents the unfolding of events in simplified form (on this, see p. 364f. below).

Once the place of writing has been determined, the following inferences can be drawn relative to the date of writing: 1 Thes must be the earliest extant letter of Paul—independent of the "absolute" chronology (see p. 340f.), since it must have originated prior to the two letters to the Corinthians, which Paul obviously wrote only after his stay in Corinth.

3. Further historical details

In 1:7f. Paul refers to the areas, that is, to the provinces of Macedonia and Achaia. From a dictionary (e.g., the *IDB*) we learn that Thessalonica was the capital of the province of Macedonia and Corinth the capital of Achaia. The mention of the name Achaia solidifies the theory that the letter had been written in Corinth. In 2:2 Paul speaks of his suffering in Philippi. Therefore, Paul had been in Philippi before Thessalonica. Again we are looking for information on this stop; at our disposal as sources are first of all Philippians, of course, and then Acts again (ch 16). The sequence of Philippi first, then Thessalonica, is also confirmed in Acts; yet, here again we see that caution is necessary when using Acts as a historical source, since none of the persons mentioned in Phil is cited in the Philippi account in Acts, and vice-versa.

1 Thes 2:9 allows a glimpse into the lifestyle of Paul: He does not draw his support from the church. But the question is why he defends himself so conspicuously at this point. Was he perhaps confronted with the accusation that he was making money through his mission?

Kümmel, *Introduction*, 258f., suspects that the Jews in Thessalonica had criticized Paul—they indeed had pursued Paul even to Berea. They intended to convince the Christian community that Paul was a "huckster" (γόης= a magician of corrupt mind). An altogether different suggestion is offered by Dibelius (p. 10f.). He argues that 2:1–12 is not to be interpreted in terms of time but in terms of motive; in other words, Paul represents the *general* situation of the Christian missionaries. Externally, their appearance was akin to that of the contemporary wandering philosophers and hucksters who indeed lived off their trade. Paul wanted to distance himself categorically from such.

2:13 begins with praise for the community and its faith and steadfastness which, in v 14 changes into a sharp attack against the Jews (the parallelism with Acts 17 is not to be ignored). A touch of anti-Jewish polemic in early Christianity surfaces here; one should consult the commentaries to understand the specifics better.

Suggested exercise:

Continue the exegesis of 1 Thes in the same format, with the question in mind: What historical details does the reader learn?

4. Theological observations

In 1:3 one discovers the triad faith-love-hope, interwoven with a corresponding concept in each case. In order to capture the essential significance of this triad, it is helpful to trace its occurrence in the NT, especially in Paul (concordance and marginal references in Nestle). 1 Cor 13 represents the most impressive example.

In the proem the community which is addressed is first of all praised for its faith, but then the scope widens and encompasses the entire church (1:8). This ecumenical style is also found in the proems of 1 Cor and Phil.

The effectiveness of the apostle's proclamation is described with the terms δύναμις and πνεῦμα (v 5; with this compare 1 Cor 2:4, "demonstration of the Spirit and power"). In 1:9f. Paul gives a brief summary of the Christian confession in which personal statements about Christ and soteriological expressions concerning the work of salvation are joined together. This reference is a good example of Paul's ability to take up and continue words and concepts found in the Jewish-hellenistic missionary literature. Thus the "idols" are juxtaposed by the "living and true God" to whom the Gentiles have been converted. Add to these the anticipation of the parousia and the christological confession that God had raised Jesus from the dead. In order to grasp the more precise details, one needs to consult the secondary literature.

The topic of chs 2 and 3 is the relationship between the apostle and the church; in it Paul emphasizes the observation that this relationship is good (3:7).

As already indicated, the sharp criticism of the Jews in 2:14–16 raises a special theological issue: How does this charge relate to the theological pronouncement on Israel which occurs later in Rom 9–11 (see p. 196 below)? Can the two statements be reconciled, or is there a break within Pauline thought? Does Paul merely use unreflected expressions of traditional, anti-Jewish polemics here? Or does this polemic for him have theological weight all the same? In the latter case, his position regarding Israel would certainly have changed radically later on. But one must be observant of the kind of charges raised against the Jews; in v 15, for instance, Paul charges that they are πᾶσιν ἀνθρώποις ἐναντίοι which agrees with the charge of the Roman Tacitus who accuses Jews of being *"hostile odium"* and Christians of being *"odium generis humani"* (*Hist.* V, 5; *Ann.* XV, 44). Paul obviously appeals to areas of commonality in the Jewish polemic of antiquity; a theologically based anti-Semitism is unthinkable.

The paraenesis begins in 4:1. Here one finds indications of the indicative—imperative schema (on this concept cf. p. 101f.). One recognizes in the remark καθὼς καὶ περιπατεῖτε that paraenesis does not necessarily always have to do with shortcomings in the community addressed. Rather, paraenesis is fundamentally necessary as an ever new instruction in the life of faith. Paraenesis is a permanent part of Christian instruction.

It is characteristic that the phrase καθὼς καὶ περιπατεῖτε is omitted in the Byzantine text. In this text type early Christian paraenesis was thought to be moralizing and one was amazed that Paul even uttered ethical exhortations, while allegedly everything was in order. Thus the respective reference was eliminated and thereby the paraenetic function "salvaged."

A new topic begins with 4:13: Eschatology, "the doctrine of the last things." A certain subdivision is marked by the twofold περί (4:13; 5:1). The first subtopic (the fate of the deceased) is precipitated by doubt which arose in Thessalonica; the second part is formulated more generally: 5:1 appears almost like a rubric in a catechism. Paul expressly emphasizes that he had already taught the church on this point.

This pericope particularly is a fine example of Paul's theological mode of operation which has already been discussed above (§ 6); a simple reference to it suffices at this point.

Suggested exercises:

1. Analyze the picture of the thief in the night (see W. Harnisch, *Eschatologische Existenz*, 1973, 84–116). The mode of expression shifts: (a) To begin with, Paul uses pictorial language—the day of the Lord comes *like* the thief. (b) But then the "day" itself is intended: You are not in darkness, in other words, you will not be surprised by the "day." (c) Since we do not live in darkness, let us watch (paraenetic expression in which the imperative is predicated upon the indicative).

2. What are the relationships of content and style in the statements about watching and being sober elsewhere in the NT? Tools: Concordance and O. Bauernfeind, s.v. νήφω, TDNT IV, 936–941. For history-of-religions comparisons, consult the commentaries.

3. Which elements of the closing of a letter are present in 1 Thes (cf. p. 29f.)?

4. It is beneficial to compile the historical and theological insights gained and thus to achieve a systematic overview of the content.

B. Second Letter

Bibliography: E. Best, *A Commentary on the First and Second Epistles to the Thessalonians*, HNTC, 1986; A. J. Malherbe, *Paul and the Thessalonians*, 1987; W. A. Meeks, *The First Urban Christians: The Social World of the Apostle Paul*, 1983; W. Trilling, *Der zweite Brief an die Thessalonicher*, EKK XIV, 1980; W. Wrede, "Die Echtheit des zweiten Thessalonicherbriefes untersucht," *TU* 42/2, 1903.

1. Comparison of the two letters

This comparison is a paradigm for practicing the questions of authenticity; in terms of method it is of special interest because both supporters and opponents of authenticity use largely the same arguments. They begin with the observation that both letters have much in common. However, they derive contrasting consequences:

(1) Based on their similarity they are the product of the same author.

(2) Based on their similarity they are not from the same author; rather, 2 Thes is an imitation.

In order to clear up the problem, both letters must be read synoptically; Wrede may be used as a guide. The following are the initial observations:

(a) The similarity applies both to the structure as well as to the overall content of the letters, even to the point of the wording.

(b) 2 Thes is entirely without the features of correspondence, that is, without the concrete reference to the relationship between apostle and community. There are no accounts, such as the one about Timothy, and even the Jewish polemic of 1 Thes 2:14ff. is not paralleled in 2 Thes.

(c) Conversely the second letter contains additional eschatological teaching. Additional information is obtained by comparing the details in both letters by means of Nestle's parallel references and of a table in B. Rigaux (*Les Epîtres aux Thessaloniciens*, EBib, 1956, 133f.; cf. Wrede [see bibliography], 24–28).

Example: The prescript of 2 Thes 1:1f. at first follows that of 1 Thes 1:1 (ἐν θεῷ occurs in the prescript of only these two letters); but in contrast to 1 Thes, the salutation in 1:2 is broadened into an ordinary form.

Eschatology as the central theme is already taken up in both proems. The treatment of this theme is not the same in the two letters; indeed, a shift becomes apparent in the method of argumentation. As we have already seen, in 1 Thes 4:5 the eschatological teaching is based on the credo, joined by a variation on the topic of "dates," together with the picture of the day, the night, and the thief. In 2 Thes 1:2, on the other hand, the emphasis is on the warning against the persecutors of the church, while the entire passage is dominated by OT allusions. Dibelius has pointed out that the transition in 2:4 is very abrupt; he assumes therefore that vv 5–10 originated in the Jewish description of a theophany into which the author merely wove some Christian supplements (vv 8, 10). However, whether or not the OT allusions actually are citations from a source cannot be established. It is also plausible to explain these findings—and they are conspicuous indeed—by referring to the possibility that the apocalyptic portrayal regained momentum in Christianity during and immediately following the era of Paul (cf. the "synoptic apocalypse" in Mk 13). It is possible that Paul himself applies this style; nevertheless, it is more likely that it was not Paul himself but one of his disciples or followers. The pericope of 2:1–10, in contrast to 1 Thes, pursues no less than the opposite tendency: In the latter the call is, "The Lord is near; he comes suddenly; therefore watch!" In the former, however, the appeal is, "Do not be confused when someone insists that the Day of the Lord has already come" (2:2).

There is an exegetical problem in 2:2: Does ἐνέστηκεν indeed denote "has come," meaning that the opponents fought in 2 Thes might have represented a gnostic, "realized" eschatology, similar to the one which is opposed in 2 Tim 2:18? Or is the meaning of ἐνέστηκεν identical with the Latin *imminet* (or, as the Vulgate reads: *quasi instet*)? In this case, the opponents would teach that the last day is imminently close; in other words, they would represent a fanatical kind of imminent expectation.

The parousia, according to the emphasis in 2 Thes, is not to be expected imminently. It must first of all be preceded by the great apostasy and the revelation of the adversary; only then will the end come. In this connection, the figure of the Antichrist (cf. Dibelius' excursus on 2:10) and the terms τὸ κατέχον (v 6) and ὁ κατέχω (v 7) represent special exegetical problems; cf. also Bauer's *Greek-English Lexicon*, 423f., and the further reading material cited there.

Result: While the parousia in 1 Thes stands for the totality of the end-time events (4:13ff.), in 2 Thes it is understood as an individual event within a whole series of endtime events. Correspondingly, the understanding of faith and eschatology seem to be formalized and "hope" is no longer part of faith itself, but denotes a merely formal anticipation of the judgment.

At the conclusion of the eschatological teaching, beginning with 2:13, there follow three uniformly structured pericopae. Each one is paralleled closely in 1 Thes (cf. 2 Thes 2:13–17 with 1 Thes 2:13f.; 2 Thes 3:1–5 with 1 Thes 4:10; 5:24f.; 2 Thes 3:6–15 with 1 Thes 5:12ff.). Each pericope contains an exhortation to the readers; in the first two it is only an allusion, while it is explicit in the third. All three pericopae merge into a ceremonious conclusion which resembles the close of a letter.

In comparison with 1 Thes, an overview of the entire letter indicates the following:

(1) Every pericope in 1 Thes—with the exception of the "correspondence" (see above)—has its counterpart in 2 Thes.

(2) Not every pericope in 2 Thes has a parallel in 1 Thes. Based on this observation, Wrede concludes that the writer of 2 Thes evidently not only had a good memory of 1 Thes, but he must have had it in front of him on his desk.

2. Historical situation

(1) If one holds 2 Thes to be authentic, it follows that Paul would have had to write to the same community twice in quick succession and with very similar content, by weaving parts of the first letter also into the second letter. Furthermore, while writing 1 Thes 5:1ff. he would have forgotten that he already instructed the community in Thessalonica concerning the Antichrist. Likewise the Thessalonians would have forgotten it; for they evidently interpreted Paul's statements with a fanaticism in the sense of a red-hot imminent expectation. After that Paul would have sent them the second letter in which he reminded them of his previous teaching, and in doing so he expressed himself as if he taught them for the first time on this subject matter.

Harnack (Das Problem des 2 Thes, SAB 1910, 560ff.) realizes the problems one encounters with the assumption that 2 Thes is authentic. He assumes, therefore, that the two letters had been directed to different groups within the community; whereas the first one was sent to the whole church, or perhaps only to its Gentile-Christian contingent, the second letter (which lacks the Jewish polemic related to current circumstances) was directed to the Jewish Christians in the community. But there are no positive indications in support of this assertion; in fact, it is virtually ruled out by the prescripts of both letters.

Kümmel, *Introduction*, 267ff., probes the eschatology of 2 Thes and concludes that it could not be explained on the basis of post-Pauline tendencies in the first century, hence the letter had to be authentic. Furthermore, 2:4 presupposes the existence of the temple in Jerusalem. It is necessary, therefore, to abide with the assumption that Paul wrote 2 Thes shortly after 1 Thes, while the first letter was still fresh in his mind. With regards to method, however, Kümmel's point of departure is incorrect: It cannot be decided at the outset whether or not the theological tendencies of 2 Thes are feasible in the post-Pauline era; the question is whether they fit into the framework of the apostle's theology as we know it from the other letters of Paul.

(2) More reasonable is the explanation that the letter was written by a disciple of Paul. In this case, his polemic would be directed against a certain type of "Paulinism" which practiced an intensive, imminent expectation and which was able to appeal to such expressions by the apostle as in 1 Cor 7:29; 10:11; Phil 4:5. 2 Thes would then claim to represent the authentic teaching of Paul over against these tendencies (cf. especially 2 Thes 2:2, 15). It is striking that the conceptualization in 2 Thes becomes more rigid when compared with 1 Thes.; thus in 1:5 the author speaks of the δικαία κρίσις and in 2:13 of the πίστις ἀληθείας—evidently the terms κρίσις and πίστις alone are no longer sufficient. In several instances 2 Thes speaks of the "Lord," where in the parallel passage in 1 Thes "God" is used. The picture of the community (1:3) and especially that of the apostle (3:7) is idealized. The apostle is both the teacher of the correct understanding and ethical standard at the same time.

Similar observations can be made in the Pastoral letters. The generation following Paul developed this idealized picture of the early church into a fixed tradition.

In addition, if one observes that the close of the letter contains two explicit affirmations that the letter is authentic (3:14, 17), it seems reasonable to assume that this is not one of Paul's letters. Rather, a follower has sought to imitate a letter of Paul in form and content and in doing so to defend the intent of Pauline eschatology against heretical deviations.

Suggested Reading:

A. Lindemann, "Zum Abfassungszweck des 2 Thes," ZNW 68. 1977, 35–47.

§ 25 Galatians

Bibliography: H. D. Betz, *A Commentary on Paul's Letter to the Churches in Galatia*, 1979; E. D. Burton, *The Epistle to the Galatians*, ICC, 1921; G. Ebeling, *The Truth of the Gospel: An Exposition of Galatians*, ET 1985; G. Howard, *Paul: Crisis in Galatia*, SNTSMS 35, 1979; J. B. Lightfoot, *The Epistle of St. Paul to the Galatians*, reprint, 1987; D. Lührmann, *Der Brief an die Galater*, ZBK NT 7, 1978; F. Mussner, *Der Galaterbrief*, HThK IX, 1974; H. Schlier, *Der Brief an die Galater*, KEK VII, [5]1971.

1. External structure and problem

The structure and content of Galatians can be worked out with relative ease if it is considered as preparatory work, as it were, for Romans. In both letters the main theme is the doctrine of justification by faith alone; in Gal it arises from the present circumstances, while in Rom it is presented and developed more as a fundamental proposition. From the theme results an analogous structure in both letters: part one, doctrine; part two, paraenesis.

Whereas Gal 1–4 represent the "dogmatic-theological" part, Gal 5, 6 represent the "ethical" part. Part one can be subdivided once again, so that one gains a three-part structure:

1–2: Historical evidence for the validity of the Pauline apostolate and hence of his preaching;

3–4: systematic evidence concerning justification by faith and freedom from the law;

5–6: ethical consequences resulting from justification;

Conclusion of the letter.

From the first glance it is clear that Gal is determined by popular polemics. The Pauline teaching of freedom from the law is being contested in Galatia. Hence the entire letter serves the argument in favor of the Pauline understanding of justification.

2. Structural details

Already the prescript is determined by the actual situation. Paul insists emphatically that he has not received his office from man, but from Christ and from God. At the same time, already in v 2 he points out that all the brothers agree with his teaching, which says indirectly that the criticism that was noised around in Galatia was unjustified. The conspicuous christological expansion of the prescript (v 4), which relates to the *sola gratia*, has the same function; here the theme of the letter is indicated already.

There is no proem, since Paul has no reason for a thanksgiving because of the current situation in the churches of Galatia. Instead, he commences with an emphatic critical-polemical θαυμάζω and defends himself and his teaching against the attacks of his opponents. In an autobiographical section (1:10–24) he clarifies the statement "not from man nor by man, but by Jesus Christ and God the Father" found in the prescript and mentions his calling in this connection (1:15f.). In doing so, however, he does not recount the Damascus experience; he restricts himself to the mention of the fact and makes central the commission he received, that of the mission to the Gentiles.

In 2:1–10 he underscores that the Christian leaders of the Jerusalem church also recognized him officially; in 2:11–21 he describes how he maintained his position when confronting Peter in Antioch. This pericope is the most important source for the "Apostolic Council"; a comparison with Acts 15 allows certain differences in the portrayal of the events to come to the fore (see § 66 below). Paul highlights the results of the council: (1) the recognition of the Gentiles' freedom from the law; (2) the de-marcation of the realms of competence: Paul as apostle to the Gentiles and Peter as apostle to the Jews; (3) the collection of a worldwide offering to support the community in Jerusalem as a visible sign of the unity of the church.

In 2:15–21 Paul already leads into the systematic presentation of his doc-trine of justification. He appeals to the OT, especially to Abraham, and delivers a kind of "scriptural evidence" in support of the argument of the Christian freedom from the law (Gal 3:4).

The ethical part of the letter begins with 5:1. The emphasis is on the fact that ethics has its basis in freedom (the "paraenetic" οὖν in 5:1 is also found in Rom 12:1). The decisive theological statement is found in 5:6. In 5:19–24 Paul contrasts the "fruit" of the Spirit of freedom with the "works" of the flesh and has the presentation merge in a catalog of vir-tues and vices. Then the classical formula in the determination of the re-lationship between the indicative and the imperative follows in 5:25: εἰ ζῶμεν πνεύματι, πνεύματι καὶ στοιχῶμεν.

6:1–10 contains general exhortations, followed by the conclusion of the letter in which Paul stresses that he had written the letter with his own hand (cf. 1 Cor 16:21 and 2 Thes 3:17; the latter possibly indicates imi-tation; see above, § 24). The conclusion is entirely in keeping with the overall tone of the letter: Paul pronounces the blessing but conveys no greetings.

According to H. D. Betz (see biblio.), Gal belongs to the genre of the "apologetic letter"; Paul uses the stylistic means of ancient rhetoric and from this perspective designed the letter as a whole.

3. Historical problems

Who the recipients of this letter were, that is, which geographical terri-tory is meant by the term "Galatia," is a matter of debate. Also debated is the theological position which the opponents who are addressed in the letter might have espoused and, hence, where they might have come from.

(1) The Galatians were Celts who invaded Asia Minor in the third cen-tury B.C. and finally settled in the area of today's Ancara (then known as Ankyra). Therefore that area was called Galatia.

On the "second missionary journey" Paul might possibly have established churches in Galatia which are otherwise unknown to us (Acts 16:6) and then visited them again (Acts 18:23) on the "third missionary journey" (on this matter, cf. pp. 242f. and 364f. below). This would harmonize with Paul's allusion in Gal 4:13 to two possible prior visits.

The crux is, however, that the Roman *province* of Galatia encompassed more than the territory of the *region* of Galatia; hence the letter could also be addressed to the churches in Pisidian Antioch, Iconium, and Lystra (consult map)—situated in the southern part of the province of Galatia—which Paul established on the "first missionary journey" (Acts 13f.). It is to be noted, however, that the inhabitants of this area were not Celts (Acts 14:11).

Since Paul does not mention the names of any city in Gal, it is not clear to begin with whether his letter is directed to the churches in the Galatian *region* (the so-called North Galatian hypothesis) or to the urban churches in the southern part of the *province* of Galatia (the so-called South Galatian hypothesis). The issue is significant not only for historical reasons, but also because of the question of whether the churches that Paul addresses were made up exclusively of Gentile Christians or whether there also were Jewish Christians among them. In other words, did the obviously Jewish Christian opponents of Paul infiltrate the churches from the outside, or had they been part of them from the beginning? There is no evidence for Jewish settlements in the region of Galatia in the first century; hence it would be reasonable to conclude that the letter was addressed to the churches in the province of Galatia (where Jewish settlements did exist). A further argument may be adduced in favor of this "South Galatian Hypothesis" (or, better, "province hypothesis"): According to 1 Cor 16:1, the Galatian churches participated in the collection for Jerusalem; yet Acts 20:4 mentions only representatives from *southern* Asia Minor as members of the delegation which brought the collection to Jerusalem. This leads to the apparent conclusion that by "Galatia" Paul had in mind the southern part of the province.

Nevertheless, this province hypothesis is to be rejected because of the weightier counter arguments. (1) The use of the term "Galatia" as designation for the Roman province is highly unusual; normally, when reference is made to the province of Galatia, the various regions are listed. (2) The list (of names) in Acts 20:4 cannot be regarded as convincing evidence since it is incomplete; the representatives from Corinth, for instance, are omitted. (3) Only with caution should one appeal to the pattern of the missionary journeys (see p. 364f. below); it cannot be established with certainty when Paul visited which area. Furthermore, it is noteworthy that while Acts 16:6 indeed speaks of a journey through Galatia, there is no mention of churches that were established there. (4) It is very unlikely that Paul addresses as "foolish Celts" (3:1) the inhabitants of the southern part of the province of Galatia who were not Celtic. (5) The omission of the names of cities favors the more rural (northern) Galatia rather than the more densely populated urban area mentioned in Acts 13f.

(2) Closely associated with the problem described above is the issue of the *date of writing* of Gal. If Paul wrote to the South Galatian churches, the letter might already have been written on the "second journey," for instance, in Corinth. In this case it could conceivably be the oldest extant letter of Paul. However, if it was addressed to the region of Galatia, the time of writing would coincide with Paul's stay in Ephesus (on the chronology, see p. 340f.). The date of writing cannot be determined more precisely. In particular the precise relation in time to the Corinthian letters remains an open issue; at any rate, the similarities, for instance, between Gal 1:6ff., 10, and 2:4 on the one hand, and 2 Cor 11:4, 5:11, and 11:26 on the other, are unmistakable. An important item of evidence is that Paul mentions in 1 Cor 16:1 that he organized the Galatian collection for Jerusalem; yet while he points out in Gal that the collection was agreed upon at the Apostolic Council, he does not write anything about the organization of the collection. This may indicate that Gal had been written before 1 Cor. It is also possible, of course, that the collection was in jeopardy because of the situation in Galatia; hence Paul does not mention it. But even if this is the case, it does not constitute solid evidence that Gal was not written until after 1 Cor.

(3) The *recipients* of Gal are Gentile Christians (4:8; 5:2f.; 6:12f.). But there are people among them who must have penetrated from outside and carried on Judaizing propaganda. These "Judaizers" are Christians who claim that the Mosaic law—whether they have in mind the whole law or primarily the circumcision ordinance, cannot be discerned—was binding for all Christians, including Gentile Christians. Obviously their demand for circumcision did not lack a positive response. The Judaizers further assert that Moses is the mediator (3:19f.) and that the law mediates the Spirit (3:2).

According to Gal 5:7, 10; 6:3, the agitation is apparently led by an individual. The argument that the allusion points to Peter (so Lietzmann, et al.), is entirely out of the question (cf. 1:18; 2:11ff. does not point in this direction either); it is more feasible that the opponents appeal to James (similar to the incidents described in 2:12). At any rate, the opponents may have been closely connected with the "false brothers" in Jerusalem (2:4). Evidently they are denying Paul's position as apostle; the same happened with the agitators of 2 Cor 10–13 who appeal emphatically to Jerusalem, that is, to the traditional leadership of the church. However, in the light of Gal 1:19 it is quite unlikely that James indeed supported them.

Apart from circumcision, the opponents apparently also demand the observance of certain times ("dates," 4:10) and the veneration of the cosmic elements (4:3, 9). Does this mean that they understand the law and Christ in the sense of a cosmic-redeemer doctrine, such as the argument that the redeemer is embodied in the cosmic elements? Based on these references, Schmithals assumes that the opponents were not Judaizers but gnosticizing Jewish Christians, that is Judeo-Christian Gnostics ("The Heretics in Galatia," in *Paul and the Gnostics*, ET 1972, 13–64). This is the reason why they did not demand the observance of the whole law; instead, they demanded only circumcision, which they viewed as a ritual to obtain liberation from the flesh, as well as the observance of other related rituals. Now Paul clarifies that to be circumcised means to yield to the whole law (5:3). But the very sweeping argumentation in Gal 3 and 4 shows that the Galatian conflict revolves around the law as a whole; on the other hand, no *specifically* gnostic tendencies are evident (cf. p. 155f.).

Based on Paul's warning against misusing freedom (5:13ff.), it is argued that Paul must have fought on two battle fronts, namely, against Judaizers as well as against libertine enthusiasts. But the statements of 5:13ff. are in keeping with the emphasis which Paul places upon the positive theological relationship between freedom and ethics; there is no polemic per se behind it.

4. Basic theological ideas

The doctrine of justification or, to phrase it differently, the relationship between faith in Christ and the Jewish law, constitutes *the* issue in Gal. In Gal 3, 4 Paul unfolds the theological principle that man is not justified by the law but by faith. In order to substantiate the point, he appeals to the OT in 3:6ff.: Abraham's faith was reckoned to him as righteousness; therefore Christians, for whom faith is likewise decisive, are Abraham's children. The argument that to be under the law means to be under the curse is of paramount significance; the connection between law and curse is made via Dt 27:26, whereas the quotation from Hab 2:4 serves to establish the connection between faith and life (Gal 3:10f.). The question of what meaning the law might have, given these preconditions, arises inevitably and is answered with a salvation-history argument. The law was given 430 years after Abraham (3:17); its task is not to annul the promise but to magnify sin even more. Here the following differentiation is made: The law *could* make alive, in which case righteousness *would* indeed come from the law (3:21); however, everything that has to do with the law belongs de facto to the realm of sin. The law is the παιδαγωγὸς εἰς Χριστόν (3:24), which does not mean that it is the trainer pointing to Christ, i.e., a pedagogical means of preparation; rather, the law is man's taskmaster until the coming of Christ. Since then we are free from this taskmaster (3:25; the idea of freedom is given more depth in 5:1ff.).

In Gal 4:21–31 Paul demonstrates an example of allegorical interpretation of Scripture. Abraham's two wives, Hagar and Sarah, are the mothers of the enslaved and of the free respectively. Christians understand themselves to be children of the promise, hence descendants of Sarah.

Suggested exercise:

Determine the theological function of the paraenesis (5:6) within the letter. What is the relationship between freedom from the law on the one hand and ethical norms on the other? In this context, compare Luther's "Sermon von den guten Werken" (Clemen I, 227–298).

§ 26 Philippians

Bibliography: F. W. Beare, *The Epistle to the Philippians*, 1959; J. B. Lightfoot, *St. Paul's Epistle to the Philippians*, reprint 1987; "Der Philipperbrief als paulinische Briefsammlung," in *Ges. Aufs.* IV, BEvTh 53, 1971, 195–205; M. Dibelius (see § 24); J. Gnilka, *Epistle to the Philippians*, ET 1981.

1. Problem and external structure

(1) Philippi was one of the regional capitals of Macedonia, a Roman colony (Acts 16:12). The city's fame came from the battle of Philippi in 42 B.C. in which Mark Anthony and Octavian defeated the murderers of Caesar; as a result the final collapse of the Republic became apparent.

In Philippi Paul established his first community on European soil. To be sure, the account in Acts 16 is quite legendary, which is already apparent from a comparison between the references to individuals there as well as in Phil.

(2) Even in a cursory reading of the letter the prominence of the terms χαίρω, χαρά is striking. Obviously Paul's relationship to this church is unencumbered; one also notices this from the fact that he accepts their financial support (4:10ff.), while he declines that of the Corinthian community (2 Cor 11:9). Philippians lacks a clear structure. Only the proem is clearly defined (1:3–11); it is followed by a reference to the apostle's current situation of imprisonment (1:12ff.). Paul assumes that martyrdom awaits him at the end of this imprisonment (1:19–23); on the other hand, he still reckons with the possibility of travelling to Philippi once again (1:24–27). In 1:27–2:4 he exhorts the Philippians to unity, followed in 2:6–11, and introduced by v 5, by the famous Christ hymn which relates to the situation of the church, as the context indicates. After a few amiable exhortations (2:12–18), there follows the correspondence in view of the current situation (2:19–3:1a).

The new beginning in 3:2 is very surprising. After a severe polemic which is apparently directed against Jewish Christians, Paul offers an auto-biographical, retrospective glance. He stresses that his calling to be an apostle was in no sense a deliverance from inner crisis, but on the con-trary, that as a Jew he considered himself free from all flaws. In his con-version he did not relinquish some inner misery, but precisely his pride, his self-accomplished righteousness. In 3:12–16 Paul describes his present situation, followed by exhortations to unity and to firmness in the faith in 3:17–4:9. The passage of 4:10–20 contains additional correspondence; Paul is primarily expressing his gratitude for their assistance. Final greet-ings close out the letter.

2. Literary questions

The extremely rough transition from 3:1 to 3:2 continues to provoke lit-erary investigations. 3:1 sounds like the introduction to the close of a let-ter; that 3:2 follows immediately ("Watch out for those dogs") is surprising, to say the least. Therefore, many exegetes assume that 3:1 was originally followed immediately by ch 4, while 3:2–4:1 represented a polemical let-ter written at a later date. Subsequently both letters were combined by a redactor.

J. Gnilka (see bibliography) distinguishes between the prison letter A (1:1–3:1a; 4:2-7, 10–23) and the letter of conflict B (3:1b–4:1, 8f.). W. Schmithals (*Paul and the Gnostics*, 1972, 75ff.) sees as many as three letters in Phil: Letter A (4:10–23) as a brief thank you letter; letter B which was written later (1:1–3; 4:4–7) and deals with the confrontation with the false teachers which is already beginning to take shape (cf. 1:15, 17, 28); letter C (3:2–4:3), finally, was written by Paul after the conflict had broken out fully.

It is unlikely that an originally independent letter lurks behind 4:10–23. Nevertheless, the difference in tone and mood between Phil 2 and 3 is significant indeed. But is this observation sufficient for a hypothesis of division? It is at least conceivable that Paul closes the essentially unpo-lemical part of the letter in 3:1a and in 3:1b prepares for the polemic which begins in 3:2. At any rate, there is no absolutely certain evidence for the notion that ch 3 actually presupposes a different external situation from that of the first part of Phil. There is no change in the essentially positive attitude towards the church, and the tensions within the church have already been mentioned in 1:15, 28; 2:21. Therefore (in contrast to the first and second [German] editions of this book), it is not possible to say with sufficient certainty whether or not Phil represents a literary unity.

3. Time and place of writing

Regardless of whether one regards Phil as one letter or not, its dating must in any case be determined, to begin with, on the basis of the first two chapters. According to 1:12–26, Paul is imprisoned—and that in Rome, following tradition. In this case, Phil would have been written relatively late, shortly before Paul's execution. The following external factors at first seem to favor Rome: Paul mentions the praetorium (1:13), that is, the praetorian barracks, and "those who belong to Caesar's household" (4:22), a reference probably to slaves of the emperor. Yet, these do not constitute clear evidence in favor of Rome as the place of writing; in the province, the praetorium is located in the palace of the governor (Mk 15:16) and there were also imperial slaves in the provinces.

A theological argument is also adduced in support of Rome as the place of writing and, at the same time, in support of a late date. Compared with 1 Cor, for instance, Phil contains a radically different eschatological conception. Whereas in the former Paul anticipated the resurrection of all Christians together at the parousia, he assumes in the latter that he would enter the new life immediately upon his death (1:23). A. Schweitzer (*The Mysticism of Paul the Apostle*, ET [2]1953, 136ff.) bases this difference in Paul's conception not on his changed conception but on his expanded procedure, as it were. Paul expects the martyr to be received into heaven at once, on account of his sacrificial death, while the other believers, by contrast, have to wait until the general resurrection of the dead. It is to be noted, however, that Paul also anticipates the parousia in Phil (3:20; 4:5) and that he does not speculate on the interval between death and resurrection in the earlier letters either. Therefore, the conceptions in 1 Cor 15 and Phil 1:23 do not need to be viewed as contradictory.

An important factor regarding the time and place of writing is the fact that, according to 2:24–26, there seems to have been frequent contact between Paul and the community. Not only is the correspondence frequent, but Paul announces his intention to travel to Philippi after his release. In the opinion of many exegetes, this indicates that the letter could not have originated in Paul's Roman imprisonment, since the distance between Rome and Philippi was simply too great to allow for such close connections. Furthermore, Paul had expressed his intention in Romans to travel from Rome to Spain (and not back to the eastern part of the empire). Thus it is necessary to look for another place where Paul, as a prisoner, could have written the letter (Phil 1:1ff.).

E. Lohmeyer (*Philipper*, KEK IX/1,3) surmises that the letter was written during the two years of imprisonment in Caesarea (Acts 24–26). However, the supporting arguments are inadequate: The distance from there to Philippi is no less than from Rome. The change in the travel plans over against their announcement in Romans is quite understandable given the fact that the church in Philippi is threatened by heresy.

Currently it is often argued that the letter was written in Ephesus. The frequent back and forth movement of news would indeed find a fairly simple explanation, given the relatively short distance between Ephesus and Philippi; however, there is no explicit support for an Ephesian imprisonment of Paul. Yet, Paul does indicate in the Corinthian correspondence that he had been exposed to extremely severe perils in Ephesus (1 Cor 15:32; 2 Cor 1:8; in Acts 19 the danger has obviously been played down). Hence, Phil—or, if one wants to subdivide it, the "first" letter of Phil—may have been written at about the time of 1 and 2 Cor (which means that the "second" letter (3:2–4:3) presumably was written shortly afterward). But neither the question of the time of writing, nor that of the place of writing, can be answered satisfactorily; nevertheless, the assumption of Ephesus seems to be most compatible with the conditions recognized in Phil.

A further concern in dating Phil (and Phlm; see p. 178f. below) arises when the connection with Col and Eph is considered. Both of these also claim to be prison letters and, if they are Paul's, must belong to the end of his life, on account of their peculiarities in style and theological thought. In contrast, Phil is "normally" Pauline in all of its parts; in other words, it can hardly have been written at the same time as Col and Eph. Actually the problem is solved if one views Col and Eph as deuteropauline (see p. 199ff. below).

4. Theological motifs

Paul's theological thrust can be recognized most lucidly in the second part (or: letter B): With greatest pungency Paul argues polemically, in 3:2–4:3, against the notion of a righteousness derived from the law. From this the conclusion is often drawn that the opponents who are criticized demanded circumcision, hence, like the opponents who are resisted in Gal, they are Judaizers. But this cannot be deduced from 3:2ff.; Paul is not concerned with the circumcision of *Christians*; but the opponents themselves are recognized as circumcised, that is, they are Jews (or Jewish Christians). They characterize themselves as "perfect" (3:12–16); hence they apparently are enthusiasts, possibly with gnosticizing tendencies. The Pauline line of argument takes up both viewpoints. On the one hand the apostle refers to his own immaculate keeping of the law and thereby pulls the rug from underneath the Jewish criticism; on the other hand, he points to the ethical conduct in keeping with the Christian confession and so combats Christian fanaticism.

This theological motif is particularly evident in 2:6ff. (letter A?) in the Christ hymn which Paul quotes. This hymn serves to substantiate the paraenetic exhortations by means of a reference to the example of Christ. The example here is not the mindset of the earthly Jesus, but the obedience of the pre-existent and incarnate Christ. Instead of following Luther's introductory formulation, "let everyone have the mindset which Jesus Christ also had," v 5 ought to be translated as "aspire to that to which one aspires in Jesus Christ." This means that the function of the hymn is not to propagate an *imitatio Christi*, rather it is designed to make clear that Christian existence is realized in the renunciation of power. In no way does this eliminate the idea of example; the picture of Christ's obedience is etched too graphically for that to happen. But Christians are not called upon to imitate particular modes of action on Jesus' part.

Between the Christology of this hymn and the theological intention of Paul there is a tension. The hymn focuses on but the incarnation of the pre-existent one, on his death and his exaltation; the central expressions in Pauline Christology are the cross and the resurrection (note that the conception of exaltation and resurrection are not identical). For this reason Paul accentuates the hymn with a clarifying addition which emphasizes the death on the cross (cf. p. 97f. below).

Suggested exercises:

1. Exegete the closing paraenesis of 4:8f. as an example of how early Christian ethics followed public standards. What is the significance of the expressions employed? What are the resultant consequences? Read: K. Barth, *Erklärung des Phil*, loc. cit.; J. Gnilka, *Phil*, loc. cit.

2. Analyze 3:2–11, especially vv 7ff. This passage is an ideal example for the "double conceptuality" in Paul. His arguments are cast both in the mold of the doctrine of justification and in that of the categories of mysticism and/or Gnosticism. (a) Which concepts should be associated with the two respective categories? (b) How are the two categories correlated with one another?

Gather the arguments in favor of and against the unity of Phil. Tools: J. Gnilka (see bibliography), 5–25; U. B. Müller, *Prophetie und Predigt im NT*, StNT 10, 1975, 205–211.

§ 27 *Philemon*

Bibliography: J. Gnilka, *Der Philemonbrief*, HThK X/4, 1982; E. Lohse, *Colossians and Philemon*, ET 1971; P. Stuhlmacher, *Der Brief an Philemon*, EKK, 1975.

1. Problem and theme of letter

Phlm is the only letter of Paul to an individual which is generally considered to be authentic. It belongs to the category of the letters of recommendation (cf. Dibelius-Greeven, *Phlm*, HNT 12, supplements 7 and 8: The plea of Pliny the Younger for a freed slave, as well as a warrant against two escaped slaves). The content of Phlm is understandably simple. Onesimus the slave escaped from his Christian master, Philemon, and fled to Paul, where he apparently became a Christian. Paul sends him back to Philemon but pleads in virtually adjuring terms not to punish the slave. In v 22 he announces his upcoming visit to Philemon's house.

2. Time and place of writing

Phlm, like Phil, was written in prison (v 1), hence the same places of writing need to be considered: Rome, Caesarea, or Ephesus. The recipient, Philemon, seems to reside in Colossae; at any rate, Archippus (v 2) is also mentioned in Col 4:17, and so is Onesimus in Col 4:9. That Colossae is the letter's destination is also underscored by the fact that Paul obviously does not know Philemon personally (v 5), since Paul himself has never been in Colossae. If this is correct, the likely place of writing is once again Ephesus, for a slave's escape from Colossae to Caesarea, or even to Rome, and his subsequent return, in any case, is hard to imagine.

3. Theological tendency

The letter has special significance regarding the question of the social setting and/or of the political disposition of early Christianity. Paul is often sharply criticized because of this letter: His attitude of not liberating the slave from the dependence upon his master but rather sending him back into slavery, only indicates that (early) Christianity had been on the side of the powerful from the beginning. At least this much is clear, Paul had been very conservative in his socio-political attitude. This criticism, however, is invalid. First off, one needs to take into consideration that Paul certainly expects the relationship between the slave Onesimus and his master Philemon to change fundamentally (v 16). Furthermore, one fails to think historically if Paul's position is evaluated based on today's convictions without considering the historical situation of the first century and especially Paul's theological presuppositions. His position on the issue of slavery is in keeping with the eschatological world view, as he delineated in 1 Cor 7. The world is coming to a close; therefore it would be senseless, if not dangerous, to change the conditions programmatically because such a transformation of the world would only result in another world—a world which no longer has a future. Naturally, this view of things cannot be transferred to the present situation but, conversely, we learn from Phlm as well as from 1 Cor 7 that no change in the social and political conditions will cause the world to cease to be world, neither will it usher in paradise-like conditions, i.e., "salvation."

Suggested Reading:

E. Lohse (see bibliography). In addition, cf. J. Lähnemann/G. Böhm, *Der Phm, Handbücherei für den Religionsunterricht* 16, 1973. The debate over the relationship between early Christianity and slavery has been waged, in part, with great fervor; the following contributions are representative: S. Schulz, "Hat Christus die Sklaven befreit? Sklaverei und Emanzipationsbewegungen im Abendland,"

EvKomm 5, 1972, 13–17 (containing a severe critique of Paul); on the opposite position: E. Schweizer, "Zum Sklavenproblem im Neuen Testament," EvTh 32, 1972, 502–506. Detailed information and bibliographic references are found in Gnilka's excursus, "Die Sklaven in der Antike und im frühen Christentum" (see bibliography), 54–81; of related interest, see in English, S. S. Bartchy, *ΜΑΛΛΟΝ ΧΡΗΣΑΙ: First Century Slavery and the Interpretation of 1 Corinthians 7:21*, SBLDS 11, 1973.

§ 28   1 Corinthians

Bibliography: C. K. Barrett, *The First Epistle to the Corinthians*, HNTC, 1968; H. Conzelmann, *1 Corinthians*, Hermeneia, ET 1975; E. Fascher and Chr. Wolff, *Der erste Brief des Paulus an die Korinther*, ThHK VII/1.2, ²1980; G. D. Fee, *The First Epistle to the Corinthians*, NIC, 1987; J. C. Hurd, *The Origin of 1 Corinthians*, ²1983; H. Lietzmann and W. G. Kümmel, *An die Korinther 1, 2*, HNT 9, ⁵1969; W. Schmithals, *Gnosticism in Corinth*, ET 1971.

1. Historical situation and structure

(1) Acts 18 informs us concerning Paul's stay in Corinth. Corinth was a Roman colony; 100 years after its destruction in 146 B.C., the city was rebuilt by Rome. Neither of the letters to the Corinthians makes reference to this special status, but this is of little significance since Phil likewise mentions nothing about the status of Philippi as a *colonia* (but cf. Acts 16:12). As capital of the province of Achaia, Corinth was an important center in Greece; its harbor and commerce gave the city its prominent role. Paul stayed in Corinth for a considerable length of time and wrote 1 Thes from there (see § 24). From Acts 19 we learn that Paul proceeded from Corinth to Ephesus; apparently he wrote 1 Cor while there (cf. 1 Cor 16:8).

(2) The letter is structured loosely. Paul discusses problems pertaining to the life of a Christian community without a topical order that follows particular points of view. Paul clearly responds to several questions from Corinth; the tenor of these questions can usually be detected indirectly from the Pauline περί which introduces several sections (7:1, 25; 8:1; 12:1; 16:1). But even in the earlier chapters, Paul already deals with problems in the Corinthian community. The series is opened in 1:10 with the term σχίσματα; likewise the issues of chs 5 and 6 (ethics of sexual conduct) are popular in Corinth and Paul raises them for this reason. From the profusion of further topics, chs 13 and 15 protrude like two pillars; in these chapters Paul deals with "love" and with the "resurrection" in terms of fundamental propositions.

K. Barth (*The Resurrection of the Dead*, ET 1933) interprets all of 1 Cor on the premise of ch 15: Eschatology is the secret theme from the very beginning, thus the letter presses towards the close as its climax. In his discussion of Barth's book,

R. Bultmann suggests the contrary (*Faith and Understanding*, ET 1969, 66–94): Although the eschatological theme is indeed the center of the letter, it does not find its purest expression in ch 15 (where it is rather eclipsed by apocalyptic conceptions) as much as in ch 13 in the description of love as eschatological existence.

In the various positions Paul is taking concerning the situation in Corinth, there is indeed a unified theological position which emerges: the theology of the cross. The existence of Christians is determined by the fact that their Lord revealed himself at the cross, in lowliness rather than in glory.

2. Structural details and basic theological thought

More than any other document of early Christianity, 1 Cor provides us with insight into the problems and processes of life in a hellenistic church. An understanding of the letter can best be established by attempting to discover behind Paul's statements the difficulties which in fact existed in Corinth and then to trace them back to a possible underlying theological-ideological position.

(1) Ch 1:10–4:21: Certain groups ("factions") developed in the community, each pledging its allegiance to a religious leader, as 1:12 indicates. Some of the issues, however, are not clear: (a) Does Paul enumerate four or only three different groups? Does the claim ἐγὼ δὲ Χριστοῦ represent the slogan of a fourth faction which seeks to outdo the other three by making Christ himself the hero of their group? Or does Paul relate this statement to himself, so that it means, "I, Paul, belong to Christ," or, "This is the only viable slogan for the Christian, for he cannot fall prey to a human leader?" The wording of v 12 as well as the line of argument in v 12f. indicate that the presence of a "Christ party" in Corinth was indeed likely. (b) The second question has to do with the views which the individual groups represented. Various hypotheses have been argued by scholarship, such as the opinion that the adherents of Apollos practiced "wisdom" (cf. Acts 18:24f.), while those of Christ were enthusiasts, meaning that they boasted of a special, immediate relationship with Christ. But all of this is speculation: Paul has nothing to say about the character of the respective "parties"; rather, he criticizes their existence altogether. (c) Lietzmann has argued the point that the existence of a Petrine faction proves that Peter had personally been in Corinth. But this has little to commend itself since Paul, in ch 3f. speaks of his and Apollos' appearance in Corinth, but says nothing of Peter's appearance.

The theme in 1:18ff. is the relationship between wisdom and foolishness. Paul develops the argument that the wisdom of God is foolishness in comparison to the world's wisdom; in other words, God's deed contradicts man's self-understanding. This is further developed in 1:26ff. through the reference to the social composition of the community—and concretely of Corinth as a major city: God has chosen the lowly; he is unencumbered by human standards in his choice. "Wisdom" as a topic concludes positively in 2:6–16 with the observation that through the Spirit it is possible for man to know the wisdom of God; in other words, Paul overcomes the Corinthians' religious ideology in the realm of pneumatology.

Ch 3 addresses the essential unity of the church, with the emphasis given to the aspect of ministry. The goal of the argument is in vv 22f.: "All things are yours." In exemplary fashion Paul here interprets the Christian existence with regard to Christ, i.e., from the vantage point of Christ crucified. Ch 4 delineates the demonstration of the Pauline apostolate as an example of the Christian life in general. This is the theme that is developed later in 2 Cor 10–13.

(2) Chs 5–7: Beginning with 5:1 Paul returns to the situation in the Corinthian community in which the problem of πορνεία apparently plays a major part. Its background is apparently to be found in another principle in the Corinthians' world view: The Spirit (πνεῦμα) liberates, knowledge (γνῶσις) liberates, hence the moral norms are no longer applicable. Paul affirms the principle that "all things are permissible" (6:12). But he points out that freedom must not invalidate itself. Freedom is predicated upon salvation in Christ, and in matters of freedom, the Christian life must be in accordance with this presupposition.

In ch 7 Paul deals with marital problems, in the process of which he incorporates a word of Jesus—a rare practice for him—in his argument (vv 10f., concerning divorce). In 7:29–31 he goes beyond the immediate issue; the eschatological relationship of the free to the world is described by the ὡς μή, "possessing things as if one did not possess them."

(3) Chs 8–10 have to do with meat sacrificed to idols; this is quite obviously the second area in which the Corinthians demonstrate their Christian freedom. By their conduct with reference to the pagan cult and, at the same time, to the object of their worship, everyone is to recognize that idols are non-existent as far as Christians are concerned. In the community there are apparently some who are "strong," who place special importance on this viewpoint. If the pagan idols are nothing, they are not able to defile anyone; hence, it is appropriate to participate in meals held in pagan temples (8:10). This raised two questions for the Corinthian community: (a) Is the Christian allowed to eat meat from animals used in sacrifice? The sole issue here is the food, a substance which, for the Christian, is "unholy" in principle. (b) Is the Christian allowed to participate in meals which are pagan-sacral in character? In this case the primary question of food ultimately becomes one of participation in the pagan cult.

Here again Paul brings the particular question back to the fundamental issue: Yes, Christians do have liberty, but liberty does not exist in the ab-

stract sense; instead, it is found concretely only in the fellowship of believers. Thus freedom becomes perverted into its antithesis when it is directed against the brother in the community. If the fundamental statement
that Christ died for the brother (8:11) is true, nothing should be allowed
to transpire which might endanger the (weak) brother. Partaking of meat
sacrificed to idols, therefore, is not prohibited in principle, i.e., because
of the cultic quality of the meat, but because of consideration for the weak
brother, i.e., only for the sake of the actual offense. The shift in the point
of the argument in 10:1–22 is peculiar. Here the participation in a pagan,
cultic meal is strictly forbidden because the Christian sacrament makes
possible an exclusive relationship to the Lord, whereas the sacrifice to
idols, the participation in the pagan cult, inevitably leads to fellowship
with demons.

It cannot be overlooked that there is a certain tension between ch 8 and
10:23–11:1 on the one hand, and 10:1–22 on the other. For this reason,
some scholars suggest that these two sections, which are undoubtedly
Paul's, came from different letters. This would also facilitate the explanation of the fact that ch 9, where Paul deals with his role as an apostle,
functions like an excursus or like an interpolation. In spite of the tension
within the Pauline argument, however, it is possible to understand the
whole as an entity in terms of content, considering the concrete situation
in Corinth. Paul concurs with the fundamental position of the Corinthians; in other words, he first sides with the strong but exhorts them to
take the "weak" into consideration (ch 8). The following chapter, especially vv 19–23, is tied to what has just been said (despite the rough transition in 9:1). In the course of the exposition of 10:1ff., however, the
problem of the relationship between "inner disposition" and "outward
behavior" becomes apparent. These two elements cannot be severed in
theoretical, abstract fashion, as the Corinthians evidently practiced it.
Hence Paul's warnings follow in 10:14–22; these, of course, do not change
anything in Paul's basic position (10:23–11:1).

(4) In chs 11–14, once again responding to abuses, Paul deals with questions pertaining to the community's life together, especially its worship.
The issue in 11:17ff. is the misuse of the Lord's Supper, which the church
interprets in the sense of enthusiasm; its characteristic of a communal
meal has all but vanished while the individual's religious enlightenment
is moved into the limelight. In vv 23–26 Paul argues by appealing to the
words of institution (cf. Mk 14:22–24): The Lord's Supper is the meal of
the Lord whereby the death of Christ is proclaimed. Therefore, there is
no room for an individualistic misuse of this meal in the community.

The gifts of the Spirit, the πνευματικά, constitute the theme of chs 12
and 14. Ecstasy, understood as immediate manifestation of the Spirit, is
flourishing in Corinth. Again, Paul agrees to begin with, since he is an

ecstatic himself (14:18). But he strongly emphasizes that ecstasy alone does not at all prove the working of the Spirit. Rather, the former is to be tested critically by the objective standard of the confession (12:3).

Incidentally, 1 Cor 12:2f. shows that pagan ecstasy was also found in Corinth. At any rate, Paul believes the Corinthians to be capable of continuing to think in the categories of the mysteries.

The application of this confession means far more than a mere formal principle. By examining someone on the basis of this criterion it must come to light *who* is revered in the ecstasy, whether Christ or the spiritually elevated individual himself. Furthermore, ecstasy must also be evaluated by whether or not and by what it contributes to the "upbuilding" of the community (14:5). But when this upbuilding becomes the decisive standard, ecstasy loses its particular worth; *every* effort for the community—e.g., the work of administration as well—becomes a manifestation of the Spirit. Behind this correction of the Corinthian pneumatics, again, we find Paul's fundamental theological position: Ecstasy fails to translate the Christian into a heavenly frame of mind but instead remains under the eschatological proviso. It must be measured against the three "abiding" gifts, among which love is the greatest (13:13).

Ch 14 contains the famous pericope *"mulier taceat in ecclesia"* (vv 33b–36, let the women keep silent). There are strong indications, however, that these explanations are later insertions into the letter: They interrupt the train of thought and their content contradicts 11:2ff. where the public appearance of women in the community is presupposed. Cf. Conzelmann (see bibliography), 246f.

(5) In the fifteenth chapter of the letter, Paul gives an extensive treatment of the resurrection of the dead. The procedure in the argument is similar to that of 1 Thes 4:13ff. He discusses the issue as a commentary on the credo (vv 3–5), for he presupposes that the confession is not disputed in Corinth. Thus his discourse on the resurrection is not primarily predicated upon apocalyptic ideas; rather, he understands it in terms of interpreting the Christ event. Nevertheless, apocalyptic images and conceptions also play a part (vv 23–28; 51–53); yet Paul establishes the fundamental proviso that the heavenly existence of those raised from the dead is categorically not visual (extensively developed in vv 35–49). The apocalyptic expressions, then, yield nothing new in this matter.

Once again, the question of what position was actually held in Corinth is a special concern. Based on v 12, the assumption seems reasonable that the resurrection of the dead in general is being rejected. But is such a position even conceivable in a Christian community which believes in the resurrection of Christ? One needs to take into account, after all, that the community practices a substitutionary baptism for the dead (v 29), which means that life after death is apparently presupposed. What is the explanation for such a contradictory situation?

The following interpretations are suggested: (a) It is not simply life after death which is rejected in Corinth, but rather the resurrection of the *body*. (b) It was asserted enthusiastically in Corinth that they were already living in the state of the resurrection (cf. 4:8, as well as the characterization of the false teachers by the author of 2 Tim 2:18). To the extent, therefore, that Paul held the Corinthians to be skeptics without realizing that they rejected the resurrection on the basis of their enthusiasm, he misunderstood them. But the arguments adduced by Paul seem to favor the correctness of the second interpretation. The eschatological proviso is being rejected in Corinth; in other words, salvation is understood as an already present reality, therefore, there can be no further resurrection. Against this, Paul emphasizes that the resurrection was still future and that Christian existence takes place not in heaven but on earth.

(6) The concluding sixteenth chapter contains correspondence (personal notes) and greetings.

3. Literary criticism

The question whether the letter is to be understood as a literary unit is debated vigorously. There are indeed several areas of tension. 10:1–22 conflicts with ch 8 and 10:23ff. (see above); the position of ch 13 between ch 12 and 14 is wooden, and the transitions in 12:31 and 14:1 are clumsy in any case; in the context of the entire letter, ch 15 appears isolated. But stylistic arguments alone are not sufficient for literary operations; rather, it is essential to discover various situations behind the respective parts of the letter. Schmithals offers a few indicators in this regard. According to 1:11 Chloe's people are presently with Paul, whereas in 16:17 an altogether different group is mentioned. Following 16:17, Stephanas is currently with Paul, but according to 1:16, where he is also mentioned, one does not get the impression that he is present. 5:9ff. could represent a further point in favor of a fragment hypothesis; here Paul refers to a letter which he wrote earlier. Could it be that this "first" letter to the Corinthians was merged with another letter to become our current 1 Cor?

Dinkler, RGG IV, 18, suggests the following divisions: Letter A: 6:12–20; 9:24–10:22; 11:2–34; 12–14. Letter B: 1:1–6:11; 7:1–9:23; 10:23–11:1; 15–16. In the compilation the prescript of letter A was eliminated in order to avoid duplication.

Dinkler's relatively uncomplicated fragment hypothesis at first seems indeed quite obvious and ingenious. But the decisive presupposition for such a theory of partition is not at all a division which is as ingenious as possible; instead, the only decisive issue would be the evidence that differing external situations have to be presupposed in the various parts of the letter and that the letter cannot be explained as a homogeneous unit. Anyone arguing for a fragment hypothesis must also demonstrate how the extant letter originated. It is quite reasonable to interpret 1 Cor as an entity; various situations cannot be demonstrated convincingly.

4. Historical and theological issues

(1) It follows from 1 Cor 16:8 (cf. 15:32) that the letter was written during the stay in Ephesus (or vicinity). Whether or not it was written before or after Gal cannot be stated with certainty (see § 25 above). Kümmel, *Introduction*, 278f. (cf. p. 304) assumes that the letter was written shortly before Gal (and the latter at about the same time as 2 Cor).

(2) Which basic position is to be sought behind the Corinthian views? In 4:8 Paul characterizes their attitude with the ironic remark that they had already "come to reign" (βασιλεύειν); from this one may draw the conclusion that fundamentally they obviously were enthusiasts who considered the heavenly glory an already present reality. They appealed to the confession of the resurrection of Jesus (15:1ff.) while interpreting it in a particular way, that of enthusiasm. Christ is exalted in heaven and from this is deduced the anthropological consequence that we too, as believers who share in his glory, are already beyond this world. In the Spirit we have already left the earthly way of life behind us and in ecstasies we experience our "riches" (12:14).

Likewise, the abuses which Paul criticizes did not arise by accident, or due to negligence. Instead, they can be traced back to a deliberate ideological basis, as indicated by the slogans "everything is permissible" or "we have knowledge" (in 6:12; 10:23 and 8:1 Paul quotes his opponents' assertions). The teaching maintained in Corinth apparently sounded something like this: The knowledge we have as Christians makes us free in every respect (e.g., in the realm of sexuality), including religious matters (e.g., with regards to idols).

Schmithals expanded the enthusiasm hypothesis in a particular way: the Corinthians were not only enthusiasts but gnostics who adhered to the doctrine of a mythical redeemer (on the term gnosis, see pp. 149ff.). But the letter contains nothing that suggests that the Corinthian Christians held a truly gnostic position.

In general, caution is necessary relative to an overly precise determination of the theological position of the opponents. One cannot simply deduce the actually existing conditions from Paul's polemic, since Paul, for instance, could have been informed inadequately and might not have been accurate in determining the situation with his polemic. In any case, Paul's argument is indeed anti-enthusiastic in 1 Cor but not specifically anti-gnostic. The cross must not be ignored in favor of exaltation; wisdom is not captured in the enthusiastic upsurge, but in the recognition of the foolishness of the cross. Against the *theologia gloriae* of the Corinthians, Paul postulates the Christian *theologia crucis* (1:18–2:16) which is the common denominator throughout his argument.

Suggested exercises:

1. Analyze and exegete 1 Cor 8:1–6 (tool: Conzelmann). What is the essential meaning of γνῶσις in 1 Cor?

2. What is the meaning of the slogan πάντα ἔξεστιν (a) for the Corinthians? (b) for Paul?

3. Analyze 1 Cor 14:33–36. Is it possible to consider this pericope as Pauline within 1 Cor? What are the indicators which favor the view that this passage is an interpolation?

§ 29   2 Corinthians

Bibliography: C. K. Barrett, *The Second Epistle to the Corinthians*, HNTC, 1973; G. Bornkamm, "Die Vorgeschichte des sogenannten zweiten Korintherbriefes," *Ges. Aufs.* IV, BEvTh 53, 1971, 162–194; R. Bultmann, "Exegetische Probleme des zweiten Korintherbriefes," *Exegetica*, 1967, 298–322; idem, *The Second Letter to the Corinthians*, ET, 1985; V. P. Furnish, *II Corinthians*, AB 32A, 1984; D. Georgi, *The Opponents of Paul in Second Corinthians*, ET 1986; E. Käsemann, "Die Legitimität des Apostels," in *Das Paulusbild in der neueren deutschen Forschung*, ²1969, 475–521; H. Lietzmann (see § 28); R. P. Martin, *2 Corinthians*, WBC 40, 1986; W. Schmithals (see § 28); H. Windisch, *Der zweite Brief an die Korinther* KEK VI ⁹1924 (reprint 1970).

1. Historical presuppositions

A working knowledge of the problem of the origin of 2 Cor can be gained by comparing, first of all, the travel plans presented in 1 Cor 16 with the statements of 2 Cor 1. In 1 Cor Paul explains that he intends to reach Corinth from Ephesus via Macedonia, to collect the offering, and to send it to Jerusalem or take it there himself. In 2 Cor 1:15f., by contrast, he mentions a different plan which was not put into effect. From Asia (=Asia Minor, hence likely Ephesus) he intended to travel directly to Corinth and from there to Macedonia, and finally to reach Judea, again via Corinth. Certain developments in Corinth about which 2 Cor provides some hints have prevented the realization of this plan. The situation in the church necessitated an immediate trip to Corinth; in scholarship it is known as the so-called intermediate visit. We know from 1 Cor 4:17 and 16:10 that Paul had sent Timothy to Corinth on account of the situation there; however, his visit was obviously unsuccessful. Meanwhile a new situation had developed: a group of anti-Pauline agitators had entered the church. It is also for this reason that Paul's "intermediate visit" ended in failure; a serious confrontation ensued (cf. 2 Cor 2:1ff.; 7:12), and Paul returned to Ephesus, from where he wrote a letter "with many tears" (2:4) and sent Titus in order to settle the crisis. While Titus was still in Corinth, Paul travelled to Macedonia (2:12f.) where they met one another. Titus brought him good news: The community once again stands with Paul (7:5ff.). As a sign of reconciliation Paul wrote 2 Cor (or a part of it, if the latter is to be viewed as a composite of several letters [see below]).

2. Structure of the letter

The letter's main theme accords with its occasion. It has to do with Paul's apostolate and its paradoxical "glory" (ch 4). Time and again Paul defends himself against accusations levelled against him (1:13f.; 3:1; 4:2f.; 5:11ff.; 6:3ff.; 7:2; 10–13). The overall structure of 2 Cor, however, is obscure and invites attempts at literary dissection (see below). Nevertheless, the individual divisions can be delineated fairly clearly. After prescript and proem, Paul immediately goes on the defensive (1:12–2:4) by explaining the change in his travel plans. In 2:5–13 he refers to the events in Corinth which led to the writing of the present letter. However, in 2:14 this train of thought is interrupted. He commences an apologetic of the apostolate which does not end until 7:4 (and in 7:5 he resumes the description of the prehistory of the letter). The discussion of the apostolate is sustained by the argument that the δόξα of the apostle is paradoxical. Suffering for the sake of the task (4:7–5:10) is a necessary part of the divine commission (2:14–4:6). In 5:11–6:13 he summarizes both of these: God's mandate, the ministry of reconciliation, the proclamation of the gospel, leads directly into suffering and persecution (6:3–10); yet, precisely herein is the paradoxical "power" of the apostle as servant of God made manifest. 6:14–7:1 interrupts the continuity: this is a general and peculiarly formulated warning against fellowship with unbelievers. In 7:2–4 Paul returns to the previous topic of 6:11–13. In 7:5–16 he describes his joy concerning the settlement of the conflict with the Corinthians.

Chs 8 and 9 are two sequences dealing with the continuation of the collection for the church in Jerusalem; likewise, joy and gratitude are the dominant emphasis here. All the more surprising is the sudden turn in ch 10 where Paul defends himself very vehemently against personal attacks which have been voiced in Corinth. On his part, Paul remonstrates against his opponents by pointing to his accomplishments and his suffering (chs 11 and 12). Finally, he announces his third visit (13:1) which is clearly meant to be a threat. Thus the markedly peaceful conclusion in 13:11–13 comes as a total surprise.

3. Historical and theological issues

As in 1 Cor, the decisive issue for the understanding of the letter is the question of the opponents with whom Paul is dealing. Are they identical in both letters (so Schmithals) or has a new group emerged which has come from outside the church (so Bornkamm and Georgi)? Is it conceivable that these new opponents are gnostics?

2 Cor 5 proves that they hold to the same enthusiastic eschatology, the correction of which Paul had already emphasized in 1 Cor 15 by means of the eschatological proviso of the "not yet" of the final salvation. Paul uses this argument in 5:7 by referring to the alternative of believing vs. seeing. As in the case of 1 Cor, it cannot be established that the opponents maintain specifically gnostic ideas. On the other hand, it is clear that they deny Paul's apostolic office on the basis of the argument that he could not demonstrate any corresponding spiritual accomplishments (10:10). The opponents place considerable emphasis on the fact that they are Jews (11:22); however, they do not make any Judaizing claims, so that they have nothing in common with the opponents Paul fought in Gal. Therefore, Käsemann's assumption is hardly appropriate; he argues that the opponents were official representatives from Jerusalem who endeavored to keep the principle of office and tradition in high regard. In any case, the theology which they advocated in Corinth does not correspond with the position of James (cf. Gal 2; see p. 172 above). It is important to note that the events in Corinth apparently did not impair, let alone sever, the relationship between Paul and Jerusalem.

Paul employs every means of polemics against the opponents. They accept money (2:17; 11:20; compare this with 12:16–18, where Paul has to defend himself against the identical accusation—this seems to be one of the consistent issues in the polemic); they want to make a good impression in Corinth by means of letters of recommendation (3:1; 10:12, 18), and they claim to belong to Christ in a special, exclusive way (5:16; 10:7; 11:23). Against their claim to the office of an apostle (11:5, 13; 12:11) and against their appeal to Judaism and to Jerusalem (11:22), Paul derides them as "superapostles" (11:5; 12:11) who infiltrate foreign mission territory and are "boasting" (10:12f., 15f.). Then Paul moves to the counter offensive: They are lying apostles (11:13), servants of Satan who proclaim a different God and a different Christ (11:4). He explains that he, too, could demonstrate being a pneumatic and he, too, is a miracle worker and ecstatic (12:12; 12:1ff.); but he rejects predicating his position and labor upon his personal abilities and accomplishments and making them the object of his preaching. His true position is brought to light in the way he connects the paradoxical praise of self (11:16ff.) with the catalog of suffering (*Peristasenkatalog*; 11:23ff.). His life, as well as his—successful!—

ministry, is lived out under the sign of the Lord's strength which is being fulfilled in weakness (12:9).

4. Literary problems

The lack of uniformity in the letter, which is conspicuous even at first glance, has spawned numerous literary hypotheses.

(1) There is a break between 2:13 and 2:14 which not only includes the train of thought (in which case the break might be explained psychologically) but in a primary sense also the assumed situation.

Whereas the critical situation is apparently viewed in *retrospect* in the first part, concluding with 2:13, the next part, namely 2:14–7:4 (on 6:14–7:1 see below), can only be understood against the backdrop of the still existing conflict. But in 7:5, where we find another break in the immediate context, the description from 2:12f. is continued; Paul came to Macedonia to await Titus, upon whose arrival there is great joy.

In light of these findings, the question must be asked whether 2:14–7:4 constitutes a part of an earlier letter which has been inserted into a later one.

(2) In the essentials, chs 8 and 9 are parallel. Both chapters begin abruptly; each comprises a self-contained description of the collection. However, while the Macedonian communities are lauded as models for the Achaians in 8:1, the churches in Achaia are presented as models for the Macedonians in 9:2. Could it be, then, that these two chapters belong to different letters?

(3) Chs 10–13 stand in sharp relief to what preceded; this is true not only because of the abrupt opening in 10:1, but also on account of their overall drift. These four chapters are a unit of their own, but they do not fit the situation after the reconciliation which is clearly presupposed in 7:5–16. On the contrary, Paul here is engaged in a fierce battle against hostile intrigues. We may assume that this is the "letter of tears" (or part of it) mentioned in 2:4; moreover one may ask whether the segment of 2:14–7:4 did not also belong to this letter of tears. Of course, against this the objection is raised that 2:14ff. requires a situation different from that in 10–13. Whereas Paul still hopes to win the community back in 2:14ff., he has given up this hope in ch 10ff.; hence these chapters are to be viewed as a part of yet another letter. Nothing definite can be decided on this matter. It is clear, however, that chs 10–13 cannot have come from the same letter that contained 1:1–2:13 and 7:5ff. Favoring this assumption is also the fact that in 12:14, 13:1, 10 Paul threatens to come to Corinth shortly for a *third* visit and that he will then no longer spare the opponents. However, based on 1:15f., 2:1f. he does not seem to anticipate an imminent trip to Corinth.

Further evidence that the present letter is no longer extant in its original form is found in the fact that certain names must have been expunged from 8:18, 22; 9:3 (cf. 9:5); 12:18. After the mention of the "brother" in the present text, one needs to add an "NN." The editors of 2 Cor were quite obviously interested in suppressing the name or names originally cited.

(4) Kümmel, *Introduction* 290ff., opposes all theories of division. Since 12:18, as much as 7:5, is a retrospective glance to the visit of Titus, it is quite feasible that both sections are part of one and the same letter. Since the event described in 2:3ff. is not taken up in 10–13 (although that would have been expected), and conversely, since the church's reaction to the extremely heavy attack of 10–13 is not mentioned in 2:3ff. and 7:8ff., it is hardly conceivable that these chapters at one time were part of a self-contained "intermediate letter." But these are psychological arguments from silence; Kümmel actually does not explain the breaks within the letter.

(5) Anyone who argues for one of the hypotheses of division must indeed explain how the present, strange construction of the letter with its polemical concluding section came about. To begin with, the present "letter" gives the impression that Paul had failed completely in Corinth. Hence one might question whether the Corinthian church, which later was proud to claim Paul as its founder, was indeed interested in compiling several Pauline letters or fragments of letters from their archives in such a way that the loudest dissonance between them and Paul remained as the conclusion. Bornkamm takes up this argument only to dismiss it, arguing that anyone who reads Paul's failure out of the concluding chapters of the extant 2 Cor has succumbed to a modern optical illusion. The generations following Paul were shaped by their battle against heresy. One of the crucial means used in this battle was to preserve the apostle's legacy, to impress his image upon their memory, and to highlight especially his suffering and his battle against false teachers (cf. the Pastorals). It is this picture which is etched in the present shape of 2 Cor. This is the decisive manner in which Paul overcame his enemies at that time.

(6) A further literary-critical problem is presented in the pericope consisting of 6:14–7:1. Not only does it rupture the context (note how well 7:2 follows 6:13; see above), but it also is non-Pauline, especially in matters of style and in matters of content as well. It represents a dualistically defined paraenesis, reminiscent of the Qumran texts with regards to terminology and content. This pericope is to be viewed as a probable interpolation; evidently the editor took it to be a Pauline polemic against the false teachers and a continuation of the exhortations in 6:11–13. At any rate, the existence of an extensive gloss, such as this, underscores the character of 2 Cor as a "conglomerate of letters."

Suggested Exercise:

Exegete 2 Cor 3:4–18. Tools: M. Rissi, *Studien zum 2. Korintherbrief*, AThANT 56, 1969, 13–41; Ph. Vielhauer, "Paulus und das AT," in *Oikodome. Aufsätze zum NT* II, 1979, 196–228, esp. 210–213; H. Windisch (see bibliography), 107–131; R. Bultmann (see bibliography), 75–98.

Control questions: How does Paul use the OT? Does Paul establish a temporal ("salvation-history") connection between the Old and the New Covenant?

What eschatological perspective is behind this pericope?

§ 30 Romans

Bibliography: G. Bornkamm, "Der Römerbrief als Testament des Paulus," *Ges. Aufs.* IV, BEvTh 53, 1971, 120–139; C. E. B. Cranfield, *The Epistle to the Romans*, 2 vols., ICC, 1975, 1979; E. Käsemann, *Commentary on Romans*, ET 1980; G. Klein, "Der Abfassungszweck des Römerbriefes," *Ges. Aufs.*, BEvTh 50, 1969, 129–144; H. Lietzmann, *An die Römer*, HNT 8, [5]1971; P. S. Minear, *The Obedience of Faith: The Purposes of Paul in the Epistle to the Romans*, SBT Second Series 19, 1971; H. Schlier, *Der Römerbrief*, HThK VI, 1977; W. Schmithals, *Der Römerbrief als historisches Problem*, StNT 9, 1975; U. Wilckens, *Der Brief an die Römer*, EKK VI/1–3, 1978–1982.

1. Problem and structure

(1) Romans is Paul's most important letter as well as the most significant theological document of Christendom. It is the only letter of Paul addressed to a church which he himself did not establish (on Col, see p. 200ff. below), which is to say that in doing so Paul oversteps his self-imposed limits.

Rom especially demonstrates the dialectical elements of the diatribe; in many places it has more in common with a theological tract than with a letter. Yet, against this common characterization it is argued that some of the important themes of Christian doctrine, such as ecclesiology, are bypassed in Rom, while others, such as eschatology, are barely touched on, let alone developed. It is incorrect, therefore, to accord this letter a "foundational" character. But this argument is inappropriate. It is correct to say that Rom is not a dogmatic compendium in the modern sense of the term; nevertheless, in matters of layout and accomplishment it far exceeds the other letters. This is made particularly clear in a comparison with Gal, where Paul deals with the same subject matter, but not nearly with the same precision and thoroughness.

(2) At the same time, these observations point to the possibilities of finding access to Rom.

(a) It is possible to begin with the main theme of justification and to interpret the letter consistently from this point of reference. This approach would help to understand why Rom became the most significant biblical document in the Reformation (cf. Luther's lectures on Romans and especially his preface to Rom in the German Bible) and why the first more or less systematic summary of the Reformation teaching, Melanchthon's *"loci,"* was based on the major concepts of Rom.

(b) It is possible to begin with Gal and to compare the two letters with one another. At first one notices an analogous arrangement: A. Doctrinal part, Rom 1–11 (paralleled by Gal 1–4); B. Ethical part, Rom 12–15 (paralleled by Gal 5–6); the concluding chapter of Rom 16 must remain outside our purview (see pp. 197f. below). A more detailed examination, however, points up important elements in Rom that are without parallel in Gal, such as the exposition of the ὀργὴ θεοῦ in 1:18–3:20, the portrayal of the existence of the justified in the world (Rom 5–8), and the discussion concerning the relationship between God and Israel (Rom 9–11).

(c) The structure of the first part of the letter (chs 1–8) is subject to debate; some exegetes divide it as follows: chs 1–5—justification, chs 6–8—sanctification. Yet, the crucial turning-point clearly comes after 4:25; the portrayal of justification by faith is followed by the delineation of the consequences of justification (this emerges clearly in 5:1). The pattern of justification-sanctification does not so much accord with Pauline theology as with post-Reformation dogmatics.

2. Structural details and basic theological thought

(1) Both the prescript and the proem already hold considerable theological importance. 1:3f. represents a christological expansion of the prescript and in 1:16f. the proem ends in the formulation of the overall theme of the entire letter: the righteousness of God is made manifest in the gospel.

Subsequently, this theme unfolds in two directions: first negatively, the ὀργὴ θεοῦ in 1:18–3:20, then positively, the δικαιοσύνη θεοῦ in 3:21–31.

ὀργή does not denote "wrath" as an emotion of God, as much as it means judgment; this is even apparent from the observation that Paul never speaks of God as angry, but always only in a substantival sense of his ὀργή. The reference to the ἡμέρα ὀργῆς in Rom 2:5 (cf. 1 Thes 1:10), therefore, is to the day of God's judgment.

It is important to note that for Paul, "righteousness" and "judgment" are not synonyms but opposites. Paul does not say, "Because he is righteous, God judges men," but he says instead, "God's judgment comes upon sin and upon the sinner, but God demonstrates his righteousness by unconditionally extending his grace to man." Hence, "righteousness" is not an abstract concept but describes salvation in a positive way: The righteousness of God is demonstrated in that he declares righteous (that is, he justifies). In this connection, the difference in terminology between 1:18 and 1:17 is striking: Whereas the judgment is revealed "from heaven," righteousness is revealed in "the message of the Gospel."

(2) Paul deals with the topic of sin in 1:18–32 and shows clearly that immorality, which is labelled "sin" in the popular Christian sense, is actually the *judgment* of sin. Sin itself is a particular attitude toward God, the confusion of creator and creature, the worship of the world and of its elements as divine entities; immorality is the consequence of this sin (v 26ff.).

In ch 2 Paul defends the position that works are the *only* premise upon which judgment will be meted out (2:6); in view of his doctrine of justification by grace alone, this is a rather surprising statement at first sight. The contradiction is cleared up, however, if the conception of judgment is tied in strictly with the doctrine of justification. Precisely because the judgment is exclusively based upon works, man is dependent upon grace and cannot appeal to any works whatsoever before God.

Suggested exercises:

1. Read Rom 1:18ff. and 1 Cor 1:18ff. in parallel. What are the objective theological agreements? Tools: commentaries.

2. Is it plausible to consider Rom 1:18ff. as a basis for a "natural theology"? The latter begins with the presupposition that man is capable of knowing God through nature (rather than through revelation alone). Which viewpoint does Paul represent? Tools: G. Bornkamm, "Die Offenbarung des Zornes Gottes. Röm 1–3," *Ges. Aufs.* I, 9–33; R. Bultmann, "The Problem of 'Natural Theology,' " *Faith and Understanding*, ET 1969, 313–331.

(3) The presentation of 1:18–3:8 is followed by the conclusion that Gentiles and Jews alike are subject to judgment (3:9–20); thereupon follows the positive assertion of righteousness by faith in 3:21ff. The premise for the Pauline argument is to be sought in the pre-Pauline formula of 3:25f., which Paul expands in characteristic fashion with the important introductory expression χάρις in v 24 and with the plainly deliberate insertion of διὰ πίστεως into the formula itself (v 25). Here Paul clarifies what he means by "righteousness of God": God is righteous and he makes righteous, i.e., he declares righteous the one who believes in Jesus (v 26). This series of arguments concludes with the foundational confession εἰς ὁ θεός, which is both Jewish and Christian (v 30).

But Paul does not base his doctrine of justification exclusively on the confession; he adds the "evidence from Scripture." Abraham, too, was declared righteous because of his faith (Rom 4; cf. Gal 3). The focal point of the chapter is found in the formula of v 25, the content of which is then explained in chs 5–8 and is introduced with the fundamental declaration that, as people who have been made righteous through faith, we have peace with God. Notice the arc which Paul describes here: The last few verses of ch 8 refer back to the beginning of ch 5 ("circular composition"), which further points to the correctness of the structure proposed above.

Rom 5:1 presents an interesting text-critical problem: The majority of witnesses read ἔχωμεν, rather than ἔχομεν. If the former is correct, we have here an example of the indicative-imperative pattern (that is, of justification-sanctification). We are justified, therefore we *ought* to maintain peace with God. The context indicates, however, that the reading which is attested by fewer manuscripts is the "better" reading; chs 5–8 continue to deal with the gift of salvation and not with the ethical consequences; besides, "peace with God" is not the subject of paraenetic demand. Hence the reading εἰρήνην ἔχομεν is to be preferred for reasons of subject matter (see p. 22f.).

(4) Of course, the declaration that we have peace with God must also be established against the external facts; for sin and death continue to rule in the world which is seemingly untouched by the salvific event. Paul addresses this problem as follows:

(a) In 5:1–11 he introduces the idea of hope in the framework of the triad of faith-hope-love. In this connection, attention needs to be given to the "chain" in 5:3ff.: It does not say we are able to endure θλίψεις through hope; instead, Paul states that it is θλῖψις which brings about hope through endurance.

In 5:12–21 Paul is in the realm of mythological thought. Death is understood as inherited, that is, as doom on account of Adam's fall. But the mythological idea is eliminated at the point where it is crucial. The fall is not traced back to a mythological cause; thus, Paul evades the notion of inescapable original sin. Death came upon all men on account of Adam's sin; nevertheless, all have sinned (v 12).

(b) In contrast, Paul restates positively in ch 6 what he has already said; freedom from sin is appropriated by baptism. In this context, baptism is interpreted with the aid of the credal statements: Christ died and has been raised, hence the one baptized has likewise died "with Christ" and *will* (notice the shift to the future tense) be raised "together with him." The expression συζήσομεν αὐτῷ in v 8 has the same function as the presentation in 1 Cor 15; the eschatological proviso is thereby clarified. The ultimate salvation is not a present reality—it is yet to come.

(c) Ch 7 outlines the idea of freedom from the law, which actually directs man to death, for the law leads him into contradiction with itself. Paul's use of the first person singular in 7:7ff. is peculiar. Is he pointing to himself thereby, in a type of personal testimony? Or is the pronoun ἐγώ to be understood rhetorically, meaning that Paul intends it to address all people? Connected to this question is a second one, that of whether the "I" here denotes the pre-Christian or the Christian self. For the Reformers, 7:14ff. provided evidence for their theological argument that the Christian is always *simul iustus et peccator*, that is to say, even the believer continues to be tempted. But 7:25a and especially ch 8 indicate that Paul has in mind man "under the law," hence, man before faith— every individual at that, not only himself. Even when this text is used in preaching, the crucial thing is the realization that Paul does not describe the subjective perceptions of man living under the law; on the contrary, such an individual may feel quite comfortable and does not necessarily sense anything of the conflict described in 7:7ff. This, in fact, is Paul's argument, that man under the law actually does not know his true situation at all; rather, only the Gospel uncovers that situation for him.

(d) The issues treated thus far are summarized in ch 8. Christian liberty is the life in the Spirit. 8:29f. touches on the topic of predestination, which is further developed in chs 9–11. The hymnic intensification of the concluding statements in vv 31–39 is noteworthy. These verses show clearly that the Christian does not leave the world behind him in mystical or ecstatic surge and thus effectively denies sin and death. Instead, Paul begins with the premise that God's grace and love are experienced through the encounter with death and peril and are held fast by faith (on this, cf. H. Conzelmann, *Outline of the Theology of the NT*, § 35).

(5) Chs 9–11 present a new portrayal of the doctrine of justification, especially as it pertains to Israel's existence; 9:18 contains the notion of double predestination and this, ultimately, is the basic issue of all three chapters. They articulate that the doctrine of predestination is not human speculation about God's secret will, but it represents the other side of the doctrine of grace and means that the sinner receives the grace of God without merit. Thus Israel will also be saved, though it is now hardened (11:33–36). The pivotal point of this passage is the statement that Christ is the end of the law—not in the sense of abstract salvation history but concretely "for everyone who believes" (10:4).

(6) Chs 12–15 contain the paraenesis. 12:1f. formulates the "ethical principle" which E. Käsemann has correctly interpreted under the concept of "serving God in the world's daily life." Style and content of 12:3ff. are in keeping with traditional proverbial ethics and, like the Pauline paraenesis as a whole, this section offers nothing radically new in comparison with the average ethical conviction in contemporary philosophy. Whereas the Christian's relationship to the state, understood as "authority," is located in 13:1–7, vv 8–14 emphasize the relationship between ethics and eschatology. Chs 14 and 15 need to be read in context with 1 Cor 8–10, keeping in mind that in Rom Paul does not argue polemically, based on actual situations; hence his argument is also less combative. Beginning with 15:14, the correspondence proper focuses on the planned visit in Rome.

Suggested exercises:

1. Rom is replete with confessional formulas (1:3f.; 3:24ff.; 4:25; ch 6; ending of ch 8; 10:9; 14:1ff.). What functions do these formulas fulfill within the letter as a whole? What is their significance in the context of Paul's theology in general?

Tools: H. Conzelmann, *Outline of the Theology of the NT,* 186f.; K. Wegenast, *Das Verständnis der Tradition bei Paulus und in den Deuteropaulinen,* WMANT 8, 1962, 70–82.

Note: In each case one needs to observe the immediate, as well as the broader context.

2. Exegete Rom 13:1–7. This pericope is frequently used as evidence for Paul's conservative political conviction. In this connection, interpreters often make the mistake of divorcing these statements from their historical context and applying them directly to contemporary situations. Tool: E. Käsemann, "Grundsätzliches zur Interpretation von Römer 13," *Ges. Aufs.* II, 204–222.

3. Literary-critical problems

In contrast to the Corinthian correspondence, there are but a few unsolved literary-critical problems in Rom.

(1) The list of greetings in ch 16 is unique on account of its length. How did it come about? What is its significance? Scholarship offers two solutions: (a) Since Paul wrote to a church with which he was not familiar, he listed all the names of those he and his fellow-workers knew in the Roman church. (b) The list of greetings in Rom is actually a fragment of an otherwise lost letter addressed to Ephesus; especially the names of Aquila and Prisc(ill)a point in this direction. Furthermore, it is highly unlikely that Paul would have directed his polemic of v 17ff. to a church unknown to him. But the reference to Aquila and Prisca in this context is not conclusive; after all, they came from Rome and may have returned to this city after the death of the Emperor Claudius, whose edict against the Jews drove them from Rome. There is no unequivocally clear case for excising ch 16 from Rom.

(2) Some exegetes consider some references to be later additions (glosses); Bultmann singles out 7:25b; 8:1 and 2:1; 13:5; 2:16 and 6:17b as secondary glosses. It is recommended to read the respective essay critically (*Exegetica,* 278–284).

According to Schmithals (see bibliography), apart from some codicils (e.g., 5:1–11 13:1–7), Rom consists of three letters. By means of letter A (1–11; 15:8–13) Paul intended to establish a church according to his model among the Christians in Rome; via letter B (essentially 12–15) he announces his visit to Rome and discusses the subject of "the strong and the weak;" 16:1–20 is a letter addressed to Ephesus. But the topic of "the church" is not mentioned at all in "letter A"; besides, the structure of Rom clearly parallels that of Gal. Most of all, Schmithals does not show the plausibility of why a redactor should have combined "letter A" with "letter B."

4. External conditions relative to the composition of Romans

The passage in 15:14ff. provides some important information. Paul deems his work in the eastern part of the empire to be completed because the communities are established to such an extent that they are able to continue to exist on their own. At the back of this is Paul's understanding of missions. The issue for Paul is not the salvation of a few individual souls but "world mission." The decisive matter is not Paul's personal effort but the proclamation of the gospel everywhere. Therefore, Paul now considers himself to be in a position to leave the east and move his realm of ministry to Spain (rather than to Rome!—he does not work where there are already Christian communities). En route he desires to visit the capital and, of course, to preach there (1:9–13). Prior to this he wants to bring the collection to Jerusalem. In this connection, he expresses a gloomy prognosis in 15:30f. which in fact proves to be true: He reaches Rome only as a prisoner (cf. Acts 21ff.).

Therefore, Rom was written shortly before the trip to Jerusalem, during Paul's last stay in Corinth (cf. Acts 20:2f.). Perhaps it is the last extant letter from the apostle.

5. Tendency and purpose

Rom is more emphatically theoretical than Gal and both 1 and 2 Cor. However, there is a polemic to be found all the same. In 2:1ff. Paul resists the "critic" who argues that he is able to hold his own before God; in 3:1ff. and similarly in 6:1ff., he rebuts the attacks against his doctrine of justification which are based upon deliberate misunderstandings. It cannot be recognized clearly, however, whether Paul refers to actually voiced criticism, or to a fictitious criticism which is possible in principle. The scholarly attempts at explanation are diverse:

(a) Paul recounts his discussion with the Jews, or more correctly, with Judaism. He is concerned with refuting Jewish objection to his teaching (cf. 7:1). (b) Paul debates Jewish *Christianity* which wants to adhere to the law in principle (on the concept of "Jewish Christianity," see p. 226f. below). 7:1 would fit this explanation as well. (c) Paul does not at all argue against Jewish or Jewish-Christian opposition; instead, he argues against libertinism, against which he has to defend himself because he is considered antinomian because of his teaching on the law. Therefore he rejects the anti-Jewish polemic (3:1ff.) and stresses the ethical consequences arising from baptism (6:1ff.).

All three hypotheses have the drawback that they claim to know more than they do know. Paul's explanations are fundamental in character; nothing can be recognized of a polemic which refers to a concrete—much less real—situation. We know very little about the Christian community in Rome at that time. We also do not know how precise Paul's knowledge of this church was; there are no concrete reference points in this regard. It is necessary, therefore, to desist from establishing theories with too many details.

Still, some of the conditions in the church can be discerned: Whereas a part of the community is of Jewish origin (4:1, 12; 7:1; 9:10), most of the Roman Christians are non-Jews (1:5, 13; 6:19; 9:3ff.; 10:1ff.; 11:13ff.; 15:15f.). From this it has frequently been deduced that the "strong" in ch 14f. are Gentile Christians, while the "weak" who insisted on adhering to food regulations, were Jewish Christians. It would then be possible to infer further that Paul actually was relatively well informed about the tensions within the church, and yet chose not to intervene directly and explicitly. But already a comparison with 1 Cor 8–10 indicates that the equation "weak" = Jewish Christians is not permissible. It may indeed be necessary to be satisfied with the assumption that Paul's reasoning is as propositional in this case as it is in the development of his doctrine of justification and that he refers to and refutes hypothetical Jewish as well as Jewish-Christian arguments against his teaching.

Suggested exercise for advanced students:

Rom 9–11 is of special significance for scholarship. Some exegetes view this section as a salvation-historical sketch which traverses the entire panorama from the Exodus out of Egypt to the final, future conversion of Israel. Other exegetes see in the example of Israel in Rom 9–11 the unfolding of the doctrine of justification (cf. N. Walter, "Zur Interpretation von Römer 9–11," *ZTkK* 81, 1984, 172–195). For the Reformers, this was the *locus classicus* of the doctrine of predestination.

It is helpful to work through these three chapters with the aid of a commentary and one of the monograph studies (such as U. Luz, *Das Geschichtsverständnis des Paulus*, 1968, or H. Hübner, *Gottes Ich und Israel*, 1984).

II. DEUTEROPAULINE LETTERS

Bibliography: K. Aland, "The Problem of Anonymity and Pseudonomity in Christian Literature of the First Two Centuries," *JTS* n.s. 12 (1961): 39–49; H. R. Balz, "Anonymität und Pseudepigraphie im Urchristentum," *ZThK* 66 (1969) 403–436; H. J. Holtzmann, *Kritik der Epheser- und Kolosserbriefe*, 1872; A. Lindemann, *Paulus im ältesten Christentum*, BHTh 58, 1979, 36–49, 114–149.

Preliminary remark

The letters transmitted under the name of Paul, presented in § 31–33, are surely unauthentic and are designated as "deuteropauline" for this reason. Nevertheless, the Pauline authorship is assumed hypothetically in the respective chapters for reasons of methodology. Cf. also p. 32ff.

§ 31   Colossians

Bibliography: J. Lähnemann, *Der Kolosserbrief. Komposition, Situation und Argumentation*, StNT 3, 1971; A. Lindemann, *Der Kolosserbrief*, ZBK NT 10, 1983; E. Lohse (see § 27); E. Schweizer, *The Letter to the Colossians*, ET 1982.

1. Problem and structure

(1) Colossae is situated in the Lycus valley (Asia Minor), near Laodicea and Hierapolis (Col 4:13). These churches were not established by Paul, but by Epaphras, as Col 1:7 seems to convey. The relationship between these churches appears to have been quite intimate; at any rate, Col 4:16 indicates that the letters addressed to them were to be circulated among them.

(2) The external structure of Col is very clear: Chs 1–2 contain instruction (and polemic) and chs 3–4 paraenesis.

(a) The proem is clearly marked only at its beginning (1:3); its primary ending is in v 8, but then it extends farther to v 20 without any indication of a content-related turning-point. There seems to be a confessional formula in 1:13f.: Salvation comes about by transposing the Christian into the kingdom of the Son and through forgiveness of sins. One notices the non-Pauline terminology used. Paul does not speak of the "kingdom of the Son" but always of the "kingdom of God" (but cf. Eph 5:5); likewise the phrase ἄφεσις ἁμαρτιῶν is not Pauline (but cf. Eph 1:7). The formula represents the introduction to the hymn cited in vv 15–20, in which Christ is described as the "image" of God (cf. 2 Cor 4:4). The concept of "image" in this context does not merely denote likeness but mode of existence. Hence this is a hypostatic concept.

The concept of hypostasis denotes the personification of a characteristic or of a specific virtue of a deity in which the hypostasis itself becomes a divine being. We are familiar with the hypostatization of OT-Jewish wisdom. To begin with, it is the wisdom of Yahweh which becomes evident in creation but is then described as God's primal creature and as his assistant in creation (Sir 24; Prov 8:22–31). On this issue as a whole, cf. Ringgren, RGG III, 504ff.

According to the hymn, the work of redemption is understood as establishing the reconciliation of the world; the revealer-redeemer is the mediator in creation and the cosmos is construed as his body. The author of Col, possibly Paul, has corrected the text in such a way that the church, rather than the cosmos, is the body of Christ the redeemer (1:18). This is in keeping with Pauline ecclesiology, as it is also encountered in 1 Cor and Rom.

1:24–2:5 draws the picture of the suffering apostle and, at the same time, exhorts to steadfastness in the faith. 1:24–27 is a good example of the stylistic peculiarities of this letter: intertwined, complicated sentences, as well as a sharp increase in the linking of genitives.

In 2:6–15 the author develops the nature of Christian existence which is "in Christ" (v 10f.); here the allusion is particularly to baptism, by means of which Christians share in the death and resurrection of Christ (v 12f.).

2:16–23 contains a solid polemic against false teachers; in terms of content and language, however, the details are quite obscure. In any case, it is not possible to recognize the particular teaching against which the author is directing his comments.

(b) The paraenesis begins with a deliberate paradox. Precisely because Christians are resurrected, they are to seek what is "in heaven above" (3:1). This means that, in spite of the "resurrection," the earth, not heaven, is the place of action and of faith. 3:5–17 lists a catalog of virtues and vices (see p. 102f. above), each containing five elements. This particular arrangement stems from Iranian religion. Likewise of Iranian origin is the peculiar conception that man's vices or virtues are his members, that is to say, he is literally comprised of vices and virtues and his existence is built upon deeds.

In Iranian religion this is expressed mythologically with the picture of the heavenly double which man will encounter after his death and with which he will then become identical; after all, that double is his own self.

3:18–4:1 constitutes a series of household admonitions (*Haustafeln*), similar to those found in Eph 5:22–6:9, as well as in 1 Pet 2:18–3:7. The norms contained in these admonitions are not specifically Christian, rather, like Christian ethics in general, they come from their environment, especially from the ethics of popular philosophy (cf. p. 103 above).

The close of the letter contains greetings (4:7ff.).

2. *Stylistic and theological distinctives: The question of authorship*

(1) It has already been mentioned that Col has some special stylistic features. Of course, in a detailed analysis only those references are subject to evaluation which the author himself—hence possibly Paul—has formulated. The hymn of 1:15–20, for instance, cannot be included in the evaluation for the same methodological reasons as those governing the exclusion of the hymn of Phil 2:6–11 in the evaluation of the style in Phil. There are indeed linguistic peculiarities to be identified even in the pericopae which are undoubtedly shaped by the author himself. The following serve as examples: the enormous expansion of compound sentences (1:9–12), the combination of several substantives with related meaning (1:27), and the increase in participial phrases which is in keeping with the liturgical style (1:3–14; 2:12f.). It would be wrong, however, to deny Pauline authorship of the letter based solely on features of style; change in an author's style is a fairly common phenomenon in antiquity.

(2) The essential theological relationship between Col and the (remaining) letters of Paul is far more pertinent in terms of the question of authenticity. While the description of the church as "body of Christ" (see above) occurs in Col, a comparison with 1 Cor, for instance, shows that the understanding of the concept has been modified. Thus the "body," the church, becomes attached to Christ, the "head," a concept which has not been stated in the earlier letters. Yet, even this shift need not signify an absolute break; it is possible for Paul to have developed his ideas further. More conspicuous is the observation that the common soteriology of the church occurs more frequently in Col; one finds such concepts as "forgiveness of sins" (1:14) as well as a greater emphasis on the idea of the propitiatory death of Christ (1:22) than (elsewhere) in Paul. But this, too, is not radically new; Paul uses formulas elsewhere, as in Rom 1:3f. for instance, which are not fully in accordance with his own theology.

(3) Of special significance, however, is the essential eschatological reorientation. For instance, the term "hope" is not understood temporally as a forward look into the future; rather, in Col hope is construed spatially as an upward glance. Hope is stored up in heaven (1:5). In the development of the baptismal understanding in 2:6–15, first of all, certain associations with Rom 6:1–11 are not to be overlooked (in addition, there is a related passage in Eph 2:4–10). But a study of the concept of the resurrection contained in these verses indicates some clear differences over against the text in Rom. All in all, several stages can be distinguished in the development of the tradition:

(a) At the outset there is the confession, "Christ died and has been raised."

(b) In Rom 6 Paul comments on this by saying that in baptism, Christians died with Christ and will be raised with Christ (future tense!).

(c) In Col 2 this statement is modified by moving the expression of the resurrection from the future tense to the past tense: We did die with Christ and have already been raised. (A fourth stage emerges in Eph where the reference to dying with Christ has been eliminated entirely and the only remaining statement is that of the resurrection which has already occurred, Eph 2:5ff.). Those exegetes who insist on the authenticity of Col want to explain the obvious difference between Col and Rom by arguing that the new ideas need to be understood in the context of the actual polemic of the letter. Since the opponents must be met on their own turf, Paul meets them halfway. But this argument ignores the fact that it is precisely the pericope of 2:6–15 which is completely void of all polemic.

The most striking peculiarities are consistently found in the non-polemical sections (1:9ff.; 1:24–29; 2:6–15; 3:1ff.). It may be true to say about the eschatology of Col in general that the prominent feature is no longer the temporal, but the spatial aspect; the theme is no longer present and future but world and Überwelt. In a merely formal way the anticipation of the parousia is still noticeable (3:4), but it no longer determines the world view—nor the paraenesis. The watchword now is, "Seek that which is above" (3:1), and the theological basis is that we have already been raised (2:6ff.).

From all of the above, we may indeed draw the conclusion that in all probability, Col was not written by Paul. A number of indicators, however, such as the connection with Rom 6 and the ecclesiastical relationship, support the notion that the author is part of Paul's environment and that he possibly even was one of his immediate disciples. Likewise, the names cited in the letter point to the vicinity of Paul, as does the fact that the founding of the communities addressed (Colossae and Laodicea) can be traced back to Ephesus, Paul's mission center.

3. Theological opposition

The obscure passage 2:16-23 allows only marginal conclusions regarding the teaching held by the opponents. Apparently they claim that one should venerate the elements of the world (as did the opponents in Gal 4:8-10) as personal beings (demons, powers, 2:10, 15, 18). They seem to insist that these beings are elements of the cosmic Christ. From this type of cosmology they derive certain cultic obligations which are applicable to Christians, such as the celebration of cosmic-cyclical festival days, the adherence to rigid food regulations, the veneration of angels, and the acceptance of certain rituals. Apparently the teaching of these opponents is syncretistic, in other words, it is an amalgamation of numerous different religious and philosophical elements. A considerable Jewish tendency is not absent either, manifesting itself especially in the association with certain foods; this is not to say, however, that the opponents are to be viewed as Judaizers. They were more likely part of the broad stream of early gnosis.

The teaching of the opponents is described as φιλοσοφία in 2:8. In Hellenism this term designates not only classical philosophy proper, but also religious and mythical teaching. The antiphilosophical influence of certain theological streams cannot be proven from Col 2:8.

The author of Col turns against this gnosticizing syncretism by stressing the Christian freedom from these powers and by reminding them of the common use of the gifts of nature (2:22). At the same time he exhorts the Christians to love one another.

In spite of this, the question needs to be asked whether the author does not himself argue for a Christology of gnostic coloration in ch 1, as well as for a gnostically influenced doctrine of redemption, or eschatology, in ch 2 ("the resurrection has already taken place"). It can hardly be ignored that the author—perhaps intentionally—positions himself in the immediate vicinity of the teaching that he essentially opposes.

Nevertheless, at the crucial point there is a fundamental difference between Col and gnosis. The paraenesis makes clear that the sphere of Christian existence is not the supra-world to which one ascends in meditation, but the earth (hence the emphatic paradox in 3:1; see above). The author of Col utilizes a gnostically colored language, has largely eliminated the Pauline concept of time, and instead is thinking in more pronounced cosmological categories. But the fundamental assertions of Paul's theology are also maintained in Col. The world is the realm of faith; Christian faith is not the spirit-related conquest of the world, but world-related existence in love. The Christian life is life in freedom, which is not to be construed as freedom in isolation from one's brother but as freedom to exhibit neighborly love. In Col the Christian continues to be on the way and does not yet live in the consummation.

Suggested exercises:

1. Compare the lists of greetings in Phlm and Col. Which names are mentioned? What conclusions does this allow to be drawn? Tool: E. Lohse (see bibliography), 246ff.

2. The concept of hope fulfills a different function in Col than in Paul. What is the difference? Tool: G. Bornkamm, "Die Hoffnung im Kol," *Ges. Aufs.* IV, 206–213.

§ 32 *Ephesians*

Bibliography: M. Barth, *Ephesians*, 2 vols., AB 34, 34A, 1974; J. Gnilka, *Der Epheserbrief*, HThK X/2. 1971; A. Lindemann, *Der Epheserbrief*, ZBK NT 8, 1985; H. Schlier, *An die Epheser*, ⁶1968; R. Schnackenburg, *Der Brief an die Epheser*, EKK X, 1982.

1. Recipients

For several years Ephesus, situated in Asia Minor, was the center of Paul's missionary activity. From here he addressed his letters to the Corinthian community; there are some indications that Phil and Phlm were also written here (see above). The local Christian community was established by Paul (Acts 18:19ff.; 19:1, 8ff.). When these facts are considered in the exegesis of Eph, some peculiarities become noticeable. The author of Eph does not seem to know the recipients of his letter (3:2); the letter is also void of all correspondence and especially of the conveyance of greetings. The only instance where persons are cited by name (6:21f.) agrees verbatim with Col 4:7f.; hence it can in no sense be used as evidence for the author's personal relationship with the community in Ephesus. The destination of Eph (1:1) is entirely obscure. In the oldest manuscripts, i.e., P⁴⁶ and in the original hand of Vaticanus and Sinaiticus, the words ἐν Ἐφέσῳ are omitted; in other words, the letter might not have been addressed to Ephesus at all, nor for that matter to any other specific church. Some advocate, therefore, that the letter was intended as a circular letter to several churches; the reference to the location would only have been inserted at a later date. In that case, however, it is hard to explain why no further location outside of Ἔφεσος is mentioned in any of the manuscripts. Some exegetes assume that Eph had never been intended as a letter, hence the absence of any mention of destination. But one dare not overlook that Eph is definitely written in *letter form* and for that to be so, it is necessary to have an address mentioning the destination or the recipient. The simplest solution of this problem is the assumption that the reading ἐν Ἐφέσῳ in 1:1 is original. After all, the bulk of the witnesses, among them Alexandrinus, attest to it. This does not have to mean that Eph is indeed a "letter to the Ephesians;" instead, a fictitious address is quite plausible, provided the letter was not written by Paul himself. Perhaps a disciple wanted to remedy the situation that Paul had not written a letter precisely to the church with which he was most closely associated; therefore he addressed his theological treatise, which he cast in the mold of a letter "to the Ephesians."

2. Structure and theme

Like Col and Phil, Eph claims to be a prison letter. Regardless of the evaluation of its authenticity, the letter must by all means be placed in the proximity of Col. The structure corresponds with that of Col: doctrine, chs 1–3 (Col 1–2); paraenesis, chs 4–6 (Col 3–4). In addition, even in the formulation of individual sentences there are considerable parallels and agreements.

Suggested exercises:

1. Read both letters side by side (Col first, contrary to the canonical sequence). What agreements or similarities are there, for instance, between Col 2:6–15 and Eph 2:4–12; Col 3:18ff. and Eph 5:22ff.?

2. What differences are there between the two letters? Which segments are more elaborate in Eph than in Col? Tools: C. L. Mitton, *The Epistle to the Ephesians*, 1951; M. Barth, *Ephesians*, 2 vols., AB 34, 34A, 1974.

The prescript (see above) is followed by a double proem. 1:3–14 is in the form of a eulogy, while 1:15–23 is shaped as a thanksgiving. This doubling is not Pauline and may betray the style of an imitator who found both the thanksgiving (e.g., 1 Cor 1:4ff.) and the eulogy (e.g., 2 Cor 1:3ff.) in Paul. In 2:1–10 the author delineates the soteriological consequences of the redemptive event that pertain to the individual; one notices considerable similarities with the respective statements in Col (1:21–23; 2:12ff.), in addition to the use of concepts from Pauline theology which almost take the character of slogans (Eph 2:5b, 8, 9; cf. the parallel passages cited by Nestle). The passage of 2:11–22 contains a portrayal of the essence of the church, described as a cosmic unity (2:14–16). Ch 3:1–13 emphasizes that the church is founded upon the apostolic teaching (cf. already 2:20). The didactic part closes with thanksgiving in 3:14–21.

The paraenesis of Eph is worked out extensively and encompasses more than half of the entire letter. Some pericopae are particularly conspicuous, e.g., the ethical sayings of ch 4; the household code of 5:22ff., which has been expanded considerably compared to Col; and the dualistic battle ethics (*Kampfethik*) of 6:10ff., whose style is reminiscent of the expressions in the Qumran writings. In terms of content, the paraenesis does not surpass that of the (other) letters of Paul, but its foundation has shifted; the paraenesis is not based on justification but on the believers' belonging to the church, that is, on being incorporated in the body of Christ. The latter reaches all the way to heaven, hence the Christians' existence is determined by their ascent to heaven which has already occurred (2:5ff.). They are admonished to walk in those good works which God prepared in advance (2:10). The ethics of Eph rests upon this systematic presupposition.

3. History-of-religions problems: World view

Eph has a peculiar world view: The world is not three-storied (heaven—earth—netherworld; cf. e.g., Lk 16:23), but is principally viewed as bipartite. The earth is below (since there is no netherworld), and above is the expanse of "the heavens," which are divided into different realms. In the lowest realm are the devil and his cohorts (2:2; 4:9f.); people project into this realm and thus are exposed to the influence of those powers. In the heaven above this realm are to be found God and Christ as the "head" of the church which projects into this very realm (1:21). As people "in Christ," Christians are removed from the influence of the devil; they, too, are in heaven (2:3–6), face to face with the powers, yet no longer vulnerable to them (2:7). There are similarities between this world view and certain conceptions in gnostic writings. Yet another aspect is of central significance for the gnostic world view: Above the atmosphere, hence above the lower heaven, there is a wall which separates the dark "world" from the "world of light"; only the gnostic is able to overcome this wall with the help of the redeemer. In scholarship it is a matter of debate whether certain elements of this idea are also found in Eph. This may very well be the explanation for 2:14; in Christ the cosmic wall is removed and for Christians the cosmos has become united (cf. 1:23). The body of Christ reaches from the head, which is in heaven, all the way down to the earth; within the body Christians are still vulnerable to the attacks of the powers, but they are assured of the victory (6:10ff.; 2:7; further, compare the sketch by A. Lindemann [see bibliography], p. 132).

4. Authorship question: Relationship to Colossians

According to 1:1, Eph was written by Paul. But the accuracy of this statement is in question. In comparison with the (older) letters of Paul, Eph not only contains some new theological ideas, but the meaning of some of the concepts used in both categories has changed (cf. also p. 201f. above). Therefore, particularly Schlier's attempt to understand Eph as Paul's "mature work" proves to be untenable. It is hardly conceivable that only a few years after the writing of 1 Cor or of Rom, Paul would have completely changed his fundamental views, especially on ecclesiology and eschatology.

An important factor in dealing with the authenticity of Eph is the clarification of the relationship between Eph and Col. There are numerous points of contact between the two letters. The question is whether they are directly dependent upon one another, or whether both letters, independent of one another, picked up a common tradition. In case there is indeed a direct relationship between them, one needs to determine which letter was written earlier and thus has priority.

Some references, especially Eph 1:1/Col 1:1 and Eph 6:21f./Col 4:7f., can only be explained under the assumption of a direct dependence. A similar assessment may also be necessary for Eph 1:15f./Col 1:4, 9; Eph 1:7, 20/Col 1:14, 20; Eph 2:20; 3:17/Col 2:7; Eph 1:19f./Col 2:12; Eph 3:2ff./Col 1:24ff. and Eph 4:16/Col 2:19. In an analysis of each individual reference and of the letters as a whole, the following results emerge: (1) It is not possible for both letters to have originated independently of one another. (2) Priority belongs to Col because it deals concretely with a specific church and its problems, while in Eph no real occasion can be discerned for its writing. Hence, Eph is a reworking of Col in its "fundamental ideas," as it were; at the same time, a certain development in the theological intent can also be observed. Furthermore, this shows conclusively that Eph cannot have been written by Paul, regardless of whether or not Col is held to be Pauline.

Some exegetes maintain that the similarities between Eph and Col do not allow the conclusion of a literary dependence, rather, they can be accounted for by arguing that both letters, in part, cite the same liturgical texts or hymns. But this is highly unlikely; for, it is precisely the clearly hymnic text of Col 1:15-20 which has no parallels in Eph. On the other hand, apart from the "call to awake" in 5:14, Eph has only *one other* text, i.e., 2:14-16, which can be traced back to an earlier source with some certainty. This analysis indicates that the additions to the supposed source correspond with certain statements in Col, but that there is no trace of a parallel per se in Col which serves as source. In all the other texts which some exegetes consider to be liturgical or hymnic citations (1:3-12; 1:17-23; 2:4-10), this identification is doubtful. On the analysis of 2:14-16, cf. A. Lindemann, *Die Aufhebung der Zeit*, 1975, 157-159, and the literature cited there.

5. Theological character

Eph is not a letter in the proper sense of the term; rather, it is a theological tractate fashioned in the form of a letter. Ecclesiology is its main theme. Every time the author emphatically refers to the salvation event, he mentions the church which is thus given a particularly outstanding significance (1:22f.; 2:14–18; 3:5, 9f.; 4:4–6; 5:25f.). Throughout, the term ἐκκλησία does not signify the local community but the universal church whose foundation is the apostles and prophets (2:20). This line of thought, which is hierarchical and based on the recognition of tradition, plays an important part in Eph. Especially the apostles and prophets, rather than all believers, are the recipients of the revelation of God (3:5); for her part, the church is the mediator of the divine wisdom over against the cosmic powers (3:10). In many instances Eph contains gnostic motifs; as a whole, its theology also shows gnostic influence. This is true not only of the world view (see above), but even of its Christology. Christ has cosmic dimensions (4:10); as the heavenly man he gathers his own (2:15; 4:13) and in his body leads them upward to himself (4:7–11; 2:4ff.). In this pursuit, the historical aspect of the redemptive event is completely eliminated; the theology of the cross and the futuristic eschatology no longer fulfill a concrete role and thus are only mentioned in passing. Only in the context of 2:14–16 does one find references to the death of Jesus; here the author virtually attempts to apply a Pauline "gloss" to a text before him.

Likewise, the anthropology of Eph happens to be in close proximity to gnosis. The Christian actually is no longer exposed to the world; rather, in Christ he has been withdrawn from the influence of the powers (2:7). Although he continues to be in conflict with the world, the outcome of this battle is assured from the beginning; the victory belongs to the Christian because he is guarded by God's weapons (6:10ff.).

Suggested exercises:

1. Similarities exist not only to Col, but also to 1 Pet. The question is whether there is also a literary correlation with the latter. Compare Eph 1:20f./1 Pet 3:22ff.; Eph 2:20ff./1 Pet 2:4ff., and Eph 4:8–10/1 Pet 3:19f. Is the common denominator in these parallels to be sought in literary dependence or in the use of similar traditions?

2. The most important ecclesiological concept in Eph is that of the "body of Christ." What is its function within the framework of the letter's theology? How does this teaching compare with Paul's ecclesiology? Tool: H. Schlier, *Christus und die Kirche im Eph*, BHTh 6, 1930, 37–60.

For the advanced student: How is the "body of Christ" notion to be derived from the history of religions? Tools: H. Schlier (see above); K. M. Fischer, *Tendenz und Absicht des Eph*, FRLANT 111, 1973, 54–78.

3. What is the function of eschatology in Eph? Tools: A. Lindemann, *Die Auf-hebung der Zeit*, 1975; F. J. Steinmetz, "Parusie-Erwartung im Eph? Ein Vergleich," *Bib* 50, 1969, 328–336.

4. For the advanced student: To date, the most significant commentary on Eph continues to be that by H. Schlier (see bibliography). We recommend its reading on several pericopae (e.g., 2:1–10; 5:22–33). (a) Certain hermeneutical principles seem to emerge. Schlier uses a "phenomenological interpretation" which fore-goes the evaluation of the historical tendency from the text to the interpreter. Rather, Schlier endeavors to let the text speak "directly," as it were. At the same time he proffers a psychological explanation for the development from the (early) Pauline letters to Eph; thus he is able to maintain the authenticity of Eph (cf. p. 207 above). The most recent Catholic exegesis (Gnilka), however, has relinquished the argument of authenticity.

(b) How feasible are Schlier's hermeneutical principles in the context of the historical-critical exegesis? For example, compare Schlier's interpretation of Eph 2:2f. with that of Gnilka.

§ 33 *Pastoral Letters*

Bibliography: N. Brox, *Die Pastoralbriefe*, RNT 7/2, [4]1969; M. Dibelius and H. Con-zelmann, *The Pastoral Epistles*, Hermeneia, ET 1972.

1. *Problem and content*

(1) The designation "Pastoral epistles" which is customarily used to-day for the letters to Timothy and Titus, already describes something of their content: they address the issue of leadership in the office of the shepherd in the church. Some of the particulars concerning the recipients mentioned in the letters can be ascertained from a concordance. Timothy is one of Paul's important co-workers who is mentioned in most of Paul's letters as well as in Acts. Whereas Titus is not mentioned in Acts, he ful-fills an important function in 2 Cor and in Gal (see p. 188 above). It can-not be ruled out a priori that Paul could not have addressed letters to both of these close fellow-workers, since Phlm demonstrates that Paul did write to individuals as well.

(2) *1 Tim* presupposes that Paul came from Ephesus and is currently in Macedonia, while Timothy remained in Ephesus. Paul announces his return; nevertheless, he gives Timothy instructions on how he is to set the church in order during his absence. It is striking that the instructions are not concerned with the concrete problems in Ephesus, such as com-batting the opponents; rather, 1 Tim contains a thoroughgoing church order which essentially applies to all churches. In this connection, the

idea of tradition is very significant, not in the sense of an apostolic succession already in view, but in the sense that the acknowledgement of the received teaching is at the same time the guarantee of the church's orthodoxy (1:15f.). There is an established order of offices in the church. At the helm are the bishop and the presbyter, and below them the deacons (1 Tim 3). Likewise, there are fixed forms of ordination (1 Tim 4:14; 5:22; 6:12). Apparently the monarchical episcopate is not yet in existence. In any case, no concrete difference can be recognized between the bishop and the presbyters; it is possible that the bishop is only *primus inter pares*. The references relative to the conduct of the believer reflect a conservative civic disposition (2:8–15; 5:1–16). 1 Tim assumes that the Christian's relationship to the world is no longer eschatologically determined in the original Pauline sense, but that they are now to settle down in the world (2:1f.; in this regard, cf. the excursus in Dibelius/Conzelmann [see bibliography], in loc.). The letter also combats false teachers; however, their position is not sufficiently clear. In this connection it is striking that in his anti-heretical polemic, the author is not concerned with refuting the theology of the opponents; instead, he rejects it summarily by appealing to the teaching handed down (6:20).

(3) The external situation in *Tit* is similar to that in 1 Tim. Together with Titus, Paul had evangelized the island of Crete; he has meanwhile left the island while Titus has remained there. From Nicopolis (likely located in Epirus) Paul requests his co-worker to come to him (3:12). As in 1 Tim, Paul at the same time gives instructions concerning the internal and external order of the church, with the emphasis on the traditional teaching again being prominent (2:1). On all other matters there are no substantial differences from 1 Tim.

(4) The situation presupposed in 2 Tim, however, is altogether different. Paul is obviously imprisoned in Rome (1:17); furthermore, he has already been tried. All of his fellow-laborers, except for Luke, have turned away from him (1:15; 4:11, 16); one of them even caused him substantial harm (4:14f.). Paul has sent Tychicus to Ephesus (4:12) and Trophimus remained in Miletus sick (4:20). Acts mentions both of them as co-workers of Paul. In 2 Tim, Paul requests Timothy to come to Rome as soon as possible and, en route, to pick up his books and a coat (4:13) which he left behind in Troas (south of the Hellespont). He anticipates his imminent death (4:6–8) and therefore urges (Timothy) to hurry (4:9).

The actual content of 2 Tim corresponds with that of the other Pastoral letters, but it has a more personal tenor than the others. From a literary perspective, 2 Tim has the form of a "testament" (cf. 2 Pet). What subsequent generations are to have impressed upon them through 2 Tim is not only the teaching, but also the portrait of the (suffering) apostle. But this is a tendency which is characteristic of the writings of the middle of the second century (on the genre of "testament," see p. 109 above).

2. Evaluation of the historical situation presupposed in the Pastorals—the question of authenticity

(1) 1 Tim may have been written during the journey through Macedonia, as described in Acts 20:1ff. But Paul had Timothy alongside of him on that journey and there is no record of a later journey following the same route; one has to reach the conclusion, therefore, that 1 Tim cannot be accommodated within the pilgrimage of Paul as it is known to us.

(2) The same applies to Tit as well: Elsewhere we do not hear of a missionary endeavor on Crete, and in Acts the island is mentioned only in connection with the transportation of prisoners to Rome (27:7ff.).

(3) The situation in 2 Tim is obscure; from Acts 20:4ff., and 21:29 we gather that Paul was indeed accompanied by Trophimus and Timothy on his journey to Jerusalem. 2 Tim presupposes, however, that Paul has been in Rome for some time; in other words, following the Acts account, at least two years must have elapsed since Paul's separation from his companions. And yet, Paul urges Timothy in 2 Tim to follow him quickly and to bring along some small items he had forgotten in Troas—a situation like this is highly unlikely. But even if this situation were not deemed impossible, the information of 2 Tim 4:10ff. can simply not be reconciled with the otherwise extant chronology of Paul. Apparently by means of some commonly known names and dates, the author of 2 Tim construed a situation in order to give the writing a Pauline life setting (*Sitz im Leben*). In any case, it seems to be clear that none of the three Pastorals can be accommodated within the life of Paul as it is known to us.

(4) Some scholars voice concerns against this evaluation. They suggest that it is possible to maintain the authenticity of all the Pastorals if one starts with the assumption that 2 Tim is the oldest letter of this group. Paul wrote it in Rome. Upon his release from prison and contrary to the plans he had expressed in Rom, he travelled to the East once again and there wrote 1 Tim and Tit. Later he was apprehended again and subsequently was executed. At this point they appeal to Rom and 1 Clem 5:7, one of the letters attributed to the "Apostolic Fathers," which had been sent from Rome to Corinth around A.D. 90–100 (see § 45). In Rom Paul had indicated he wanted to leave the East for good and to move to Spain via Rome. It says in 1 Clem 5:7 that Paul had reached "the boundaries of the West"; if this referred to Spain, this letter would presuppose that Paul had been acquitted at his trial in Rome. Therefore, the writing of the Pastorals after Paul's first stay in Rome is historically conceivable.

(5) But the arguments against the authenticity of the Pastorals are weightier. First of all, an investigation of the context of 1 Clem 5:7 shows that this letter at least does not have a clear conception of Paul's assumed trip to the West, nor is it aware of two Roman imprisonments of Paul. In addition, we learn from Acts 20 that Paul never saw his churches in the East

again (Acts 20:25, 38). It is to be noted, finally, that the Pastorals themselves presuppose that Paul died at the end of his first imprisonment—they know nothing of an acquittal in Rome.

The assessment of the authenticity of the Pastorals, which is based on the historical setting, is further confirmed by the exegesis of the texts. In the Pastorals one notices new theological terms that play an important part but which are not found in the older letters, such as "a good conscience" or "sound doctrine." On the whole, the style of the Pastorals is smoother and simpler than Paul's; additionally, one gets the impression at various points that Pauline expressions from older letters are all but imitated (cf. 1 Tim 1:12–16/Gal 1:13–16 and 1 Cor 15:9f.; 2 Tim 1:3–5/Rom 1:8–11).

A further argument to be adduced is that of the attestation of the Pastorals in the transmission of the text. They are lacking in P[46], and Marcion does not have them in his canon. On this basis many exegetes go to the extent of concluding that the Pastorals were not written until the time of Marcion; the warning against the antitheses of the "ideas of what is falsely known as gnosis" (1 Tim 6:20) refers to Marcion's book, "Antitheses." This would mean that the letters were only written about 80 years after Paul's death. But this assumption is unlikely because the teaching which the Pastorals oppose, in contrast to Marcion (see p. 20f. above), utilizes the OT positively (Tit 1:14; 1 Tim 1:7). Elsewhere, nothing at all indicates an anti-Marcionite front in the Pastorals.

It is therefore virtually impossible that the Pastorals were written by Paul himself or during his lifetime. On the other hand, it may not be appropriate to date them too late; they were probably written toward the end of the first or at the beginning of the second century.

3. Literary characteristics and theological opposition

(1) The most important theme of 1 Tim and Tit is that of church order. One notices in this connection that some of the statements have more in common with a household code, i.e., with paraenesis, than with church order (cf. e.g., 1 Tim 2:9f. with 1 Pet 3:3ff.). There is no clearly discernible arrangement of the individual sections; instead, they seem to be strung together in a somewhat disorderly fashion: 2:1ff.—worship; 3:1ff.—bishops and deacons; 5:3ff.—widows; 5:17ff.—presbyters; 6:1f.—slaves. It is feasible, therefore, that the regulations were not drafted uniformly but that they are a collection. The author has placed them directly in the framework of combatting the heretics. The definition of correct doctrine and of proper order in the church signifies the demarcation over against heresy (just as it is true, conversely, that such confrontations only precipitate the necessity of developing a fixed order). This interrelationship is especially clear in Tit 1:9f.

2 Tim serves a different function. It is the "testament" of Paul who offers paraenetic exhortations to his "beloved child Timothy" and who presents himself as an example of suffering in order to motivate Timothy to endure in the same manner. In reality, of course, the author's purview includes the entire church (3:12).

(2) All three of the Pastorals are dealing with an actual confrontation with false teachers whose status is not clearly defined. It seems that they adhere to gnostic teaching with a Jewish slant; for, on the one hand they practice spiritualism (2 Tim 2:18), a retreat from the world (1 Tim 4:3; Tit 1:14), and "gnosis" (1 Tim 6:20), while on the other hand demanding conformity (1 Tim 1:7; Tit 1:10, 14; 3:9); finally, they seem to be intensely occupied with myths and genealogies (1 Tim 1:4; 4:7; Tit 3:9). The Pastorals oppose them by stressing first of all that the appearance of false teachers is a sign of the beginning of the endtimes (1 Tim 4:1; 2 Tim 3:1); hence they must be countered with tenacity. The false teachers are told that the world is God's creation (1 Tim 4:3-5) and that for this reason Christians can associate with the things of the world. While special emphasis is placed on the demand that the moral conduct of the leaders of the community be irreproachable (1 Tim 3:2-12), the "heretics" are conversely charged with gross immorality—a topic common to polemics (1 Tim 6:3-10).

For one, the starting point for such polemics is libertinism, which is in fact practiced in some groups, is based on a certain world view, and is assailed in 1 Cor, Jude, and 2 Pet. For another, the starting point is the notion taken from Judaism that false religion must necessarily be accompanied by false morals (Wis 13-15; cf. Rom 1:18ff., 1 Jn).

In this sense the Pastorals also maintain the continuous validity of the law (1 Tim 1:8-11) because it does not address the righteous as much as it does the lawless who disregard "sound doctrine."

Proper tradition is the decisive criterion in the evaluation of the heresy. In this context we find the first occurrence of the notion of inspiration (*theopneustia*); the "Scripture"—which apparently already includes some Christian writings—is God-breathed (2 Tim 3:16). With regard to the tradition, there is a significant difference here in comparison to Paul; while Paul assimilates the tradition by incorporating it in his theological framework, it is merely practiced in the Pastorals, that is, it has been accepted as authoritative. The second extremely important perspective in the Pastorals is the church order. The church that is intact and orderly is the guarantor of orthodoxy; this is an idea that pervades all three of the Pastorals.

Suggested reading:

G. Haufe, "Gnostische Irrlehre und ihre Abwehr in den Past," in *Gnosis und NT* (ed. K.-W. Tröger), 1973, 325-339.

III. SYNOPTIC GOSPELS AND ACTS

§ 34   Gospel of Mark

Bibliography: (For commentaries, see pp. 41 above) H. C. Kee, *Community of the New Age. Studies in Mark's Gospel*, 1977; D.-A. Koch, *Die Bedeutung der Wunderer-zählungen für die Christologie des Markus-Evangeliums*, BZNW 42, 1975; W. Marx-sen, *Mark the Evangelist*, ET 1969; R. Pesch, ed., *Das Markus-Evangelium*, Wege der Forschung 411, 1979; V. K. Robbins, *A Socio-rhetorical Interpretation of Mark*, 1984; J. M. Robinson, *The Problem of History in Mark and other Marcan Studies*, 1982; V. Taylor, *The Gospel According to St. Mark*, ²1966; W. Wrede, *The Messianic Secret*, ET 1971.

1. Problem and structure

Mark is the oldest of the three synoptic Gospels and served the other two as a source (see § 7). A working knowledge of the content and, at the same time, of the theological intent can be gained by taking note of the basic structure. Part one (Mk 1–9) deals with Jesus' ministry in Gali-lee; part two (Mk 11–15) with Jesus' passion in Jerusalem. The tenth chapter, which links the two, is an account of Jesus' journey to Jerusalem (cf. 10:1, 17, 32, 35, 46; 11:1). The concluding chapter, 16:1–8, contains an account of the tomb.

One notices at once that the second part is disproportionately long, con-sidering the external events that are presented. More than a third of the book is given to the account of the passion, although the events occur-red within the course of only a few days. Based upon this peculiar cir-cumstance is also evident to a lesser extent in the other Gospels, M. Kähler has come to the conclusion that the Gospels are to be taken as "passion stories with an extended introduction" (*The So-called Historical Jesus and the Historic, Biblical Christ*, ET 1964, 80). But this view is one-sided be-cause it ignores the fact that the words and deeds of Jesus have their own significance in each of the Gospels and that they are not be viewed merely as "introduction."

In Mk this is moreover apparent from the way he parallels the arrange-ment of the geographical reference points with a christologically defined sketch. It is emphasized over and over in the first part that Jesus' mes-siahship is to be kept hidden from the public (see p. 219f. below). In the presentation of the passion in part two, however, the confession of Jesus as the Messiah is expressed publicly—among the disciples to begin with, then before the Jewish Council, and finally in public under the cross. Hence, the geographical-biographical arrangement and the christological structure of the Gospel clarify one another. The *public* ministry of Jesus in Galilee is carried out by disguising his messiahship; however, his glory is revealed in Jerusalem, i.e., in the passion and at the cross, for at this juncture it can no longer be misunderstood. It is for this reason that 8:27–10:52, which to some extent is still part of "Galilee," i.e., of the travel narrative, continually points ahead to the passion, such as is done in Peter's confession, in the scene of the transfiguration, and especially in the three predictions of the passion in 8:31; 9:31; 10:33f. (see p. 220 below). This acute emphasis of the theology of the cross is actually Mark's theological center.

2. Important stages in the presentation

(1) Ch 1:1–13 clearly functions as a prelude: John the Baptist, the baptism and, peripherally, the temptation of Jesus. In terms of salvation history, the horizons of the ministry of Jesus are set at the beginning. In doing so, Mark appeals to OT prophecies but not to Jewish history as a whole. Hence, the history of Jesus preceding the Baptist is not important for Mk, although the material he processed certainly contained the notion of preparation in terms of salvation history (cf. 12:1–11). A thematic summary of the proclamation of Jesus is found in 1:14f. In its present form, this "summary" (see p. 59f. above) is the work of the evangelist, of course, and not the verbatim rendering of the sermons of Jesus. The foundational themes are the kingdom of God, repentance, and forgiveness of sins.

(2) 1:16–5:43 informs us about the appearance of Jesus in Galilee. The vicinity of the Sea of Galilee, and especially the town of Capernaum, constitute the center. The entire first chapter takes the shape of a paradigm for Jesus' public appearance in general. In it Mk repeatedly links the miracle stories that were passed on to him with references to the *teaching* of Jesus and its effect upon the hearers (see above). In the same way, the subsequent chapters are not arranged biographically but topically; chs 2 and 3 contain a series of disputes, followed by the chapter of parables (Mk 4) and, finally, by a collection of extensive miracle stories (Mk 5).

(3) Mk 6–9 describe the ministry of Jesus in Galilee and in the immediate vicinity. The geographical conceptions presupposed here are quite obscure. The individual pieces of tradition are but loosely joined together. It has been assumed that this section might possibly have been inserted into the Gospel at a later date, since the subject matter, for the most part, is not found in Lk. It is possible that Lk had not read this passage in Mk (see p. 50ff.). But an analysis of the redactional elements in the passage indicate that Mk is the author. Besides, it is incorrect to jump to the conclusion of secondary interpolations at the sight of nonsensical aspects in the presentation.

(4) In ch 10 Mk describes the journey of Jesus through Transjordan to Jericho, while it has already been made clear that Jesus actually is on his way to Jerusalem.

(5) Mk 11–13 are a prelude to the passion. Jesus' entry into Jerusalem represents the first public demonstration of his messiahship. Yet, as soon as he reads the passion predictions, the reader of the Gospel knows that this entry does not lead to glory but instead to the cross. The public effectiveness of Jesus draws to a close with the cleansing of the temple and the ensuing disputes (Mk 11f.). The discourse on "the last things" (Mk 13), as esoteric teaching, addresses the disciples exclusively.

The separation of public and esoteric teaching is established categorically in Mk 4. There we are told that while parables are related in public, their content is interpreted for the good of the disciples (4:10–12, 33ff.).

The position of Mk 13 within the Gospel as a whole is in keeping with the traditional position of eschatology in early Christian doctrine; the "last things" constitute the final part of the catechism (see above).

(6) The passion of Jesus is the topic of ch 14f.: Arrest, condemnation, execution. Mk has cast the duration and sequence of the passion event in Jerusalem into a weeklong scheme (Mk 11ff.). Jesus' entry into the city takes place on a Sunday, the cleansing of the temple on Monday, the debates of Mk 12 on Tuesday, the Feast of Unleavened Bread (14:12) begins on Thursday, the crucifixion takes place on Friday, and the discovery of the empty tomb after the Sabbath, occurs, again, on Sunday (16:1).

The sequencing of the hours of the day of his death is ordered in the same schematic manner. The early morning hour, as well as the third, sixth, and ninth hour are specified emphatically (15:1, 25, 33, 34).

(7) The presentation of Easter (16:1–8) conspicuously has only the one scene at the empty tomb. Appearances of the resurrected one are heralded (16:7; 14:28); however, there follows no account of them.

This points up the frequently discussed problem of the Markan ending. Why does Mk not contain any appearance narratives, in spite of the evangelist's own indication that he is familiar with such accounts (16:7 is redactional, as indicated by the likewise redactional sentence of 14:28)? Is it possible for the Gospel to end with the sentence, "They said nothing to anyone, because they were afraid?" Or has the original ending been omitted intentionally or lost accidentally? Yet, there is no conceivable reason for an intentional excision of appearance stories that were narrated originally. The loss of a leaf—which can happen quite easily in the case of ancient manuscripts—would have to have occurred as early as with the autograph; for Mt and Lk are acquainted with Mk only up to 16:8, and there is no trace of a continuation in the oldest manuscripts. The search for the "lost" ending of Mark is based on the assumption that a continuation is absolutely essential after v 8. But this assumption is a *petitio principii*. It is certainly conceivable to understand the 16:1–8 passage as a deliberate "punchline" of the Gospel. Mk indeed knows of the appearances of the risen one, hence he mentions them in 14:28 and 16:7. But he does not have to narrate them specifically. From the account of the transfiguration (9:2ff.) the reader is already informed concerning the destiny of Jesus after his death. In addition, it is important to note that *narratives* about the epiphanies of Jesus emerge relatively late, as Paul's negative report indicates (cf. esp. 1 Cor 15:3ff.).

Suggested reading:

A. Lindemann, "Die Osterbotschaft des Markus," *NTS* 26, 1980, 298–317.

H. Paulsen, "Mk XVI 1–8," *NovTest* 22, 1980, 138–175.

3. Sources

In his book, Mk has without a doubt assimilated literary sources and did not just incorporate material that was handed down orally. The Markan additions (vv 22, 27a) within 1:21–28 are thus recognized without great difficulty, that is to say, the account must already have been extant in written form apart from the additions. Mk inserted 16:7 into a completed, written text; likewise, the scene narrated in 14:3–9 has been inserted into an already available context, as indicated by a comparison with the context (v 1f., 10f.). Mark already had the parable of the sower (4:1–9), with its interpretation (vv 13–20) available; the "rationale for parables" that he himself inserted (vv 10–12) is clearly recognized as a later expansion. To begin with, it is unimportant whether these verses were formulated by Mk himself or with the aid of a source (*Vorlage*); it is to the evangelist's credit that they are mentioned at this point. Yet, a comprehensive reconstruction of the sources used by Mk is not possible; particularly the scope of such sources can only be the object of speculation. We may have to be satisfied with the observation that individual accounts were already accessible to Mk in written form and were not fixed in writing only by Mk.

H.-W. Kuhn, *Ältere Sammlungen im Markusevangelium*, StUNT 8, 1971, argues for a more extensive assimilation of sources by Mk; W. Schmithals, *Das Evangelium nach Markus*, OTK 2, 1979, goes to the extent of reconstructing a comprehensive "basic writing" (*Grundschrift*) which the evangelist merely revised.

4. Language

The language of Mk is very simple; the author of literary Greek is unobtrusive. The sentence structure is decidedly primitive; parataxis, that is the simple joining together of sentences by means of καί, is standard (cf., e.g., Mk 1:16–22). Mt and Lk have endeavored to make some improvements, an example of which is Mk 14:12 and parallels. Mt and Lk also replace some of Mk's terms, which they deem to be inappropriate, with more refined terms; for instance κράβαττος in Mk 2:4ff. is replaced with κλίνη (Mt 9:2). Likewise the diminutives (5:23—θυγάτριον) that Mk occasionally uses sometimes do not fit with an elevated literary style; here again, Mt and Lk have made the necessary corrections. The fact that Mk is the shortest of the Gospels has more to do with the scope of the material he used than with his manner of presentation. On the contrary, the individual narratives generally are quite detailed and, in part, awkwardly formulated; Mt and Lk have frequently expressed their material with greater brevity (cf. Mk 4:21–43 with its parallels, and Mk 2:1–12 with Mt 9:1–8). Yet Mk is also skilled in employing narrative artifice, such as the interweaving of two or more narratives. The pericope of 3:20–35 is a good example of this. A dispute with the scribes (vv 22–27) and the logion of the unpardonable sin (vv 28–30) are woven into the scene of "Jesus and his family" (v 21f., 31ff.). Evidence of literary mastery is also seen in Mark's linking of Jesus' arrest and trial by the Sanhedrin with the scene of Peter's threefold denial (14:53–72); Peter's denial of Jesus occurs simultaneous with the soldiers' derision.

5. Authorship

According to church tradition, the Gospel was written by John Mark of Jerusalem who is mentioned in Acts. He is a relative of Barnabas and accompanied the latter and Paul on the first part of the "first missionary journey." According to Acts 13:13, he left Paul in Paphos; hence Paul refuses to take him along again (15:37–39). Yet, later he seems to be with Paul again, following Phlm 24.

Legend has it that Mark later became Peter's secretary and translator in Rome (1 Pet 5:13); based on Papias' information (see pp. 91f.), he wrote his Gospel on the basis of Peter's reports. But the text does not confirm this information. Mk has quite obviously not been written by a Jew. The author does in any case not demonstrate familiarity with the geography of Palestine (cf. the travel itinerary of 7:31 with a map of Palestine!); he knows the local conditions in and around Jerusalem just as little (11:1). He is not acquainted with Jewish customs and refers to them only from a distance (7:3f.). Evidence against the authorship of John Mark is the fact that Mk is practically uninfluenced by Pauline theology—the influence of which would surely be expected of a companion of Paul (Phlm 24; cf. Col 4:10; 2 Tim 4:11).

There is no proof for the popular assumption that the author himself was hiding behind the reference to the young man fleeing naked at the arrest of Jesus (Mk 14:51f.), nor that he was thus providing a cryptic reference to his own identity, in keeping with ancient custom.

The only thing we can state is that the author of Mk is a Gentile Christian with whom we are not otherwise acquainted.

The problem of the time of writing depends heavily upon whether the destruction of Jerusalem is presupposed in the apocalyptic discourse of Jesus (Mk 13) or whether it is assumed to be taking place in the near future. In any case, the book must have been written ca. A.D. 70, the time of the Jewish War. The only thing to be said about the place of writing is that it has to be situated outside of Palestine (see above for references to the geographical information). Based on the numerous Latinisms it is sometimes argued that Mk was written in Rome. But this argument is not valid. These are commonly used terms like centurion, legion, census, etc., which are part of the colloquial use of hellenistic Greek. Therefore, nothing can be said concerning the place of writing.

6. Basic theological ideas

Kähler's opinion that the Gospels are passion narratives with extended introductions (see above) is not even relevant for Mk. The first part, which contains the miracle stories and the presentation of Jesus' teaching, carries its own significance. It is nevertheless true that, beginning with 8:27, the focus on the passion becomes the decisive principle in the literary presentation.

The "messianic secret" is the central theological idea pervading the entire Gospel and which concretely determines its structure (see above). At first, the ministry of Jesus is carried out by veiling his true nature: (a) The demons are not allowed to say who he is (1:24f.; 1:34; 3:12). (b) Miracles are not to be talked about in public; they are not to be told to others (5:43). Clearly, the messianic secret has no historical core; instead it is a *theologoumenon*. Historically speaking, the prohibition to speak of the miracles is nonsensical; for instance, how is it conceivable that a raising of the dead could be kept secret (cf. 5:43)? (c) The disciples constantly misunderstand the meaning of Jesus' actions (6:52; 8:17 et al.). (d) With reference to the messianic secret, there is a clear turning-point in 8:27; while the secret has already been disclosed twice (2:1–12; 7:36), only now, immediately preceding the passion, does Jesus confirm that he is the Messiah. Representatively, Peter voices for all believers the confession that Jesus is the Christ. However, the basic misunderstanding persists; when Jesus announces his passion and death, Peter reacts indignantly and rebukes him. The link Mk has established between Peter's confession and the prediction of the passion makes clear that the messiahship of Jesus leads not to glory, but to the cross. For the first and the last time, in the trial scene in 14:62 Jesus states openly that he is the Son of God. It is this statement that leads to his condemnation.

The disclosure of the secret shows the theological interest at the back of Mk's conception of the messianic secret. The claim Jesus makes upon men in his proclamation is not a worldly claim to power. He is not understood until he is seen as the one accused before the Jewish Council and as the one executed on the cross (cf. 15:39). For this reason we are told repeatedly in the passion predictions that suffering and death *must* (δεῖ) come to pass, meaning that they are in accordance with God's will.

The predictions of the passion, which enjoy special significance to begin with because of their prominent positioning (8:31; 9:31; 10:32–34), are not historically the words of Jesus. They are confessional statements of the Christian community which have subsequently been credited to Jesus (*vaticinia ex eventu*). Their meaning is clear: the messiahship of Jesus can only be understood properly from the vantage point of his suffering. Mk underscores the actual significance of these statements by adding discipleship sayings to each of the three predictions of the passion: 8:34–9:1—whoever confesses Jesus must take up his cross and himself be ready to suffer; 9:33–37—he who wants to be first must be the servant of all; 10:35–40—discipleship means passion rather than glory. The destiny of Jesus also determines the destiny of his disciples, Christians whose discipleship indeed means suffering on account of the cross.

The historical problem of the messianic secret has been discovered by W. Wrede. Wrede argued that Jesus did not teach that he was the Messiah. After Easter his disciples remembered that there was nothing visibly pertaining to his messiahship in his life. Because of Easter, i.e., because of the appearances of the risen one, they believed in him as the Messiah. Thus they endeavored to approximate historical reminiscence with present faith and developed the theory that Jesus understood himself as Messiah (i.e., as Son of God) even during his lifetime but intentionally chose to keep it hidden. Hence the messianic secret reflects a certain embarrassment in the pre-Markan Christian community.

While Wrede's observations are correct, his interpretation of the data is unfounded. The materials which Mk assimilated, especially the miracle stories, do not at all indicate a nonmessianic portrait of Jesus; in fact, there is no such thing as a nonmessianic Jesus tradition. Especially the Christology of the miracle tradition sees in Jesus the θεῖος ἀνήρ, the miracle worker equipped with special powers. In comparison to this tradition, the messianic secret is a secondary and theological theory of deliberate shape, which purports that the meaning of Jesus is not disclosed to the one merely seeing the miracles, rather it is faith that sees Jesus correctly from the vantage point of the cross and the resurrection. Without a doubt, this type of idea was already known in the pre-Markan community; however, against Wrede's argument, the messianic secret as a mature theological concept is the accomplishment of Mk. He applied it purposefully to the entire Jesus tradition and thus cast into the mold of the "Gospel" what at first was an unorganized mass of traditional material. The messianic secret does not belong to the tradition but to the redactional effort of Mk. For theological reasons he even inserted it where it actually contradicts the logical course of actions (5:43; 7:36).

Suggested exercises:

1. Read Mk while asking a twofold question: (a) Where, in the ongoing course of action, are the references to the messianic secret? Where is it unveiled and what consequences are cited? (b) Where is the secret unveiled to the *reader* through the Gospel itself? Example: The parabolic theory of 4:10-12 is communicated to the reader; it is the reader, as a Christian, who understands the secret of the kingdom of God.

2. What perspectives for Christology and the understanding of faith can be gained from Mk 8:27-35; 9:31-37; 10:32-45? Tools: U. Luz, "Das Geheimnismotiv und die markinische Christologie," ZNW 56, 1965, 9-30, especially 20ff.; G. Strecker, "Zur Messiasgeheimnistheorie im Markusevangelium," in *Eschaton und Historie. Aufsätze*, 1979, 33-51.

§ 35 Gospel of Matthew

Bibliography: G. Bornkamm, G. Barth, H. J. Held, *Tradition and Interpretation in Matthew*, ET 1963; F. V. Filson, *The Gospel according to St. Matthew*, HNTC, 1960; W. Grundmann, *Das Evangelium nach Matthäus*, ThHK I, 1968; E. Klostermann, *Das Matthäusevangelium*, HNT 4, ⁴1971; J. Lange, ed., *Das Matthäus-Evangelium*, WdF 525, 1980; U. Luz, *Das Evangelium nach Matthäus (Mt 1-7)*, EKK I/1, 1985; P. S. Minear, *Matthew: The Teacher's Gospel*, 1982; E. Schweizer, *The Good News According to Matthew*, ET 1975; G. Strecker, *Der Weg der Gerechtigkeit. Untersuchung zur Theologie des Matthäus*, FRLANT 82, ³1971; M. J. Suggs, *Wisdom, Christology, and Law in Matthew's Gospel*, 1970; W. Trilling, *Das wahre Israel. Studien zur Theologie des Matthäus-Evangeliums*, StANT 10, ³1964.

1. Problems and structure

(1) Mt is a combination of Mk and Q; in addition it contains some special material. For this reason Mt is much more extensive than Mk, although the texts that Mt incorporates are frequently abridged and their intent heightened.

A synoptic comparison, especially with Mk, helps crystallize the particular methodology of Mt. The Gospel of Mt does not begin with John the Baptist, but with the genealogy of Jesus, the birth story, and some childhood narratives. Typical for Mt are the six major discourses that Mt himself has produced by using texts from all three groups of material available to him (cf. pp. 225f. below): Sermon on the Mount (Mt 5-7), commission (10), parables (13), church order (18), against the Pharisees (23), on the last things (24f.). The position of these discourses in the Gospel allows an overview of its structure. In other respects Mt is not structured as plainly as Mk.

(2) Mt begins with a genealogy by which Jesus emerges as the descendant of the Patriarchs and of King David (on the relationship between genealogy and Virgin Birth, see p. 52f. above).

Next to the fathers, some of the women from Israel's history are mentioned, i.e., Tamar, Rahab, Ruth, and Uriah's wife. It is sometimes explained that these women are mentioned because they are sinners and non-Jewesses, for the purpose of demonstrating that Jesus entered the entanglements of sin in order to break them up. But in Judaism these women were held in high esteem precisely as examples of faith.

The birth narrative shows the reader from the start that because of his miraculous birth, Jesus is by nature the Son of God, and that the divine proclamation at his baptism did not signal his "adoption" only at that point.

The actual presentation begins in 3:1 with John the Baptist; here Mt follows the lead of Mk and expands it with Q. As in Mk, this is followed by the call of the first disciples and subsequently by the inauguration of the public ministry of Jesus. Beginning with 4:12, it is possible to arrange the Gospel into three major sections:

4:12–13:58—Jesus in Galilee

14:1–20:34—travels through Galilee and Judea

21:1–27:50—Jesus in Jerusalem

In Mt, just as in Mk, the choice of the geographical scenes is given designated meaning. Galilee is the promised land in which the annunciation of the prophets is fulfilled (4:12–16). The destiny of Jesus at the cross is fulfilled in Jerusalem.

Beginning with 4:13, he departs from the Markan leitmotif; in place of the miracle stories of Mk 1:21ff., Mt has a summary (4:23–25) which is followed by the Sermon on the Mount, a catechism-like digest of paraenesis. The narrative of Jesus' activities does not follow until ch 8 and is partly based on material taken from Mk 1. From 9:1 to the end, Mt again adheres to the pattern of the Markan source, while expanding it with insertions from Q and from his special material. This arrangement, which comes to light particularly in the special position of the Sermon on the Mount, has a definite theological intent behind it: The teaching of Jesus is moved into the foreground; his deeds confirm the validity of that teaching.

(3) One ought to remember some of the passages significant for the theology of Mt:

(a) 6:9–13—the Lord's Prayer. In contrast with the text handed down in Lk, this one is expanded (the final doxology is lacking in both). Because of its place in the framework of the Sermon on the Mount, prayer is highlighted (in contrast, cf. the context of Lk 11:2–4) and given fundamental significance (cf. Mt 6:5–8).

(b) Mt 13:24–30, 36–43—the parable of the weeds among the wheat and its interpretation. Eschatological and ecclesiological motives are intertwined in the compilation of the seven kingdom-of-God parables of Mt 13. 13:24ff. shows that the Christian community is not yet the gathering of the elect; instead, they continue to be a community comprised of evil and good individuals whose separation will not take place until the final judgment.

(c) 16:17–19—the message to Peter. Particularly important here is the term ἐκκλησία, which occurs in only one additional place in the synoptic Gospels, in Mt 18:17 (discourse on church order). The use of this term shows that this is without a doubt a post-Easter saying. The power of the keys that Peter receives as apostle of the church pertains to the era between Easter and the parousia. Hence this saying reflects the concept of church in the early Palestinian community.

(d) 25:31–46—the portrait of the last judgment (contrary to popular identification, this text is not a parable). As the coming Son of man, Jesus judges all nations, the criterion being man's conduct in this life. Of course, the discourse addresses the reader of the Gospel; he is summoned to feed the hungry, to give drink to the thirsty, etc. Thus the apocalyptic scene is essentially reduced to an exhortation to Christian existence in the world.

(e) 28:18–20—the Great Commission. This contains the summary of the Gospel. The dominion of the world is given to the risen one; his disciples carry his teaching to all mankind and baptize them in the name of God. At the conclusion the emphasis is once again eschatological. The commission applies from the present until the "end of the world"; because Christ is with his disciples for this length of time, the missionary task of the church also lasts until then.

2. Sources

(1) Next to Mk and the logia source Q, Mt has used the so-called special material whose character as a source is subject to debate. B. H. Streeter (*The Four Gospels*, [9]1956, 223–270) argues that the special material comes from a third literary source. There are indeed systematically formed sections of special material in the framework of the Sermon on the Mount (Mt 5:6), into which Mt fitted material from Q whose secondary insertion can be recognized clearly. The assumption of a third, complete source of special material is predicated upon a continuous thread, woven through all of the special material of Mt. No such thread can be discerned, however.

(2) Another problem related to the source issue is that of the "formula quotations," which are particularly characteristic of Mt. In fact, they point out the Matthean conception of salvation history in that they interpret events in the life of Jesus as confirmation of OT prophecy in the pattern of promise and fulfillment: "This happened so that it might be fulfilled

what the Lord had said through the prophet . . ." (cf. 1:22f.; 2:5f.; 2:15, 17, 23; 4:14–16; 8:17; 12:17–21; 13:35; 21:4f.; 27:9f.).

K. Stendahl (*The School of St. Matthew and its Use of the Old Testament*, ²1968) sees in the formula quotations the intentional scribal effort of a "Matthean" school, styled after the ancient theological schools in Judaism. In a manner similar to that of the Aramaic version of the OT, the Targums, the wording of the quoted texts is adjusted to the interpretation which the scribes derived. The use of the OT in Christian theology indeed corresponds by and large with this hermeneutical model.

In distinction to Stendahl, Strecker (see bibliography) assumes that Mt had a source containing these formula quotations. He bases his assumption on the observation that the OT wording of the formula quotations is more akin to the Hebrew text, while Mt otherwise quotes from the LXX (Mt 4:6f. par Lk 4:10f. from Ps 90:11f. LXX). In Strecker's opinion, only the introductory formulae are usually Mt's own work.

However the inquiry into the source of the formula quotations is resolved, it is in any case certain that Mt subjected them to redactional treatment. They indicate the typically Matthean understanding of salvation history; furthermore, the direct relationship between quotation and context can be observed at several points. In this way, in 21:5 Mt modifies the account of the discovery of the she-ass (which he accepted from Mk 11:1f.) in keeping with the quotation from Zec 9:9 (joined with Is 62:11). Even in this relatively insignificant process he was able to see the confirmation of an OT prophecy. This indication cannot have come from a source.

H. D. Betz, *Essays on the Sermon on the Mount*, ET 1985, regards the Sermon on the Mount as a further source of Mt. The evangelist inserted this document of decidedly Judeo-Christian theology unchanged into his Gospel. But this argument requires further discussion.

3. Language and its peculiarities

The style of Mt is more elegant than that of Mk. On the other hand, the terminology is frequently reminiscent of Jewish ways of expression. The concept of the kingdom of God, for instance, is replaced with the specifically Jewish expression "kingdom of heaven" (βασιλεία τῶν οὐρανῶν); this reflects the Jewish endeavor to avoid the divine names (cf. J. Jeremias, *New Testament Theology*, ET 1971, 96ff.).

4. Authorship

According to the tradition of the early church, the author of the Gospel was Matthew, the "apostle" and former tax collector. Following the statement of Papias (see p. 91f. above), he had published the words of Jesus in their original "Hebrew" (which can only mean Aramaic) rendering.

The assumption of an originally semitic version of Mt has also been postulated in scholarship. But the evangelist has based his book on two *Greek
sources*; it never existed in the "Hebrew" or Aramaic language.

Nevertheless, some exegetes take pains to find a historical core in the Papias reference, arguing that Papias did not have Mt in mind but the original form of the
logia source Q. But it is doubtful that, at the time of Papias' account, Q was still
known as a self-contained book.

The time of the writing of Mt can only be approximated. Mt presupposes
Mk and thus was written after 70, to be sure, after the destruction of Jerusalem. The Matthean form of the parable of the wedding banquet points
this out clearly (cf. Mt 22:7). Conversely the Gospel must definitely have
been written prior to 110 (Ignatius), since the existence of Mt is obviously
presupposed in Ign Smyrn 1:1 (ἵνα πληρωθῇ πᾶσα δικαιοσύνη, cf. Mt
3:15).

In the church, the Gospel of Mt became the leading Gospel and, therefore, had a strong influence upon the others in the history of the text.
Time and again one finds readings in the texts of Lk and Mk which are
the result of harmonization with Mt.

5. Basic theological ideas

(1) The structure of Mt is determined by the six major discourses (see
above). Five times it says after such a discourse of Jesus: καὶ ἐγένετο ὅτε
ἐτέλεσεν ὁ Ἰησοῦς τοὺς λόγους τούτους, or something similar (7:28; 11:1;
13:53; 19:1; 26:1). This leads many exegetes to conclude that Mt arranged
his Gospel into five parts, with each part containing narrative material
to begin with and then a discourse of Jesus to conclude. In this manner
Mt wanted to intimate symbolically that his book was to take the place
of the five books of the OT Torah. Thus Jesus is presented as the new
Moses who surpasses the original Moses with his assertions, "But I say
to you" (5:21f., 28f. et al.).

But while a five-part structure of Mt is perhaps feasible based on the
expression mentioned above, the theological design of Mt does not by
any means show Jesus to be the new Moses. Although there are faint
traces of a Moses typology in the pre-history, the book itself does not
pursue these aspects further.

In the evaluation of the theology of Mt two questions are of particular
interest: Is this a Jewish-Christian Gospel or a Gentile-Christian Gospel
(see below [2])? What is the relationship between eschatology and ethics
(see below [3])?

(2) Mt is generally considered to be a document of Jewish-Christian
theology. In support of this assumption one points to the Judaistic references, such as 10:5f. and 15:24, which say that the mission of Jesus and

of his disciples was not directed to the world as a whole, but refer to Israel exclusively. It is also explained that in Mt, Jesus is understood to be the Messiah of Israel, while the church is the true Israel. Hence the critique and charge are first of all directed against the unbelief of the Jewish people and specifically against that of their pharisaic leaders. This line of argument is said to be specifically Jewish-Christian.

Several counter arguments are adduced against this view, however. The ceremonial law of Judaism is negated in the Gospel of Mt; it is to be recognized further that it is the *worldwide* mission (28:16–20) which denotes the horizon of the author's thinking. The Judaistic statements in Mt have their reason in the evangelist's assimilation of Jewish-Christian material which remained in place in the (Gentile-Christian) final redaction.

Next to these two arguments, a third one is suggested: Mt addresses Judaism neither polemically nor apologetically; rather, the recipients of his Gospel are solely the Gentiles. The anti-Jewish polemic in Mt is only concerned with the Israel of history.

It can hardly be denied that Mt has been greatly affected by the disputes between Judaism and the Christian community. In 23:1–6 the positive statements of the Pharisees are contrasted with their negative *deeds*. Yet, a *fundamental* rejection of the Jewish position of legal orthodoxy is lacking. Therefore, the answer to the question whether Mt is Gentile-Christian or Jewish-Christian in essence depends on one's definition of the concept "Jewish Christianity." The teaching of Judaism that only Jews (and proselytes) can attain salvation and that Gentiles, therefore, must begin by converting to Judaism and must adopt the law and circumcision before they are allowed to become Christians—this teaching was not espoused by the author of Mt and, to that extent, he is not a "Jewish Christian." Like Paul, however, he is a Jew by birth, and in this formal sense he is, of course, a Jewish Christian. He has an intimate knowledge of Judaism and especially of the interpretation of the law at his command; he is apparently engaged in a pressing dispute with Judaism in its legal constitution. Nevertheless, his "gospel" per se, i.e., his doctrine of salvation, is universal; ultimately his proclamation addresses the whole world.

Between the Judaistic limitations to Israel on the part of Jesus (10:5 etc.) on the one hand and the Christian proclamation of the disciples (which, in the final analysis, is world-mission oriented) on the other, Mt finds the necessary balance with the help of a concept from the history of salvation. Jesus' mission has been Israel-oriented, hence both his teaching and his deeds were directed to them alone. But Israel rejected him and thereby lost the salvation which now has been given to the Gentiles. This salvation-history sketch becomes virtually paradigmatic in the Matthean form of the parable of the wicked tenants of the vineyard (Mk 12:1–12 and Mt 21:33–46). V 43 says that the βασιλεία τοῦ θεοῦ will be taken away "from you" and δοθήσεται ἔθνει ποιοῦντι τοὺς καρποὺς αὐτῆς.

(3) Also of special significance is the question of the relationship between eschatology and ethics in Mt. Does he represent a Christian legalism—e.g., in contrast to Paul? Statements such as those of Mt 5:17–19 seem to point in this direction. Could it be that Mt maintains a two-stage ethic, as the term "better righteousness" (5:20) seems to indicate?

If one takes the entire Gospel into account, or even only the Sermon on the Mount scene, it is apparent that Mt's theology is not "legalistic," at least not in the sense that salvation can be obtained only by way of fulfilling the precepts of the law. The promise of salvation *precedes* the exhortation to keep the commandments; the Beatitudes, which express the unconditional favor of God, are positioned at the beginning of the Sermon on the Mount, followed by the demands that take their orientation from the law. Further, Mt does not represent a two-stage ethic; when he demands the "better righteousness" that exceeds that of the Pharisees, he apparently does not have in mind an ethically more valuable stage beyond the "normal" demand. Rather, the "better righteousness" is the absolute condition of salvation and is made possible because all demands are subsumed under the love commandment which, in turn, is preceded by God's pledge—his act—of salvation.

To this extent there is essential agreement between Paul's doctrine of justification and the theology of Mt; in both the pledge of salvation precedes the demand. But if law and righteousness in the theology of Mt are placed in juxtaposition to Paul's doctrine of justification, the difference is certainly substantial. Unlike Paul, Mt does not say that men are given δικαιοσύνη freely. It is not appropriate, however, to parallel the concepts too rigidly; instead, it is necessary to take note of the structure of their theological thought process. If this structure is examined in Mt and Paul, it appears that the systematic locus of δικαιοσύνη in Pauline theology corresponds to "kingdom of heaven" rather than to "righteousness" in Mt. βασιλεία τῶν οὐρανῶν in Mt and δικαιοσύνη θεοῦ in Paul denote essentially the same thing; they designate God's unconditional salvific action and God's demonstration of grace.

(4) In the Sermon on the Mount we encounter another problem relative to the ethics of Mt. Is it possible for its demands, particularly those of the antitheses (5:21–48), to be met? If so, what is their relationship to the Ten Commandments? And if not, what meaning can they possibly have?

The ethics of traditional Catholicism distinguish between the commandments of the Decalogue and the "evangelical counsel" of the Sermon on the Mount, which signifies a higher level than the former. But the text does not allow for such a differentiation. First, it is to be noted that the

demand addresses everyone, not only a few Christians who are particularly "good." Second, the phrase "but I tell you" does not imply a demand for additional performance beyond the demands of the OT
commandments already given; on the contrary, it intends to bring to light
their original intent.

To this extent H. Windisch (*Der Sinn der Bergpredigt*, 1929) is correct: The Sermon
on the Mount contains the radical Jewish ethic of obedience, which is predicated
upon the assumption that its demands can be met.

However, the opposite position has been argued in the theology of the Reformation. The sinner can by no means meet the demands of the Sermon on the
Mount; its norms, after all (according to the argument of orthodoxy), were only
established for the purpose of convicting man of sin.

Finally, A. Schweitzer postulated a third position in his book *The Mystery of
the Kingdom of God. The Secret of Jesus' Messiahship and Passion*, ET 1960, 54ff. The
demands of the Sermon on the Mount are meant to be kept, but only within a
time span that is construed to be very brief, i.e., between Jesus' teaching in the
present and the ushering in of the kingdom of God (key concept: "interim ethics").
On the whole issue, cf. § 55.

In the evaluation of the ethics of the Sermon on the Mount, it is important
to note that its content is not introduced as new material and, most of
all, is not eschatologically based (which already militates against the notion of an interim ethics). One must note further that Mt himself shaped
the Sermon on the Mount and it is in no sense identical with the teaching of Jesus. But unlike Jesus, Mt no longer reckons with the imminence
of the parousia—it is precisely for this reason that he compiles the Sermon on the Mount. This recognition has methodological implications.
The Sermon on the Mount cannot be viewed in isolation; rather, it is to
be considered in view of the whole Gospel, especially in view of the horizons of 28:16–20. In this case, the demands of the Sermon on the Mount
do not turn out to be a temporary regulation for a brief period of time;
on the contrary, they serve as abiding ethical directives for Christian existence in the world. This also means that they are certainly expected to
be met in the realm of the Christian life, for they bring to bear the actual
meaning and content of the OT commandments.

According to Betz (see p. 91), Jesus is the authoritative interpreter of the Torah
for the law-abiding community of the Sermon on the Mount; "thus the ethics
of the SM is at home in the context of Jewish piety and theology. Like all Jewish
ethics, it is an ethic of obedience to the Torah" (*Essays*, p. 123).

(5) Over against the tradition upon which he depends, especially Mk
and Q, the author of the first Gospel set his own very specific emphases.
This is seen, for instance, in the changed christological titles; next to the
terms "Christ" and "Son of man" the title "Son of God" becomes especially prominent. The same tendency is also seen in Mt's non-acceptance

of the Markan messianic secret (cf. especially Mk 6:51f./par. Mt 14:33). He does not want his Gospel to portray the veiling of the true nature of Jesus; instead, he wants it to point to the paradox of his revelation that takes place in lowliness (10:42; 11:25; 12:18ff.; 18:6, 10; 25:40, 45). A comparison of the accounts of the triumphal entry (Mk 11:1–10 par. Mt 21:1–9) points up additional important elements of the Matthean Christology. By means of a formula quotation in 21:4f., he emphasizes from the beginning that the issue now is the entry of the *Messiah*; in v 9 Mt supplements the Markan ὡσαννά with τῷ υἱῷ Δαυίδ. Jesus, who in his lowliness enters on a donkey, is openly acknowledged as Messiah.

In addition to Christology, the church's (self) understanding in Mt also changes. It is not intended as a temporary entity but has the character of permanence. As a result, the anticipation of the parousia recedes; instead, greater emphasis is placed upon the problem of the false teachers who will appear "in the last days." By the same token, the disciples are no longer reprimanded for *un*belief, as in Mk, but for their "*little* faith," their despondency (cf. Mt 8:26 with Mk 4:40). Here again, the early church setting at the time of Mt's writing is reflected.

Suggested exercises:

1. Observe Mt's methodology by means of the parallel passages, especially in Mk. Mt abridges and sharpens. Cf. Mk 2:1ff. with the corresponding text in Mt. Tool: G. Barth (see bibliography).

2. Compare the pericope of the plucking of heads of grain on the Sabbath in Mt and Mk. What purpose emerges in Mt? Tool: A. Lindemann, *WuD* NF 15, 1979, 79–105.

3. Attempt an analysis of the sources in Mt 10; 24f. Tool: R. Bultmann, *The History of the Synoptic Tradition*.

4. Determine the structure of the discourses by observing the final eschatological emphasis. Tool: G. Bornkamm (see bibliography), 15–24.

§ 36 Gospel of Luke

Bibliography: G. Braumann, ed., *Das Lukas-Evangelium*, Wege der Forschung 280, 1974; H. Conzelmann, *The Theology of St. Luke*, ET 1961; J. A. Fitzmyer, *The Gospel according to Luke, I–IX, X–XXIV*, 2 vols., AB 28, 28A, 1981, 1985; W. Grundmann, *Das Evangelium nach Lukas*, ThHK III, ⁶1971; E. Klostermann, *Das Lukasevangelium*, HNT 5, ²1929; H. Schürmann, *Das Lukasevangelium. Erster Teil: Lk 1:1–9:50*, HThK III, 1969; E. Schweizer, *The Good News According to Luke*, ET 1984.

1. Structure and problem

(1) Lk is the longest and, at the same time, linguistically the most carefully constructed Gospel. The vocabulary is more comprehensive than that of Mk or Mt, and with regard to style, Luke is on a more sophisticated level than the two other writers. Already the prologue of 1:1-4, which accords with hellenistic practice, shows that Lk makes literary claims that are foreign to the other synoptic Gospels.

The structure of Lk can be ascertained in a comparison with Mk. In place of the two-part structure of Mk, Lk divides into three parts. Part one, which (after the prehistory of Lk 1f.) is comprised of the section 3:1–9:50, narrates the journeys of Jesus in Galilee and Judea. Part two, 9:51–19:27, contains the presentation of Jesus' journey to Jerusalem. Jesus' sojourn in Jerusalem is the subject of the third part, 19:28–24:53.

Among themselves, the three parts are equivalent; in contrast to Mk, the sojourn in Jerusalem is not limited to one week, but one gains the impression that he has in mind an appearance of longer duration. A comparison with Mt also distinctly shows that Lk's methodology differs from that of Mt. While Mt causes the individual sources to blend, Lk consistently joins together entire blocks of material, either from Mk or from the non-Markan sources, i.e., Q and the special material. Up to 6:19 he follows essentially the Markan order (Mk 3:19); then, in 6:20–8:3 he brings in the so-called little interpolation from Q and from the special material. Beginning with 8:4, he adheres to the Markan source again by resuming with Mk 4:1 (in part, the materials from Mk 3:20–35 are inserted later). Lk uses the same procedure again in ch 9ff. Up to 9:50 he follows Mk (to Mk 9:41); in the so-called big interpolation of 9:51–18:14, however, he again uses material primarily from Q and from his special material, with a few exceptions. From 18:15 to the end of the passion portrayal, he uses Mk's outline. This procedure, typical of Lk and different from Mt, is also seen in that Lk assumes from Mk *and* Q both the mission discourse and the eschatological discourse. However, he does not compile the material to form a lengthy discourse, as Mt does in ch 10, but he builds them into his Gospel at various points and without assimilation (9; 10; 17:20ff.; 21).

(2) Similar to Mt, Lk also begins with the birth and childhood stories of Jesus (Lk 1f.). The action proper begins with 3:1, at which point Lk begins to join the Markan source for the most part. It is striking, however, that he departs from this source after 9:17 (par Mk 6:44); Mk 6:45–8:26 are without parallel in Lk. In 9:18 he follows the Markan source again, beginning with Mk 8:27. Why does Lk allow this gap to remain? According to one hypothesis, this passage had been lacking in (yet to be postulated!) Ur-Mk (cf. p. 47); but against this speaks the fact that Mt certainly read and assumed the same text of Mk omitted by Lk. Therefore, another view suggests that Lk apparently used a damaged copy of Mk in

which the passage 6:45–8:26 had dropped out for external reasons. But this, too, is highly unlikely, since the scene of Lk 9:12–17 and the beginning of the following pericope in 9:18 are carefully coordinated. V 18 emphasizes that Jesus is alone again with his disciples, which surely refers back to the previous scene with the crowd of people. This stylization would hardly make sense if all Lk wanted to do was bridge a gap in Mk. It is much more plausible that Lk ignored Mk 6:45ff. for essentially theological reasons. He obviously wants to eliminate Jesus' "journey into foreign territory"—i.e., his travels to Tyre and the rides across the Sea of Galilee—as much as possible. Lk deliberately omits the territories outside of Galilee and Judea as places of Jesus' ministry (exception: the healing of the Gadarene demoniac).

A section that is particularly characteristic for the Gospel of Lk is the travel narrative of 9:51–19:27. The relatively brief delineation of Jesus' journey to Jerusalem (Mk 10) is here expanded into a comprehensive and self-contained major unit.

For many exegetes the travel narrative ends already with 18:15 because Lk rejoins Mk at this point. But the character of the travel narrative is maintained to 19:27; the source issue is irrelevant to the exposition of the literary and theological intentions of Lk.

In the Passion narrative Lk again adheres closely to Mk; only at the end does he exceed the Markan source through the inclusion of appearance stories.

2. *Sources and other literary problems*

(1) Lk poses bigger problems here than the two other synoptic writers. The fundamental question must indeed be raised with regard to Lk whether the two-document hypothesis continues to be tenable in its traditional form. It is thus modified by the British exegetes B. H. Streeter (see p. 223 above) and V. Taylor, among others, who argue for the "proto-Luke hypothesis." According to this view, Lk did not take his orientation from the Markan structure and then expand it by inserting additional material from Q and from the special source (see p. 55f. above). Instead, he first synthesized Q and his special material ("proto-Luke"), and only then, in a second phase, did he insert the Markan material in blocks into this combination. This assumption is supported by the observation already outlined: while Lk indeed has "non-Markan" blocks, i.e., amalgamations of Q and special material, there are no mixtures of Q and Mk or of special material and Mk. Nevertheless, the proto-Luke hypothesis has little to commend it: (a) If the hypothesis were correct, the material from Q and the special material contained in Lk would have to result in a complete gospel. But this is not the case, for the passion section is lacking. Representatives of this hypothesis are forced, therefore, to postulate an-

other source besides Mk in the passion section of Lk, i.e., a passion story that came either from Q or from the special source. It is already established, however, that Q did not contain a passion narrative (see p. 57f. above); the situation in Mt also demonstrates this. The special material found in the Lukan passion narrative is insufficient for a second complete passion account. (b) The proto-Luke hypothesis is also militated against by the observation that the extant, purposeful structure of Lk is the result of the Markan leitmotif; the latter Gospel provided the outline for the Lukan presentation. Even the travel motif which Lk enlarged so extensively by means of Q and the special material is basically Mk's. Precisely in a "proto-Luke" the travel account would not have been a "central section" (so Taylor); only in the present form of the Gospel is this the case.

The rejection of the proto-Luke hypothesis does not yet say anything about the character of the special material in Lk. Was this material a literary source? Or was it merely Lk's collection of various oral traditions? Against the argument that it was an independent gospel (so A. Schlatter), the objection needs to be raised again that there is no evidence of a passion narrative in the special material (see above). The analysis also indicates that there was apparently no connection, in the pre-Lukan stage, between the individual units of tradition in the special material. Conversely, it is true that the special material demonstrates throughout certain distinct peculiarities. The category of example story (the good Samaritan, 10:30–35; the rich farmer, 12:16–21; the rich man and Lazarus, 16:19–31; the Pharisee and the publican, 18:10–14) is found only here; the parable of the lost Son, which is narrated in unusually detailed fashion, is given only here (15:11–32). In addition, the Lukan special material contains strangely intimate scenes (Jesus with Mary and Martha, 10:38–42; Jesus and the sinful woman, 7:36–50; cf. Mk 14:3–9). Finally, it is striking that some elements of the special material contain pointers that they were originally shaped in Jerusalem. Some statements indicate a certain familiarity with Palestinian customs and religious viewpoints (17:14). It can be assumed that the Lukan special material actually was not merely a random collection, but represented a layer of tradition which was to some extent already fixed.

(2) The beginning of the Gospel is a special literary problem (Lk 1f.) The reader notices immediately that 3:1f. resembles the beginning of a book and that the genealogy of Jesus does not appear until ch 3 (in contrast, cf. Mt). The first two chapters stand out linguistically; their style has a more pronounced Semitic flavor than the rest of Lk. Nevertheless, Lukan authorship can hardly be questioned since Lk's typical elements of style are also found in this part. But it is conceivable that Lk did not place the first two chapters in front of the entire Gospel until phase two of his work (cf. 3:1ff. with Mk 1:1ff.). This assumption is also supported

by the observation that in the framework of the Gospel beginning with ch 3, as well as in Acts (see below), the birth narrative is not important for Christology (when Lk, for instance in Acts 1:21f., speaks of the "beginning" of Jesus, he has in mind the baptism of Jesus, not his birth).

3. Authorship

As stated by tradition, the author of the third Gospel (and of Acts) was the physician Luke (who was also a "lawyer" according to the Muratorian Canon), who was a companion of Paul, according to Phlm 24 (cf. Col 4:14; 2 Tim 4:11). Dibelius defends this tradition as historically reliable, but the arguments against it are fairly weighty. At least the author of Acts (who may very well be identical with the author of Lk) does not appear to be in the immediate vicinity of Paul's life; in addition, he is barely influenced by the theology of Paul. The likelihood is minute, therefore, that Luke, the companion of Paul, was indeed the author of the two "Lukan" writings. Furthermore, we lack any and all evidence pointing categorically to another author known to us. Consequently it may be difficult to avoid the conclusion that we do not know the author of Lk. The time of the writing of Lk can only be vaguely determined. In any case, Lk knew the Gospel of Mk; equally certain is his retrospective view of the destruction of Jerusalem (21:20–24), which means that the Gospel must have been written after A.D. 70. The *terminus ad quem*, however, can only be determined in conjunction with the dating of Acts (see pp. 236f., 238f. below).

Nothing at all can be said about the place of writing of Lk; the only certainty is that the author did not know Palestine.

4. Basic theological ideas

(1) The basic theological conception can be worked out best by noting the variations from the Markan pattern, while observing the special redactional comments at the same time. In comparison to Mk, the description of Jesus' first public appearance is reshaped in programmatic fashion. The summary-like description of the proclamation of Jesus (Mk 1:14f.) and the description of the appearance of Jesus in his hometown Nazareth (Mk 6:1–6) are compiled in such a way by Lk that the now broadly shaped sermon in Nazareth becomes his very first public appearance (Lk 4:14, 16–30). It is possible that the entire scene, except for vv 25–27, is Lk's redactional work (cf. R. Bultmann, *History of the Synoptic Tradition*, 31f.).

4:13 and 22:3 represent a special kind of parenthesis. Satan vanishes from the surroundings of Jesus beginning with his first public appearance until the betrayal of Judas, that is, until the passion. The ministry of Jesus is neither assailed nor endangered. This has consequences for the exegesis of the entire Gospel. For example, when Jesus sends out the disciples "like sheep among wolves" in Lk 10:3, the emphasis is not on the danger they will encounter, but rather on the special protection they are under. This is in sharp contrast to the description of the situation of the disciples after Jesus' departure (cf. the transition from 22:35 to 22:36).

It is significant that from the beginning Lk points to the entire Jewish realm, rather than only Galilee, as the sphere of Jesus' ministry (4:44; 7:17). Conversely, any reference to an appearance of Jesus outside of this realm is categorically excluded. The intent of this tactic is to clarify the mission's sequence in terms of salvation history. Lk wants to show that the ministry of Jesus was focused entirely on Israel; only his death and exaltation lead to the mission to the Gentiles (cf. Acts 1).

Even more than in Mk and Mt, Jerusalem becomes the center for Lk. Not only is Jerusalem the place of Jesus' death as predestined in the history of salvation, it is also the place of the appearances of the resurrected one and thus the church's place of origin. The first part of Acts further points out the extent to which Lk concentrates upon the church's earliest time in Jerusalem.

(2) Lk considers himself to belong to the third Christian generation (1:1–4); thus he has at his disposal a well-developed concept of tradition. For this reason, Lukan scholarship has sometimes argued that the author of the Third Gospel should already be considered a representative of "early catholicism." Acts especially, for example, clearly indicates that the apostles became the "guarantors of the gospel tradition" and later on the "guarantors and criterion of the canonical tradition," because in the disputes about the canon and about correct doctrine, the church needed "guarantors of the reliability of their own doctrinal tradition" (E. Käsemann, "Ministry and Community in the New Testament," in *Essays on New Testament Themes*, ET 1964, 91). "So far as we can see, then, it was Luke who was the first to propagate the theories of tradition and legitimate succession which mark the advent of early Catholicism" (p. 91). But the notion of tradition as such is only one ingredient of "early catholicism"—a rather unfortunate name; more important is the linking of this notion of tradition with the succession of office. This twofold aspect is found in 1 Clem, for example. The notion of an office is by no means developed in Lk, however. In contrast with the letters of Ignatius, for instance, the structure of a hierarchy is conspicuously absent (see § 45 below). He does not tie up doctrine and Spirit with the ecclesiastical organization.

(3) One notices that Lk deliberately reflects on the tradition he received. This is especially true of eschatology. Lk does not share the common anticipation of an imminent parousia; on the other hand, he is not satisfied merely with accepting a protracted period leading to the end of the world. Rather, for him time itself becomes the object of theological reflection. He therefore develops his own special conception of salvation history. For

Lk, between the exaltation of Jesus and the parousia lies the age of the church. Jesus is the center of salvation history, for he effects the transition from the age of Israel to that of the church. The duration of the church age, however—Lk enjoins repeatedly—can in no sense be calculated (17:20f.; 19:11; 21:5-36; 22:69; Acts 1:1-11). The present is the era of the church's persecution. But the church has received the Spirit as a powerful aid to endure this age. The tradition of Jesus and of his teaching, as well as the portrait of his nature and ministry, are preserved in the church. Likewise the eschatological hope, which no longer focuses as much on the parousia as it does on the anticipation of the resurrection of the individual, is vouchsafed by this tradition.

(4) Also characteristic for Lk is a certain political apologetic. One clearly gains the impression that Lk exonerates the Roman procurator Pilate from the guilt of Jesus' death and mainly burdens the Jews with the responsibility for the execution of Jesus. Yet it is important to recognize that Lk is not primarily concerned with exonerating Pilate. He is much more concerned with viewing the role of the Jews as fulfillment of prophecy and thus as a necessary precursor in the unfolding of the history of salvation. At the same time, the political leadership of the Roman Empire needs to be shown that Jesus' claim of dominion of which Christians speak is not a political claim. This is the reason why Pilate speaks so emphatically of the innocence of Jesus (23:22) and why he does not condemn him but, instead, merely "hands him over" to the Jews.

5. Exercise in methodology: A paradigm of redaction criticism in Luke

The extensive travel narrative in the middle of the Gospel is typical for Lk. What conception lies behind this design?

In order to work out an answer, the following methodological steps are necessary:

(1) It is striking that the mention of movement from one place to another almost entirely vanishes precisely at the point where the journey to Jerusalem begins (9:51). There are merely a number of routine references that express that Jesus is en route on the journey (10:38; 13:22; 17:11). This allows two conclusions. From a *literary* perspective, this means that apparently Lk himself shaped this part of the Gospel as a travel narrative, since the respective notes are redactional, i.e., they come from the hand of Lk. This leads to the second, a *historical* conclusion that the journey as a whole is fictitious.

This does not mean that Jesus did not travel to Jerusalem; but this journey cannot be reconstructed from the account of Lk.

(2) The observation that the material (in which only the introductory scene of 9:51-56 depicts a travel situation) does not correspond with the form of its presentation leads to the question of why Lk would even cast the material he received into this mold.

Answer: Apparently Lk wants to impress upon the reader that the "face" of Jesus is now focused upon Jerusalem. The reader is to know and understand Jesus as the Messiah destined for the passion.

(3) There are three divergent christological aspects in the three parts of the Gospel which arise for the theological evaluation of the Lukan redaction. (a) Through his birth, his teaching, and his miracles, Jesus is the Messiah/Son of God. (b) He is the Messiah destined to suffer; as such, he "goes up" to Jerusalem. (c) He is the king who teaches in the temple and as a result is killed, but whom God glorifies in the resurrection.

Suggested exercise:

Eschatology is one of the important problems of the theology of Lk:

1. Analyze the apocalypse of the logia in the Lukan form in 17:20–37 and compare it with Mt (Tool: Aland's *Synopsis*, 315–318, or Huck-Greeven, 173–175). What redactional expansions are found in Lk and what is their theological function?

2. Analyze the synoptic apocalypse in the Lukan form in 21:5–36 and compare it with Mt and Mk. What literary-critical assessment can be made concerning the text? What theological tendencies can be recognized? Tool: H. Conzelmann (see bibliography), 120–132.

§ 37 Acts

Bibliography: H. Conzelmann, *Acts*, Hermeneia, ET 1987; M. Dibelius, *Studies in the Acts of the Apostles*, ET 1956; E. Haenchen, *The Acts of the Apostles*, ET 1971; F. J. Foakes Jackson and K. Lake, *The Beginnings of Christianity: The Acts of the Apostles*, 5 vols., reprint, 1979; J. Roloff, *Die Apostelgeschichte*, NTD 5, 1981.

1. Authorship and literary character

(1) It is clear at the first glance that Acts and Lk originate from the same author.

(a) Acts 1:1 refers back to the beginning of Lk (the dedication is to the same individual, Theophilus, who is unknown to us).

(b) The presentation of the historical events in Acts 1:1–11 connects with Lk 24 (ascension narrative).

(c) Both style and theological ideas of the two books are in agreement. Of course, there are differing features to be found in certain details, but those are the result of differences in the material used. Many differences are also traceable back to the fact that in the Gospel the author was more strictly bound to the sources and extant, fixed traditions. Concerning the time and place of writing of Acts, the observations made in Lk also apply to Acts; time and place cannot be determined. The only thing that is clear is that Acts was written shortly after Lk.

For the most part, Acts confirms the observation that Luke, the companion of Paul mentioned in Phlm 24, cannot be the author of the two books (see p. 233 above), since any familiarity with the peculiarities of Pauline theology is lacking (doctrine of justification, theology of the cross). The Paul of Acts is considerably different from the historical Paul as we know him from his letters.

(2) Acts is most closely related to the historical monographs of antiquity, especially with the genre of the πράξεις; on the whole, however, the agreements between them are scant. The typical stylistic elements that Lk implements (discourses, novel-like descriptions, biographical elements of style) are consistently restructured in view of the special theological interest he pursues.

Suggested reading:

A comparison with the apocryphal Acts of Paul, for instance, indicates clearly how reserved and "modern" Lk's writing is. Prolific growth of the tradition and exaggeration of content are very rarely encountered. In this connection, it is useful to read the "Acts of Paul and Thecla" in H-S II, 353–364, and to compare the miracle stories in it with the respective pericopae in Acts.

2. Structure and content

A cursory overview of the content and theme of Acts can be obtained by observing that the "Apostolic Council" that confirmed the mission to the Gentiles, who are free from the law, is at once the literary and objective center of the book. For the rest, the structure of the book is already indicated in 1:8 where Jesus promises the disciples as the final word prior to his ascension that they were to be his witnesses "in Jerusalem, in all Judea and Samaria, and to the end of the world." In keeping with this announcement, the first section, Acts 1–5, deals with the church in Jerusalem, the second part, chs 6–12, with the mission in Judea and Samaria, and the third part, chs 13–28, with Paul's "world mission," which takes him as far as Rome.

The last part can be subdivided again: (1) Acts 13–14 contains a prelude of sorts (Paul and Barnabas); (2) ch 15 establishes the theological and "canonical" basis for the mission to the Gentiles; (3) chs 16–28 deal exclusively with Paul—other figures of the church are practically no longer important.

The content of Acts can be easily grasped by observing the theological highpoints: Ch 1—ascension; ch 2—Pentecost, where a certain literary pattern is used: a miracle takes place first, followed by an explanatory mission discourse. It is interesting to look for further examples of this pattern in Acts (cf. already ch 3). Ch 4f. records the two investigations of the apostles by the Sanhedrin.

Suggested exercise:

The agreements between the accounts of Acts 4 and 5 are so considerable that one can hardly consider the possibility of two separate traditions.

1. Is Lk aware of the fact that he is recording the same account in Acts 4:5–22 and Acts 5:26–42?

2. What intent does a comparison between the two texts show?

The section composed of 6:1–8:3 describes the circumstance of the hellenistic Christian Jews in Jerusalem; the center of the presentation is the major speech and the martyrdom of Stephen (Acts 7). One notices immediately that this speech breaks out of the framework; it is not relevant to the situation but has its independent content.

Suggested exercise:

1. What is the purpose behind Stephen's speech?

2. Is the speech structured uniformly, or is one to assume that it integrates a source?

3. Is the speech to be considered historically authentic, that is, did Stephen indeed give it in this form? Or is this a literary product?

Tools: M. Dibelius, *Studies in the Acts of the Apostles,* 167–170; E. Plümacher, *Lukas als hellenistischer Schriftsteller. Studien zur Apostelgeschichte,* 1972.

In ch 9 Lk tells of the commission of Saul (Greek name: Paul); the account is repeated in 22:3–21 and 26:9–20. Acts 10 contains the paradigmatic account of the conversion of a non-Jew. Upon the initiative of the Spirit, the "missionary" is Peter who thus appears as founder of the mission to the Gentiles. Ch 11 is an account of the Gentile-Christian community of Antioch where the designation "Christians" (χριστιανοί) is used for the first time. Beginning with ch 14, the book's development is essentially determined by Paul's ministry.

In Lk's presentation, this task is carried out in the form of missionary journeys, all of which follow the pattern of the first journey (Acts 13f.); i.e., in an unfamiliar city Paul turns first to the Jews of the synagogue and by using the OT proclaims Jesus as the Christ. Eventually this leads to conflict between the Jews and this message while at the same time there is an enormous influx of Gentile hearers. Thus Paul turns away from the Jews and toward the Gentiles (cf., e.g., 13:44–46; 18:5f.; extensively detailed in 28:17–28).

By means of this "first missionary journey" of Paul, Lk brings to light the fundamental problem of the mission. Do converted Gentiles have to accept the Jewish law, especially circumcision? Or is a mission to the Gentiles that is free of the law's demands feasible? Ultimately the work of Paul can only begin after the solving of this problem—that is, immediately following the Apostolic Council in Acts 15 (on the Council, see § 66 below).

Paul's second journey (15:40–18:22) is hardly set off from the third (18:23–21:17). The significance of the apparently separate journey, discussed with curious terseness, from Corinth to Syria via Ephesus and then Antioch (18:18–23) is not clear.

The decisive points of reference of the second journey are the crossing over to Europe (16:9ff.) and the stay in Macedonia, Athens, Corinth, and Ephesus. This section likewise contains several scenes that resemble particular models. For example, Paul's appearances in Philippi, Corinth, and Ephesus are models of a political apologetic; the famous speech on the Areopagus in Athens is meant to portray the confrontation with Hellenism.

The last part of Acts narrates Paul's arrest in Jerusalem, his imprisonment and trial in Caesarea, and, finally, the transportation of Paul the prisoner to Rome. Here, too, certain scenes have been given a paradigmatic form. When in Acts 25f. the procurator Festus and King Herod Agrippa do not see any reason to take steps against Paul, the purpose of such a presentation is to show that the Roman state had no reason to take steps against Christianity.

The conclusion of Acts is strange. Nothing is said about the result of the Roman proceedings against Paul; instead, the book ends with the remark that Paul preached in Rome μετὰ πάσης παρρησίας ἀκωλύτως. If one remembers the condemnation and execution of Paul, this can hardly be in harmony with the facts. For this reason, a number of hypotheses about the ending of Acts have been argued: (a) Lk wrote the book prior to the trial's conclusion; indeed, the whole book is the written defence of Paul by Lk (the lawyer, see p. 233 above). But there is no evidence for the argument that Acts was written as a result of an actual event. Furthermore, Paul's farewell address in Acts 20 shows clearly that Lk knew of Paul's end. (b) After the trial in Rome, Paul was in fact released and died only after a second imprisonment. In favor of this hypothesis, reference is made to the existence of the Pastoral letters (see above). For one thing, however, the Pastorals undoubtedly belong to the post-Pauline era and, for another, they too know of only *one* imprisonment of Paul in Rome. (c) Lk knows full well that Paul was executed after two years of imprisonment in Rome. But he does not mention this fact because he either (i) did not want to write a biography of Paul but a history of the founding of the church, or because (ii) he was of the opinion that the description of Paul's execution by a Roman court would seriously disturb the political apologetic he pursued.

It is hard to say which of these theories is correct. The one mentioned last is the most plausible one in relative terms, but it also cannot be substantiated with absolute certainty.

3. Literary-critical problems (sources)

In the analysis of Acts one needs to utilize essentially the same methods as used in the analysis of the Synoptics (cf. §§ 7–10 above).

(1) The first question pertains to those literary sources used throughout Acts. In this regard, the historical question plays an important part (as it does in Gospel research) i.e., whether it is possible to reconstruct in this way individual events as historically reliable. Peculiarities of style are conspicuous in the reading of Acts rendering it probable that Lk used sources in the writing of it. For instance, extensive parts of the book are written in the first person plural, though Acts as a whole is not arranged as an adventure account. Certain contradictions arise in some narratives so that one gains the impression that two different sources have been integrated.

According to the theory of Harnack—and frequently accepted by other exegetes—two parallel sources with distinct character have been assimilated in the first part of Acts, one which is historically reliable and a second, historically useless source that contained numerous miracle stories (Harnack speaks of recensions A and B). The historically reliable source was comprised of 3:1–5:16 (the parallel text from recension B is handed down in Acts 2; 5:17–42) as well as the fragments of 8:5–40; 9:31–11:18; 12:1–23. This Jerusalemite-Caesarean source can possibly be traced back to the evangelist Philip. Next to it there is an Antiochan-Jerusalemite source (6:1–8:4; 11:19–30; 12:25–15:35), which is also predominantly historically reliable; it could be that Silas was its author.

It is indeed quite certain that Lk used literary sources in the writing of the first part of Acts; however, a detailed reconstruction of these sources is not possible.

(3) The situation is apparently different in the second part of Acts where an outstanding indication seems to be offered in favor of a separation of sources: the "we" sections in 16:10–17(40); 20:5–15; 21:1–18, and 27:1–28:16. It could be assumed that the author describes events of which he was an eyewitness. The "we" begins in the account about Troas (16:10) and vanishes in the course of the delineation of the stay in Philippi and only emerges again in the context of a journey from Philippi to Troas (20:5f.). Parts of the account of Paul's stay in Miletus and of the journey to Jerusalem as well as the narrative of the journey to Rome are also written in the "we" style. It could be assumed, therefore, that Lk came to know Paul in Troas and there joined him; for some reason he then remained in Philippi while Paul continued on; however, later on he must have joined him again. But as logical as this assumption seems to be at first, some textual observations clearly oppose it. First, the "we" section ceases *during* the stay in Philippi (not only in connection with Paul's departure). Second, the Philippi account is highly miraculous, hence presumably not an eyewitness account. One has the impression that the "we" section is not at all closely associated with the events described.

Incidentally, these difficulties are no less removed if one assumes that Lk did not narrate his own experiences but that he accepted a source in the "we" form here, i.e., an account of an unknown eyewitness.

In view of these circumstances, some exegetes argue that the "we" sections are neither a source nor an eyewitness account; rather, they represent a literary device of the author who thereby sought to make the events more vividly tangible to the reader. Yet this raises the question why this device is used in only such few instances and is used precisely in the description of sea voyages during which nothing important happens in terms of missions.

Ch 27f. is in this respect particularly interesting. This sea voyage is the only description of a genuine journey in Acts. It is striking, however, that the scenes in which Paul appears are easily separated from the narrative. One may ask whether Lk possibly drew up this description of the journey by himself or whether he accepted an existing narrative of a shipwreck and only subsequently built in the Pauline scenes.

It may be difficult to avoid the conclusion that the "we" sections are meant to create the impression of an eyewitness account, although this is actually not the case.

(4) The author of Acts based his work on a framework he himself created and then inserted the individual accounts available to him. Hence the routes of the journeys can in no way be accorded the character of a source; instead, they represent the redactional work of Lk (cf. p. 103f., above).

Without a doubt, in recent decades exegetical scholarship has contributed decisively to the clarification of the traditions assimilated in Acts. Nevertheless, the riddle of the sources in Acts is still not conclusively solved.

4. Unique features in the text tradition

The text of Acts contains a peculiar problem. The so-called Western text (see p. 21 above), represented by Codex D, some Old Latin mss, and the marginal notes in a Syriac version, demonstrates peculiarities that are much more pronounced than in the rest of the NT writings. It was argued, therefore, that Lk perhaps wrote two editions of Acts. But this is altogether unlikely. (1) If there are outright contradictions between the Alexandrian and the Western text, one recognizes that they cannot be two "editions" from the hand of the same author, but rather that the Western text misunderstood or even intentionally corrected the author of Acts. For instance, in 5:16, 39 he inserts explanatory paraphrases into the text. One also notices in 3:11 and 14:2ff. that he endeavors to smooth out the text. Likewise, in 15:20, 29; 16:30, 39 he obviously makes deliberate "improvements"; clearly tendentious alterations are found in 15:1ff. (2) An adequate evaluation of the textual tradition of the Western text may not be possible without referring to the Gospel of Lk next to Acts. In this way one recognizes that this text as a whole is permeated with "harmonizing variants" that frequently seek to obliterate the peculiarities of Lk and to assimilate his text with the parallels. Evidently this tendency, with its intent to harmonize things, is continued in Acts by "purifying" the text frequently from expressions that have become either offensive or unintelligible.

Suggested exercises:

1. Look up the references cited and evaluate in each case the intentionality of the Western reading. Tool: E. J. Epp, *The Theological Tendency of Codex Bezae Cantabrigiensis in Acts*, SNTSMS 3, 1966.

2. Undertake a text-critical analysis of the "apostolic decree" (cf. p. 362ff. below).

5. Theological peculiarities and the historical value of Acts

(1) The speeches and summaries in Acts are especially characteristic of the theology of Lk. It is to be noted to begin with that these are not authentic speeches. In keeping with the practice of classical historiography (cf. e.g., Thucydides), they are the author's own work and have subsequently been inserted into the presentation; it does not address the theology of the respective speakers or the setting in which the speeches possibly were given. They are neither the records of nor the excerpts from speeches that Peter, James, etc. actually gave; the only thing that can be recognized in them is the theology of Lk.

Some definite types can be pinpointed with relative ease.

(a) The speeches of Peter, shaped as missionary addresses to Jews, contain specific characteristics: continuity with the OT, christological kerygma, scriptural support and affirmation of salvation (including a call to repentance). Paul's speech in Acts 13 follows the same pattern, which incidentally, indicates that the speeches indeed do not reflect the individuality of the respective speaker.

(b) Stephen's speech (Acts 7) is a critical overview of the history of Israel; through it Lk endeavors to justify the shift of the mission to the Gentiles. The only connection to the presupposed external setting (accusation before the Sanhedrin) is found in 7:52b.

(c) In the mind of Lk, the Areopagus speech is a typical Pauline missionary address to Gentiles. At no point does it contain the characteristics of Pauline theology.

Against this opinion it is sometimes argued that it cannot be dismissed categorically that Paul had preached a missionary sermon in Athens. This is certainly true. It is nevertheless also true that it cannot have been the speech handed down in Acts. Compare the excursus in H. Conzelmann (see bibliography), 111–113.

(d) Paul's speech in Acts 20 has the features typical of a farewell address; it is Paul's only address to Christians in Acts. In the mind of Lk it signals the close of the mission and provides the hearers with the final exhortations and advice for his own continued work. This type of "testament" is also found in Jn 13–17 as well as in the post-Pauline letters (2 Tim and 2 Pet). In the exegesis of Acts 20, therefore, it is to be noted that Lk does not render a historical speech of Paul to the Ephesian elders, but that he himself addresses the Christians of his time (for instance, cf. the references to heresy in vv 29f.).

(e) Finally, the defense speeches of Paul the prisoner constitute a special type. They point out that the Christian faith and the Roman state do not touch one another and hence can easily exist side by side.

As sources, the summaries in Acts (cf. 2:42–47; 4:32–35; 5:12–16) have as little immediate value as the speeches. They do not permit a glance into the actual conditions of the early church; rather, they present the ideal picture of the church desired by the author. Lk learned this *form* of presentation from Mk (cf. Mk 1:14f., though here without idealization) and took it up both in his Gospel as well as in Acts.

(2) These observations yield some fundamental conclusions relative to the evaluation of the historical value of Acts. Acts is not a continuous source for the history of the early church. Merely some individual events (such as the dispersion of the hellenistic Jewish Christians from Jerusalem) and certain typical phenomena of the early church (such as the initial adherence to the temple cult) can be reconstructed from it. There is no cohesive presentation of the history of the early church, and probably one was never intended. The picture of the church that is drawn in the summaries is not historically authentic but represents an idealization of the early period of the kind frequently observed in classical historiography ("golden era"). A characteristic example is the illustration of Jerusalem. Its community is indeed the maternal locus of the church, but Lk enlarges the picture to the extent that the earliest community becomes the center of the church and the beginning of all ecclesiastical activity. The actual situation was different, as can be seen from the references to the Antiochene church in Acts, and especially from Gal 1 (particularly v 17).

Also historically incorrect is the traditional picture conveyed in Acts, according to which Paul's mission was carried out in the form of three missionary journeys. It is refuted especially by the Pauline letters.

This critical assessment of Acts does not mean that Acts is not to be accorded considerable value as a source, but the history of early Christianity as a whole cannot be reconstructed from Acts with historical reliability.

Suggested exercise for the advanced student:

What are the differences between the portrayal of Paul in Acts and in Pauline theology? What are the arguments for the nonlegalistic Gentile mission in Acts? What are they in Paul?

Tools: G. Klein, *Die zwölf Apostel*, 1961, 114–192; A. Lindemann, *Paulus im ältesten Christentum*, 1979, 49–68; J. Munck, *Paul and the Salvation of Mankind*, ET 1959; W. Schmithals, *The Office of Apostle in the Early Church* ET 1969; Ph. Vielhauer, "Zum 'Paulinismus' der Apg.," *Ges. Aufs.* I, 1965, 9–27.

IV. JOHANNINE WRITINGS (GOSPEL AND LETTERS)

Bibliography: R. Bultmann, *Theology of the NT*, ET 1951/1955, 2:3–92.

§ 38 Gospel of John

Bibliography: C. K. Barrett, *The Gospel According to St. John*, ²1978; J. Becker, *Das Evangelium nach Johannes*, OTK 4/1.2, 1979/81; R. E. Brown, *The Gospel According to John*, 2 vols., AB 29, 29A, 1966, 1977; idem, *The Community of the Beloved Disciple*, 1979; R. Bultmann, *The Gospel of John*, ET 1971; C. H. Dodd, *The Interpretation of the Fourth Gospel*, 1953; G. Richter, *Studien zum Johannesevangelium*, BU 13, 1977; R. Schnackenburg, *The Gospel According to St. John*, 3 vols., ET 1980–1982.

1. Structure and problem

(1) The peculiarities of Jn are best ascertained by a comparison with the Synoptics. In its broad scope, the structure corresponds with that of the first three Gospels. Part one deals with Jesus' public ministry, while part two deals with his passion in Jerusalem. In contrast to the Synoptics, however, Jesus' ministry in Jn encompasses Judea, Galilee, and Samaria. In addition, Jn records several journeys of Jesus to Jerusalem.

(2) In the details, too, one notices some considerable differences. These concern both the sequence of individual events and the whole method of presentation. In the Synoptics the teaching of Jesus is given in the form of logia and parables, and the original independence of the individual logion can still be recognized, even in the summarization of individual logia into "speeches." In Jn, however, the discourses of Jesus are clearly drawn up in larger units that are complete in themselves and that incorporate only isolated self-contained sayings. Jn has no parables at all; there are only two parabolic discourses (of the good shepherd, Jn 10, and of the vine, Jn 15), which differ very substantially from the style of the synoptic parables. Already the beginning of Jn is significant for the character of Jn, which is completely different from that of the Synoptics. Mk sees the "beginning of the gospel" in John the Baptist, while Mt and Lk begin with the birth narratives. In contrast, Jn opens his Gospel with a hymn concerning the Logos and intersperses it with references to the Baptist. Only then does the narrative of the Baptist's appearance follow (1:19–34) and, finally, the account of the calling of the first disciples—which is given an entirely different shape, of course, from that of the Synoptics.

(3) The volume of the narrative material common to both Jn and the Synoptics is relatively small: (a) The cleansing of the temple (Jn 2:13–16; cf. Mk 11:15–17 and parallels), which in Jn is found at the beginning rather than at the end of the ministry of Jesus; (b) the story of the royal official of Capernaum (Jn 4:46–54; cf. Lk 7:1–10 and parallel) which, compared to its form in Q, is much briefer in Jn; (c) the feeding of the five thousand and Jesus' walking on the water (6:1–15, 16–21; cf. Mk 6:30–44, 45–52 and parallels). In both places the two accounts are rendered together, while the context is completely different (both Jn 5:2–47 and 6:22–39 are without parallels in the Synoptics); (d) the narrative of the anointing at Bethany (Jn 12:1–8, cf. Mk 14:3–9 and parallels) where the agreements in the basic content are relatively extensive but the linguistic differences in the details are quite considerable (the contextual setting is again different in both); (e) the account of the entry into Jerusalem (Jn 12:12–19, cf. Mk 11:1–10 and parallels), which agrees with the synoptic presentation for the most part. (f) Likewise the passion narrative itself, beginning with 18:1, is largely congruent with the synoptic rendering.

(4) It is striking that Jn has no account of exorcisms, i.e., the casting out of demons by Jesus, yet all of the other types of miracle stories are represented.

The finding of common logia is also relatively rare. Jn 2:19 corresponds to Mk 14:58 and parallels (but cf. the vastly different context); Jn 3:3, 5 essentially corresponds to Mt 18:3; Jn 4:44 compares with Mk 6:4 and parallel; Jn 13:16 equals 15:20 and corresponds to Mt 10:24; Jn 13:20 to Mt 10:40; Jn 15:7 compares with Mt 7:7 and Jn 20:23 corresponds to Mt 16:19 (= Mt 18:18).

All of these observations lead to the difficult question of what the relationship between Jn and the Synoptics is (see pp. 248f. below).

2. Structural details

(1) It is not easy to gain an overview of the first part of Jn, chs 1–12, since it does not proceed in linear fashion.

The first few chapters contain some marked climaxes. Ch 1 contains a type of prelude; in ch 2 the action proper is ushered in by means of two symbolic scenes, the wedding at Cana and the cleansing of the temple. This is followed in ch 3 by the nocturnal conversation with Nicodemus about being born again and about the Spirit, and in ch 4 by the noonday conversation with the Samaritan woman about the water of life, the Messiah, and the true worship of God. Jn 5:1–16 tells of a healing at the pool of Bethesda on the Sabbath, while the second part of the chapter contains an extensive discourse of Jesus in Jerusalem. Jn 6, finally, tells of the feeding of the five thousand, of the walk on the water, and contains the discourse on the bread from heaven.

But beginning with ch 7 it is difficult to recognize any order; narratives, miracle stories, and especially lengthy discourses alternate. Yet, there seems to be an essential common denominator throughout the Gospel: the continually escalating crisis between Jesus and the world, represented by the Jews. The beginning point is the pericope of 6:66–71, the Johannine form of Peter's confession; already here Judas is signalled as traitor and the tension rises until ch 12.

Some characteristic points help in remembering the content and structure of Jn 1–12:

(a) The sequence of festivals is conspicuous. In the Synoptic presentation, Jesus goes to Jerusalem only once, at the time of the Passover when he is arrested and executed. In contrast, in Jn he makes several journeys between Judea and Galilee and thus comes to Jerusalem a total of four times, and every time for a festival (2:13; 5:1; 7:10; 12:12ff; the festivals are mentioned in 2:13; 5:1; 6:4; 7:2 and 10:22; cf. p. 251 below). The question of which presentation is closer to historical reality may remain open at this point (see pp. 294 below).

(b) The character of the miracles narrated by Jn is also striking. Some of them are identical with the miracle stories of the Synoptics (see above); others, however, by far exceed the synoptic narratives in their extent (cf. e.g., Jn 11:39). Jn recounts seven miracles in all (2:1–11—miracle of the wine at Cana; 4:43–54—royal official of Capernaum; 5:1–9—healing at Bethesda; 6:1–15—feeding of the five thousand; 6:16–21—walking on the water; 9:1–7—healing of the blind man; 11:1–44—raising of Lazarus), but this count of seven seems to be accidental; at any rate, there is no development of symbolism.

(c) Finally, the manner in which Jn joins miracles and discourses together is conspicuous. The healing from a distance of the son of the royal official of Capernaum, which follows the two parallel chapters 3 and 4, functions as a corroboration and confirmation of Jesus' authority. Conversely, chs 5 and 6 begin with miracles which are then followed by a substantiating discourse. The miraculous multiplication of bread in Jn 6:1–15 is followed by the discourse of Jesus concerning the true bread from heaven (6:32–65). Hence the discourses clearly have the function of interpreting the events symbolically; the quintessence is often summarized in the "I am" sayings (cf. 6:35, 51). The same goal is achieved, for instance, when the saying "I am the light of the world" (8:12) precedes the healing of the blind man (9:1ff.) and the declaration "I am the resurrection and the life" (11:25) precedes the raising of Lazarus (11:44).

Suggested exercises:

Study the "I am" sayings in Jn. The following questions need to be answered: 1. What is the predicate and what is the subject in these sentences? What are the respective inferences pertaining to the interpretation?

Bultmann and Schweizer: In some of these sentences, the "I" predicate is to be construed in the sense of the famous *"l'état c'est moi."* What hermeneutical principle is behind this exegesis?

2. To what type of symbols do those belong to which the Johannine Jesus refers (bread, vine etc.)? What direct self-identifications are there?

3. For advanced students:

In the light of the "I am" sayings, what does "to believe" mean in Jn? These sayings are generally followed by a statement of faith/salvation/crisis. What significance is one to attribute to these expressions?

How does Jn use the technique of misunderstanding in connection with the "I am" sayings? Cf. 11:21–27.

Tools for all exercises: E. Schweizer, *Ego Eimi*, FRLANT 56, [2]1965; R. Bultmann, *Theology of the NT*, II, 65ff.; Schnackenburg, *Gospel According to Jn*, II, 79–90.

(2) The second part of Jn, chs 13–20, can be divided formally into the farewell discourses (13–17) and the passion and resurrection story (18–20). Bultmann correctly groups both parts under the unified perspective of "revelation of the ΔΟΞΑ of Jesus before his own," first in the self-contained farewell discourses and, second, in the openly visible passion, which faith recognizes as exaltation.

The theme of the farewell discourses is elucidated characteristically in the opening scene, the farewell meal. Unlike the Synoptic accounts, Jesus in John's Gospel institutes footwashing as a sacramental act rather than the Lord's Supper; apparently the Johannine community practices footwashing as a permanent ritual. The farewell discourses themselves are concerned with the farewell of the glorified one and his return to the Father, and with the promise of the Spirit, the "Paraclete," who guides the community after Jesus' departure. They are concerned with the Father, with the Son, with the community and finally with the commandment to love one another. These ideas are summarized in the concluding "high priestly prayer" in Jn 17. There are substantial agreements with the Synoptics in the last section of Jn, especially in the passion story. But precisely against this backdrop, the insertions made by Jn appear in sharp relief. Thus Jn considerably reshaped, for instance, Jesus' trial before Pilate (Jn 18:29–38; 19:1–15) as well as the scene at the cross. The play with the double entendre of the term αἴρειν is striking and—for Jn—typical (cf. Jn 19:15; consult a concordance for the other instances). Further characteristic for Jn is the place that he accords the term "truth," especially in the passion narrative.

A special exegetical problem that cannot be probed further here is the question of how one is to explain the existing parallels in the passion account, especially with Lk.

3. Sources and other literary-critical issues

(1) Does Jn know one or more of the synoptic Gospels? Or did he author his book without direct knowledge of the first three Gospels? All of the theoretically feasible hypotheses are represented in scholarship: (a) Jn is familiar with *one* of the Synoptics (Mt, Mk, and Lk are mentioned respectively in this regard). (b) Jn knows more than one of the synoptic Gospels; various combinations are again possible: Mk and Mt; Mt and Lk; Mk and Lk—or all three of them. (c) Jn is not acquainted with any of the synoptic Gospels; instead, he, like Mk, gathers his material from oral tradition.

If one opts for one of the hypotheses cited under (a) or (b), it is necessary to explain the considerable differences between Jn and the Synoptics. In this pursuit, reference to the individual theology of the fourth evangelist will hardly suffice to explain the facts, such as that Jn would have to have arbitrarily ignored the largest part of the synoptic material. Further, one needs to explain the origin of the additional material, which is extraordinarily extensive and stratified. Two attempts at explanation are proffered: (a) Jn endeavored to *replace* the Synoptics—perhaps because he was aware, as an eyewitness, that he possessed better, more authentic material (tradition regards the disciple John as the author of Jn; see below), or perhaps because he thought he presented a better theological interpretation. But the text does not substantiate this argument; no essential polemic against the Synoptics can be discerned. (b) Jn did not intend to push the Synoptics aside, but to *augment* them; therefore he concentrated fully on the additional material not present in the Synoptics. However, this argument also cannot be substantiated from the text. It is very obvious that Jn was not drawn up as a supplement to another book (or to several other books); rather, it is to be taken as a fully adequate and comprehensive account (20:30f.). Jn does not presuppose that other books about Jesus would also have to be read. If one considers the third hypothesis cited above (i.e., that Jn was not familiar with any of the Synoptics) as correct, it is necessary to explain the unquestionable agreements between Jn and the Synoptics. British scholarship, for instance, predominantly assumes that Jn collected oral tradition directly and thus came upon partly identical material to that of the authors of the synoptic Gospels. But at least for the Johannine form of the passion narrative, this explanation is inadequate; it must have been based on a literary source closely related to the synoptic passion narrative.

Result: It is very apparent that in many instances Jn used sources unknown to us. Conversely, at least his presentation of the passion of Jesus is akin to the synoptic passion story.

(2) What types of sources, then, did Jn use? Next to a source used in the passion story, Bultmann argues for two further sources in Jn: One source with miracle stories (*semeia* source) and one with discourses, both of which Jn incorporated into his Gospel.

(a) Bultmann discerns a *miracle source* on the basis of the references in 2:11 and 4:54, indicating that the miracle stories were obviously originally numbered. Bultmann claims that this enumeration does not match the extant presentation, since 2:23 and 3:2 speak of further miracles, so that it is not appropriate to speak of the "second" miracle in 4:54. Therefore, what appears here is the source in which the healing of the royal official's son was actually the second miracle. But this argument is not valid, for the healing in 4:43ff. is also the second *recorded* miracle in the current text (the others are merely alluded to). The enumeration, therefore, may be John's own and does not have to based on a source. Bultmann's second argument, that the catchword σημεῖον belongs to the linguistic usage of the source, is likewise hardly correct. Bultmann assumes that Jn in no sense wanted to understand the miracles as "signs" because they invariably led to misunderstanding. However, the opposite may be more plausible. By means of the concept "sign," Jn is able to characterize the ambivalence of the miracles—they are signs, no more and no less. The reference of 4:48 may be a clue: "Unless you see miraculous signs and wonders. . . ." The evangelist has clearly interspersed this criticism of miracle mania within a given context; this aspect was surely foreign to the original miracle story of 4:43ff. Finally, Bultmann's assumption that the conclusion of Jn, in 20:30f. was originally the close of the miracle source cannot be sustained. The linguistic usage indicates that this could be a formulation of the evangelist (see concordance). Nevertheless, the existence of a source containing miracle stories is probable. As the stylistic analysis shows (cf. Bultmann, *John*, 98 fn. 6; 113 fn. 1), the miracle stories are written in simple Greek with semitic coloring, though this is not to be construed as translated Greek (from an Aramaic source, for instance). Johannine stylistic characteristics of style are missing in 2:1–11; 4:46–52 (except v 48); 12:1–8; 12:12–15. This shows up with special clarity in 4:43ff. (see above); Jn quite obviously inserted v 48 into a literary source. Of course, nothing can be said about the details of this source.

Compared to the synoptic miracle stories, it may be essentially maintained that there is a considerable heightening of the miraculous, such as in the raising of Lazarus as well as in the account of the feeding and in the walking on the water (cf. the respective synoptic parallels). This, too, may rather point to John's use of a source, though the notion that Jn was critical of the miracles and ultimately rejected them does not do justice to the state of affairs; after all, he accepted them in his Gospel.

(b) The second source is surely to be found within the *passion narrative*. The Johannine additions are easily discerned at some points: 18:33–37; 19:7–11. The underlying account is similar to, though not identical with, the synoptic presentation. Apparently Jn had access to an ancient form of the passion narrative that probably was still independent from Mk.

Suggested exercises:

1. With regard to the stylistic analysis of the passion source, read Bultmann, *John*, 635f.

2. Analyze Jn 18:12–28 in comparison with Mk. Where does one find insertions of the evangelist? Which differences from Mk are likely not predicated upon Johannine theology and, therefore, must be regarded as peculiarities of the source?

Tool: K. Aland, *Synopsis Quattuor Evangeliorum*.

(c) In Bultmann's opinion, the basic component of the *discourses* also derives from a source, specifically, a collection of pre-Christian, gnostic speeches of revelation that Jn augmented. Once again, the most important argument is the analysis of style, in which Bultmann deals primarily with the prologue. But the question is whether or not it is necessary to distinguish between the findings in the prologue on the one hand and the remaining discourse segments on the other. The assumption of a *pre-Johannine*—though not a pre-*Christian*—hymn is convincing in the prologue (1:1–14 [18]). The prologue's rigid characteristics of style cannot be found in the other passages that Bultmann wants to attribute to a gnostic source. In the case of several discourses, there are individual logia, introduced, for instance, by the phrase ἀμήν, ἀμήν, which serve as climaxes. Apparently Jn belonged to a particular tradition of style within his community to which he adapted the discourses of his book; he thus produced certain solemn statements to which he added didactic explanations. In other discourses the essential climax is found in Jesus' self-identification ("I am," see above): The promise is directed to the believers and the warning to the unbelievers (stylistically, both the participle [6:35; 8:12; 11:25f.] and the conditional [6:51a] are found). All of this evidence militates against, rather than in favor of, a continuous source of discourses. All in all, it may be considered probable that the discourses in Jn were formulated by the evangelist himself—by adopting certain traditional terminology, of course.

(3) Besides the source question, there are numerous other literary-critical problems in Jn.

(a) The sequence of chs 5–7 seems to be disturbed. As the geographical references indicate, 6:1 would make better sense if it followed ch 4; this would also clarify the chronology because the Passover announced in 6:4 would begin in 5:1 (in the current text 6:4 and 7:2 are colliding). The remark in 7:1 about the Jews' intention to kill also becomes clearer, if it is assumed that it was preceded immediately by 5:18. One may indeed assume, therefore, that chs 5 and 6 were originally in the reverse order; a few rough spots remain, of course, even after such a reorganization.

The switching around of pages in a manuscript was possible in antiquity; for instance, Sir 33:13b–36:16 should be placed after 30:24, and also in 1 Enoch the proper sequence had to be restored subsequently in one instance: 93:1–10; 91:12–17; 92; 94. A modern example is the alleged switching around of pages in Kant's *Prolegomena to Any Future Metaphysics*.

(b) Jn 13–17 also seems to be in disarray. One notices that the farewell discourses contain two parallel discourse sequences and that at the end of the first discourse sequence, in 14:31, there is a clearly marked closure (cf. Mk 14:42; Mt 26:46), after which 18:1 would follow quite easily. Should chs 15–17, therefore, be construed as a secondary interpolation? This is out of the question, since this passage is Johannine, both in essence and in style. The question might be asked whether Jn wrote two drafts of discourses, both of which were then adopted by the editors of the Gospel (see below). Bultmann has suggested a complicated solution: He wants to reorganize Jn 13–17 into the sequence of 13:1–30; 17:1–16; 13:13–35; 15:1–16:33; 13:36–14:31; 18:1ff.

At numerous other places, Bultmann considered it necessary to reorganize the text. For the most part, there is no train of thought to be detected in the extant text, and it is to be assumed that the editors were unskilled in stringing together individual fragments (cf. Bultmann, *John*, 236ff.; 249: Reconstruction of a discourse on the "light of the world"). It can indeed hardly be contested that Bultmann's reconstructed text is smoother and more logical than the form of Jn handed down; in most cases, however, there is no absolute necessity to reconstruct the texts.

It is to be noted further, that the "disorder" of the Johannine text would have to have arisen as early as in the first edition of the Gospel; such an accumulation of switched pages was impossible in the course of later text transmission (see K. Aland, *Studien zur Überlieferung des NT und seines Textes*, 1967, 49ff.).

(c) At the close of Jn, mention is made of the editors of the work. 21:24f. indicates clearly that it was not the author himself who published his Gospel, but that at least the final chapter represents a revision, i.e., a supplement. This is underscored in the observation that 20:30f. already contains a conclusion to the book to which the editors then added another chapter with epiphany stories. Bultmann assumes that the editors also meddled with the text in other instances; their interpolations can be recognized by their style and theological intention, and especially from their severing of the context.

In this connection, Bultmann speaks of an ecclesiastical "redaction" of Jn. This term is subject to misunderstanding, to say the least, since "redaction" generally denotes the work of the evangelist (cf. the synoptic Gospels). It is more appropriate, therefore, to speak of interpolations, if one wishes to characterize the work of the editors of Jn.

If one evaluates the secondary interpolations in Jn that Bultmann assumes, there emerges a common denominator: The editors of Jn are obviously concerned with adapting the theology of Jn to common ecclesiastical perspectives. This is seen with special clarity in the area of eschatology. Originally Jn advocated a "realized" eschatology: Now is the time of crisis, the transition to eternal life takes place now—faith has life already in the present (5:24f.). Surprisingly, in 5:28f. one finds the expectation of a future resurrection all the same, expressed in the style of traditional apocalyptic of the community (similarly in 6:39f.); according to Bultmann, this is a secondary addition. Another example, following Bultmann, is the pericope of 6:51c–58 where the traditional teaching on the Eucharist is inserted immediately following the typically Johannine discourse of the bread. In terms of style, this pericope is without a doubt an interruption. Especially striking is that beginning with v 51c, the "I am" discourse (6:35, 48, 51a) is reversed. Jesus no longer "is" the bread, instead he "gives" it, namely, as "his flesh" (v 53ff. even speaks of drinking his blood).

There is indeed much that favors Bultmann's hypothesis of an "ecclesiastical revision" of Jn. It is to be noted, though, that the special character of the "original" Jn is not at all lost through this revision. The theologically "offensive" statements, for instance, the eschatological ones, are not eliminated; they have merely been given an "orthodox" frame. It would be wrong, therefore, to suppose that the "ecclesiastical" interpolator could have been an outside censor; the Johannine community itself may have adapted its Gospel to the otherwise common ecclesiastical tradition before they "published" it (the very early fragment P[52] [see p. 18ff.] contains precisely one of those references that Bultmann views as interpolation, i.e., 18:32).

4. Authorship

According to tradition (Irenaeus), Jn was written from Ephesus by the aged John, the son of Zebedee, thus by an eyewitness of the life of Jesus.

A number of arguments militate against this tradition: Since the book makes use of source material—especially in the miracle stories, it is highly unlikely that the author was an eyewitness of the events. Furthermore, it is strange that Ignatius, who was a contemporary of Jn, who may have come from the same area and, in particular, shared his theological language, does not mention the Gospel of Jn (which would be even more serious if one assumed with Kümmel, *Introduction to the NT*, 246, that he knew John). Irenaeus considers Polycarp, bishop of Smyrna, to be the link between the son of Zebedee, whom Polycarp still knew, and himself. But this acquaintance is neither mentioned in Polycarp's own letter to the Philippians, nor in the account of his martyrdom. This means that we do not possess any historically reliable reference to the person of the author of Jn. It is inappropriate, however, to conclude that Jn might possibly not have been written until the middle of the second century. On the contrary, the discovery of P^{52} guarantees that Jn was already written around the year 100.

From the perspective of church history it is presupposed that church and synagogue have already been fully separated (9:22; 16:1ff.); "the Jews" are already addressed as a fixed, opposing entity without any need for differentiation. It is very striking that Jn polemicizes against the devotees of John the Baptist and not against John the Baptist himself. This indicates that, at the time of the writing of Jn, there were still baptist groups who appealed to John.

A. Schlatter argued that Jn came from Palestine; he had the respective geographical knowledge, and his language shows Palestinian idiosyncrasies typical of the rabbis. In this regard, Bultmann points out critically that while the specific rabbinic characteristics of style can be seen in references formulated by the evangelist himself (cf. Bultmann, *John*, 70, fn. 3; 71, fn. 4, 5; 79, fn. 1, 3), this linguistic evidence is not sufficient to locate the Gospel in Palestine. It is to be noted as well that the author wrote in Greek and not in one of the semitic languages.

This is questioned by some scholars: The semitisms are clear evidence that Jn was originally written in Aramaic. But semitisms, such as ἵνα + conditional participle + negated finite verb (3:16; 6:39; 12:46 et al.), in no sense prove an original semitic form; they only show that the author *also* spoke semitic languages. The original semitic form of a text can be demonstrated without question only when specific references in the Greek text have to be regarded unequivocally as translational errors, that is, when the current text can be understood only by referring to the original form in another language.

5. Problem of the history of religions

A comparison with the synoptic Gospels shows that Jn contains a series of unfamiliar concepts. Among these are, for instance, the statements about the λόγος, which are found exclusively in the prologue (1:1ff.), however. To be added are the words concerning the Paraclete in the farewell discourses. Also striking are: The identification of the revelation and the revealer ("I am"), the notion of the pre-existence of Jesus and the concept of his being "sent," that is, of the descent and the ascent of the Son. Also typical for Jn is the dualism of "above" and "below," as well as the dualism of light and darkness and, in this context, the combination of "light" and "life." In order to explain these concepts and terms, scholarship searches for parallels in the history of religions. In this pursuit, Jewish texts (especially from Qumran), hellenistic, and particularly gnostic texts, are adduced.

There are indeed parallels with Jn in various realms of the religious environment. The dualism of light and darkness and the call to an unconditional surrender are found in Judaism (Qumran); Philo knows and uses a λόγος-concept that is related to the Johannine prologue. But clear parallels are also found in pagan texts from the environs of gnosis, specifically from the Hermetic and the Mandaean writings. (This is similarly true of later or almost contemporary Christian texts that are more or less gnostically influenced, such as the letters of Ignatius or the Odes of Solomon).

The Mandaean question is a special problem in Johannine scholarship. The gnostic sect of the Mandaeans (manda = knowledge = gnosis) which still exists today in southern Iraq, seems to have had its beginning in the region of the upper Jordan during the time of early Christianity. The Johannine parallels are so pronounced in the Mandaean writings that it was once assumed that Johannine Christianity derived from the Mandaeans. Since then, however, it has been acknowledged that the literary form of the Mandaean texts came about much later than that of Jn. Nevertheless, these texts continue to be significant for Johannine scholarship because they contain a number of related motifs independent of Jn.

The problem of the history of religions has considerable significance for the interpretation of Jn. Bultmann takes the position that the Johannine theology and especially Christology presuppose a complete gnostic myth. This myth has a fixed pattern: The ur-man, that is, the son of God, the envoy, descends to earth in order to summon the particles of light (human beings) that have been imprisoned in the material realm on account of the Fall and to lead them back to heaven with him. The redeemer is identical in substance with the redeemed particles of light. The souls or particles of light are not from the world (matter), but from heaven (light) and are brought back to their place of origin by the envoy. On the basis of this assumption, Bultmann argues that Jn extracted the center from this myth, namely, the assertion of the soul's pre-existence and of its substantial identity with the redeemer. In contrast to Gnosticism, redemption is not tied to the existence of what is to be redeemed in Jn, but to the free redemptive act of God in his Son alone. Thus Jn proves to be a sharp critic of the gnostic teaching.

Bultmann's view, however, is untenable for historical reasons. The gnostic myth in the form described above, does not come from the early period of Gnosticism; on the contrary, it comes at the end of the development of gnostic thought. For this reason it cannot be the immediate source of Johannine thought. Jn has probably taken up individual elements, both of hellenistic Judaism and of early Gnosticism and connected them with the person of Jesus, thereby creating, in actuality, a Christian myth of his own.

Recently the view has resurfaced that Jn was much closer to the religious assertions of early Gnosticism than Bultmann thought. In fact, his Gospel must already be considered as part of Gnosticism; for, at its center is the christological assertion that the redeemer does not enter the world but is consistently separate from it. Therefore Jn represents a naive docetism (so E. Käsemann, *The Testament of Jesus. A Study of the Gospel of John in the Light of Ch 17*, ET 1968), or even a deliberate one (so L. Schottroff, *Der Glaubende und die feindliche Welt*, 1970, 228–296). Assertions within Jn that contradict this basic tendency (e.g., Jn 1:14) do not mean that this redeemer truly participated in the world through the incarnation. Jesus remains a celestial being who merely contacts the world but does not enter into it.

This argument is based upon many correct observations. Nevertheless, the assertion is not tenable that Jn is a thoroughgoing docetic (and to this extent gnostic) writing; for, a docetic Christology in principle needs a corresponding world view. The believers would have to be called upon to withdraw—at least spiritually—from the world. And this is precisely what Jn does not teach. He does not claim that the community has to flee from the world (17:15).

Suggested reading:

1. A. Lindemann, "Gemeinde und Welt im Joh," in *Kirche*. FS G. Bornkamm (ed. D. Lührmann and G. Strecker), 1980, 133–161.

2. The diverse positions relative to the history-of-religions locus of Jn are expressed vividly in the commentaries of Bultmann and Schnackenburg. Especially helpful is the comparative reading of the explanations concerning the origin of the Logos concept (Bultmann, *John*, 19–36; Schnackenburg, *John*, I, 481–493).

6. Purpose

Evidently Jn was written neither as a competitor of nor as a supplement to the Synoptics (see above). From time to time scholarship has held the view that the book is a missionary writing that addresses Israel (or, conversely, the Gentile world). Nothing in the text, however, indicates such a specific intent. Jn is not a "missionary writing" but a book of faith for the Christian community. The evangelist intends to clarify for the community the decisive assertions of the Christian confession; in other words, Jn is a theological product of the community it addresses. This community is to be strengthened in the faith that it already possesses. This community is shown how the Spirit leads it "into all truth" and thereby "abides" in the world despite all trials (cf. the special weight given to the catchword μένειν in Jn). The intent of Jn is not mission but witness, exhortation to brotherly love, by which the community is distinguished from the world, which reacts with hatred.

Suggested exercise:

There are a number of theological concepts and terms in Jn that ought to be remembered because they play a decisive role. In the following they will be cited only briefly, in order to gain an overview that may then be expanded with the help of the literature.

1. There are the typical "I am" sayings of Jesus in the realm of Christology.

2. In the realm of anthropology, the relationship of believing and knowing is characteristic for Jn.

3. Ecclesiology is dominated by the concept of brotherly love on the one hand, and of the world's hatred on the other.

4. The most important characteristic of Jn is the "realized," present eschatology (3:18f.; 5:24f.). The question here is whether the futuristic statements in Jn belong to a different layer and, hence, are a secondary interpolation, or whether both groups of expressions can be balanced in terms of their essential theology.

5. The tradition of the Christian community is altered in some instances. Thus in place of the Lord's Supper comes footwashing. Is this the work of Jn alone, or did he already find this alteration in his community?

6. Jn interprets the cross as Jesus' exaltation: Easter, Ascension, Pentecost, and the parousia are gathered up into one.

7. The notion of pre-existence takes on significance in Christology. In this context, one of the crucial questions is the relationship between Jesus and the figure of the Paraclete.

8. The miracles are a special problem. On the one hand, Jn contains the most spectacular miracle stories as well as the most convincing epiphany stories; on the other hand, these events are sublimated to "signs" (see above). Is this a contradiction, or can both aspects be reconciled with one another?

Appendix: The Disciple Whom Jesus Loved

Three times in Jn a disciple is mentioned of whom it is said emphatically that Jesus loved him (13:23; 19:26; 20:2, using the terms ἀγαπάω or φιλέω; cf. 21:7, 20); but his name is never given. It is generally assumed that it refers to John, the son of Zebedee; and those who maintain that he was the author of the Gospel regard this as evidence for their assumption. Only a genuine companion of Jesus could refer to himself in this manner. Others are of the opinion that the references are fictitious. In this way the son of Zebedee is to appear as authority of the book and, at the same time, as the patron of the church in which it arose.

Against this Bultmann and Kragerud (*Der Lieblingsjunger im Joh,* 1959) argue that the "disciple whom Jesus loved" was not a historical person; it is a symbol for the circle to which the book belongs (Bultmann: The symbol of Gentile Christianity in contrast to Petrine Jewish Christianity; Kragerud: The symbol of the church of the Spirit in contrast to the church of the ecclesiastical office [*Amtskirche*]). But such interpretations cannot be read out of the text. It is especially important to bear in mind that the appendix of the book (21:23) takes a retrospective glance at the death of this disciple and that it does refer, therefore, to a historical person. Kümmel (*Introduction,* 238) considers it to be most likely that the author of Jn attached value to being able "to adduce as guarantor of his account of the passion of Jesus someone who was adjudged worthy of the title 'the disciple whom Jesus loved.'" Kümmel points out emphatically that this assumption is not sufficient to settle the question of authorship.

§ 39 *Johannine Letters*

Bibliography: R. Bultmann, *The Johannine Epistles,* Hermeneia, ET 1973; W. Nauck, *Die Tradition und der Charakter des ersten Johannesbriefes,* WUNT 3, 1957; R. Schnackenburg, *Die Johannesbriefe,* IIThK XIII/3, ⁴1970; G. Schunack, *Die Briefe des Johannes,* ZBK NT 17, 1982; R. Brown, *The Epistles of John,* AB 30, 1982; idem, *The Community of the Beloved Disciple,* 1979.

Preliminary remark:

A working knowledge of the letters of Jn can best be achieved by considering them in relationship to the Gospel. A number of aspects affirm that Jn and the Johannine letters are closely related to one another. First, the introduction to 1 Jn (1:1-4) emphatically refers back to the Gospel of Jn; second, there is a clear affinity with regard to language and thought. Since 2 Jn is connected to 1 Jn, and 3 Jn, in turn, to 2 Jn, it is initially necessary to treat all three letters as an essential unit—regardless of the question of authorship.

First John

1. Problem

The basic problems in 1 Jn are identical with those of the Gospel of Jn. As in the Gospel, Bultmann finds here the source of the discourses of revelation. Nauck and Haenchen deny its existence in both. Bultmann also finds additions in 1 Jn that he bases upon "ecclesiastical redaction" (he includes 1:7b; 2:2, 28; 4:10b; 5:7–9; 5:14–21, and possibly parts of 3:2; 4:17b). The question of authorship is a matter of debate: Is the author of 1 Jn identical with Jn the evangelist, or is he not?

2. Structure and character

1 Jn is not a letter. This is already indicated in the introduction, which is not suitable for a letter but for a theological treatise. Likewise, the conclusion does not have the character of a letter (regardless of whether one considers either 5:21 as the conclusion or 5:13, as Bultmann does). Conversely, the readers are addressed directly, that is, the author seems to have specific readers in mind and does not address "the church" at large.

The whole writing is determined by the continuous alternation between dogmatic (christological) passages on the one hand, and paraenetic sections on the other. In this context, the intent is clear: knowing and doing are to be understood as inseparably related; fellowship with God (understood as walking in the light) and the fellowship of Christians with one another belong together as much as do fellowship with God and obedience to the old but, simultaneously new commandment.

The sequence "dogmatics"—"ethics" corresponds to the pattern of the Pauline letters in which the indicative and the imperative follow one another.

Otherwise, however, it is not possible to discern a clearly organized structure. 1 Jn may perhaps be characterized as a compilation of ideas on the basic theme portrayed: faith and love.

3. Literary-critical problems

(1) There are a number of analyses that attempt to isolate sources, or at least material that has been used in 1 Jn.

(a) In the pericope of 1:5–2:11 Bultmann sees tensions between style and content: On the one hand, dogmatic statements are formulated in poetic form, while there are, on the other hand, pastoral statements in prose style. Therefore, Bultmann proposes the following analysis: 1:5–10 belong to the poetically formulated source (except vv 7b, 9, which were inserted by the author or perhaps not until the "ecclesiastical redaction"; both of these sections of verses do, in fact, depart altogether from the context in terms of content and terminology). 2:1 is a homiletical application of what preceded, given by the author himself, and is then further augmented in v 2 by the ecclesiastical redaction (see below). Beginning with v 3, the author ushers in the new topic of "knowledge of God" by returning to the source in 2:4f. in order to add his own explanations once again in 2:6–8. The antignostic assertions of vv

9–11, which are shaped dualistically, are taken from the source again, according to Bultmann. Originally the letter concluded with 2:27 in Bultmann's opinion; the following part, 2:28–5:13, is to be viewed as a subsequent composition from individual fragments from the first part, leaving open the question whether this addendum (i.e., section 1:5–2:27) was constructed by the author of the letter himself or by one of his disciples.

(b) Nauck, too, sees considerable stylistic differences within 1 Jn and wants to associate them with different layers. Unlike Bultmann, however, he maintains that all of these layers come from the author himself. The explanation of this circumstance is that the author later commented on the "source" that he himself had created.

(c) In contrast, Haenchen (see p. 261) disputes altogether the possibility of distinguishing different layers and forms of style. Rather, the author of 1 Jn formulated the entire text consistently in prose. Haenchen explains the combination of apodictic and homiletical language within the letter by arguing that the author was a disciple of the author of Jn whose work depended on the Gospel with regard to theology and style. This assumption may indeed be the simplest and, therefore, the most probable solution.

(2) Bultmann argues that some sentences in 1 Jn are to be attributed to the subsequent "ecclesiastical redaction." But the substantiation of this argument is far less convincing here than in the Gospel of Jn. Those references Bultmann isolated (see above) indeed contain uniquely traditional, theological assertions that are not otherwise common in the Johannine writings. In most cases, however, they cannot be isolated from the context but remain an integral part; in other words, their character as a gloss remains entirely unlikely.

The conclusion of 1 Jn, however, is a different matter: The writing clearly seems to indicate that its goal is reached in 5:13. Thus 5:14–21 could be a secondary expansion; this is all the more likely since the pericope looks like a terse summary of what preceded.

4. Linguistic and theological peculiarities

(1) Theologically and linguistically 1 Jn has close affinities with the Gospel of Jn. For one, this is seen in the terminology used (in spite of some remarkable differences; see below); for another, it emerges with special clarity in the commonality of the "realized" eschatology found in both writings, as a comparison between Jn 5:24f. and 1 Jn 3:14 shows.

There is a certain essential tension between 1 Jn 3:14 and 3:2; 4:17. For this reason, Bultmann wants to isolate certain fragments of the two references mentioned above as glosses; in the final analysis, however, this is an inadequate premise for a literary-critical operation.

(2) Conversely, despite all formal and essential similarity, 1 Jn also exhibits considerable differences compared to the Gospel of Jn. In the Gospel, *Jesus* is designated as "the light of the world," whereas 1 Jn 1:5 designates *God* as light (in 4:8 as love). Differences are also seen in the comprehension of some concepts found in both writings: Thus, in Jn 1:1, ἀρχή denotes the absolute beginning of creation, whereas in 1 Jn 1:1 it describes the beginning of the church with Jesus. In the Gospel, the "Paraclete" is the Spirit, while in the letter it is Jesus himself (1 Jn 2:1). On the whole, the meaning of the term πνεῦμα in 1 Jn—in contrast to the Gospel—is not plain: For instance the false, non-Christian spirit is also called πνεῦμα (1 Jn 4:1ff.). The term πνεῦμα alone no longer suffices to designate clearly the power of salvation; instead, for this purpose the author uses the term χρῖσμα (2:20, 27), which is unknown in the Gospel.

In comparison to the Gospel, 1 Jn introduces some new ideas. There is the special emphasis, for instance, upon the atoning death of Christ, upon his "blood" (1:7b, 9; 2:2; cf. Bultmann's analysis), as well as an emphatic reference to the possibility of repeated forgiveness of sins and, at the end, the distinction between sins that lead to death and less serious sins (5:16ff.; but this reference is perhaps secondary in nature (see above).

In connection with the issue of "sin," one notices a distinct tension within the text: While 3:6–9 asserts that believers are without sin, 1:10 states conversely that the one who claims sinlessness is a liar. Does this tension result from the differences between one of the sources and the author? Or is it simply that the author was remiss in his argumentation? The tension is resolved, however, if both statements are given a strictly theological interpretation: Believers are without sin on account of Christ (3:6ff.);, but they cannot appeal to that as a position before God and the brothers (1:10).

The most striking difference between 1 Jn and the Gospel of Jn is the fact that concrete polemic against heresy and false teachers plays an important part in 1 Jn. In the NT, 1 Jn is *the* document dealing with the awareness of "orthodoxy and heresy" within the Christian church. All of the theological arguments in 1 Jn, the realized eschatology, as well as the paraenesis, serve the polemic against the heretics. The adversary of the endtimes, the antichrist, has appeared in the heretics—that is the thesis of 1 Jn (2:18ff.). The denial of the incarnation is the central teaching of these heretics; they claim that Jesus was not truly human (cf. 2:23 and 4:2). In order to refute them, the author uses as a weapon the confession of faith, sharply focused in the decisive christological argument that Jesus is the Christ, the Son of God (4:3, 15; 5:1, 5). A further criterion of orthodoxy is ethical behavior: Knowing and doing (love) belong unequivocally together; he who does not love (one's neighbor) has not known God (4:8).

5. Authorship

In the course of the explanations thus far, it has become clear that the author of 1 Jn is probably not identical with the author of the Gospel of Jn. Quite obviously, however, he comes from the "school" of the evangelist of Jn; he probably wrote shortly after the latter, in the first half of the second century. In all probability, the two other letters of Jn were written at about the same time.

Suggested exercises:

1. Compare the Christology of the Gospel of Jn with that of 1 Jn. Which christological expressions are usually emphasized? What function does Christology have in both writings?

Tool: R. Bultmann (see bibliography), 82–87.

2. Compare the language of 1 Jn with that of the Gospel of Jn: What agreements and differences are there?

Tool: E. Haenchen, *Ges. Aufs.* II, 1968, 238–242.

Special attention is to be given to the insignificant words: The word οὖν is lacking in 1 Jn, while it occurs 194 times in the Gospel of Jn; παρά with the genitive is found 25 times in the Gospel of Jn, not at all in 1 Jn. There are no semitisms in 1 Jn, such as the Johannine ἵνα and ὅτι to denote the Aramaic ר; compound verbs, like ἀναγγέλλω, occur much less frequently in 1 Jn than in the Gospel of Jn.

Of the typical, theologically "loaded," Johannine catchwords, the following are not found in 1 Jn: σῴζειν, ἀπολλύναι, πέμπειν, κρίνειν/κρίσις, εἰρήνη.

3. Exercise in textual criticism: Evaluate the "Comma Johanneum," 1 Jn 5:7f.

Second John

1. General matters

2 Jn is the letter of a πρεσβύτερος to a "chosen lady." In contrast to 1 Jn, this is a genuine letter which corresponds with the form of a hellenistic private letter, even if it has a certain official character in terms of content. Jülicher and others consider 2 (and 3) Jn to be deliberate imitations of the Johannine writings. On the other hand, Kümmel points to the unpretentiousness of both texts: It cannot be determined why it was necessary for the author of 2 (and 3) Jn to imitate the Gospel and 1 Jn.

The content of 2 Jn is simple: It contains an appeal to walk in love and a warning against false teachers.

2. Special problems

(1) The question is asked whether the author who designates himself as πρεσβύτερος (2 Jn 1), is a presbyter (elder) or simply an old man ("the old one"). Perhaps πρεσβύτερος is indeed to be understood as a title; in this case it could possibly be a member of that circle of presbyters which is regarded as guarantor of the Christian tradition in Papias, Irenaeus, and Clement of Alexandria. If this is correct, the presbyter John (see above), mentioned by Papias, could actually be the author. It has to be noted, however, that the name "John" is not found in the letter!

(2) The meaning of "lady," in the address, is not clear. The question arises whether the letter is addressed to a woman or to a church. Since there is evidence that the term κυρία is a designation for "cities" in Hellenism (cf. W. Foerster, TDNT III, 1095), it is more likely that the letter is addressed to a church and not to an individual, all the more since a proper name would have been given in this case.

Third John: The Problem of Heresy

3 Jn is also a letter of the "presbyter," in this case addressed to an otherwise unknown Gaius. The author polemicizes against a certain Diotrephes; hereby we gain an interesting glimpse into the intra-church conflicts of the second century.

(1) The letter has caused exegetes to postulate a number of arguments that continue to be discussed in scholarship.

(a) A. Harnack (*Über den dritten Joh*, TU 15/3, 1897) explains: There are not only personal rivalries between the presbyter and Diotrephes; rather, in this conflict emerge the two major streams of the early history of the church: the Spirit-oriented church (*Geistkirche*) and the office-oriented church (*Amtskirche*). On the one side there are the charismatics, the itinerant missionaries who were authorized by the presbyter but otherwise are not subject to any permanent organization. On the other side is Diotrephes; he is the representative of the locally resident "office" and thus does not trust those itinerant preachers. Harnack argues that Diotrephes is the "first monarchical bishop whose name we know" (p. 21). This is made particularly clear in that Diotrephes is by no means accused of heresy by the presbyter and hence cannot be considered as part of the group of heretics by the author (Bultmann concurs, *The Johannine Epistles*, ET 1973, 95).

(b) According to W. Bauer (*Orthodoxy and Heresy in Earliest Christianity*, ET 1971, p. 93f.), 3 Jn is evidence for the argument that there was no clear distinction yet concerning orthodoxy and heresy in the early phase of the history of the church. Diotrephes is a heretical bishop, according to Bauer, who excommunicated other Christians and for this reason was assailed by the presbyter.

(c) E. Käsemann ("Ketzer und Zeuge," *Ges. Aufs.* I, 168–187) notes that the converse is likely the case. It is not Diotrephes but the presbyter who is on the side of heresy; in any case, the bishop suspects him as an adherent of gnostic doctrines.

(2) All three interpretations are very hypothetical and by far exceed what can be gathered directly from the text. There is nothing to be found on either side of heresy and excommunication. The only thing that can be inferred is that Diotrephes takes a position in the church which, from the presbyter's viewpoint, does not befit him at all. Whether there is a fundamental canonical dispute behind it, cannot be determined.

V. HEBREWS

§ 40 Hebrews

Bibliography: E. Käsemann, *The Wandering People of God*, ET 1984; O. Michel, *Der Brief an die Hebräer*, KEK XIII, [13]1976; H. W. Montefiore, *The Epistle to the Hebrews*, HNTC, 1964; G. Theissen, *Untersuchungen zum Hebräerbrief*, StNT 2, 1969; H. Braun, *Der Hebräerbrief*, HNT 14, 1984.

1. Problem and structure

Heb is not a letter but a theological treatise. It does indeed contain some concrete allusions to the situation of the readers, who are occasionally addressed directly (5:11f.; 6:10; 10:32–34; 13:7, 18f., 23), and it even has an elaborate epistolary conclusion (13:24f.); but the letter form is lacking at the beginning.

Heb is a theological treatise whose writing came at a time when the church dealt with Judaism primarily along theoretical, i.e., literary lines. Besides Heb, the speech of Stephen in Acts 7 and, outside of the NT, the letter of Barnabas (see § 45), are further examples of this phase of the development.

It is characteristic of the structure of Heb to find alternating christological and paraenetic sections (2:1–4; 3:7–4:11; 4:14–16; 5:11–6:12; 10:19–39; 12:1ff.; 12:12ff.; 13:1ff.). In this case the paraenesis is presented as consequence of the christological statements; thus, the indicative-imperative pattern is dominant here as well. The question is posed repeatedly in scholarship, Which part does the author of Heb emphasize— the christological prerequisites or the ethical consequences (at the present time, the tendency is toward the latter)? This debate ignores, however, that there is no alternative for Heb at all at this point. If one examines the pericope of 5:11–6:20, a clear, purposeful integration of paraenesis and Christology/soteriology becomes evident: In terms of form, there is paraenesis, but in terms of content the author moves from the baptismal catechism (5:12; 6:1–4) to the πνεῦμα ἅγιον, hence to soteriology. By means of the catchword Melchizedek (7:1) he then refers back to 5:10.

There is also an ongoing debate concerning whether Heb was structured in three, four, or five parts, thus in keeping with a rhetorical pattern of antiquity (Windisch). It is also debated in this context whether the primary division is to be seen in 10:18 or in 10:31. In both cases, however, the dispute is ultimately pointless: Divisions of form are not factual; rather, they may serve the purpose of pointing to possibilities of observation.

Probably it is simplest to make a threefold division:
(a) 1:1–4:13—God's revelation in his Son far exceeds any other revelation.
(b) 4:14–10:18 (or 10:31)—Jesus himself is the perfect high priest.
(c) 10:19 (or 10:32)–13:25—Paraenetic instructions and (epistolary) conclusion.

2. Literary and history-of-religions problems

The question has been raised whether the author of Heb assimilated fixed doctrinal expositions in his work. Evidence of this is found in Heb 1f.; 5:1–10; 7:1–10:8, and in ch 11. But since the entire "letter" has pronounced didactic features, there are no adequate criteria for isolating individual sections.

Some exegetes argue that a Jewish source was used in Heb 11. It is indeed striking that v 39 does not fit the flow of the text but has the effect of a later insertion. But it is doubtful whether this is a sufficient criterion for the separation of sources.

Conspicuous in Heb are some traditional forms of Jewish interpretation of Scripture that are otherwise not found in the NT. Thus Heb 3:7–14 is a midrash of Ps 95 and Heb 7:1–25 is a midrash of Ps 110 and Gen 14:17–22. On the whole, Heb uses concepts, ideas, and methods of hellenistic Judaism extensively; its affinity to Philo is especially close: In both cases Melchizedek is understood as King of Righteousness, and in both cases the exegesis is typological and allegorical (allegory in Heb: 11:13ff.; 13:11ff.). Still, there are decisive differences: Typology in Heb has the history of salvation as its focus; prominent are such categories as the old and the new covenant. By contrast, Philo's thinking is ahistorical; thus for him, paradise is the timeless realm of virtues, and OT individuals represent (timeless) types of the path to God. In contrast to Heb, Philonic teaching contains no eschatology. It may be stated with some certainty, therefore, that there is no *literary* relationship between Heb and Philo.

In the manner in which Heb establishes the relationship of the "Son" with the "sons" (2:10–18), E. Käsemann perceives a link with the gnostic idea of an identity between the redeemed and the redeemer. But this is improbable; Rom 8 indicates that the concept of son/sons can also be understood without the specific hypothesis of Gnosticism.

3. Style and linguistic characteristics

From a literary perspective, Heb is the most carefully developed writing of the NT. As far as style is concerned, it demonstrates the best Greek of any NT writing; this can be recognized, for instance, in its elaborate compound sentences (1:1–4; 2:2–4, 14f.; 7:20–22, 23–25), which are rarely found elsewhere in the NT. The structure of Heb is analogous to that of the writings from the hellenistic diatribe; certain affinities exist with such writings as the Wisdom of Solomon or those of Philo (see above). Likewise with regards to content, Heb largely corresponds with hellenistic-Jewish erudition, as we know it from Alexandria, again especially from Philo.

4. Historical questions

In the early church, Heb was frequently held to be a Pauline writing; in P[46] it is situated between Rom and 1 Cor. However, both style and theological content rule out the possibility that it was actually a Pauline work. Its idea of the church, Christology (Heb does not take the "resurrection" as its orientation, but the "exaltation" of Christ), and eschatology are entirely different from the Pauline teaching. Despite the mention of Timothy in 13:23, the assumption that Heb came from the Pauline school, can be dismissed. The statement in 13:7, about the "leaders" whose example is to be followed and who had proclaimed the word of God, further indicates clearly that the apostolic era already belongs to the past. Likewise, the difference between Jewish Christians and Gentile Christians is quite obviously already history; the dispute with Jewish Christianity is merely theoretical.

Beyond these general observations, the parameters for the time of writing of Heb can be somewhat established: (a) There are references to a persecution (6:10f.; 10:32f.), the specific details of which must remain open, however. (b) Mention is made of "those from Italy" (13:24). (c) 1 Clem, which was probably written during the reign of Domitian, around A.D. 90, apparently presupposes the existence of Heb (cf. 1 Clem 17:1; 36:2–5). Therefore, Heb must have been written no later than in the last decade of the first century, but probably after the deutero-pauline letters Col and Eph.

While the time of writing can still be established with some certainty, the remaining introductory questions remain practically unanswerable. The quest for the author is as hopeless as that for the recipients. The title "To the Hebrews" is secondary in any case; it is the result of the character of the writing which has been influenced strongly by hellenistic Judaism. Nothing can be said about the place of writing; if the reference to persecution refers to Domitian's campaign against the Christians, Heb would have been written in northern Asia Minor, but there is nothing certain about that.

5. Basic theological ideas

The theology of Heb is determined by the idea of the "wandering people of God." In it, Käsemann even saw the leading motif of the entire writing. In contrast, A. Oepke (*Das neue Gottesvolk*, 1950, 57–74) stressed that the emphasis was not so much on the wandering itself but on the church—which is indeed construed as being on a pilgrimage—as the *new* people of God. Reference to the wandering is made especially in the paraenesis, with 3:7–4:13 serving as the best example. The believer must battle and is able to battle against weariness which occurs on a prolonged pilgrimage by contemplating the future, that is, the destination of the pilgrimage, the heavenly rest in the heavenly city. This image shows at the same time that the eschatology is developed both temporally and spatially in the pattern of below/above. Those wandering are further exhorted to be reassured of the present: The description of the way, which helps their orientation, eases the toils. Even the retrospective glance upon the already covered stretch of the journey is meant to help. The weary are reminded of the old covenant, of the promises of that time, whereby the forward glance at the destination is once again indirectly underscored.

With the help of this wandering motif, the basic concepts of Heb can be ascertained. Faith is understood as remaining in the fellowship of the wandering people; sin is to fall behind, and to grow weary, hence to fall into unbelief and apostasy; finally, hope is the view of the destination along the journey. On the one hand, the promise is already fulfilled; the people of God are already en route. On the other hand, the end is not yet; the destination has not yet been reached and the people continue to need strengthening. The assurance of hope has its basis in the work of salvation, in the sacrifice of Christ, the true high priest (4:14–7:28). Against the backdrop of the OT example of Melchizedek, Christ the priest arises in bold relief as the perfect high priest whose ministry and sacrifice surpass by far everything pertaining to the OT. The relationship between the old and the new covenant is determined in the same manner (8:1–10:18); the second covenant is better by far (8:6). In terms of typological interpretation, the old and the new covenants are related to one another like symbol and reality or like promise and fulfillment; in other words, the new covenant both supersedes and surpasses the old.

Suggested exercises:

1. Interpret the concepts πίστις and ἐπαγγελία in connection with the idea of the "wandering people of God."

Tools: E. Käsemann (see bibliography); E. Grässer, "Der Glaube im Hebr," *MThSt* 2, 1965, 13–63; idem, "Rechtfertigung im Hebr," in *Rechtfertigung* (FS E. Käsemann), 1976, 79–93.

2. In 6:4–8 the author takes the theological position that a Christian who has fallen away from Christ has no possibility to obtain forgiveness by way of a second repentance. How is one to view this teaching?

Tools: H. Windisch, *Taufe und Sünde im ältesten Christentum bis auf Origenes*, 1908, 294–312; E. Grässer, *Der Glaube im Hebräer*, 1965, 192–198.

VI. THE "CATHOLIC LETTERS"

Preliminary remark

The "catholic letters" do not address specific recipients as much as the entire (="catholic") church. This group of seven letters also encompasses the three Johannine letters which have already been discussed in part four.

§ 41 James

Bibliography: P. Davids, *The Epistle of James*, NIGTC, 1982; M. Dibelius, *James: A Commentary on the Epistle of James*, Hermeneia, ET 1976; S. Laws, *The Epistle of James*, HNTC, 1980; F. Mussner, "Der Jakobusbrief," in: H. Balz/W. Schrage, *Die katholischen Briefe*, NTD 10, 1973, 5–58; H. Windisch/H. Preisker, *Die katholischen Briefe*, HNT 15, ³1951, 1–36.

Preliminary remark

James is not a true letter either. Whereas it opens with an introductory salutation of a single clause and, hence, is Greek in its form (see p. 27f. above); the epistolary format is missing at the end. In Heb (see p. 263 above) the converse is the case.

1. Structure and literary-critical problems

A fixed structure cannot be recognized. The introductory salutation (1:1) is followed by paraenetic elements and wisdom sayings that are loosely strung together. In terms of form and content, section 2:14–26, concerning the relationship between faith and works, is given central significance. All in all, however, there is no orderly arrangement and no continuous sequence of thought (cf. e.g, the jump from 1:2–18 to 1:19ff.).

The groups of sayings in ch 2 are very similar to those found in Jewish aphoristic ethics, as a comparison of the parallels cited in Nestle will show (1:5 with Prov 2:3–6; Wis 9:6; Jas 1:13 with Sir 15:11ff. etc.). The topic of ch 1 is the πειρασμός (with the meaning of the term shifting from "trial" to "temptation"). At the back of it is the Jewish idea that God actually tests man in terms of a method of divine pedagogy.

The middle part contains three minor essays (Dibelius: diatribes) concerning the problems of poor and rich (2:1–13), faith and works (2:14–26), and the issue of the misuse of the tongue (3:1–12). These three sections are structured fairly regularly: (a) name of the issue; (b) illustration by examples; (c) refutation of the objections of an imaginary opponent; in addition, 2:14–26 mentions (d) support from Scripture. There is, however, no correlation of ideas from section to section.

Only in the last part of the letter does the author establish a connection between two sections; 4:13–17 and 5:1–6 are a parallel treatment concerning man's (futile) planning for the future and concerning the rich. The conclusion of Jas contains words of consolation and exhortation, as well as specific regulations for individual situations (5:7–20).

A. Meyer ("Das Rätsel des Jac," *BZNW* 10, 1930, 240–305) postulates a completely different argument regarding the structure of Jas. He begins with the observation that there are hardly any Christian traces in Jas. Apart from the salutation, Jesus is mentioned only in 2:1 where the sentence structure is next to impossible. It is not out of the question that this reference to Jesus is interpolated. Therefore, Meyer argues that Jas was based on a Jewish writing whose structure followed a specific principle; the author simply gave this writing a slight Christian retouching. This basic document belongs to the genre of the "Testaments of the (twelve) Patriarchs." "James" originally meant the OT patriarch Jacob; his name and those of his sons were interpreted allegorically, namely, with reference to fortunes, manners of conduct, virtues or vices (cf. Test XII, Philo, rabbinic writings). Thus Meyer deciphers one section after another: The name James is interpreted to mean "temptation" in 1:1–16. The term ἀπαρχή in 1:18 points to Reuben, the firstborn; section 1:19–27, concerning hearing and serving God, refers to Simeon and Levi etc.

Some of these interpretations are undoubtedly meaningful in themselves. But in many instances the allusions ascertained by Meyer can be discovered only by forcing things. Meyer does indeed see this problem. He attributes the difficulties this brings for his interpretation to the fact that the Christian editor truncated his source; thereby the allusions became very unclear in part.

But Meyer's argument does not do justice to the text of Jas as a whole. Especially the middle part cannot be understood as a reduction of a source, but only as the deliberately shaped work of the author. With this realization, however, the entire hypothesis collapses.

2. Historical questions: Author and recipients

(1) In 1:1 the author introduces himself as "James, a servant of God and of the Lord Jesus Christ"; in all probability, this refers to the brother of Jesus. Should the authorial reference of James be reliable, this would mean that Jas was written prior to A.D. 62 (James' death in Jerusalem).

Some scholars attempt to underscore this assumption by pointing out that the letter indicates that at the time of its writing the tradition of Jesus was still in the oral stage and not yet in the literary stage (cf. Jas 5:12 with Mt 5:34–37). But this argument is not valid because the oral tradition doubtlessly continued even after the Gospels were fixed.

The assumption of the authenticity of Jas is settled quickly, however, when it is seen that historically the letter does not fit the time of the Lord's brother James. In addition, it becomes clear from section 2:14–26 that the dichotomy Jewish Christians—Gentile Christians, which stands in the limelight of the early church's dispute, is no longer present. But if the letter were authentic, precisely this issue would have to be central. Furthermore, there would at least have to be traces of the dispute between Christians and Jews in view of the threat of the Jewish War, but none of it can be seen. Further, nothing in the letter indicates that the author knew Jesus personally. Finally, especially 2:14–26 makes it clear that the author very obviously polemicizes against Paul, that is, perhaps more correctly, against a more developed "Paulinism." For him, the law has again become a positive entity (cf. the expression "the law of liberty" in 2:12). In conclusion, the relatively fine Greek in the framework of the NT as well as the use of the LXX also militates against James as author; both of these could hardly be expected from a Jew from Jerusalem.

(2) The letter mentions the twelve tribes in the Diaspora as the recipients; without a doubt, this refers to the whole church (not only Jewish Christianity). The use of the term "diaspora" has its explanation in that the world is foreign territory for Christians (cf. Phil 3:20; Heb 13:14; 1 Pet 2:11). Thus Jas belongs to the genre of Diaspora letters.

(3) Scholarship searches for literary relationships to other writings which might shed light on the actual writer of Jas. Thus one compares Jas 4:6–10 with 1 Pet 5:5–9, or Jas 1:5–8 with Herm Man IX, 1-7. However, in neither of these cases is there a direct relationship. This means for us that the author remains completely shrouded in darkness. The time (ca. A.D. 100) and place of writing must also remain open.

3. Basic theological ideas

Meyer's argument that Jas was virtually devoid of Christian elements (see above), is untenable. There are no Jewish parallels, for instance, for the statement in 1:9; the saying of 1:18, which is reminiscent of Jewish wisdom literature, can readily be given a Christian interpretation, that is, in view of those who are born again. 2:7 can only be understood with the Christian baptism in mind; anointing (5:14) is not a Jewish ritual. There are also allusions to sayings of Jesus—apart from 5:12 (see above) also in 1:5, 17 (cf. Mt 7:7ff.) and in 4:12 (cf. Mt 7:1, yet see also Rom 2:1). More than anything else, Jas emphasizes the observation that the distinction between poor and rich is not permissible within the community (2:1–13; 5:1–6), and this is a typical trademark of the Christian community (cf. 1 Cor 1:26; Gal 3:28).

Section 2:14–26 is of decisive importance for the determination of the theological position of Jas. It can hardly be doubted that the theology of Paul is presupposed here, especially his formulation of the doctrine of justification and its demonstration in the figure of Abraham. According to Pauline theology, especially as developed in Gal and Rom, man is justified by God and before God by faith alone, apart from the works that the law demands (Rom 3:27). Therefore Gentiles are not obligated to receive the law, because there is only one God (Rom 3:30), that is, because his justifying grace applies not only to the Jews but also to the Gentiles. For Paul, Abraham is the model for this understanding of faith (Rom 4). Jas very obviously refers to this Pauline position and criticizes it. If someone has only faith and no works, faith is in vain. Faith without works is dead faith. The demons also believe that εἶς ἐστιν ὁ θεός (2:19; with this, cf. the entirely different interpretation of this statement by Paul in Rom 3:30). Man is justified by works and by no means by faith "alone." Once again it is Abraham who serves as model for this comprehension of faith and works.

How is the unavoidable dilemma—that two NT theologians maintain such diametrically opposed positions by using identical conceptual materials—to be explained?

(a) It could be that the historical James, as a major representative of Jewish Christianity, polemicizes directly against Paul, whose attack of the law he repudiates. Whether he understood Paul correctly in this context, remains an open question.

(b) It could be that the historical James opposes degenerate Paulinists, as it were, such as libertinists, who appeal to Paul to justify their behavior.

While both solutions may indeed be feasible in themselves, they are to be dismissed because Jas, without doubt, was not written by the historical James, the brother of Jesus (see above).

(c) The imaginary James might carry on a polemic directly against Paul and the recognition his doctrine of justification enjoys within the church.

(d) The imaginary James might carry on a polemic against a degenerate Paulinism that interprets the Pauline teaching as abrogation of all ethical norms.

It is likely that Jas does not target a later caricature of Pauline theology, but Pauline theology itself; the affinity between Jas 2:19 and Rom 3:30 allows little room for doubt in this regard. Nevertheless, it is to be assumed that he does not combat Paul in retrospect (e.g., against his recognition as apostle). Apparently, his adversary is a contemporary form of a developed Paulinism. It is striking in any case, that Jas does not give consideration to the peculiarities of the Pauline understanding of faith;

thus the position of the law within the framework of the entire problem finds no explicit reference. At the back of the argument of Jas, that only the cooperation of faith and works (and not faith alone) is necessary for salvation, is obviously the misunderstanding that faith is a purely intellectual effort. The Pauline understanding of faith is not encountered thereby, of course.

Suggested reading:

A. Lindemann, *Paulus im ältesten Christentum*, 1979, 243–252 (and the literature cited there).

His position on eschatology is significant for the situation of Jas relative to the history of the church and of theology. While the old forms are still repeated (5:7f.), they no longer have any concrete theological significance. The Christianity of Jas belongs to the era of the Apostolic Fathers (see § 45 below). That the ceremonial law is no longer binding for Christians is a matter of course for Jas; yet the ethical norms retain their value (cf. 2:12). Most of all, the law has again become the way of salvation; for, indirectly, the regard for works is at the same time the recognition of the law.

Suggested exercise:

The relationship of Jas to Pauline theology poses the question of whether theologically the NT canon makes sense if within this canon there are two opposite positions taken in a decisive question of faith or theology. In his preface to Jas, Luther has taken the contrast to Paul as pretext to deny Jas any theological significance as such. Is such a verdict absolutely necessary, or are there options to incorporate both the position of Paul and of Jas into the overall frame of a NT theology?

Tools: G. Eichholz, "Jakobus und Paulus. Ein Beitrag zum Problem des Kanons," *ThEx* NF 39, 1953; E. Lohse, "Glaube und Werke. Zur Theologie des Jakobus," *Ges. Aufs.*, 1973, 285–306; U. Luck, "Die Theologie des Jakobusbriefes," *ZThK* 81, 1984, 1–30.

§ 42   1 Peter

Bibliography: E. Lohse, "Paränese und Kerygma im 1. Petrusbrief," *Ges. Aufs.*, 1973, 307–328; N. Brox, *Der erste Petrusbrief*, EKK XXI, 1979; J. H. Elliott, *A Home for the Homeless. A Sociological Exegesis of 1 Peter, Its Situation and Strategy*, 1981; J. R. Michaels, *1 Peter*, WBC 49, 1988; E. G. Selwyn, *The First Epistle of St. Peter*, ²1947; W. Schrage, in: H. Balz and W. Schrage, (see § 41), 59–117; H. Windisch and H. Preisker (see § 41), 49–82.

1. Theme and thought pattern

After the prescript and praise (1:1–2, 3–12), the first part of 1 Pet exhorts Christians to holy conduct. This presupposes that they are already redeemed (1:22–2:10); "holy conduct" is consequently not understood as a means of self-justification. The message of the second part is a comprehensive household code (2:11–3:12) in which Christians are called upon to let their conduct be commensurate with their respective position. In 3:13–4:11 Christians are exhorted to appropriate conduct in suffering in keeping with the example of Christ's suffering (this is repeated in 4:12–5:11). A brief epistolary ending follows in 5:12–14. Similarly to Heb, paraenesis and soteriology also alternate in 1 Pet.

Of vital significance for the theological understanding of the letter is the fact that the setting of persecution (cf. the term "suffering" above) leads to a reactivation of the eschatology that has been all but eliminated in the deutero-pauline letters (cf. also Rev). While there is no specific section on eschatology to be found in 1 Pet, there are comments with an eschatological content in several references (2:12; 4:5, 7; 4:13, 17; 5:8; i.e., especially in the context of statements regarding the sufferings of Christians).

2. Literary problems

In its external form, 1 Pet is a letter. Ch 1:1 cites the recipients who reside in a specific area of Asia Minor. But the first major part of 1:3–4:11 is almost devoid of any concrete reference that would allow for conclusions about an actual relationship between sender and recipients. It is probable, therefore, that 1 Pet is not a letter but a theological essay without reference to concrete situations. The manner in which the paraenesis is presented, also demonstrates this: There are no allusions to actual situations.

It is argued that 1 Pet is a baptismal liturgy; in the back of it some exegetes see a Passover liturgy (seeing a relationship between the expression πάσχω and the concept of the Passover; however, there is no evidence for this connection as early as the first century). These arguments exceed what can in fact be ascertained; the individual passages are not liturgical in form and no carrying out of a liturgical act can be discerned.

An important literary problem appears in 4:11; for, this reference has the makings of a liturgical conclusion. It is also striking that the references to the situation of persecution and suffering are more frequent in the continuation of 4:12ff. than in the first part. On the basis of this, some exegetes conclude that there is a literary seam between 4:11 and 4:12; whereas the discussion has to do with a potential persecution up to 4:11, section 4:12ff. presupposes an actual situation of persecution. It is necessary, therefore, to speak of two parts that were written at different times. Section 1:3–4:11 was originally a baptismal homily that was supplemented with concrete references after the persecution began (4:12ff.) and was reshaped into a letter (1:1f. and conclusion). But this argument is not tenable. In no wise are the allusions to baptism the dominant theme of the entire section to 4:11; rather, they are found almost exclusively in 1:3–2:10. Furthermore, the assertions in 4:12ff. do not have to be traced back to a situation of the church that is different from that for the first part.

Suggested exercise:

Analyze the two hymns of 2:21–24; 3:18–22.

Tool: R. Bultmann, "Bekenntnis- und Liedfragmente im ersten Petrus," in *Exegetica*, 1967, 285–297.

In the second hymn the following is to be noted: If 3:19f. is bracketed, one recognizes that the hymn originally dealt with the ascension. Only by means of the reference to the fallen angels (Gen 6) and to Noah's contemporaries did it become a description of Christ's descent into hell—the only one of its kind in the NT.

3. Historical setting

The letter claims to be written in "Babylon" by Silvanus (5:12f.). Acts 15–18 frequently speaks of this Silvanus (Silas); in addition, Paul mentions him as a fellow sender in 2 Cor 1:19 and in 1 Thes 1:1 (cf. 2 Thes 1:1). Since Babylon definitely refers to Rome, the "letter" presupposes that Peter and Silvanus were in Rome at the time of a persecution and, from there, addressed the communities of the "Diaspora" in Asia Minor with words of comfort and exhortation (on the term "Diaspora," see p. 269 above). Indeed, already by A.D. 100 it is held without doubt that Peter had resided in Rome (Ignatius; 1 Clem), though there is no clear information about it.

All the same, several indications militate against Peter's writing of 1 Pet. For one, there is no evidence that the author knew Jesus personally. For another, the use of the LXX indicates that the author came from the Greek-speaking territory. A further argument against its "authenticity" is the designation of "Babylon" for Rome (5:13), which did not arise until after the Jewish War. It is to be noted further that the persecution of which 1 Pet speaks, threatens the entire church, not only individual communities in particular areas; this scenario does not apply until the reign of the emperor Domitian (cf. 1 Clem). Finally, 1 Pet demonstrates the influence of Paul at several points: The prescript corresponds with the Pauline epistolary form (however, one is to note the modification of εἰρήνη πληθυνθείη); the idea of the Christians' participation in the sufferings of Christ is as likely derived from Pauline theology as the conception of righteousness effected by the death of Christ (2:24; 3:18). 1 Pet contains one of the rare references to the doctrine of justification outside of the *Corpus Paulinum*. In this context, it is also striking that the recipients addressed in 1:1 in part live in the mission territory of Paul—this also speaks against the authorship of Peter. This does not mean that the letter is to be dated very late. After all, Polycarp already quotes 1 Pet, and the author of 2 Pet also knows of the existence of 1 Pet (see comments on 2 Pet 3:1 below).

Some interpreters point out that there are certain agreements between 1 Pet and Eph, as well as Jas; they attempt to derive out of this a literary relationship. But these agreements merely consist of a few traditional expressions that the authors quite obviously adopted independently of one another.

All of these items favor a writing of 1 Pet around 80–90, from Asia Minor.

Suggested exercise:

Compare 1 Pet 2:13–17 with Rom 13:1–7.

Tools: W. Schrage (see bibliography), 87–90; idem, *Die Christen und der Staat nach dem Neuen Testament,* 1971, 50–68.

§ 43 Jude and 2 Peter

Bibliography: T. Fornberg, *An Early Church in a Pluralistic Society,* 1977; W. Grundmann, *Der Brief des Judas und der zweite Brief des Petrus,* ThHK XV, 1974; E. Käsemann, "An Apologia for Primitive Christian Eschatology," in *Essays on NT Themes,* ET 1964; K. H. Schelkle, *Die Petrusbriefe, der Judasbrief,* HThK XIII/2, [3]1970, 137–239; W. Schrage, in: H. R. Balz and W. Schrage (see § 41), 118–149, 217–232; H. Windisch and H. Preisker (see § 41), 37–48, 83–105.

Preliminary remark

These two letters need to be discussed jointly. With regard to content, they are not very important, but they are very suitable as exercises for literary-critical observations. A parallel reading shows similarities to the point of verbal agreements which renders the question of literary dependence upon one another inescapable.

1. The problem of mutual dependence

(1) If Jude 4–16 and 2 Pet 2 are read side by side, the conclusion is inevitable that the author of one letter must have known the other letter. The agreements are found not only in the wording of individual references (this could be explained via usage of a common tradition), but especially in the order of the sayings. Thus, in both cases the reference to the disobedient angels is followed by the allusion to Sodom and Gomorrah (Jude 6f., 2 Pet 2:5f.). Jude 7–9 corresponds largely with 2 Pet 2:10f.; however, the reference to the righteous in 2 Pet 2:7–9 is not paralleled in Jude. Moreover, even a glance at the marginal reference in the Nestle text indicates how pervasive the structural agreements are.

This poses the question of priority. The names of the authors in both letters offer no help. Of course, Jude, the brother of Jesus, might have written his letter at about the same time as Peter, the disciple of Jesus. But both letters are without a doubt pseudonymous writings. In Jude this is demonstrated in that for him the apostles represent a group already belonging to the past (Jude 17)—always a sure sign of a relatively late origin of a text. In 2 Pet the pseudonymity becomes clear especially in 2:1–3:12ff., because the warning against heresy, which is initially intended as prophetic utterance, in reality focuses on the present (v 15 even uses the past tense; cf. p. 277 below). In addition, 2 Pet 3:16 shows that a collection of the Pauline letters is already available (they are apparently used especially by false teachers of a gnostic provenance and for their own purposes). All of these characteristics and circumstances could not possibly be explained in the framework of "authentic" letters of Jude and of Peter.

(2) The question of which letter is to be accorded priority can easily be answered by comparing the differences between the parallels of the two writings. The following picture results: (a) Jude and 2 Pet generally adduce examples from the history of the OT. Thus Jude 5–7, mentions Israel in the wilderness, then the fallen angels, and finally Sodom and Gomorrah (in this order); 2 Pet 2:4ff. contains references to the angels, the flood, and Sodom and Gomorrah—hence, the order in which these stories are told in Genesis is maintained in 2 Pet, whereas it was changed in Jude. (b) Mythological references are found in both letters, but while they are very explicit in Jude, they are only faintly implied in 2 Pet. In this context, it is especially striking that Jude, at some points, contains references to apocryphal writings, while there are no references to such writings in 2 Pet. One needs to compare Jude 6f. (cf. 1 Enoch 12:4; 10:4) with 2 Pet 2:4, as well as Jude 9, which contains a reference to a lost piece from the Assumption of Moses (As Mos), with 2 Pet 2:11, and, finally, Jude 12f. (cf. 1 Enoch 18:11ff.; 21:3) with 2 Pet 2:17. In Jude 14f. Enoch is mentioned explicitly, but this reference is likewise missing in 2 Pet.

These observations lead to the conclusion that Jude is the older letter and that 2 Pet is dependent on it. The author of 2 Pet has quite obviously sought to correct the "deficiencies" he saw in Jude, such as the imprecise rendering of the biblical accounts and the citation of non-canonical books. Furthermore, he expanded Jude at both ends by using materials from Jude even in the expanding chapters 1 and 3. One may compare 2 Pet 1:5 with Jude 3; 2 Pet 1:12 with Jude 5; 2 Pet 3:2 with Jude 17 (Jude 16 was assimilated, in the end, in 2 Pet 2:18); and 2 Pet 3:14 with Jude 24. In any case, this is the more plausible assumption than the reverse, that Jude is a condensation of 2 Pet. (Control question: Based on what criteria should such a condensation have occurred?)

2. The problem of the date

It can hardly be stated with adequate precision when Jude and 2 Pet were written. The only certain thing is that 2 Pet must have been written after Jude and that 1 Pet was also already known (see below). The fact that a collection of the Pauline letters was already in existence when 2 Pet was written (3:15f.), allows the conclusion that 2 Pet originated in the first half of the second century.

3. Content of Jude and 2 Peter

(1) The assumption of the priority of Jude that resulted from the literary comparison between Jude and 2 Pet is confirmed by comparing their contents. Whereas Jude, as a whole, represents one single polemic against heresy, 2 Pet has limited and sharpened the same, in ch 3, for combatting the denial of the imminent parousia.

The battle against false teachers employs the same tactics used in the Pastorals. One does not learn the nature of the heretics' teaching; only very vaguely are they alluded to as dreamers (Jude 8) or as unspiritual (*Psychiker*) (v 19), hence they were likely gnostics. Just like the "Paul" of the Pastorals, Jude appeals to tradition against the false teachers (vv 3, 20); he stresses that their appearance is a sign of the endtimes and is in keeping with ancient prophecy (cf. 1 Tim 4:1; 2 Tim 4:3). Their special characteristic is their personal immorality (Jude 10ff.). Cain and Balaam (v 11), for instance, are prototypes of the heretics; Jude 14f. refers to 1 Enoch 1:9, 60:8, where the appearance of the heretics in the endtime and their judgment are prophesied.

(2) 2 Pet is not merely a revision of Jude; besides Jude the author also knows 1 Pet. This can be deduced from the imitation of the prescript of 1 Pet (1:1f.) and from the retrospective reference in 3:1. The hellenistic terminology in 1:3–11 is characteristic for 2 Pet: The concepts of virtue (1:3, 5; cf. the list of virtues in 1:5–7) and of knowledge (1:2, 3, 5f., 8) play a significant part. There is also the idea that salvation meant man's participation in the divine nature (1:4). The warning against myths (which means invented stories of deities) is clearly conveyed as Peter's legacy (1:15f.; Peter's death is presupposed here). Conspicuous is the manner in which the story of Jesus and the disciples is passed on in 2 Pet: The narrative of the transfiguration on the "holy mount" (1:16b ff.) has all the features of a sacred story, the knowledge of which itself already denotes an element of salvation's realization.

Similar to 2 Tim, 2 Pet is shaped as a "testament"; both person and teaching of the apostle are to be passed on to future generations (1:15).

In comparison to Jude, there is a clear intensification in the polemic; the false teachers are not merely opposed, but there is an emphatic demand for separation from them (3:17). And while Jude generally explains that the appearance of the heretics was prophesied, in 2 Pet this "prophecy" is created by attributing it to Peter, thereby shaping it into an exhortation which reaches from the past into the present. In short, it could be expressed like this: Jude himself polemicizes directly against contemporary heretics; 2 Pet has Peter polemicize against future heretics (that this is fiction can be seen in the wrong choice of the tenses in 2:10, 12ff., 18; on the other hand, cf. 2:1–3).

4. The problem of the eschatology of 2 Peter

2 Pet is a document of the famed problem of the "delay of the parousia." At the end of the first and the beginning of the second century, the church was faced with the problem of whether or not and in what way it should maintain the idea of the imminent coming of Christ as the eschatological judge of the world. A. Schweitzer and subsequently especially M. Werner (cf. *Die Entstehung des christlichen Dogmas*, [2]1953, 105–125) were of the opinion that solving this problem was *the* decisive theological task of the early church, but this is a modern conception. Although there are traces of a corresponding debate in the texts of this era, it is not possible to speak of a foundational crisis. The solution to the problem that 2 Pet proposes, is startling in its clarity and simplicity: The imminent expectation continues to apply, he explains, because one needs to note that to God a thousand years are like one day (3:8; apparently the author does not realize that this saying can also be used as an argument against the imminent expectation). Käsemann has posed the question whether the existence of 2 Pet in the canon is indeed pertinent.

Suggested readings:

E. Käsemann (see bibliography); C. H. Talbert, "II Peter and the Delay of the Parousia," *Vig Chr* 20, 1966, 137–145.

VII. THE APOCALYPSE

§ 44 Apocalypse of John

Bibliography: W. Bousset, *Die Offenbarung Johannis* (KEK XVI, 1906), [7]1966; G. B. Caird, *The Revelation of St. John*, HNTC, 1966; A. Y. Collins, *The Combat Myth in the Book of Revelation*, HDR 9, 1976; idem, *Crisis and Catharsis: The Power of the Apocalypse*, 1984; H. Kraft, *Die Offenbarung des Johannes*, HNT 16a, 1974; E. Lohmeyer, *Die Offenbarung des Johannes*, HNT 16, [2]1953; E. Lohse, *Die Offenbarung des Johannes*, NTD 11, [3]1971; J. Roloff, *Die Offenbarung des Johannes*, ZBK 18, 1984.

Preliminary remark

The Rev (of John) is the only work in the NT belonging to the genre of apocalypse. In order to familiarize oneself with them, it is essential to be informed about the character of this literary genre (cf. pp. 31f. and 280f.)

1. Structure and problem

(1) To begin with, the visionary framework of the entire book is established in Rev 1; Rev is the result of a personal revelation of Christ to John (1:1). The pattern by which the entire book is structured is cited in 1:19: The first part describes the present—"that which now is"—and encompasses chs 2 and 3 with the seven letters; the second part, dealing with the future—"that which will be," contains a broad presentation of the apocalyptic drama (chs 4–22). The letters to the seven churches are uniform in their structure: (a) The seer receives the commission to write (τῷ ἀγγέλῳ . . . γράψον); (b) the introduction of the letter (τάδε λέγει) with a more precise presentation of the one who gave the commission; (c) praise or rebuke of the church with a corresponding exhortation or warning; this is followed either by (dᵃ) a formulaic challenge to hear (ὁ ἔχων οὖς ἀκουσάτω) which closes letters 4–7, or by (dᵇ) the saying concerning "overcoming," which makes up the close of the first three letters (2:1–17).

(2) The structure of the second part of Rev is more complicated. The framework is delineated first of all in Rev 4f.: The visionary sees the handing over of the book with the seven seals to the Lamb. 6:1–8:1 represents the overture, as it were, to the events of the end: The first six seals are opened; the 144,000 chosen from Israel and the great multitude of martyrs appear before God's throne. The climax is in 8:1, namely, the great silence that commences in the whole universe with the opening of the seventh seal. But then it is strange that beginning with 8:2 it is not the content of the book that is shared; instead, new symbols (seven trumpets, seven "bowls of wrath") take the place of the book.

Ch 7 is comprised of two parts that have nothing to do with the vision of the seals itself. The first scene with the 144,000 elect (cf. 14:1–5) is a piece of tradition that the author has moved to this point; the second scene with the innumerable multitude of martyrs, in contrast, is obviously the interpretation of the author, who transfers the picture of the 144,000 of Israel to the church.

8:2–11:19 and 15:1–16:21, in two parallel sequences, tell of seven trumpets and of seven bowls of wrath respectively. In particular, however, one notices abrupt changes and breaks. Thus in 8:12 three woes are announced, but only two of them are actually carried out (9:12; 11:14). The story of the seven trumpets is interrupted twice in chs 10 and 11; ch 10 gives an account concerning the further unfolding of the events and gives the reason for additional material to follow (10:11). On the one hand, the view is retrospective to ch 1 (appearance of the angel and summons to prophesy); on the other hand, however, the view is prospective to ch 17 via reference to the kings. The second such interruption is in 11:1–14 where the "two witnesses" are introduced. In this context, it is unclear whether this is a presentation of a historical event in apocalyptic disguise (such as the martyrdom of Peter and Paul) or whether the text is apocalyptic in the true sense of the word, meaning that no historical allusions are behind it. In any case, the Jewish War in which the temple was occupied by the Zealots is presupposed in 11:1f.; the author has interpreted temple and altar in terms of the Christian community.

In 11:15–19 the author resumes the pattern of the number seven: The seventh trumpet sounds. Thereby the last act of the drama should actually be introduced, but something else happens once again. In chs 12–14 follow concise mythological expressions, whose details to a large extent cannot be interpreted at all (e.g., the garment of the woman, or certain characteristics of the beasts, see p. 272ff. below).

Rev 14 contains in vv 1–5 the reminiscence of the 144,000 (ch 7), in vv 6–13 the introduction to a judgment scene, a fragment of which is still discernible in vv 14–20.

Rev 15–18 almost have the effect of revising the material covered in chs 8–14; one only needs to remember the relationship between chs 12f. and 17f. (the contrast is also to be noted, of course: the heavenly queen in the former, the harlot in the latter). It is not necessary here to elaborate on the details of the fate of the great city Babylon (meaning Rome, of course).

In some way 19:1–21 is parallel to 14:1–20, for the judgment upon the earthly powers is meted out. The seer sees the assault of the nations and finally the victory over the "beast" (19:19–21).

The dawn of the millennium (20:1–6) is in keeping with the concepts of the messianic kingdom in Jewish apocalyptic (4 Ezra 7:28f.; 1 Enoch 91:12ff.; 93)—in both 4 Ezra and 1 Enoch there is a final battle against the kingdom of God, the ultimate victory and the final judgment (20:7–13).

In 21:1–8 the seer describes the new heaven and earth and in 21:9–27 the new Jerusalem. Characteristically, this new world is without time; moon and sun no longer exist. Furthermore, there is no more sea (symbol of the powers of chaos) in the new world, but trees of life are planted at the river of life (22:1–5). The external shape of the new Jerusalem is cubic, which is to say that its shape is ideal.

Rev closes in 22:6ff. with the assurance that what it described is truthful, and with a reference to the fact that the drama of the end described is imminent (22:10–12). The conclusion is comprised of a warning against any attempt to alter the text (22:18f.), a request for the parousia of Jesus, and the benediction.

2. Literary and history-of-religions problems

(1) The apocalyptic part of the book (ch 4ff.) begins with the description of heavenly worship. In scholarship this is tied to the argument that the entire book follows the procedure of a heavenly worship service that is paralleled by the earthly events. But this argument ignores that the pattern of Rev is apocalyptic: It is the anticipated unfolding of the world events that provides the basis for its arrangement.

Other exegetes take the position that Rev as a whole was based on a Jewish writing that the author reworked. However, attempts at reconstructing a continuous source are met with failure. Yet, there are indications that complete fragments have been incorporated in some instances.

Brief hymns are found everywhere in Rev: 4:8, 11; 5:9f., 12, 13; 7:12; 11:17f.; 12:10ff.; 15:3f.; 19:1f.; 19:6ff. Are they to be understood as hymns associated with public worship that the author has modified? Apparently this is not the case, for when their contextual setting is examined, it follows that the hymns are consistently shaped with the context in mind; in other words, they prove to be the work of the author of Rev himself.

(2) Peculiarities relative to the history of religions are found especially in the highly mythical chs 12 and 13. At the back of the image of the "birth of the child" (12:1–6) is the conception of the heavenly queen of the astral myths whose son is protected from the pursuits of the dragon by God himself. Michael's struggle with this dragon, described in 12:7ff., is a new, separate topic. The external flow of action is the persecution, flight, and ultimate rescue of the woman who, in keeping with the purpose of Rev, symbolizes the church. The backdrop is given in two mythical complexes: For one, the myth of the birth, persecution, and victory of the sun god, for another, the conception of the onslaught and fall of the dragon of chaos. Likewise, the language of ch 13 has mythical models: The two beasts originally were Leviathan and Behemoth, with the details (such as the ten horns) coming from the book of Daniel (cf. Dan 7). However, the apocalyptic writer has interpreted the traditional picture historically: The sea, for example, is not only the original mythical sea which symbolizes chaos, but, at the same time, is concretely the Mediterranean Sea, the *mare nostrum* of the Roman Empire. The "authority" is not merely mythical but also the concrete power of Rome, of the emperor. Behind 13:3 is also the idea of a Nero redivivus (with an additional reference in 17:8). The numbering of the emperors in Rev 13, however, remains unclear; likewise, in spite of all speculation, the number 666 (Rev 13:18) cannot be deciphered.

(3) Rev belongs to the same genre as Jewish apocalypses; yet there are fundamental differences. The most important one is the fact that Rev is not pseudepigraphic in its design; it does not appeal to a figure from antiquity and contains no "prophecy" of a "future" history (of the world;

see p. 31f.). In keeping with the program of 1:19 (see above), the author is concerned with the Christian communities that are externally threatened and with the announcement of the future of God which overcomes every hostile power. The letters of Rev 2 and 3, which are Christ's literal dictates (cf. the vision in 1:12–18), contain assessments of the actual situation in Asia Minor; the second part of Rev describes in the form of a heavenly vision what is to take place on earth "shortly" (cf. 4:1 with 22:6–20). In spite of the strong echoes of the themes found in Jewish apocalyptic, which was experiencing a revival at this time, it seems that John has to be understood as standing within the tradition of the prophets (1:9–11, 19f. function like a commissioning account; cf. also 1:3; 22:9).

3. Authorship

Without further elaboration, the author calls himself John (1:1–4). Following the ancient tradition of the church, this refers to John the son of Zebedee, who is also held to be the author of the Gospel of Jn and of the letters of Jn. But both language and theological ideas, particularly in the area of eschatology, are completely divergent in John and in Rev. Against authorship by the son of Zebedee speaks the fact that no knowledge of the historical Jesus can be discerned. This means that we have no knowledge of the author of Rev.

Based on a few indications, the time of writing of Rev can be ascertained with fair certainty. The emperor cult (which the Christians reject; 13:8, 15) is already developed, and there is an organized persecution of the church in Asia Minor (6:9–11). Both aspects apply in the era of Domitian (81–96), and this temporal setting is confirmed by Irenaeus (*Adv Haer* V 30:3). Thus it is very likely that Rev was written in Asia Minor towards the end of the first century.

4. Theological problem

Probably for no other NT book has such an intensive search been conducted for an interpretive key as for Rev. Prophecies concerning the history of the church, as well as a precise prediction concerning the end of the world's course, have been read out of Rev. To this day, Rev plays a uniquely significant part among certain Christian groups and sects, because they claim to interpret and explain from it certain phenomena, past and present, and to be able to calculate the end of the world. But an explanation of Rev in terms of the history of both the church and the world is not truly an exegesis of the text, but, as a matter of fact, is an "application" of the text to the particular situation. For instance, the "beast" of ch 13 has always been applied to individuals of the present time, such as Hitler, and thereby the attempt is made to qualify the present at once also as endtime. This is not tenable

as exegesis of the text. Many pericopae in Rev require a historical interpretation that reflects a veiled description of the author's present time.
This type is common, for instance, in the interpretation of Daniel (see
above). With reference to Rev, this means that one needs to see an emperor, such as Nero or Domitian, in the beast of Rev 13. Babylon, which
is situated on the seven hills (17:9), denotes Rome, of course.

While these interpretations are undoubtedly accurate, they still do not
explain everything. The mythical figures certainly also have their own
meaning which cannot be exhausted historically. It is necessary, therefore, to supplement the historical interpretation with a strict history-of-
religions interpretation. One needs to ask the question of where the figure of the "beast" originated and what its intrinsic meaning was before
the author of Rev used it historically. One also needs to ask about the
theological meaning of temporal events that can be interpreted in such
a manner, namely mythically.

The author is not interested in a historical interpretation of the apocalyptic images available in the tradition. Rather, he wants to interpret his
own history in the sphere of the supra-historical and the transcendent
that is expressed in these images.

(2) Closely associated with the answers to these questions is the basic
theological outlook of Rev. Bultmann and other interpreters argue that
the theology of Rev was merely a slightly retouched Judaism. But this
view is too critical. While the author of Rev is a Jewish Christian, it is
not appropriate at all to consider him as an adherent to Judaism. For example, he does not postulate the validity of the law for Gentile Christians. His book is also shaped by a Christian universalism: According to
5:9, the redemptive act of Christ applies to people from all nations, and
according to 7:9ff., people from all nations come to the throne of the Lamb
(Christ). Yet, 14:6 could be interpreted in such a way that the organized
mission of the Gentiles is withheld from the endtime and is virtually God's
own work and not the church's task.

Christology and ecclesiology are developed uniformly within Rev; it is
interesting that from the story of Jesus only his death and exaltation are
mentioned (1:5). Otherwise, the past is of no interest. The history of Israel is meaningless; despite endless allusions to the OT, there are no literal
quotations. Likewise, the history of the church, from Jesus to the present
time of the author, is not taken into purview.

Suggested reading:

Read 1 Enoch, especially the similitudes and the apocalypse of the ten weeks
(Charlesworth, I, 29–50; 73–74), as well as 4 Ezra, especially ch 11–14 (Charlesworth
I, 548–555), in comparison with the Rev of John.

Tool: E. Lohse, "Apokalyptik und Christologie," in *Die Einheit des NT* (*Ges. Aufs.*),
1973, 125–144.

VIII. APPENDIX

§ 45 Writings of the "Apostolic Fathers"

Preliminary remark:

The writings of the "Apostolic Fathers" originated at approximately the same time as the later NT books. It is appropriate, therefore, to discuss them within the framework of this survey of the NT writings, since, like the latter, they are part of the early Christian literature.

Text editions: Early Christian Writings I: J. A. Fischer, *Die Apostolischen Väter*, 1966; II: K. Wengst, *Didache* (Apostolic Teaching). *Barnabasbrief. Zweiter Klemensbrief. Schrift an Diognet*, 1984 (text and German translation with extensive explanations); F. X. Funk and K. Bihlmeyer, *Die Apostolischen Väter*, 1956 (Greek); J. B. Lightfoot, *The Apostolic Fathers*, 1900 (text and English translation with extensive explanations) *Apostolic Fathers*, 2 vols., trans. K. Lake, LCL, 1912, 1913 (Greek text with English translation).

Bibliography: R. Knopf, H. Windisch, and M. Dibelius, *Die apostolischen Väter* I–IV, HNT suppl. vols., 1920–23; W. Bauer and H. Paulsen, *Die Briefe des Ignatius von Antiochia und der Polykarpbrief*, HNT 18 (Die Apostolischen Väter II), ²1985; W. R. Schoedel, *Ignatius of Antioch*, Hermeneia, 1985; R. Bultmann, *Theology of the NT*, ET 1955, II, 100–111.

1. Letters

(1) The *first letter of Clement* was sent to the church in Corinth from Rome. Clement, who is held to be the author since the second century, is listed in the Roman register of bishops as the (alleged) second or third successor to Peter. Later he became the patron of an extensive body of writings, the Pseudo-clementines. From 1 Clem it may be gathered that there was a conflict in Corinth: A certain group within the church rose up against the presbyters (1:1; 3:2–4; 44:5f.), and now the Roman church demands the restoration of the old order. The letter reflects a setting of persecution, but this is probably not a reference to the events in Rome at the time of Nero (6:1f. views him in retrospect, already from some distance), but is probably a reference to Domitian (81–96). It is to be noted that 1 Clem was in any case written *after* that persecution. This letter is the first document to mention the martyrdoms of Peter and Paul. At the same time, it demonstrates a clear shaping in church order and especially in the idea of tradition which for the first time is connected with the concept of an apostolic succession (44:1–3). To this extent it is true to say that the earliest traces of "early catholicism" are found in 1 Clem. Far beyond the immediate purpose (bringing order into the Corinthian situation), the letter contains broad expositions on faith and ethics in which the OT plays a

significant part as a moral textbook (cf. Heb 11). The conclusion is particularly valuable because it contains an extensive prayer—probably from the liturgy.

(2) The seven letters of *Ignatius*, the bishop of Antioch, which are addressed to churches in Asia Minor as well as to Rome and to Polycarp, the bishop of Smyrna, were written around 110, during the reign of Trajan. Whereas their authenticity was questioned for a long time, it is hardly subject to doubt today. Ignatius was brought to Rome as a prisoner and there was condemned to death by being thrown to the animals in the arena.

The Ignatian letters indicate an advanced development of the ecclesiastical hierarchy. The three levels, bishop—presbyters—deacons, are construed as a type of the heavenly hierarchy; the monarchical episcopate, however, still seems to be more theoretical than practical reality. The emerging sacramentalism is striking: Ignatius conceives of the sacrament in terms of the metaphor φάρμακον ἀθανασίας (Ign Eph 20:2). By means of a strong emphasis of the incarnation, Ignatius combats docetism; at the same time one notices a particular emphasis on the notion of martyrdom: A martyr is someone who experiences the sufferings of Christ in his own body.

(3) The letter of *Polycarp* of Smyrna, who became known through his martyrdom, is addressed to the church in Philippi; it may be composed of two letters. In terms of the history of the church, it has little significance.

Polycarp was the recipient of one of the letters of Ignatius who came to Philippi en route to Rome from Smyrna via Troas. The local church asked Polycarp to forward the Ignatian letters, and in honoring this request Polycarp attached a letter of his own.

(4) The letter of *Barnabas* is a doctrinal writing which does not yield any historical dates. Barn was probably written in Egypt. The author is unknown. Clement of Alexandria voices the assumption that Barn was written by Barnabas, the companion of Paul, but the writing indicates no affinity with Pauline theology.

2. Didache

The "Teaching of the Twelve Apostles" should be required reading. The first part of the Did (1–6) is a catechism, developed according to the pattern of the "two paths" (path of life, path of death); content-wise it is essentially based upon Jewish ethics. The identical catechism is also found in Barn 18–20. An analysis indicates that the catechism has been revised in the Did; in the Did it has been augmented with materials from the synoptic tradition, which is not yet the case in Barn. The second part, Did 7–15, contains an order for liturgy and community, especially the order governing baptism and the Lord's Supper which is of vital importance for the history of the Lord's Supper. Did 8:2 has the Lord's Prayer in the Matthean form, including the closing doxology which becomes traditional later. Yet, the only complete Greek manuscript of Did that has been preserved comes from the year 1056, after the closing doxology had long been accepted as a part of the Lord's Prayer in Mt (the same is not the case for Lk).

Significant for the history of the church is the fact that church order in Did does not reflect knowledge of presbyters, as much as it does of bishops and deacons (cf. the situation in Paul), plus itinerant apostles and prophets. The ecclesiastical structure is obviously still in its initial beginnings.

At the end of Did there is a brief apocalypse.

The dating of Did is particularly difficult, since there is no mention of historical events—which, according to title and content, is not to be expected. Yet, the church situation which is described or, better, presupposed, favors a relatively early origin, perhaps ca. 100–130, from Syria.

3. Second Clement

2 Clem is not a letter, but an early Christian sermon (homily). It has nothing in common with 1 Clem (see above). 2 Clem is apparently closely associated with Jewish Christianity and in a few instances cites apocryphal gospels. Similar to Herm (see below), it deals with the problem of a second repentance (2 Clem 8; on this issue, cf. p. 266 above). Authorship and time of composition can no longer be determined.

4. Shepherd of Hermas

Herm consists of three parts: Five visions (*visiones*; Herm Vis), twelve "commandments" (*mandata*; Herm Man), and ten "parables" (*similitudines*; Herm Sim). In terms of its content, Herm is a penitential homily; in its form, however, it is an apocalypse. Similarly to Heb, Herm is concerned with the question of the possibility of a "second" repentance. He reaches the conclusion that there is another, but only *one* more, chance to repent for those who have denied their faith (Man IV, 1). This writing probably originated in Rome, in the middle of the second century.

Suggested reading:

Detailed information on the non-canonical writings is offered by Ph. Vielhauer, *Geschichte der urchristlichen Literatur. Einleitung in das Neue Testament, die Apokryphen und die Apostolischen Väter*, 1975 (beginning with § 31).

PART FOUR: JESUS OF NAZARETH

§ 46 The Problem of Scholarly Inquiry

Bibliography: R. Bultmann, "Das Verhältnis der urchristlichen Christusbotschaft zum historischen Jesus," *Exegetica*, 1967, 445–469 (and further bibliography in loc.); H. Conzelmann, "Zur Methode der Leben-Jesu-Forschung," *Ges. Aufs.*, BEvTh 65, 1974, 18–29; L. Goppelt, *Theology of the NT I. The Ministry of Jesus in Its Theological Significance*, ET 1981; F. Hahn, "Methodologische Überlegungen zur Rückfrage nach Jesus," in K. Kertelge (ed.), *Rückfrage nach Jesus*, 1974, 11–77; J. Jeremias, *NT Theology. The Proclamation of Jesus*, ET 1971; W. G. Kümmel, *Dreissig Jahre Jesusforschung (1950–1980)*, 1985; J. M. Robinson, *A New Quest of the Historical Jesus*, 1959; J. M. Robinson and H. Koester, *Trajectories through Early Christianity*, 1971; A. Schweitzer, *The Quest of the Historical Jesus*, ET 1964; W. Wrede, *The Messianic Secret*, ET 1971.

(1) In the scholarly inquiry into Jesus, his life, and his proclamation, three tasks have to be accomplished:

1. The sources providing information on the history of Jesus must be subjected to a critical analysis.

2. Based on source analysis, an attempt must be made to reconstruct this history.

3. The question of the extent to which this reconstructed history of Jesus is relevant for the Christian faith must be answered. This final task is particularly significant because the reconstruction is not allowed to remain a mere review of a historical teaching. Indeed, this is what poses the theological problem of why the Christian faith is not identical with the faith, that is, with the proclamation of Jesus. One needs to explain why, apart from the Gospels, all early Christian literature all but completely ignores both the teaching and the history of Jesus.

(2) The reconstruction of the teaching and life of Jesus posed no particular problem for scholarship as long as the premise was accepted that at least the synoptic Gospels offered a reliable summary of Jesus' life and teaching. It was the traditional conviction that (a) the Gospels yield authentic historical accounts, and (b) that there is full agreement in the essentials between the historical Jesus and the dogmatic portrait of Christ; in other words, the Jesus of the dogma, such as the Apostles' Creed or the Nicene Creed, is the Jesus of the Gospels. He is the supernaturally incarnate being of God who demonstrated his essential oneness with God in his discourses and miraculous deeds and who, in the end, was inaugurated as Lord of the church through death, resurrection, and ascension.

With its principle of reason, the enlightenment tested the Gospels and the dogma that was handed down by the church. Thus the miracle accounts were subjected to a rationalistic interpretation by accepting them as given and then asking in what sense they were "rational." Accounts like the walking on the sea and the calming of the storm were sought to be explained as natural processes (e.g.: At the shore the water glistened in the morning sun so that it appeared as if Jesus walked across the lake).

This approach was demolished by D. F. Strauss. He demonstrated that rationalism ignored what the texts stated. He proved that the texts reported unequivocally about miraculous deeds and of wondrous happenings beyond reason. Historically they were therefore "myths"—products of fantasy, i.e., "history-like forms of early Christian ideas."

Literary source criticism reached a completely different conclusion, especially on the basis of the two-document hypothesis. Now the Gospel of Mark was regarded as a reliable presentation of Jesus' *appearance*, while the logia source Q was viewed as an authentic rendering of Jesus' *teaching*. In terms of content, the result of this presumed objective reconstruction of the history of Jesus was a customized Jesus patterned after the requirements of the 19th century. Sayings that appeared to be odd or offensive were eliminated "critically." Jesus became the representative of a bourgeois religiosity and morality whose goal it was to call people to turn around into the kingdom of God (Mk 1:14f.) and thus "to establish an inner realm of the mind's transformation."

The history-of-religions inquiry has shown that this view does not do justice to the facts in the case. It no longer compared Jesus' teaching primarily with the OT but especially with the texts of contemporary Judaism, such as the apocalypses, and thereby discovered that like Jewish apocalyptic Jesus also anticipated the collapse of the existing world and the creation of a supernatural, new world. Jesus' statement that the kingdom of God was "at hand," did not announce an "inner realm of the mind's transformation," as much as the imminent end of the world. It became clear at the same time that the Jesus portrayed by liberal theology was not at all the objective result of a methodologically proven analysis of sources. The sources have nothing to say about Jesus' character; therefore, this lacuna was simply filled with psychological assumptions—which were in keeping, of course, with the authors' own ideal with regard to personality. This created a portrait of the character of Jesus that was not based on the evidence of the sources but on the respective religious and moral conceptions. If one bracketed the assumptions that the authors expressed in the "life-of-Jesus" presentations and summarized only what the sources truly yield, there would be only scant material left for a life of Jesus.

Now the question arises whether the sources—namely Mk and Q—are historically reliable. Wrede (see p. 219ff. above) has shown that this question has to be answered negatively. The sources do not present the historical Jesus, but they portray Jesus from the vantage point of post-Easter faith as the Son of God, the Messiah. Wrede explained that Jesus did not consider himself to have been the Son of God, as can be recognized from the "messianic secret" in the synoptic Gospels.

Wrede takes this messianic secret to be a hypothesis of church dogmatics: The supernatural nature and the messianic features of Jesus' life were first attributed to him by the church; the historical traditions of Jesus had no knowledge of such.

Form criticism established that the Gospels are presentations that already have their own theological character and, therefore, cannot be viewed as trustworthy historical witnesses. But this posed a new problem: Does not the fact that we know so little about the founder of Christianity have certain consequences for the Christian faith? This was answered negatively by the "dialectical" school of theology, which is closely connected with form criticism at this point. Faith is not interested in a special apprehension of the life and proclamation of Jesus, because the former does not rely on the knowledge of certain historical facts but is established by the appearances of the risen one; these are the pristine elements of the Christian confession. So then, is faith dependent upon assertions made by people we do not know and whose experiences we cannot repeat? Is it indeed possible to have assurance of faith under these circumstances? Does this not reduce faith to an acceptance of miraculous processes and metaphysical or mythological conceptions as truth?

Does not dialectical theology merely look for a desperate escape from the historical malaise when it asserts that faith could disregard the person of Jesus? Does this assessment of the Gospels not ignore their self-understanding? It is precisely Luke's intention, for instance, to present the witness of faith as an historical account (Lk 1:1–4).

But that is precisely what characterizes the gospel genre, i.e., makes it distinct from the historical monograph (see § 5 above). The Gospels are not the result of attempts to reconstruct the vita of Jesus. Rather, they intend to awaken faith and to strengthen already existing faith. In this they obviously do not distinguish between authentic Jesus tradition and secondary formation by the community, that is to say, they are not at all interested in what is currently called "the quest for the historical Jesus."

(3) It would be wrong to conclude from the realization that the Gospels want to be witnesses of faith, that they are not to be used as historical sources. To be sure, A. Schweitzer and W. Wrede have been successful in their attack against the liberal "lives of Jesus" and the theology associated with them. They demonstrated that the reconstruction of the life and teaching of Jesus, by the latter, was not based on sources

but on psychological assumptions. Therefore, one is able to read occasionally that the inquiry into the life of Jesus has received the death-knell. But this is not correct. The endeavor to develop a life-of-Jesus theology and to depict Jesus, as a person, as the object of faith, has failed. But the critical effort to establish and delineate especially the teaching of Jesus continues. In the concluding chapter of his book, Schweitzer himself sketched the essential direction:

"The historical Jesus of whom the criticism of the future, taking as its starting-point the problems which have been recognised and admitted, will draw the portrait, can never render modern theology the services which it claimed from its own half-historical, half-modern, Jesus. . . . Recognized in the particular definiteness of his conceptions and actions, he will be to our time a stranger and an enigma" (398f.).

Information on the beginnings of the more recent scholarly inquiry into Jesus which, in part, is very diverse, can be gathered in the essays of the following volume: *Jesus Christus in Historie und Theologie* (FS H. Conzelmann), 1975, ed. G. Strecker; and in J.M. Robinson, *New Quest of the Historical Jesus*, 1959.

§ 47 Sources

Bibliography: *Section 1*: J. Klausner, *Jesus of Nazareth; His Life, Times, and Teaching,* ET 1964, 17–62; J. Maier, *Jesus von Nazareth in der talmudischen Überlieferung,* EdF 82, 1978.

Preliminary remark
The situation of the sources is relatively clear at first glance. While the synoptic Gospels present extensive Christian material, the few non-Christian sources are unproductive and do not add anything new. Monumental sources such as inscriptions and coins, which might shed light on Jesus' appearance, are non-existent.

1. Non-Christian sources

(1) The testimony of Tacitus in *Annals* XV, 44 is famous. In his account on the fire of Rome under Nero he also mentions the blow against the Christians in the capital by the latter and remarks: *Auctor nominis eius* (namely of Christianity) *Christus Tiberio imperitante per procuratorem Pontium Pilatum supplicio affectus erat* (cf. Barrett, 15–16). Of course, this fact could be gathered from wherever Christians lived. Tacitus obviously had no further information about the life of Jesus beyond this. He considers "Christus" to be a proper name, while he is apparently not acquainted with the actual name.

(2) It is not certain whether Suetonius refers to "Christ" when he writes (Claudius 25): (Claudius) *Iudaeos impulsore Chresto assidue tumultantes Roma* *expulit.* It is possible that Suetonius is under the impression that this Chrestos (Jesus?) himself was in Rome at the time of Claudius.

(3) Likewise from Jewish texts we learn little more about Jesus than from the two early Roman sources. In *Ant.* XX, 200, Josephus reports that Ananos (Annas II), the high priest, had James, "the brother of Jesus, the so-called Christ" executed in A.D. 62. As a Jew, Josephus knows that "Christ" is not a proper name but a title.

The so-called testimonium Flavianum in *Ant.* XVIII, 63f. is of an entirely different character than the first reference (text in H-S I, 436f.). Here one finds exultant praise of Jesus, indeed a confession of adherence to him such as can hardly be expected from a non-Christian Jew. It has been maintained for a long time, therefore, that this represents a Christian interpolation. The only thing that remains open is whether one of Josephus' original notations has merely been given a Christian supplement or whether this is entirely a Christian insertion into the text of Josephus. In any case, Josephus does not increase our knowledge of Jesus.

(4) The same is also true of the (few) rabbinic texts that mention Jesus. There one finds mostly polemical references to Jesus' criticism of the Torah; in addition, there are allusions to his miraculous activity, which is viewed as witchcraft, as well as to his execution on the eve of the Passover. The search for his father is characteristic of the style of the rabbinic concern with Jesus: In some instances, Jesus is called Jeshu ben Pantera (or something like that) because he is alleged to have been the son of the soldier Pantera. There may indeed be no discriminating intention behind this naming to begin with; only later this Pantera is alleged to be the lover of Mary and, hence, Jesus becomes an illegitimate child. These remarks cannot be accorded any historical value. (The material is found in Billerbeck I, 36–39.)

2. Christian sources

We are thus dependent on the Christian sources for a reconstruction of the life and teaching of Jesus. But the question arises here, whether or not and how the Christian tendency has shaped the portrait of Jesus and thereby has possibly distorted the historical facts. That this tendency exists is no longer debated today; only the extent to which they are to be considered trustworthy is evaluated differently. Earlier the question was often asked whether greater reliability was to be accorded to the Synoptics—especially to Mk—or to Jn. This is a significant question, indeed, because the character of the public appearance of Jesus is entirely different in the synoptic presentation than in Jn. For instance, while the parables of Jesus play a key role in the Synoptics, Jn records not a single parable. The duration of the public appearance of Jesus is different in both. Furthermore, Jn mentions a different day for the death of Jesus than the Synoptics. Meanwhile, however, the question of the essential priority has been made very clear: It is almost exclusively the synoptic Gospels that are taken into consideration as sources for the life and teaching of Jesus.

Additional sayings of Jesus are handed down within the NT as well as in post–NT Christian literature, i.e., in Lk 6:5 (only in uncial D), Jn 7:53–8:11 (although this pericope is found in a large number of manuscripts, at least within Jn it has to be regarded as secondary, without assessing its historical value thereby, of course), Acts 20:35; 1 Thes 4:15; 1 Cor 7:10. Further non–NT sayings of Jesus ("agrapha") are collated and critically analyzed in J. Jeremias, *Unknown Sayings of Jesus*, ET 1964.

§ 48   *External and Internal Chronology*

Bibliography: J. Finegan, *Handbook of Biblical Chronology*, 1964, 214 301. On Section 3: J. Jeremias, *The Eucharistic Words of Jesus*, ET 1966, 36–41.

1. Year of Jesus' birth

It is certain that Jesus was born during the reign of Octavian (Augustus), as indicated in Lk 2:1. It is unclear, however, whether the additional reference in Mt 2 and Lk 1:5 is correct, according to which the birth of Jesus occurred during the administration of Herod the Great. Following our chronology, Herod died in 4 B.C. (= *ab urbe condita* of Roman chronology). In this case, Jesus would have to have been born "before Christ."

Yet, the Christian chronology was not established until the 6th century by the Roman monk Dionysius Exiguus who fixed the year 754 *ab urbe condita* as year of Jesus' birth and then designated it as year 1. Dionysius could have miscalculated, in other words, it is by all means possible that Jesus could have been born during Herod's reign.

It is to be noted, however, that the reference to Herod is found only in the legendary birth narratives and thus may not require a historical basis.

In any case, the dates given in the birth legends do not yield anything with reference to the calculation of the year of Jesus' birth, all the more so since they partially contradict one another. According to the legend of the slaughter of children in Bethlehem, Herod had all children up to two years of age murdered (Mt 2:16); this means that Jesus' birth had to occur no later than between 6 and 4 B.C. Compared with this, the census mentioned in Lk 2:1f. would have to be fixed considerably later: According to Josephus, *Ant.* XVIII, 1f., a general census was taken in A.D. 6, following the deposition of Archelaus. It was by no means worldwide but was limited to Judea (in other words, it did not even encompass Galilee with Nazareth).

Any dating according to the star of the magi is impossible. While there was a special astral constellation in 7/6 B.C., Mt. 2:9 describes a wandering "miracle star" rather than a real astronomical phenomenon.

When Lk 3:23 says that Jesus was "about 30 years old" at his first public appearance, in context with Lk 3:1f. (see below) this means that Jesus must have been born in one of the final years "before Christ"; in any case, the precise year of birth is unknown.

2. Public appearances

The NT contains a single, fairly accurate, and probably reliable date in conjunction with the life of Jesus, namely, the "synchronism" of Lk 3:1f. It says that John the Baptist appeared in the fifteenth year of Tiberius, approximately in A.D. 28. (For details on this problem, see Finegan, 259ff.). The additional reference to Annas, who is said to have been the high priest at that time, is incorrect; Caiaphas was the current high priest. It is not clear how Luke obtained this date. Did he have a source or is it his own calculation?

If one accepts A.D. 28 as a more or less reliable date for John, the question still remains of how extensive was the interval in time between John and the public ministry of Jesus. Presumably, this interval was relatively brief, so that it can be said that the time of Jesus' public ministry falls somewhere around A.D. 30.

3. Year of death

(1) The situation is similar with regards to the dating of the death of Jesus: Whereas the *precise* date can no longer be pinpointed, the approximate *time frame* can be delineated with adequate precision. It is certain that the crucifixion of Jesus took place during the administration of Pilate, the Roman procurator, and of Annas, the high priest. The Gospel references concerning the officiating high priest are somewhat confusing, indeed: Mk does not mention any high priest's name, while Mt mentions Caiaphas. In the passion narrative, Lk (like Mk) offers no name but provides the following reference in Lk 3:2 (cf. Acts 4:6): "under the high priest (singular!) Annas and Caiaphas"—which is impossible, of course. Jn also mentions both names in 11:49 and 18:13–24; apparently he found the name Annas in his source but knew that Caiaphas was the correct one; thus he added the latter without eliminating the former. Conclusion: The literary sources do not make precisely dating the year of Jesus' death feasible.

(2) It has been attempted, therefore, to use astronomy to establish the point of time of his death more accurately. Jesus died during a Passover festival; the Jewish calendar established that the Passover was to be cele-

brated on the evening of the fourteenth day of Nisan, the month of spring. All of the Gospels report that the day on which Jesus died was the last day prior to the Sabbath, i.e., a Friday. According to the synoptic presentation, Jesus ate the Passover meal with his disciples on the previous evening, which means that he would have died on Friday, the fifteenth of Nisan. The question is: In which year around A.D. 30 did the fifteenth of Nisan fall on a Friday?

The situation is more complicated yet, for two reasons:

1. According to Jn, Jesus already died in the hour in which the Passover lambs used to be killed (hence in the afternoon of the fourteenth of Nisan. The meal is then eaten in the evening; thus, in Jn in any case, Jesus' last supper with his disciples is *not* a Passover meal). Jn also presupposes that this fourteenth Nisan was a Friday. Dibelius regards the date given by Jn as correct; for, it is also presupposed in Mk 14:1f., which states that Jesus is not to be executed on the festival. Furthermore, such an execution date is very unlikely. But the note in 14:1f., as well as the reference of 14:12, is inaccurate and, therefore, cannot be adduced as evidence.

The suggestion of the use of different calendars within Judaism—for example, the fact that in some instances the Pharisees and Sadducees differed from one another in the dating of the Passover (Billerbeck)—yields absolutely nothing. Likewise lacking in evidence is the argument that Jesus adhered to the Qumran calendar in the Passover meal, while Jn dated the event according to the normal calendar. First of all, the divergent calendars of the Sadducees and Pharisees are late constructions and, second, there is no evidence at all that Jesus adhered to any of the rules of Qumran.

2. It must be asked whether the reference to "Friday" is correct historically and was not calculated subsequently by dating the resurrection "on the third day" (i.e., Sunday as the first day of the week).

The question of which year it was when the fifteenth (or fourteenth) Nisan fell on a Friday, essentially cannot be answered by means of astronomical calculations, since the beginning of Nisan was not fixed astronomically. The first Nisan was always considered to be that day when the "new light" could be observed after the preceding last new moon of winter; and this observation naturally was contingent upon the cloud-cover. This rendered a definitive dating impossible.

Given these provisos, the following can be said: Jesus died at the approximate age of 30. Assuming that he was born roughly in 4 B.C., he would have died in one of the years following A.D. 26. If this is linked to the synoptic references that the day of death was a Friday, the following arise:

Friday, fifteenth Nisan: Likely the year A.D. 27, possibly also 30, 31, or 34. If the references are linked to Jn, the result is as follows:

Friday, fourteenth Nisan: Likely the year 30 or also 33, possibly 27.

In general one may bear in mind that Jesus died around A.D. 30.

4. Internal chronology

The internal chronology of the life of Jesus, or the duration of Jesus' public ministry, is a matter of debate. According to the Synoptics, the public ministry of Jesus began after the imprisonment of John the Baptist (Mk 1:14), but nothing at all is said about its duration. The account given refers merely to the beginning, then to individual events during the ministry of Jesus and, finally, to the journey that leads to Jerusalem, to the passion. The Synoptics do not fix the time frame of his appearance to about one year, as one is able to read occasionally; in fact, they do not determine it at all.

John's presentation differs (cf. p. 246 above). According to 3:22f. the time of Jesus' public appearance overlaps with the ministry of the Baptist. And, following the Johannine presentation, Jesus does not travel to Jerusalem only once, but several times: In 2:13 to the Passover, in 5:1 to an undetermined festival (the text is not certain), in 6:4 a Passover is mentioned again (if one reverses chs 5 and 6, as Bultmann suggests, 5:1 would refer to this Passover); according to 7:1 Jesus goes to the Feast of Tabernacles, and following 10:22 he stays in Jerusalem during the Feast of Dedication. As in the case of the Synoptics, the death of Jesus occurs during the Passover time in Jn. Should this reference to three Passover festivals be historically reliable, it would mean that Jesus' public ministry lasted at least two full years. It is not possible, however, to use Jn for the internal chronology of Jesus, since his presentation is not based on ancient tradition but belongs to the redaction of the evangelist.

§ 49   Descent, Birth, and Home of Jesus

Bibliography: R. E. Brown, *Birth of the Messiah*, 1977; M. Dibelius, "Jungfrauensohn und Krippenkind. Untersuchungen zur Geburtsgeschichte Jesu im Lukas-Evangelium," in *Botschaft und Geschichte* I, 1953, 1–78; H. Schürmann, *Das Lukas-Evangelium 1:1–9:50*, HThK III/1, 1969, 140–145; K. Stendahl, "Quis et Unde? Eine Analyse von Mt 1–2," in J. Lange (ed.), *Das Matthäus-Evangelium*, WdF 525, 1980, 296–311.

Preliminary remark
Only Mt and Lk contain narratives of the birth and childhood of Jesus. To begin with, a comparison between the two yields some agreements: Both Gospels have a genealogy of Jesus (although in Lk it does not occur until 3:23–38; see p. 232f.), both mention the virginity of Mary, both mention Joseph, and both presuppose, that is, they report emphatically that Jesus was born in Bethlehem during the time of Herod (in contrast, Mt does not mention any involvement with Bethlehem on the part of Jesus). But otherwise, the presentations of Mt and Lk differ widely.

1. *Nativity of Jesus according to Mt 1–2*

The two introductory chapters of Mt contain four parts that were originally self-contained: The genealogy, the account of Jesus' birth, the story
of the magi, and the account of the slaughter of children in Bethlehem.
Whether these individual sections were already connected by a prede-
cessor or only by Mt remains an open question. They contain legendary
material but are mixed extensively with theological reflections. In Mt they
are summarized under the following theme: Who Jesus is and where he
comes from. Evidence is to be adduced that, in terms of descent and
home, Jesus is the Messiah from the family of David.

(1) The genealogy, Mt 1:2–17, indicates that Jesus descends, via Joseph,
in direct line from Abraham and David. In this it was originally presupposed, of course, that Joseph was the father of Jesus; a contradiction resulted from the combination of the genealogy with the motif of the virgin
birth.

Yet, this combination must have come about previously at a relatively early date,
since it is also found in Lk (see p. 296f. below).

What historical value does the reference that Jesus was the son of David
have? The earliest evidence for this claim comes from the pre-Pauline form
of Rom 1:3f.; but in Rom 1:3f. Davidic sonship is probably not intended
to be understood genealogically, rather, it is meant as a dogmatic observation: Jesus is the Messiah, hence he is the descendant of David. Moreover, even if the references to the Davidic sonship had a historical basis,
this would only prove that Jesus, i.e., his family, claimed such descent
for themselves and would express nothing about the actual data.

In Jn 7:41f., 52, the Davidic origin of Jesus and, at the same time, his birth are
questioned, though perhaps not on the basis of a more reliable historical understanding, but on the basis of Johannine Christology (cf. R. Bultmann, *John*, 305, 310f.).

(2) The account of the birth of Jesus, given in Mt 1:18–25, is self–
contained and is not predicated upon the genealogy. It is striking that
the text is actually not given a narratival shape following the style of a
legend. Thus, while the wondrous birth is announced, it is not narrated.
These are apparently reflections with an apologetic designed to ward off
hostile suspicions concerning the more detailed circumstances of the birth
of Jesus. The main point in the text is the name of Jesus, particularly its
meaning as "savior." Jesus is understood and presented as the fulfillment of the OT promises (cf. the quotation reflecting this in v 23).

(3) The story of the magi, Mt 2:1–12, was also self-contained originally.
It is not predicated upon the preceding text but, instead, competes with
it, since it contains the motif of the legend of the "recognition of the child."
It is precisely the tenor of the legend of the magi that the child, who has

not been recognized in his uniqueness thus far, is revealed by a wondrous star—to pay homage is the story's purpose. (Since Joseph is not
mentioned, one may ask whether this is a legend of a virgin; so Dibelius).

The following is to be noted: Even if the story of the star were shaped in commemoration of the astral constellation of 7/6 B.C., no factors can be derived for
the dating of the event (see p. 292 above).

Some commentators claim that the magi are representatives of superstition which is thus to be opposed indirectly. But the presentation is completely void of such tendencies; indeed, the magi fulfill more of a
revelatory function.

(4) In its present form, the narrative of the slaughter of the children
(2:13–23) is interwoven with the story of the magi; initially it may well
have been self-contained, since the story of the magi is not laid out with
such a "bloody epilogue" (Dibelius) in mind. The narrative of the slaughter
of the children contains the classic motif of the endangering and rescue
of the subsequently important child (there are similar legends about
Moses, cf. Ex 1:15–2:10, as well as about Sargon of Akkad, Cyrus, and
Augustus). The flight to Egypt is also reminiscent of Moses. Finally, in
v 23 the place-name of Nazareth is biblically "anchored" by means of a
(fictitious) quotation.

Suggested reading:

1. M. Hengel and H. Merkel, "Die Magier aus dem Osten und die Flucht nach
Ägypten (Mt 2) im Rahmen der antiken Religionsgeschichte und der Theologie
des Matthäus" (FS J. Schmid), 1973, 139–169.

2. Suetonius, *Vit Augusti*, ch. 94.

2. Prehistory of Jesus according to Lk 1–2

As far as style is concerned, the narratives of Lk 1f. are legends; to this
extent they are clearly distinct from Mt 1f.

The present form of the first two chapters of Lk contain a so-called syn-
crisis, or a comparative presentation of the wondrous birth of the Baptist
and of Jesus. An analysis demonstrates, however, that the two strands
of narrative were not originally related to one another: It is not necessary
to know one strand in order to understand the other. Likewise, in itself,
the Jesus strand is not a unit in the history of tradition; rather, it can be
divided into individual stories.

(1) The birth of John the Baptist is announced in Lk 1:5–25. Three motifs stand out: The long barrenness of Elizabeth (in the OT the same is
reported of Sarah as well as of the mothers of Samson and of Samuel;
cf. Gen 17:15ff.; Jdg 13:2ff.; 1 Sam 1); the appearance of an angel (cf. Jdg
6:22) with the call of "fear not!" which is typical in such epiphanies; and

finally the announcement of the birth of the infant savior. It can be recognized clearly that the child is not meant to be the forerunner of one
greater than he, but is himself destined to be the eschatological savior.
John will be the bringer of joy (v 14), he will be called "great" (v 15), he
is *God's* forerunner—hence not of the Messiah, that is, he is identical with
Elijah (v 17). A further typical motif is the sign of confirmation: Zechariah's
muteness (v 20) is not the punishment for his doubt, but serves as a witness.

(2) The message to Mary interrupts the story of John. Is it self-contained
or is it predicated upon the latter? Schürmann assumes that the pericope
is a reproduction of vv 5–25, hence that the reference to the Baptist had
been known from the beginning. And the agreements are lucid indeed.
In both cases a marvelous birth is announced, and in both the name and
character of the child are already revealed in the announcement: He will
be called "Son of the Most High."

The text does pose certain difficulties: V 26f. appear overloaded, so that
it must be asked whether the reference to Joseph was possibly inserted
secondarily. Thus Dibelius assumes that, in the narrative's original form,
the angel Gabriel was sent to a virgin from the house of David. But this
hypothesis is not credible: The tradition has the Davidic descent of Jesus
pass through Joseph (this does not change until Ignatius).

A second difficulty is found in vv 34–37. According to Bultmann (*History
of the Synoptic Tradition*, 295), Lk himself created this passage; in the original announcement of Jesus' birth (1:26–33, 38), then, Mary was not
presented as a virgin at all (cf. the actual birth narrative of 2:1ff. in which
the virgin motif is not found). Dibelius (*From Tradition to Gospel*, 124), rejects this idea by indicating that it was precisely the miraculous which
had been part of the narrative from the outset. Nevertheless, he also considers v 27 to be secondary; the association with the narrative of John
had originally been lacking. Whether this association was only created
by Lk, or prior to him, remains an open issue. On the whole, it can be
said that in its essence the narrative of Lk 1:26–38 had also been self-
contained originally and that the correlation with the narrative of John
was made later.

(3) The encounter of the two women, 1:39–56, is not as much an actual
story as it represents a secondary merging of the two scenes; the "Magnificat"
inserted here, may originally have been a psalm stemming from the community of the Baptist, since it contains no explicit references to Jesus.

(4) The birth of John (1:57–80) would continue smoothly following v 25.
This narrative makes it clear as well that the entire story about John is not
laid out in terms of his subordination to a subsequent one who is greater.

(5) The narrative of the child in the manger, 2:1–20, presupposes neither
the story of John nor the angel's announcement to Mary. Rather, Joseph
and Mary are regarded as the parents of Jesus and apparently also as a

couple (only through the addition of τῇ ἐμνηστευμένη αὐτῷ in v 5, does Mary become the betrothed one). The child is not distinguished by a miraculous conception, but by the epiphany of the angels and by the distinctive sign, the manger (cf. Mt 2:1–12; see above).

3. Summary

The analysis of the birth stories in Mt and Lk has shown that they are made up exclusively of legendary material. Still, indirectly, some light is shed on the heritage of Jesus as well as on his place of birth.

(1) The theologoumenon of the virgin birth occurs in only a few passages within Mt 1f. and Lk 1f.; in Lk 2 it is clearly secondary. Paul does not know this concept at all (Gal 4:4, "born of a woman" merely denotes "human"; on this expression, cf. Job 14:1); Jn 1:45 and 6:42 flatly contradict it (cf. R. Bultmann, *John*, 62, fn. 4). It may be assumed, therefore, that this comprehension is secondary and, furthermore, is initially disputed in early Christianity.

(2) The birth stories report that Jesus was born in Bethlehem. This conflicts with the evidence of the rest of the NT where Nazareth is consistently regarded as place of birth (Mk 1:9; 6:1; Jn 1:45f.; on the whole, cf. the designation Jesus "of Nazareth"). Evidently, Bethlehem as the place of birth is required only by a certain perspective of the Messiah (Mt 2:6); Jesus may indeed have been born in Nazareth. The means by which the event is moved to Bethlehem is decidedly artificial in Lk: What is the purpose of a census which is not held in the place of residence and of work, but in the hometown of the family?

Suggested exercises:

1. Analyze Lk 2:21–52. Tools: See bibliographic references.

2. Read one of the comparative texts, such as Virgil's Fourth Ecologue. For more in-depth reading, consult the bibliography.

§ 50   John the Baptist

Bibliography: J. Becker, *Johannes der Täufer und Jesus von Nazareth*, BSt 63, 1972; C. H. H. Scobie, *John the Baptist*, 1964; Ph. Vielhauer, Article on Johannes der Täufer, RGG III, 1959, 804–808; W. Wink, *John the Baptist in the Gospel Tradition*, SNTSMS 7, 1968.

(1) Material concerning the life and proclamation of John the Baptist is offered in Mk, the logia source Q, Jn, and Josephus. Some references are also found in Acts. The status of the sources makes it probable from the start that the portrait of John which is handed down, is given an extensive Christian gloss. The birth story in Lk is legendary (cf. § 49), as is probably also the descent from a priestly family—a claim that is found only here. The question of whether John indeed saw himself as the Messiah's preparer of the way or whether it also was a Christian interpretation is subject to debate. As we have seen, the original form of the birth legend presupposes that John was God's preparer of the way, hence the final voice before the end. This birth story very likely comes from the Johannine circle of disciples. It does not correspond with the self-understanding of the historical John; for, it can be gathered from Mt 3:11 and parallels, that John announced the coming baptizer with fire, hence a transcendent figure. It is likely that John's reference to the coming one who is stronger, represents a historical fact and not Christian interpretation.

(2) It is fairly certain that John was the first one to introduce the *one-time* baptism, in contrast to the purification rituals of Judaism which had to be repeated again and again. This is already indicated by the fact that he is called the "Baptist." Apart from Josephus, this term is found only in Christian writers and refers to John exclusively. Therefore, he was obviously conspicuous by his baptismal practice. John understood his baptism to be eschatological. The interpretation is Christian, therefore, when he describes his baptism as merely a baptism with water which is of a lesser order than the Spirit baptism to come.

Probably neither John nor Jesus speak about the "Spirit"; it is the Christian community that speaks of the Spirit on the basis of its own experience of the Spirit. Two hypotheses are generally postulated concerning the presuppositions upon which John developed his baptismal understanding: (a) John follows the example of the Jewish proselyte baptism. (b) John adheres to the rituals of Jewish baptismal sects in the Jordan valley (such as the Qumran community or of early forerunners of the Mandaeans). But both hypotheses are on shaky ground: Witnesses testifying to the existence of proselyte baptism come from a later time. Furthermore, this baptism has as its purpose the attainment of cultic purity; there is no eschatological referent. Among the Jewish sects along the Jordan River, purification rites became prominent; yet a *one-time* baptism was foreign to them. Only the place of the Baptist's activity, namely, the Jordan valley, relates him to Qumran. The question of the history-of-religions presuppositions for John's baptism may likely not be answered satisfactorily. The important question concerns the *meaning* that John's baptism had. It is debated occasionally whether it was a (efficacious) sacrament or only a symbolic act. But the latter alternative misses the point, since mere ritualistic symbolic acts without immediate or mediate efficacy are unknown in antiquity. But John emphasized that his baptism did not work mechanically, but that repentance was the condition for the purifying efficacy of baptism. Whether or not one wishes to designate it as a sacrament, ultimately is a question of how the term "sacrament" is defined; in any case, John understands his baptism to be an efficacious penitential rite in view of the coming judgment.

Practice illustration:
Following Mk, John's baptism effects forgiveness of sins. Is this the Baptist's own interpretation, or does it represent a Christian interpretation?

It is to be observed that Christianity endeavored to differentiate between Christian baptism and John's baptism by distinguishing between Spirit baptism and water baptism. There is little likelihood, therefore, that early Christians would have granted the efficacy of the forgiveness of sins of their own accord had it not already been part of the tradition. Mt eliminates the reference to the forgiveness of sins!

Suggested reading:

H. Thyen, *Studien zur Sündenvergebung*, FRLANT 96, 1970, 131–145.

(3) John baptizes in the wilderness: The reference is likely to the lower Jordan valley (cf. Josephus, *War* III, 515). For John, this location has symbolic meaning; the wilderness time is Israel's uncorrupted time, the time of Moses, of the covenant, of the giving of the law. Hence the Qumran community also moved into the wilderness because Israel's eschatological redemption was to come to pass there (cf. Hos 2:14ff.). This symbolism, which John therefore chose deliberately, is further underscored with references to the Baptist's food and clothing (Mk 1:6). Generally 2 Kgs 1:8 and Zec 13:4 are used as parallels with the explanation that, with this prophetic cloak, John intended to pattern himself after Elijah. But the coincidence with the description of Elijah is marginal at best and applies only when the LXX is used. The reference to the Baptist's dress and food in Mk 1:6 is meant to characterize him simply as a desert dweller and thereby to underscore the wilderness symbolism.

(4) When all of the Gospels (and Q) present John as allied with Jesus, it is clearly understood to be a Christian interpretation. The same intention lies also behind the Scripture citation of Mk 1:2f. (according to Is 40:3; cf. this with the original text!).

What is the temporal relationship between the appearance of the Baptist and of Jesus? The references in the Synoptics and in Jn contradict one another. According to Mk and Mt, Jesus appears in public only after the imprisonment of John (Mk 1:14 and parallel in Mt 4:12). Is this to be construed as historical or as history of salvation oriented? Conversely, Jn states in Jn 3:22ff. that the proclamation of the two was concurrent, at least for some time. Is one to see a reminiscence of some old, reliable tradition in this? Or is it Jn's intent to highlight especially the fact that Jesus succeeded John (cf. 3:30)? We may have to be content with the following observations: Jesus was baptized by John (Mk 1:9), that is to say, his preaching convinced Jesus. Jesus himself developed further the notion of the kingdom of God which is at hand (see § 54 below), but then he went his own way. He did not remain in the wilderness and did not practice asceticism (Lk 7:34). He indeed acknowledged that Jn was the prophetic goal (Lk 16:16 and parallels), but he was obviously convinced that it was inappropriate to stop with his proclamation.

Herod Antipas probably imprisoned John and sentenced him to death for political reasons (Josephus, *Ant.* XVIII, 116ff.). But the account of Salome's dance, given in Mk 6:21, is a legend (on the motif of granting a special wish, cf. Herodotus IX, 109ff.).

(5) The Baptist movement associated with his name did not end after John's death. In competition with the Christian communities, the Johannine disciples apparently also developed a sort of "Johannine Christology," the upshot of which is still reminiscent in Lk 1 (see § 49 above). In some instances Jn reflects a clear polemic, not against John himself, but against his followers who declared him to be the Messiah (1:19ff. et al.).

§ 51 Public Appearance of Jesus

Bibliography: G. Bornkamm, *Jesus of Nazareth*, ET 1960; H. Braun, *Jesus of Nazareth: The Man and His Time*, ET 1979; R. Bultmann, *Jesus*, 1926 (⁵1983; UTB 1272); M. Dibelius, *Jesus*, ET 1949.

1. Biographical problem

Form-critical analysis has shown the impossibility of reconstructing a cohesive biography of Jesus, because the "frame of the story of Jesus" in the synoptic Gospels proves to be secondary. Besides, almost all of the details necessary for a biography are lacking. We are indeed told that he was a carpenter, i.e., a carpenter's son (Mk 6:3) and that he had brothers and sisters. But no information is offered about the environment in which Jesus grew up or about the education he received. Hardly any mention is made of his father, from which it is occasionally inferred that he must have died early. But Jesus' mother, who outlived her son, does not play a major part in the sources either. We learn from 1 Cor 9:5 that Jesus' brothers (and perhaps his mother as well) were converted to the Christian faith after his death. James, one of the brothers of Jesus, is cited explicitly in 1 Cor 15:7 as a witness to the epiphany of the risen one.

The parabolic material allows certain conclusions about the milieu from which Jesus came, namely, the rural world of Palestine: The sower, the housewife who searches extensively for a small coin, the *one*-room house. In contrast to Paul, not even a trace can be found of the culture of the neighboring hellenistic towns.

Most of the details, however, which might be of interest biographically, are lacking altogether: No description is given of the appearance of Jesus; neither does the reader of the Gospels learn anything about his character (certain remarks in the Gospels, e.g., that Jesus was provoked, are always redactional and thus without value as a source). It is particularly conspicuous that the sources do not say anything about the internal maturation of Jesus, though such description should have elicited the keenest interest. The accounts of the heavenly voice at his baptism, of his temptation by Satan, and of the transfiguration on the mountain, contain *theologoumena* that are clearly post-Easter, hence they are to be recognized as legends. Therefore, no references to Jesus' particular self-consciousness can be drawn from them.

2. Public ministry of Jesus

(1) At the outset, Jesus was probably associated with John the Baptist (see § 50 above). He adopts certain elements of John's preaching (repentance, anticipation of judgment), but he goes beyond that by proclaiming God's salvation, rather than primarily judgment, *in his person*. The question of where this self-consciousness originated, must remain open. Even if one assumes that Jesus became aware of his special nature because of his experience of the gift to heal the sick, one needs to note that he never makes his "inner life" the object of his teaching.

(2) The features of his proclamation can already be derived from some external characteristics. In contrast to John, Jesus does not stay in the wilderness; he does not call people to come out to him, but he goes to the people he wishes to address. The characteristic form of his appearance, according to everything the sources have to say, is his journeys through the villages and towns of Palestine, especially of Galilee. Yet, the routes mentioned in the Gospels do not divulge anything regarding the actual process of the proclamation; the references are redactional throughout. Apparently Capernaum is somewhat of a center of his ministry and (as a result?) becomes a seat of local traditions; at a later time a very important Christian community existed there. From Mk 1:29 we gather that Peter owned a house in Capernaum, and one may ask, after all, whether Jesus also had a permanent residence in this town (cf. Mk 2:1?).

Suggested exercise:

Reconstruct the routes of the journeys of Jesus according to the Gospels. If, following Lk, Jesus stays exclusively in Galilee and Judea, but not in foreign territory, whereas Mk speaks of excursions to Phoenicia and to the Decapolis, what is the theological concept behind the former? What does it mean when Jn tells of journeys through Samaria?

Tools: On Mk, W. Marxsen, *Mark the Evangelist*, ET 1969, 54–95, and D.-A. Koch, "Inhaltliche Gliederung und geographischer Aufriss im Mk," *NTS* 29, 1983, 145–166; on Lk, H. Conzelmann, *The Theology of Luke*, ET 1961, 27–94; on Jn, K. Kundsin, *Topologische Überlieferungsstoffe im Johannesevangelium*, FRLANT 39, 1925.

(3) The impression Jesus made upon his hearers is captured in "summaries" (e.g., Mk 1:14f.), which, of course, are secondary formations of the redactors. For this reason we know very little about the actual effectiveness of Jesus' preaching. The only fact assured historically is that there was a group of adherents at the time of his death. Whether Jesus had already set apart a more intimate circle of twelve from those, or whether this circle was only built as a result of the appearances of the risen one, is a matter of debate. The number refers symbolically to the eschatological, "true" Israel; it is questionable whether this notion played any part in the proclamation of Jesus. As far as can still be derived from the text, the followers who accompanied Jesus were more numerous in any case and, most of all, were not intentionally limited.

One needs to note that the title of an apostle in no wise originated with Jesus; besides, "the twelve" and "the apostles" were not identical originally (see p. 346f. below).

The interest in the disciples, of course, grew in the course of the history of the early church. In many narratives of the synoptic tradition, miracle stories, apophthegms, disputes, etc., they were lacking at first and were added to the text only later, perhaps via redactional notes in the margin (cf. e.g., Mk 1:21ff.; see p. 41 above).

3. Appendix: Psychological interpretation of Jesus

The following is a popular portrait: At the outset, Jesus' appearance had been most successful (evidence: the feeding of the five thousand demonstrates that Jesus gathered great multitudes of adherents and hearers around him); later the masses turned away from him in disappointment. In this crisis, Jesus retreated into solitude with the few remaining loyalists; here, on behalf of the disciples, Peter confessed him as the Messiah. Encouraged thereby, Jesus was determined to induce an ultimate decision in Jerusalem. Amidst the jubilation of the faithful as well as of the populous, he entered the capital as messianic pretender; however, the people soon realized that their hopes were dashed once again, for Jesus did not prove to be the bringer of salvation. Hence there was another turn of events and these ended in his conviction and execution.

This portrait is predicated upon a synthesis between Jn and the Synoptics. In Jn 6:66 there is indeed a crisis in the public ministry of Jesus; it is wrong, however, to import this presentation into the synoptic Gospels. Peter's confession in Mk 8:27 was not intended to serve as psycho-logical motivation for the subsequent conduct of Jesus; rather, in the frame-work of the Christology of Mk, it represents the decisive transition, because for the first time Jesus reveals himself to his disciples as the Mes-siah. On principle this pericope could also be placed elsewhere in the Gospel, in other words, it does not constitute evidence for a historical development and, instead, fulfils a theological or christological function.

§ 52 Method of Reconstructing Jesus' Teaching

Bibliography: *Section 2:* G. Bornkamm, H. Braun, R. Bultmann, M. Dibelius (see § 51); H. Conzelmann, Article on "Jesus Christus," RGG III, 1959, 619–653; D. Flusser, *Jesus*, 1968 (Rowohlt's Monographs 140); E. Schweizer, *Jesus*, ET 1971, 13–64. *Section 3:* F. Hahn (see § 46); J. Jeremias, "Kennzeichen der ipsissima vox Jesu," in *Abba* (*Ges. Aufs.*), 1966, 145–152; N. Perrin, *Rediscovering the Teaching of Jesus*, 1967.

1. General matters

Considerably more important and profitable than the reconstruction of the biography of Jesus is the attempt to delineate Jesus' teaching. For this reason, the literature on this subject is voluminous.

Even a cursory overview indicates that the nineteenth-century presentations of the teaching of Jesus generally are very extensive. Since the beginning of the twen-tieth century, i.e., concurrent with the rise of more precise exegetical methods, the books have generally become rather thin, because the opinion about what is truly certain historically has undergone change.

How does one extract the material necessary for reconstructing Jesus' teaching, i.e., what are the criteria according to which statements within the synoptic tradition (and outside of it) turn out to be historically re-liable sayings of Jesus? Bultmann's proposal that regards only those say-ings of Jesus as definitely "authentic" which (a) are unthinkable in the framework of Judaism and (b) are not part of the post-Easter situation of the church may serve as an initial, minimal criterion. On this premise one may search for similar sayings that are connected with those already accepted as authentic. One needs to take into account, of course, that the proclamation of Jesus may have coincided largely with Jewish teach-ing, such as wisdom. In this case, however, it is not possible to arrive at a trustworthy verdict of authenticity (cf. p. 306f. below).

2. Problem of the presentation of Jesus' teaching

(1) The perspectives by which the proclamation of Jesus is to be struc-tured and presented are by no means only significant in terms of form.

Rather, it must be shown what the reason was for selecting precisely these topics and why they were presented in exactly this sequence.

Two alternatives present themselves: (a) One may take an exegetical-analytical approach and ask: Which statements can be traced back to Jesus himself? Is it possible to organize these statements within the framework of specific themes? What is the relationship between the particular themes, such as eschatology and ethics or theology and ethics? (b) One may take a systematic-synthetic approach by beginning with individual, theologically relevant themes and test whether it is possible to find authentic sayings of Jesus to that end.

A third alternative is taken by the Jewish NT scholar D. Flusser. He begins with the basic theological themes and issues of Judaism and asks to what extent Jesus assumed or changed these.

(2) According to what criteria is the proclamation of Jesus presented in the various more recent scholarly volumes on Jesus?

(a) Bultmann divides his book on Jesus into the following three parts: [1] the coming of the rule of God; [2] the will of God; [3] the transcendent and imminent God. It is striking that there is no section on the self-consciousness of Jesus (cf. with Bultmann's *Theology of the NT*).

(b) The presentation of Dibelius also begins with eschatology ([1] the kingdom of God; [2] the signs of the kingdom) and is followed by a presentation of the self-consciousness of Jesus ([3] the Son of man), and concludes with the development of the ethics of Jesus ([4] Man before God).

(c) Bornkamm chooses a similar outline: [1] eschatology, [2] ethics, [3] self-consciousness of Jesus.

These three presentations show considerable agreement: Eschatology and ethics are considered to be particularly important themes in Jesus' teaching, hence they are consistently discussed in this order.

One distinction, however, is striking: Bultmann treats Jesus' theology proper separately, whereas Dibelius and Bornkamm treat it as part of ethics. It is worthwhile pondering these different positions.

Three further, more recent treatments depart from those already cited:

(d) Schweizer moves "Jesus' claim," i.e., the presentation of his self-consciousness, into first position, followed by eschatology, ethics, and finally, the problem of the miracles of Jesus.

(e) Braun likewise places eschatology in front position, but then follows with a chapter on the call to repentance ("conversion"), an extensive section on ethics, and concludes with two parts on the topics of "Jesus' authority" and "God."

(f) Flusser chooses the exactly opposite order: ethics, eschatology, self-consciousness of Jesus.

(3) Which order is the relevant one? Most authors seem to be compelled to begin with the presentation of the eschatology of Jesus. First, it can be best supported from the sources; second, it obviously constitutes the foundational theme in the proclamation of Jesus from which all other themes are derived. This position is certainly legitimate, for methodological and objective reasons; however, it does raise a special problem: Where is theology proper to be included? Does it belong somewhere between the realms of eschatology and ethics? Or should it be positioned in the forefront as a sort of foundation?

We propose here to begin the presentation of Jesus' teaching with the doctrine of God, followed by eschatology (kingdom of God) and ethics (will of God). The question of the self-consciousness of Jesus no longer pertains directly to the realm of the problem of Jesus' teaching, since Jesus did not make his self-consciousness a theme of his proclamation.

This order is advisable in the analytical procedure, if one intends to ascertain first the reliable materials. The situation is different, however, if one intends to present the teaching of Jesus in a random collection. In this case, the question of the self-consciousness of Jesus must be given priority, since the specifics of his teaching are seen only against the backdrop of this self-consciousness. Cf. H. Conzelmann (see bibliography).

3. Advice for using criteria of authenticity

(1) While the basic materials of the parables can be regarded as authentic (see p. 71f. above) and, conversely, the apophthegms generally prove to be "ideal scenes" (see p. 68 above), the determination of the authenticity of the logia of Jesus is considerably more complex. The following methodological steps are required:

(a) Does the logion to be evaluated express a particularly unique self-understanding of Jesus? If so, does it reflect a tendency that has not only been shaped by the Christian belief in the resurrection of Jesus, but which applies exclusively to the situation before his death? Only in the latter case is it possible that the logion originated with the historical Jesus.

(b) Are the sayings that thematically speak of the person of Jesus to be viewed as self-expressions? Or do they represent christological statements of the community that were subsequently reshaped into sayings of Jesus? Example: How are words of the type of "I have come . . . " to be viewed? Are these actual words of the earthly Jesus? Or are these words intended to summarize the whole of the redemptive work? If the latter were true, the words would certainly be formations of the community.

(c) Finally, is the logion to be assessed typical or atypical of the proclamation of Jesus? Can it be explained more easily in the context of his preaching or rather in connection with the Christian kerygma?

A proverbial saying, for instance, must clearly be regarded as atypical, for it is not possible to assess with certainty whether Jesus adopted the proverb or whether the community later attributed it to him. This is especially true of those proverbs which received their specifically Christian sense only as a result of the context (cf. Mk 8:35 in the framework of the pericope of 8:34–9:1); this proverb *may* have been used by Jesus, but there is no evidence for this assumption.

(2) Apart from the parables, the following may be considered as "authentic" with some degree of certainty: The call to repentance (especially in its particular radicality); sayings such as Mk 10:15 (children and kingdom of God); sayings about outward and inward purity (Mk 7:15); eschatological sayings, such as Mk 3:27; Lk 11:31f.; and pronouncement sayings of conflict, such as Mt 23:16–19, 23f., 25f. The authenticity of the saying "but I say to you . . . " in the antitheses of the Sermon on the Mount is a matter of debate (see p. 313f. below).

Suggested reading:

N. Perrin (see bibliography), 15–53.

(3) The question posed above (p. 290f.), regarding the layer of sources that is to be accorded priority relative to the reconstruction of the life and teaching of Jesus is now answered. It is impossible to solve the problem of authenticity on the basis of a wholesale assessment of the sources. Neither Q, nor Mk, nor the special material in Mt or in Lk can be regarded as the sole bearer of authentic tradition. Rather, it is necessary to apply the criteria cited above for the evaluation of each individual logion or parable handed down as a saying of Jesus independently of the source in which that saying occurs.

§ 53 *Jesus' Teaching about God*

Bibliography: J. Becker, "Das Gottesbild Jesu und die älteste Auslegung von Ostern," (FS H. Conzelmann), 1975, 105–126; P. Hoffmann, "Er weiss, was ihr braucht . . . ," in *"Ich will euer Gott werden"* (SBS 100), 1981, 151–176; J. Jeremias, "Abba," in *Abba (Ges. Aufs.)*, 1966, 33–67; W. G. Kümmel, "Die Gottesverkündigung Jesu und der Gottesgedanke des Spätjudentums," *Ges. Aufs.*, 1965, 107–125; N. Perrin, *Rediscovering the Teaching of Jesus*, 1967; idem, *The Kingdom of God in the Teaching of Jesus*, 1963.

(1) Are the emphases Jesus makes in his teaching about God decisively new? Or does he essentially adhere to the Jewish understanding of God he received? There are two basic positions juxtaposed: According to

K. Holl ("Urchristentum und Religionsgeschichte," *Ges. Aufs.* II, 1928, 1–32), Jesus did indeed introduce a new concept of God in the teaching that God favors the sinner. This fundamental assertion, which is new in comparison to Judaism, at the same time establishes a new, non-Jewish ethics. In his review of Holl's work, R. Bultmann rejected this formulation (*ThR* NF 4, 1932, 1–21): Jesus did not bring a new "concept of God," rather, he speaks concretely of the God who is to come. What is important *now*, is to hear God's demand.

The proclamation of Jesus undoubtedly presupposes the Jewish understanding of God. Following the OT belief, God is the creator and ruler of the world; yet, as the author of the covenant and of the law, he also is at the same time the one who chooses, keeps, and delivers Israel. Therefore, the devout Jew is summoned to obedience to God and to God's commandments. At the same time, he admits he is a sinner before God because he is incapable of keeping the commandments (this idea is realized radically in Qumran). In Jewish apocalyptic, God is first of all the future judge; the individual human being is challenged to expect the judgment to come and to conduct himself accordingly. This leads to a more pronounced individualism: Belonging to Israel as God's elect people does not save; only an individual's righteous effort, i.e., God's acceptance of that effort, saves. These elements of the Jewish doctrine of God are also found in Jesus. But the emphasis is different: The notion of the people of God recedes almost entirely; belief in God as the creator is presupposed, but not really developed. Jesus' message of repentance and its related promise of forgiveness presuppose belief in God as judge. In this connection, primacy is given to the offer of salvation, for "now" Jesus announces God's coming, which holds the possibility of salvation for man. In his proclamation Jesus teaches that God's free gift precedes the demand and is therefore not the result of human effort. Thus man does not have to shield himself against God, but instead is able to hear God's commandment on the basis of the already promised salvation.

Jesus views man's relationship to God from a twofold perspective: He is God's creature—and a sinner at the same time. Hence God provides for him—and grants him his forgiveness at the same time. As a result man is freed from anxiety; man is summoned to imitate God's free giving and to be ready to forgive and reconcile. This aspect of Jesus' understanding of God is particularly prominent in the Lord's Prayer (Mt 6:9ff.) and in the parable of the unmerciful servant (Mt 18:23ff.).

There is no theory of the origin of sin in the proclamation of Jesus; it is simply established—"You who are evil . . . " (Mt 7:11). Likewise it is simply verified that man is exposed to temptation (Mt 5:30), without moral criticism. Its intention is clear: God causes the sun to rise over the good and the evil, and in this unconditional gift his attitude becomes man's norm and example.

Jesus modifies the traditional Jewish conception that God punishes an individual's sins already in the life here and now—for instance through sickness or misfortune. In man's misfortune Jesus does not see God's punishment of the individual's failures, but they point up for him the sinfulness and weakness of man. For this reason it says: "Unless you repent, you too will all perish" (Lk 13:1–5).

For Jesus it is certain that we may bring our petitions to God and that we may be assured of his granting them. This entails an explicit and theologically pertinent paradox: God has preordained everything—yet we may entreat him to do something unforeseen; God knows what we need—yet we are to pray. This paradox is resolved when we interpret it in the context of an immediate relationship to God: In that God offers us to petition him, we recognize our unconditional dependence upon him.

Suggested exercise:

The Lord's Prayer needs to be examined more closely as a typical example of the nature of intimacy with God. A literary-critical comparison (Mt-Lk) is necessary: Which form is older and may possibly be traced back to Jesus? What can be drawn from a comparison with a similar Jewish prayer, such as the Eighteen Benedictions? Finally, the theological questions are: What does the Lord's Prayer essentially mean? Into what relationship to God is the pray-er drawn when God is "offered" this prayer?

Tool: A. Vögtle, "Der 'eschatologische' Bezug der Wir-Bitten des Vaterunser," in *Jesus und Paulus* (FS W. G. Kümmel), 1975, 344–362.

(2) A special historical (and theological) problem is the address of God as father. It is explained that this terminology indicates Jesus' special understanding of God and his self-consciousness. Jesus shows that he understands God in the exclusive sense as his father and thus himself as son. In the history of religions, "father" is a common designation for deity. Zeus is the "father of gods and men"; likewise in the mystery religions, "father" is a common address of deity (cf. G. Schrenk, TDNT V, 953f.). In the OT, as well as in intertestamental Judaism, God may be called the "Father of Israel" (citations from the pseudepigraphical writings are provided by Billerbeck I, 392f.); the individual expression ("my father," "our father") occurs very rarely (Ps 89:27). Jesus ben Sirach prays: "Lord, father and master of my life" (Sir 23:1; cf. 51:10). Only one instance is found in Qumran, 1 QH IX 35. In later times it becomes a common Jewish designation for God (cf. Billerbeck I, 394).

In the synoptic Gospels God is frequently described as the *father of men* ("your father"); among these, Mt 5:45 and 5:48 (parallel Lk 6:36) are certainly authentic. By contrast, the designation of God as the *father of Jesus* ("my father") presupposes the Christology of the community in which Jesus is understood to be the Son of God (the evidence is delineated and critiqued in H. Braun, *Radikalismus* II, 127f., note 2).

An exception is Mk 14:36 where the address "abba" is attributed to Jesus. It is indeed clear that this cannot represent a historically authentic case, for who would have been witness to it (cf. v 35)? Nevertheless it is feasible that this preserves the reminiscence of the divine predicate which Jesus used frequently. However, Rom 8:15 and Gal 4:6 indicate that "abba" is the church's address used in prayer and thus could easily have been used in Mk 14:36. In any case, nothing supports the view that this was an address exclusively used by Jesus.

§ 54 Jesus' Proclamation of the Kingdom of God

Bibliography: H. Conzelmann, Article "Reich Gottes (im NT)," RGG V, 1961, 912–918; C. H. Dodd, *The Parables of the Kingdom*, 1961; G. Friedrich, *Utopie und Reich Gottes. Zur Motivation politischen Verhaltens*, o. J. (1974), Kleine Vandenhoeck-Reihe 1403; W. G. Kümmel, "Die Naherwartung in der Verkündigung Jesu," *Ges. Aufs.*, 1965, 457–470; idem, *Promise and Fulfillment*, SBT 23, ET ²1961; N. Perrin, *The Kingdom of God in the Teaching of Jesus*, 1963; idem, *Jesus and the Language of the Kingdom*, 1976; W. Schmithals, "Jesus und die Weltlichkeit des Reiches Gottes," in *Jesus Christus in der Verkündigung der Kirche*, 1972, 91–117; Ph. Vielhauer, "Gottesreich und Menschensohn in der Verkündigung Jesu," *Ges. Aufs.* ThB 31, 1965, 55–91; W. Willis, ed., *The Kingdom of God in 20th-Century Interpretation*, 1988.

(1) What has been true of his teaching about God also applies to the eschatology of Jesus: It is predicated upon the eschatological anticipation present in contemporary Judaism. Hence there is no need for Jesus to define the concept kingdom of God; rather, he assumes in the parables, for instance, that the hearer essentially knows what the kingdom of God is.

The extensive terminology associated with the concept of the kingdom of God is only infrequently documented in Judaism. Yet, some very diverse meanings can be found. The OT speaks of both the *future* kingdom of the Son of man (Dan 7:13f.) and the *present* kingdom of God over the universe (Ps 103:19; 145:11-13), using the Hebrew term מלכות (LXX: βασιλεία). Both the present (1 QM XII 7) and the future connotation (1 QM VI 6) are found in Qumran. In rabbinics, the expression מלכות יהוה does not denote "kingdom of God" at all, but the noun is to be understood as a circumlocution of the expression מלך יהוה: "God reigns." The saying has an eschatological meaning: God's dominion is not made manifest in the world, but this itself demands a decision on the part of the hearer now. Neither the idea of the people of God nor that of the Messiah are important in this context (see p. 134f. above).

These findings raise the question whether an objective rendering of βασιλεία τοῦ θεοῦ should be taken to mean "kingdom" or "rule" of God in the synoptic Gospels. The translation "kingdom" is probably preferred, since it also refers to a realm that is conceived spatially. Around the turn of the century, liberal theology construed βασιλεία τοῦ θεοῦ to mean the "inward" realm of faith and morality. On the basis of the texts, however,

J. Weiss and A. Schweitzer made clear that it denotes a condition that is understood as future and apocalyptic. In turn, C. H. Dodd raised objections against this by developing the notion of a "realized eschatology": The kingdom of God as Jesus proclaimed it is already present in the coming of Jesus. Dodd bases his argument primarily on Lk 11:20 and Mt 12:28.

Kümmel considers neither of these two positions as appropriate. Instead, Jesus reckoned with an interim between the present *working* of the kingdom in his own proclamation and the ultimate *realization* of the kingdom after his death.

(2) A critical analysis of the synoptic material concerning Jesus' proclamation of the kingdom of God results in the following findings:

1. The kingdom of God *is coming* (cf. the Lord's Prayer); in other words, the world does not evolve, for instance, through a historical process, towards the kingdom, which might then be understood as mankind's ultimate, ideal state, but the kingdom of God breaks into this world from "beyond." This means at the same time that the kingdom does not develop in the world—by "leavening" it, as it were, as the parable of the leaven (Mt 13:33) might suggest; rather, the kingdom is imminent. It is announced in the message of Jesus, so that the hearer's instantaneous decision might be elicited by the sign of salvation. The paradox also applies here (see p. 308f. above): The coming of the kingdom is certain; yet man may pray all the same that the kingdom may come "soon."

Mt 13:33 (cf. also Mk 4:30–32 and parallels) is concerned with the contrast between the phase of the beginning and of the end: The present and the kingdom of God are related to one another like the small piece of leaven to the leavened batch of dough.

As far as the time of the kingdom's arrival is concerned, there are two parallel groups of statements: According to Lk 17:20; 17:24 and parallel Mt 24:27, the kingdom breaks in unannounced; according to Lk 12:56, however, its signs can already be recognized and must be taken seriously. In the same vein, the judgment is depicted as a present act of separation between good and evil on the one hand (parable of the weeds, or of the net, Mt 13:24–30, 47–50; cf. especially Mt 24:40f. and parallel), and as an eschatological court session in which man will have to give an account of his works on the other hand (Mt 25:31ff.). What is the relationship between these two groups? Is it possible that the contradiction is irreconcilable, meaning that one of the two groups has to be secondary? This is clearly not the case. On the contrary, both agree in their basic structure in that they confront man with the same situation: They require an immediate disposition in view of what is to come and that is already now at work in the proclamation. Thereby the decision is not only demanded, but is indeed made possible in the first place (cf. Lk 9:60).

2. As we have seen, the aspect of time is a pivotal problem. Especially the meaning of ἤγγικεν is disputed in this connection: Does this term mean that the kingdom of God "is at hand," or that it is "already here" (so C. H. Dodd)? The literal meaning of ἐγγίζειν indicates that it refers to the immediate future and not to the present. Conversely there is one instance which speaks of the kingdom having already come: ἔφθασεν (Mt 12:28; Lk 11:20). How do these two assertions relate to one another? Some exegetes assume that they are different translations for the same Aramaic term; but since the Aramaic equivalents are unknown, a hypothetical reference back to the language of Jesus serves no purpose. Furthermore, it is inappropriate to base a factual opinion on the meaning of one single (and even unknown) word. If all of the material is taken into account, especially that presented in the parables of the kingdom of God, it is clear that the kingdom of God in the proclamation of Jesus is a future entity. Likewise the logia that address entrance into the kingdom (Mk 10:15; 10:23ff.; Mt 7:21; 21:31) refer to the conditions for entrance in the *future*. Of course, the aspects of future and present belong inseparably together: The future is already at work in the present (Mk 3:27); its present signs belong to the imminent, coming kingdom (cf. the Beatitudes). This is not contradicted by the fact that Jesus refuses the demand made upon him for signs; Jesus rejects signs on which judgment can be passed neutrally, without an individual's personal decision. He himself is the most important sign, together with his miracles and his preaching. Both point to the future of the kingdom already in the present (Mt 12:28).

Suggested exercise:

What relationship is there between the future and the present of salvation: (a) in Jesus; (b) in Qumran?

Tool: H. -W. Kuhn, *Enderwartung und gegenwärtiges Heil*, 1966, esp. 189ff.

(3) What is the relationship between Jesus' eschatological proclamation and his self-understanding? Does he consider himself to be the eschatological fulfillment, the Messiah or Son of man, or does he wait for someone else, for the coming Son of man? There is some support for the argument that Jesus never spoke of an eschatological bringer of salvation, neither in regard to himself, nor in regard to another. Such a figure cannot be found in his eschatological parables.

As Ph. Vielhauer has made clear, there was no room at all for a Messiah or a Son of man, in Jesus' proclamation of the kingdom of God. In the oldest layer of the synoptic tradition of the sayings of Jesus, there is no correlation between the "kingdom of God" and the "Son of man." Jesus understood the kingdom of God that he proclaimed as the beginning of God's direct rule. He takes his own appearance as a sign that the kingdom of God that is at hand is influencing the world already in the present.

(4) What is the relationship between individual and people of God, that is, the idea of the church. Is belonging to an organization a precondition for salvation, according to the teaching of Jesus? The famous words to Peter (Mt 16:18f.) might point in this direction; but this clearly mirrors the ecclesiology of the church and not the teaching of Jesus. But regardless of one's evaluation of the authenticity of this logion, the overall findings indicate that Jesus did not view adherence to a concrete group as a condition for salvation. He did not hand his disciples an organization with regulations and norms. His call to repentance is not directed to a "holy remnant" which he is yet to elect, but it is directed to all of Israel.

One may ask whether the image of sitting on twelve thrones (Mt 19:28) is authentic, hence whether Jesus assumes that he is gathering the representatives of the true, eschatological Israel (so Bornkamm, *Jesus*, 138). The agreement of this image with the church's self-understanding renders it plausible that this picture was formed by the church.

Universalism is given de facto, though not yet in theory, in the individualization of the gift of salvation, itself already typified in the notion of repentance in Judaism. For Jesus it is certain that God will gather all peoples at the end of time.

(5) Jesus shares with the Pharisees the expectation of a resurrection from the dead. For him this idea is an obvious prerequisite of his anticipation of salvation and judgment, and therefore it does not become a specific issue for discussion (possibly with the exception of Mk 12:18ff. and Mt 12:41ff.). In this connection it is also striking that the illustrations of salvation are reduced considerably in comparison with the respective Jewish material.

§ 55   The Will of God (Jesus' Ethics)

Bibliography: In general: H. Bald, "Eschatologie oder theozentrische Ethik," *VF* 24, 1979, 35–52; R. Banks, *Jesus and the Law in the Synoptic Tradition*, SNTSMS 28, 1975; H. Braun, *Spätjüdisch-häretischer und frühchristlicher Radikalismus. Jesus von Nazareth und die essenische Qumransekte*, II. *Die Synoptiker*, BHTh 24, ²1969; W. Schrage, *Ethics of the New Testament*, ET 1988. Section 1: H. Hübner, *Das Gesetz in der synoptischen Tradition*, 1973. Section 3: H. D. Betz, *Essays on the Sermon on the Mount*, 1985; Chr. Burchard, "Versuch das Thema der Bergpredigt zu finden," (FS H. Conzelmann), 1975, 409–432; R. A. Guelich, *The Sermon on the Mount*, 1982; J. Jeremias, "Die Bergpredigt," in *Abba* (Ges. Aufs.), 1966, 171–189; idem, *The Sermon on the Mount*, 1963; E. Lohse, "Ich aber sage euch," *Ges. Aufs.*, ²1976, 73–87; U. Luck, *Die Vollkommenheitsforderung in der Bergpredigt*, ThEx 150, 1968; E. Schweizer, *Die Bergpredigt*, 1982 (KVR 1481); G. Strecker, *Die Bergpredigt. Ein exegetischer Kommentar*, 1984; A. N. Wilder, *Eschatology and Ethics in the Teaching of Jesus*, 1950; H. Windisch, *The Meaning of the Sermon on the Mount*, ET 1937.

1. Jesus and the law

(1) The appropriate role of ethics in the proclamation of Jesus is discussed largely in terms of a dispute regarding the interpretation of the Sermon on the Mount. The latter contains a number of ethical assertions originating with Jesus himself, but it also contains material coming from the continued work of the community or directly from the pen of Mt. It would be inappropriate, therefore, to hastily reconstruct the ethics of Jesus from the Sermon on the Mount. Instead, the initial task is to analyze critically the Sermon on the Mount (or its assumed precursor, the Sermon on the Plain handed down in Lk). This analysis will not be undertaken here; we will merely refer to some aspects. The basic core of the Beatitudes (Lk 6:20f. and parallel) most likely had its origin in Jesus; they indicate that Jesus' ethical claim was based systematically upon the promise of salvation. Likewise, in terms of content, the claims made in the antitheses (Mt 5:21ff.) are in keeping with Jesus' proclamation.

Yet it is important to differentiate between the "primary" and the "secondary" antitheses: In the primary antitheses in which the antithesis is directly related to the thesis and is made intelligible only on the basis of the latter, an OT commandment is usually surpassed (Mt 5:21f.; 5:27f.; 5:33–37). The Sermon on the Plain in Lk lacks the parallels of these primary antitheses; hence they belong to the special material of Mt. In the secondary antitheses (Mt 5:31f.; 5:38–41; 5:43–48), the "antithesis" is intelligible without the preceding thesis. They are essentially self-contained claims that do not surpass but which correct the OT commandment. Lk does have parallels for these secondary antitheses, though not in the antithetical *form* ("but I . . . "). This form is found only in Mt, who probably did not create it himself but found it already in use. This can be ascertained in that the given pattern ("it is said . . . but I tell you") is broadened in some instances; one speaks of "broken patterns."

Do the antitheses in their form derive from Jesus himself? This is a matter of debate. The phrase "but I . . . " occurs in the theological discussion of the rabbis' interpretation of a given Scripture reference. In analogical fashion it was perhaps attributed to Jesus by the community. In their essence, however, the antithetical claims likely originated with Jesus.

Suggested exercise:

The alteration of the original meaning of a saying by the tradition of the community can be shown in a comparison of Mt 5:25f. with Lk 12:58f. Tools: J. Jeremias, *Parables of Jesus*, ET 1969, 43ff.; G. Klein, "Die Prüfung der Zeit (Lukas 12:54–56)," *ZThK* 61, 1964. 373–390.

(2) The ethical teaching of Jesus can only be understood against the backdrop of Judaism. Jesus does not intend to introduce new commandments, neither does he insist on supplementing those already in place. Rather, he wants to establish the uncorrupted intent of the commandments of God and for this reason removes the additions made by the pharisaic interpretation. He is even capable of taking a position contrary to the authority of Moses, who acquiesced to divorce on account of "the hardness of your hearts" (Mt 19:8). Thus Jesus does not demand the "intensification" of the Torah, but interprets the commandment radically as the will of God and dismisses any reinterpretation.

In comparison to the Jewish understanding of the law, there is only one completely new idea: Jesus teaches the possibility "that seriousness and obedience to the law could be dangerous for man" (so Braun, *Jesus*, 50). Jesus argues that in stringent obedience to the letter of the law, it is possible for man to withdraw from God's claim by ignoring, in formal obedience to God, the intent of the law, namely, the fact that it applies to the "whole" man. It is in harmony with this context that Jesus never cancels the Jewish legal norms in principle. For instance, occasionally he breaks the Sabbath regulations, yet he never pleads for the general abolition of the sanctification of the Sabbath (Mk 2:23–28). Far from being a compromise, behind it is Jesus' critique of any formal legalism; the abolition of the Sabbath commandment could mean man's escape from the "whole" obedience which God intends for him, just as much as his formal adherence to the Sabbath regulations does. But for Jesus the main thing is to understand God's claim as a radical claim upon man at any given moment.

(3) The same applies to the ceremonial regulations: Jesus does not deny that fasting, for instance, can be an exercise of piety; but he resists the hypocrisy demonstrated in the public display of personal piety (Mt 6:1–4, 5–8). Finally, Jesus' disposition with regard to material possessions points up matching concerns (Mk 10:17ff.): He threatens the rich but does not claim a general denial of possessions; in other words, he does not make poverty the condition for obtaining salvation. Nor does Jesus merely proclaim man's "inward freedom" with regard to possessions: Under certain circumstances, radical obedience to God could mean one's relinquishing of all possessions.

The characteristic difference in the Qumran community was its general demand to renounce personal property. The one who enters the order hands over his possessions to them and, in turn, receives the order's assurance that his material existence is secure. But this means that obedience is taken care of with one single act, while Jesus demands, in a given situation, the unmitigated surrender of security which results from the confidence in God's provision. This lack of principle (*Ungrundsätzlichkeit*, Braun) on the part of Jesus calls into question the legalistic piety of Judaism at its very core.

(4) In an attempt to determine the relationship of Jesus to Judaism, it is necessary to warn against misconstruing the Jewish understanding of

the law. In Judaism, commandment and obedience are not primarily formal entities either; rather, they are related to one's total relationship with God. Obedience to God's commandment is not an external, obligatory exercise for the Jew, but is by all means related to all of his thoughts and desires. For this reason D. Flusser is readily able to say that the Jesus of the synoptic Gospels did not violate the authentic Jewish practice of the law anywhere. Where he opposes Jewish customs (as in Mt 15:11), he does not abrogate the commandment as such but is merely critical of the pharisaic overzealousness.

There are indeed numerous agreements between the ethics of Jesus and the average Jewish ethics, as presented in summary form in Sir 27:30–28:7, for instance. A comparison with the rabbinic sayings likewise points up remarkable parallels, even to the point of vocabulary: Mk 2:27, "The Sabbath was made for man, not man for the Sabbath," is paralleled by Mekh Ex 31:13 (Billerbeck II, 5): "The Sabbath is given to you, not you to the Sabbath." Mt 6:34, "Therefore do not worry about tomorrow, for tomorrow will worry about itself;" this is paralleled by *Sanh* 100[b] (Billerbeck I, 441): "Do not be anxious about the trouble of tomorrow, for you do not know what the day (of today) will bring forth." Compare Mt 5:23f. with *Yoma* VIII 8: "Transgressions between a person and his neighbor are not atoned for by the Day of Atonement, unless he appeases his companion."

It is argued at times that even if there is a Jewish parallel to a saying of Jesus, it can be demonstrated that the Christian form indicates a higher moral. The "golden rule" is adduced as example (Mt 7:12; Lk 6:31) for which there both Jewish and Greco-Roman parallels. In this connection it is argued popularly that Jesus uses the rule positively ("and this you will do") while the Jewish rabbis formulate it negatively (for instance Rabbi Hillel: "What you do not want"); the positive formulation, naturally, is of higher ethical value. It is necessary to point out in this regard, however, that the positive formulation is also found outside of Christianity and, furthermore, that both denote the same in terms of content: They express the naive egotism of popular wisdom ("*do ut des*"). The saying receives a specifically Christian sense only in the context of the overall understanding of salvation, namely, by understanding the rule in the context of the all-inclusive love commandment that relinquishes worrying for oneself, on account of God's provision and forgiveness.

(5) Materially, therefore, Jesus' ethics are Jewish ethics:

What is new lies not in the individual claims but in the fact that the claim is preceded by the offer of salvation. This is the systematic requisite for the claim to be rendered absolute and summarized in the love commandment. For Jesus, the love commandment is not the sum, or the crowning conclusion of the individual commandments, as it were; instead, every commandment represents an aspect and a concrete form of the love commandment and can only be understood in this framework.

Note: (a) Even the commandment to love God and the neighbor comes from the OT (Dt 6:5; Lev 19:18). (b) The double form of the commandment (Mk 12:30f.) is not evidenced in the OT, however. In its essence, it is a pertinent rendering of Jesus' teaching, though the form of the double commandment probably did not originate with Jesus. This construction is not extant in the rabbinic material and only barely so in hellenistic Judaism. In any case, Mk 12:30f. may be the result of Jewish-hellenistic influence. (c) Jesus renders the commandment absolute by emphatically incorporating the love for one's enemies (Mk 5:44).

2. Specific problems

In connection with the ethics of Jesus a number of difficult problems arise which we shall outline briefly as follows:

(1) It is a matter of debate whether it is appropriate at all to speak of Jesus' "ethics." But this is a fruitless dispute. Many issues, such as the political and social configuration of society and the whole realm of culture, are not addressed; to this extent there surely is no such thing as an ethic of Jesus in a systematic sense. But if by "ethics" one only means the postulation of certain claims of oughtness, it is certainly appropriate to speak of the ethics of Jesus.

(2) According to a term which H. Braun has coined, the ethical proclamation of Jesus is determined by the "intensification of the Torah." This is a fair concept, as long as it is not made absolute and made dogma, as it were (which Braun himself is not guilty of doing); it is not true that Jesus sharpens and radicalizes the demands of the law in particular. The concept "intensifying of the Torah" points to specific aspects of Jesus' proclamation, for instance, his attempt to understand the law not casuistically but radically as the absolute will of God. Intensification of the Torah, then, means that Jesus divests the commandments of their interpretive meanings and brings them back to their essential core. Even as far as the individual commandment is concerned, God requires man's obedience, not in part but in full.

(3) The often expressed argument that Jesus conceived himself as the "bringer of the messianic Torah" is inappropriate. By means of the antithetical "but I tell you" he sets himself above Moses and thus acts as Messiah (see p. 323f. below). First, the notion of a messianic Torah does not exist in Judaism and, second, Jesus does not compare himself with Moses. Furthermore it is not certain whether the antithetical form dates back to Jesus after all (see p. 314f. above). This does not deny that Jesus' conduct and teaching express a well-defined self-consciousness that is not at all congruent with the patterns given in the Jewish religion.

3. Problems in the interpretation of the Sermon on the Mount

(1) Subject to discussion is the question whether the demands of the Sermon on the Mount are capable of being met at all; in this case the object of discussion is no longer the teaching of Jesus, but the extant form of the Sermon on the Mount as Mt shaped it by means of his redactional work. In particular, the positions taken are diverse:

(a) H. Windisch explained that the ethic of the Sermon on the Mount is Jewish (albeit radical) and is indeed realizable. But even if this is correct, the question remains whether it is truly realizable. (b) But the opposite position is also argued: The demands are deliberately shaped in a way that they cannot be met; in this way man is to be convicted of his guilt before God. But this raises the question whether an ethical claim that is deliberately structured in such a way that it cannot be met deserves to be taken seriously. (c) A compromise between the two positions is also feasible (and has been argued by exegetes): It pertains to the special ethics of the kingdom of God or the special ethics for the disciples, specifically, the regulations for the life of believers in the church. But this theory ignores the text: It is clearly recognized that the statements of the Sermon on the Mount refer to life in the world and that they are outlined as presenting the will of God for *every* human being. For this reason, the Sermon on the Mount cannot be interpreted in the sense of (d) two-level ethics, as if the commandments of the Decalogue were binding upon all people, while Jesus teaches the possibility of practicing a higher level of obedience. Mt. 5:19f. indicates that the Sermon on the Mount will not permit such a differentiation. (e) Based on his fundamental point of departure ("thoroughgoing eschatology"), A. Schweitzer takes the assertions of the Sermon on the Mount to be an "interim ethics": Jesus expects the imminent end of the world and for the brief time that still remains he gives radical ethical instructions that are to be kept only in this brief time frame. It must be asked, however, whether the individual instructions, in fact, do refer only to a brief period of time. Are they not instead very clearly formulated as commonly valid rules of behavior? One needs to take into account especially that the claims are by no means substantiated by the nearness of the kingdom of God; in contrast to the call to repent which is indeed anchored in the announcement of the kingdom of God, the commandments of the Sermon on the Mount are not eschatologically based. At the back of them is the appeal to reasonable judgment: "Who among you is . . . ?" or: "Consider the lilies. . . ."

The question of the feasibility of living out the demands of the Sermon on the Mount must be seen in the overall concept of the proclamation of Jesus, for only then does the intent behind them become clear. The absolute demand is the love commandment, and this is made intelligible precisely in its absoluteness: God does not merely want *something* from me, but he wants *me* (Bornkamm), which means that God's commandment is not to be interpreted casuistically.

It is significant in this connection that the tradition in Mt 5:44f. is probably authentic. But it is also important to note that Jesus did not coin the love commandment himself but that it originated in the OT (see p. 316f. above). By adopting it, Jesus stresses that God never intended anything other than love with his commandments; the individual commandments merely make this central commandment concrete. (On the correlation of love of God and of neighbor [Mk 12:28ff.], see p. 316f. above).

(2) It is of crucial importance to observe the fact that the gift, namely, that of forgiveness, precedes the demand. This signifies that the question of carrying out the commands cannot be separated from the question of forgiveness. The commandment convicts me only if I am able to grasp why God wants precisely love and not selfishness and why he wants forgiveness rather than vengeance. In other words: The commandments are in keeping with the nature of the giving God—only then do they not remain foreign to man, only then is it possible for my will to agree with God's will, only then is man's inward resistance against the commandments overcome.

The precedence of the promise of salvation to the demand has another consequence: The possibility does not exist for man to ponder the question of what he does *not* have to do. There is no "exempted" realm in which man might be free from God and his demands. There is no such thing as a holy inactivity—such as by appealing to cultic requirements. The Sabbath, for instance, does not alter the obligation to render help.

(3) Of theological significance is the question whether or not the ethical teaching of Jesus contradicts the Pauline teaching of justification by faith alone; it appears that Jesus does indeed teach a rigorous justification by works (Mt 5:20). But this is the wrong impression: Jesus does not teach that God rewards man's good works appropriately and that the relationship of God to man is thus contingent upon human effort. Jesus teaches God's absolute sovereignty by which he expects good works from man (Lk 17:7-10), and in keeping with this he teaches that God grants his grace independent of human effort (Mt 20:1-16). This means that the relationship between God and man is not abstract; rather, man may indeed expect from God what is good. Conversely, nothing arbitrary is expected of man, but his actions—if they are good—have a redemptive effect which affects him personally.

Suggested exercise:

Analyze Mk 10:17ff.: What disposition to possessions can be gathered from (a) Jesus, (b) the community, (c) Mk himself? What is the relationship between possessions and salvation in the various levels of tradition? Tool: J. Gnilka, *Das Evangelium nach Markus*, EKK II/2, in loco.

4. Criticism of the ethics of Jesus

The ethic of Jesus and within it the ethics of Christianity as a whole have been subjected to criticism by various positions. Friedrich Nietzsche called it "morality of slaves," behind the tacit humility of which there is actually hiding a particularly subtle type of desire to rule. It is the morality of those who are dependent upon "masters" (such as a deity). At the same time it is a morality of vengeance which uses evil so that it might itself appear to be good. Behind the outwardly demonstrated willingness to forgive and to be merciful is actually the secret desire to prove oneself to be good and righteous before a higher authority.

Nietzsche demanded the "will to power" which seeks itself.

This will is "beyond good and evil" (not: good and bad) and to this extent is an expression of radical freedom.

Suggested reading:

F. Nietzsche, *The Genealogy of Morals*. First Essay: "Good and Evil," "Good and Bad," ET 1956, 158–188.

The Marxist criticism of Christian ethics was based upon nineteenth-century-religions criticism. Marx espoused Feuerbach's argument that God is a projection of man. Accordingly there can be no ethics which appeals to the will of God. Rather, in its present forms and contents, Christian ethics are nothing other than the glorification of bourgeois conceptions of value and, at the same time, are an instrument of the ruling class to maintain its power. The rise of the classless society as the domain of liberty necessarily signifies the end of such ethics, for the total self-responsibility of man replaces the determination of ethics by something foreign.

More recent Marxism, as reflected in Bloch for instance, also more strongly emphasizes (next to the positivistic-mechanistic element in Marxist thought) the idealistic tendency in the philosophy of the younger Marx. Thus Bloch interprets God not simply as the transcendence of man's claims to power but as the hypostatized ideal of man who has not yet come to identify with himself (cf. *Prinzip Hoffnung* III, 1523). Hence Bloch endeavors to pick up the eschatological core of early Christianity; in this connection he explains that the Sermon on the Mount and its ethics could not be understood without this apocalyptic frame. Christian ethics is a "dream of the absolute" which will also find its place in the history to come.

The interpretation of the Sermon on the Mount cannot be undertaken from the materialistic nor from the idealistic vantage point. Instead, the ethic of Jesus can be understood in its essence only when it is understood in its theological framework, that is, only if one recognizes that its assertions are referring strictly to man's relationship with God. If one attempts to derive explicit political or individual instructions for conduct from the Sermon on the Mount and thereby to eliminate the discussion of God, the "ethical" claims are perverted into a call for an ethic of performance. Only if one understands them as the claim of a gracious God can they truly prove to be a call to act in freedom.

§ 56   The Question of Jesus' Self-consciousness

Bibliography: G. Bornkamm, *Jesus of Nazareth*, ET 1960; H. Conzelmann, "Das Selbstbewusstsein Jesu," *Ges. Aufs.*, 1974, 30–41; J. Jeremias, "παῖς (θεοῦ) im Neuen Testament," in *Abba* (*Ges. Aufs.*), 1966, 191–216; B. Meyer, *Aims of Jesus*, 1979; R. Otto, *Kingdom of God and the Son of Man*, ET 1957, 159–261; E. Schweizer, "Der Menschensohn (Zur eschatologischen Erwartung Jesu)," *Ges. Aufs.* I, 1963, 56–84; H. E. Tödt, *The Son of Man in the Synoptic Tradition*, ET 1965; Ph. Vielhauer, "Jesus und der Menschensohn," *Ges. Aufs.*, ThB 31, 1965, 92–140.

1. General matters

The problem of understanding the self-consciousness of Jesus, is more difficult than that of understanding Jesus' teaching. For one, the evidence of the sources is quite uncertain: Which self-designations of Jesus are authentic and which ones are traced back to the Christian community? For another, the issue is encumbered by the dogmatic tradition.

The traditional concept of the self-consciousness of Jesus is determined by the assertions of the church's Christology. Jesus is the pre-existent Son of God who became man; he is the suffering servant of God and Son of man who will come again to judge; he is true God and true man, the second person of the Trinity. Some of these assertions about Jesus are substantiated in the synoptic Gospels. The question is: Did they originate with Jesus in full or in part? There are two methodological alternatives to clarify these questions:

(1) Form criticism opts for the analytical alternative. It begins with the texts and seeks to trace them back to their origin. Its goal is to assess the possible authenticity of the individual assertions and then to collect what has been acknowledged as authentic. In this connection, special attention is given to the investigation of whether the traditional messianic designations were used by Jesus himself with regard to his own person, hence whether he understood himself to be the Son of God or the Messiah. The conclusion reached relative to the question of the self-consciousness of Jesus can be radical: The messianic titles of Jesus possibly originated in the Christian community and cannot be traced back to Jesus. The question whether Jesus possibly considered himself as a prophet or as a teacher within the framework of Judaism naturally remains open.

(2) The ability of form criticism to pass judgment on matters of authenticity is being contested. The analytical method has to be replaced with the synthetic one. It is necessary to begin with specific models that are familiar from the history of religions, such as the type of the (OT) servant of God or the type of the (apocalyptic) Son of Man. The question to be asked of the texts is whether it is possible to detect a self-consciousness of Jesus that matches these types (or a synthesis of them). The evidence for the accuracy of such an assumption is established when a comprehensive picture emerges that is complete in itself and parallels the thought forms of that time.

Example: It is argued that Jesus viewed himself as the suffering servant according to Is 53. Hence it is asked: What statements within the synoptic Gospels can be fitted into this framework of this self-understanding? Answer: The predictions of suffering, for instance. Therefore we have no reason to doubt their authenticity.

There is no doubt that the synthetic method leads to a more complete picture of the self-consciousness of Jesus than the form-critical analysis is capable of producing. A well-known example is the book on Jesus by R. Otto (*Kingdom of God and Son of Man*). For Otto it is also clear, of course, that the dogmatic categories of the homoousia and of the doctrine of the two natures cannot be traced back to Jesus; in other respects, however, he is of the opinion that many of the features of the traditional portrait of Jesus do in fact have a basis in the person of the historical Jesus. Jesus did indeed believe that the notion of the Son of man was merged in his person with the concept of the servant of God; this brought about the unity of the eschatological consciousness and that of suffering. Nevertheless, the alternative of the analysis of the individual texts upon which form criticism has embarked is to be preferred because it alone leads to methodologically verifiable results.

2. Problem of messianic titles

The decisive question concerning the problem of Jesus' self-consciousness is whether Jesus used particular messianic titles in reference to his own person. Three titles emerge prominently in this regard: (1) Messiah, (2) Son (of God), (3) Son of man. The question is whether Jesus himself used them or whether they were attributed to him by the community only after Easter.

The following steps are required in an analysis: Where does the title come from? What is its significance in the pre-Christian linguistic usage? How is it to be interpreted if the pre-Easter, historical Jesus already laid claim to this title for himself? What is its significance if the community did not use it with reference to Jesus until after Easter?

(1) *Messiah:* The Messiah expected in Judaism is not conceived as a supernatural person, but as a mortal, this-worldly person. His political function is in the foreground: The Messiah will gather and liberate Israel. Jewish writings contemporary with Jesus only rarely refer to the Messiah, of course. The title occurs frequently in the synoptic Gospels, i.e., in the Greek translation of Χριστός (Μεσσίας occurs in the NT only in Jn). In this context, one of the most important references is Mk 8:27ff.: If this reference, that is Peter's confession of him as the Christ (Messiah), which Jesus does not decline, is historical; if it has any historical core, it would almost be established with certainty that Jesus at least did not reject the designation of Christ—though in a new, nonpolitical sense, compared to Judaism. At the same time this reference would indicate that he demanded (initial) secrecy of this fact.

The analysis of Mk 8:27ff. indicates agreements with the confession of faith formulated by the Christian community. The pericope contains no concrete, historical material but turns out to be a sort of credal presentation in the form of a scene: that which the whole community believes, Peter voices as representative of all. The pericope Mk 12:35-37 is to be treated similarly. Jesus declares himself to be not the son, but the Lord of David and substantiates it with a reference to Ps 110:1. This likewise presupposes the Christology of the community. As man Jesus was the son of David, that is, the Messiah; but with his exaltation he was made the Lord of David. This Christology roughly approximates that of Rom 1:3f.

The assumption that Jesus did not designate himself as Messiah is further evidenced by the silence of the sources concerning Jesus' effective discussion with the traditional Jewish idea of the Messiah. If Jesus had understood himself as Messiah, one would have expected him to juxtapose the old messianic portrait with his own new conception, but nowhere does one hear anything about that.

By itself such an argument from silence is weak; however, together with the other arguments cited above, it is nevertheless weighty.

What then is the situation with the other synoptic texts in which the messianic title (or one related to it) is used of Jesus? Of course, the cry of Blind Bartimaeus ("Son of David") is no historical datum, since it is a question of an introduction to a miracle story, hence a question of a formation by the community. Precisely at the point crucial for us, namely, in the eschatological rejoicing of the multitude, the narrative of the entry into Jerusalem proves to be a messianic legend of the community. The scene is inconceivable as a historical event. The concept of the Messiah also occurs during the trial of Jesus before the Sanhedrin (Mk 14:61): Jesus replies yes to the question of whether he was the Christ, the Son of God. But here it is likewise clear that this scene is devoid of a historical core, for the presentation of the trial is altogether determined christologically.

The question of the high priest presupposes that the designations Messiah and Son of God are ultimately identical—a linguistic usage that is foreign to Judaism. The reference of Mk 14:61f. was very obviously drawn up as a compendium of the community's Christology; it is intended to show that all of the messianic titles—Messiah, Son of God, Son of man—are of equal value.

That Jesus moved to Jerusalem at the end of his life, fully cognizant of the threat of danger there, is frequently regarded to be strong evidence for the messianic consciousness of Jesus. This decision must indeed be viewed as evidence for Jesus' "consciousness of mission"; of course, nothing is said thereby about his messianic claim. Yet, the final argument is decisive: Even if Jesus designated himself as Messiah, nothing at all is expressed thereby relative to the structure of his self-consciousness. Given everything we know of Jesus, it is precisely the concepts that traditionally have been associated with this title that he did not adopt.

(2) *Son (of God):* This has become the most common title in the Christian church. As a designation of the eschatological bringer of salvation, it does not occur in Judaism; the evidence is scant for the adoption of the prophecy of Nathan (2 Sam 7:13f.) on the part of Judaism (cf. E. Lohse, TDNT VIII, 360–362; differently M. Hengel, *The Son of God*, ET 1976, 63–66).

Suggested exercise:

What is the situation in the Synoptics? Is 2 Sam 7:14 cited there? Tool: Nestle's appendix in which has a list of the OT citations in the NT.

The demons address Jesus as Son of God (Mk 3:11); but this is the community's formation, as is the trial before the Jewish Council, as we have already seen. And the same applies ultimately also to the two epiphany narratives of the baptism and of the transfiguration: They too are legends.

The absolute term "the Son" is to be distinguished from the title "Son of God" (Mk 13:32; Mt 11:27 and parallel Lk 10:22). In both instances "the Son" is clearly in relationship to "the Father"; especially in connection with Mk 13, a clear subordination can be recognized. It is frequently expressed that such a term could not be invented: The community would never have subordinated Jesus to God in this manner; therefore behind this saying must be seen the authentic self-consciousness of Jesus. But Mk 13:32 reflects the early Christology of the church.

At any rate, the reference to the alleged inability to invent a saying is questionable. In its tradition, the early church did not consciously distinguish between authentic sayings of Jesus and secondary formulations of the community. It is incorrect to suppose that dogmatically offensive statements were handed down only out of pious respect for the tradition that goes back to the historical Jesus.

Mt 11:27 is also an expression of community Christology (cf. the affinity with Mt 28:18). It is more difficult to assess the situation in Mk 12:1ff.:

At issue is a parable in which the absolute form of "the Son" is used. Is not Jesus' claim to be the Son (of God) recognized in this instance (though in cryptic form)? The parable under discussion is an allegory of the history of God with Israel, formulated in retrospect of the death of Jesus. If one attempts to reconstruct an original parable of Jesus by excising the allegorical features, all that would remain is merely a parable concerning the fate of the owner of a vineyard and of his son; even then the text would not answer the question of whether Jesus laid claim to the title Son (of God).

Conclusion: As far as it can be recognized, Jesus did not designate himself as Son of God.

(3) *Son of Man:* The first question to be answered with regard to the expression "Son of man" is whether the latter is a title at all or whether it was understood as such. Could it not be that this is simply another designation for "man" (cf. the frequent use of בן אדם in Ezk where it does not represent a title either)? The titular sense would then only have come about as a result of a misunderstanding in the translation from Aramaic to Greek. One can test this by probing the situation in Jewish apocalyptic: Is "Son of man" used as a title there? The famous reference of Dan 7:13 indicates *no* titular usage, whereas in 1 Enoch a certain movement towards the titular sense can be detected (71:14, 17). Yet, pre-NT Judaism is lacking any explicit evidence. It is necessary, therefore, to take up the entire synoptic contribution in order to arrive at a solid conclusion regarding the question of the meaning of the Son-of-Man concept.

Suggested exercise:

Look up all of the references in a synopsis (tool: concordance) and then analyze the following: Where is the title inserted secondarily (e.g., by Mt, in contrast to Mk)?

In which source layers is it handed down primarily (Mk, Q, special material of Mt, or special material of Lk)?

The material may be organized according to essential perspectives. Some references (Mk 2:10, 28; Mt 8:20 and parallel Lk 9:58) speak of the Son of Man on earth; here the question may indeed be asked whether or not these actually discuss man and his earthly destiny. It is also conceivable that the term is a circumlocution for "I" when voiced by Jesus, without alluding in any way to a particular honor or majesty: "The Son of man (I) has no place to lay his head," or: "But that you may know that I (the Son of man) have authority on earth to forgive sins . . . " (cf. Mt 9:8; Mk 2:10). This style would have been perfectly normal in the Aramaic language of Jesus; the expression would have been attributed the titular sense only in the translation into Greek.

But this supposition ultimately leads us no further. There can be no doubt that the Synoptics know the expression Son of man as a *title* (e.g.,

Mt 10:23; Mk 2:28; Mk 8:31, 38 et al.). There are no criteria for the assumption that the Synoptics, or the tradition on which they are based, knew of a twofold usage (titular and non-titular). This means that as far as we can determine, the term Son of man denotes a title of majesty throughout the synoptic Gospels. Consequently, the problem can be reduced to the following question: Did *Jesus* use the Son-of-Man title with regard to his own person?

Three groups of Son-of-Man sayings are to be distinguished:

(a) Sayings concerning the parousia of the Son of man; (b) sayings concerning the suffering Son of man; (b) sayings concerning the Son of man's "having come."

(a) If the statements about the parousia of the Son of man (Mk 8:38; 14:62) were to be viewed as authentic, one would have to assume that Jesus expected his own future transformation into the Son of man; but this construct can in no wise be derived from the texts.

Some exegetes, including Bultmann, attempt to solve the problem by supposing that Jesus expected not himself but another to be the coming Son of man. Based on this assumption it is conceivable that the second group of Son-of-Man sayings originated with Jesus himself. But this argument ignores that no difference of style can be recognized between these and all the other Son-of-Man sayings: Jesus consistently speaks of the Son of man only in the third person. There is no methodologically identifiable evidence for the supposition that it was precisely in the sayings concerning the coming Son of man that he had in mind someone else.

It is conceivable, of course, that Jesus spoke of someone else as the coming Son of man. If so, the community would have interpreted this by saying that Jesus did refer to himself and would have added further sayings (of the earthly, suffering Son of man). But this calls for evidence of a methodological and especially of a form-critical nature: It would be necessary to see stylistic differences between the "genuine" and the secondary Son-of-Man sayings emerging—and that proves to be an impossible feat.

The sayings that speak of the coming Son of man probably point back to Dan 7:13f. and were subsequently applied to Jesus by the community.

(b) There are sayings that speak of the suffering Son of man (Mk 8:31) but, as we have already seen, these are likewise formulations of the community (see p. 220 above).

(c) Did Jesus designate himself as the Son of man "who has come"? Schweizer (*Ges. Aufs.* I, 72) affirms this with reference to Mt 8:20 and parallel: This constitutes Jesus' authoritative call to discipleship, and it is inconceivable that the church would have spoken of Jesus in this form, had the saying not been authentic (on the argument of the "uninventability" of a logion, see p. 324 above). Vielhauer (*Ges. Aufs.*, 123f.) is correct in his objection that the statement, attributed to Jesus as a description of the actual situation, is an "extravagant exaggeration" and thus is in no wise to be taken literally. The statement becomes meaningful when it is understood as the community's retrospective glance upon the overall ministry of Jesus; only from this vantage point does it take on meaning as a call to discipleship. It is probable, therefore, that this understanding of the Son-of-Man concept originated only in the church.

It is striking that the title Son of man also plays a part in Jn. Like in the Synoptics, the term occurs only in Jesus' sayings, never where he is addressed, nor in a narrative. But Jn provides it with a special character by broadening the scope of meaning of the concept in keeping with Johannine Christology: The Son of man is pre-existent (Jn 3:13).

Conclusion: As far as we can discern, Jesus used none of the christological titles mentioned in the Synoptics in connection with his own person. Consequently it is impossible to reconstruct the self-consciousness of Jesus from the christological titles of the synoptic tradition. But it follows from the message of his preaching and from his ministry (healings) that he understood himself, as well as his appearance, as the sign of the kingdom of God that is at hand. Any statements that go beyond this are nothing more than mere supposition.

Suggested reading for advanced students:

The history of the christological titles in early Christianity is delineated in F. Hahn, *Christologische Hoheitstitel*, FRLANT 83, [4]1974.

Detailed information on the history-of-religions and exegetical questions related to the messianic titles "Son," "Son of God," and "Son of man" can be found in the article υἱός κτλ. (P. Wülfing von Martitz, G. Fohrer, E. Schweizer, E. Lohse, W. Schneemelcher), TDNT VIII, 334–397, as well as in the article υἱὸς τοῦ ἀνθρώπου (C. Colpe), TDNT VIII, 400–477.

§ 57 The End of Jesus (The Passion)

Bibliography: J. Blinzler, *Der Prozess Jesu*, [4]1969; H. Conzelmann, "Historie und Theologie in den synoptischen Passionsberichten," *Ges. Aufs.*, BEvTh 65, 1974, 74–90; M. Dibelius, *Das historische Problem der Leidensgeschichte, Botschaft und Geschichte* I, 1953, 248–257; E. Lohse, *History of the Suffering and Death of Jesus Christ*, ET 1967; P. Winter, *On the Trial of Jesus*, Studia Judaica 1, [2]1974.

1. General matters

(1) The question of why Jesus moved to Jerusalem with his disciples is clearly answered *theologically* in the synoptic Gospels' predictions of suffering. He "must" (δεῖ) go; the way to glory through suffering was

determined for him by God. At the same time, this christological statement has anthropological and thus also ecclesiological consequences: The
suffering of Jesus at once also determines the way for his followers (Mk
8:34ff.).

But it is very difficult to answer the question of what the real reason
was for Jesus' going to Jerusalem. Since the sources are glossed heavily
with Christian tradition, we are left to suppositions concerning Jesus' motives. Apparently Jesus wants to take his announcement of the kingdom
of God and his call to repentance to the Jewish people; on the occasion
of a major feast, therefore, he enters the capital because he is able to reach
a particularly large crowd there.

Of course, this notion, too, remains merely a supposition. Only one
thing is established historically: For whatever reason, Jesus did, in fact,
move to Jerusalem, and he was crucified there.

The question is whether it is possible merely to make assumptions concerning the reasons for his crucifixion, or whether we have more precise
information available to us. To begin with, it is necessary to establish the
evidence of the sources.

(2) The passion accounts of the four Gospels do not agree on all points.
At least two versions have been handed down, that of Mk (adopted by
Mt and Lk) and one which is to be reconstructed from Jn which, while
related to Mk, nevertheless contains additional and divergent material.

It is debatable whether a third passion narrative emerges in Lk, in which case
it is asked whether it originated in Q or in the special material of Lk. In this context, see p. 231f. above.

Form-critically the passion is completely different from the first part of
the Gospels, for unlike the case of the first part of the Gospels, the framework of the passion is a given. The sequence of the crucial events—arrest,
trial, execution—can hardly be changed. An outline of this sequence is
found in Mk 10:32–34 (the final and most detailed prediction of suffering
in Mk) which clearly presupposes the complete passion narrative.

The fact that the external framework was essentially intact obviously
does not rule out that the course of the narrative could be augmented
with additional episodes and with individual diversity. At any rate, one
would misunderstand the passion narrative(s) if they were regarded to
be an attempt to reconstruct the course of events with historical accuracy.
Just as in the earlier part of the Gospels, the christological interest predominates here as well: The passion story interprets the Christian confession and has been shaped exclusively with this interest in mind. The
christological meaning is further underscored by the adoption of OT motifs and quotations (cf. the description of the entry into Jerusalem, the
compensation of the traitor Judas, the casting of lots for the garment of
Jesus, the sayings of Jesus on the cross—OT elements throughout).

2. Passion story of Mark

The observations made thus far do not mean that the passion story does not also have a historical core. By means of a form-critical analysis of the Markan leitmotif, we will nonetheless attempt to establish an approximation of such a core.

(1) Mk 11:1-10—Entry into Jerusalem:

That Jesus came to Jerusalem is a historical fact. But the form of this narrative as the messianic entry of the Son of David is legendary. The details mentioned elucidate this: The narrative of the procuring of the animal is spun from Zec 9:9 (cf. Mk 11:2-6 with Mt 21:5); in its narrated form, this process is inconceivable as a historical event.

In terms of methodology it is to be maintained once again: Naturally it cannot be ruled out that Jesus rode on a donkey at his arrival in Jerusalem. But it is not the reminiscence of a possibly historical event of this kind that is behind the account of Mk. The narrative ties into the OT and not into historical events.

Likewise the description of the reaction of the multitude can hardly be in keeping with what actually transpired: What is heard is the eschatological rejoicing (underscored by the OT quotations). One may ask upon what historical basis is the account ultimately constructed. It is conceivable, of course, that Jesus entered Jerusalem together with a crowd of pilgrims in anticipation of the imminent breaking in of the kingdom of God (so Bornkamm, Jesus, 144f.), but this is nothing more than speculation.

The scene of Mk 11:12-14 was not connected with the passion story originally; neither nor was the continuation of 11:20-25.

(2) Mk 11:15-19—Cleansing of the temple:

The OT saying in v 17 that forms the center of the current scene plainly indicates that this is an ideal scene, constructed as an apophthegm. Yet, it is obviously possible that there is a historical core behind it. The recent trend—especially in popular literature—to interpret the temple cleansing as a sign of the revolutionary mind set of Jesus, or even as a signal for an uprising, has to be accepted with extreme caution. Is it possible that this scene could have transpired in this fashion? The temple area was very extensive; why did neither the temple police nor the Roman troops whose barracks were at the northern end of the temple intervene? But it is especially important to ask whether the narrative was initially part of the passion story. In the presentation itself, at least, there are no such indications; therefore Jn was readily able to move it to the beginning of the public ministry of Jesus. It is clear that the pericope is tied to Jerusalem as the arena. With regard to the outline of Mk, therefore, it could only be used within the framework of the passion story, since Jesus did not stay in Jerusalem prior to the passion. But it can no longer be said whether this pericope has always been part of this framework.

The dialogues and speeches of Jesus in 11:27–13:37 are certainly built into the passion narrative secondarily. They have nothing in common with Jerusalem and with the situation of the passion. Mk has artificially connected the discourse "of the last things" (Mk 13) with the context; its placement at this particular locus is due to the fact that Mk intended to present the eschatology of Jesus as the conclusion of his teaching.

(3) Mk 14:1–11—Beginning of the passion:

The narrative motif of Mk 14:1f. is continued in v 10; in between, vv 3–9 are inserted secondarily and only subsequently have been interpreted with reference to the death of Jesus by means of the augment (v 8). The framework of vv 1f. and 10f. was already available to Mk.

(4) Mk 14:12–25—Lord's Supper:

Already in the oldest tradition (1 Cor 11:23) the Lord's Supper has been presented as Jesus' last meal with his disciples before he "was handed over." Within the Markan frame it appears as the Passover meal, but this impression is a secondary product. Originally the narrative of the Lord's Supper was a cult legend without temporal constraints and without reference to the Passover festival, for such a connection is made neither in the Pauline nor in the Markan form (there indeed was such a tradition which can still be discerned in Lk). If one asks about a possible historical core, it is essential to be reminded again of the methodological principle already mentioned: Certainly Jesus did have a last common meal with his disciples, but the account of the Lord's Supper does not contain the historical reminiscence of this last meal. Rather, this account is deliberately shaped as sacramental institution, for it presupposes Jesus' death. Within the Last Supper is found the reference to Judas' betrayal of Jesus; the motif—at least in this form—has been derived from of Ps 41:10 (cf. Jn 13:18). Whether a reminiscence of a historical event is to be sought behind it cannot be determined. Likewise from the OT comes the motif that all the disciples will forsake Jesus (Mk 14:26–31; cf. with v 53f. and v 66ff.).

(5) Mk 14:32–43—Gethsemane:

Time and again this narrative has invited the attempt to interpret Jesus' behavior psychologically. But it is clear that this account is legendary as well; there was no eyewitness or auricular witness at all of the described events (Mk 14:35–40).

(6) Mk 14:43–52—Arrest:

This narrative may originally have followed v 31, for its goal is the fulfillment of the prophecy (v 27) in v 50. As a sign of the betrayal the "kiss of Judas" is legendary. Even if it can be deemed historical that one of his followers was a participant in the arrest of Jesus, it has to be maintained, nonetheless, that nothing can be said concerning his motives. Any suppositions in this regard, such as that he wanted to force Jesus to reveal his glory and then committed suicide on account of his disillusionment regarding the outcome of things, are pure fantasy.

(7) Mk 14:53f., 66–72—Peter's denial:

This has to do with the fulfillment of the second part of the prophecy of 14:30 (see above). The threefold character is in harmony with a popular narratival motif; otherwise, though, it is possible that there is a historical core in the account.

(8) Mk 14:55–64—Trial before the Sanhedrin:

The question of the historical premise arises once again. Is the messianic claim that Jesus makes a capital offense according to Jewish law of that time? Is it to be taken as blasphemy against God? From all we know, this was not the case. Rather, the scene is an example of the christological shaping of a narrative: The focal point is a compendium of Christology (v 61f.) Its intent is to make clear that Jesus was condemned on account of his messianic claim (hence Bultmann and others consider vv 57–59 as "secondary"). The whole scene of the trial is not based on an eyewitness account but has been shaped from the perspective of the believing post-Easter community.

Therefore the question is not: What charge did the high priest bring against Jesus? Instead: What does the Christian narrator allow him to say? It is not possible to assess with historical reliability whether or not an official trial before the Jewish council actually transpired (or under the given specific conditions).

(9) Mk 15:1–27—Trial before Pilate:

The time sequence (v 1, 25, 33ff.; cf. v 42) is redactional. V 2 is in competition with vv 3–5; after the open self-designation of Jesus as "king of the Jews," the continuation of the trial (in which the royal title or claim is not addressed) makes little sense. Therefore, v 2, as well as its corollary of v 26, may likely be secondary.

There is no doubt that a trial of Jesus before the representative of the Roman government actually did take place. But the historical details can no longer be reconstructed. In any case, the episode with Barabbas is a secondary insertion from a literary standpoint. As far as content is concerned, it is to be regarded as legendary, for outside the Gospels nothing is known of a corresponding Passover custom.

(10) Mk 15:24–32—Scoffing:

The episode has been derived from Ps 22:19 and 22:8.

(11) Mk 15:33–39—Death:

This scene contains distinct legendary features. Vv 34, 35, and 36b are secondary padding of Jesus' wordless cry of v 37. V 39 is also secondary and represents a redactional comment of Mk, who consciously suspends the messianic secret, in a conclusive manner, under the cross of Jesus who died, by allowing the Roman centurion to express the confession of Jesus as the Son of God publicly for the first time.

(12) Mk 15:40f.—Women as witnesses:

These verses are clearly secondary. The women have taken the place of the disciples (who fled) and represent the necessary (Christian) witnesses.

(13) Mk 15:42–47—Burial:

Bultmann does not see any legendary features here; but even if vv 44f. and 47 are bracketed (cf. Bultmann, *History of the Synoptic Tradition*, 274), the remainder is hardly based on a historical core. Probably the scene has been drawn in prospect of the Easter narrative and thus is altogether part of the complex of the tomb stories.

The historical basis of the entire tradition of the passion proves to be relatively thin: Much more than the fact of the sentencing and of the crucifixion cannot be secured historically.

3. *Historical problem of the sentencing of Jesus*

The question of the year in which Jesus was crucified has already been discussed (see p. 292f. above). Two problems remain, however: On the basis of what judicial code was it possible to sentence Jesus to death? And, in conjunction with this: Who sentenced Jesus?

The Gospels agree that the Sanhedrin and the authority of the Roman occupation (Pilate) collaborated, with Pilate pronouncing the actual sentence. Does this presentation agree with the historical facts?

In order to be able to answer this question, it is first of all necessary to clarify whether the Jewish Sanhedrin at that time even had the judicial authority to impose capital punishment.

Some exegetes suppose that while the Jewish council was allowed to pass the death sentence, it was not allowed to execute it without Roman consent. It is further debated whether the trial proceedings described in the Gospels were properly carried out in keeping with the ordinances of Jewish criminal law, or whether the latter were violated in the process. However, this discussion leads nowhere, because the legal ordinances embedded in the Mishnah are developed as ideal law, and that at a time when the Jews no longer had jurisdiction over their own affairs. In any case, these ordinances were not in force at the time of Jesus.

One question still remains: Was the verdict of the death sentence voiced by the Sanhedrin and merely confirmed by Pilate? Or does the sentence itself go back to Pilate? The type of execution shows unequivocally that Jesus died as a result of a Roman death sentence, for the crucifixion is not a Jewish, but a Roman method of execution. Furthermore, it is to be noted that capital trials in Jerusalem were always conducted before the tribunal of the Roman procurator, if the latter resided in the city (E. Lohse [see bibliography], 74ff.). Therefore, Jesus was not only executed in keeping with Roman instruction, but he was also sentenced by the Romans.

The description of the Gospels that Jesus was sentenced both by the Sanhedrin and by Pilate has no historical background; like the entire scene of the trial before the Jewish council (see above), it is determined by christological interest. Cf. D. Lührmann, "Markus 14:55–64. Christologie und Zerstörung des Tempels im Mk," *NTS* 27, 1981, 457–474.

But why was Jesus condemned? Or, putting the question like this: On the premise of what accusation did the Jews hand him over to the Roman government? This point should be a matter of certainty. It must have been a political accusation that was levelled against Jesus, for the Romans did not concern themselves with purely religious questions. Yet, the so-called *titulus* on the cross (Mk 15:26) cannot be adduced as evidence in support of this argument, since the motive behind this *titulus* was a christological one without historical background. Contrary to the assertion argued occasionally, there is no evidence for affixing such inscriptions above the head of the one sentenced to death as a Roman custom.

4. Question of the "guilt" for Jesus' death

(1) The question discussed from time to time concerning who bears the "guilt" of Jesus' death is historically absurd and to be rejected on theological grounds. It is historically absurd to inquire into the guilt on the part of the Jews living today, and that quite apart from whether one poses this question in terms of an attack or in terms of an apologetic attempt to absolve them from the accusation of being "murderers of God." "The Jews" do not need such defense. The whole question is theologically perverse because in so doing a historical situation and a faith statement are being mixed up and interchanged. The historical evidence is unequivocal: A political suspect was executed by the Romans, with the cooperation of Jewish circles. The Christian belief says: Jesus had to die as Son of God. These two statements cannot be reduced to a common denominator.

(2) If one inquires into the evidence of the Gospels, it is to be noted at the outset that the passion story is a testimony of faith. This leads to the perspective from which the opponents of Jesus are viewed and described. The Gospels constantly emphasize the innocence of Jesus; at the same time they are apparently endeavoring—though with varying distinctiveness—to offer an interpretation of the role of Pilate. Are the evangelists thereby pursuing anti-Semitic, or pro-Roman (i.e., political) motives? Evidently this is not the case.

Rather, their assessment of the Jews is based on their view of salvation history (cf. also 1 Thes 2:14–16): By their attitude in relationship to Jesus, the Jews have rejected the eschatological fulfillment of the prophetic utterances. Political-apologetic motifs certainly play a part in the description of Pilate; the tendency to exonerate Pilate can be detected especially in Lk. But the Gospels' portrait of Pilate essentially has less to do with fear of the Roman state than with the fact that the Christian communities are not (yet) actively engaged in an altercation with Rome. According to the evangelists, Christianity initially has nothing to do with Rome and with Roman religion; but it has to do with Jewish religion, for it claims to be the fulfillment of the latter.

One needs to observe that, in any case, for Mk, Lk, and Jn, the Jews of Palestine were a distant entity; Mt is likely living among Jews, but he, too, is separated from the time of Jesus by the Jewish War. Hence the synoptic presentation of the end of Jesus is less in keeping with a historical reminiscence or a "moral" valuation of the Jews of that time than with the theological valuation demanded by the situation of the time.

5. The verdict of Jewish scholars concerning Jesus

For Jewish scholarship (and for Judaism in general) Jesus poses a special problem. On the one hand, the Christian church has fully claimed Jesus. On the other hand, he is a Jew in his life and teaching and there are no historically anchored indications that he essentially departed from the premise of Judaism. The critical point is always the question of why the Jewish leaders had an interest in the execution of Jesus at all, under these conditions.

J. Klausner, (*Jesus von Nazareth. Seine Zeit, sein Leben und seine Lehre*, 1930) argues that Jesus himself had been a pharisaic teacher who made the Pharisees his enemies, obviously, due to his association with tax collectors and sinners. Furthermore, he roused the Sadducees against himself because of his cleansing of the temple.

P. Winter (see bibliography) explains that Jesus himself was a Pharisee and that the Gospels' presentation of the conflicts between him and the pharisaic party was essentially incorrect. The accusation against Jesus was raised by the Sadducees, and only because it was no longer the Sadducees but the Pharisees who were the representatives of Judaism at the time of the writing of the Gospels did the latter move into the limelight altogether and appeared as the accusers of Jesus. In truth, the Gospels did not at all describe the conflict between Jesus and his Jewish contemporaries, but the struggle between the church and (pharisaic) Judaism.

D. Flusser (see bibliography, § 52) argues similarly to Winter that Jesus was not in conflict with the scribes and Pharisees but with the hyperpious, with institutional Judaism which the Pharisees also rejected.

A. Finkel (*The Pharisees and the Teacher of Nazareth*, AGSU 4, 1964) differentiates even more sharply: Jesus' charges had been directed especially against the rabbinic school of Shammai and against their extreme intensification of the purity code.

Suggested reading:

Read one of the Jewish presentations of Jesus (Flusser's is the most accessible [see bibliography on § 52]). Control question: How can his arguments be controlled methodologically?

A detailed overview of the older Jewish scholarship on Jesus is provided by G. Lindeskog, *Die Jesusfrage im neuzeitlichen Judentum*, ASNU 8, 1938; reprint with epilogue, Darmstadt, 1973. Information on Jewish literary works on Jesus is also found in E. Grässer, "Motive und Methoden der neueren Jesus-Literatur," *VF* 2/1973, esp. 30–34, and in G. Baumbach, "Fragen der modernen jüdischen Jesus-forschung an die christliche Theologie," *ThLZ* 102, 1977, 625–636.

PART FIVE: HISTORY OF EARLY CHRISTIANITY

Bibliography: R. Bultmann, *Primitive Christianity in its Contemporary Setting*, ET 1956; H. Conzelmann, *History of Primitive Christianity*, ET 1973; L. Goppelt, *Apostolic and Post-Apostolic Times*, ET 1970; H. Lietzmann, *A History of the Early Church*, vol. I, ET 1961; W. Schneemelcher, *Das Urchristentum*, UT 336, 1981.

§ 58 Essentials Regarding Terminology

The history of primitive Christianity is frequently organized schematically. Knopf, Lietzmann, and Goppelt, for instance, distinguish generally between the "apostolic" and the "post-apostolic" eras. There is relative justification for his division: Whereas we are fairly well informed about the first few decades of the early church, we know virtually nothing about the events of the history of the church subsequent to the death of the first Christian generation (approx. A.D. 60) until about A.D. 100, despite the fact that with the exception of the authentic letters of Paul almost all of the NT writings emerged during this time. If reference is made to this period of time, the division of apostolic/post-apostolic may be used carefully. But it is capable of implying a distorted historical picture, such as suggesting that the "apostolic" era was the pure, unadulterated primitive time of the church, while the "post-apostolic" era signals its decline. The overall concept is itself questionable; while "the apostles" are difficult to define as historical entities, the idea of the "twelve apostles" does not arise until the third generation, whose concept of history seeks to understand the "first" generation as a complete entity. Even if one depends only on the fairly identifiable figures—Peter, Paul, James—and their death signals the end of the "apostolic" era, there is no common criterion that arises. The role of James is limited, and we know hardly anything about the significance of Peter outside of Palestine. On the other hand, Paul's death does not denote a particular turning-point in the history of the church. A certain point in time is marked by the Jewish War, especially by the conquest of Jerusalem in A.D. 70. It is important to note, however, that this war played no decisive role outside of Palestine, either for Jews or for Christians. The war represented an extremely decisive event only for Palestinian Judaism.

The second equally useless division employed occasionally is "New Testament" and "post-New Testament" era. As far as the time of writing is concerned, canonical and non-canonical writings overlap; for instance, (canonical) 2 Pet was written considerably later than (non-canonical) 1 Clem.

It is best to use the neutral concept "primitive Christianity" and to establish and set its parameters according to criteria that have been drawn from the sources themselves. In this case, the epoch of primitive Christianity ends where Christians consciously set themselves off from the primitive time, that is, from the era of the "eyewitnesses," and where they explicitly inquire into the reliability of the received traditions and, at the same time, undertake the shaping of tradition by collecting and sorting what has been received. The classic document of the period immediately *following* primitive Christianity understood in this manner, is Luke's two-fold work (Lk and Acts) with the programmatic prologue of Lk 1:1–4.

Such differentiations as Jewish Christianity—Gentile Christianity, or early church—hellenistic church, are inappropriate as patterns of division because the transitions are fluid throughout.

Much debated is the notion developed by the expert of ecclesiastical law, R. Sohm, according to whom the early church led by the Spirit is to be distinguished from the later church led by office. Originally the church knew no fixed organization, instead it was directed by charismatic leaders. 1 Clem points up the end of, as well as the transition from, this independent church to the church led by office. Sohm attached a value judgment to this notion: Only the charismatically led church is truly church; ecclesiastical law is self-contradictory. In contrast, A. v. Harnack pointed out that from the very beginning the church knew a certain legal regulation.

According to R. Bultmann, this controversy arises from a different understanding of the church in Sohm and Harnack. Harnack's argument is established on the premise that the church is a historical phenomenon; Sohm, on the other hand, views the primitive church from the perspective of its own self-understanding. In reality, however, legal ordering within the church contradicts the nature of the church only when the former is no longer understood as the church's regulation but as the entity that constitutes the church. It is clear, in fact, that in primitive Christianity the work of the Spirit itself regulates the church (cf. 1 Cor 14).

Suggested reading:

R. Bultmann, *Theology of the NT,* ET 1951/55, II, 95–118.

§ 59 *Sources for the Reconstruction of the History of Primitive Christianity*

1. NT *and other Christian writings*

(1) The NT writings, especially the authentic Pauline letters and Acts, constitute the most important sources.

The council of Jerusalem serves as an example of the critical comparison of sources. It represents a historical event (re. dating, see below) recounted in two sources: Gal 2 and Acts 15. It is clear that the account of Paul, as a participant in this conference, has greater value as a source than the Acts presentation, since the latter itself possibly depends on sources that have been assimilated. However, to acknowledge this does not yet mean to attribute unqualified reliability to the account of Gal. It is certainly conceivable that Paul's presentation is itself biased.

Suggested exercise:

A synoptic reading and a critical comparison of Gal 2:1–14 and Acts 15. Tools: Commentaries on Gal and Acts.

The following are further examples of the character of Paul's letters as sources: 2 Cor 11f.; Gal 1—for the biography; Rom 15—for his travel plans; 1, 2 Cor and Gal—for the arguments with his theological opponents. Likewise the deutero-pauline letters serve as historical sources: From Col we learn about the existence of Christian communities in Asia Minor and about the nature of theological arguments in that locale. Though it is a fictitious writing as a whole, the letter to Titus permits the conclusion that the Christian mission reached Crete. Despite its secondary nature in comparison to the letters of Paul, Acts must be considered as an indispensable source. The analysis (see § 37 above) has shown that the book was written around A.D. 80/100 and hence is already relatively distant from the events it reports. Nevertheless, its presentation of the history of primitive Christianity is not based on pure fiction, for there is evidence that contemporary sources have been assimilated in Acts. While this may not yet be true of the first community of Jerusalem, the (Gentile) Christian community of Antioch apparently did produce sources.

Of course, Acts is not to be used as a presentation of the history of "the apostles," for, beginning with ch 16, it pursues the ministry of Paul almost exclusively, while the work of the other apostles and missionaries and, accordingly, the non-Pauline mission territories, are not addressed. Even so, Acts is the most important source for the history of primitive Christianity. Events in the history of the church are also reflected in the Gospels, such as persecutions, arguments within the churches, events of the Jewish War (especially the destruction of Jerusalem). But the Gospels can hardly be considered as sources for particular historical facts.

(2) Extrabiblical Christian sources also play a certain part in the reconstruction of the history of primitive Christianity. In some instances, historical events can be derived from the writings of the "Apostolic Fathers" (see § 45 above). Special value as a source for the history of primitive Christianity is accorded to the church history of Eusebius of Caesarea, although it was not written until the beginning of the fourth century. In actuality, Eusebius drew from abstracts of older works which, in part, are lost. Of special importance is the material which his work contains regarding the history of the church of Jerusalem: The death of James, the church's escape from the city at the outset of the Jewish War, the church's post-war situ-

ation. In the evaluation of this data it is always necessary to consider that not all reports are entirely reliable. Therefore, they must be evaluated carefully and individually.

2. Non-Christian sources

These are less valuable for us by far. Josephus mentions the death of James, the Lord's brother; in his *Annals,* Tacitus briefly touches on the persecution in Rome under Nero; it is mentioned in Suetonius that, at the time of Nero, there were disturbances in Rome among the Jews—these were possibly connected with the advance of Christianity. Finally, in his tenth letter, Pliny the Younger provides a glimpse into the tactics of the Roman authorities against the Christians in Trajan's era (in the province of Pontus which Pliny governed, at any rate). For the rest, however, we learn nothing about the earliest history of the church from non-Christian, and especially from Jewish sources.

Suggested reading:

Read Tacitus, *Annals* XV, 44, and Pliny's 10th letter (English texts in H. Conzelmann, *History of Primitive Christianity,* ET 1973, 166–170).

§ 60 Chronology

Bibliography: J. Finegan, *Handbook of Biblical Chronology,* 1964, 302–325.

1. General observations

Jesus was crucified in approximately A.D. 30 (see p. 292 above). In addition, what further dates in the history of primitive Christianity can be established with relative certainty? The NT contains but few datable items or references to persons or events or that we know more closely from other sources.

In Acts 11:28 reference is made to a worldwide famine during the reign of Emperor Claudius. While we know of famines during his tenure, nothing is known of a worldwide one. Josephus mentions a famine in Palestine which ravaged the country in A.D. 46/48; one may ask whether the reference in Acts is connected with this and thus represents a generalization.

Acts 12 records that Agrippa I had James the son of Zebedee executed and shortly afterward died. Since Agrippa reigned over all of Palestine from 41 until his death in 44, the execution of James took place within this time frame.

Acts 18 reports about the couple Aquila and Priscilla, who had been evicted from Rome on account of the edict of Claudius concerning the

Jews. The Christian historian Paulus Orosius (5th cent.) dates this edict in 49, whereas the Roman writer Dio Cassius apparently dates it in 41. The dating remains uncertain.

2. Chronology of Paul

The most important evidence for a date in the history of primitive Christianity is the Gallio stone, an inscription from Delphi, which indicates that the Roman proconsul Gallio resided in Corinth in the year 50/51 (or 51/52 at the latest; Barrett, 48f.). Acts 18:12ff. mentions that Paul worked in Corinth during the administration of Gallio—it is not clear, of course, whether this happened at the outset of Gallio's activity (hence possibly as early as A.D. 50) or only towards its end. But it is possible to state with certainty that Paul resided in Corinth around A.D. 50.

On the Gallio inscription, cf. G. Lüdemann, *Paul: Apostle to the Gentiles*, ET 1988, 163–164 (with further bibliography). In addition, Lüdemann argues for a theory of the Pauline chronology that is significantly different from the one delineated here (cf. p. 358f. below).

This historical date offers the possibility of organizing the biography of Paul, and hence the history of primitive Christianity, with greater chronological precision.

The first two chapters of Gal contain some important data regarding the life of Paul: Three years after his commission he went to Jerusalem for the first time; after fourteen years he was in Jerusalem again, specifically for the purpose of the Apostolic Council.

The references are not unambiguous: "After" three or fourteen years does not have to denote "after completion of" this number of years, but can also mean "in the third" etc. year. Furthermore, it is not clear whether the fourteen years mentioned are to be added to the three years mentioned initially, or whether they are already contained in the former. Hence it is either X (year of commission) + 3 (or 2) + 14 (or 13) years, or X + 14 (or 13) years until the Apostolic Council.

With this in mind, the following possible chronology can be reconstructed: The council took place before Paul came to Corinth during the "second missionary journey," hence prior to A.D. 50, possibly 48 or 49. Thus one can calculate backward:
Stay in Corinth, 50/51
Apostolic Council, approx. 48
Commission, 32/35.
From the same point one can also calculate forward:
Stay in Ephesus, 52/56
Transport to Rome, 58
Imprisonment in Rome until approx. 60.

There remains a fundamental uncertainty, for the Pauline presentation in Gal 1f. does not agree with the Acts account of Paul's journeys to Jerusalem. According to Acts 9:26, Paul was already in Jerusalem immediately following his commission, and 11:30 refers to a journey of Barnabas and Paul to Jerusalem on behalf of the Antiochan community. Some exegetes suggest that this was the journey to the council which, therefore, must already have taken place before Agrippa's death, thus, no later than A.D. 43. If this assumption were made the premise for the remaining data in Gal, one would, in the extreme case, arrive at 43 minus 17 years, i.e., A.D. 27, as the date for Paul's commission.

With reference to Paul's death there also is a method of dating that departs from the calculations suggested above. According to tradition Paul was executed in A.D. 64, during the Neronian persecution; therefore the trip to Rome and the imprisonment there would have taken place in A.D. 62 (and not in 58; see above). However, the sources have nothing to say about Paul perishing during the Neronian persecution. On the contrary, it is probable that he died earlier, for Acts specifically presupposes a situation that was judicially fixed and not a situation of persecution.

From the time after 60, two dates can be established historically: James, the brother of Jesus, was executed in 62 (Barrett, 199f.), and the Jewish War took place in 66–70.

§ 61   The Rise of the Christian Church

Bibliography: H. v. Campenhausen, *Der Ablauf der Osterereignisse und das leere Grab*, [3]1966; H. Grass, *Ostergeschehen und Osterberichte*, [4]1970; W. Marxsen, "Die Auferstehung Jesu als historisches und als theologisches Problem," in *Die Bedeutung der Auferstehungsbotschaft für den Glauben an Jesus Christus*, 1966, 9–39; idem, *Die Auferstehung Jesu von Nazareth*, 1972; U. Wilckens, "Die Überlieferungsgeschichte der Auferstehung Jesu," in *Die Bedeutung* (see above), 41–63.

Some traditions trace the founding of the church back to Jesus himself, as does the famous saying to Peter in Mt 16:17–19; it is also presupposed in the account of the institution of the Lord's Supper ("as often as you do this"). But these accounts are without exception of a later date and are certainly not reliable historically.

The decisive primary source for the rise of the church is the early Christian credo in the form of 1 Cor 15:3ff. Peter is the first recipient of an appearance of the Risen One (likewise Lk 24:34); in other words, *historically* Peter is the founder of the church, which presupposes that faith considers this founding to be the deed of the resurrected Jesus. 1 Cor 15:5b reports on an appearance to the twelve (and to "all the apostles," v 7, not, however, to the "twelve apostles"). Several problems arise with this: Why did a group of twelve people assemble? Had this group already been organized by Jesus and now gathers again—perhaps prompted by Peter's initiative? In this case, the appearance to all would virtually signify the group's legitimation by Jesus himself, while at the same time underscoring the idea of the church as expressed in the number twelve: The twelve are the representatives of the elect people of God.

Much, however, militates against the assumption that Jesus himself gathered the circle of the twelve (see p. 303 above). Thus the rise of the church probably has to be explained via Peter's vision, which stands at the beginning. It was Peter who concluded from the appearance "to him" that he was to constitute God's eschatological people, through the twelve as representatives of the church. And this decision would then have been confirmed explicitly by the appearance to this new circle. In any case, it is clear that the appearances at once constituted a community. All of the recipients of a revelation of the Risen One immediately understand it as a mandate to missions. The self-understanding of the new Christian community expresses itself, among other things, by establishing itself in Jerusalem (without detriment to the existence of further communities in Galilee) and immediately begins with the mission among the Jews.

It is characteristic that the appearances of the Risen One are not *described* in this oldest tradition. Nothing is said about how he appears, what orders he issues, and what immediate impression the visions made upon the recipients. It is particularly important to note the fact that none of the eyewitnesses remained neutral, as it were, and that none left behind a description of his experience (the Acts accounts of Paul's Damascus experience are legends of a later date).

The Easter narratives of the Gospels as well as the stories of the ascension and of Pentecost in Acts are secondary sources, narratival descriptions of the faith that Jesus lives, that the Risen One founded his church. Nevertheless, theological positions can be drawn from the geographical localization of these narratives. Mk, who does not have any appearance account and, instead, has only an angelophany, in 14:28 and 16:7 points ahead to appearances in Galilee. Whether Mk originally also contained accounts of such appearances is subject to debate, but may be questioned for good reasons (see p. 216 above). Apart from an appearance of Jesus in Jerusalem, Mt informs especially of one in Galilee; Lk, however, exclusively relates appearances in Jerusalem. Jn 20 tells of appearances in Jerusalem and the postscript, chapter 21, of the same in Galilee. What historical insights (not about the place of the appearances, but) about the place of origin of the Christian community can be derived?

It is to be noted that the Easter stories originally were individual stories and that their combination into a group of legends is secondary. A combination of the data in the Gospels, thus a synthesis of Galilee and Jerusalem into a sequence of events (cf. Jn), is impossible, unless one assumes the hurried march of the disciples from one place to the other, which cannot be supported from the texts, of course.

On account of this situation, one has to resort to hypotheses.

(1) One assumption says that the disciples fled from Jerusalem to Galilee after the arrest of Jesus and saw the Risen One there. Because of this event they returned to Jerusalem where the appearances then continued. One may indeed assume that the vision of James, the Lord's brother, came in Galilee. Otherwise, however, this hypothesis raises problems: No source reports the disciples' flight to Galilee and of their corresponding "return" to Jerusalem.

And furthermore: Had the Risen One appeared in Galilee, would not Galilee (and not Jerusalem) have to be regarded as the place of eschatological salvation; in other words, would the Christian communities not have been formed in Galilee to begin with?

(2) The differing localizations of the appearances can be attributed to the side-by-side existence of two "primitive communities" (in Jerusalem and in Galilee). However, we have no other evidence of such a primitive Galilean community.

(3) It is argued that the first and possibly also all other appearances occurred in Jerusalem; the appearance to Peter is likely bound up with this place. Against this the objection is raised that the localization in Jerusalem is favored by special interests, but not so the localization in Galilee. Hence in the history of tradition the latter is primary.

One may, with all reservations, consider it to be probable that the first appearances occurred in Jerusalem. The rise of the Christian church which was constituted on account of these appearances is clearly bound up with this city.

There is a certain rivalry between the appearance narratives and those of the empty tomb. While both strands of tradition are already connected together in Mk, this intertwining is secondary. It is possible that the tomb stories originally were a result of the belief that the Risen One was taken up into heaven immediately and then had angels announce his rapture on Easter morning. This would also tie in with the fact that the ascension narrative did not emerge until relatively late, when believers were no longer directly cognizant of the initial character of the tomb stories.

The decisive theological question is what significance the Easter stories have for the Christian faith.

(1) The question of whether the resurrection of Jesus is a "historical event" is to be rejected from the start. "The only thing that can be established historically is that certain people asserted an experience they made after the death of Jesus which they described as seeing Jesus, and the reflection on this experience then led these people to the interpretation: Jesus has been raised" (Marxsen, *Bedeutung* [see bibliography], 24).

(2) It is of crucial significance that there is no neutral witness to an appearance. Each appearance immediately resulted in faith.

(3) It is not permissible to make the mistake of attempting to explain the visions psychologically. We know absolutely nothing about the emotional state of the disciples after the death of Jesus. It is to be noted further that former companions of the historical Jesus are not the only ones having a vision; Paul, the opponent of Christians, who did not know Jesus in his lifetime, has a vision as well. Paul denies emphatically that he did not come to believe in Christ because of disappointing experiences with the Jewish religion (Phil 3:5ff.).

(4) Paul, the only eyewitness whose authentic statement we possess on this matter (Gal 1; 1 Cor 15:8), is silent on the type and manner of his experience.

Conclusion: It is methodologically incorrect to engage in psychological assumptions; rather, what matters is the question of the issue itself: What were these appearances, that is, what did they signify? The answer can be drawn from the conclusions reached by those affected: They are convinced that God raised the crucified Jesus and that they themselves constituted the eschatological people of God on earth. For Christians, belief in the resurrection of Jesus denotes the missionary task of proclaiming God's salvific act in all the world.

§ 62   *Primitive Community and the Development of Jewish Christianity*

Bibliography: H. v. Campenhausen, *Ecclesiastical Authority and Spiritual Power in the Church of the First Three Centuries*, ET 1969, 12–29; J. Jeremias, *The Eucharistic Words of Jesus*, ET 1966; G. Klein, *Die zwölf Apostel. Ursprung und Gehalt einer Idee*, FRLANT 77, 1961; W. Schrage, "'Ekklesia' und 'Synagoge.' Zum Ursprung des urchristlichen Kirchenbegriffs," *ZThK* 60 (1963) 178–202; E. Schweizer, *Church Order in the NT*, ET 1961, 34–88.

1. Community in Jerusalem

(1) Acts is the primary source for the scope and organization of the community in Jerusalem; besides Acts there are a few references in Paul. Once again it is to be noted in principle that the Acts account comes from a second hand, that is to say, it was revised by Lk and therefore must be analyzed critically.

It is clear that the Jerusalem community is Judeo-Christian and hence is comprised exclusively of Jews who, in keeping with their own self-understanding, remain Jews, even as Christians. Among them one finds Jewish Christians both of Palestinian and of hellenistic background (Acts 6).

The portrait that Acts paints of this church, shows idealistic features: The Spirit governs the community, hence the believers are intimately unified. They celebrate common meals with (eschatological) rejoicing; the outward sign of loving one another was that they had all things in common. The Lord himself grants the community rapid growth (2:47).

An analysis, especially of the summaries in Acts, indicates that this portrait is to a large extent the product of Luke's redactional effort.

Example of an exercise:
The early Christian "communism," that is, the believers' holding of property jointly, is mentioned in Acts 5 (cf. 2:42ff.) and appears to be illustrated in the narrative of Ananias and Sapphira. In principle, such communistic communities were feasible in the Judaism of that time, as the Qumran community shows. However, this does not yet constitute evidence of a similar tendency in the Christian church. On the contrary, it is possible that the original account was given an idealistic coloration precisely in dependence upon such models (such communism is also reported of the "primitive community" of the Pythagoreans). An analysis, especially the comparison between the summaries on the one hand and the concrete information in Acts on the other hand, does indeed indicate that the (redactional, hence secondary) summaries tend to idealize. While the narratives inform us of endowments made to the community (Barnabas; the account of Ananias also deals with such a voluntary bequest), nothing is said of a general and compulsory, mandated commonality of property. In fact, the renunciation does not become a general demand.

It is nevertheless correct that the community in Jerusalem is governed by a particular self-understanding which can be deduced from the self-designation of "saints" (Rom 15:25; 2 Cor 8:4; 9:1). This has to do with an eschatological concept. For Paul, of course, the Christians of Corinth, Rome, and Philippi, are also "saints."

(2) The word ἐκκλησία represents the most important ecclesiological term. Both etymology and meaning of the term are subject to debate. The question is: What understanding of church is indicated when Christians use this term with reference to their community? Methodologically, two questions are of help:

(a) What is the term's prehistory in the OT and in Judaism? Which is its Hebrew or Aramaic equivalent?

(b) What is the statistical finding in the NT? Does the term ἐκκλησία denote the church as a whole or the individual community? How frequently are the singular or plural forms used?

The following positions are argued in scholarship:

(i) The model is to be sought in the OT קהל (Dt); the church is to be understood as the renewal of the gathered community (in the Sinai desert). Evidence: Acts 7:38.

(ii) Its equivalent is כנישתא, meaning synagogue. The Christians organized themselves as their own synagogue within Judaism, which would certainly have been feasible from a legal standpoint (so K. L. Schmidt).

(iii) The term ἐκκλησία did not come into use in Jerusalem but, instead, in the hellenistic community. In Greek, ἐκκλησία denotes the political assembly, and the Christian community specifically adopted this secular-political sense, thereby signalling its distance from the Jewish cult and law (W. Schrage).

(iv) The etymological significance is popular: ἐκκλησία, derived from ἐκκαλέω, describes the community of those whom God has "called out." But there is no evidence that the first Christian century was still aware of this etymology.

The term ἐκκλησία may designate the individual community which gathers for worship (Acts 5:11; 15:22) or simply the respective local community (Acts 16:5; cf. 1 Cor 16:1, 19). Yet, ἐκκλησία also denotes the whole church as a unity (Gal 1:13; Mt 16:18). This apparently signifies that "the church" finds its concretion in the individual community; this is made clear in the prescripts of the letters to the Corinthians: "The church which is in Corinth."

The church is taken to be God's called community in the world. Its claim is exclusive: It is not possible to be a Christian and, at the same time, belong to another religious fellowship (in contrast to the mystery religions, for instance). In this context emerges the church's self-understanding as an eschatological entity.

According to the traditional conception, the "twelve apostles" were at the helm of the primitive community of Jerusalem; among these, Peter's position was that of *primus inter pares*. This is the backdrop to the scene of Acts 1:15ff. which recounts the election of Matthias to complete the number of twelve. Although they only receive a cursory sketch in Acts, these twelve emerge as the bearers of the mission and teaching in the community; furthermore, they are the leaders of public worship (6:4) and of the community's organization (6:1ff.). The question must be raised, however, whether this picture corresponds with the actual historical realities.

First, it is necessary to be reminded once again that "the twelve" are to be distinguished from "the apostles." There is practically no information about the role of the twelve. While it is clear that they are to symbolize the eschatological nature of the church as the true Israel, virtually nothing is said about what they do in practical terms. Peter is apparently the only one who advances the mission outside of Jerusalem; occasionally, like a shadow, one finds John at his side. Otherwise, however, any traces of the twelve vanish rapidly; not even their names are handed down uniformly.

Even more difficult to grasp is the threesome of Peter, John, and James, the son of Zebedee (cf. Mt 26:37).

From Gal 1f. we learn that the three "pillars," Peter, John, and James, the *Lord's brother*, constitute the leadership of the community at the time of the Apostolic Council. Their relationship to the twelve, however, remains altogether unclear. At any rate, nothing is said of the twelve at the Apostolic Council (Gal 2), and it appears that James, alone, supported by a group of elders, was at the head later.

It is certain, then, that there existed no "officially" defined areas of competence in the administration of the community in the early years. Active in the primitive church were prophets, that is preachers (Acts 11:27f.; 13:1-3; 15:32), and in the hellenistic and Gentile-Christian communities there were apostles, prophets, and teachers (1 Cor 12:28). It cannot be determined at what point in time the institution of the elders emerged; perhaps James was responsible for this institution.

(4) The summaries in Acts list specific elements of community life: Common meals in the houses of the members of the community (in this context, cf. also 1 Cor 11), the apostles' teaching ministry, breaking of bread, and prayer. It is argued that the object of the summaries is not at all the life of the community as a whole, but especially the public worship, in other words, they reflect the sequence of an early Christian worship service. But this argument ignores the literary character of the summaries: Luke does not want to describe the sequence of an early Christian worship service; rather, he wants to point out what in his mind are the enduring elements of community life of primitive Christianity.

As far as public worship itself is concerned, it likely followed the model of the *synagogue*: No sacrificial ritual, but "ministry of the Word" with prayer, Scripture reading, and teaching. Some of the early liturgical elements include the eschatological exclamation *maranatha*, the address *abba* in prayer and, of course, (christological) confession. Already very early on one begins to find traces of the shaping of an elemental "catechism." One is received into the community through baptism, the precursor of which is the baptism of John (see p. 298ff. above). This is indicated by the tradition following which Jesus was baptized by John. The confession of sins is part of the baptismal rite, for baptism effects forgiveness; and the confession of faith also belongs here, for it is carried out in the name of Jesus.

(5) The Lord's Supper has been the subject of numerous hypotheses. One of these maintains that there were two types of Lord's Supper, namely, the breaking of bread as non-sacramental act and the actual Eucharist. The breaking of bread, which is also known as the agape meal, was merely the continuation of the communal meal Jesus celebrated with the disciples, whereas the Eucharist (as it came to be known) was the meal commemorating Jesus' death. The only thing that can be said, however, is that the Lord's Supper was celebrated in the context of the communal meal. No tendencies by the primitive church to trace the communal meal back to Jesus can be detected.

It is not known how frequently the Lord's Supper was celebrated; the argument that it was held in every early Christian gathering, cannot be established (in the context of this issue, it is important to read 1 Cor 11:17–34 and Did 10; cf. Bornkamm, *Ges. Aufs.* II, 138–176).

The assertion is made frequently that there are Jewish models for the Lord's Supper. But it is certain that while Judaism is acquainted with very festive meals, it does not know of sacramental meals. The relationship of the Lord's Supper to the Jewish Passover was only established secondarily.

If one compares the Lord's Supper with the meals with bread and "wine" reportedly held in the Qumran community (1 QSa 2:18), it becomes apparent quickly that the similarity is but an external one.

Suggested exercise:

One may attempt a reconstruction of the primitive form of the words of institution of the Lord's Supper. The following steps are necessary:

(1) Compare the four wordings in Mt, Mk, Lk, Paul (1 Cor 11).

(2) Inquire into the literary relationship: Mt is dependent upon Mk; Lk, however, appears to know of a further tradition whose fragments can still be recognized (in this connection one has to inquire into the priority of either the text's length or brevity).

(3) Compare Mk and 1 Cor 11 keeping in mind the question of the underlying oldest tradition.

(4) Are the words of the Lord's Supper translated from a Semitic language, or have they always been formulated in Greek? What is the significance of the interpretive elements? Tools: J. Jeremias, *The Eucharistic Words of Jesus*, ET 1966; G. Delling, Article "Abendmahl" II, TRE I, 1977, 47–58.

2. Further development of Jewish Christianity

Even after the Apostolic Council the Jerusalem community remains a strictly Jewish-Christian community which seeks to maintain the association with Judaism, especially by observing the legal code. James, the Lord's brother, takes Peter's place as its representative; at the outset he enjoys the respect of all because of his piety. On account of the intensification of Jewish nationalism—Zealotism prior to the Jewish War, however, the community is subjected to more intense pressure; during a vacancy in the Roman procuratorship, James is stoned to death in A.D. 62 at the hands of the Sadducean high priest Ananos (Hannas II). Four years later, according to a reference by Eusebius (*Church History* III, 5:3), at the outset of the Jewish War the community fled to Pella in the Transjordan. The accuracy of this information is disputed, of course.

The law-abiding element of Jewish Christianity in the West was reduced to a peripheral existence rather quickly. Justin (ca. A.D. 150) considers Jewish Christians who declare their teaching to be binding upon the Gentile

Christians as well to be heretics. Irenaeus (ca. A.D. 180) was the first to mention the "Ebionites," who, besides the OT, acknowledge only Mt and categorically reject especially the letters of Paul. By contrast, in the East there are law-abiding Jewish-Christian groups until the fifth century; after that, however, they are no longer able to survive between the church at large and the synagogue.

An overview of the history of scholarship since F. C. Baur is provided by G. Lüdemann, *Paulus, der Heidenapostel*. II, FRLANT 130, 1983, 13–55. On the Pella tradition, cf. idem, 265–286.

§ 63 Hellenists in Jerusalem

Bibliography: A. v. Harnack, *The Mission and Expansion of Christianity in the First Three Centuries*, Harper Torchbook 92, 1962; M. Hengel, *Between Jesus and Paul*, ET 1983, 1–29 (with extensive bibliography); H. Kasting, *Die Anfänge der urchristlichen Mission. Eine historische Untersuchung*, BEvTh 55, 1969, 61–123; M. Simon, *St. Stephen and the Hellenists in the Primitive Church*, 1958.

According to the portrait of Acts, the Christians in Jerusalem are of "one heart and one mind." But at one point, almost inadvertently, a shadow is cast upon this ideal picture. It is reported that in caring for the poor, the widows of the "hellenists" are overlooked and that leads to confrontations (Acts 6:1). What historical development might be at the back of this reference?

To begin with, the meaning of the term Ἑλληνισταί is not clear; prior to this reference, this term does not occur anywhere. Two possibilities are feasible: Either they are Greek-speaking Jews or simply Greeks. The context of Acts indicates that Lk had Greek-speaking Jews in mind; for, the first Gentile, in keeping with Luke's schema of the history of the church, is not received into the church until later (Acts 10). Historically this is also accurate, since the rise of this group precedes the transition to the Gentile mission. Stephen is not stoned as an adherent of a new religion, but as a renegade Jew (Acts 6:11–15). Jews who came from the Diaspora lived in Jerusalem (Billerbeck II, 663: Synagogue of the Alexandrians in Jerusalem; Deissmann, *Light from the Ancient East*, 378ff.: Synagogue of Theodotus in Jerusalem with Greek inscription), and it is likely, therefore, that hellenistic Jews joined the Christian church. Now the question is why it was specifically the widows of these hellenistic Jews—and only they—who were collectively overlooked in the community's care for the poor. Did they live as a separate group? It is conspicuous that all of the seven deacons (*Armenpfleger*) appointed by the twelve as a result of this incident had Greek names (Acts 6:5) and hence were apparently also "hellenists." Yet, their task encompasses the entire community.

If one examines the information in the text more closely, it appears that the seven were not deacons at all. The portrait of Stephen has less in common with that of a "deacon" than with that of an "evangelist"— and that to a far greater extent than in the case of the twelve. One of the seven, Philip, as much as bears the title of "the evangelist." It is the seven and not the twelve who stir up the public (Acts 6:8–15). Thus it is probable that the seven hellenistic "deacons" were actively engaged in missions. Philip's activity in Samaria after the scattering of the hellenists from Jerusalem also points in the same direction. It is indeed conceivable that a separate hellenistic group arose within the Christian community, under the leadership of Stephen, analogous to the rural associations of synagogues among the Jews (Billerbeck II, 661ff.), though, of course, we have no detailed knowledge of this group's views. But one may conclude from these events that, in contrast to the other Jewish Christians, they no longer held the cultic law to be binding (6:13f.). The core of Stephen's "speech" (Acts 7:1ff.) may possibly be based upon the traditions of this group of hellenists. Whether this group continued Jesus' criticism of the law, must remain open. In any case, Paul's statement that he persecuted Christians on account of his zeal for the traditions (law) of the fathers (Gal 1:13f.), proves that there were Jewish Christians who obviously had been emancipated from the law. The special position of the hellenistic Jewish Christians was apparently recognized by the public. At any rate, they alone took the brunt of the effects of Stephen's execution and of the dispersion from Jerusalem. The consequence, however, was the expansion of the mission outside of Jerusalem and of Palestine by maintaining the historical relationship of the church with Israel, of course, and by acknowledging the ties with the primitive community of Jerusalem.

Suggested exercises:

1. Analyze Acts 6–8, especially the speech of Stephen. It seems to consist of two layers: (a) Devotional treatment of the history of Israel; (b) Polemical application. Question: Does it allow for the theology of the hellenists to be discerned?

2. What type of action is used against Stephen? Is it a matter of mob-rule or of the official procedure of the authorities? Is the note about Paul in keeping with the actual situation, or is it a secondary addition?

Tools: Commentaries on Acts.

§ 64 *First Phase of Christianity's Expansion and its Public Position*

Bibliography: H. Kasting, *Die Anfänge der urchristlichen Mission. Eine historische Untersuchung,* BEvTh 55, 1969.

1. Primitive Christian mission

(1) Acts is virtually the exclusive source at our disposal; in addition, there are some brief references in Paul which indicate that outside of Jerusalem there were also Christian communities in Judea (Gal 1:22; cf. 1 Thes 2:14). That Paul the persecutor of Christians experienced his commission near Damascus (Gal 1:17; cf. 2 Cor 11:32; cf. Acts 9) indicates that there were already Christian communities in Syria as well. Paul knows the apostles (cf. 1 Cor 15:7), as well as the brothers of Jesus (1 Cor 9:5), as missionaries.

Some of the summaries in the Gospels (Mk 3:7-12; cf. Mt 4:24f.; Lk 6:17-19) represent indirect testimonies of the expansion of the church. From the Gospels one also learns something about the methodology of missions (cf. the discourse on the commissioning for the mission, Mt 10) that still shows traces of a fundamental difference concerning the question of the mission to the Gentiles (Mt 10:5f.).

Such arguments are also found in Acts (10, 11), which pictures the following developments: (a) To begin with, there is a rapid expansion in Jerusalem (2:42; 5:14; 6:7—the reference to the number is fanciful, of course); (b) then follows the successful mission in the surrounding area (5:16), and (3) finally the expansion into Samaria and to the coastal regions precipitated by the dispersion (Acts 8, 9). The external development described above is matched by concrete internal progress: (1) At its outset, the mission is directed to the Jews, then (2) to the Samaritans as Jewish heretics, with the emphasis that this advance was brought about and justified by the Spirit. Acts 8:14-17 explains emphatically that the Spirit did not come to the Samaritans until their community was approved by Jerusalem. (3) The next step is the baptism of a foreigner—the Ethiopian official, whose religious status Lk keeps intentionally ambiguous. Here it is likewise the Spirit who brings about the event (Acts 8:29). (4) The first baptism of a Gentile, in principle, constitutes the conclusion of the development; it is also occasioned by the Spirit (Acts 10), who characteristically comes through Peter. This legitimizes the mission to the Gentiles and, at the same time, establishes their close relationship with Jerusalem. Ch 11 reflects further on Jerusalem's tensions regarding the mission to the Gentiles.

For the most part this Lukan presentation of the development likely corresponds with the actual historical situations. But one may have to imagine the development as less systematic and less structured. It is clear that there were only Jewish Christians at the beginning, but it can hardly be the case that Peter initiated the first step towards the mission to the Gentiles; rather, it may have been taken by the hellenists.

A trace of this can be recognized even in Acts in that the hellenist Philip comes to Caesarea Maritima even before Peter.

Besides, there are gaps in the presentation: In Acts 9 the existence of a community in Damascus is presupposed without prior mention of a missionary thrust into Syria.

Suggested exercise:

What historical core can be established from the Pentecost narrative? Many exegetes are of the opinion that it represents the appearance of Jesus to more than five hundred brothers reported in 1 Cor 15. But it must be asked whether Acts 2 does indeed deal with an appearance story. This is obviously not the case. Two questions are significant:

1. Does Lk speak of speaking in tongues or of a miracle of language?

2. Could it be that two different accounts have been combined?

Tool: Commentaries.

(2) It may also be historical reality that Christianity early on developed in a northerly direction, along the Phoenician coast; the mention of Phoenician place names in the Gospels also points to this. The second great Christian center emerges in the major city of Antioch. Here the mission is no longer directed to the Jews only; rather, Gentiles are also accepted into the community. In Antioch the public also recognizes the peculiarity of Christianity over against Judaism: Possibly they receive the name Χριστιανοί (Christiani), which is a Latinized derivation of Χριστός, from the Roman authorities.

Occasionally it is assumed that an Antiochan source with authentic information from this community has been incorporated throughout Acts. While this cannot be established conclusively, the pericopae of 11:19ff. and 13:1–3, which Luke edited, undoubtedly contain valuable ancient references. In connection with Antioch, the analysis indicates a tension in the overall structure of Acts: According to Acts 11:19ff. it looks as if Gentiles were accepted into the church for the first time, which of course conflicts with ch 10. Still, it is possible to uncover the actual development. It was undoubtedly the hellenists who, on the basis of their attitude to the law, were prepared to accept Gentiles into the community; that began not only with Antioch. But Lk was especially interested in connecting this step with Peter and with the primitive church. Hence he moved the Cornelius account up in the outline of Acts. It is nevertheless possible to gather from his presentation that the first large community comprised of both Gentile and Jewish Christians existed in Antioch.

2. Attitude of the Christians in Jerusalem

Acts' portrayal of Christians in the public life is oddly conflicting. On the one hand, it speaks of persecution drives against Christians while, on the other hand, the progress in the community's expansion seems to be relatively undisturbed. In the accounts of the hostile measures against Christians, there is a distinct difference between the conduct of the authorities and the attitude of the people, or between the reaction of the Pharisees and that of the Sadducees. According to Acts 5, Gamaliel the Pharisee stands up for the release of the arrested apostles; there is a certain tension between this and the statement that Paul, the persecutor of Christians, had been a disciple of Gamaliel. The persecution undoubtedly played a considerable part. This is also pointed out in the persecution sayings in the Gospels (Mk 13:9ff.). The information about the extent, however, is contradictory. According to Acts 8:1-3 the persecution encompasses the whole community, while only the apostles are allowed to remain in the city; the public protest apparently is directed exclusively against the hellenists (outside of Palestine the action also targets only this group to begin with). In this connection one notices that the action in Damascus described in Acts 9 is considered to be organized by the Jewish council. Paul himself, however, depicts his activity as voluntary action out of "zeal." In any case, the Jewish council had no legal jurisdiction for the measures in Damascus.

In time the situation intensifies: During his administration of Jerusalem, between 41-44, Agrippa I takes action against the Christians. It was then that James, the son of Zebedee, was executed (Acts 12:1f.).

Some scholars argue that John, the son of Zebedee, was also executed at this time. This argument is predicated upon Mk 10:39, where Jesus announces the martyrdom of both sons of Zebedee, assuming that this is a case of vaticinium ex eventu. Should this assumption prove to be true, it would affect the dating of the Jerusalem council. In Gal 2:9 John is said to be present at the council. This would lead to the conclusion that the council was not held in 48 but, instead took place no later than 43, still during the administration of Agrippa. But Mk 10:39 in no wise purports that the martyrdom of James and of John had to be concurrent; whether or not the reference is to be construed as vaticinium ex eventu, that is, as "retrospective prophecy," is of no concern at all.

It is likely that Peter had to leave Jerusalem at a later time, while James was able to remain in the city until his execution in 62.

§ 65 *Hellenistic Christianity and the Beginning of Paul's Activity*

Bibliography: G. Bornkamm, *Paul*, ET 1971; W. Bousset, *Kyrios Christos. A History of the Belief in Christ from the Beginnings of Christianity to Irenaeus*, ET 1970, 69-152; R. Bultmann, *Theology of the NT*, ET 1951/55, I, 63-183; Chr. Burchard, *Der dreizehnte Zeuge. Traditions- und kompositionsgeschichtliche Untersuchungen zu Lukas' Darstellung der Frühzeit des Paulus*, FRLANT 103, 1970; G. Klein, "Der Synkretismus als theologisches Problem in der ältesten christlichen Apologetik," *Ges. Aufs.*, BEvTh 50, 1969, 262-301.

1. Pre-Pauline hellenistic Christianity

Based on the sources we know relatively little about the form of Christianity that Paul the Jew persecuted at first, then joined, and in which he finally developed his specific theology. There are no direct witnesses from pre-Pauline, hellenistic Christianity; for its reconstruction, therefore, one is dependent upon the Pauline letters and partly upon even later texts (Acts).

From the form-critical analysis of the letters of Paul we learn that in many instances Paul adopted statements belonging to pre-Pauline, hellenistic Christianity. The Christ hymn of Phil 2:6-11 (see pp. 97f., 177f. above) is a particularly obvious example.

Further significant for the reconstruction of pre-Pauline, hellenistic Christianity are expressions that are presented as obvious Christian expressions both in Pauline and non-Pauline writings, but which cannot be traced back to the primitive community of Jerusalem on account of their hellenistic coloring. A paradigm for continuity, as well as for the new beginning in the hellenistic-Christian theology, is the title κύριος given to Christ. When the Palestinian community speaks of Jesus as the "Lord" (cf. the cultic exclamation maranatha; see p. 101 above), it looks ahead to his future parousia in glory. The hellenistic community, which adopts this title, retains its traditional significance but expands its "scope of application." The κύριος is pre-existent, his incarnation occurs in a cosmic framework (Phil 2:6ff.). The acclamation κύριος Ἰησοῦς (1 Cor 12:3) becomes the foundation of the Christian worship service.

The organization of the church likewise continues to be simple in hellenistic Christianity. There is no supra-church leadership. Although the Jerusalem community continues to enjoy special recognition, its position is not established legally. This can be seen, among other things, in that Paul indeed maintains contact with it but does not acknowledge its superiority; neither is he apparently required to do so (cf. the process and result of the Apostolic Council; see § 66). The individual communities understand themselves as part of a church, but this unity is not demonstrated in an organizational union.

Occasionally it is argued that the early church knew a "twofold organization": The church as a whole was subject to a charismatic leadership through the apostles and prophets (cf. Eph 2:20, e.g.); the individual community, however, knew fixed offices (teachers, bishops, deacons; cf. 1 Cor 12:28; Phil 1:1). But 1 Cor 12 indicates that precisely the charismatic "offices" are associated with the individual community. Conversely the special status of the apostles and prophets had no organizational significance whatsoever.

2. Primitive Christianity as syncretistic religion

The beginning of Paul's public ministry within the church must be seen against this backdrop.

Prior to the recognition of the significance of the pre-Pauline, hellenistic community, Paul and his theology had consistently been compared directly with Jesus himself. Thus developed the tendency to distinguish the simple "religion" of Jesus from the "theology"—especially the "doctrine" of justification—of Paul, the former Pharisee. In addition one noticed that the proclamation of the historical Jesus had no part to play for Paul. The reason for this was seen in that the religious consciousness of Paul, his "personality," was interested in a Christ "mysticism"; by contrast, the historical Jesus was concerned with an "ethically" motivated "religion."

Suggested reading:

O. Pfleiderer (in: W. G. Kümmel, *The NT. The History of the Investigation of its Problems,* ET 1972, 207–210).

This aspect was not overcome until the history-of-religions school introduced the sociological aspect into the analysis of Pauline theology. It recognized that Paul was not original in the development of his basic theological thought; rather, essential expressions of his teaching were preformed in hellenistic Christianity in which he lived and worked after his commission. The exclusion of the proclamation of the historical Jesus from Christian teaching, for instance, was not only the work of Paul, rather Paul found that to be the pattern already in the hellenistic community. Its object of faith was not the historical Jesus and his proclamation, but the exalted Lord, the κύριος. The Christ myth was not created by Paul but by the hellenistic community. And the influence of hellenistic thought upon Christianity was not only made possible through Paul; rather, he himself found Christianity to be a syncretistic and hellenistically influenced product already.

There is a significant theological problem at the back of the argument, first formulated by H. Gunkel, that Christianity was a syncretistic religion: What does it mean for the Christian faith if Paul's expressions, in part, are not original at all but instead derive from the Jewish or hellenistic pagan environment? Does this not affect the "truth" of Christianity, of the Christian faith? If so, the truth (of faith) would be bound up with a historically demonstrable originality.

Primitive Christianity came into being upon the soil of Palestinian Judaism. The latter had adopted numerous non-Jewish concepts into its teaching, such as the belief in the resurrection of the dead, which probably originated in Iran. There is practically no evidence for this idea in the OT, and even later it still was subject to debate (see p. 130 above; cf. Acts 23:6f.). In early Christian theology or eschatology this became one of the decisive themes. Elements of form and content in the sacramental celebrations of primitive Christianity were influenced by the hellenistic mystery religions, as for instance the interpretation of baptism as a "dying together with Christ" as the cult deity (Rom 6). Likewise the communal celebration of the Lord's Supper as a sacramental meal was influenced by hellenistic ideas.

It would be wrong to attempt to view these elements as foreign to the nature of Christianity and hence to discard them. Rather, they are an intricate part of the Christian faith of that time and to that extent do not need to be interpreted any differently from other primitive Christian teaching. "Truth" of belief and historical originality are in no wise contingent upon one another. Rather, they exist upon two different levels. "The truth of Christianity, like that of any other religion or philosophy, is always a matter of personal decision, and the historian has no right to deprive any man of the responsibility" (Bultmann, *Primitive Christianity,* 11f.). In other words: Neither does originality prove nor does the recognition that Christianity is a syncretistic religion disprove the truth of the Christian faith. Therefore, faith does not need to defend itself against the historical knowledge that primitive Christianity has adopted certain expressions and elements of thought from other religions.

3. Reconstruction of the life and work of Paul based on his letters and on Acts

Any attempt to comprehend the life of Paul raises a methodological problem: Acts cannot be used as a primary source because it yields, in many instances, a tendentious presentation of the ministry of Paul and then colors it with a legendary hue; furthermore, its chronological references are incomplete. Yet the letters of Paul themselves do not make possible a complete reconstruction of the *vita Pauli* either. The only feasible attempt, therefore, is to present individual aspects.

(1) The year of Paul's birth is unknown. He does indeed refer to himself as an old man in Phlm 9, but that is a relative matter, of course. Acts mentions the Cilician provincial capital, Tarsus, as his place of birth. Paul himself does not divulge his place of birth; yet it is certainly possible that the reference to Tarsus is predicated upon an ancient tradition.

We learn only from Acts that Paul used the Jewish name Saul; in the letters he always identifies himself by the Greek (actually Latin) name Paul. But it was certainly common for Jews to have a double name in this fashion (cf. Col 4:11).

From 1 Thes 2:9 and 1 Cor 4:12 we are able to infer that Paul was an artisan (or perhaps a small businessman?). His missionary work presupposes the availability of considerable finances; yet he stresses that he did not become a financial burden to the communities (with the exception of Philippi: Phil 4:10ff.; cf. 2 Cor 11:8).

Little can be said about the general education of Paul. The city of Tarsus was a significant educational center. Nothing is apparent, however, of a philosophical education in the sense of the Greek educational tradition; the Jewish mindset is always in the foreground (one only needs to compare Rom 1f.). The famous speech on the Areopagus in Acts 17, with its explicit correlation with Stoic philosophy (17:28), is no testimony of Paul's education, for the speech is shaped by Luke (see p. 242f. above). Paul writes in a deliberate, non-literary Greek but does make use of some rhetorical artistry (see pp. 15, 160 above).

We also learn only little about Paul's theological education. The information of Acts 22:3 that he had been a student of Gamaliel I in Jerusalem is hardly reliable. But Paul himself explains in Phil 3:5 that he was a Pharisee. His letters indicate indeed that he is very much shaped by Jewish theology. This has primarily to do with the hellenistic Judaism of the Diaspora, of course; yet it is to be noted that the transitions between Palestinian and hellenistic Judaism were fluid (see p. 118f. above).

It is characteristic that Paul says something about his own person only when he deems that necessary in the context of a theological argument. Thus in Phil 3:5 he refers to himself as a Jew, a "Hebrew of Hebrews" (in this regard, cf. W. Gutbrod, TDNT III, 393; J. Gnilka, *Der Philipperbrief*, ad loc.), from the tribe of Benjamin, a Pharisee who was a persecutor of the church for the sake of the commandments of the Fathers (Phil 3:6; cf. Gal 1:13; 1 Cor 15:9). The reason for this self-presentation is the sharp polemic against the representatives of the circumcision (see p. 177f. above), thus, Paul here illustrates in his own person the value and, at the same time, the problem of a religion of works.

Paul says that as a Jew he fulfilled every condition of strict Judaism. Hence, his conversion did not liberate him from inner strife or from remorse. Rather, the opposite is true: His conversion liberated him from the outwardly fully legitimate pride in his own efforts. The sentence passed in Phil 3:7ff., therefore, is in no sense the necessary consequence of a ruined life; rather, it denotes the reversal of the value structure that he had recognized thus far.

(2) Paul sketches his fortunes and accomplishments following his commission in 2 Cor 11f., where some of the expressions are particularly notable. Paul has visions (2 Cor 12:1ff.); in his "revelations" he receives concrete instructions (Gal 2:2) or answers to concrete requests (2 Cor 12:8f.). However, Paul rejects the notion of making such experiences the topic of his proclamation or of according them a special ability to legitimize the truth of his teaching (cf. 2 Cor 12:1, 11). On the contrary: From 2 Cor 10:10; 11:6 we learn that he was blamed for being an insufficiently qualified pneumatic because he was lacking in eloquent rhetoric. Hence when he points to his special qualities in his counter-move, he does so with the explicit intent not to laud himself but to defend polemically the issue he stands for, namely, the gospel.

The reference in 1 Cor 15:1–11, recounting the "seeing" of the risen Lord that was granted to him personally, serves the same purpose. This is the appropriate introduction to the chapter on the theology of the resurrection.

According to 2 Cor 12:12, Paul has the gift of performing miracles (in this regard, cf. 2 Cor 12:9f.); likewise he has the gift of speaking in tongues (1 Cor 14:18)—without wanting to attribute special significance to it, of course (v 19). Quite mysterious is 2 Cor 12:7, which points to a physical affliction. What kind of sickness it was cannot be recognized. At any rate, "medical" attempts at determining it remain pure speculation.

In 1 Cor 9:1 and 15:8 Paul mentions his calling; in addition, he names the location Damascus in Gal 1:16f., but he does not relate what happened there. For this reason the accounts of Acts, with its tendency to color in the details, clearly prove to be secondary. This circumstance has concrete consequences for the interpretation of the conversion or of the commission: It is wrong to inquire into Paul's personal experience on the way to Damascus. Rather, what needs to be crystallized is the objective content of the experience. Outside of Damascus Paul becomes an adherent to and defender of the Gentile mission which is free from the law.

(3) The details of Paul's commission, therefore, remain obscure. In Gal 1:11f., 15ff., he himself emphasizes strongly that his commissioning to be a missionary to the Gentiles came directly from the Lord and, hence, not through human mediation or by means of a subsequent, intellectual explanation of his experience. Rather, his conversion was synonymous with the commission to be an apostle.

Hypothetically the commission may be construed as follows: Paul persecuted Jewish Christians who were liberated from the ceremonial law, that is to say, he already knew of Christianity which was free from the law. When Christ himself thwarted this persecution (in what form this happened, remains open), it signified to him that God aligned himself with the crucified Jesus and, at the same time, that the freedom from the law which the Christians practiced was endorsed by God. Consequently the law could no longer be viewed as the condition for salvation. But in this case salvation was not only for the Jews but for all mankind—and thus Paul had his task.

We know little about the initial phase of his ministry as apostle. According to Gal 1:17 he went to Arabia immediately after his commission. But this does not mean that he went into the "desert," hoping there to work through his experience by meditation. "Arabia" is not the desert, but the territory of the Arabic Nabataeans. The notion that the Nabataeans took certain measures against Paul, as 2 Cor 11:32 implies, is only plausible under the assumption that he was active as a missionary there. However, no traces of this mission have been preserved. According to Gal 1:18f. (cf. Acts 9:26ff.), Paul then travels to Jerusalem, followed by his labor in Syria and Cilicia (Gal 1:21). He bypasses the matter of how he arrived at Antioch and what he did there (in contrast, cf. Acts 11:25ff.; 13:1–3). Yet, his position there does not seem to have been insignificant, for together with Barnabas he is a delegate of this community at the Apostolic Council. In Jerusalem he is acknowledged as *the* representative of the mission to the Gentiles.

It is striking that we have no extant Pauline letters from the time prior to the Apostolic Council. The information handed down by Luke in Acts 13f., appears to be the only—though secondary—source for this part of the Pauline mission. One hypothesis that departs from the common chronology of Paul is developed by G. Lüdemann, *Paul:*

Apostle to the Gentiles, ET 1988: During the thirteen years mentioned in Gal 2:1 Paul had already been active as a missionary in Greece. The writing of 1 Thes occurs during the time prior to the council. For a critique of this argument, cf. A. Linde-mann, *ZKG* 92, 1981, 344–349.

(4) In addition to Paul's own references, Acts contains further information; however, it is difficult to distinguish between what is reliable, what comes from ancient tradition, and what is legendary.

Acts informs us, for instance, that Paul had grown up in Jerusalem (22:3) and had relatives there (23:16). But these references may well be reflective of Luke's endeavor to show Paul's association with Jews closely connected with Jerusalem.

Later on, Jerome even knows that Paul's family originally came from Gishala in Gal-ilee and from there emigrated to Tarsus.

We are further told that Paul was a citizen not only of Tarsus (21:39), but, more importantly, from his birth he also was a citizen of Rome (22:28). Most scholars consider this to be a reliable reference. Such dual citizenship was indeed possible (see p. 116f. above), but at least on the basis of 2 Cor 11:23–25, it is very unlikely. In any case, Paul himself does not mention his cit-izenship anywhere.

Acts indicates his profession as "tent making," which would correlate with Tarsus being an important center for the textile industry (18:3; the meaning of the rare term σκηνοποιός is not clear; it could also mean leather worker). This too remains uncertain, of course.

Like Paul himself, Acts reports of his active participation in the persecu-tion of Christians. According to Acts 7:58 he began such in Jerusalem itself, but if this were the case he would probably have been known "personally" by the churches in Judea, which he denies categorically in Gal 1:22.

As stops subsequent to his commission (see above), Acts mentions a brief involvement as proclaimer in Damascus, followed by a first journey to Je-rusalem and the community there (9:26), and the withdrawal to Tarsus, con-cerning which no details are given (9:30). The stay in Tarsus is clearly construed as a pause (cf. 9:30 with 11:25; against it Gal 1:21). Later Bar-nabas finds Paul in Tarsus and takes him to Antioch, and together they undertake the "first missionary journey" (Acts 13f.).

Quite incidentally, during this journey Lk changes the apostle's name: "Saul" be-comes "Paul." This "change" of name (see p. 356 above) is in no way connected with his commission, but occurs merely in external association with the name of the gov-ernor, Sergius Paulus (Acts 13:9).

The success of this first journey, namely, the founding of purely Gentile-Christian communities, presents the problem of the law as virulent. Hence the story-line of Acts follows this incident with the Apostolic Council, where this problem is discussed and solved.

§ 66   Apostolic Council

Bibliography: M. Dibelius, "The Apostolic Council," in *Studies in the Acts of the Apostles*, ET 1956, 93–101; G. Klein, "Gal 2:6–9 und die Geschichte der Jerusalemer Urgemeinde,": *Ges. Aufs.*, BEvTh 50, 1969, 99–128; W. G. Kümmel, "Die älteste Form des Aposteldekrets," *Ges. Aufs.*, 1965, 278–288.

Preliminary Remark

The essentials regarding the intrinsic problems of dating the council, have already been addressed in § 60. Gal 2 is the primary source for its process and result. While Paul's presentation of the events is recognizably tendentious and polemical, it is nevertheless possible to begin by saying that it was necessary for Paul to relate the external facts with exactitude precisely in order to not play down the value of his argumentation with the Galatians. For this reason Acts 15 as a secondary source is to be corrected throughout, based on Gal 2.

However, it remains a matter of debate whether or not Lk used a literary source in Acts 15.

1. Occasion and course of the council

(1) The problem that occasioned the council, was brought about by the mission to the Gentiles. The pivotal question was: Must Gentiles acknowledge the claims of the Jewish law as necessary for salvation, hence adopt the law before they can be eligible for baptism?

In favor of this claim it was possible to point to the salvation-history connection between the church and Israel and to the continued importance of the OT in the church. And Acts 15:1 and Gal 2:4 indicate that this understanding was indeed advocated in the church. On the other hand, without theological reflection upon this situation it is necessary to recall that the Gentile-Christian communities were initially free from the law.

For Paul, the claim of freedom from the law was not made imperative because of practical missions considerations. Rather, for him it arose directly from his understanding of the event of salvation (see p. 363 below): God grants man salvation unconditionally; the only "condition" is faith, that is, the acceptance of the offer of salvation. If keeping the law were declared to be a further condition for salvation, "Christ would have died for nothing" (Gal 2:21).

(2) According to his own presentation in Gal 2—and that, as he points out emphatically, on account of a revelation—Paul, together with Barnabas, comes to Jerusalem. Thereby he stresses his independence, which does not rule out, by the way, that he is the official delegate of the Antiochan community, as presented in Acts 15:2f. Paul takes along Titus, the Gentile Christian (who is not mentioned in Acts, although he was very important to Paul). Since the latter was not forced to be circumcised in Jerusalem, this meant

that the Gentile Christians' freedom from the law was acknowledged; it was probably Paul's intent to demonstrate this (cf. Gal 2:3). Against the protests of the "false brothers," an agreement is reached in Jerusalem between Paul and the three "pillars." In this connection, the role of Barnabas remains undetermined (in 2:9 he is mentioned as well, but not in 2:6).

(3) The Apostolic Council served not only to acknowledge Paul's missions endeavor, but also his apostolate.

Nevertheless, his account raises several questions:

(a) To begin with, the text of Gal 2:1ff. poses problems; some manuscripts read in v 5: "for the moment we gave in," which in conjunction with v 3 could mean that while Titus was not immediately "forced" to be circumcised, he consented to it of "his own volition." However, this assertion would contradict the flow of the account as a whole. Furthermore, the external attestation of this reading is poor, so that it may not be appropriate to ascribe any claim of originality to it.

(b) It is not clear why Paul emphasizes so strongly that he was not concerned about what "they," namely, the "pillars," were "formerly." Was the authority of the companions of Jesus played off against the new-comer Paul in Galatia? Or did those in Jerusalem at first attempt to pressure Paul with this argument?

(c) Why does Paul expressly write in v 6 that no further obligations were imposed upon him? Did others claim that the council agreed to more than Paul wanted to admit, for instance, the apostolic decree which Paul does not even mention (see below)?

(d) What is the significance of the division of labor between Peter and Paul? Is it to be understood geographically, in the sense that Peter was responsible for Palestine, whereas Paul was responsible for the rest of the world? In practical terms this is hardly conceivable and, furthermore, conflicts with the fact that Peter comes to Antioch later (Gal 2:11ff.). Or is the division meant objectively: Peter is to be responsible for the Jews and Paul for the Gentiles in the whole world? But this is not practically feasible either; furthermore, Paul engages in missions among the Jews as well. This agreement apparently is only intended to express the equality of the mission to the Gentiles alongside that among the Jews; probably no organizational principle should be sought behind it.

(e) What is the function of the collection mentioned in Gal 2:10 (cf. 2 Cor 8f.)? Some exegetes interpret it to mean that Paul thereby officially acknowledged Jerusalem's primacy of position as the location of the church. For Paul, however, it is strictly a token of the church's unity and not an element of "the church's right" (on this, see p. 366).

(4) Additional problems arise because the Acts account differs from the Pauline presentation at several points. Acts depicts it as if the council were occasioned by Judaistic opposition in Antioch. According to its account, the council's participants were the apostles (Gal speaks only of the three

"pillars"), plus the elders, as well as "the whole church assembly" (Acts 15:12). Paul and Barnabas merely play a passive role; their account of God's mighty deeds among the Gentiles is mentioned, but its specific content is not rendered. The decision in favor of the Gentile mission apart from the law is brought about by the votes of James and Peter. In this connection the argument is used that the law is an unbearable burden which ought not to be imposed upon the Gentiles. This perspective is non-Jewish, however (and non-Pauline: Paul does not reject the law because it is difficult to keep but because the way of works of the law, as the way of salvation, is erroneous). Finally, it is striking that the collection for Jerusalem in conjunction with the Apostolic Council is ignored and is only mentioned in passing in 24:17, while conversely the "apostolic decree," which Paul fails to mention, takes center stage in Acts.

2. Apostolic decree

The "apostolic decree" (Acts 15:23–29) is the cardinal problem of the Acts account of the council, objectively as well as historically. In terms of Paul's presentation, this decree cannot have been issued by the council, for, according to Gal 2:6 Gentiles have been excused from any obligations. But when did it originate, then? Could it be that it does not represent a meeting of the minds between Paul (i.e., the community of Antioch) and the pillars? Could it possibly be a one-sided claim made by those from Jerusalem? These questions cannot be answered independently of the text tradition. The decree has been handed down in two very distinctly divergent forms: According to one form, it contained certain *cultic* stipulations, such as the minimal obligations for non-Jews that began to make it possible for Jews to live together with Gentiles (they are the stipulations of Lev 17f.; cf. also Billerbeck II, 729–739). According to the other form, the decree contained *ethical* obligations. How are these two forms of the text to be assessed?

Apparently the "ethical" form of the decree, which has been handed down in the "Western" text, originated later than the "cultic" one, namely, at a time when the church was de facto already Gentile-Christian. It no longer needed the cultic stipulations and by then no longer understood their meaning. Yet it is probable that the cult-oriented decree likewise did not come from an early phase in the history of the church. The issues of this decree—sacrifices to idols, fornication—are discussed, by Paul in 1 Cor, without even mentioning the decree. This means: Either Paul did not know this decree, i.e., it did not exist at this time, or Paul does indeed know about its existence but does not recognize it, i.e., at least for him it did not have any canonical relevance.

Otherwise H. Lietzmann: The conflicts in Corinth came about precisely because of their acquaintance with the decree. But then one would expect Paul to mention it all the more.

The "decree" probably originated in a mixed Jewish-Christian/Gentile-Christian context, and that obviously precisely because the problem of the direct association of Jews with Gentiles in a Christian community was *not* solved by means of the council's decision concerning the division of the mission territories and concerning the mission to the Gentiles apart from the law. One may even assume that this association at any rate became a problem only as a result of the Jerusalem decision. Whereas Jews and Gentiles were apparently able to be members of the same community without complications until then, now the Jewish Christians could be obligated to strict adherence of the law. Only thereby did they encounter the conflict of how they were to conduct themselves over against the Gentiles in the community. A strict interpretation of the decision that Gentile Christians were not to adopt the law, while Jewish Christians were not to abolish it, could make living together a practical impossibility for both groups—surely not a consequence that Paul desired.

How is one to explain the contradictions between Gal 2 and Acts 15? How do the two presentations relate to one another in terms of content? The Acts portrait that shows Paul and Barnabas as the recipients of a mandate is quite obviously Lukan; it is Luke's intention to accord the prime position to the primitive church. The further development indicates that, in reality, Paul was recognized as equal. This confirms the argument that Paul's account is perhaps more in keeping with the actual events than the Acts account.

One may ask whether the decision of Jerusalem was not—from Paul's view at any rate—an inconsequential compromise. Is it in keeping with Pauline theology when the validity of the law was nevertheless recognized for Jewish Christians? Based on the doctrine of justification, would Paul not have had to demand freedom from the law for Jewish Christians as well?

For Paul the appropriation of salvation occurs *sola gratia*, that is, everyone is called for who he is; he does not have to produce any prior effort whatsoever. The Gentiles does not have to become a Jew; conversely, however, the Jew must not relinquish his Jewishness, even as a Christian, but may maintain both circumcision and the essence of the demands of the law. It is true for the Jew as well, of course, that the law as a means of salvation is out of the question (cf. 1 Cor 9:19–23). From this vantage point the decision reached at the council is indeed not a compromise as far as Paul is concerned, but the full theological consequence of the understanding of faith.

Suggested exercise:

Undertake a text-critical reconstruction of the two forms of the "apostolic decree" in Acts 15:23–29. What essential function does the decree have in both forms?

Tool: E. Haenchen, *Acts*, 468–472.

§ 67 Paul and the Pauline Communities

Bibliography: D. Georgi, *Die Geschichte der Kollekte des Paulus für Jerusalem*, ThF 38, 1965; B. Holmberg, *Paul and Power: The Structure of Authority in the Primitive Church as Reflected in the Pauline Epistles*, 1980; W.-H. Ollrog, *Paulus und seine Mitarbeiter*, WMANT 50, 1979; E. Schweizer, *Church Order in the NT*, ET 1961, 89–112.

1. Basic features of the Pauline mission

(1) We know far more about Paul's public ministry after the council than about the first phase of his missionary activity. The (authentic) Pauline letters serve as our primary sources, while Acts once again serves as secondary source which is almost exclusively concerned with Paul from 15:35 to the end.

In this time frame one generally distinguishes between the second and third missionary journeys (15:40–18:22; 18:23–19:40 or 21:17); but even in Acts the separation between the two journeys can barely be recognized—and the division into "missionary journeys" has no essential significance anyhow (see p. 243 above).

The Acts account is incomplete; it focuses extensively upon Paul alone, thus making his fellow workers appear as mere afterthoughts. Although the latter frequently labor quite independently, as one is able to learn from the Pauline letters, Acts completely ignores their activity outside of the large centers. For instance, the mission and the establishing of communities in the Lycus valley (Colossae) is not mentioned in Acts. Particularly striking is the fact that a co-worker as important as Titus is not mentioned at all in Acts.

Likewise the missionary activity of Paul himself is simplified in Acts. Thus the negotiations that Paul carries on with the Corinthian community during his Ephesian stay (cf. the Corinthian correspondence) is not mentioned at all; the founding of the Galatian communities is only hinted at (on this problem see § 25 above). We learn nothing about the internal crises that we know about from the Pauline letters (Corinth, Galatia).

(2) The missions presentation in Acts follows a fixed pattern: In every town Paul enters, he first of all turns to the Jews and preaches in the synagogue. Only then does he go to the Gentiles—as reaction to the Jews' rejection of his message. In its essence this presentation may well be in line with the actual events: The Jews and their sympathizers (proselytes and "God fearers") likely were the initial converts to Christianity outside of Palestine as well. But in Luke's presentation, his salvation-history program is the backdrop for this strategy of Paul's: Salvation is proclaimed to the Gentiles because the Jews have not accepted it (cf. Acts 13:46 and the close of the book).

In Acts Paul is presented as a man who earns his livelihood with manual labor. This agrees with Paul's own references but is nevertheless inaccurate in its generalized form presupposed in Acts. We learn from the letters that in certain instances Paul did indeed accept support from the community (cf. 1 Thes 2:9; 1 Cor 4:17; 9:1ff.; Acts 18:3 with Phil 4:10ff., on the one hand, and with 2 Cor 11:7ff. on the other). One might ask whether Luke had no information to this effect, or whether he ignored it intentionally.

It is sometimes argued in scholarship that Paul was an apocalyptic, as indicated by the method of his missionary activity. Under the pressure of the parousia which he believes to be imminent, he scurries across the countries in order to reach the uttermost parts of the inhabited earth with his mission before the end of the world. Rom 15:28, for instance, is cited as evidence. But Paul actually indicates no such thing—quite the contrary is true. It is typical that Paul indeed allows for time in his mission; for instance, he remains in the same city for more than a year (Corinth, Ephesus).

His mission strategy can be reconstructed indirectly: He enters especially the major cities; there he works until the community is able to exist (and evangelize) on its own (cf. 1 Cor 16:19; 2 Cor 1:1; 1 Thes 1:8, as well as Phlm and Col).

(3) On the whole one may follow the presentation of Acts 15–20 for the historical sequence of events; in many instances, however, a critique based on the Pauline letters is necessary. For instance, the Acts presentation of the events between the mission to Thessalonica and the one to Corinth differs from Paul's account in 1 Thes. According to Acts 17f. Paul left Thessalonica after a brief stay, because of a tumult, and travelled alone, without his companions Silas and Timothy, via Berea and Athens to Corinth. Over against this, the situation in the Thessalonian community, as far as can be ascertained from 1 Thes, allows for the assumption that Paul may have stayed in the city longer than only three weeks. Furthermore, Paul writes in 1 Thes 3 that he sent Timothy back to Thessalonica from Athens; in other words, contrary to the Acts presentation, the latter must have accompanied Paul all the same. (In addition, cf. the account concerning the mission to Philippi, Acts 16:12ff. with the statements of Phil; on this, see p. 174f. above).

But then there are also extensive agreements between Acts and the letters of Paul. Acts 18:2 reports that Paul had met Aquila and Priscilla in Corinth (cf. 1 Cor 16:19). They were not baptized by Paul (cf. 1 Cor 1:14ff.), which means that they were Christians already before Paul came to Corinth. Therefore, Paul was not the first one to bring Christianity to Corinth, but he was the founder of the local Christian *community* (cf. 1 Cor 3:6ff.; 4:15).

The Asia Minor city of Ephesus was a further mission center. In broad presentation Acts 19 reports of events which threaten the safety of Paul; this too agrees with Paul's own references (1 Cor 15:32; 2 Cor 1:8). Nevertheless, the danger does not appear to be as serious according to the description in Acts as it is for Paul. Yet even in Acts the actual situation still shines through indirectly (20:17ff.): On his last journey to Jerusalem Paul meets with the representatives of the Ephesian community in Miletus, which means that he apparently either cannot or is no longer allowed to enter Ephesus.

Suggested exercise:

Compare the Acts pericope of 19:1–21:17 with the presentation in 2 Cor (2:1; 12:14; 13:1). The outline of the itinerary is identical in both instances, but it is simplified in Acts.

Acts 20:1ff. speaks of Paul's last visit to Corinth. Following that he wants to travel to Jerusalem with the collection that has been completed in the meantime (cf. 2 Cor 8f.), and subsequent to that he plans to travel to Spain (Rom 15:24). However, Paul is imprisoned in Jerusalem and is moved to Caesarea, the residence of the Roman procurator, from where he is handed over to Rome two years later.

In Rome Paul was executed. The Acts account of Paul's final days must be approached guardedly. The account of the voyage to Rome is highly legendary; the presentation of his stay in Rome may not agree with the actual circumstances either. It is particularly striking that Acts has nothing to say about Paul's death, although it knows about it (cf. the farewell address in Miletus which is clearly shaped as a "testament" in 20:17ff.; on this, see p. 210f. above).

At this point we again need to mention the hypothesis that initially Paul had been released from his Roman imprisonment and then travelled to Spain in keeping with his original plans. This argument does not fit into what we know of Paul from the sources known to us (on the detail, see p. 205f. above).

2. Nature and polity of the church

(1) One of the foundational elements of the Pauline concept of the church can be demonstrated on the basis of the collection for the poor in Jerusalem, which is gathered in the Pauline communities as a result of the Apostolic Council. This collection is not merely a charitable deed, but a reflection of the idea of the church: In all its communities, the church is one unit, hence all of its members practice solidarity among themselves. At the same time the collection indicates that Paul maintains the relationship, in terms of the history of salvation, of the entire church (including the Gentile-Christian communities) with Israel, though without linking this relationship with a juridical understanding of the primitive community as a kind of final ecclesiastical authority. The argument that this collection was a type of church dues is untenable in the first place because it was a one-time gift and not a regular tribute (cf. Rom 15:25f.; 2 Cor 8f.).

(2) The organization and social composition of the Pauline communities cannot be reconstructed from Acts. As indicated in the Pauline letters, there were no "elders" in the communities (otherwise the presentation in Acts 14:23; 20:17); there was no supra-church organization. Paul consistently understands the church as a unity, but this unity is not produced and secured by legal means. In the communities he does indeed have apostolic authority, but every time he has to regain his authority with respect to each issue he advocates. Hence he can never appeal in his letters to a juridically fixed position or demand the recognition of such from the communities.

Yet there certainly are "offices" within the communities: Apostles, prophets, and teachers (1 Cor 12:28), or bishops and deacons (Phil 1:1). But this has to do with a charismatic order of offices: It is the Spirit who leads and builds up the church, just as, conversely, every contribution to the upbuilding of the church is understood as the work of the Spirit.

The either/or debate of whether the church is ordered by the Spirit or by ecclesiastical law (controversy between R. Sohm and A. v. Harnack; see p. 337 above) is therefore fallacious from the start. The Spirit himself works justice, according to primitive Christian understanding; the pneumatic contributes something to the upbuilding directly and thereby also to the structure of the church.

From the Corinthian letters we gain some information concerning the social makeup of the communities. 1 Cor 1:26ff. indicates that the members of the church come primarily from the lower strata; it is said of the Macedonian communities that they were very poor (2 Cor 8:2).

In principle, the question of slavery was no problem: Both slave and slave owner could belong to the Christian community without having to change their social status (cf. the problem of Phlm; on this, see § 30). When 1 Cor 1:16 speaks of a "household," it presumably includes the slaves as well (cf. 1 Cor 7:21ff.); an important piece of evidence is the list of greetings in Rom 16 which contains several names typical of slaves.

The reason for this relative indifference to the social conditions is eschatological: Being part of, or not being part of a societal group does not bear upon salvation. Therefore Paul does not develop a theologically or Christian motivated social program; but at the same time he rejects categorically any Christian eschatology that results in a withdrawal from the world's problems. The entire letter of 1 Cor is concerned with the enthusiastic retreat from the world, for eschatological and mystical reasons, as propagated in Corinth. Specifically Paul is not decreeing that the daily problems of Christian existence in the world are irrelevant; rather, he addresses these problems and seeks to clarify them. An example of this is the pericope of 1 Cor 7:1-17 dealing with the issue of marriage or divorce. The remarkable objectivity and realism with which the subject is addressed is striking here. A theologically exaggerated glorification of marriage has as little place as does hostility to sexuality for which Paul is frequently blamed.

The paraenetic sections of the letters of Paul indicate that the content of Christian ethics conforms largely with the average ethics of Judaism and of hellenistic popular philosophy; Rom 12:3ff. and Phil 4:8 particularly serve as examples. What is new in Christian ethics is not to be found in its message, but in its christological and eschatological foundation (cf. Rom 12f.; 1 Cor 7:31): Ethics is the consequence of the gift of salvation in Christ, not its prerequisite.

This tendency is seen both in the disposition on the question of slavery and in the non-ideological statement about the state (Rom 13). It would be wrong to attempt to read the basic elements of a Christian doctrine of government out of Rom 13. In Paul's situation under the domain of the emperor Nero at the beginning of the second half of the first century, the argument of Rom 13 represented a reasonable and pertinent answer to the question of what ought to be and may be the Christian's relationship to the authority of the state. In no wise must it be overlooked that Rom 13 does not represent the juridically fixed relationship of a fully developed church to the authority of a state that is intent on preserving Christianity as a moral agent supporting the state. Rather, this text presupposes in principle that the disposition of Christians to the authorities was to accord with that which may be expected of everyone (cf. 13:1).

1 Cor 8–10 provides a particularly interesting glimpse into the problem of the existence of Christian communities in a pagan environment. In antiquity civil life is linked directly with the religious forms of life. For Christians this leads to the question of whether they were to reject these life patterns inwardly while, at the same time, accepting them outwardly, or whether they were also to examine their civil existence on the basis of their attitude towards pagan religion. Paul's argumentation shows that there were divergent viewpoints in the community on this issue and that his own position quite obviously was not entirely firm either.

Suggested reading:

E. Käsemann, "Grundsätzliches zur Interpretation von Röm 13," *Ges. Aufs.* II, 204–222; W. Meeks, *The First Urban Christians*, 1983; W. Schrage, *Die Christen und der Staat nach dem Neuen Testament*, 1971; H. v. Soden, "Sakrament und Ethik bei Paulus," in *Das Paulusbild in der neueren deutschen Forschung*, [2]1969, 338–379; G. Theissen, *The Social Setting of Pauline Christianity*, ET 1982, esp. 27–174.

§ 68 Establishing Paul's Theology

Preliminary remark:

It cannot be the task of this book to delineate and develop in detail Paul's theological position. Such a presentation in brief would be necessarily incomplete and would raise more questions than it is able to answer. We refer, therefore, to the presentations of Pauline theology, especially as found in the various theologies of the NT.

R. Bultmann, *Theology of the NT*, ET 1951/55, I, 185–352 (bibliography!); H. Conzelmann, *An Outline of the Theology of the NT*, ET 1969, 155–286; W. G. Kümmel, *The Theology of the NT According to its Major Witnesses: Jesus—Paul—John*, ET 1973, 137–254; E. Lohse, *Grundriss der neutestamentlichen Theologie*, Theologische Wissenschaft 5, ³1984, 74–111; K. H. Rengstorf (ed.), *Das Paulusbild in der neueren deutschen Forschung*, Wege der Forschung 24, ³1982.

It is the purpose of this chapter to point to ways and means by which the basic theological assertions in the Pauline letters—and thus the basic features of Pauline theology—can be ascertained. In this context it is presupposed that this task is itself already theology. In other words, it does not suffice to establish the historical, exegetical situation; instead, it is important to show the essential import of the reconstructed assertion. It is not permissible to stop with the question: What did Paul mean by faith? What did Paul mean by freedom? etc., but one has to continue with the question: What *is* faith, freedom, given the exegetically established theological position of Paul? In this regard, it is important to guard against the fallacy of wanting to discover in the time-conditioned "shell" of the Pauline argumentation something like a timeless "kernel" which is to be ascertained and translated into contemporary theology. Theological statements are only meaningful when they are historically tied to their respective milieu; in other words, it is not possible to have the kernel without the shell. Hence it is necessary to ask why Paul presents a particular issue in this particular way and not in any other, and why he argues in precisely this manner and not in another.

This also applies especially to problems in the history of religions. It is not sufficient to note that Paul interprets baptism in Rom 6 by means of some categories that he borrowed from the mystery religions. Rather, one has to ask: Why does Paul do this? What functions do these categories have in his teaching on baptism as a whole?

There are a variety of ways to establish Paul's theology. For one, it is possible to begin with the Jewish assumptions, similar to establishing the teaching of Jesus (§ 52): Which aspects of faith does Paul retain from Judaism? Which does he discard? What does he reconstruct? What could possibly be so commonplace for him that he does not see a need to address it in detail at all? Conversely, which theological assertions are completely new over against those from the OT and from contemporary Judaism?

Examples: Among the issues that Paul takes as given because of their historical relationship with Israel are the doctrine of God, the recognition of the authority of the Bible, the idea of Israel's election, and the anticipation of the resurrection of the dead. He only needs to delineate these issues specifically when he intends to invest them with a particular emphasis in conjunction with Christian teaching (classical examples: 1 Thes 4f.; 1 Cor 15; Rom 9–11).

On the other hand, certain theological notions and concepts that are of fundamental importance for Paul have no OT tradition behind them, such as the idea of freedom or the notion of conscience. Yet both concepts play a significant role in Jewish-hellenistic theology and in philosophy (cf., e.g., Philo's thought). Here one has to ask: Where does the Pauline understanding of these concepts come from? What functions do they have in the framework of his theology?

And finally a third possibility: Paul reshapes Jewish concepts. For instance, he adopts the traditional Jewish assertion that God is wise and just. But he furnishes it with a new form, predicated upon the Christian confession: God has revealed himself on the cross, that is to say, Christ is the wisdom of God, Christ is the righteousness of God. This is the essential foundation for his doctrine of justification, and thereby Christology becomes the key for Pauline theology.

This method of beginning with the Jewish assumptions and from there pointing up the peculiarities of Pauline theology is methodologically possible and necessary. A different approach is crucial, however: It is possible to recognize that Paul begins his theology with the Christian confession. This is meant literally: The form-critical analysis shows that in many instances Paul delineates his ideas in conjunction with the confession of faith (cf. the basis of 1 Cor 15:3ff.: Christ died and has been raised; cf. Rom 10:9). The decisive question is *how* Paul interprets this confession. Two positions are juxtaposed: According to A. Schweitzer, Paul's theology is determined by the notion of being "in Christ" (Schweitzer's term: Christ myth). This formula does indeed play such an important part in Paul (cf. Rom 6:11, 23) that one has to inquire into its essential meaning in Pauline theology as a whole. But R. Bultmann, for instance, argues that this was not Paul's central assertion. He is of the opinion that the doctrine of justification is the center of Pauline theology; thereby the Christian confession relates to the existence in the world of those justified. This position, which was also held by the Reformers, has been criticized, however, by pointing out that Paul's teaching of justification in reality was merely an apologetic against the narrowing of the idea of grace in Judaism; since its support in fact comes only from Gal and Rom, it can in no wise be considered as the basis of Pauline theology.

Suggested exercise:

The following question is the methodological paradigm for determining the key to Pauline theology: Does Paul interpret the confession in the direction of the Christ myth? Or does he relate it to justification? With these questions in mind, analyze Rom 3:21ff.; 4:25ff. on the one hand, and Phil 3:2-14 on the other hand.

It is undoubtedly correct that the concept of the doctrine of justification by no means occurs in all of the Pauline letters; the Corinthian letters, for instance, are almost devoid of any reference to it. But it is to be noted that it is not sufficient merely to rely on the term's statistical findings. More important and ultimately decisive is the question of the dominant understanding of God and man in all of Paul's theology. It becomes apparent, then, that the doctrine of justification in Rom and Gal designates the exact same relationship between God and man, and the same destiny of man in this world, as the theology of the cross in the Corinthian letters.

This essential position represents the pivotal point for all of Paul's theology. In the *doctrine of God* which he assumes from Judaism, Paul establishes a corresponding emphasis: God is the Father of Jesus Christ, i.e., the Father of the crucified one. Thus the understanding of God has received a new quality in that it stands itself as critique of works-oriented religion.

Paul's *Christology* is predicated upon confession, just as also is the orientation of faith in the resurrected one (and not in the historical Jesus); furthermore, the anticipation of the parousia and the idea of the pre-existence of Christ are also presupposed. While Paul adopts these christological assertions, he does not treat them as equally important but places the emphasis clearly upon the idea of the cross (cf. Phil 2:6–11; on this, see p. 97f. above). In general it may be said that Paul did not further develop the presuppositional aspect of Christology (via further expansion of the notion of pre-existence, e.g.), but that he understands Christology as interpretation of human existence (cf. 1 Cor 1f.).

Suggested exercise:

It is not the confession of faith that is contested between Paul and the Corinthian community (1 Cor 15:1ff.), but the interpretation varies, indeed, is juxtaposed. The Corinthians interpret it in terms of enthusiasm: We follow the exalted one in his ascent. But Paul underscores: We know the exalted one only as the crucified one (cf. 1 Cor 1:2). Faith does not call us to a mystical ascent into heaven, but holds us securely in the world. Ch 15 in its entirety can be interpreted on this premise.

The *ecclesiology* is not developed along theoretical lines. But from the term ἐκκλησία it can be deduced that the unity of the church is understood dialectically. Plural and singular are used so as to clarify that the individual community is not subordinate to the church as a whole but represents the latter, as it were (cf. p. 344f. above). This aspect is also the premise for the typically Pauline concept of the church as the body of Christ (cf. 1 Cor 12).

His *soteriology* and *anthropology* are particularly good examples of Paul's theological endeavor. Certain soteriological interpretations of the death of Jesus were already available to him, as in the Lord's Supper tradition, for instance: Jesus died as propitiatory sacrifice; his death was a substitutionary sacrifice, or a covenant sacrifice for the forgiveness of sins (Rom 3:25; cf. 1 Cor 11:24f.). Yet Paul sees the limits of the notion of sacrifice: The latter leaves the redemptive event in the past and its scope is limited in showing how salvation determines the present—for instance with the aid of such ideas as the renewal of the covenant or of the new covenant people. Paul is not concerned only with the eradication of the past ("forgiveness of past sins"; plural!), but with the liberation from sin in the present (singular!), in view of man's future. It is for this reason that Paul emphasizes the proclamational character of the salvific event so strongly: Justification and reconciliation procured in Christ are becoming reality today through the word that proclaims reconciliation to man (cf. especially 2 Cor 5:11–6:10).

It is characteristic for Pauline anthropology that man is always found in certain relations. Man is God's creature. But at the same time he is subjected to sin and thus doomed to die (the key word σάρξ is the typical term to characterize this state of affairs). For Paul, "sin" or "flesh" represent supra-personal powers from which man is not capable of delivering himself because any attempt at self-liberation is caught up in the sphere of σάρξ from the start. Man can gain freedom only through God's gracious deed and through the gift of the Spirit. Grace bestows justification and the Spirit bestows the power for a new life in freedom that is concretely: the possibility of love. The only precondition for this is faith, which receives justification and thus leads into the new life.

Suggested exercises:

What theological-systematic place does *eschatology* have in Paul? Does Paul take his orientation from apocalyptic images? What is the relationship between the eschatological and christological assertions?

Note: Eschatology is faced with the same problem found in all endeavors to render doctrines and conceptions objective: It seeks to grasp the future by means of an image of the future, in other words, it explains things future and other-worldly through images of the present and this-worldly. However, eschatology can be understood radically only when any attempt at objectivizing is relinquished and is replaced with a total absence of visualization, with a genuine openness to the future.

1. Exegete 1 Cor 15 in comparison with 1 Cor 7. Which eschatological understanding is prominent?

2. Exegete Rom 5:1ff. What is the relationship between Christology and hope?

§ 69   *Development of the Church until* A.D. *100*

Bibliography: K. Aland, *A History of Christianity*, ET 1985; W. Bauer, *Orthodoxy and Heresy in Earliest Christianity*, ET 1971; L. Goppelt, *Christentum und Judentum im ersten und zweiten Jahrhundert. Ein Aufriss der Urgeschichte der Kirche*, BFChTh II/55, 1955, 71–267; A. Lindemann, *Paulus im ältesten Christentum*, BHTh 58, 1979; U. B. Müller, *Zur frühchristlichen Theologiegeschichte*, 1976.

1. External development

(1) The external events of the history of the church are practically unknown, for there are virtually no Christian sources relative to these events. The most important insight comes from a non-Christian document, a letter written around A.D. 110 by Pliny the Younger to the emperor Trajan, concerning the proceedings against the Christians.

On the other hand, the development of the church's teaching and in part its ecclesiastical organization are fairly well known. Almost all of the NT writings, with the exception of the letters of Paul, originated during this time, between A.D. 60 and 110; some writings, of course, came from an even later period.

(2) The expansion of Christianity can be discerned by way of the particular names mentioned in the sources. The summaries of the Gospels mention Idumea and the Transjordan, as well as Tyre and Sidon (cf. Mk 3:8). According to Acts 15:39, Barnabas engages in missionary work on Cyprus; Titus establishes communities on Crete, while Heb presupposes communities in Italy. 1 Pet 1:1 provides a sweeping overview of the dissemination of Christian communities in Asia Minor. Finally, Pliny's letter mentioned above proves that by the year 100 Christianity had already pushed back the pagan cult in Bithynia and Pontus to a considerable degree. Meanwhile the communities established in the first phase of the mission have continued to develop. Thus the Antioch community enjoyed an exceptional position, as the special significance of their bishop Ignatius indicates; likewise at the time of the writing of Eph (§ 32), the Christian community in Ephesus was held in high regard: It is mentioned in both letters to Timothy, in several of the Ignatian letters, as well as in Acts. Tit speaks of churches in Dalmatia; in his letter to the Philadelphians, Ignatius (11:1) mentions a Christian community in Cilicia, and 1 Clem, as well as the letter to the Philippians by Polycarp of Smyrna, prove that the communities in Corinth and Philippi established by Paul, are flourishing.

Suggested exercise:

Determine the expansion of Christianity based on the recipients of 1 Pet, the seven letters in Rev, and the letters of Ignatius.

2. *Theological tendencies*

(1) The spiritual condition of the church remains anything but uniform. Nevertheless, certain lines can be drawn up: The (deutero)Pauline and the Johannine "school," as well as the synoptic tradition. But only in the succession of Paul—and even there only in part—is it possible to trace a historically continuous line (on the details, see Lindemann [bibliography]).

It is the common characteristic of the writings of this period that the contrast between Jewish Christians and Gentile Christians is no longer relevant, such as Eph demonstrates. The orientation of the church is now de facto Gentile-Christian. Accordingly, freedom from the law—except in Jewish Christianity (see p. 348f. above)—is no longer contested; conversely the OT is clearly recognized as Holy Scripture. The early Christian writers endeavor in a variety of ways to solve the contradiction that to some extent is found there: Mt develops the schema of promise and fulfillment; Heb brings to blossom the typological significance of the OT; Barn also interprets it typologically. 1 Clem understands the OT as a book of ethical examples. The Christian community has completely shed the cultic law (cf. the "Western" text of the apostolic decree; see p. 362 above).

(2) A second important issue is the development of eschatology: 2 Thes, which claims to be written by Paul, opposes an exaggerated imminent return which—apparently also in the name of Paul—laments the "delay of the parousia"; it would be wrong, however, to overestimate the significance of the problem. In fact, the non-arrival of the parousia did not precipitate a sweeping crisis; traces of such a crisis can only be found in 2 Thes and in 2 Pet as well as in some statements of the Synoptics. On the whole, however, this crisis was averted because certain new theological concepts appeared. In the theology of Col and especially in that of Eph there prevails a pervasive disregard for a future-oriented eschatology, a removal of the time factor from theological thought. In its portrait of the wandering people of God, Heb forges a synthesis of the expectation of the parousia and of the experience of its absence; finally, Jn solves the problem by eliminating the cosmological-apocalyptic elements from theology altogether.

On the other hand, the "extending" of time raises a further problem: What is the situation with the sins committed after baptism? Can there be a second forgiveness of sins after baptism? Or is a "second repentance" no longer possible? The problem is addressed in Heb and in Herm with differing solutions: Heb rules out a second repentance (see p. 266 above); for Herm, however, a second repentance and forgiveness of sins (but not a third one!) is considered possible. 1 Jn and 1 Clem distinguish between forgivable and unforgivable sins.

(3) The Pastorals endeavor to establish church order and at the same time to preserve the Pauline tradition. There is an increased tendency in the writings of this era to establish the foundations of the Christian faith

in the warding off of "heresy." But this does not yet establish the nature
of what constitutes orthodoxy and of what is heresy (so the basic argument of W. Bauer). In the course of expanding the consciousness of tradition, the various theological schools and directions want to collect the
heritage they received; the apostles are considered to be fixed entities of
the past, while the writers already clearly consider themselves to be the
third Christian generation (cf. especially Lk 1:1–4). By means of this collection and through the establishing of the tradition, in the course of a
historical process, one gains the criteria whereby it is believed to be possible to determine orthodoxy and heresy.

It is extremely instructive to read the synoptic Gospels as documents
of this development. Here Jesus is consciously portrayed as a teacher;
faith is deliberately tied to the history of Jesus in order to establish a measuring stick for the Christian life.

(4) Even in the post-Pauline era there is no central church organization.
Some interpreters, however, believe that the Pastorals reflect the emergence of such an overarching organization in the form of a monarchical
episcopate: Timothy and Titus are to install bishops—hence they themselves must be some sort of archbishops. But this cannot be derived from
the text of the Pastorals: There is not a word of an installation of an overarching *organization*; indeed, Timothy and Titus are but fictional representatives of the "apostolic" Pauline tradition. What is correct, however,
is that within the communities a fixed order of offices has replaced the
charismatic ministry in the community. The office of elders, for instance,
also begins to be the norm in the communities established by Paul (only
Did does not yet know of presbyters). Yet, the monarchical bishop apparently does not yet appear in the Pastorals; not until Ignatius is he mentioned explicitly. Here one also finds the first three-level hierarchy that
distinguishes between bishop, presbyters, and deacons in the form of an
order of rank. But it is possible that this hierarchy is still more of a wish
on the part of Ignatius than it is concrete reality in the communities (so
W. Bauer's argument).

(5) We are familiar with a wealth of intra-church traditions from this
period of time: In public worship the Scripture (i.e., the OT) is read and
then interpreted in paraenesis and doctrine (1 Tim 4:13); Did and 1 Clem
contain prayers used in public worship. The liturgy of the early Christian
celebration of the Lord's Supper is known from Did 9, 10, 14. Meanwhile
the laying on of hands has become an established practice in the bestowal
of the Spirit (Acts 8:17; 1 Tim 4:14), and even fasting has found entrance
into the church (Did 8). The celebration of the first day of the week is
characteristic for Christian living (1 Cor 16:2; Acts 20:7; Eph 1:10; Did 14:1).
Pliny's letter to Trajan says that Christians gathered on a specific day before
dawn, in order to offer up songs of praise to Christ, their God; on the
same day they gather for a second time to partake in a common meal.

Suggested reading:

Pliny's letter to the emperor Trajan (see p. 339 above).

(6) This era of the history of the church is frequently burdened with the label "early catholicism"; this has connotations of a certain depreciation—at least in Protestant circles. What, then, are the criteria for using this concept? Is the idea of office by itself, or the principle of tradition per se already the identifying mark of early catholicism?

It is advisable to use this concept—if at all—only when the idea of tradition is linked with the notion of the succession of office; and this is not the case until 1 Clem. In addition, in Ignatius there are indications of tying the salvific effect of proclamation and sacrament to the office.

Suggested exercise:

Read H. v. Campenhausen, *The Formation of the Christian Bible*, ET 1972, 1–146; E. Käsemann, "Paulus und der Frühkatholizismus," *Ges. Aufs.* II, 239–252.

§ 70   The Church in the Roman Empire

Bibliography: K. Aland, *A History of Christianity*, ET 1985; idem, "Relationship between Church and State and Early Times," *JTS* 19, 1968, 115–127; O. Cullmann, *State and Church in the NT*, ET 1956; W. H. C. Frend, *Martyrdom and Persecution in the Early Church*, 1965; R. M. Grant, *Sword and the Cross*, 1955; idem, *Early Christianity and Society*, 1977; P. Ketesztes, "The Imperial Roman Government and the Christian Church," *ANRW* 23/2, 247–315, 375–385; R. Klein (ed.), *Das frühe Christentum im römischen Staat*, WdF 267, 1971; R. MacMullen, *Enemies of the Roman Order*, 1966; J. Moreau, *Die Christenverfolgung im Römischen Reich*, 1961; R. Wilken, *The Christians as the Romans Saw Them*, 1984; A. Wlosok, *Rom und die Christen. Zur Auseinandersetzung zwischen Christentum und römischem Staat*, 1970.

First-century Christianity presents itself to the Greeks and Romans as one of the many novel religions which stream into the West from the East (cf. § 20). Of Christianity's competitors, only two are mentioned in the NT: The disciples of John the Baptist, who claim the latter to be the revealer (Jn 1:6; 3:25ff.), and Simon Magus (Acts 8). Simon appeared as God incarnate and was quite a sensation in Samaria and apparently also in Rome. Acts presents him as a charlatan—apparently on purpose, in order to disparage him. Later his followers developed Simon's teaching into a gnostic system (Simonian Gnosis; texts in W. Foerster, *Gnosis* I, 27–33). Only indirectly do we learn of other ancient religions—with the exception of Judaism, of course—from the early Christian writings. Paul undoubtedly knows some of the teachings of the mystery religions (cf. Rom 6); Col contends with early forms of Gnosticism and Eph has incorporated some of the thought conceptions of the latter into its theological system. Pagan polytheism is presupposed in the speech on the Areopagus (Acts 17:22–31), as well as in 1 Cor 8:1ff.; there is no deliberate argumentation with it, however.

Persecutions of Christians occur relatively early, not in the entire Roman Empire at first, but in particular areas only. In corresponding manner, the cause and forms of such sanctions are not uniform. At first the proceedings against Christians are not instigated by the authorities of the state or of the city, rather they were merely public riots. Acts 19 cites the loss of business, which the Ephesian merchants of devotional relics incurred on account of non-cultic Christianity, as motive for their fury against Christians. Frequently the sanctions are also instigated by the Jews (as in Thessalonica). According to the Acts account, they point to the political aspect by implicating the position of the emperor (Acts 17:7). Given such indicators, the authorities can no longer afford to remain passive, but have to at least investigate the matter. But this means at the same time that for the Roman authorities, Christianity is not a religious problem, but a political one. They are concerned with the security of the Roman dominion and in particular with maintaining public order, especially in the major cities. There are precedents for such in earlier Roman sanctions against foreign cults that are considered to be superstition (cf. Suetonius, *Tiberius* 36; Tacitus, *Annals* II, 85). In his letter to Trajan, Pliny asks about what in Christianity should be regarded as punishable: Is it being a Christian per se (*nomen ipsum*), or only the crimes associated with it (*flagitia nomini cohaerentia*)? Trajan's answer does not provide a theoretical definition of the legal status but recommends a "principle of opportunity": The authorities are not on their own to seek out Christians. If Christians are informed against and convicted, they are to be punished. But if one of them adduces evidence that he is not a Christian by revering the gods, he is not to incur any harm. In no wise are they to investigate anonymous accusations, for this would not be in keeping with the spirit of the age. Thus the legal situation remains largely unclear.

In the older literature the question is asked whether the sanctions against Christians came about via formal criminal proceedings, based on existing laws or via *coercitio* by the police, hence practically on the basis of acts of despotism. This alternative does not agree with the actual legal situation: Emperor and senate were not obligated to adhere to the existing laws, but depending upon the situation were able to establish new penal evidence. Furthermore, it is to be taken into consideration that in the provinces the jurisdiction was vested in the governmental task of the proconsul and hence depended upon his personal assessment of the situation.

In principle, a court of law was only allowed to convict Christians of being guilty if they refused to venerate the gods as ordered by the state or to sacrifice to the emperor's image. Yet one must not overestimate the significance of the emperor cult in the early era: To begin with, it hardly plays a role in daily life, and only Rev alludes to it as an immediate reason for the persecution of Christians.

The assertion that Christians who were to articulate the confession κύριος καῖσαρ but instead answered with the confession κύριος 'Ιησοῦς, cannot be established from the available sources (still otherwise H. Conzelmann, "Was glaubte die frühe Christenheit?" 1955, in *Ges. Aufs.*, 112).

When Pliny demands a sacrifice from the Christians in the province of Pontus which he governed, he does not expect a token of their loyalty to the state but their denial of Christianity. For Christians to bring this sacrifice, therefore, is out of the question.

All in all it is appropriate to say that the community is continually subject to the threat of persecution, while the concrete sanctions remain limited in time and location. The well-known Neronian persecution after the fire of Rome (Tacitus, *Annals* XV, 44) is directed only against the Christian in the capital. Likewise the Roman measures taken by Domitian (cf. 1 Pet; Rev; 1 Clem) and Trajan (cf. Ignatius) in no way encompass the whole empire; rather, they essentially involve only Pontus and Bithynia.

In this context, the relationship between Christianity and Judaism is a further important problem. The Jews enjoy certain privileges (see p. 136f. above); it is necessary to ask, therefore, whether Christians did not (also) attempt to make use of these privileges—for instance by referring to themselves as the true Israel. Occasionally it is argued that Acts is pursuing this tendency in order to commend Christianity to the Roman state in this manner. But this cannot be substantiated. The world around them recognized very early on the Christians' special position over against the Jews (cf. Acts 11:26)—a Christian apologetic in this direction would have been totally in vain.

Lk is not at all arguing in Acts that Christians are the true Israel and therefore are entitled to the protection of the Roman authorities. He emphasizes much more that Christianity makes no political claims and therefore poses no threat to Rome. The same tendency is also seen in Jesus' dialogue with Pilate in Jn 18:28–40.

The Christians' reaction to persecution is in accordance with their confession: On the one hand, the death and resurrection of Jesus, and on the other hand eschatology, are the basis of their attitude. The world moves towards its end and is the place where truth is persecuted. The Christians look for the parousia of their Lord and for the resurrection to come. Hence the NT is permeated with the idea of "joy in suffering"— indeed more intensified: Joy on account of suffering. In this way Stephen's speech (Acts 7), Rev, and later Ignatius, and especially the martyr documents of the second century, develop the idea of martyrdom as the suffering ordained by God. This does not mean, however, that martyrdom is sought after. But for Christians, being disciples of Jesus effectively signifies acceptance of the suffering of Jesus (cf. Mk 8:27–9:1), something that is capable of formulation as a fixed rule (Acts 14:22). A classic document of the Christian attitude in this situation is the commissioning discourse of Mt 10 (especially v 23).

Spiritual or even armed resistance against Rome is forbidden for Christians on account of their faith. 1 Pet calls for obedience to the authorities precisely in the face of persecution; in the same situation 1 Clem calls for prayer for the authorities. The only means of defence is the evidence that Christians are objectively innocent and are persecuted unlawfully. Furthermore, Christians pray for protection against persecution.

On the further developments, cf. A. Lindemann, "Christliche Gemeinden und das Römische Reich im ersten und zweiten Jahrhundert," *WuD* 18, 1985, 105–133.

Glossary of Greek terms

The following is an index of frequently used Greek (and Hebrew) terms (with transliteration and English translation):

ἀδελφός	adelphos	brother
αἷμα	haima	blood
ἀλήθεια	alētheia	truth
ἁμαρτία	hamartia	sin
ἄνθρωπος	anthrōpos	man
ἀπόστολος	apostolos	apostle
βασιλεία (τοῦ θεοῦ)	basileia (tou theou)	kingdom of God
γινώσκειν	ginōskein	to know
γνῶσις	gnōsis	knowledge
γραμματεύς	grammateus	scribe
δικαιοσύνη	dikaiosynē	righteousness
δοῦλος	doulos	slave
εἰρήνη	eirēnē	peace
ἐκκλησία	ekklēsia	church
ἐξουσία	exousia	authority, power
εὐαγγέλιον	euaggelion	gospel
εὐλογεῖν	eulogein	to praise
θάνατος	thanatos	death
θεός	theos	God
θλῖψις	thlipsis	tribulation
κύριος	kyrios	Lord
λόγος	logos	word
νόμος	nomos	law
ὁμολογεῖν	homologein	to confess
ὀργή	orgē	wrath, judgment
οὐρανός	ouranos	heaven
παραβολή	parabolē	parable

πιστεύειν	pisteuein	to believe
πίστις	pistis	faith
πνεῦμα	pneuma	spirit
πορνεία	porneia	fornication
σταυρός	stauros	cross
χάρις	charis	grace
ψυχή	psychē	soul, life
משל ל	mashal le	saying about
קבל מן	kibbel min	to receive from (someone)
מסר ל	masar le	to deliver to (someone)

The following is an English translation of the letter forms cited on p. 28:

"Apion to Epimachus his father and lord many greetings," (Deissmann, *Light from the Ancient East*, 180).

"And continually do I pray that thou art in health. I make intercession for thee day by day to the lord Serapis," (Deissmann, 188).

"There saluteth thee my life's partner, Auphidia and Maximus my son," (Deissmann, 184).

Dan 4:1—"King Nebuchadnezzar to all the peoples, tribes, and tongues who dwell in all the earth: Peace be multiplied to you."

INDEX OF NAMES AND SUBJECTS

INDEX OF SCRIPTURE REFERENCES
(New Testament)

Only text references that have been addressed in some depth are listed; texts that are referenced in Part Three (Overview of the NT Writings) have been included in the index only if the case warranted it. On texts outside of the NT, see the Index of Names and Subjects.